The American People in World War II

The Oxford History of the United States

C. Vann Woodward, *General Editor*

The American People in World War II

Freedom from Fear
Part Two

DAVID M. KENNEDY

OXFORD
UNIVERSITY PRESS

OXFORD

UNIVERSITY PRESS

Oxford   New York
Auckland   Bangkok   Buenos Aires   Cape Town
Chennai   Dar es Salaam   Delhi   Hong Kong   Istanbul   Karachi
Kolkata   Kuala Lumpur   Madrid   Melbourne   Mexico City   Mumbai
Nairobi   São Paulo   Shanghai   Taipei   Tokyo   Toronto

Copyright © 1999 by David M. Kennedy

First published by Oxford University Press, Inc., 1999
198 Madison Avenue, New York, New York 10016
www.oup.com
First issued as a one-volume Oxford University Press paperback, 2001
First issued as a two-volume Oxford University Press paperback, 2004

Oxford is a registered trademark of Oxford University Press

Library of Congress Cataloging-in-Publication Data
Kennedy, David M.
Freedom from fear / David M. Kennedy.
p. cm. — (The Oxford history of the United States ; v. 9)
Originally published as one vol. in 1999.
Includes bibliographical references and index.
Contents: Pt. 1. The American people in the Great Depression —
Pt. 2. The American people in World War II.
ISBN-13: 978-0-19-516893-8 (pbk.)
1. United States — History — 1919–1933.
2. United States — History — 1933–1945.
3. Depressions — 1929 — United States.
4. New Deal, 1933–1939.
5. World War, 1939–1945 — United States.
I. Title.
II. Series.

E173.O94 vol. 9
[E801]
973 s — dc22
[973.91]   2003058491

6 7 8 9 10

Printed in the United States of America
on acid-free paper

This book is for Ben, Bess, and Tom
qui laetificant vitam meam.

Contents

Maps

Preface

While Americans struggled throughout the decade of the 1930s to find an exit from the seemingly endless agonies of the Great Depression, a still more menacing threat was brewing abroad. Adolf Hitler's unappeasable lust for war in Europe, coupled with the vaulting ambitions of militarists in Japan and abetted by the imperial yearnings of the Italian Fascist dictator, Benito Mussolini, eventually ignited history's most dreadful and destructive conflict, World War II. The war claimed some fifty million lives and inflicted ghastly punishment on vast regions of the planet, culminating in the nuclear devastation of Hiroshima and Nagasaki in August 1945. The years of fighting also defined the historical crucible in which the modern world was formed. The war extinguished the menaces of Fascism and Naziism, undermined centuries-old colonial regimes, starkly exposed mankind's bottomless capacity for cruelty and evil, spawned fearsome new military technologies and new war-fighting doctrines, and ironically left the victors edgily facing each other in what turned out to be a four-decade-long stand-off known as the Cold War. World War II also banished the Depression from the United States and ushered in a half-century of American prosperity and global economic expansion on scales previously unimaginable. And the war worked a lasting geopolitical revolution. A long historical era of European centrality in the world's affairs came to a finish, as did the stubborn tradition of American isolationism. At war's end, Winston Churchill rightly declared, the victorious United States stood "at the summit of the world," a position it effectively occupied for at least half a century thereafter.

This volume tells the story of America's ascent to that summit. It is in many ways a highly improbable story. No sane observer in America's last full peace-time year, 1940, would have dared to predict what history had in store for the American people just five years over the horizon of the future. Nineteen-forty was the eleventh year of the Great Depression (an ordeal recounted in Part One: *The American People in the Great Depression*). For more than a decade, millions of hands willing to work had found no gainful employment. Huge tracts of America's vaunted industrial establishment lay idle, silently rusting away in a sorry spectacle of economic paralysis about which Adolf Hitler mercilessly mocked President Franklin Roosevelt. From such a stricken nation, what did the dictators have to fear? From such a seemingly ineffective leader, what could the friends of democracy hope?

What was more, in the two decades since the First World War had ended, the American people had repeatedly demonstrated their studied determination to keep their distance from the troubles that were convulsing other nations. They shunned membership in the League of Nations; choked immigration down to a trickle; effectively dropped out of the international economy after the Depression descended in 1929; neglected to maintain their armed forces; and applauded warmly as Congress on five occasions during the 1930s passed formal Neutrality Acts designed to insulate the United States from the growing threat of global military conflict.

In those circumstances, who in 1940 could have foreseen that the United States was about to snap out of its Depression doldrums and astonish the world with a "production miracle" that managed to lift the American standard of living in wartime even while spewing out prodigious quantities of the munitions of war: some 1,500 naval vessels, 88,000 tanks, nearly 300,000 aircraft, more than 600,000 jeeps, over 2 million trucks, 6.5 million rifles, and 40 billion bullets? Who could possibly have foretold that this deeply isolationist nation would field a multimillion-man military and naval force—many times larger than it had mustered in World War I—that would project overwhelming power onto three continents and two oceans? Or that in the course of the war the United States would forsake a century and half of diplomatic diffidence and step forward as a phenomenally energetic international leader—leader of the Grand Alliance with Britain and the Soviet Union; founder of the United Nations, the successor to the discredited League;

architect of the International Monetary Fund and the World Bank, designed to revive and stabilize the same world economy that Americans had scorned in the pre-war years; creator of the General Agreement on Tariffs and Trade, which would morph in the last years of the century into the World Trade Organization, committed to liberalizing trade among all countries; author of the Marshall Plan to rebuild war-smashed Europe?

The pages that follow seek to explain those electrifying developments. I do not presume that any of them were inevitable. Franklin Roosevelt himself succumbed to isolationist sentiment on occasion, and even after his own internationalist principles crystallized—by 1935, I argue, and certainly no later than 1938—he had to toil exhaustively to convince his wavering countrymen that their nation had a stake in the great contest of arms and ideas that was taking shape. How Roosevelt shepherded his reluctant people to stand alongside Britain, the Soviet Union, and China in their stand against Nazi and Japanese aggression constitutes a remarkable episode in the annals of political leadership—one of those rare instances in history when the power and presence of a single personality measurably determined the course of events (Winston Churchill's wartime leadership of Britain is another).

The Japanese attack on Pearl Harbor on December 7, 1941, squashed all lingering debate in the United States about the necessity to take up arms, but in my view that debate had been effectively concluded months earlier, when Congress passed the Lend-Lease Act in March 1941, allocating $7 billion (more than twice the entire federal budget when Franklin Roosevelt first took office) for aid to embattled Britain. If anything, the Pearl Harbor assault did not so much clinch the case for war as it threatened momentarily to undermine the foundational premise around which all the Anglo-American war planning was organized: that the truly strategic adversary was not Japan, but Germany, and that the major American war effort must be waged not in the Pacific, but in Europe. As FDR put it: "defeat of Japan does not defeat Germany," while "defeat of Germany means defeat of Japan." The weight and centrality of that premise are themselves sufficient to refute any speculation that Roosevelt might have deliberately risked the fleet at Pearl Harbor in order to bait the Japanese to war—a war that in the larger framework of American strategic thinking was the wrong war, at the wrong time, in the wrong place, and against the wrong enemy.

The Japanese-American confrontation in the Pacific was a war of startling innovations—notably the displacement of the battleship by the aircraft carrier as the centerpiece of naval combat, and of course the advent of nuclear weapons—and it would also prove to be inordinately cruel, with both sides guilty of repugnant atrocities. But the Pacific theater of action was always subordinate to the main event in Europe. There the United States relied primarily on air power to carry the battle to its German adversary. Only relatively late in the day—just eleven months before the European war's conclusion, on D-Day, June 6, 1944—did the long-anticipated but much-delayed Allied invasion force storm onto the beaches of Normandy.

This volume chronicles the fighting on land, sea, and in the air from Guadalcanal in the Southwest Pacific in 1942 to the Battle of the Bulge in Northwest Europe in late 1944, and beyond. It examines in depth the diplomatic maneuvering and strategic planning that framed the fighting. It offers fresh perspective on controversial political and military developments like the decision to delay the opening of the "second front" against Germany in western Europe, which engendered the bitter frustration of Soviet leader Josef Stalin and effectively determined the political map of postwar Europe; President Roosevelt's surprise announcement of the "unconditional surrender" formula at Casablanca in 1943; the strained relationship between the Soviets, who bore most of the military burden of the war against Hitler, and their wary British and American allies; and the "decision," if that is what it can be called, to drop the two atomic bombs on Japan at war's end.

The American People in World War II probes other long-running historical controversies as well, including the deeply vexed question of what Americans knew about the Nazi persecution of the Jews that eventually led to the systematic genocide of the Holocaust, and whether the United States could have taken more effective action to stop it. I have also devoted considerable attention to the forced internment of some 120,000 Japanese-Americans, and to the lesser-known harassment of Italian-Americans and German-Americans, some 5,000 of whom were taken into custody.

The "home front" figures prominently in the following account, including analyses of the long-term effects of the war's employment opportunities for women, and its shattering impact on the Jim Crow regime of segregation that had imprisoned African-Americans in society's basement for generations since the end of the Civil War, even while the government largely refused to allow black troops to serve in combat. I also examine the far-reaching effects of the great wartime demographic reshuffling that put millions of blacks as well as whites into motion, shifting the centers of population and power in the postwar United States to the newly energized Sunbelt.

Many outsized characters stride across the pages that follow. In addition to the commanding figures of Roosevelt, Churchill, and Stalin, and the diabolical Adolf Hitler, they include the silky diplomat Sumner Welles, who helped to convince FDR that in Churchill Britain had at last found a leader who would not genuflect before the Nazis; Admiral Isoroku Yamamoto, the reluctant architect of the Pearl Harbor attack; George C. Marshall, the "organizer of victory" whose unflappable demeanor and methodical planning skills wrought order out of the gargantuan sprawl of the American war effort; the deceptively genial Dwight D. Eisenhower, plucked from obscurity at the war's outset to command the greatest assembly of combined arms in history; George C. Patton, Eisenhower's flamboyantly profane subordinate; and the haunted theoretical physicist Robert Oppenheimer, who for better or worse brought the "Manhattan Project" to a successful conclusion with the production of history's first atomic weapons.

This volume concludes with an examination of the world that World War II made and the memories it left behind. National mythology has enshrined the great conflict as the "good war," fought by the "greatest generation," and if any war can be said to be good, so it was in terms of the justice of its ends and the courage of the citizen-soldiers who waged it. More than 400,000 of them died. But though they represented proportionately far fewer combat deaths than suffered by any other major belligerent, and though their sacrifice helped to deposit the United States at the summit of the world in 1945, their mute tombstones remind us still of the terrible wages of a war that mankind can only wish had never happened.

Acknowledgments

In writing this book I have drawn on a rich body of scholarship and imposed on the kindness of a great many colleagues, friends, and kin. I want to say a special word of appreciation for the pioneering work on the New Deal era by a remarkable generation of scholars, including John Morton Blum, James MacGregor Burns, Kenneth S. Davis, Frank Freidel, William E. Leuchtenburg, and Arthur M. Schlesinger Jr. Though I sometimes disagree with their emphases and evaluations, they laid the foundation on which all subsequent study of that period has built, including my own. I also learned much about World War II from the veterans with whom I traveled to battlefields in Italy, the Solomon Islands, and Normandy. For their service to their country, and for their generosity to me, I thank them.

Several research assistants have given me invaluable help: Leslie Berlin, Elizabeth Kopelman Borgwardt, Mark Brilliant, Kyle Graham, Tom Jackson, Sean Malloy, John McGreevy, and Jonathan Schoenwald. Their contributions and the comments of participants in Stanford's faculty–graduate student American History Workshop have greatly improved this book.

Stanford University granted me two research leaves, one spent at the Center for Advanced Study in the Behavioral Sciences, the other at the Stanford Humanities Center, both partly financed by the National Endowment for the Humanities, which greatly facilitated my research and writing. The Harmsworth Family, the Faculty of Modern History, and the Provost and Fellows of Queen's College, Oxford, provided material support and stimulating collegiality during a year I spent as the Harmsworth Professor of American History at Oxford University. A seminar I co-taught there with John Rowett of Brasenose College proved particularly helpful in shaping my thinking about the New Deal.

I am especially indebted to Jack Beatty of the *Atlantic Monthly*, James T. Patterson of Brown University, and James J. Sheehan of Stanford University, each of whom read the entire manuscript, rescued me from innumerable errors and infelicities, and challenged me to think harder and write more clearly. Co-teaching a course on World War II with my Stanford colleague Jim Sheehan has contributed substantially to my work on this project, not least because of his example of deeply thoughtful scholarship and inspired teaching. I also want to thank others who acceded to my requests to comment on various parts of the manuscript: Barton J. Bernstein, Lizabeth Cohen, Paul David, Peter Duus, James Kloppenberg, Karen Sawislak, and Gavin Wright. Henry Archer rescued me from countless mistakes.

Sheldon Meyer at Oxford University Press first asked me to undertake this book, and his wisdom and counsel, not to mention patience, cheer, and good company, have sustained me over the years of work on it, as have the invariably thoughtful commentaries of the general editor of the Oxford History of the United States, C. Vann Woodward. Joellyn Ausanka, India Cooper, and Susan Day provided the excellent editorial support for which Oxford Press is justly renowned.

My wife, Judy, read the entire manuscript, endured life as a writer's widow, and provided unflagging support. Our three children, Ben, Bess, and Tom, grew up with this book, and to them I lovingly dedicate it, with the hope that this history may prove useful to their voyage, and their generation's, into the future.

Stanford, California   David M. Kennedy
July 4, 1998

Editor's Introduction

The brief period from 1929 to 1945 is unique in American history for its complexities of change and violence of contrasts. People who lived through the years of the Great Depression, the New Deal, and the Second World War—only half the years normally assigned to one generation—experienced more bewildering changes than had several generations of their predecessors. These changes included a transition from economic and social paralysis to unprecedented outbursts of national energy, the emergence from wretched years of poverty to unparalleled levels of prosperity, and the repudiation of a century-and-a-half of isolation as America entered World War II.

Events of this magnitude and global significance make extraordinary demands upon the historian. Fortunately, David M. Kennedy is richly endowed with the talents and skills required by his challenging task—plus gifts as a writer. He is not the kind of historian who dwells upon abstract "forces." His emphasis is upon *people*—not only leaders but followers and opponents as well as victims and beneficiaries. Readers of *Freedom from Fear* will encounter vivid portraits not only of American statesmen and commanders, but of their foreign counterparts as well. Their decisions, errors, blunders, and such measures of luck as shaped the course of history are given due attention, but not to the neglect of the people who suffered or endured the results.

It is the people who suffered in the Great Depression who receive David Kennedy's primary attention, and more of them did suffer, and more deeply, and longer, than has been generally assumed. Southern white sharecroppers, for example, averaged an annual cash income of $350, black sharecroppers $294. At wages of $1 a day miners subsisted on a diet suggesting that of domestic animals. Emaciated children who never tasted milk wandered the streets, some shoeless in winter, too poorly clad to go to school. Milch cows dried up for lack of feed, and starving horses dropped in their harnesses. More surprising than the people's despair was their prevailing submissiveness. Their creed of individualism may account for much of this: If success and prosperity were due to merit and striving, failure and poverty must be due to the lack of them. Much more common than rebellion among Americans of those years was a sense of shame and a loss of self-respect. Year after year of depression went by with little or no sign of the recovery promised by politicians.

Franklin D. Roosevelt and his New Deal have been both credited with recovery from the depression and blamed for the failure of recovery. David Kennedy refuses to settle for either simplification. He traces the complex interplay between continuing economic stagnation and Roosevelt's remarkable programs of social and economic reform, new ones almost every year until 1938. Granting the inconsistencies, contradictions, and failures of the New Deal, Kennedy nevertheless summarizes its "leitmotif" in a single word: security. Its programs extended security not only to vulnerable individuals, races, and classes but to capitalists and consumers, bankers and homeowners, workers and employers, as much security and freedom from fear as democratic government might provide. FDR set out, he once declared, "to make a country in which no one is left out." Without resort to revolution or abandonment of the Constitution, the New Deal constructed an institutional framework for such a society as its main heritage. What it did *not* do was to end the Great Depression and restore prosperity. That proved in the end to be the incidental and ironic work of a terrible war.

It was a war — really two wars — that the will of the people as expressed repeatedly by congressional majorities wanted no part in. As for the quarrelsome Europeans, let them settle their differences themselves this time, as American intervention had failed to do in the previous war. And as for the Japanese, let the vast Pacific Ocean serve as our shield. Appeals and threats from both sides of the globe seemed only to increase the zeal of American isolationists and the stubborn resistance to intervention. What military preparation the country made (and it started virtually from scratch) must be limited to the protection of national rights and property. Increasingly, however, the survival of Britain, and then of the Soviet Union, came to be seen as crucial to America's own survival. After years of agonizing neutrality, war eventually came to America with the Japanese attack on Pearl Harbor.

In the half of his book that deals with the war, its coming and its conduct, Kennedy exhibits remarkable talents in discussing diplomacy, especially relations with Churchill and Stalin. He also shows unusual skills in analyzing and depicting modern warfare in two hemispheres, including naval war and air combat. Readers are not spared accounts of the most gruesome and brutal atrocities, especially in the savage Pacific War. Without neglecting any essentials of military history, including the greatest naval battle ever fought and the development and use of the most powerful weapon ever made, *Freedom from Fear* also gives us a superb account of what the war did to the hundreds of millions of noncombatants on the homefront. Their lives were as much revolutionized as the lives of those in uniform. Women replaced or joined men in the work force; blacks gained jobs and skills; southerners moved north, easterners moved west. The whole population was profoundly shaken up and the American way of life deeply changed.

This volume of the Oxford series covers an incomparable period of American history, a period of extraordinary challenges and demands upon the historian, demands that David Kennedy has met surpassingly well.

C. Vann Woodward

Abbreviated Titles Used in Citations

C&R   Warren F. Kimball, ed., *Churchill and Roosevelt: The Complete Correspondence*, 3 vols. (Princeton: Princeton University Press, 1984)

Cantril   Hadley Cantril, ed., *Public Opinion, 1935–1946* (Princeton: Princeton University Press, 1951)

Churchill   Winston S. Churchill, *The Second World War*, 6 vols. (Boston: Houghton Mifflin, 1948–53)

Craven and Cate   Wesley Frank Craven and James Lee Cate, *The Army Air Forces in World War II*, 6 vols. (Chicago: University of Chicago Press, 1953)

Dallek   Robert Dallek, *Franklin D. Roosevelt and American Foreign Policy, 1932–1945* (New York: Oxford University Press, 1979)

Davis   Kenneth S. Davis, *FDR*, 4 vols. (New York: Random House, 1985–93)

FRUS   *Foreign Relations of the United States* (Washington: USGPO, various years)

HSUS   *Historical Statistics of the United States*, 2 vols. (Washington: USGPO, 1975)

Ickes Diary   Harold L. Ickes, *The Secret Diary of Harold L. Ickes,* 3 vols. (New York: Simon and Schuster, 1953–54)

L&G, *Challenge*   William L. Langer and S. Everett Gleason, *The Challenge to Isolation, 1937–1940* (New York: Harper and Brothers, 1952)

L&G, *Undeclared*   William L. Langer and S. Everett Gleason, *The Undeclared War, 1940–1941* (New York: Harper and Brothers, 1953)

Morgenthau Diary   John Morton Blum, *Roosevelt and Morgenthau* (Boston: Houghton Mifflin, 1972)

Morison   Samuel Eliot Morison, *The Two-Ocean War* (Boston: Little, Brown, 1963)

PDDE   Alfred D. Chandler Jr. et al., eds., *The Papers of Dwight David Eisenhower*, 19 vols. (Baltimore: Johns Hopkins University Press, 1970–)

PPA   *The Public Papers and Addresses of Franklin D. Roosevelt*, 13 vols. (New York: Random House and Harper and Brothers, 1938–50)

Schlesinger   Arthur M. Schlesinger Jr., *The Age of Roosevelt*, 3 vols. (Boston: Houghton Mifflin, 1956–60)

Spector   Ronald H. Spector, *Eagle Against the Sun: The American War with Japan* (New York: Free Press, 1985)

Stimson Diary   Diary of Henry L. Stimson, microfilm, Green Library, Stanford University (original in Sterling Library, Yale University)

The American People in World War II

1

The Agony of Neutrality

*If we are conquered, all will be enslaved and the United States will be
left single-handed to guard the rights of man.*
— First Lord of the Admiralty Winston S. Churchill,
November 12, 1939

While German dive-bombers screamed over Warsaw and German tanks
crunched through the stubble of the freshly harvested grain fields in
Polish Silesia, the world briefly and vainly held its breath, hoping against
all reason that the war that had come at last might somehow not really
have come at all. But on September 3, after Hitler had rejected British
and French ultimata to withdraw from Poland, futile hope expired.
Seated in front of a microphone at Number 10 Downing Street, Chamberlain announced to his countrymen on September 3 that "this country
is at war with Germany." In Paris, Prime Minister Edouard Daladier
followed suit a few hours later.[1]

In Washington, Roosevelt's first public pronouncement on September
1 was a plea to all the belligerents to refrain from "bombardment from
the air of civilian populations or of unfortified cities" — an appeal that
bespoke the terror of air power then obsessing every mind, and a declaration that eventually made for ironic reading in the light of the war's
nuclear climax at Hiroshima and Nagasaki nearly six years later. On the
evening of September 3, Roosevelt also took to the radio to deliver another of his now familiar Fireside Chats. "Until four-thirty o'clock this
morning I had hoped against hope that some miracle would prevent a
devastating war in Europe and bring to an end the invasion of Poland

1. James W. Gantenbein, ed., *Documentary Background of World War II* (New York:
Columbia University Press, 1948), 409.

1

by Germany," the president said. Now that war had irreversibly come, Roosevelt announced, "[t]his nation will remain a neutral nation." But, Roosevelt emphatically added, "I cannot ask that every American remain neutral in thought as well. . . . Even a neutral cannot be asked to close his mind or close his conscience."[2]

The president's statement contrasted starkly with Woodrow Wilson's appeal at the outbreak of the Great War in 1914 that his countrymen should be "impartial in thought as well as in action." By late 1939 few could doubt where American sympathies lay. The mind and conscience of America were decidedly anti-Hitler. A Gallup poll in October found that 84 percent of respondents were pro-Ally and only 2 per cent pro-German. But as it had for half a decade of troubled peace, so now in wartime moral sympathy stopped well short of armed support. Though Roosevelt might have conceded, even encouraged, American alignment with Britain and France in his Fireside Chat, he also declared that "the United States will keep out of this war. . . . Let no man or woman," he said, "thoughtlessly or falsely talk of America sending its armies to European fields."[3]

Meeting with his cabinet on the afternoon of September 1, Roosevelt clung reflexively to the "methods-short-of-war" approach he had outlined some eight months earlier. Over and over he insisted, "We are not going in." When War Department planners proposed raising an army large enough to support a possible American Expeditionary Force in Europe, Roosevelt cut them off: "You can base your calculations on an army of 750,000 men [the army's strength was then about 175,000], for whatever happens, we won't send troops abroad. We need only think of defending this hemisphere."[4]

Roosevelt needed also, of course, to think about how, exactly, he might supply Britain and France with the tools to fight Hitler. Munitioning the democracies was the heart of the methods-short-of-war policy. Finding the means to do so was the major foreign policy problem with which Roosevelt had been wrestling since his unsuccessful attempt

2. PPA (1939), 454; Russell D. Buhite and David W. Levy, eds., FDR's Fireside Chats (Norman: University of Oklahoma Press, 1992), 148–51. Buhite and Levy use transcriptions of Roosevelt's actual radio addresses, which sometimes differ slightly from the official versions published in PPA.

3. Public Opinion Quarterly 4 (March 1940):102; Buhite and Levy, Fireside Chats, 149.

4. Joseph Alsop and Robert Kintner, American White Paper: The Story of American Diplomacy and the Second World War (New York: Simon and Schuster, 1940), 64–65.

to modify the first Neutrality Act in 1935. The president had long since made his own general intentions clear to European leaders, though he was notably less candid with the American people, and for that matter aggravatingly unrealistic in his signals to the Europeans. In late 1938, in the wake of the Munich debacle, he had privately promised Prime Minister Chamberlain that "in the event of war with the dictators he had the industrial resources of the American nation behind him," though he knew as well as Chamberlain did that formidable legal and political obstacles stood athwart any serious effort to make good on that promise. At about the same time, meeting secretly at Hyde Park with the French financier Jean Monnet, Roosevelt sketched an elaborate, even fantastic, scheme for evading the American Neutrality Act: in the event of war, Roosevelt suggested, American factories at Detroit and Niagara Falls would ship motors and airframes across the border to Canada, where they could be assembled and flown away as combat-fitted aircraft. Implementing that ploy would violate the presidential oath to enforce the law and would almost surely expose Roosevelt to demands by isolationists for his impeachment. That Roosevelt even entertained such notions is a measure of the desperation to which isolationist strictures had driven him.

The same obsession with air power that informed Roosevelt's plea to avoid city-bombing had also guided much of the president's thinking about American strategy. It was said of Roosevelt that he played with the navy as another man might play with toy trains. He had served as assistant secretary of the navy, adorned his White House office with prints of historic naval vessels, and routinely commandeered navy ships for presidential "vacations" at sea. Yet for all his doting upon the navy, Roosevelt was if anything an even more enthusiastic advocate of the air arm. Air power—especially air power delivered to the European democracies from American factories—seemed the ideal instrument with which the historically isolationist and chronically depressed United States could implement the short-of-war strategy. Even more effectively than ships, wide-ranging airplanes could patrol the ocean vastness and keep the fighting far from the New World's shores. Deep-penetration bombing raids could strike much farther into the enemy heartland than even the biggest naval guns could reach. A few thousand bombers, flown by several thousand airmen, could inflict damage at many times the rate of a million-man ground force, and at a lower cost in human life. And building the bombing machines for a vast air fleet would invigorate the American economy, giving employment to countless workers.

Ever receptive to novelty, Roosevelt had easily succumbed to the seductive logic of aerial warfare. At the time of the Munich crisis he had mused that "pounding away at Germany from the air" would crack the morale of the German people. "This kind of war," Roosevelt claimed, "would cost less money, would mean comparatively few casualties, and would be more likely to succeed than a traditional war by land and sea."[5] At a momentous meeting with his military advisers at the White House on November 14, 1938, Roosevelt had laid out his extraordinarily ambitious plan to develop an American aircraft industry sufficient to equip the British and French and to maintain a ten-thousand-plane American air force. To him, the lesson of Chamberlain's humiliation at Munich was clear. As William Bullitt had tersely put it, "The moral is: If you have enough airplanes you don't have to go to Berchtesgaden." Roosevelt agreed. "Had we had this summer 5,000 planes and the capacity immediately to produce 10,000 per year, even though I might have had to ask Congress for authority to sell or lend them to the countries in Europe," said Roosevelt, "Hitler would not have dared to take the stand he did." Army Air Corps General H. H. "Hap" Arnold exulted at this presidential endorsement: "Airplanes—now—and lots of them!" was Arnold's summation of Roosevelt's position. "The President came straight out for air power. . . . [Expanded American ground forces] would not scare Hitler one blankety-blank-blank bit! What he wanted was airplanes."[6] Pursuant to that aim, Roosevelt asked Congress in January 1939 for a special appropriation of $300 million for aircraft construction. That request marked the decidedly modest origins of a rearmament program that would in time pour forth an avalanche of weaponry.

As the shooting war began, the full impact of that avalanche still lay well over the horizon of the future. Roosevelt's overtures to Chamberlain and Monnet in 1938, as well as his extravagant plans to expand the American aircraft industry, had come to little by late 1939. The president's clandestine offers of aid to Britain and France precluded any deterrent effect on Hitler, as the historian Donald Watt has acidly observed, for the simple reason that "deterrence and secrecy are largely

---

5. Ickes Diary 2:469.
6. Orville H. Bullitt, ed., *For the President: Personal and Secret, Correspondence between Franklin D. Roosevelt and William C. Bullitt* (Boston: Houghton Mifflin, 1972), 288; Morgenthau Diary, 273; Arnold quoted in Michael S. Sherry, *The Rise of American Air Power: The Creation of Armageddon* (New Haven: Yale University Press, 1987), 80.

incompatible notions."[7] What was more, Roosevelt's lavish ambitions for the air corps flummoxed most American military leaders, with the conspicuous exception of Hap Arnold. They preferred a balanced force, its ground, sea, and air arms all proportionately developed and deployed in concert. "What are we going to do with fifteen thousand planes?" Army Chief of Staff Malin Craig angrily queried. They worried even more about the president's impatience to deliver planes to the Europeans, at a time when American forces were pathetically under strength. "Don't you think so, George?" Roosevelt asked chummily of Malin's deputy chief, General George C. Marshall, at the conclusion of the presidential pitch on November 14, 1938, for delivering airplanes to Europe. "I am sorry, Mr. President, but I don't agree at all," Marshall frostily replied. It was the last time Roosevelt ever addressed Marshall, a studiously formal man, by his first name.

George Marshall was in the habit of speaking bluntly to his superiors. As a young captain with the American Expeditionary Force in France in 1917, he had dared to correct General John J. Pershing in front of a group of fellow officers. Pershing responded by making Marshall his principal aide. But despite his anointing by the legendary Pershing, Marshall, in common with almost all officers in the interwar years, had languished in the missionless peacetime army, where promotion was slow and action rare. He remained a lieutenant colonel for eleven years. He uncomplainingly accepted a series of apparently dead-end assignments: with the tiny U.S. Army garrison in Tientsin, China; with the Illinois National Guard; and even with the Civilian Conservation Corps. Yet everywhere he made a consistent impression as an outstanding soldier. His directness, his keen analytic mind, his unadorned speech, and his granitic constancy evoked admiration that bordered on reverence. More than one of his commanding officers, answering the routine efficiency report question of whether they would like to have Marshall serve under them in battle, replied that they would prefer to serve under his command—the highest of soldierly compliments. Marshall was just shy of six feet tall, ramrod-straight, invariably proper, impeccably self-controlled, and determinedly soft-spoken. Most associates saw only fleeting glimpses of his potentially volcanic temper. "I cannot allow myself to get angry," he once told his wife; "that would be fatal." In 1938, at the age of fifty-eight, Marshall became the head of the War Plans

7. Donald Cameron Watt, *How War Came: The Immediate Origins of the Second World War, 1938–1939* (New York: Pantheon, 1989), 130.

Division, then deputy chief of staff under Craig. On the signal date of September 1, 1939, Roosevelt elevated him to army chief of staff. He was by then a shrewd, even ruthless judge of men. He proceeded to winnow the army's senescent officers corps to identify the leaders who could fight and win the next war. He also determined that he could not do his job properly if he allowed himself to be seduced by the fabled Rooseveltian charm. He reportedly made a solemn vow never to laugh at the president's jokes.[8]

Marshall's stony riposte to Roosevelt on November 14, 1938, began a protracted debate between the president and his service chiefs about the competing needs of the Allied and the United States armed forces for the still-limited output of American war materiel. Many factors conspired to keep that output small: the persistent belief that the conflict was far away and somebody else's business, or that it might yet be averted altogether; the hair-trigger sensitivity of congressional isolationists to anything that hinted at a more active American international role; and the constraints of traditional fiscal orthodoxy. All those considerations had long precluded any request on Roosevelt's part for substantial military and naval budgets. The total national defense appropriation in fiscal 1940 was just $1.3 billion, a 50 percent increase over 1939, but still only about one-seventh of the federal budget. In January 1940 Roosevelt asked for a small increase to $1.8 billion for the 1941 fiscal year, and Congress immediately proceeded to whittle away even at that modest sum. In any case, the Nye Committee's sensational accusations of World War I profiteering left many corporations gun-shy about accepting orders for armaments. The 1939 defense budget provided funding for just 250 B-17 "Flying Fortresses," designed in 1935 as the premier American long-range bomber, and the army placed orders for only seventy B-17s in fiscal 1940. Actual production lagged even further behind the president's grand vision of a mighty air fleet. Exactly fifty-two B-17s were available for service as late as May 1940.[9]

As for foreign purchases, despite Roosevelt's active encouragement, European orders for aircraft remained exceedingly modest in scale. The Allies were understandably skittish about becoming reliant on a source of critical supplies that would statutorily dry up the instant formal hos-

8. Eric Larrabee, *Commander in Chief: Franklin Delano Roosevelt, His Lieutenants, and Their War* (New York: Harper and Row, 1987), 96ff.
9. Sherry, *Rise of American Air Power*, 89; Mark Skinner Watson, *United States Army in World War II: Chief of Staff: Prewar Plans and Preparations* (Washington: Department of the Army, 1950), 305.

tilities commenced. Looking toward a protracted war, and doubly debarred (by the Johnson debt-default law and the cash-and-carry provisions of the Neutrality Act) from seeking credit in the United States,
they also hesitated to exhaust their precious dollar and gold reserves.
They worried too about the political implications of provoking an isolationist backlash if they appeared to be stretching the spirit of the Neutrality Act. By mid-1939 the French and British together had contracted
for only about fifteen hundred aircraft.[10] As the war began, the United
States was itself unarmed and was making only a piddling contribution
to munitioning the European democracies. The result, said Undersecretary of State Sumner Welles, was a "nightmare of frustration." The
government "had no means whatever," Welles explained, "short of war,
to which American public opinion was overwhelmingly opposed, of diverting or checking the world cataclysm and the threat to the very survival of this country."[11] The short-of-war strategy, in other words,
amounted in practice to not much of a strategy at all.

Exercising the scant discretion that the law permitted him, Roosevelt
delayed official recognition of the European war until September 5,
1939, to permit Britain and France to clear some previously ordered
supplies from American ports. Then he issued two Neutrality Procla-
mations, one, like Wilson's in 1914, in accordance with traditional international law, the other mandated by the Neutrality Act of 1937. The
latter declaration clamped an iron-bound embargo on all "arms, ammunition, or implements of war," including "aircraft, unassembled, assembled or dismantled," as well as "propellers or air screws, fuselages,
hulls, wings, tail units [and] aircraft engines." Now the Allies could not
legally buy so much as a single cartridge in the United States, let alone
vast swarms of combat aircraft.

From London, Ambassador Kennedy reported that British officials
were "depressed beyond words" that the Neutrality Act had been invoked. From Paris, Bullitt wrote: "It is, of course, obvious that if the
Neutrality Act remains in its present form, France and England will be
defeated rapidly." Repealing the act now became Roosevelt's highest
priority. "I am almost literally walking on eggs," Roosevelt wrote, "saying
nothing, seeing nothing, and hearing nothing" as he tried to ease neutrality revision through the treacherous legislative process. On September 13, nearly two weeks after the fighting had erupted in Poland, and

---

10. Craven and Cate 6:302.
11. Sumner Welles, *The Time for Decision* (New York: Harper and Brothers, 1944), 148.

after delicate politicking with key legislators, he called for a special session of Congress to convene on September 21 to consider neutrality revision.[12]

Despite the president's measured caution, the announcement of a special congressional session instantly galvanized the champions of isolation. Senator Borah broadcast a lurid warning on September 14 that tampering with the neutrality law would surely lead to eventual American belligerency (a prediction that was to prove correct). On the following day, the celebrated aviator Charles Lindbergh made the first of several impassioned radio addresses against neutrality revision. "The destiny of this country does not call for our involvement in European wars," Lindbergh said. "One need only glance at a map to see where our true frontiers lie. What more could we ask than the Atlantic Ocean on the east and the Pacific on the west . . . ? An ocean is a formidable barrier, even for modern aircraft." Lindbergh, Father Charles Coughlin, and several isolationist senators filled the airwaves with denunciations of Roosevelt's impending request to amend the 1937 statute. In a matter of days, their campaign swamped congressional offices with more than a million antirevision telegrams, letters, and postcards.[13]

After six weeks of contentious debate, Congress at last sent a revised neutrality bill to the White House. Voting on the bill illustrated the momentous shifts in political geometry that had occurred since the glory days of the New Deal. In the Senate, most of Roosevelt's erstwhile progressive Republican allies on domestic policy deserted him. In the House, southern Democrats voted 110–8 in favor of revision, vividly highlighting the degree to which the president's foreign policies now depended not on the liberal coalition that had legislated the New Deal but on the traditionally conservative southern core of his party, which was largely hostile to further domestic reform.

12. Kennedy quoted in Dallek, 200; Bullitt's remark is in Bullitt, *For the President*, 369; Roosevelt in Elliott Roosevelt, ed., *FDR: His Personal Letters, 1928–1945* (New York: Duell, Sloan and Pearce, 1950), 2:934.

13. Charles A. Lindbergh, "Appeal to Isolationism," *Vital Speeches of the Day*, October 1, 1939, 751–52; Dallek, 200ff. Lindbergh, an attractive personality celebrated as the first man to fly solo across the Atlantic, was a particularly sharp thorn in Roosevelt's side. He had visited Germany several times in the 1930s and had been decorated by the German government in 1938, prompting Roosevelt to conclude that more than simple, home-grown isolationism motivated Lindbergh's crusade against neutrality revision. "If I should die tomorrow, I want you to know this," Roosevelt exploded to Secretary Morgenthau in May 1940: "I am absolutely convinced that Lindbergh is a Nazi." Frank Freidel, *Franklin D. Roosevelt: Rendezvous with Destiny* (Boston: Little, Brown, 1990), 323.

Roosevelt signed the revised Neutrality Act on November 4, 1939. He beamed for the newsreel cameras as he affixed his name to the document and made a show of handing the ceremonial pens to the bill's congressional sponsors. Despite this presidential bravado, however, the new Neutrality Act represented at best only a partial victory for the methods-short-of-war strategy. The act did lift the arms embargo. Belligerent powers could now place orders for war material, including combat aircraft, in the United States. But congressional isolationists still had sufficient strength to exact a heavy price for that concession: they restored the 1937 law's cash-and-carry provisions, which had expired in May 1939. Credits to belligerents were absolutely prohibited, from the U.S. Treasury and from private bankers alike. Purchasers of arms and ammunition had to make full cash payment and take title before the goods left American docks, and shipments could move only in foreign vessels. Further underscoring the implacable determination of American lawmakers to avoid a war-precipitating incident, the new law forbade American merchant ships from transiting a broad "danger zone" that embraced most of the sea lanes to western European ports, neutral as well as belligerent. The North Atlantic was Britain's historic lifeline and America's traditional shield. With the flourish of his pen on November 4, Roosevelt swept that sea more cleanly of American ships than a thousand torpedoes could have done.

This limited revision of the neutrality law accurately reflected the precarious equilibrium in which American diplomacy was now suspended. Public opinion and official policy alike hung quivering between hope and fear—hope that with American help the Allies could defeat Hitler, and fear that events might yet suck the United States into the conflict. Roosevelt, for one, did not deceive himself about the terrifying implications of a Nazi triumph in Europe, but neither did he suffer any illusions about the temper of his countrymen. "What worries me," Roosevelt confided in late December 1939 to a fellow internationalist, Kansas newspaperman William Allen White, "is that public opinion over here is patting itself on the back every morning and thanking God for the Atlantic Ocean (and the Pacific Ocean). We greatly underestimate the serious implications to our own future. . . . Therefore, my sage old friend, my problem is to get the American people to think of conceivable consequences without scaring the American people into thinking that they are going to be dragged into this war."[14]

14. E. Roosevelt, FDR: His Personal Letters 2:968.

THE EERY LULL that settled over much of Europe after the German invasion of Poland compounded Roosevelt's problem in late 1939 and early 1940, as he faced the task of educating Americans about the real and present danger they faced. Fulfilling the secret protocols of the Nazi-Soviet pact, Stalin gobbled up eastern Poland in mid-September and invaded Finland at the end of November. But those were relatively minor clashes on Europe's distant eastern periphery. In the western European heartland, the fearsome German *Wehrmacht*, the truly great menace to the peace of the Old Continent, lay mysteriously idle. The *Blitzkrieg*, or "lightning war," that had crushed Poland in three weeks gave way to six months of *Sitzkrieg*—a curious "sitting war" during which Hitler consolidated his gains but launched no new military adventures.

Hitler kept Paris and London off balance during this interval with seductive but ultimately bogus peace feelers. For their part, the Allies showed no inclination to seize the military initiative. France marked time, deluded by its faith in the supposedly impenetrable Maginot Line. Britain contented itself with leaflet raids on German cities. As the closing days of 1939 stretched to weeks and then to months, and still no blow came in the west, Europe relaxed a bit. English children who had been evacuated from London under the threat of air raids in September were returning home by Christmastime. Even so bellicose a Briton as Winston Churchill, appointed in early September as first lord of the British admiralty in Chamberlain's cabinet, continued to think of the war more as an imminent prospect than a present reality. As late as Christmas Day 1939, he telegraphed to Franklin Roosevelt: "Generally speaking, think war will begin soon now."[15]

As 1940 opened, there was still no war in the west—or only what Senator Borah sneeringly called the "Phony War," yet another saber-rattling stand-off between the blustering Nazis and the craven democracies, but nothing for the United States to worry about. Among Americans, the British ambassador reported from Washington, there was a feeling "of boredom that the tremendous drama of unlimited aerial war in Europe which they had been educated to expect is apparently not going to come off."[16]

15. *C&R* 1:29. Interestingly, Churchill wrote Chamberlain on the same day that he considered Roosevelt Britain's friend, "but I expect he wants to be re-elected, and I fear that isolationism is the winning ticket." Rock, *Chamberlain and Roosevelt*, 243.
16. Rock, *Chamberlain and Roosevelt*, 224.

The Phony War's strange calm appeared momentarily to enchant even Franklin Roosevelt with the mirage of a negotiated settlement before the dreaded wider war exploded. The recent history of appeasement gave him little basis for confidence that either Britain or France would muster the political will to stand up to Hitler for long. Nor did he have much reason to believe that the British or the French military would prove any kind of match for the Nazi juggernaut once it started to roll. Bullitt sent several warnings from Paris that France would be subdued by German air power well before the French could build their own air arm, with or without American help. From London, Ambassador Kennedy repeatedly emphasized the morale-sapping effects of Berlin's suggestions of a settlement. Chamberlain, Kennedy believed, might yet cut a deal with Hitler. Kennedy himself, in fact, was inclined to favor such a deal as the best that outgunned and underfinanced England could hope for. "Make no mistake," Kennedy wrote the president on November 3, "there is a very definite undercurrent in this country for peace. . . . Although everybody hates Hitler, [the British] still don't want to be finished economically, financially, politically, and socially, which they are beginning to suspect will be their fate if the war goes on very long."[17]

The better to gauge the European mood, Roosevelt announced on February 9, 1940, that he was dispatching Undersecretary of State Sumner Welles on an ostensible "fact-finding" mission to Rome, Berlin, Paris, and London. The deeper purpose of Welles's trip the president did not feel free to state publicly: to explore the possibility of an American-mediated peace settlement negotiated with Hitler — surely, Roosevelt felt, a preferable course to a peace settlement dictated by Hitler.

What Welles found unnerved him. Though many Italian officials were anxiously seeking a way to avoid war, Mussolini was clearly Italy's supreme boss, and Welles concluded that there was not "the slightest chance of any successful negotiation" with *Il Duce*.[18] In Berlin, where he saw Polish prisoners of war glumly shoveling snow from the streets, Welles sat icily through a two-hour harangue from German foreign minister Joachim von Ribbentrop, the minister's eyes continually closed, "the pomposity and absurdity of his manner" accentuating the impression that "the man is saturated with hate for England." Welles came

17. Bullitt, *For the President*, 380, 391; Kennedy quoted in Rock, *Chamberlain and Roosevelt*, 236, and Dallek, 213.
18. L&G, *Challenge* 374.

away from an interview with Hitler on the following day "thinking to myself as I got into the car that it was only too tragically plain that all decisions had already been made. The best that could be hoped for was delay, for what little that might be worth." In Paris, motoring through the streets where he had spent much of his privileged childhood, Welles received abundant confirmation of the grim reports that Bullitt had been filing about the state of French morale. He saw only "sullen apathy" in people's faces. "[O]nly in the rarest instances . . . did I obtain the impression of hope or vigor, or even, tragically enough, of the will to courage."

In England, the picture was different. "There was no resemblance between the impressions which I obtained in London and those which had been forced upon me in Paris," Welles later recalled. Many writers have played down Welles's sojourn in London as mere "window dressing" to mask his allegedly more serious mission to Rome and Berlin. But in fact it was Welles's visit to England that had by far the more important consequences, for the simple reason that Welles there confronted in person the stiffening English spirit of defiance — a spirit that Ambassador Kennedy's doom-laden reports had done little to convey. The British, Welles momentously concluded, "would fight to the last ditch. . . . There appeared to be a determination that rather than live once more through the experiences that they had suffered since the autumn of 1938, they would see it through to the end no matter how far off that end might be, nor how bitter the progress toward it might prove." The attitudes of two men in particular made a deep impression on Welles. Anthony Eden, the once and future foreign secretary now in the Dominions Office, forcefully expressed his stark conviction "that nothing but war is possible until Hitlerism has been overthrown." Still more emphatically, Winston Churchill, once and present first lord of the admiralty and soon to become prime minister, bathed Welles in "a cascade of oratory, brilliant and always effective, interlarded with considerable wit." Wreathed in cigar smoke and gesturing with a glass of whiskey and soda (not his first of the day, Welles surmised), Churchill declaimed: "There could be no solution other than outright and complete defeat of Germany [and] the destruction of National Socialism."

Welles returned to Washington at the end of March and submitted his report to the president. His journey had demolished two illusions. On the one hand, his discussions with Mussolini and Hitler conclusively established that the quest for a negotiated peace was "a forlorn hope." On the other hand, contrary to what the history of the Chamberlain ministry and the assessments of Ambassador Kennedy had long suggested, England was not entirely devoid of the will to resist the Nazis. Welles had found among at least some leaders in England, Churchill most conspicuously, a fierce resolution to make war to the end against Hitler. On that resolution, and especially on Churchill's ability to sustain it and to convince others, the Americans above all, of its depth and durability, much history would turn.[19]

NO SOONER had Welles arrived back in the United States than Hitler shattered the false calm of the European standstill. On April 9 Germany occupied Denmark, and German troops swarmed with astonishing speed across southern Norway and into several ports along the fjord-serrated Norwegian coast. An Anglo-French force scrambled to dislodge the invaders, but within weeks the Germans overran the country, and the humiliated Allies withdrew. As the Royal Navy evacuated British units from collapsing Norway in early May, Chamberlain's government finally fell. (In France, Daladier had been replaced by a new prime minister, Paul Reynaud, some seven weeks earlier.) "In the name of God, go!" one backbencher shouted at Chamberlain, quoting Cromwell's words to the Long Parliament in the seventeenth century. "You have sat too long here for any good you have been doing. Depart, I say, and let us have done with you." On May 10 Winston Churchill became prime minister. "I felt as if I were walking with Destiny," Churchill recollected, "and that all my past life had been but a preparation for this hour and for this trial."[20]

The swift subjugation of Norway was but a prelude to the long-delayed attack in the west. On May 10, the same day Churchill clasped Destiny's hand in Britain, the full ferocity of *Blitzkrieg* detonated over Holland, Belgium, and Luxembourg. German airborne troops nullified the Netherlands' historic defense of flooding the invasion routes. Luftwaffe bombers flattened the center of Rotterdam. Panzer (mechanized) divisions raced toward Brussels. On May 14, eighteen hundred German tanks roared out of the Ardennes woods, well north of the useless Maginot Line, and scythed clockwise toward the sea, cutting off the French and British columns that had advanced to check the initial German thrust into the low countries. Luxembourg was unceremoniously overrun. Holland surrendered on May 14, Belgium on May 28. On May

19. Welles, *Time for Decision*, 91, 99, 109, 121, 134, 77.
20. Churchill 1:659, 667.

15, French premier Paul Reynaud telephoned Winston Churchill. "We have been defeated," he said, speaking in English. When a stunned Churchill made no reply, Reynaud went on: "We are beaten; we have lost the battle," a declaration that proved premature by only thirty-two days.

In that chaotic thirty-two-day interval, amid scenes of indescribable pandemonium, including exchanges of gunfire between French and British troops scurrying for the evacuation ships, Britain managed to rescue some 338,000 troops (including over a hundred thousand Frenchmen) from the northern French port of Dunkirk—making, with Norway, two evacuations of an Allied force from the European continent in as many months. Left abandoned on and about the gravelly Dunkirk beaches was all the British Expeditionary Force's heavy equipment— "the whole equipment of the Army to which all the firstfruits of our factories had hitherto been given," Churchill lamented, including ninety thousand rifles, seven thousand tons of ammunition, and 120,000 vehicles.

Churchill's distress reflected his keen understanding of the inexorable economic logic of modern warfare, when machines, and the speed and volume of their manufacture, mattered at least as much as men, and the swiftness and precision of their maneuver, in determining the battle's outcome. The pell-mell retreat from Dunkirk had stripped the British army of the bulk of its implements of war. "Many months must elapse," Churchill brooded, "before this loss could be repaired." On the sea and in the air, the Royal Navy and the Royal Air Force remained viable fighting forces. But on land, Britain was now all but defenseless.[21]

Once the departing British and French troops disappeared across the Channel, the remainder of the French army crumpled before the German onslaught with little more than a flourish of the matador's cape. The panzer columns rolled over obsolete antitank obstacles as if they were tin cans and swept across the Meuse River "as if it did not exist," an awed Bullitt reported. Even the battle-seasoned Churchill was agape at the speed and crushing completeness of the Nazi victory. "I did not comprehend," he later reflected, "the violence of the revolution effected

21. Churchill 2:42, 141–42. One British soldier remembered moving with his artillery regiment to take up defensive positions in Yorkshire. "The total equipment of the 65th Field Regiment, Royal Artillery, at that historic moment was one commandeered civilian truck and a few dozen rifles," he recalled. Ronald Lewin, *Ultra Goes to War* (London: Grafton 1988), 73.

since the last war by the incursion of a mass of fast-moving heavy armour."

On June 10, playing "the role of jackal to Hitler's lion," in Harold Ickes's trenchant phrase, Mussolini declared war on reeling France, and for good measure on Britain as well. *Il Duce* thus dashed any lingering hopes that Italy might yet be detached from its German ally. A week later, on June 17, France asked for an armistice. On June 22, 1940, in the same railway car in which the Germans had been forced to capitulate in 1918, Hitler gleefully accepted the official French surrender. By the terms of the surrender document, Germany occupied all the French Atlantic coastline and the French interior to a demarcation line south of the Loire River. A vassal government, headed by the authoritarian patriarch Marshal Philippe Pétain and installed at the spa town of Vichy, was allowed to preside over the rump French state. "The Battle of France is over," Churchill told a somber House of Commons. "I expect that the Battle of Britain is about to begin." England, Pétain sourly predicted, "will have her neck wrung like a chicken."[22]

The French surrender fundamentally altered the military calculus, whether the equations were plotted in London or Washington. Until the French defeat, British planners had counted on France to absorb the initial shock of a German attack, allowing Britain time to rearm. American strategic doctrine, such as it was, had in turn implicitly rested on the triad of French land power, British sea power, and American industrial power, especially aircraft production for the European democracies. Now France lay prostrate under the Nazi boot. Could Britain, alone and largely disarmed after the Dunkirk debacle, long survive?

Ambassador Bullitt had warned that France would collapse with unseemly haste in the face of German invasion. The events of May and June 1940 had confirmed his worst premonitions. Ambassador Kennedy had been issuing similar warnings about England. In the wake of Dunkirk, a disaster he had accurately foretold, Kennedy repeated his prediction that the Germans, having expelled England from the Continent and conquered her most important ally, would make London a peace offer it could not refuse. Who could now confidently rebut Kennedy's prophecy? And if Britain fell, what then would—or could—America do? If Britain were defeated, Churchill ominously intoned, "then the whole

22. Bullitt, *For the President*, 416; Churchill 2:42, 43, 141; Ickes Diary 3:203; Pétain quoted in Davis 4:560.

world, including the United States, including all that we have known and cared for, will sink into the abyss of a new Dark Age." Speaking at Charlottesville, Virginia, Roosevelt concurred. The United States could not survive as "a lone island in a world dominated by the philosophy of force," Roosevelt said. "Such an island may be the dream of those who still talk and vote as isolationists," but that fatuous and dangerous dream "represents to me," said the president, "the nightmare of a people lodged in prison, handcuffed, hungry, and fed through the bars from day to day by the contemptuous, unpitying masters of other continents. . . . On this tenth day of June 1940, in this University founded by the first great American teacher of democracy, we send forth our prayers and our hopes to those beyond the seas who are maintaining with magnificent valor their battle for freedom."[23]

It was now urgently incumbent on Churchill to vindicate that faith in British valor. He had not only to rally his own countrymen but also to convince the Americans that England had put all the temptations of appeasement behind her. Ultimately, of course, Churchill also hoped to bring the United States into the war at England's side. He made scant secret of those intentions in a famous peroration to a speech at the time of the Dunkirk evacuation, a speech as remarkable for its frank cry for help as for its hypnotic rhetorical flights. South African premier Jan Smuts once remarked of Churchill's speeches that "Every broadcast is a battle."[24] This one, delivered on the floor of the House of Commons on June 4, was at once Churchill's Trafalgar and his Agincourt, a soaring triumph of the orator's art. Speaking in lyrical Elizabethan cadences, Churchill addressed himself as much to Americans as to Britons (though Americans had little idea that it was not Churchill's voice but the recorded voice of his designated impersonator, Norman Shelley, that rumbled into millions of their homes via transatlantic radio):

> We shall go on to the end, we shall fight in France, we shall fight on the seas and oceans, we shall fight with growing confidence and growing strength in the air, we shall defend our island, whatever the cost may be, we shall fight on the beaches, we shall fight on the landing grounds, we shall fight in the fields and in the streets, we shall fight in the hills; we shall never surrender . . . until in God's good time, the

23. David Cannadine, ed., *Blood, Toil, Tears and Sweat: The Speeches of Winston Churchill* (Boston: Houghton Mifflin, 1989), 177; PPA (1940), 261, 263–64.
24. Martin Gilbert, *Churchill: A Life* (New York: Henry Holt, 1991), 690.

new world, with all its power and might, steps forth to the rescue and the liberation of the old.[25]

With those words, Churchill resoundingly confirmed Sumner Welles's estimate of the British leader's bellicosity and tenacity. "It was a great speech," the usually dour Ickes noted in his diary. Roosevelt thought the speech was "firmness itself." "The President and I," wrote Secretary of State Hull, "believed Mr. Churchill meant what he said. . . . There would be no negotiations between London and Berlin." Like a sorcerer's incantation, Churchill's words literally spoke open the door to American cooperation. "Had we had any doubt of Britain's determination to keep on fighting, we would not have taken the steps we did to get material aid to her," Hull later wrote.[26]

Yet not all Americans swooned so readily under the British leader's spell, nor were all doubts about Britain's prospects for survival so swiftly laid to rest. Churchill had charmed open the door to Anglo-American partnership, but only a crack. The winds of war and anxiety could easily slam it shut again. Churchill's toils, verbal and otherwise, were just beginning.

Winston Spencer Churchill was peculiarly suited to the task of summoning the New World to the salvation of the Old. The son of an English father and an American mother, he was the very incarnation of Anglo-American unity. The mysterious caprices of character and the purgatories of his sixty-four years had combined to gird him by 1939 with an impressive armamenture of mettle, guile, and prowess. Graced as well with superbly honed rhetorical gifts, Churchill was a formidable suitor for the hand of his American cousins. On them, he knew, everything depended. All of his wile and wit Churchill now directed to the task of persuading the Americans to become England's comrades-in-arms.

While he courted the American public over the radio, Churchill also cultivated Franklin Roosevelt by telephone and telegraph. They had met only once, in London in 1918. In the early days of the New Deal, Churchill had sent to the White House a copy of his biography of his ancestor John Churchill, the first duke of Marlborough. He inscribed it "with earnest best wishes for the success of the greatest crusade of modern

25. Cannadine, *Blood, Toil, Tears and Sweat*, 165; for the impersonator's role, see *C&R* 1:42.
26. Ickes Diary 3:202; Lash, *Roosevelt and Churchill*, 150.

times." The two men had no further contact until September 11, 1939, just days after Churchill had joined Chamberlain's cabinet as first lord of the admiralty, when Roosevelt sent a personal note: "It is because you and I occupied similar positions in the World War [when Churchill had been first lord of the admiralty and Roosevelt assistant secretary of the navy] that I want you to know how glad I am that you are back in the Admiralty. . . . What I want you and the Prime Minister to know is that I shall at all times welcome it if you will keep me in touch personally with anything you want me to know about." That brief message laid the foundation of a remarkable personal and political relationship.[27]

With Chamberlain's full approval, Churchill had seized the opportunity to open a direct line of communication with the American president. Not the least of the Englishmen's reasons was their desire to offset what they knew were Ambassador Kennedy's increasingly dark assessments of Britain's prospects. Kennedy, one British diplomat observed, was "malevolent and pigeon-livered." Another called the American ambassador "a very foul specimen of double-crosser and defeatist." Given the pessimistic reports that he knew Kennedy to be filing, Churchill shrewdly intuited "that it was a good thing to feed [Roosevelt] at intervals," and to feed him more bracing fare than he was being served by Kennedy.[28]

In Roosevelt, Churchill found a resonant soulmate for his own uncompromising spirit. During the preceding half decade, the president had sometimes been as annoyed with British appeasement as the British had been dismayed with American isolation. "I wish the British would stop this 'we who are about to die, salute thee' attitude," Roosevelt had written exasperatedly to a Harvard historian in early 1939. "What the British need today is a good stiff grog, inducing not only the desire to save civilization but the continued belief that they can do it. In such an event they will have a lot more support from their American cousins." Churchill might well be the man to brew that grog. As for Kennedy, Roosevelt had long since taken his ambassador's measure. "Joe Kennedy . . . has been an appeaser and always will be an appeaser. . . . [H]e's just a pain in the neck to me," Roosevelt exclaimed to Morgenthau in October 1939.[29]

27. C&R 1:23, 24.
28. Rock, Chamberlain and Roosevelt, 277; Lash, Roosevelt and Churchill, 138.
29. Freidel, Rendezvous with Destiny, 312–13; John Morton Blum, From the Morgenthau Diaries: Years of Urgency, 1938–1941 (Boston: Houghton Mifflin, 1965), 102.

Yet Kennedy's reports could not be so easily dismissed. The messenger may have been a pain in the neck, but his message had a sobering plausibility. Britain might indeed be about to die, or at least to bow subserviently before Hitler's overbearing force, however hearty the drafts of rhetorical grog that poured from Churchill's prodigious oratorical well. Even Roosevelt thought on at least one occasion in the spring of 1940 that "the English were going to get licked."[30] Just as Kennedy surmised, influential members of the British government, even at this late date, still entertained the idea of reaching an understanding with Hitler, not least because they continued to despair of American assistance. "U.S. looks pretty useless," Alexander Cadogan, senior adviser to Lord Halifax, still the foreign secretary in Churchill's government as he had been in Chamberlain's, noted at the time of the French collapse. "Well, we must die without them," Cadogan concluded.[31] At a secret meeting of the five-member War Cabinet on May 28, 1940, Halifax, prince of appeasers, urged taking up Mussolini's offer to mediate a settlement. Chamberlain, stripped of the premiership but still a political force to be reckoned with, agreed. He admonished his colleagues that they should be "ready to consider decent terms if such were offered to us." These sentiments outraged Churchill, whose overriding goal was to purge them and all their vestiges from the British body politic. Speaking to the full cabinet moments later, the new prime minister administered a potent verbal emetic: "[E]very man of you would rise up and tear me down from my place if I were for one moment to contemplate parley or surrender," Churchill fulminated. "If this long island history of ours is to end at last, let it end only when each one of us lies choking in his own blood upon the ground." Churchill "was quite magnificent," one minister wrote in his diary. He was "the man, and the only man we have for this task."[32]

The new prime minister also proffered a bracing round to Roosevelt on May 15, just five days after assuming office. Coyly styling himself "Former Naval Person," a transparent reference to his previous stints at the admiralty and an uncharacteristically labored attempt to emphasize his common ground with Roosevelt, Churchill penned a chillingly frank overview of the British situation and initiated what would become a

30. Dallek, 220.
31. David Dilks, ed., *The Secret Diaries of Sir Alexander Cadogan* (New York: G. P. Putnam's Sons, 1972) 299.
32. Gilbert, *Churchill: A Life*, 651.

cascade of importunings for American help. Through all of Churchill's bravura, Roosevelt could hardly fail to register the prime minister's tone of desperation.

"Although I have changed my office," Churchill ingratiatingly began, "I am sure you would not wish me to discontinue our intimate, private correspondence." Then he quickly got down to cases:

> As you are no doubt aware, the scene has darkened swiftly. The enemy has a marked preponderance in the air. . . . The small countries are simply smashed up one by one, like matchwood. . . . We expect to be attacked here ourselves, both from the air and by parachute and air borne troops in the near future, and are getting ready for them. If necessary, we shall continue the war alone and we are not afraid of that. But I trust you realize, Mr. President, that the voice and force of the United States may count for nothing if they are withheld too long. You may have a completely subjugated, Nazified Europe established with astonishing swiftness, and the weight may be more than we can bear. . . . Immediate needs are: first of all, the loan of forty or fifty of your older destroyers. . . . Secondly, we want several hundred of the latest types of aircraft. . . . Thirdly, anti-aircraft equipment and ammunition. . . . Fourthly, [we need] to purchase steel in the United States. This also applies to other materials. We shall go on paying dollars for as long as we can, but I should like to feel reasonably sure that when we can pay no more, you will give us the stuff all the same. Fifthly . . . , the visit of a United States squadron to Irish ports, which might well be prolonged, would be invaluable. Sixthly, I am looking to you to keep that Japanese dog quiet in the Pacific.

This was an extraordinary communication from one head of government to another. It bordered on the presumptuous in its naked candor and nearly abject pleading. Churchill soon grew more brazen still. Just five days later he wrote to Roosevelt that though he personally intended to fight to the finish, should things go badly, "[m]embers of the present administration would likely go down [and] if members of the present administration were finished and others came in to parley amid the ruins, you must not be blind to the fact that the sole remaining bargaining counter with Germany would be the fleet, and if this country was left by the United States to its fate no one would have the right to blame those then responsible if they made the best terms they could for the surviving inhabitants. Excuse me, Mr. President, putting this nightmare bluntly. Evidently I could not answer for my successors who in utter despair and helplessness might well have to accommodate themselves to the German will." Churchill conjured this dark prospect again on June 15: "I know well, Mr. President, that your eye will have already searched these depths but I feel I have the right to place on record the vital matter in which American interests are at stake in our battle." A pro-German government might come to power in England and turn the British Isles into a "vassal state of the Hitler empire," making a gift of the British fleet to Germany in the process. At that moment, said Churchill, "overwhelming sea power would be in Hitler's hands."[33]

From another man's pen, or in another man's eye, these forebodings could have been taken for blackmail. Indeed, a British Foreign Office memorandum at the time so described them: "blackmail, and not very good blackmail at that."[34] But Roosevelt chose to ignore the uncloaked threat that if America failed to act, appeasement might yet dictate England's fate, with consequences for America that needed little spelling out. Instead, the president immediately assented to almost all of Churchill's requests. The day after receiving the prime minister's list of needs of May 15, Roosevelt replied that he could not transfer destroyers without authorization from Congress (a rationale that would soon evaporate) but that he was doing his utmost on the other items. Aircraft deliveries were being expedited; antiaircraft equipment and ammunition would be sent; so would steel; he would take under advisement the proposed fleet visit to Ireland; and he had already dispatched the main body of the U.S. fleet to Hawaii, as a warning signal to Japan. On the matter of whether the United States would "give us the stuff all the same," when Allied dollar reserves were exhausted, the president was studiously silent. "The best of luck to you," Roosevelt genially concluded.[35]

The same day, Roosevelt made a dramatic appearance before a joint session of Congress to ask for a supplemental defense appropriation of nearly $1.3 billion. The funds were to begin building what was soon dubbed a "two-ocean navy." No less boldly, the president called for a production goal of "at least 50,000 planes a year"—a truly fantastic leap when measured against the niggardly output of military aircraft since Roosevelt's rather ineffective call for "airplanes—and lots of them" in 1938. Finally, in a clear reinforcement of his short-of-war strategy, Roosevelt insisted that the lion's share of that hugely increased aircraft production should be delivered to overseas buyers. "For the permanent

33. C&R 1:37–38, 40, 49.
34. Lash, Roosevelt and Churchill, 135.
35. C&R 1:38–39.

record," the president pointedly declared, "I ask the Congress not to take any action which would in any way hamper or delay the delivery of American-made planes to foreign nations." Unknown to the general public, Roosevelt had already quietly directed that the Allies would have "first call" on the planes then beginning to roll, with painful slowness, off American assembly lines. Just weeks earlier, Britain and France had placed the first substantial orders for aircraft—five thousand airframes and ten thousand engines of the most advanced design.[36]

Roosevelt's ready agreement to Churchill's requests, and his emphasis on producing arms for foreign buyers, pitched the president once again into a bitter confrontation with his own senior diplomatic and military advisers. Ambassador Kennedy cabled on the very day of Churchill's historic supplication that complying with the British demands would "leave the United States holding the bag for a war in which the Allies expected to be beaten. . . . It seems to me," Kennedy concluded, "that if we had to fight to protect our lives, we would do better fighting in our own back yard."[37] Several key American military leaders emphatically seconded Kennedy's opinion. Their ingrained martial habits of prudence combined with their singular commitment to American defense to produce a cast of mind that was deeply, fearfully skeptical of the president's initiatives. They found Roosevelt's key assumption—that Britain would hold out—dubious, to say the least. They saw their supreme obligation as recruiting, training, and fielding an *American* fighting force, which at that moment scarcely existed and which could not be created without arms and equipment. American production, they argued, must flow to American soldiers, sailors, and airmen, not be tossed away across the sea in a vain farewell gesture to the drowning British. George C. Marshall was reminded of the so-called amalgamation controversy in World War I, when General Pershing had resolutely resisted incessant Allied demands to incorporate American troops directly into Allied units, demands that threatened the very existence of an independent American army. Marshall was not about to cave in where Pershing, the most celebrated living American military hero and

36. *PPA* (1940), 202. For Roosevelt's decision to give the Allies "first call" on American production, see Ickes Diary 3:84–85, describing a conversation with Postmaster General Jim Farley in December 1939. What would happen, Farley asked, if England or France wanted airplanes and we wanted them at the same time? "The President said that it was a matter of confidential information, but that, up to a certain number at any rate, we would let England and France have the first call."

37. L&G, *Challenge*, 481–82.

his own revered mentor, had stood firm. Marshall worried especially that shipping aircraft to England would cripple the American pilot-training program. Air corps head Hap Arnold estimated that the transfer of a hundred aircraft to the Allies would replace only three days' supply at the rate they were then being shot down but would set back the pilot-training schedule in the United States by six months. "It is a drop in the bucket on the other side and it is a very vital necessity on this side, and that is that," Marshall briskly concluded, and he so advised the secretary of war on May 18: "I regret to tell you that I do not think we can afford to submit ourselves to the delay and consequences involved in accommodating the British Government."[38]

Roosevelt himself agonized over the precariousness of his position that maximum possible aid should go to England. "I might guess wrong," he confided to Ickes on June 4, 1940, in a rare revelation of the doubts that must have besieged him, "and it is nothing more than a guess. And if I should guess wrong, the results might be serious. If we should send some destroyers across, they would be of no particular use to the Allies but they might serve further to enrage Hitler. We cannot tell the turn that the war will take, and there is no use endangering ourselves unless we can achieve some results for the Allies." Ickes, appreciating "that the President was in a delicate position," agreed. "If you do send some help with bad consequences to ourselves, the people will blame you just as they will blame you if you don't send the help and the Allies are crushed." Ickes's concurral was cold comfort — but he described with chiseled accuracy the awful dilemma that Roosevelt faced, a dilemma whose perplexities and dangers vastly deepened when France fell.[39]

Through May and June 1940 the president stuck unflinchingly with his risky bet. Sometimes he had to cudgel his subordinates into backing his high-stakes gamble. Three questions were at issue. First, should the Allies have prior claim on new American aircraft production? Second, could the U.S. Army transfer from its own arsenals to Britain sufficient arms to make good the losses at Dunkirk? Third, could the U.S. Navy release the destroyers that Churchill had requested? Roosevelt answered yes to all three and brooked no opposition. When Secretary of War Harry H. Woodring, a Kansas isolationist committed to a "Fortress America" strategy, balked at releasing aircraft for overseas delivery, Roosevelt ordered him either to go along with the program or resign. Informed

38. Morgenthau Diary, 318–19.
39. Ickes Diary 3:200.

that Hap Arnold continued to complain about the devastating impact of Roosevelt's priorities on the army air corps, Roosevelt said brusquely, "Well, if Arnold won't conform, maybe we will have to move him out of town," perhaps to the career burial-ground of Guam. Arnold soon bowed to the presidential will. When Secretary of the Navy Charles Edison reported that the navy's judge advocate general considered any destroyer transfer to be unlawful, Roosevelt denounced the navy's highest legal officer as nothing but a "sea lawyer" and advised Edison to send the troublesome subordinate away on a vacation. "If the man next in line didn't know any more law, he should also be sent on a vacation, and so on down the list." Edison persisted in presenting the Judge Advocate General's case. "[F]orget it and do what I told you to do," the president snapped. Within weeks, Roosevelt shoved both Woodring and Edison out of the Cabinet. A newly potent, decisive Roosevelt was emerging, a different man from the president who had been politically wounded and checkmated through much of his second term. Now he was ready to play the lion, and he appeared to relish the role.[40]

Virtually commanding his military chiefs to declare certain items as "surplus," the key to their legal release, Roosevelt forced some of the arms transfers through. Churchill's question about the destroyers still remained unanswered, but on the night of June 11, New Jersey stevedores began handling some six hundred freight-car loads of Enfield rifles, machine guns, 75mm field guns, and over one hundred million rounds of ammunition onto British ships. The military men who grudgingly expedited the shipments were aghast at the spectacle unfolding on the New Jersey docks. "[I]f we were required to mobilize after having released guns necessary for this mobilization and were found to be short in artillery materiel," one army officer warned, "everyone who was a party to the deal might hope to be found hanging from a lamp post."[41]

Roosevelt could not indefinitely continue stuffing his undefended hunches down the throats of his cabinet secretaries and his senior military and naval commanders. On June 13, 1940, searching for system and consensus, he set down his strategic assumptions on paper. He requested the army and navy chiefs to assess the reasonableness of his premises and to comment on the economic, political, military, and psychological implications of his aid-to-Britain policy. This meager and imperfectly prophetic outline, penned just two days after the forced arms

40. Morgenthau Diary, 301–32; Ickes Diary 3:202.
41. Watson, *Chief of Staff*, 312.

shipments of June 11 and less than a week before the fate of France was finally sealed, set off an even angrier round of controversy that reverberated through the frantic summer of 1940 and beyond.

Peering with as much confidence as he could muster into the future, Roosevelt laid out his vision of the world six months hence. He ventured six predictions:

1. Time. Fall and winter of 1940.
2. Britain and the British Empire are still intact.
3. France is occupied, but the French Government and the remainder of its forces are still resisting, perhaps in North Africa.
4. The surviving forces of the British and French Navies, in conjunction with U.S. Navy, are holding the Persian Gulf, Red Sea and the Atlantic from Morocco to Greenland. The Allied fleets have probably been driven out of the Eastern Mediterranean, and are maintaining a precarious hold on the Western Mediterranean.
5. Allied land forces are maintaining their present hold in the Near East. Turkey maintains its present political relationship to the Allies.
6. Russia and Japan are inactive, taking no part in the war.
7. The U.S. active in the war, but with naval and air forces only. Plane production is progressing to its maximum. America is providing part of Allied pilots. Morocco and Britain are being used as bases of supplies shipped from the Western Hemisphere. American shipping is transporting supplies to the Allies. The U.S. Navy is providing most of the force for the Atlantic blockade (Morocco to Greenland).[42]

Army Chief of Staff Marshall and his counterpart, Chief of Naval Operations Admiral Harold Stark, took this presidential prognosis under intense advisement for the next several days. At a White House meeting on June 22 they presented Roosevelt with their own considered response. On the crucial point—Britain's survivability—they took strong issue with the president's assumptions. They agreed instead with Ambassador Kennedy that "[t]he actual invasion and overrunning of England by German military forces" appeared to be "within the range of possibility." Consequently, they advised that "to release to Great Britain additional war material now in the hands of the armed forces will seriously weaken our present state of defense and will not materially assist the British forces"—an opinion they had long held and now stated of-

42. Maurice Matloff and Edwin M. Snell, *United States Army in World War II: The War Department: Strategic Planning for Coalition Warfare, 1941–1942* (Washington: Department of the Army, 1953), 14.

ficially. They also took the occasion to criticize Roosevelt's decision to keep substantial portions of the fleet at Pearl Harbor, a move they judged too feeble to deter Japan but belligerent enough to antagonize her, and in any case a deployment that dangerously weakened American naval strength in the far more important Atlantic theater. American unreadiness in all arms was so great, Marshall and Stark counseled, that the United States should carefully husband its own resources and scrupulously avoid provoking any of its potential adversaries. Meanwhile, the administration should look to hemispheric defense by strengthening relations with South America, adopting conscription as a step toward "complete military and naval mobilization" and taking all means to speed up arms production, including putting workers onto seven-day overtime shifts in the major arms plants.[43]

Roosevelt listened respectfully but rejected his chiefs' advice. On their last point, the president vigorously demurred. With unemployment still high, he would tolerate no changes in the standard five-day workweek. So long as the Depression lingered, jobs were more important than expedited arms production, though Roosevelt surely appreciated that increased arms production eventually meant more jobs, and lots of them. Nor did he assent to the recommendation to shift fleet elements to the Atlantic. He accepted the necessity for conscription, though he downgraded the goal of "complete" mobilization to "progressive" mobilization. Most important, Roosevelt mulishly reconfirmed his commitment to keep aid flowing to Britain.

Given the formally declared opposition of his military and naval chiefs, not to mention, in this election year, the preponderantly contrary opinion of the American public, two-thirds of whom believed Britain was about to go down, Roosevelt acted with remarkable boldness — or with wanton recklessness. Former NRA director Hugh Johnson, now an outspoken isolationist and still a fountain of invective, charged that Roosevelt was irresponsibly "shooting craps with destiny."[44]

For their part, the British knew on what rolls of the dice their destiny depended. "The degree to which the U.S.A. will come to our assistance rather than concentrate upon the defence of her own hemisphere," a Foreign Office official observed, "depends in the highest degree upon our ability to prove that we are vigorously prosecuting the war." No one

43. Matloff and Snell, *Strategic Planning for Coalition Warfare, 1941–1942*, 14; Watson, *Chief of Staff*, 111.
44. Dallek, 231.

appreciated that logic more acutely than Churchill. Speaking at a secret session of the House of Commons on June 20, he dwelled at length on the attitude of the United States and how Britain might affect it. No formal record was kept, but his surviving notes capture his themes: "The heroic struggle of England best chance of bringing them in. . . . A tribute to Roosevelt. It depends upon our resolute bearing and holding out until Election issues are settled there."

Churchill soon found a dramatic opportunity to demonstrate British resolution. Elements of the French fleet, nominally under Vichy's control by the terms of the French-German armistice but clearly vulnerable to German seizure, lay at anchor, fully combat-ready and with their French crews still aboard, at the naval base of Mers el-Kebir, near Oran in French Algeria. Taking care to apprise Roosevelt in advance, Churchill ordered a Royal Navy task force to steam for Mers el-Kebir. The British arrived on July 3 and demanded that the French commander either surrender or scuttle his ships. When he refused to do either, the Royal Navy gunners opened fire, sinking several French vessels and killing 1,297 French sailors. The British seamen took little pleasure in this attack on their erstwhile allies. But however distasteful to the men who executed it, the Mers el-Kebir incident gave bloody punctuation to Churchill's belligerent pronouncements. Mers el-Kebir was "the turning point in our fortunes," Churchill later remarked. "[I]t made the world realise that we were in earnest in our intentions to carry on."[45]

Mers el-Kebir ruthlessly displayed Britain's ability to deliver a punch. There soon followed a test of the far more consequential matter of her ability to take one. The Battle of Britain, predicted by Churchill at the time of the French-German armistice, opened on July 10, 1940. Great German aerial flotillas, wave after wave of Heinkel and Junkers bombers accompanied by phalanxes of Messerschmitt fighters, began bombing British coastal installations, preparatory to a cross-Channel invasion. "The Führer has ordered me to crush Britain with my Luftwaffe," German air minister Hermann Goering told his generals. "By means of hard blows I plan to have this enemy . . . down on his knees in the nearest future."[46] But this enemy, uniquely in Hitler's experience to date, declined to genuflect. Against forbidding odds, the Royal Air Force struggled instead to drape a ragged protective curtain of Spitfire and Hurricane fighter planes over the British Isles. Aided by the new

45. Lash, *Roosevelt and Churchill*, 151, 165; Gilbert, *Churchill: A Life*, 667.
46. John Keegan, *The Second World War* (New York: Viking, 1989), 91.

technology of radar, which gave advance warning of German bombing runs, and by the cracking of the top-secret German "Enigma" codes, which provided further intelligence about the tactics and targets of the attackers, British Fighter Command managed to keep the Germans at bay through July. Goering shifted his targeting to RAF airfields in August, and then to terror-bombing of London in September—the "Blitz," Londoners soon named this phase of the battle. Americans followed the drama keenly, tuning their radios to Edward R. Murrow's nicotine-lubricated voice reporting from BBC House. "London is burning," Murrow began nightly in his trademark funereal tone, and Americans anxiously awaited the apparently inevitable announcement of Britain's final subjugation.

As the Battle of Britain raged, Churchill dunned Roosevelt anew for aid. On July 16, Enigma cryptanalysts, working in tweedy academic surroundings in the Buckinghamshire village of Bletchley, the priceless value of their top-secret unit implied in their operation's code name—Ultra—furnished him with a copy of Hitler's Führer Directive No. 16: "I have decided to prepare a landing operation [code-named Sealion] against England," Hitler instructed his generals. This intercepted message confirmed Churchill's worst fears. It now "seemed certain," he later recalled, "that the man was going to try." With invasion imminent, Churchill pleaded again for the destroyers he had first requested on May 15. "Mr. President," he cabled to Roosevelt on July 31, "with great respect I must tell you that in the long history of the world, this is a thing to do now. . . . I am sure that with your comprehension of the sea affair, you will not let this crux of the battle go wrong for the want of these destroyers."[47]

The requested destroyers were ostensibly intended to help screen the English Channel against the expected German amphibious assault. But Roosevelt and Churchill alike understood that the American vessels had more psychological and political utility than they had naval value. The ships in question were four-funneled World War I–era heirlooms, barnacled old battlewagons in no condition for modern naval warfare. It would take months to refit them for use by the Royal Navy. If invasion were indeed as imminent as Churchill believed in July, they would never be ready on time and might in any event prove more a liability than an asset on the battle line. But both leaders also knew that morale and perception were scarcely less important than metal and firepower

47. Churchill 2:296, 302; C&R 1:57.

at this pivotal moment. Delivering the destroyers to Britain would bolster British spirits, signal Hitler that the patience of the neutral Americans was wearing thin, and, most significant, help drive home to those same Americans their stake in the struggle against Nazism. For those reasons, at least as much as for his "comprehension of the sea affair," Roosevelt was determined to transfer the vessels.[48]

AS ROOSEVELT WELL KNEW, however, even presidential determination is not always dispositive. With the aircraft sales and arms transfers of the preceding weeks, Roosevelt had stretched his constitutional prerogatives to their outermost boundaries. He had also risked his own political neck. Now, in the summer of 1940, his neck was more than ever on the block.

It is a quirk of the American constitutional system that presidential elections come by the calendar, not by the crisis. By awkward coincidence, the quadrennial American political ritual of nomination, campaign, and election fell amidst the abounding crises of the desperate summer and fall months of 1940. Britain's fate hung by what Churchill described as "a slender thread," a makeshift gossamer woven of flimsy planes and a handful of valiant but green pilots. As if persistent isolationism and the uncertain outcome of the Battle of Britain were not enough to vex his calculations in that excruciating moment, Roosevelt also had to reckon with the inevitable electoral season.

Just when Roosevelt decided to seek a third term as president remains a puzzle. He kept his own counsel more closely than usual. Even Eleanor did not know for certain what his intentions were or by what process he eventually shaped them. Custom dictated that he give up the office; no man before him had dared breach George Washington's two-term example. As 1940 opened, Roosevelt gave every appearance that he would follow tradition and retire to his beloved Hyde Park estate. There he was actively supervising the construction of Top Cottage, a snug stone-and-timber hideaway in a remote corner of the sprawling grounds. He seemed already to be looking to his place in history, setting a precedent of his own with the erection at Hyde Park of the nation's first presidential library, a repository for the records of his administration and a place where he could edit his papers and perhaps write his memoirs. He was looking to bolster his personal financial future as well. In

48. Some of the destroyers, it turned out, were scarcely seaworthy, barely able to make the Atlantic crossing. See Lash, *Roosevelt and Churchill*, 272.

January he signed a contract with *Collier's* magazine to produce a series of articles after leaving office, for a fee of seventy-five thousand dollars a year, his presidential salary. "I do not want to run," he confided to Morgenthau at that time, but then added, "unless between now and the convention things get very, very much worse in Europe."[49]

Things got infinitely worse, of course, and, though the particulars of Roosevelt's thinking remain obscure, the European crisis surely provided the ultimate explanation for his eventual decision to try to shatter the two-term tradition. The European scene weighed not only on Roosevelt's mind but also on the strategy of his political adversaries. Had it not been for the collapse of France, the Republican Party might well have nominated for president one of its powerful senatorial barons, such as Ohio's Robert Taft or Michigan's Arthur Vandenberg. But both those midwestern senators were unyielding isolationists. When the Republican convention was gaveled to order in Philadelphia on June 24, just two days after the French surrender, the delegates were in no mood to nominate a candidate as parochial as Taft or as insular as Vandenberg, for all the senators' standing in the Grand Old Party. Instead, in one of the most astonishing surprises in the history of American presidential politics, unmatched for its sheer improbability since the Democratic nomination of Horace Greeley in 1872, the Republicans chose an erstwhile Democrat and rank political amateur, Wendell Willkie.

Open-faced and tousle-haired, the boyish, plain-spoken, forty-eight-year-old Willkie was a rumpled and charismatic Hoosier who had made good as a corporate attorney and utilities executive, prompting Harold Ickes's impish description of him as "a simple barefoot Wall Street lawyer." As head of Commonwealth and Southern Corporation, a public utility holding company with extensive interests in the South, Willkie had dueled with Roosevelt's TVA over the issue of public power. By the late 1930s he had emerged as a leading spokesman for those in the business community who felt themselves aggrieved by the New Deal. Yet Willkie was no old-fashioned conservative. He gave his blessing to most of the New Deal's social legislation and conspicuously refrained from endorsing right-wing Republican preachments about the virtues of unbridled laissez-faire. Instead, he denounced the Democrats as having acquired a vested political interest in the Depression and therefore as having willfully throttled the wealth-making and job-creating potential of private enterprise — the nut of the political case that the Republicans

49. Freidel, *Rendezvous with Destiny*, 328.

would make against the Democrats for a generation or more to come, and an argument that marked the seismic shift in American politics that the New Deal had wrought. Until just a few years earlier Willkie himself had been a registered Democrat. Former Indiana Republican senator James E. Watson, on hearing that the ex-Democrat Willkie was his party's nominee, fumed: "If a whore repented and wanted to join the church I'd personally welcome her and lead her up the aisle to a pew. But, by the Eternal, I'd not ask her to lead the choir the first night."[50]

Most important, Willkie was an unshakeable internationalist. He had publicly criticized Nazi aggression and had spoken out eloquently in favor of repealing the arms embargo and in support of aid to Britain. Just for those reasons he appealed strongly to eastern, Anglophilic Republicans, who saw Willkie as an instrument with which to contain their party's formidable isolationist wing. Backed by internationalist Republicans like the influential and deep-pocketed publishers Henry Luce and Roy Howard, a Willkie-for-president organization had formed as early as 1939. On the sixth ballot at Philadelphia, Willkie won the nomination. In one of the shotgun marriages typical of presidential politics, his running mate was Oregon's Senator Charles McNary, who favored public power projects as fervently as Willkie condemned them.

Enigmatically refraining from any specific statement of his intentions, Roosevelt remained at the White House while the Democrats prepared for their own July convention in Chicago, the sentimental site of Roosevelt's first nomination in 1932 and, more important, a city firmly under the fist of Mayor Edward J. Kelly, the local Democratic boss. Kelly could be counted on to pack the galleries with Roosevelt enthusiasts and to help orchestrate a supposedly spontaneous surge to draft Roosevelt. Sphinx-like, Roosevelt still made no overt move to seek the nomination as the conventioneers poured into Chicago. His precedent-breaking third-term candidacy must have the appearance, at least, of responding to enthusiastic pleading from the delegates. In reality he was by now determined to have the nomination. The delegates, however, threatened to flub their designated roles. They appeared to be going about the chore of nominating Roosevelt, one newspaper observed, with all the gusto of a chain gang. At the critical juncture, as the presiding officer read a statement from Roosevelt that the delegates were free to vote for whomever they pleased, Kelly ordered a pro-Roosevelt demonstration to begin. From the loudspeakers an unidentified voice bellowed, "We want

50. Davis 4:582.

Roosevelt," and the demonstrators mimicked and swelled the cry, chanting it for nearly an hour. Meanwhile, a reporter tracked the mysterious voice to the convention hall's basement, where he found Mayor Kelly's superintendent of sewers seated at a microphone, surrounded by amplification equipment and a detailed script for stimulating the "spontaneous" spectacle on the floor above.

Thanks to the "voice from the sewer," the charade of a "draft" was at least momentarily sustained, and Roosevelt was nominated on the first ballot. In a provocative move, he designated as his running mate Agriculture Secretary Henry Wallace, a former progressive Republican who had first registered as a Democrat only in 1936. Wallace was an unreconstructed liberal reformer and an unflinching New Dealer, qualities that recommended him to Roosevelt. But old-guard Democratic Party regulars deeply distrusted Wallace as an apostate Republican and as a doe-eyed mystic who symbolized all they found objectionable about the hopelessly utopian, market-manipulating, bureaucracy-breeding New Deal. Boos echoed through the Chicago convention hall when Roosevelt's choice of Wallace was announced. The delegates appeared to be on the brink of mutiny. Roosevelt later tried to appease Democratic conservatives by naming RFC director Jesse Jones, an archconservative Texan, as secretary of commerce. But for the moment, it was only after Roosevelt threatened to decline his own nomination if Wallace were not on the ticket, and after a conciliatory speech by Eleanor Roosevelt, the first wife of a nominee ever to address a national political convention, that the delegates grudgingly yielded. Their grumpy acquiescence and the soon-to-be-announced Jones appointment provided yet more proof of the deep ideological divisions in the Democratic Party.

When he named Wallace his vice-presidential partner, Roosevelt flung a farewell bouquet to the old progressive wing of the Republican Party — the wing of George Norris, Hiram Johnson, and Robert La Follette Jr. — with whom he had once hoped to forge a lasting partnership for liberalism. In a far more telling pair of appointments in June, unmistakably signaling that foreign policy, not domestic reform, was now his urgent priority, Roosevelt had extended his hand to an altogether different Republican constituency. In the process, he cut some important political ground out from under Willkie. Remembering the sad fate of his old chief, Woodrow Wilson, whose foreign policies had been unraveled by partisan wrangling, Roosevelt named two prominent Republicans to his cabinet just four days before the GOP gathered in Philadelphia. Frank Knox now became secretary of the navy and Henry L. Stimson secretary of war (to replace the argumentative Charles Edison and the recalcitrant Harry Woodring, respectively). Knox was a onetime Rough Rider, a well-known Chicago newspaper editor, the Republican vice-presidential nominee in 1936, and a vociferous internationalist.

Stimson was an elder statesman of impeccable personal and political pedigree. Born to wealth, he had been educated at Andover, Yale College, and Harvard Law School. Effortlessly assuming his station in what passed for the American aristocracy of his day, he had served as secretary of war in William Howard Taft's administration and as secretary of state under Herbert Hoover. The arc of Stimson's career traced the breathtaking transformations in American life in the near-century since the Civil War had ended. Born during Reconstruction, Stimson was seventy-three years old in 1940, a man who had lived out his boyhood in the bow-and-arrow era of the Plains Indian wars and was destined to help direct a thoroughly modern world war to its shattering nuclear conclusion. Shaped by the values of the nineteenth century, Stimson was a paragon of probity, both public and private (the Stimsons did not entertain divorced persons). He was also the very model, indeed monument, of internationalist Republicanism, a figure of towering prestige and unflappable self-possession that immunized him against the inevitable accusations that he had betrayed his party by accepting Roosevelt's invitation to join the cabinet. Stimson was, if anything, an even more ardent and outspoken internationalist than Knox. In the months leading up to his appointment, he had grown increasingly uncomfortable with his isolationist associates in the Republican Party. On the very eve of his cabinet appointment, Stimson delivered an earnest radio address urging maximum possible aid to Britain, including U.S. Navy escorts to shepherd the great British merchant convoys bearing munitions across the Atlantic — a position that Roosevelt himself had not dared to take publicly.

The appointments of Knox and Stimson bespoke Roosevelt's high-minded intention to seek bipartisan consensus in a time of grave national crisis. "Not since that titanic conservative, Alexander Hamilton, handed the election of 1800 to his hated rival, the liberal Jefferson, to save and unite the nation in a time of crisis," wrote Dorothy Thompson in the *New York Herald Tribune*, "has a political leader of America made a more magnanimous and wholehearted gesture." The Knox and Stimson appointments had a less edifying partisan logic as well. Roosevelt knew that these two high-profile cabinet nominations would drive a wedge into Republican ranks on the issue of aid to Britain, isolating the isolationists and thereby weakening the hand of whoever was the Republican presidential candidate.[51]

Willkie thus commenced his already curious political career with considerable handicaps. He attempted to overcome them by campaigning with muscular and sometimes madcap eccentricity. An energetic but amateurish speaker, he often ad-libbed witlessly—as when he promised to replace social worker Frances Perkins with a new secretary of labor drawn from labor's own ranks, and then added gratuitously, "and it won't be a woman, either." He frequently grew so animated at the podium that he jittered away from the fixed microphone—a fatal mistake in the radio age.

Yet whatever his crotchets as a campaigner, Willkie shared enough of Roosevelt's own internationalist convictions that his candidacy, along with the Knox and Stimson appointments, helped to neutralize foreign policy as an issue for much of the campaign. Roosevelt, for example, had hesitated to embrace the Burke-Wadsworth selective service bill, a bipartisan proposal then making its way through Congress, though its provisions fitted well with his own declared policies. In defiance of Marshall's and Stark's call for "complete mobilization," and in keeping with Roosevelt's short-of-war thinking, the selective service bill mandated just one year of service for draftees and forbade their deployment outside the Western Hemisphere. The bill would nevertheless impose the first peacetime draft in American history, and its potential electoral fallout chafed on Roosevelt. Even "a limited form of selective draft," he told a correspondent, "may very easily defeat the Democratic National Ticket."[52] But when a reporter advised Willkie that "if you want to win the election you will come out against the proposed draft," Willkie shot back: "I would rather not win the election than do that." Selective service, Willkie declared in a campaign speech, "is the only democratic way in which to assure the trained and competent man-power we need in our national defense."[53] With the backing of both presidential candidates, the bill passed on September 16. One month later, more than sixteen million men between the ages of twenty-one and thirty-five were registered on the draft rolls.

The vexed and long-delayed destroyer transfer was a different matter.

51. *New York Herald Tribune*, October 9, 1940, 25.
52. Dallek, 249.
53. Ellsworth Barnard, *Wendell Willkie, Fighter for Freedom* (Marquette: Northern Michigan University Press, 1966), 204–5.

By early August, Roosevelt thought he had hit upon a device for getting the destroyers into Churchill's hands. He proposed to exchange the warships for a gift from Britain to the United States of two naval bases in Newfoundland and Bermuda and ninety-nine year leases on additional bases in the British West Indies. In this form, the destroyers-for-bases deal could be presented as a means of upgrading hemispheric defense, thus shrewdly blunting isolationist criticism and neatly sidestepping a statutory prohibition on the release of equipment deemed essential for national defense.[54] The exchange provisos of the deal also constituted a shaky but arguably supportable legal basis on which to ask Congress for authorization to make the transfer. Would Willkie use his good offices with congressional Republicans to facilitate the transaction? Roosevelt sent his personal emissary, journalist William Allen White, head of the Committee to Defend America by Aiding the Allies, to put the question to Willkie, then campaigning in Colorado. "Willkie ducked," White reported, "for various good reasons. . . . [H]e feels a natural diffidence about assuming Congressional leadership before his ears are dry." But, White told the president, "It's not as bad as it seems." Willkie would not endorse the deal, but neither would he condemn it outright. Bereft of Willkie's help with Congress, Roosevelt brooded that he "might get impeached" if he proceeded with the transfer.[55] But reassured that Willkie would not make the destroyer-bases deal a major campaign issue, Roosevelt eventually bypassed Congress altogether and ordered the exchange on his own executive authority. It was consummated on September 2.

The destroyer-bases deal was a ringing triumph for Churchill. In a speech honoring the airmen waging the Battle of Britain — "Never in the field of human conflict was so much owed by so many to so few," he said, coining the soubriquet ("the Few") by which the RAF pilots would forever be known — Churchill also extravagantly hailed the

54. The National Defense Appropriation Act that Roosevelt had just signed on June 28, 1940, contained a clause that reflected the mounting American concern that Roosevelt was doing to America by policy what Dunkirk had wrought upon Britain by retreat — exhausting the nation's already meager weapons stockpile. The act permitted the transfer only of equipment that had been certified as not essential for national defense. Since the understrength navy had just declared even its aging World War I–vintage ships indispensable for that purpose, the act's language appeared to present an insuperable obstacle to transferring the destroyers to Britain.

55. L&G, *Challenge*, 754; David E. Lilienthal, *The Journals of David E. Lilienthal* (New York: Harper and Row, 1964), 1:209.

destroyer-bases agreement. Well he might have. The deal helped bring closer to realization the vision that had guided all Churchill's foreign policy since assuming office. It signified, he said, the deepening of a process whereby "the English-speaking democracies, the British Empire and the United States, will have to be somewhat mixed up together in some of their affairs for mutual and general advantage. For my part, looking out upon the future, I do not view the process with any misgivings. I could not stop it if I wished; no one can stop it. Like the Mississippi," Churchill artfully concluded for the benefit of his American audience, "it just keeps rolling along. Let it roll. Let it roll on full flood, inexorable, irresistible, benignant, to broader lands and better days."[56]

The destroyers themselves did not roll on with comparable inexorability. By the end of the year, only nine of the promised fifty had reached Britain, where the admiralty found them even less seaworthy than expected. In any case, on September 17, just two weeks after the destroyer-bases deal was announced, Enigma decrypts confirmed that Hitler had indefinitely postponed Operation Sealion, the expected invasion against which the destroyers were to have been deployed.[57] It was "the Few," not American ships, that had won the Battle of Britain. But as Churchill understood, the compelling logic for the destroyer-bases exchange had always been more political and psychological than military. The deal's true payoff lay in the future. It was to be measured not in its contribution to the defense of Britain in the summer of 1940 but in its catalytic effect on cementing the Anglo-American alliance — and in edging the United States closer to belligerency.

Willkie confined himself to denouncing the executive order that implemented the destroyer-bases deal as "the most arbitrary and dictatorial action ever taken by any President in the history of the United States" — a sweeping charge, to say the least, but also a hollow and ironic one, since Willkie could have made himself the instrument of congressional involvement had he chosen.[58] In any event, Willkie's criticism was restricted to the method, not the substance, of the destroyers-for-bases swap. The archisolationist *Chicago Tribune*, in contrast, damned the deal as "an act of war." Churchill put the matter more temperately but essentially agreed with that assessment. "The transfer to Great Britain of fifty American warships was a decidedly unneutral Act," he later wrote.

56. Cannadine, *Blood, Toil, Tears and Sweat*, 192.
57. Ronald Lewin, *Ultra Goes to War*, 95.
58. Freidel, *Rendezvous with Destiny*, 352.

"It would, according to all the standards of history, have justified the German Government in declaring war upon [the United States]. . . . [I]t was the first of a long succession of increasingly unneutral acts in the Atlantic which were of the utmost service to us. . . . All the world," Churchill concluded, "understood the significance of the gesture."[59]

In the closing days of the campaign, Willkie's mounting political desperation and the abrasive nagging of isolationist Republicans like Vandenberg temporarily eclipsed the candidate's internationalist convictions, not to mention his poise. Abandoning the civil tone that had informed his early campaign statements, Willkie took to stridently denouncing Roosevelt as a warmonger. "We do not want to send our boys over there again," he said in a speech in St. Louis. "[I]f you elect the third-term candidate, I believe they will be sent."[60] In an increasingly emotional series of speeches on Willkie's behalf, Charles Lindbergh bruited the same theme. So did John L. Lewis, who endorsed Willkie and damned Roosevelt in a nationwide broadcast on October 25. For good measure, Lewis threatened that if the nation's industrial workers repudiated his advice, he would resign as president of the CIO.[61]

The Lindbergh and Lewis endorsements and Roosevelt's clear vulnerability on the warmongering charge unsettled the Roosevelt camp in the campaign's closing days. "This fellow Willkie is about to beat the Boss," presidential adviser Harry Hopkins fretted.[62] Roosevelt remained in the White House for most of the campaign, but at the end of October, appearing presidential and statesmanlike, he at last took to the campaign trail. As with Willkie, the rising political stakes as election day neared clouded Roosevelt's usually careful judgment. At first he contented himself with reminding audiences that Willkie's was also the party of "Martin, Barton, and Fish," three notoriously isolationist congressmen whose names formed a catchy trinomial chant with which Roosevelt worked Democratic crowds into paroxysms of partisan enthusiasm.[63] But as he

59. An excellent brief account of the destroyers-for-bases deal is in L&G, *Challenge*, 742–76. Churchill's remarks are in Churchill 2:404. Contrary to much mythology, the destroyers were hardly, as the title of one melodramatic account claims, *Fifty Ships That Saved the World* (by Philip Goodheart; Garden City, N.Y.: Doubleday, 1965).

60. Lash, *Roosevelt and Churchill*, 237.

61. As good as his word, Lewis resigned after the election returned Roosevelt to the White House.

62. Lash, *Roosevelt and Churchill*, 235.

63. Joseph Martin was from Massachusetts; Bruce Barton and Hamilton Fish were from New York. All three were Republicans.

headed for a crucial speech in Boston on October 30, Roosevelt was manifestly worried. Neither for the first time nor the last, he requested from Churchill a gesture that would give him a boost with American voters, a statement, he instructed Morgenthau, "in Churchill's own language — he is a writer — that the president can use to the Boston Irish."[64] But Churchill's word-mill failed him on this occasion. Roosevelt, left to his own devices in Boston, zestfully invoked the now familiar litany of "Martin, Barton, and Fish." He also ventured a reckless promise: "I have said this before, but I shall say it again and again: Your boys are not going to be sent into any foreign wars." Conspicuously, Roosevelt omitted the qualifying phrase that he had used on previous occasions: "except in case of attack."[65]

Listening on the radio, Willkie exploded: "That hypocritical son of a bitch! This is going to beat me."[66] He was half right. Willkie was decisively beaten, to be sure, but it was not Roosevelt's tortuously hedged promises to stay out of foreign wars that carried the president to his unprecedented third-term victory. Public opinion surveys indicated that it was in fact the looming reality of American involvement in armed conflict, not Roosevelt's seductive assurances about peace, that hurt Willkie the most. Asked how they would vote if there were no war, voters favored Willkie by a 5.5 percent margin, reflecting disillusion with the New Deal and disaffection over the third-term issue. But when confronted with the possibility of fighting, they preferred Roosevelt by a far larger percentage. By election day many voters had obviously made their reckoning with the dread prospect of war. They had decided it was no time to exchange the reliable Roosevelt they had known through eight years of depression, reform, and ratcheting international tensions for the edgy Willkie they had seen in the campaign. The Republican candidate prevailed in just ten states — the traditional Republican strongholds of Maine and Vermont and eight more in the isolationist Midwestern heartland. Roosevelt's winning margin was his narrowest yet. Willkie polled five million more votes than Landon had four years earlier, a

64. Warren F. Kimball, *The Most Unsordid Act: Lend-Lease, 1939–1941* (Baltimore: Johns Hopkins Press, 1969), 84.

65. *PPA* (1940), 517. In previous campaign speeches, Roosevelt had added the words "except in case of attack" to his promise not to send Americans into "foreign wars." When an adviser remarked the absence of that qualifier in the Boston speech, Roosevelt testily replied, "If somebody attacks us, then it isn't a foreign war, is it?" — a pettifogging cavil that betrayed the president's uneasiness on this most volatile of all issues. See Freidel, *Rendezvous with Destiny*, 355.

66. Barnard, *Wendell Willkie, Fighter for Freedom*, 258.

THE AGONY OF NEUTRALITY   39

telling index of how far Roosevelt's popularity had diminished from the triumphal referendum on the New Deal in 1936. But in the last analysis, Willkie owed his defeat to anxiety about his inexperience—and to the faint signs of returning prosperity.[67]

Roosevelt had in fact devoted most of his speech in Boston not to fatuous promises of peace but to a somewhat callous recitation of the good economic news spawned by the British war orders. "You good people here in Boston know of the enormous increase of productive work in your Boston Navy Yard," he reminded his listeners. At the same time he spoke, through the radio, to the "citizens of Seattle—you have watched the Boeing plant out there grow." Similarly, he addressed listeners in southern California, Buffalo, St. Louis, Hartford, and Paterson, New Jersey—all communities where war orders were terminating a dreary decade of mass unemployment. Roosevelt well understood the cold political logic of rising employment. "These foreign orders mean prosperity in this country and we can't elect a Democratic Party unless we get prosperity and these foreign orders are of the greatest importance," he had said privately some eight months earlier, when the big Allied aircraft contracts were starting to come in.[68] Thanks largely to British weapons purchases, by election day nearly 3.5 million more workers were employed than in the trough of the Roosevelt Recession of 1937–38. Unemployment had shrunk by the end of 1940 to 14.6 percent, its lowest level in ten years, and was swiftly trending lower still.

In Britain, meanwhile, by the time of Roosevelt's reelection more than ten thousand Londoners had perished in the Blitz, six thousand in October alone. Those rising death tolls made a somber contrast with falling American unemployment statistics, a contrast that foretold much about the different destinies that the gods of war had in store for America and for its eventual allies, not to mention the fates that awaited their common enemies. The contrast was hardly lost on Winston Churchill. He grumbled privately that the Americans were "very good in applauding the valiant deeds done by others," but to Roosevelt he was the soul of graciousness. "I prayed for your success," he cabled to Roosevelt after the election. "I am truly thankful for it. . . . Things are afoot which will be remembered as long as the English language is spoken in any quarter of the globe."[69]

67. Dallek, 250.
68. Morgenthau Diary, 302.
69. Gilbert, *Churchill: A Life* 672; *C&R* 1:81.

2

To the Brink

We must be the great arsenal of democracy.
— Franklin D. Roosevelt, Fireside Chat,
December 29, 1940

The supreme geopolitical fact of the modern era, Prince Bismarck is alleged to have remarked, is that the Americans speak English. Winston Churchill, with his incessant references to the common ideals and interests of the "English-speaking peoples," exploited that theme shamelessly. On it, indeed, he based his strategy for Britain's survival. But for all the apparent inevitability of Anglo-American cooperation against the Nazi threat, in actual practice the transatlantic partnership was devilishly difficult to forge. Churchill's anxieties and often cunning manipulations, as well as Roosevelt's own hesitations and evasions, his wary deference to the isolationists, and his frequently cagey misrepresentations to the American public, all testified to the abundant difficulties that impeded collaboration between Britain and the United States — not to mention the even more formidable obstacles that blocked full-blown American belligerency.

As 1940 drew toward a close, an especially complicated difficulty arose. With flatfooted lack of ceremony, Lord Lothian, the British ambassador to the United States, announced the problem on November 23, upon his return from a brief trip to London. Alighting from his plane at New York's La Guardia Airport, Lothian declared to the waiting reporters: "Well, boys, Britain's broke. It's your money we want."[1]

Lothian's statement surely lacked diplomatic subtlety, but it just as

1. Warren F. Kimball, *The Most Unsordid Act: Lend-Lease, 1939–1941* (Baltimore: Johns Hopkins University Press, 1969), 96.

40

surely came as no surprise. The British themselves had long anticipated their impending insolvency. In early 1939, even before the war's outbreak, the British treasury had begun to seize control of all gold holdings, foreign securities, and dollar balances held by British nationals. Further to conserve precious dollar reserves, and to the annoyance of American business interests, the London government had curtailed certain American imports, including fruit, tobacco, and Hollywood films. But those measures only postponed the inevitable. The day of reckoning was now at hand.

It was no easy thing for Americans accustomed to thinking of Britain as the swaggering master of a global empire now to believe the assertions of British bankruptcy. Many American observers had special difficulty grasping the crucial distinction between Britain's still-formidable sterling reserves and her meager stock of dollars, dwindled by a decade of constricted U.S.-British trade. Meeting to analyze the British financial situation on December 3, 1940, at Woodley, Secretary of War Stimson's Washington home, several officials squinted in puzzlement at the figures that Treasury Department specialists scrawled across the blackboard. The inescapable conclusion of the complicated mathematical exercise was that Britain would exhaust its gold and dollar balances within weeks, just to pay for orders already placed. The dollars to pay for future orders were nowhere in sight. At length Secretary of the Navy Knox asked simply, "We are going to pay for the war from now on, are we?" To which Treasury Secretary Morgenthau replied: "Well, what are we going to do, are we going to let them place more orders or not?" On the response to that question hung Roosevelt's short-of-war strategy, which relied on an adequately supplied Britain to carry the battle to Germany. On it, too, depended the reviving health of the American economy, stimulated since mid-1940 by accumulating British war orders. Aware of those facts, Knox and the other leaders in the room did not need long to ponder the implications of Morgenthau's question. "Got to. No choice about it," Knox answered.[2]

There may have been no choice, but neither were there readily apparent means for the United States to facilitate further British purchases. The Johnson Act of 1934, prohibiting loans to countries in default on their World War I debts, remained on the books; so did the cash-and-carry provisions of the neutrality legislation of the preceding decade. Legally, not to mention politically, Uncle Sam's hands seemed to be

2. L&G, *Undeclared*, 229.

tied. The only recourse, Morgenthau confided to his diary, was to trust in Franklin Roosevelt's inventive mind. "It gets down to the question of Mr. Churchill putting himself in Mr. Roosevelt's hands with complete confidence," Morgenthau wrote. "Then it is up to Mr. Roosevelt to say what he will do."[3]

On December 9 a navy seaplane feathered down through the balmy Caribbean air to deliver a packet of mail to President Roosevelt, cruising aboard the USS *Tuscaloosa* on a postelection vacation. The mail pouch contained a historic letter from Churchill, one that has been described as "the most carefully drafted and re-drafted message in the entire Churchill-Roosevelt correspondence" and that amounted to what the historian Warren Kimball calls an "epitaph to the British Empire as [Churchill] knew it."[4] Perhaps understandably, Churchill took up several other matters before facing the moment of fiscal truth. "It takes between three and four years to convert the industries of a modern state to war purposes," Churchill began. By that reckoning, the United States would need at least two more years to reach "maximum industrial effort." During that preparatory interval, Britain alone would "hold the front and grapple with Nazi power until the preparations of the United States are complete." But two dangers threatened Britain's ability to persevere. Both of them could be alleviated only by the repeal of the American cash-and-carry provisos. Churchill first elucidated the "carry" problem. There was "mortal danger," Churchill warned, in "the steady and increasing diminution of sea tonnage." If shipping losses continued at their present rate, Churchill predicted, the results would be "fatal," for Britain as well as the United States, because "we may fall by the way and the time needed by the United States to complete her defensive preparations may not be forthcoming." Only American merchant ships, and ultimately armed escorts of merchant convoys by the U.S. Navy, could keep the Atlantic lifeline intact.

The shipping problem was grave, but the second threat was even more urgent. It was the one that Lothian had already advertised and the one that especially galled Churchill to discuss: Britain's lack of cash. The prime minister got to it only in his closing paragraphs: "Last of all I come to the question of finance. The more rapid and abundant the flow of munitions and ships which you are able to send us, the sooner will

3. L&G, *Undeclared*, 231.
4. C&R. 1:88, 111.

our dollar credits be exhausted. . . . The moment approaches when we shall no longer be able to pay cash for shipping and other supplies." Contemplating the liquidation of centuries' accumulation of imperial wealth, the prime minister suggested that it would be wrong if "Great Britain were to be divested of all saleable assets so that after victory was won with our blood, civilization saved and time gained for the United States to be fully armed against all eventualities, we should stand stripped to the bone. . . . We here would be unable after the war to purchase the large balance of imports from the United States. . . . Not only should we in Great Britain suffer cruel privations but widespread unemployment in the United States would follow the curtailment of American exporting power."[5]

Back in Washington a week later, tanned and rested from his Caribbean cruise, Roosevelt gave his answer to Churchill at a press conference. Confirming his view that "the best immediate defense of the United States is the success of Great Britain in defending itself," Roosevelt went straight to the financial question. "I have read a great deal of nonsense in the last few days by people who can only think in what we may call traditional terms about finances," Roosevelt said airily to the reporters crowded around his desk on December 17. "Now, what I am trying to do," Roosevelt continued, is to "get rid of the silly, foolish old dollar sign." The president illustrated his point with what became a famous parable. If a neighbor's house was on fire and he needed your garden hose to put it out, you wouldn't haggle about the price; you would loan him the hose, and he would return it when the blaze was extinguished. By the same token, Roosevelt proposed, the United States would provide Britain whatever supplies she needed, "with the understanding that when the show was over, we would get repaid something in kind, thereby leaving out the dollar mark in the form of a dollar debt and substituting for it a gentleman's obligation to repay in kind. I think you all get it."[6]

Roosevelt drove the point home twelve days later. In one of his most memorable Fireside Chats, on December 29, 1940, he offered his countrymen a basic primer on American national security policy. "If Great Britain goes down," he explained, "the Axis powers will control the continents of Europe, Asia, Africa, Australasia, and the high seas — and they will be in a position to bring enormous military and naval resources

5. C&R 1:102–9.
6. PPA (1940), 604–8.

against this hemisphere. It is no exaggeration to say that all of us, in all the Americas, would be living at the point of a gun." To prevent that result, "we must have more ships, more guns, more planes—more of everything. . . . We must be the great arsenal of democracy." The nations already contending against Hitler, Roosevelt insisted, "do not ask us to do their fighting. They ask us for the implements of war. . . . Emphatically we must get these weapons to them in sufficient volume and quickly enough, so that we and our children will be saved the agony and suffering of war which others have had to endure."[7]

That last statement reflected Roosevelt's continuing public adherence at the end of 1940 to the short-of-war strategy. For the record, he was proposing that America should be an arsenal, not become a combatant. Yet the president's military advisers were already giving him reason to believe that he could not indefinitely adhere to his carefully measured strategy of pro-British nonbelligerency. "We cannot permanently be in the position of toolmakers for other nations which fight," thought Henry Stimson.[8] In the new year that was dawning, events soon threatened to shove the United States to the forwardmost edge of the combat zone, especially in the embattled North Atlantic.

The release of "surplus" military supplies in the summer of 1940 and the destroyer-bases deal in September of that year had been consummated as executive actions. Roosevelt's new proposal to supply Britain without reference to the dollar sign, soon popularly known as "Lend-Lease," would not be—indeed, could not be—an executive action, since Lend-Lease required an initial congressional appropriation of some $7 billion. "We don't want to fool the public; we want to do this thing right out and out," Roosevelt said to Morgenthau.[9] Lend-Lease would now be the subject of a "Great Debate," conducted publicly, noisily, lengthily, and for the most part responsibly, but not always with the unvarnished candor that Roosevelt claimed.

The president inaugurated the debate in his annual message to Congress on January 6, 1941, when he announced that he was sending the Lend-Lease Bill to Congress. He ended with a ringing flourish in which he defined the "four essential human freedoms" that his policies were ultimately aimed at securing: freedom of speech and religion, and free-

7. PPA (1940), 633–44.
8. Kimball, *Most Unsordid Act*, 129.
9. L&G, *Undeclared*, 255.

dom from want and from fear. These Four Freedoms, promulgated in every then-known medium, including a sentimental painting and poster by the popular artist Norman Rockwell, soon became a sort of shorthand for America's war aims. They could be taken, too, especially the concepts of freedom from want and fear, as a charter for the New Deal itself. At this level of basic principle, there was unmistakable continuity between Roosevelt's domestic policies during the Great Depression and his foreign policies in the world war.

Congressional hearings on the Lend-Lease bill—the House version cleverly numbered H.R. 1776—opened on January 10, 1941. Beyond the Capitol, in blue-collar bars and paneled clubrooms, in classrooms and church basements and around kitchen tables, over the airwaves and in editorial columns, the bill was ventilated, analyzed, criticized, probed, and praised. Fortunately for the president's purposes, the debate over Lend-Lease took place at a favorable moment. England's apparent victory in the Battle of Britain had fended off the threat of immediate invasion, and Roosevelt's recent electoral victory had freshened his political popularity. As the debate began, public opinion polls showed solid majorities behind the president's Lend-Lease policy.[10]

Leaving nothing to chance, Roosevelt sent both Harry Hopkins and Wendell Willkie to England to coach Churchill on how best to support the Lend-Lease legislation. Hopkins helped to draft one Churchill speech that was both disingenuous and, even by the prime minister's own occasionally mawkish standards, more than a little treacly. Churchill declared: "We do not need the gallant armies which are forming throughout the American Union. We do not need them this year, nor next year; nor any year that I can foresee. But we do need most urgently an immense and continuous supply of war materials and technical apparatus of all kinds. . . . We need a great mass of shipping in 1942, far more than we can build ourselves." Churchill next directly addressed his American listeners with a passage from Longfellow that Roosevelt had copied out in longhand and asked Willkie to deliver:

> Sail On, O Ship of State!
> Sail on, O Union, strong and great!
> Humanity with all its fears,
> With all the hopes of future years,
>   Is hanging breathless on thy fate!

10. Cantril, 409–11, 588.

Then, more than a little misleadingly, Churchill concluded: "Give us the tools, and we will finish the job."[11]

American isolationists were not so easily taken in by this display of Churchillian charm. The prime minister's soothing assurances that Britain needed only American materiel, not men, they branded as transparently counterfeit. They believed that Lend-Lease was not just another measure to aid Britain. By openly committing the United States government to financing the British war effort, America became Britain's co-belligerent in all but name. If Lend-Lease passed, it was only a matter of time until American naval and military forces would be engaged in a shooting war. In all this, events proved the isolationist critics to be quite correct.

Fear of Lend-Lease's eventual consequences even attracted some new adherents to the anti-interventionist cause. Roosevelt's former supporter William Allen White, head of the Committee to Defend America by Aiding the Allies, created a year earlier to promote aid to Britain, resigned from the committee in protest over Lend-Lease, which he thought ran too close a risk of precipitating American belligerency. America's motto, White declared, should be "The Yanks Are Not Coming." Mothers, coated against the January chill, knelt on the Capitol steps to pray histrionically: "Kill Bill 1776, not our sons." Other opponents of Lend-Lease voiced additional criticisms. The America First Committee, organized several months earlier in the wake of the destroyer-bases deal, argued that funneling Lend-Lease resources to Britain would criminally retard America's own rearmament program. Spokesmen for the German-American Bund predictably denounced the bill as wantonly provocative. So did representatives of the Communist Party, still slavishly in thrall to the tortured party line that Nazi Germany,

11. David Cannadine, ed., *Blood, Toil, Tears and Sweat: The Speeches of Winston Churchill* (Boston: Houghton Mifflin, 1989), 202–13. Churchill's disingenuousness went further still. He encouraged Hopkins to believe that the Germans might invade any day, going so far as to tell Hopkins that he had already devised the peroration for his speech announcing the German landings: "The hour has come; kill the Hun." Hopkins reported to Roosevelt on January 28: "The most important single observation I have to make is most of the Cabinet and all of the military leaders here believe that invasion is imminent." What neither Churchill nor anyone else told Hopkins was that on January 12 a Bletchley decrypt of a German order shutting down the Continental wireless stations necessary to an invasion had confirmed that Operation Sealion had been canceled. See Robert E. Sherwood, *Roosevelt and Hopkins* (New York: Grosset and Dunlap, 1950), 257, and Martin Gilbert, *Churchill: A Life* (New York: Henry Holt 1991), 688.

as an ally of Moscow since the Molotov-Ribbentrop Pact, should not be antagonized. One Irish-American congressman from Cleveland, Ohio, gave vent to the Anglophobia that pervaded many American communities by penning a new stanza for "God Bless America:"

> God save America from British rule:
> Stand beside her and guide her
> From the schemers who would make of her a fool.
> From Lexington to Yorktown,
> From blood-stained Valley Forge,
> God Save America
> From a king named George.[12]

In the isolationist capital of Chicago, the ever-pugnacious Robert R. McCormick fulminated against the bill. Along with his cousin Joseph Patterson's New York *Daily News* and his cousin Cissy Patterson's *Washington Times-Herald*, McCormick's two-penny, million-circulation *Tribune* had long numbered among the biggest megaphones for isolationist pronouncements. The internationally minded publisher Henry Luce called the cousins "the Three Furies of Isolation." Roosevelt called them "the McCormick-Patterson Axis." Together the cousins brewed up a gale of complaint against Lend-Lease. The *Daily News* ran cartoons showing a ghoulish figure of World War II as "Uncle Sap's new girlfriend." From McCormick's archconservative *Tribune* (as well as from the Communist *Daily Worker*) came the dark pronouncement that H.R. 1776 was a "Dictator Bill" designed "to destroy the Republic." In testimony before the Senate Foreign Relations Committee, McCormick flatly asserted: "I do not think [Britain] needs anything." When Wendell Willkie testified in favor of Lend-Lease, the *Tribune* took to referring to him as "the Republican Quisling."[13] Some other critics were rougher still. Roosevelt's onetime progressive ally Montana senator Burton Wheeler, now his implacable adversary in foreign policy, charged that the Lend-Lease legislation was the New Deal's "triple-A foreign policy; it will plough under every fourth American boy." Roosevelt called that accusation "the rottenest thing that has been said in public life in my generation."[14]

---

12. Kimball, *Most Unsordid Act*, 186–87.
13. Richard Norton Smith, *The Colonel: The Life and Legend of Robert R. McCormick, Indomitable Editor of the* Chicago Tribune (Boston: Houghton Mifflin, 1997), 403–4. Vidkun Quisling was the Norwegian collaborator who helped the Germans prepare the conquest of Norway and became the premier of Nazi-occupied Norway in 1942.
14. L&G, *Undeclared*, 258–59.

To counter isolationist criticism, Roosevelt reasoned, Britain must be seen to have exhausted all its dollar resources before receiving American aid. The administration made a particular point of requiring Britain to use her remaining dollar reserves to finance the capital costs of the plant expansion necessary to servicing her future war orders. Accordingly, and to Churchill's extreme consternation, Roosevelt seized some British assets and compelled the sale of others. When a U.S. naval vessel showed up in Cape Town to collect some $50 million in British gold reserves, Churchill penned a stinging note protesting that the American action had "the aspect of a sheriff collecting the last assets of a helpless debtor." It was "not fitting that any nation should put itself wholly in the hands of another," the prime minister complained, but on sober second thought he decided that supplication and scolding did not gracefully mix, and refrained from sending the letter.[15] By late January 1941 the British treasury agent in New York, under intense American pressure, was liquidating Britain's American securities holdings at the rate of some $10 million per week. When London protested, Secretary Morgenthau explained: "[W]hat is in the mind of the ordinary citizen is that England yet hasn't gone far enough. . . . It is a matter of—well, convincing the general public of the determination, of just how far the English businessman is ready to go. It is a psychological matter as much as anything else."[16] Psychological indeed. Eventually the Reconstruction Finance Corporation arranged for loans to finance the plant expansion necessary to service the British—and American—war orders, ending the need for Britain to sell off her remaining direct investments in the United States. But the public spectacle of forced British sales in the early months of 1941 helped see the Lend-Lease bill through to congressional passage.

The isolationists were strong enough to attach several amendments to the Lend-Lease bill. By far the most consequential of them anticipated the issue over which administration policymakers were to agonize for much of the remainder of 1941: the question of providing U.S. Navy escorts on the Atlantic to ensure the safe arrival of the convoys carrying Lend-Lease goods to Britain. (In naval parlance, a warship "escorted" a convoy of merchant ships; but among laymen, including the legislators in Congress, the term "convoy" was often used in place of "escort.")

15. C&R 1:120; see also Gilbert, *Churchill*, 687.
16. L&G, *Undeclared*, 230. Morgenthau had additional motives for promoting the sale of British securities. "The tie-up between the so-called 'City' in London and our own Wall Street is terribly close," he remarked when one important sale was consummated. "I consider this a great New Deal victory." Kimball, *Most Unsordid Act*, 225.

"Nothing in this Act," the relevant clause read, "shall be construed to authorize or to permit the authorization of convoying vessels by naval vessels of the United States."[17] The administration accepted that amendment, but here, too, there was an element of evasion. In their congressional testimony, both Secretary Stimson and Secretary Knox publicly acquiesced in the no-convoy clause while maintaining that the president already had the constitutional authority as commander-in-chief to order naval escorting. Whether the president himself believed that he had the constitutional power—and, no less important, the political license—actually to implement escorting remained an open question. At a press conference on January 21, Roosevelt denied that he had even thought about naval escorts. Escorting could lead to shooting, he said, "and shooting comes awfully close to war, doesn't it? That is about the last thing we have in our minds."[18]

In early March Congress passed the amended Lend-Lease bill by substantial majorities: 60–31 in the Senate and 317–71 in the House. Almost all the opposition was Republican, and it was heavily concentrated in the still staunchly isolationist Midwest, the great land-island dominated by Robert McCormick's Chicago. But in the rest of the country, the Great Debate over Lend-Lease had produced a rough consensus of the sort that Roosevelt had long sought. Two-thirds of respondents told polltakers in January 1941 that they approved of the Lend-Lease bill. Before the Lend-Lease debate, the most that Americans would commit themselves to was aid to the democracies short of war. Now, despite Roosevelt's studied reluctance to cross all his *t*'s and dot all his *i*'s, he had edged them closer to a commitment to aid the democracies even at the risk of war.[19]

Roosevelt signed the Lend-Lease bill on March 11. Congress obligingly appropriated $7 billion to fund the first shipments. The *New York Times* hailed Lend-Lease as marking "the day when the United States ended the great retreat which began with the Senate rejection of the Treaty of Versailles and the League of Nations. Our effort to find security in isolation has failed. By the final passage of the lend-lease bill we confess its failure."[20] The president quickly established an independent

17. Thomas A. Bailey and Paul B. Ryan, *Hitler vs. Roosevelt: The Undeclared Naval War* (New York: Free Press, 1979), 113–14.
18. *The Complete Presidential Press Conferences of Franklin Delano Roosevelt* (New York: Da Capo, 1972), 17:86–87 (January 21, 1941).
19. Cantril, 410.
20. *New York Times*, March 12, 1941, 20.

Office of Lend-Lease Administration, briefly headed by Harry Hopkins and later by businessman Edward Stettinius. Lend-Lease mooted the "cash" portion of cash-and-carry. Restrictions remained in force against sending American ships into a designated war zone. Thus it was mostly British vessels that began hauling munitions, foodstuffs, and other supplies away from American ports, the first of nearly $50 billion of American aid, most of it directed to Britain, that would flow from American assembly lines, mills, refineries, and farms during the war. Fittingly enough, given the homely analogy with which Roosevelt had inaugurated the Lend-Lease debate, the first consignment to Britain included nine hundred thousand feet of fire hose.[21]

Lend-Lease effected a kind of "common-law alliance" between Britain and the United States. As in many such unions, attraction and suspicion commingled in sometimes volatile proportions. Churchill told the House of Commons that Lend-Lease was "the most unsordid act in the history of any nation." He telegrammed his thanks to Roosevelt: "Our blessings from the whole of the British Empire go out to you and the American nation for this very present help in time of trouble." More grandiloquently, he capped a radio broadcast on April 27 with yet another paean to American generosity:

> In front the sun climbs slow, how slowly,
> But westward, look, the land is bright.

Yet in private Churchill grumbled that the terms of the legislation, especially the forced sales of British assets that had preceded the bill's passage, meant that "we are not only to be skinned, but flayed to the bone." More calculatingly, he crowed to a British treasury official that after months of angling for American support, he had the Yanks almost where he wanted them: "I would like to get them hooked a little firmer," he said, " but they are pretty on now." Old suspicions died hard, however. Within the Foreign Office, some officials even now doubted that the Americans were safely hooked. Roosevelt's continued fidelity in public to the short-of-war strategy and his manifest reluctance to embrace the manifestly necessary tactic of naval escorts left "many of us here" a senior Foreign Office official noted, with "an uneasy feeling." America, he speculated, "may in her turn yet rat on us." That decidedly ungrateful attitude had its counterpart on the American side. An Army War Plans Division report in the month following the Lend-Lease Act's signing

21. Kimball, *Most Unsordid Act*, 229n.

revealed that American planners, too, had not yet submerged all their anxieties about Britain. The ghost of Neville Chamberlain's sorry ministry still chilled American ardor for embracing the British common-law bride. The danger still loomed, the report warned, of "a material change in the attitude of the British Government directed toward appeasement."[22]

　　ROOSEVELT HAD COMMITTED the United States to becoming the "great arsenal of democracy." Now it remained to stock that arsenal, a herculean task after years of willful neglect of military preparedness. Time was the most precious of military assets, and America had already squandered much of it. "Dollars cannot buy yesterday," Admiral Harold Stark had said in pleading for the "two-ocean navy" bill in 1940, but 1941 saw a flood of dollars directed toward buying the weapons for a tomorrow that was approaching with hurricane speed.[23] By this date money was no problem. As Senator Henry Cabot Lodge Jr. declared to General Arnold: "[I]t is the general feeling of the Congress, and as far as I can gather, among public opinion throughout the country, to provide all of the money necessary for the National Defense, so all you have to do is ask for it."[24] Ask the administration did: for $7 billion in Lend-Lease authorizations and for $13.7 billion in requisitions for the army and navy before 1941 was over—a mammoth increase over the paltry $2.2 billion appropriated for defense in 1940.[25] That rising tide of military spending began at last to float the wallowing hulk of the economy out of the slough of depression. As nearly one million draftees filed into hastily hammered, green-timbered military training camps, and as war orders poured into the big industrial centers, unemployment sank below 10 percent for the first time in more than a decade.

　　But if money was no problem, other obstacles still impeded the stocking of democracy's arsenal. Among them, ironically, was prosperity itself.

22. Kimball, *Most Unsordid Act*, 236; C&R 1:143; Gilbert, *Churchill: A Life*, 692; Frank Freidel, *Roosevelt: A Rendezvous with Destiny* (Boston: Little, Brown, 1990), 362; Joseph P. Lash, *Roosevelt and Churchill: The Partnership That Saved the West* (New York: Norton, 1976), 291; Mark Skinner Watson, *The United States Army in World War II: The War Department: Chief of Staff: Prewar Plans and Operations* (Washington: Department of the Army, 1950), 389.
23. Morison, 30.
24. Watson, *Chief of Staff*, 166.
25. Figures are for calendar, not fiscal, years. They are taken from Harold Vatter, *The U.S. Economy in World War II* (New York: Columbia University Press, 1985), 9.

Contemplating the prospect of their first substantial profits in years, many manufacturers resisted conversion from civilian to military production. "In the beginning most of our industrialists were rather cautious about having their companies undertake war work," RFC head and Secretary of Commerce Jesse H. Jones recalled. "They didn't want to invest a lot of their own funds in equipment to manufacture things they believed would not be in demand after the shooting ceased."[26] The case of the automobile industry exemplified the stiffening competition between civilian and military demands on the economy. Detroit was anticipating sales of some four million cars for 1941, a million more than it had sold in 1939. When United Auto Workers vice-president Walter Reuther proposed utilizing the remaining estimated 50 percent idle capacity in automobile plants by converting them to the manufacture of military aircraft under government contract, the Detroit carmakers flatly refused. Turning a motor vehicle plant to the making of airplanes was not simply a matter of having a different product roll off the end of the assembly line, the automakers insisted. Expensive new investment, the hiring of new designers and engineers, retooling, retraining of workers, and, above all, diversion of resources from that hungrily contemplated four-million-car sales target would all prove necessary. What was more, Reuther's plan would squarely deliver the automobile industry into the clutches of a single powerful customer, the federal government. After years of being badgered by New Deal reformers, the automakers had little desire to clasp the hand of their nemesis and place themselves at the mercy of such an unequal and unpredictable business partner.

A further problem was organizational, or, more precisely, political. Roosevelt could not easily envision any coordinating body powerful enough to organize economic mobilization that would not repeat the distasteful experience of the War Industries Board of World War I, which wrapped private businessmen in the mantle of government authority and effectively licensed them to control the nation's economy. Because those very businessmen, or their successors, had been his stoutest adversaries through the New Deal years, Roosevelt now groped for ways to rationalize economic mobilization without empowering his political opponents. (The New Dealers, Hugh Johnson growled, that "pack of semi-communist wolves," did not "intend to let Morgan and Du Pont men run a war.")[27]

26. Jesse H. Jones, *Fifty Billion Dollars* (New York: Macmillan, 1951), 320.
27. Richard Polenberg, *War and Society: The United States, 1941–1945* (Philadelphia: Lippincott, 1972), 7.

Roosevelt began his fumbling effort to wring a measure of order out of the economic chaos of the budding war economy in May 1940, when he revived another World War I–era agency, the National Defense Advisory Commission (NDAC). The NDAC was a weak and ineffective body that was replaced by the only slightly less weak and ineffective Office of Production Management (OPM) in January 1941. OPM had not one director but two: General Motors head William Knudsen and Amalgamated Clothing Workers president Sidney Hillman. Beyond the fact that they were both immigrants — Knudsen from Denmark and Hillman from Lithuania — they had little in common, but their joint appointment signaled the administration's commendable ambition to reconcile the interests of both capital and labor as the job of moving the economy onto a war footing went forward. Roosevelt blithely described OPM's duo as "a single responsible head; his name is Knudsen and Hillman," but the most conspicuous fact about OPM under Knudsen and Hillman was how little responsibility Roosevelt allotted them.[28] Their operational weakness was soon illustrated when Roosevelt supplemented OPM with two additional agencies: the Office of Price Administration and Civilian Supply, under New Deal economist Leon Henderson, as well as the Supply Priorities and Allocation Board, headed by Sears, Roebuck executive Donald Nelson.

This proliferation of mobilization agencies kept economic organization out of the hands of the dreaded businessmen — indeed, effectively out of anyone's hands save possibly Roosevelt's. But it also violated all the rules of sound administrative practice and vastly complicated the task of sorting out all the competing claims on the nation's economy. Confusion as to the country's eventual purpose in the war and the means it might bring to bear to achieve that purpose was by no means new. But as 1941 opened, the continuing irresolution of those questions was becoming painfully acute. It threatened to confirm Nazi foreign minister Joachim Ribbentrop's sneering comment that "American re-armament was the biggest bluff in the world's history."[29] Lend-Lease exacerbated the confusion. Did the British or the American military have first claim on production? Did the president really believe the short-of-war strategy would work? If so, then for what purpose was the American military and naval buildup intended? What would be the overall scale and duration of American mobilization? Would the United States be called upon to field a ground force or not? If it did, when and where would it be

28. *PPA* (1940), 684.
29. L&G, *Undeclared*, 495.

deployed? What would be its size and the composition of its various arms—infantry, armor, artillery? Should the ground, air, or naval services receive priority in development?

AT BOTTOM, the inefficiencies that beset economic mobilization in 1941 were due to the persistent confusion over American strategy. "How much munitions productive capacity does this country need and how rapidly must it become available?" Knudsen had asked as early as June 1940—a businesslike question to which a businesslike answer might have been forthcoming if only politics were as simple as business. Well into 1941 the stubborn fact was that at the highest political levels no firm answers had yet been determined about "the nation's main objective"—or at least none that could be publicly declared and hence made available to shape the mobilization effort.[30]

In the last weeks of 1940 Roosevelt had reviewed one notable attempt to set down a comprehensive strategic vision that might guide future planning. Its basis was a memorandum prepared by Admiral Harold Stark, the chief of naval operations. Stark laid out four options for American military and naval policy but strongly advocated the fourth, listed as item D in Stark's summary, or "Plan Dog," in the signalmen's jargon by which it was ever after known. Plan Dog essentially ratified an older strategic doctrine, code-named Rainbow 5, one of the American military's many contingency plans drafted in the prewar years. Rainbow 5 had anticipated waging war simultaneously against two or more enemies, Germany and Japan in particular. It assumed cooperation with Britain and France and envisioned sending American ground forces to Europe. Rainbow 5's premises, revised now to take account of France's defeat and the looming menace that Japan posed in the Pacific, deeply informed Plan Dog and constituted the foundation of all American strategic thinking from this date forward.

30. Watson, *Chief of Staff*, 174, 177, 308. Roosevelt frequently seemed oblivious to the fact that short-term needs were directly competitive with long-term plans. When George C. Marshall, for example, asked in December 1940 whether Roosevelt's order allocating half of aircraft production to Britain referred to half of the planes already delivered or half of those scheduled for future delivery, and exhibited a chart illustrating the considerable difference between the two calculations, Roosevelt waved him off, saying, "Don't let me see that chart again." Not for nothing did Stimson remark, "Conferences with the President are difficult matters. His mind does not follow easily a consecutive chain of thought but he is full of stories and incidents and hops about in his discussions from suggestion to suggestion and it is very much like chasing a vagrant beam of sunshine around a vacant room." Stimson Diary, December 18, 1940.

Stark began by emphasizing the indispensable importance of Britain's survival — a tacit but generous endorsement of Roosevelt's wager on Britain during the preceding summer, a wager against which Stark himself had then recommended. "[I]f Britain wins decisively against Germany we could win everywhere," Stark reasoned. But "if she loses the problem confronting us would be very great; and while we might not lose everywhere, we might, possibly, not win anywhere." From that simple starting point, weighty conclusions followed. The United States should devote its principal effort to the European theater, remain strictly on the defensive in the Pacific, and take care to avoid open conflict with Japan. For the foreseeable future, all possible aid should flow to Britain. As for longer-term developments in Europe, Stark minced no words: naval blockade and aerial bombardment might weaken Germany, but certain victory could come only "by military successes on shore." Britain was essential not only as a comrade in arms but, no less importantly, as an indispensable piece of real estate, an unsinkable aircraft carrier and a safe marshaling yard "from which successful land action can later be launched." Finally: "For making a successful land offensive, British man power is insufficient. Offensive troops from other nations will be required. I believe that the United States, in addition to sending naval assistance, would also need to send large air and land forces to Europe or Africa, or both, and to participate strongly in this land offensive. The naval task of transporting an army abroad would be large." In those few, spare sentences, Stark accurately foretold much of the story of American military and naval participation in World War II.[31]

Plan Dog had passed under Roosevelt's eyes well before he launched the Lend-Lease debate, but because he remained wary about the degree of candor that public opinion permitted him, he was scrupulously noncommittal about Stark's plan and breathed no syllable about it in public. ("Less than 1% of our people," he confided to Norman Thomas in May 1941, understood the lessons of the war then being fought. "It takes several generations," Roosevelt said, "to understand the type of 'facts of life' to which I refer.")[32] But he agreed sufficiently with Stark's prognosis that he authorized a further and momentous step, as Stark had recommended: joint staff talks between British and American military and naval planners.

In mid-January, the British battleship *King George V* hove into the Chesapeake to deliver the new British ambassador, Lord Halifax, to

31. Matloff and Snell, *Strategic Planning for Coalition Warfare, 1941–1942*, 25–27.
32. L&G, *Undeclared*, 441.

Washington. (He replaced Lothian, who had died unexpectedly a month earlier.) The *King George* also debarked five senior British officers, dressed in mufti and listed on the ship's manifest as "technical advisers" to the British Purchasing Commission. A few days later, Marshall and Stark welcomed the "advisers" in Washington. The Americans stressed the need for secrecy, warning the Britons that public knowledge of their presence "might well be disastrous" for the Lend-Lease bill being debated at that very moment in Congress. With those preliminaries, the American and British officers launched their discussion, known by the code name ABC-1, American-British Conversation Number 1.[33]

Less than a year earlier, wary British officials had refused Sumner Welles's request to visit the British Expeditionary Force in northern France. Now the British planners opened their arms and their briefing books to their American colleagues. Prior to their arrival Roosevelt had outlined his own strategic views in a meeting with his secretaries of war, navy, and state, as well as his two service chiefs, Marshall and Stark. Roosevelt's directions for the American positions in the upcoming talks showed the imprint of Plan Dog: continued aid to Britain; for the moment a defensive posture in the Pacific, with no squandering of scarce resources, not even for naval reinforcement of the Philippines. As for ground forces, the president wished to avoid any commitment "until our strength had developed." Meanwhile, the planners should consider "the possibility of bombing attacks against Japanese cities." When it came to naval escorts in the Atlantic, which Roosevelt was publicly denying even thinking about, the President advised that "the Navy should be prepared to convoy shipping in the Atlantic to England."[34]

Meeting from January 29 to March 29, the Anglo-American planners hammered out substantial agreements along those lines. Most important, they agreed that in the event of a two-front war in both Asia and Europe, Germany must be defeated first, even at the risk of serious reverses in the Pacific theater. As Marshall put it: "Collapse in the Atlantic would be fatal; collapse in the Far East would be serious but not fatal."[35] Yet at the conclusion of the talks, three questions remained unresolved: What, in light of Lend-Lease's passage, would be the precise allocation of production between British and American needs? Could the United States in fact undertake to provide naval escorts for the mer-

33. Matloff and Snell, *Strategic Planning for Coalition Warfare, 1941–1942*, 33.
34. Watson, *Chief of Staff*, 124.
35. Watson, *Chief of Staff*, 397.

chant convoys bearing arms to Britain? And how, exactly, might the United States "keep that Japanese dog quiet in the Pacific," as Churchill had earlier put it, without provoking a shooting war with Japan?

Military and economic officials struggled through the spring of 1941 to make headway within these broad and imperfect guidelines. Then, as the summer officially began, Adolf Hitler introduced a new variable that threatened to scramble all of the planners' already labile equations. On June 22, 1941, he launched Operation Barbarossa, an attack on his supposed ally the Soviet Union. With 153 divisions numbering some 3.6 million troops and thousands of aircraft and tanks, Barbarossa was Hitler's boldest military venture to date, and indeed one of the most gigantic military operations in history. As the awesome wave of the *Wehrmacht*'s men and machines rumbled eastward toward Moscow, opinion divided sharply in the United States about the implications of this new phase of the war. In many ways, the debate over America's relationship to the now belligerent Soviet Union was a reprise of the long-running controversy over aid to Britain, though further complicated by deep ideological estrangement. Would the Soviets be able to survive the German onslaught, or would they crumple like all of Hitler's previous victims, save only England? If the Russians somehow managed to stay in the field, how could the United States lend them material support—indeed, given the communist character of the Soviet state, *should* the United States make common cause with the Russians? "If we see that Germany is winning we ought to help Russia, and if Russia is winning we ought to help Germany, and that way let them kill as many as possible," said Missouri senator Harry S. Truman, expressing in his own unvarnished, show-me, Missouri idiom the feelings of many of his countrymen. "[A]lthough," Truman added, "I don't want to see Hitler victorious under any circumstances."[36]

From London, Churchill extended the hand of comradeship-in-arms to Stalin. "No one has been a more consistent opponent of Communism than I have for the last twenty-five years," the prime minister declared in a radio broadcast on June 22. "I will unsay no word that I have spoken about it. But all this fades away before the spectacle which is now unfolding. . . . Any man or state who fights on against Naziism will have our aid. . . . [W]e shall give whatever help we can to Russia and the Russian people."[37] American officials, however, were more cautious.

36. David McCullough, *Truman* (New York: Simon and Schuster, 1992), 262.
37. Churchill 3:371–72.

Secretary of War Stimson forwarded to Roosevelt the army's estimate that the Russians would last three months at the most and could conceivably collapse within four weeks.[38] Roosevelt's own thinking at first reflected the uncertainty bred by these conflicting appraisals: "Now comes this Russian diversion," he wrote to Ambassador William D. Leahy in Vichy, a description of the events in eastern Europe that suggested the president's agreement with Stimson's and the army's assessment. But, Roosevelt added: "If it is more than just that it will mean the liberation of Europe from Nazi domination."[39]

Like Churchill, Roosevelt had no illusions about the essential nature of the Soviet state. Several months earlier, he had somewhat reluctantly agreed to Eleanor's request that he address a gathering of the Communist-sponsored American Youth Congress. "The Soviet Union," said the president to the young people assembled on the White House lawn, "as everybody who has the courage to face the fact knows, is run by a dictatorship as absolute as any other dictatorship in the world." Boos arose from the crowd of leftist students.[40]

But however ideologically unsavory the Soviets might be, in time of danger, the old saying went, it was permissible to walk with the devil. Just as he had repudiated the counsel of his military chiefs that Britain could not endure, Roosevelt now discounted their pessimistic evaluations of the Russian situation and edged cautiously toward cooperation with Stalin. He may well have reasoned that Operation Barbarossa presented him with a unique, heaven-sent opportunity to clinch the tenuous logic of his short-of-war strategy. Keeping a Russian army in the field would certainly delay, and might even make entirely unnecessary, sending American troops to Europe. The suspicion that Roosevelt coldly calculated just that possibility festered in Stalin's mind in the months and years ahead.

Whatever his reasoning in the uncertain summer of 1941, the president invited the Soviet ambassador, Konstantin Oumansky, to draw up a list of items that the United States might supply to the Soviet armed forces. Within a week the Russian diplomat submitted a detailed request. Significantly, it included industrial materials such as machine tools, rolling mills, and petroleum-cracking plants for the manufacture of aviation

38. Sherwood, *Roosevelt and Hopkins*, 303.
39. Elliot Roosevelt, ed., *FDR: His Personal Letters, 1928–1945* (New York, Duell, Sloan and Pearce, 1950), 2:1177.
40. Freidel, *Roosevelt*, 325.

gasoline. Those items, looking to the long-term support of a mechanized army, strongly indicated the Soviets' intention to fight a lengthy war. That impression was soon emphatically confirmed by Harry Hopkins, who traveled to Moscow as Roosevelt's personal envoy in late July and reported positively on Stalin's resolve, just as Sumner Welles had helped Roosevelt to take the measure of Churchill's will to fight in 1940. Soon Roosevelt was putting even more American eggs in the Russian basket. In early August he ordered the delivery of a hundred fighter planes, even if they had to be taken from the U.S. Army. "Get the planes right off with a bang next week," he instructed an aide. "[U]se a heavy hand and act as a burr under the saddle. . . . Step on it."[41] Even though Churchill warned him candidly in September that British officials negotiating with the Soviets "could not exclude the impression that they might be thinking of separate terms," Roosevelt persuaded Congress the following month to include the Soviets in the Lend-Lease program, opening the door to an eventual total of some $10 billion in aid.[42]

"It is ridiculous," thundered McCormick's reliably outraged *Chicago Tribune*, "that sane men should have the slightest faith that . . . the supreme monster . . . Bloody Joe . . . , who brought on the war by selling out the democracies, will not sell them out again and make another deal with Hitler."[43] More temperately, the *New York Herald Tribune* opined: "A Hitler victory over Russia and Britain means . . . the triumph of totalitarian barbarism throughout the world. A victory of Great Britain, the United States and Communist Russia holds out no such prospect. Even if Communist totalitarianism survives the strain in Russia, the fact that it would only do so in association with victorious democracy in Britain and the United states would give it no such untrammeled prestige and power as success would bring to Nazi totalitarianism. An essentially democratic world would still be possible."[44] In such an atmosphere of wary suspicion and cynical calculation, and on such a bed of fragile hopes, the "Grand Alliance" was conceived.

Roosevelt's decision to join hands with Stalin raised new logistical nightmares for the beleaguered American planners. They continued to be frustrated by the timidity of civilian manufacturers and were still racked between the pull of their mandate to expand the American armed

41. James MacGregor Burns, *Roosevelt: The Soldier of Freedom* (New York: Harcourt Brace Jovanovich, 1970), 115.
42. C&R 1:238
43. L&G, *Undeclared*, 819.
44. L&G, *Undeclared*, 544.

forces and the tug of the president's insistence on sending Lend-Lease supplies to Britain, and now to Russia as well. Just a few months earlier, thanks to Roosevelt's order to divide B-17 production "fifty-fifty" with Britain, one general had complained: "We have a school at Shreveport, instructors, schedules, students, everything except planes." The slowdowns in the pilot-training program drove even the stolidly professional Marshall to the brink of insubordination. In late 1940 he had instructed his air chief, Hap Arnold, to "see if there is anything more we dare do" in frustrating implementation of the president's "even-Stephen" directive. "What will this do in blocking training of pilots?" Marshall asked rhetorically. "If the British collapse there are certain things of theirs we can seize," said Marshall, "but we can't seize trained pilots. We will be the sole defenders of both the Atlantic and the Pacific. What do we dare do in relation to Britain?" Now Roosevelt's response to the Russian requests threatened to make Marshall's job all but impossible. "I think the President should have it clearly pointed out to him," Marshall noted crisply to Stimson, "that Mr. Oumansky will take everything we own." Things were already bad enough, Marshall emphasized: "We have planes on the ground because we cannot repair them." Stimson agreed. He thought that "this Russian munitions business thus far has shown the President at his worst. He has no system. He goes haphazard and he scatters responsibility among a lot of uncoordinated men and consequently things are never done." Besides, Stimson personally regarded Oumansky as "nothing but a crook" and "a slick, clever little beast." The secretary therefore readily joined Marshall in yet another supplication to Roosevelt to clarify his overall strategic plan.[45]

On July 9 the president responded. He instructed his war and navy secretaries to undertake a systematic survey of "the overall production requirements required to defeat our potential enemies. . . . From your report we should be able to establish a munitions objective indicating the industrial capacity which this nation will require. . . . I realize," the president wrote, "that this report involves the making of appropriate assumptions as to our probable friends and enemies and to the conceivable theaters of operation which will be required."[46] This was not precisely the concrete strategic directive that Marshall and Stimson wanted,

45. Watson, *Chief of Staff*, 307, 329; Stimson Diary, August 4, 5, 1941.
46. Watson, *Chief of Staff*, 338–39. On August 30 Roosevelt added further instructions, stipulating that the final plan provide for "all reasonable munitions help" to Russia. Nevertheless, the planners appear not to have weighed Russian requirements heavily in their calculations. Watson, *Chief of Staff*, 348–49.

but it was useable enough. The president had now empowered the military to come up with a reasonable estimate of the material and logistical needs of the defense program, based on specified assumptions about allies, adversaries, and likely battlefields. Here at last was a license to think comprehensively about the complex relationship between America's likely commitments and schedule of deployments in the event of war, the probable scale and composition of the American armed forces, and the financial and industrial means required to equip them.

The assignment to draft the plan fell principally on the shoulders of Major Albert Wedemeyer in the army's War Plans Division. "I never worked so hard on anything in my life," Wedemeyer later recalled. "We were spending billions on arms without any clear idea of what we might need or where and when they might be used. I went to every expert in the Army and the Navy to find out the ships, the planes, the artillery, the tanks we would require to defeat our already well-armed enemies."[47] The document Wedemeyer and his team produced, soon known as the "Victory Program," reached the White House in late September. From the planners' perspective, it was still an imperfect work-in-progress, not yet firmly grounded on specific strategic commitments and defined war objectives, and therefore riddled with more uncertainties and contingencies than were comfortable. "The estimate is based upon a more or less nebulous policy," the War Plans Division observed, "in that the extent to which our government intends to commit itself with reference to the defeat of the Axis powers has not as yet been defined."[48] Nevertheless, Wedemeyer's team drew up a remarkably extensive survey, which for better or worse served thereafter as the basic planning matrix for American mobilization. The Victory Program comprised a bulging sheaf of reports canvassing possible theaters from the Atlantic to the Mediterranean and from western Europe and Siberia to the islands and seas of the far western Pacific. Among the welter of the report's minutiae several items stood out starkly:

- the first major objective of the United States and its associates ought to be the complete military defeat of Germany
- it will be necessary for the United States to enter the war
- only land armies can finally win wars
- July 1, 1943 [is] the earliest date when US armed forces can be mobilized, trained, and equipped for extensive operations.

47. *American Heritage* 38, no. 8 (December 1987): 66.
48. Watson, *Chief of Staff,* 341.

To accomplish its objectives, the Victory Program report concluded, the U.S. Army would eventually have to field 215 divisions, totaling some 8.7 million men (this estimate assumed that the Russians would no longer be in the war by 1943, the single greatest forecasting error in the entire document). Equipping that force and supplying the Allies in the meantime would require at least doubling current production plans, at the previously unimaginable expense of some $150 billion (this figure also turned out to be far off, as the war's eventual cost approached $300 billion). "Ultimate victory over the Axis powers," one planner wrote presciently, "will place a demand upon industry few have yet conceived."[49]

F.D.R.'S WAR PLANS! screamed the headline of McCormick's *Chicago Tribune* on Thursday, December 4, 1941. GOAL IS TEN MILLION ARMED MEN; HALF TO FIGHT IN AEF. PROPOSES LAND DRIVE BY JULY 1, 1943, TO SMASH NAZIS. PRESIDENT TOLD OF EQUIPMENT SHORTAGE. The following story quoted liberally from the Victory Program report. It even reproduced verbatim the president's letter ordering the preparation of the plan. The German chargé in Washington radioed to Berlin: "Report confirms that full participation of America in war is not to be expected before July 1943. Military measures against Japan are of defensive character."[50]

The *Tribune*'s scoop was one of the most sensational and potentially damaging news leaks in the history of American journalism. Whoever leaked the Victory Program to the *Tribune*, Henry Stimson said, was "wanting in loyalty and patriotism." Publication of the report made liars out of those administration spokesmen who had been denying the possibility of sending American troops overseas. Yet however mortifying to some political leaders, the *Tribune* story proved to be the isolationists' last hurrah, a final attempt to sabotage the preparedness effort. By now, most Americans had accepted the necessity of the military buildup and were expressing a willingness to countenance armed intervention. Even in Chicagoland, McCormick's grandstand stunt outraged many readers. Thousands of them took up the anti-McCormick cry of "Millions for defense, but not two cents for the *Tribune*," and canceled their subscriptions. However sensational, the *Tribune*'s effort to spike the mobilization

49. Watson, *Chief of Staff*, 350. The excerpts from the Victory Program plan are drawn from several sources: Watson, *Chief of Staff*, 331–66; L&G, *Undeclared*, 739ff.; and Sherwood, *Roosevelt and Hopkins*, 410–18.
50. *Chicago Daily Tribune*, December 4, 1941, 1; William L. Shirer, *The Rise and Fall of the Third Reich: A History of Nazi Germany* (New York: Simon and Schuster, 1960), 894–95n.

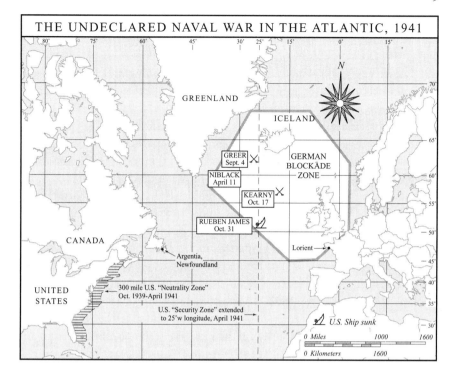

THE UNDECLARED NAVAL WAR IN THE ATLANTIC, 1941

program was also by this date largely irrelevant. Just three days later, the United States was at war.[51]

THE LEND-LEASE ACT also aggravated the controversy over naval escorts on the Atlantic. There was little sense in spending $7 billion for Lend-Lease goods that ended up at the bottom of the ocean. In alarmingly mounting volume, that was just where the munitions and other materiel leaving America's East Coast ports in 1941 were headed. German attacks were sinking British ships at nearly five times the rate that new construction could replace them. At that rate, the British merchant marine, the steel bridge of gray-hulled vessels on which America's strategy and England's very life depended, would soon vanish altogether.

The deadliest marine weapon, responsible for over half the lost

51. Cantril, 976; *American Heritage* 38, no. 8 (December 1987): 65. Though the FBI investigated the matter, the leaker of the *Tribune* story was never discovered. Some writers have speculated that it might have been the president himself who released the document, as a way of provoking Hitler into a declaration of war. No convincing evidence has been adduced to support that claim.

tonnage, was the U-boat (from the German word for submarine, *Unterseeboot*). The architect of Germany's U-boat campaign was Erich Raeder, commander-in-chief of the German navy; its resourceful executor was Karl Dönitz, head of the U-boat service. Raeder had long dunned the reluctant ex-soldier Hitler to commit more resources to the naval war. Raeder especially wanted to unleash his U-boats into the three-hundred-mile deep U.S. Neutrality Zone, proclaimed by Roosevelt in October 1939 to keep warships out of North America's offshore waters. After the introduction of the Lend-Lease bill, Raeder redoubled his efforts, with notable success. On 6 February 1941 Hitler directed that Germany's main objective in the war against England would now be to achieve "high losses in merchant shipping inflicted by sea and air warfare."[52] In Churchill's words, the Battle of Britain now gave way to the Battle of the Atlantic. Hitler stopped short of allowing Raeder to penetrate the American Neutrality Zone, but on March 25, 1941, he reacted to the passage of the Lend-Lease bill by extending the German naval combat area far out into the Atlantic, to the eastern coast of Greenland.

From their pens on the Nazi-occupied Atlantic coast of France, Dönitz's U-boats now swarmed into the midocean "gap" south of Greenland where British air reconnaissance was thinnest and little or no escort was available. By early 1941 Germany was producing four new submarines per month, including the long-range type IX boats, with a cruising range of at least 10,500 miles. Armed with a complement of twenty-two torpedoes, they packed nearly twice the firepower of earlier models. Soon Dönitz commanded a fleet of more than two hundred boats, of which he could keep thirty-six at sea, operating routinely as far westward as the line of forty degrees west longitude, and occasionally prowling beyond.

Dönitz's growing fleet also allowed him to perfect a new tactic—the so-called wolf-pack attack. Directed by radio from Dönitz's headquarters at Lorient, in Britanny, several U-boats would converge on a convoy. One would fire a torpedo into the flank of the formation of merchant ships, typically a diagonal shot to maximize the chance of a hit. Escorting vessels, if any, would then break away to pursue the attacker or rescue survivors, leaving the disrupted and defenseless merchantmen at the mercy of the several other raiders that had taken up positions athwart the convoy's path. In April 1941 alone these tactics claimed more than 650,000 tons of shipping.

52. Dan Van der Vat, *The Atlantic Campaign: World War II's Great Struggle at Sea* (New York: Harper and Row, 1988), 177.

"The decision for 1941 lies upon the seas," Churchill warned Roosevelt. On the outcome of the Battle of the Atlantic "the crunch of the whole war will be found." More ships and better protection for them on the transatlantic passage were absolutely necessary, and "only the United States can supply this need."[53]

Only the United States could not — at least not legally. The vestiges of the neutrality laws still on the books banned American cargo ships from entering a declared war zone. Worse, the Lend-Lease statute unambiguously declared: "Nothing in this Act shall be construed to authorize or to permit the authorization of convoying vessels by naval vessels of the United States." Faced with those obstacles, Roosevelt resisted the advice of "all-outers" like Henry Stimson, Henry Morgenthau, Harold Ickes, and his top naval commanders, who urged him to deploy the newly designated Atlantic Fleet, recently trained in antisubmarine warfare, for escort duty. Failure to do so, argued the all-outers, would mean feeding Lend-Lease aid to the fishes, would render ABC-1 a mere thinking exercise, and might well leave Britain with no choice but to surrender. (As late as September 1941, Harry Hopkins was still worrying that under worsening war conditions "the British appeasers might have some influence on Churchill.")[54] But authorizing armed escorts, Roosevelt fretted, would vitiate both his and Churchill's promises that Lend-Lease was sufficient to guarantee British victory without risking further American involvement. Committing U.S. Navy ships to escorting would confirm the most dire predictions of the isolationists and expose the president to potentially vicious political reprisals. "I realized from the first," declared Senator Wheeler on April 2, "after the Lend-Lease bill was passed, that the next step would be that the warmongers in this country would cry for convoys, and everyone recognizes that convoys mean war."[55] (Roosevelt himself had said as much in his press conference of January 21.)

Opinion polls reinforced Roosevelt's assessment of his political vulnerability. Bare majorities supported escorting, even at the risk of war, but even stronger majorities continued to oppose entering the war altogether, and 70 percent of respondents felt that the president had already done enough or too much by way of helping Britain.[56] Such

53. C&R 1:103, 107.
54. Sherwood, Roosevelt and Hopkins, 374.
55. L&G, Undeclared, 443.
56. Cantril, 973, 1128; Dallek, 267.

ambivalence formed a poor basis for a risky policy initiative like escorting. A further constraint on Roosevelt's ability to deploy American ships
in the Atlantic was the need to maintain naval elements in the Pacific
as a check on Japanese ambitions. Legally, politically, and operationally,
there seemed to be no way that the U.S. Navy could offer protection
to the precious Lend-Lease convoys. Admiral Stark, for one, appreciated
the president's awful predicament. "The President has on his hands at
the present time," Stark wrote in mid-April, "about as difficult a situation
as ever confronted any man anywhere in public life."[57]

Roosevelt writhed on the horns of this dilemma through the spring
and summer of 1941. Needled by conflicting counsel and buffeted by
irreconcilable demands, he flipflopped, dodged, waffled, and dissem-
bled. In early April he approved Hemisphere Defense Plan No. 1. It
called for the transfer of three battleships, an aircraft carrier, and several
supporting vessels from the Pacific to the Atlantic and for active escorting of England-bound convoys. Scarcely a week later he rescinded those
orders, leaving the ships in the Pacific and settling for a policy of "patrolling" rather than escorting. Even this limited policy he embraced
gingerly. He explained in a telegram to Churchill on April 11 that he
was extending the coastal American security zone into the distant mid-
Atlantic — to west longitude twenty-five degrees, which took in virtually
all of Greenland and, not insignificantly, overlapped the western third
of Hitler's recently expanded German combat zone. But the navy's role
in this newly defined American security zone was to be something less
than what Churchill and the all-outers wanted. "[I]n great secrecy," Roosevelt explained to the prime minister, American naval vessels patrolling
within the new hemispheric defense belt would notify the British about
any enemy ships or aircraft sighted. The implication of "patrolling" was
that the U.S. Navy would do no shooting but serve only as a reconnaissance arm for the Royal Navy and Air Force. Moreover, Roosevelt
added, "it is important for domestic political reasons . . . that this action
be taken by us unilaterally and not after diplomatic conversations between you and us. . . . I believe advisable that when this new policy is
adopted here no statement be issued on your end. It is not certain I
would make specific announcement. I may decide to issue necessary
naval operations orders and let time bring out the existence of the new

57. Eric Larrabee, *Commander in Chief: Franklin Delano Roosevelt, His Lieutenants,
and Their War* (New York: Harper and Row, 1987), 63.

patrol area." The patrols were "a step forward," Roosevelt somewhat sheepishly explained to the all-outers. "Well, I hope you will keep on walking, Mr. President. Keep on walking," urged Stimson. But for the moment, Roosevelt remained planted where he stood.[58]

Roosevelt did announce on April 10 that the United States was occupying Greenland, an orphaned Danish colony at risk of German seizure now that Denmark itself lay under Nazi occupation. Summarily defining the remote, snow-cloaked Danish colony as part of the Western Hemisphere, and hence subject to the Monroe Doctrine's protection against intervention by a European power, the president waved aside an issue that had stumped generations of cartographers. Two months later, Roosevelt sent a scratch force of some four thousand marine regulars to occupy Iceland, having bent the geographers' logic still further by declaring Iceland to be part of the New World as well, thereby deftly sidestepping the Selective Service Act's prohibition on stationing draftees outside the Western Hemisphere.

In Berlin, Raeder insisted that these new American moves meant war. He pleaded again for authorization to carry the fight directly to the Americans. But Hitler, about to launch Barbarossa against the Russians, wanted no distractions. He was "most anxious to postpone the United States entry into the war for another one or two months," he told Raeder. Naval encounters with the Americans should be avoided "as far as possible."[59]

As Roosevelt anticipated, time soon brought the existence of the expanded Atlantic patrols to the American public's attention. Reporters at the president's press conference on April 25 pressed for clarification: "Can you tell us the difference between a patrol and a convoy?" one journalist asked. Just as much difference as between a cow and a horse, Roosevelt opaquely answered. Could the president define the functions of the patrols? "The protection of the American hemisphere," Roosevelt replied, repeating that answer three times, without further elucidation. Exactly how far would the new patrols extend? "As far on the waters of the seven seas as may be necessary for the defense of the American hemisphere," said the president. The reporters persisted: "Mr. President, if this patrol should discover some apparently aggressive ships headed

58. C&R 1:166; Stimson Diary, April 25, 1941.
59. *Fuehrer Conferences*, in Rear-Admiral H. G. Thursfield, ed., *Brassey's Naval Annual, 1948* (London: William Clowes and Sons, 1948), 221.

toward the Western hemisphere, what would it do about it?" "Let me know," Roosevelt joked.[60]

In the meantime, Hitler was scoring spectacular gains in the Mediterranean. In April German troops pushed British forces back across the North African desert to the borders of Egypt. Other elements of the *Wehrmacht* swept through Yugoslavia and expelled the British army from Greece. On May 3 Churchill abandoned all restraint and frankly begged Roosevelt for an American declaration of war. Roosevelt demurred. The losses in the Mediterranean were regrettable, he said, but "this struggle is going to be decided in the Atlantic."[61]

Yet in the Atlantic the Americans were still doing no more than conducting reconnoitering patrols. "I am not willing to fire the first shot," Roosevelt told his cabinet.[62] Some of the all-outers were disgusted. "The President is loath to get into this war, and he would rather follow public opinion than lead it," an exasperated Morgenthau noted in mid-May. If the president would not ask for a declaration of war, Morgenthau suggested, "how about doing something internally first?" Two weeks later, seizing upon the news that the German battleship *Bismarck* had got loose on the Atlantic and had sunk the *Hood*, the obsolescent pride of the Royal Navy and the biggest battleship afloat, Roosevelt took up Morgenthau's suggestion and "did something internal." He gave a Fireside Chat that one of its authors described as "calculated to scare the daylights out of everyone"—but, he added, "it did not do much else."[63] Speaking from the White House on May 27 to an estimated audience of eighty-five million radio listeners worldwide, Roosevelt declared an "unlimited national emergency." But what did that mean in practice? At a press conference the following day, the president bewildered the reporters by suggesting that it meant very little. He had no intention of asking for neutrality revision, he explained. As for aggressive naval escorts, he breezily opined that they were "outmoded." Stimson fumed that the press conference was "one of his worst and almost undid the effect of his speech. . . . The President shows evidence of waiting for

60. PPA (1941), 132ff.
61. C&R 1:184.
62. Ickes Diary 3:523.
63. Dallek, 266. The British succeeded in sinking the *Bismarck* a few days later, after she had been sighted from the air by Tuck Smith, an American pilot on loan to the British Coastal Command.

the accidental shot of some irresponsible captain on either side to be the occasion of his going to war."[64]

Other all-outers shared Stimson's dismay. "My own feeling," Harold Ickes wrote in his diary, "is that the President has not aroused the country; has not really sounded the bell . . . , does not furnish the motive power that is required. . . . In his speech [of May 27] the President said that we would do everything necessary to defend our own land [and] he also left the way clear to convoy ships carrying food, merchandise, and arms to England. . . . But we really are in the same *status quo* . . . it seems that he is still waiting for the Germans to create an 'incident.' "[65]

In the spring of 1941, at least two incidents had already gone unused. The U.S. destroyer *Niblack*, steaming five hundred miles southwest of Iceland on April 11, picked up a sonar contact with what it thought was a U-boat and dropped several depth charges. Sometimes labeled the first hostile act of World War II between U.S. and Axis naval forces, the *Niblack*'s depth bombs were proved by postwar investigation to have exploded in an empty sea. No U-boat was in the area. Had Roosevelt seized on this "incident" to wage war against Hitler, he would have egregiously compounded the folly of relying for a *casus belli* on "an accidental shot of some irresponsible captain."[66]

On May 21 a U-boat sank the American freighter *Robin Moor* well outside the declared war zone, midway between the bulge of Brazil and the bight of Africa in the South Atlantic. In violation of international conventions, the U-boat captain cast the freighter's crew adrift in life-boats with meager rations and without radioing their position to nearby ships that might come to the rescue. When the first survivors were picked up on June 9 and told the story of the *Robin Moor*'s illegal sinking and the abandonment of its crew, the head of the British Purchasing Mission in the United States was not alone in praying for some "dividends" from the episode. The American all-outers also urged Roosevelt to seize upon this "incident," far more concrete and outrageous than the *Niblack*'s shadowy encounter of the previous month, to transform the Atlantic reconnaissance patrols into aggressive escorts. Roosevelt once again disappointed such hopes. He used the occasion only to close the remaining German consulates in the United States. Hitler's reaction to the *Robin Moor* incident, expressed on the very eve of

64. Stimson Diary, May 23, 29, 1941.
65. Ickes Diary 3:526–27.
66. See the account in Bailey and Ryan, *Hitler vs. Roosevelt*, 129–32.

Barbarossa, was once more to admonish Raeder "under all circumstances" to "avoid any possibility of incidents with the U.S.A." until the outcome of the Soviet invasion "becomes clearer, i.e., for a few weeks."[67]

As spring passed into summer in 1941, the Nazi juggernaut appeared unstoppable. With stunning successes in the Mediterranean and the Atlantic and with Barbarossa gaining lethal momentum, Hitler seemed about to sweep all before him. His adversaries in the emerging Grand Alliance looked on in dismay. Stalin anguished as the *Wehrmacht* rolled eastward into Russia, gobbling up miles of Soviet territory daily and carving a path of mayhem and destruction unparalleled in the annals of warfare. Churchill brooded over the losses in North Africa and the Balkans and the even more appalling losses of British ships in the Atlantic. He worried if he would ever succeed in coaxing his American cousins to take up arms. Roosevelt fretted over the competing demands of the Pacific and Atlantic theaters and struggled to get a grip on industrial mobilization.

The president also faced a nasty fight in the Congress over the extension of the Selective Service Act. Particularly nettlesome was a clause extending draftees' tour of duty for eighteen additional months beyond the twelve months specified in the original legislation of 1940. The recruits called up under that act a year earlier, chafing under the unfamiliar military discipline, confused about their part in a war that the president was still insisting they would never have to fight, were scrawling OHIO on the walls of their encampments. Had the fledgling troops in fact melted away—either by statutory release from duty, or by mass desertion, as the ubiquitously chalked code for "Over the Hill in October" threatened—the army would have had to start all over again, inflicting catastrophic delays on the Victory Program's timetable. Congress on August 12 approved the extension of service (while retaining the prohibition on deployment outside the Western Hemisphere) by a margin of a single vote in the House. The threatened desertions did not occur, and the army continued to grow, but the perilously thin margin in the House vote provided a sobering reminder of the nation's continuing reluctance to move to a full war footing.

The congressional vote on selective service came just as Churchill and

67. A good account of the *Robin Moor* episode is in Bailey and Ryan, *Hitler vs. Roosevelt*, 138–47. At about the same time, another near-incident occurred in the North Atlantic, when U203 mistook the U.S. battleship *Texas* for a British warship and shadowed her for 140 miles but failed to get into proper firing position. See Bailey and Ryan, *Hitler vs. Roosevelt*, 148–49.

Roosevelt were rendezvousing for their first face-to-face meeting as prime minister and president. On August 9 HMS *Prince of Wales*, bearing Winston Churchill, steamed into Placentia Bay, offshore of Argentia, a defunct Newfoundland silver-mining camp. The British battleship sidled up to the U.S. cruiser *Augusta*, aboard which Roosevelt awaited Churchill's arrival. The two ships rode at their anchors off Argentia for three days as the two leaders engaged in strategy sessions and camaraderie.

The Argentia meeting's most publicized accomplishment was a document that became known as the Atlantic Charter. Initiated by Roosevelt partly as a way of assuaging American anxieties that a war in alliance with Soviet Russia might contaminate democratic ideals, the charter pledged the two Western leaders to seek a postwar world that would honor the principles of self-determination, free trade, nonaggression, and freedom of the seas. The charter made vague reference to "the establishment of a wider and permanent system of general security." The two leaders also sent a message to Stalin pledging their assistance and proposing high-level political and military discussions at an early date.

Almost as soon as they settled into their chairs in the *Augusta*'s wardroom on the first evening of their talks, Churchill again pressed Roosevelt for an American declaration of war. "I would rather have an American declaration of war now and no supplies for six months than double the supplies and no declaration," he said. Roosevelt, certain that Congress would balk, again demurred. The president did agree at last that the U.S. Navy would provide armed escorts as far as Iceland. How he would announce such a bold step to the American public and to Congress remained a problem. As Churchill later explained to his War Cabinet, Roosevelt "said he would wage war, but not declare it, and that he would become more and more provocative. . . . Everything was to be done to force an 'incident.' . . . The President . . . made it clear that he would look for an 'incident' which would justify him in opening hostilities."[68]

Soon after the two leaders steamed away from Argentia on August 12, an "incident" presented itself. True to his pledge to Churchill aboard the *Augusta*, Roosevelt quickly grasped it, indeed substantially distorted it, as the occasion for his long-deferred announcement of armed escorts. On September 4 the U.S. destroyer *Greer*, proceeding toward Iceland with mail and supplies for the tiny marine garrison, received a blinker message from a patrolling British aircraft that a U-boat had been sighted ten miles ahead on the *Greer*'s course. The destroyer captain, conscious

68. Dallek, 285.

of his standing orders not to shoot but only to trail and report, rang up full speed and zig-zagged toward the U-boat, making sonar contact at a range of two thousand yards. The *Greer* locked on her quarry and assumed a narrow-target, bow-on orientation to the submarine. She held that position for over three hours while continuously reporting the U-boat's position to the British plane circling overhead. When the aircraft, running low on fuel, inquired if the U.S. ship was going to attack and got a negative reply, the pilot released four depth charges and flew away. The U-boat commander, knowing only that he was under attack and that as much of the *Greer*'s profile as he could see suggested she was one of the type of ships transferred to the Royal Navy in the destroyer-bases deal, loosed two torpedoes at the *Greer*. Both missed. The *Greer* retaliated with a pattern of eight depth charges, then a second pattern of eleven charges. None was effective, and U-652 eventually slipped away unharmed, as did the *Greer*.

A week went by, ample time for Roosevelt to get the facts of this encounter straight. But on September 11 he took to the radio and announced with studied hyperbole that an American warship had been the innocent victim of a wanton attack. "I tell you the blunt fact that the German submarine fired first upon this American destroyer without warning, and with deliberate design to sink her," the president misleadingly said. "These Nazi submarines and raiders are the rattlesnakes of the Atlantic," he went on, and then announced what was soon called the "shoot-on-sight" policy: "American naval vessels and American planes will no longer wait until Axis submarines, lurking under the water, or Axis raiders on the surface of the sea, strike their deadly blow. . . . From now on, if German or Italian vessels of war enter our waters . . . they do so at their own peril."[69] Six days later, off Newfoundland, Canadian escorts handed over a fifty-ship convoy eastbound from Halifax to five U.S. destroyers, who safely shepherded the merchantmen across the North Atlantic and into the hands of a Royal Navy squadron waiting just south of Iceland. The North Atlantic, remorselessly transforming with the autumn's waning light into a gloomy, frigid hell of mountainous seas, howling winds, and gathering danger, began slowly to fill with U.S. destroyers, warily flanking the precious merchant convoys.

Roosevelt's prolonged indecision and his ultimate deviousness in implementing the escort policy have exercised generations of critics. With

69. PPA (1941), 384.

respect to his indecision, it might be said that if statecraft were chemistry, the president's actions between March and September of 1941, and indeed in the periods before and after those dates, could be described as titrating—a series of experiments with various policy reagents to measure the volume and concentration of the isolationist acid that remained in the American body politic. Much polling data supports the argument that in fact Roosevelt took the wrong measurements from those experiments, that a majority of the American people were prepared to accept escorting well before the president's dubious rendition of the *Greer* episode.[70] But Roosevelt was more alchemist than chemist. His tools were the sorcerer's arts of politics, not the deceptively tidy algorithms of science. He was also true to the democratic politician's creed when he worried about the political necessity of creating a consensus among the American people as he brought them to the brink of war. As the historian Robert Dallek persuasively concludes, "it is difficult to fault Roosevelt for building a consensus by devious means. . . . [I]f he had advised the public of the fact that the U-boat had fired in defense and that Hitler did not then seem intent on attacking America's Atlantic traffic . . . he would have risked having to wait for the collapse of Russia and Britain's near demise before gaining broad national support for a resort to arms. . . . [T]hat would have been a failure of his responsibility as Commander in Chief."[71] It is also important to note that whatever Roosevelt's duplicity concerning the *Greer*, he used the incident not to take the country into full-blown war but only to secure the much more limited policy of an armed response to Hitler's U-boats.

As for Hitler, his restraint had all along matched Roosevelt's hesitation, and it lasted longer. Even after the *Greer* speech and Roosevelt's announcement of a state of virtual naval warfare in the Atlantic, *der Führer* continued to reject Raeder's advice to attack American ships. Instead, he ordered his submariners "to avoid any incidents in the war on merchant shipping before about the middle of October"—when he apparently expected the Soviet invasion to be wrapped up.[72]

Incidents nevertheless ensued. U-boat commanders making spot decisions in the sweat of battle were less punctilious than their superiors

---

70. Robert A. Divine, for example, concludes flatly that "Roosevelt could have begun convoys months earlier with solid public support." Divine, *The Reluctant Belligerent* (New York: John Wiley and Sons, 1965), 144.

71. Dallek, 289.

72. *Fuehrer Conferences on Matters Dealing with the German Navy* (Washington: U.S. Office of Naval Intelligence, 1947), 2:33 (September 17, 1941).

calmly calibrating policies in the security of headquarters. On October 17 U568 put a torpedo into the bowels of the U.S. destroyer *Kearny*, which limped into Iceland, escorted by the now notorious *Greer*, bearing eleven dead sailors, the first American casualties of the still undeclared war. On October 27, Roosevelt responded with an exceptionally belligerent address. "America has been attacked," he proclaimed. "The U.S.S. *Kearny* is not just a Navy ship. She belongs to every man, woman, and child in this Nation. . . . I say that we do not propose to take this lying down. . . . [W]e Americans have cleared our decks and taken our battle stations." To justify his bellicosity, Roosevelt charged that he had seen a document laying out Hitler's "plan to abolish all existing religions — Catholic, Protestant, Mohammedan, Hindu, Buddhist, and Jewish alike." No less wildly, and with even less basis in fact than his account of the *Greer* attack, Roosevelt alleged that he had in his possession a "secret map" showing the Nazi plan to divide all of South America into "five vassal states."[73] But the president still declined to ask for a declaration of war. Instead, Roosevelt merely asked for the authority to arm American merchant vessels and to allow them to enter combat zones — in effect repealing the "carry" provisions of the neutrality laws. Congress obliged him in early November.

Just three days after Roosevelt's egregiously inflammatory remarks of October 27, six hundred miles west of Ireland, U552 sent a single torpedo into the midship ammunition magazine of the USS *Reuben James*. The American destroyer broke in two and sank almost instantaneously, killing 115 seamen. Despite these escalating provocations from both sides, America still remained officially neutral. The Germans and the Americans faced each other in the North Atlantic through periscope and gunsight in a tense standoff. With Germany absorbed in the east and with America still largely unarmed, neither side was prepared to take the next step toward a formal declaration of all-out war. So things might have remained indefinitely save for another "incident," replete with drama and consequence, that exploded not in the gray expanse of the wintry Atlantic but in the blue waters of the tropical Pacific.

IF THE TANGLED SKEIN of events that eventually led to war between Japan and the United States could be summed up in a single word, that word would be "China." From the 1890s onward, Japan had

---

73. *PPA* (1941), 438ff. The maps and documents that Roosevelt referred to were almost certainly forgeries. See Bailey and Ryan, *Hitler vs. Roosevelt*, 203.

cast covetous eyes on China, especially on the fertile, resource-rich region of Manchuria. There Japan longed to pursue its own imperial destiny, in emulation of the Western powers that had already laid claim to much of Asia and threatened the integrity of China itself. Following the Meiji Restoration of 1868, Japan had embarked on an astounding program of modernization, leaping from feudal insularity to advanced industrial status in scarcely more than a generation, and whetting an imperial appetite commensurate with its growing economic heft. In 1905 Japan spectacularly demonstrated both its economic achievements and its surging ambitions by waging a successful war against czarist Russia, Japan's foremost rival for control of Manchuria and, along with Britain, for supremacy in East Asia. The Russo-Japanese War's climactic naval battle at Tsushima Straits also offered a prophetic glimpse of Japan's mastery of naval warfare, then the most technologically sophisticated branch of combat. Victory over Russia made Japan the first non-Western state ever to achieve military success against one of the traditional European "great powers," an exhilarating triumph that further fed Japan's imperial aspirations.

The United States, however, had stepped in as the spoiler of Japanese dreams as early as 1905. Theodore Roosevelt arbitrated a settlement of the Russo-Japanese conflict that denied the Japanese claim for a large indemnity payment from the czar and rejected the full menu of territorial concessions in Manchuria that Tokyo demanded. In Japanese eyes, the pattern was thus early established of inexplicably gratuitous American resistance to Japan's just deserts, as well as American refusal to accept Japan as a legitimate imperial power in Asia — such as the United States itself had recently become, with its annexation of the Philippine Islands in 1898. In the years that followed, again and again Japan watched the United States assume the spoiler's part, the American role often colored with an ugly tincture of racial condescension that exacerbated Japanese resentment. The Americans shut off further immigration from Japan to the United States in the so-called Gentlemen's Agreement of 1908; they declined in 1919 to accept the Japanese proposal for a declaration of racial equality in the Versailles peace treaty, forced unwanted naval limitations on Japan in the Washington Naval Disarmament Conference of 1922, permanently debarred from American citizenship the tiny Japanese immigrant community in the notorious "national origins" immigration law of 1924, and, most provocative of all, refused to extend diplomatic recognition to the Japanese military takeover of Manchuria in 1931.

Japan had a huge stake in Manchuria. Manchuria promised salvation from the ills of the Great Depression, which had closed many traditional markets to Japan and heightened the sense of vulnerability that came from its lack of raw materials and adequate foodstuffs. Tokyo installed a puppet government in Manchuria, renamed the territory the state of Manchukuo, and dispatched half a million Japanese colonists to settle there, including 250,000 farmers to relieve the island kingdom's dependence on foreign food imports. America's response was the Stimson Doctrine, proclaimed in 1932 by Herbert Hoover's secretary of state, the same man who in 1940 became Franklin Roosevelt's secretary of war. Stimson's manifesto declared that the United States would not officially recognize the Manchukuo regime, nor any other arrangements imposed on China by force.

The Stimson Doctrine served as the foundation of American policy regarding China and Japan for the following decade. It provided the political and ideological framework for the unfolding events that eventually led to war. The doctrine irritated and baffled the Japanese, as it did some Americans. It was a statement of high principle but based on no concrete American material stake in China—certainly nothing to match the substantial Japanese investment there, and for that matter nothing to match the scale of America's trade with Japan. Under neither Hoover nor Roosevelt did Washington choose to back the Stimson Doctrine with economic or military muscle. The Stimson Doctrine represented "an attitude rather than a program," the historian Herbert Feis concluded. As events were to prove, mere attitudes were dangerous guides to foreign policy, especially when they were premised on morally charged and uncompromisable principles rather than on negotiable material assets. But for better or worse, the Stimson Doctrine remained the cornerstone of American policy in Asia. And in 1940 the man who had laid that stone once again took his seat in the highest councils of the American government.

Japan's renewed assault on China in 1937 exposed both the hollowness and the rigidity of the Stimson Doctrine. "We have large emotional interests in China, small economic interests, and no vital interests," William Bullitt reminded Roosevelt. For those reasons, Bullitt urged the president to take a more conciliatory tone with the Japanese, especially in light of the very tangible American interests that needed attending to in Europe, the historically paramount theater of American concern. Roosevelt instead loudly condemned Japan's action—but he did little more than that. He extended some token aid to Chiang Kai-shek, the head of China's Nationalist, or Kuomintang, government, though Chiang seemed undecided whether his principal foe was the Japanese invader or his Chinese Communist opponents. Simultaneously, Roosevelt continued to allow American exports to flow to Japan, including the steel and petroleum products that fueled the Japanese army's brutal subjugation of China's coastal cities and its occupation of the valleys of the Yangtze and Yellow rivers. The "China Incident," as the Japanese incursion was called, threw into high relief the four-decades-old central paradox of America's Asian diplomacy: the United States wanted to champion Chinese sovereignty and to control developments in Asia, even in the absence of any substantial American interests on the ground; at the same time, Washington resisted the commitment of any appreciable economic, diplomatic, or military resources to the region. Here was a perilous disconnect between American aspirations and American means, a gap between the national wish and the national will. In that dangerously inviting space, Japan dared to seek its advantage.[74]

By 1940 the China Incident was three years old. Its continuation was a burden, even an embarrassment, to the Tokyo regime. Japanese troops, spearheaded by the quasi-independent Manchurian occupational force, the Kwantung Army, had inflicted appalling hardships on the Chinese. The war had also wrung ever-greater sacrifices from the Japanese people themselves, but the army had not yet succeeded in quelling Chinese resistance. Chiang Kai-shek withdrew deep into the Chinese interior, established a new capital at Chunking in Szechwan province, and waited for Tokyo to tire of its costly China adventure. Frustrated by those tactics, Japanese military leaders sought with increasing desperation to resolve the incident once and for all. They groped for ways to insulate China from outside help. They simultaneously sought to liberate island Japan from dependence on foreign sources of supply, perhaps by widening the arc of conflict to include Siberian Russia or Southeast Asia. But the Americans, still somewhat incomprehensibly in Japanese minds, continued to oppose Japanese designs. "In particular, after the entry of Stimson into the Government," a Japanese diplomat explained to the German foreign minister in 1940, "Japan had to be very careful in regard to America in order not to provoke that country into taking severe measures against Japan." The Americans had by that time already put themselves on the road to taking severe measures: in January 1940 they

---

74. Donald B. Schewe, ed., *Franklin D. Roosevelt and Foreign Affairs* (New York: Clearwater, 1969), 2d ser. 7:349.

abrogated their 1911 commercial treaty with Japan, opening the way at last to the possible imposition of trade embargoes.[75]

The Japanese military's gnawing impatience to find a way to break the stalemate in China brought down Japan's government in July 1940. It was the third Japanese cabinet to fall in less than two years—strong evidence of the tension and uncertainty besetting the Japanese leadership. Prince Fumimaro Konoye, prime minister when the Sino-Japanese war had begun in 1937, and notoriously opposed to any negotiated settlement with Chiang, formed a new cabinet pledged to "expedite the settlement of the China Incident" and "solve the Southern Area problem." A docile aristocrat, Konoye was destined to be Japan's last prewar civilian prime minister.

Konoye's government included General Hideki Tojo as war minister. Tojo was a second-generation professional soldier whose reputation as a ruthless disciplinarian had earned him the nickname "the Razor." As chief of staff of the Kwantung Army in 1937, he had been a major architect of the Chinese incursion. He was among the hardest of Japan's legions of hard-liners. Like Konoye, he opposed any diplomatic compromise with Chiang Kai-shek. He believed that only a crushing application of military force could bring the China Incident to an end. Unlike Konoye, Tojo did not flinch from facing additional enemies, including the Soviet Union, Britain, and the United States, if that would bring success in China, and secure Japanese paramountcy in Asia.[76]

Tojo now wielded fearsome power, not least because of the peculiar role of the Japanese military in the scheme of Japanese civil government. By political convention and, after 1936, by law, the ministers of the army and navy were chosen not from civilian ranks but from the senior officer corps of the respective services. Thus by refusing to nominate a candidate or by withdrawing its officer from the cabinet, either of the armed services could topple a government. Moreover, the military reserved unto itself "the right of supreme command," by which it could deal directly with the emperor, bypassing the civilian government altogether. Konoye was thus Tojo's hostage, and the Razor quickly bent the pliant, melancholic prime minister to his will.

Until 1940, the Japanese invasion of China had been a regional event.

75. Herbert Feis, *The Road to Pearl Harbor* (Princeton: Princeton University Press, 1950), 77.
76. Scott D. Sagan, "The Origins of the Pacific War," in Robert I. Rotberg and Theodore K. Rabb, *The Origin and Prevention of Major Wars* (Cambridge: Cambridge University Press, 1988), 326.

It convulsed Asia, to be sure, and proceeded in worrisome parallel with the quickening pace of aggression in Europe, but it remained essentially an isolated affair, unlinked to the other fateful moves being played out on the great game board of global strategy. But Hitler's *Blitzkrieg* conquest of France and the Netherlands and the onset of the Battle of Britain in the summer of 1940 rearranged that game board and rewrote the geopolitical rules. Tojo and other Japanese imperialists now saw prospects opening before them that they had not earlier dared to dream. Hitler's successes, American ambassador to Tokyo Joseph Grew observed, had "gone to their heads like strong wine."[77]

With the colonial powers under Hitler's guns in Europe, Japan brought pressure to bear on French Indochina and the Dutch East Indies to supply Japan with rice, rubber, oil, and basing rights, as well as on British Burma to close the Burma Road, cutting off Chiang's principal supply route. In one of his rare recorded criticisms of the militarists' policies, Emperor Hirohito likened those initiatives to the actions "of a thief at a fire."[78] Tojo was unmoved. With broad support from both military and civilian leaders, Tojo breathed defiance at the distracted British and the meddlesome but weak and unarmed Americans and began negotiating a formal alliance with Nazi Germany and Fascist Italy. These steps in mid-1940 set events on the pathway to a *world* war.

Washington had two means of restraining Japan: either by bolstering China, as it was bolstering Britain, or by imposing economic sanctions on Japan—a policy instrument all but useless against virtually self-sufficient Germany but potentially highly effective against import-dependent Japan. As for direct aid to China, the simple facts were that China was not Britain, and Chiang Kai-shek was no Churchill. China's military performance was pitiful and deteriorating, and Chiang's inability to shape an effective government inspired little confidence. Roosevelt did extend modest credits to China. He also allowed American military pilots to resign their commissions and join Colonel Claire Chennault's Flying Tigers, a volunteer combat air squadron that flew for the Chinese. Eventually a trickle of Lend-Lease aid reached Chiang. But Washington's principal tool for restraining Tokyo was economic sanctions against Japan.

By 1940 Japan depended on the United States for a long list of indispensable strategic materials, conspicuously including oil; 80 percent

77. Leuchtenburg, 309.
78. Feis, *Road to Pearl Harbor*, 95.

of Japan's fuel supplies came from America. Roosevelt knew that Japanese dependence on American sources of supply gave him a powerful club. He also knew that it was a dangerous weapon to use. "If we once start sanctions against Japan we must see them through to the end," Ambassador Grew warned Roosevelt in the autumn of 1939, "and the end may conceivably be war. . . . [I]f we cut off Japanese supplies of oil . . . [Japan] will in all probability send her fleets down to take the Dutch East Indies."[79]

On July 26, 1940, Roosevelt forged an important link in the chain of events that would lead to war. Seeking to restrain Japanese pressure on the European colonial possessions in Southeast Asia, he declared an embargo on the shipment to Japan of premium grades of scrap iron and steel, as well as high-octane aviation gasoline. That move nettled the Japanese but did not deter them. Tokyo landed troops in northern French Indochina, with the Vichy government's compliant approval, and officially joined the Axis by signing the Tripartite Pact with Germany and Italy in September. By terms of the accord, the signatories pledged "to assist one another with all political, economic and military means when one of the three contracting Parties is attacked by a power at present not involved in the European War or in the Sino-Japanese Conflict."[80] An additional clause specifically exempted the Soviet Union from that last description—making it unmistakably clear that the pact was intended above all to cow the United States into remaining neutral by menacing the Americans with the prospect of a two-ocean war. Washington responded to the Tripartite Pact with a further turn of the economic screw, extending the list of embargoed items to include *all* iron and steel shipments.

Both Japan and the United States by this point had settled into the rhythm that would characterize their relationship for the next year. Each stepped through a series of escalating moves that provoked but failed to restrain the other, all the while lifting the level of confrontation to ever-riskier heights. Tokyo calculated what aggression it could pursue without precipitating open conflict with Washington. The Americans gambled that they could pressure Japan by economic means without driving Tokyo to war. For each side, however, the attitude of the other remained

79. Grew quoted in Daniel Yergin, *The Prize: The Epic Quest for Oil, Money, and Power* (New York: Simon and Schuster, 1991), 310.
80. *Documents on German Foreign Policy, 1918–1945* (Washington: USGPO, 1960), Series D (1937–1945), *The War Years*, September 1, 1940–January 31, 1941, 204–205.

a secondary consideration. Japan's highest priority was still China. America's was Europe.

Conspicuously absent from the expanded American embargo list in September 1940 was the most vital of Japan's needs: oil. Other than aviation gasoline, petroleum products remained unembargoed thanks largely to the influence of Secretary of State Hull. Within the American government, a Great Debate over policy toward Japan raged from the summer of 1940 virtually until the outbreak of open hostilities in December 1941. This debate was much less publicly audible than the discussion of aid to Britain, but no less portentous. Not incidentally, the two struggles to define American policy, in Europe and in Asia, were also virtually synchronous. Many of those who favored all-out assistance to Britain also lined up in favor of strong measures against Japan. They included the quietly aggressive Morgenthau, Ickes, who truculently branded any lesser policy "appeasement," and of course the stiffly principled Stimson. Hull, on the other hand, with the strong backing of the U.S. Navy, as well as the generally consistent support of Ambassador Grew in Tokyo, argued that broader sanctions would simply prod the Japanese into seeking alternative sources of supply, by military force if necessary, in French Indochina, British Burma and Malaya, the Dutch East Indies, and even the Philippines. Those moves the United States would be powerless to prevent, especially given the American commitment, embedded in Plan Dog, ratified at ABC-1, and reaffirmed at Argentia and in the Victory Program, to give priority to the struggle against Hitler. An armed confrontation with Japan, in the view of Hull and the senior military leaders, would be the wrong war, with the wrong enemy, in the wrong place, and at the wrong time. For a long season, Hull's views prevailed, if only partially.

Hull by this date had grown accustomed to partial victories. Born in a log cabin in 1871, he had soldiered his way up through the political ranks in his native Tennessee. He had served first in the state legislature, then for more than two decades as a congressman. His fellow Tennesseans sent him to the U.S. Senate in 1930, but he cut his term short in 1933 to accept appointment as secretary of state. Roosevelt always dominated him and frequently undercut him, most notoriously at the London Economic Conference in 1933. Another man might have resigned after that humiliation, but Hull plowed on, pushing his special interests in the Good Neighbor Policy and in free trade and swallowing the further humiliation of watching his undersecretary, Sumner Welles, enjoy better access to the president than he himself did. Roosevelt did not consult Hull about Welles's mission to Europe in 1940 and excluded Hull from the Argentia Conference, the ABC-1 talks, and the Lend-Lease negotiations. Dogged, conscientious, and dull, Hull was a plodding bureaucrat, a predictable thinker, and a boring public speaker. He worked six full days a week plus Sunday mornings, took a briefcase of papers home every evening, and shunned the capital's social life. His only recreation was an occasional game of croquet on the lawn of Henry Stimson's estate. Washington insiders called him "Parson Hull."

That Hull enjoyed such influence as he did in shaping policy toward Japan indicated how relatively unimportant Roosevelt considered the entire Pacific region to be. When it came to Europe, Roosevelt handled matters himself. To Hull he left the decidedly lesser matter of negotiating with the Japanese. Hull succeeded for a time in dampening the tempo of economic warfare against Japan, but the coil of sanctions was nevertheless tugged progressively tighter. In December 1940 Washington added iron ore and pig iron to the prohibited list; the following month, copper and brass, and additional materials on a regular basis thereafter — but still not oil.

The closing cinch of the American embargo only slightly reined in the Japanese, but it worried them greatly, especially as they contemplated the ever-present threat of its extension to oil. In early 1941 Tokyo sent a new ambassador to Washington, Kichisaburo Nomura, an earnest naval officer and former foreign minister who had some acquaintance with the United States and a serviceable, but halting, command of English. In March he began a series of what would be some fifty meetings with Hull, many of them conducted in the secretary's suite at the Wardman Park Hotel. Nomura labored under heavy handicaps from the outset. Unknown to him, American cryptanalysts had cracked the highest Japanese diplomatic codes. Thanks to Magic — the code name for this intelligence breakthrough — they were able to brief Hull on Nomura's positions even before the Japanese ambassador presented them, and often with greater clarity than Nomura's broken English could manage. (He insisted on working without a translator, a practice that also led to his frequent misunderstanding of what Hull was saying.) Beyond that, Nomura was hobbled by the policies he was compelled, somewhat against his own better judgment, to defend and by his despair over the accelerating momentum for war in Tokyo. He poignantly expressed his discomfort. "I deeply fear lest I should make a miscalculation at this moment, and besides, there is a limit to my ability," he wrote to his superiors in Tokyo. "I am unable to perceive the delicate shades of the policy of the Government, and am quite at a loss what to do."[81]

In reality, Nomura's government's policy was not so much delicately shaded as it was intractable, a disagreeable fact that Nomura struggled to downplay but could not in the end evade. On his side, Hull, too, represented a government that was inflexibly committed to the one thing Nomura could not possibly concede—a Japanese withdrawal from China. Time and again through 1941 Nomura indicated that Japan might be willing to back off from pressuring Southeast Asia if the Americans would stop aiding China and lift the trade sanctions. Time and again Hull replied that Japanese withdrawal from China was the precondition for further negotiations. Throughout their tedious, repetitive conversations, each of the two negotiators did little more than affirm his opinion of the other's intransigence. Through the spring and summer the one goal they shared was to gain time, to postpone the moment of confrontation until, in Nomura's case, cooler and wiser heads might prevail, or, in Hull's case, until the American naval and military buildup might alter the balance of forces in the Pacific.

Hitler stepped forward in June 1941 as the thief of time. Just as it shattered so many other assumptions and plans, Operation Barbarossa broke the temporizing stalemate in Hull's hotel room. In a callous exhibition of his opportunistic attachment to the Tripartite Pact accord, Hitler launched Barbarossa without forewarning his Japanese "ally." His attack on the Soviet Union surprised the Japanese as much as it did the Russians. It also triggered a fateful argument within the Japanese government. "Northerners" who favored joining Hitler's attack on the Soviet Union were pitted against "southerners" who argued that now was the time, while the Soviet-German death struggle secured Japan's Siberian flank, to plunge into the rice paddies and rubber plantations of Indochina and Malaya and the coveted oil fields of the Dutch East Indies. The southerners invoked weighty arguments. Seizing Southeast Asia would girdle much of China's periphery with Japanese power, seal Chiang off from outside help, and thereby seal his fate. Moreover, the southerners argued, Japan had only a two-year reserve of oil, eighteen months under war conditions, and the American spigot could be turned off any day. Now was the moment to seize the rich Dutch East Indian oil fields and end Japan's humiliating dependence on the Americans for

81. L&G, *Undeclared*, 657.

essential fuel supplies. If Japan were ever to end the China Incident, claim industrial self-sufficiency, and make good on its promise of creating an "Asia for the Asians," cleansed of the Western colonial powers, then the time was now.

The most aggressive of the northerners, Foreign Minister Yosuke Matsuoka, urged Japan to join Hitler's attack on the Soviet Union, thus extinguishing for all time the age-old Russian threat. "He who would search for pearls must dive deep," Matsuoka told the cabinet. "The outbreak of war between Germany and the Soviet Union presents Japan with a golden opportunity such as comes only once in a thousand years," declared another of the northerners, mindful of Japan's historic contest with Russia for hegemony in East Asia.[82] But by this time the northern option looked decidedly unattractive. The Kwantung Army was still smarting from its mortifying defeat by Soviet forces in the summer of 1939 at Nomonhan, a speck of an outpost on the Halha River, which defined the frontier between Soviet Mongolia and Japanese-controlled Manchukuo. Remembering Nomonhan, chastened Japanese army generals refused to take the offensive against a Soviet force unless they enjoyed overwhelming numerical superiority. Stalin's daring decision not to shift his Siberian garrisons to the defense of Moscow, along with evidence of stiffening Soviet resistance against the Germans, robbed the northerners of their "golden opportunity." At a conference in the emperor's presence on July 2, the southerners carried the day. The decision to go south was confirmed. "We will not be deterred by the possibility of being in a war with England and America," the conferees confidently recorded. Before the month was out, Japanese troops, already ensconced in northern Indochina, had moved into southern Indochina, clearly a preparatory move for the leap into British Malaya and the Dutch East Indies.[83]

Thanks to Magic, officials in Washington were able to follow closely these deliberations in Tokyo. "[T]he Japs are having a real drag-down and knock-out fight among themselves," Roosevelt told Harold Ickes, "trying to decide which way they are going to jump—attack Russia, attack the South Seas . . . , or whether they will sit on the fence and be more friendly with us. No one knows what the decision will be but, as

82. Hosoya Chihiro, "The Japanese-Soviet Neutrality Pact," in J. W. Morley, ed., *The Fateful Choice: Japan's Advance into Southeast Asia, 1939–1941* (New York: Columbia University Press, 1980), 97, 101.
83. Feis, *Road to Pearl Harbor*, 216.

you know, it is terribly important for the control of the Atlantic for us to help keep peace in the Pacific." As for what, precisely, to do in the face of this new Japanese threat, Roosevelt was less sure. His preoccupation with "the control of the Atlantic" was a heavy constraint on any show of force against the Japanese. "I simply have not got enough Navy to go round," Roosevelt complained, "and every little episode in the Pacific means fewer ships in the Atlantic."[84]

While Roosevelt tried to devise a response to Japan's southward thrust, the American naval chiefs counseled prudence. An embargo on oil was the obvious step to take, and the American hard-liners were warmly urging such a step. But the War Plans Division of the navy cautioned the president on July 21, 1941, that "an embargo would probably result in a fairly early attack by Japan on Malaya and the Netherlands East Indies, and possibly would involve the United States in early [the implication was "premature"] war in the Pacific. . . . Recommendation: That trade with Japan not be embargoed at this time."[85]

On July 26 Roosevelt announced the American response. He declared an immediate freeze on all Japanese assets in the United States, requiring any further Japanese purchases to be cleared through a government committee that would unblock dollars to pay for the exports. Despite much misunderstanding then and later, this was not a total embargo on trade with Japan. Roosevelt was merely unsheathing that ultimate economic weapon, not yet plunging it into the vitals of his foe. He conceived of the freeze on assets as a temporary and complicating device, one more click of the trade-sanction ratchet, a carefully measured policy consistent with the slowly escalating restrictions that had gone before. The American hard-liners were disappointed. "Notwithstanding that Japan was boldly making this hostile move," a frustrated Ickes noted in his diary, "the President . . . was still unwilling to draw the noose tight. . . . [He] indicated that we would still continue to ship oil and gasoline." Over the objections of cabinet members who wanted "a complete job as quickly as possible . . . , [the President] thought that it might be better to slip the noose around Japan's neck and give it a jerk now and then."[86] Freezing Japanese assets was, in the last analysis, intended to be but another instance in Roosevelt's continuing policy of "appeasement" toward Japan that so infuriated Ickes and other hard-liners. They soon

84. Ickes Diary 3:567.
85. Feis, *The Road to Pearl Harbor*, 232.
86. Ickes Diary 3:588.

found a means to turn the president's latest pronouncement to their own purposes.[87]

The goal of Roosevelt's move was to cultivate maximum uncertainty in Japan about future American intentions. More uncertainty in Tokyo meant more time for American shipyards and aircraft plants, and more apprehension about the future of trade relations with America should breed a greater Japanese willingness to yield something at the negotiating table. Certainly Roosevelt did not envision the freeze as a provocation to war. All to the contrary, America's "chief objective in the Pacific for the time being," Sumner Welles told his British counterpart at the Argentia Conference just days later, "was the avoidance of war with Japan."[88] But in one of those striking vignettes that illustrate the contingent character of history, the freeze was promulgated on the eve of Roosevelt's departure for Argentia, and in his absence poorly instructed and temperamentally aggressive government officials refused to thaw any Japanese assets at all, for any purchases whatever. Roosevelt learned only in early September, after his return from Newfoundland, that his intended temporary freeze had congealed into the glacial hardness of a total embargo. By then it would have been a sign of weakness to back down. Contrary to the president's original intention, all American trade with Japan was now cut off. "The vicious circle of reprisals and counter reprisals is on," a gloomy Grew recorded in his diary in Tokyo, lapsing into the Latin that came naturally to the Groton-and Harvard-educated diplomat: "Facilis descensus averni est," the descent into hell is easy.[89]

The Japanese now watched with envy and anger as heavily laden American tankers plowed through La Perouse Strait between Hokkaido and Sakhalin, headed for Vladivostok with oil for the Russians, while the last Japanese tankers churned away high-hulled and empty from the American West Coast. The clock now measured time differently in To-

---

87. See the excellent account of this episode in Waldo Heinrichs, *Threshold of War: Franklin D. Roosevelt and American Entry into World War II* (New York: Oxford University Press, 1988), 133ff.

88. Dallek, 300.

89. Feis, *Road to Pearl Harbor*, 248. Assistant Secretary of State Dean Acheson played a crucial role in transforming what Roosevelt had intended to be a temporary measure into an airtight (and war-breeding) embargo. Acheson later unapologetically defended his behavior: "whether or not we had a policy, we had a state of affairs," he wrote in his memoirs. See Acheson, *Present at the Creation: My Years in the State Department* (New York: Norton, 1969), 26.

kyo and Washington. The Americans still wanted more of it. The Japanese worried that it was rapidly running out on them. They felt, said one Japanese leader, "like a fish in a pond from which water was gradually being drained away."[90] The Imperial Navy calculated that in the event of war it had an eighteen-month oil reserve and that it would enjoy no more than a two-year period of superiority over the U.S. Navy in the Pacific, given the pace of the naval building program then proceeding in the United States. The window of opportunity was narrow and closing rapidly. The Americans had thrown down the gauntlet. The challenge had to be accepted soon.

On September 6 a Japanese Imperial Conference stipulated that if a reversal of the American policy were not achieved through diplomatic means by early October, Japan should launch the "Southern Operation." Its main strategic objective would be the oil of the Dutch East Indies. As Japanese war games had repeatedly demonstrated, however, for the Southern Operation to be successful Japan must first knock out the huge British naval facility at Singapore, deny the Americans the use of the Philippines as a forward basing area, and venture far out into the Pacific to cripple the main elements of the American Pacific Fleet at Pearl Harbor, Hawaii. The plan was hugely ambitious but not insane. Its slender logic resided largely in the hope that the Americans would be so stunned by Japan's lightning blows that they would lose the will to fight a protracted war and accept a negotiated settlement guaranteeing Japan a free hand in Asia. All the Japanese planners understood that a conventional victory, ending in the complete defeat of the United States, was an impossibility. Admiral Takijiru Onishi was one of the few voices warning that an attack on Pearl Harbor might make the Americans "so insanely mad" that all hope for compromise would go up in flames. If the Americans should choose to fight a war to the finish, all knew, Japan was almost certainly doomed. The emperor, a diminutive figure revered by his people as the son of God, a taciturn man who usually sat impassively during these ritualized conferences, appreciated the perils ahead. He sharply reminded his military leaders that China's extensive hinterland had cheated Japan of victory on the Asian mainland and that "the Pacific was boundless." To that cryptic utterance he added nothing more, and the plan was approved.[91]

90. Satō Kenryō, quoted in Heinrichs, *Threshold of War*, 182.
91. Gordon W. Prange, *At Dawn We Slept: The Untold Story of Pearl Harbor* (New York: Penguin, 1981), 261; Feis, *Road to Pearl Harbor*, 266.

Prime Minister Konoye made one last bid to prevent war. On the evening after the September 6 Imperial Conference he invited Grew to dine, taking elaborate precautions to keep the occasion secret: using a friend's home, removing the license plates from his car, dismissing the servants. Over the sake and rice, Konoye pressed for a personal meeting with Roosevelt, perhaps in Honolulu. Grew vigorously supported the idea, but when it became clear that the Americans still insisted on Japanese abandonment of China as a precondition for such a meeting, the proposal collapsed. On October 16 Konoye was ousted as prime minister. Tojo replaced him.

In both capitals the measured language of diplomacy could no longer muffle the rising beat of the military tatoo. On November 5 another Imperial Conference directed that war plans should go forward, to be confirmed on November 25 if a last diplomatic effort failed. Ironically enough, on that same date of November 5, the American Joint Board of the Army and Navy reaffirmed that the primary objective of the United States "is the defeat of Germany." Therefore, the Joint Board concluded, "[w]ar between the United States and Japan should be avoided." Even further Japanese offensives in China "would not justify intervention by the United States against Japan." In short, American military planners were conceding their inability to affect events in China and were still looking for ways to avoid an Asian distraction when their main concern was Germany.[92]

Well might the question be pondered: Why did the American government not publicly accept the logic of this reasoning? Why not acquiesce, however complainingly, in the Japanese action in China, reopen at least limited trade with Japan, and thereby deflect Tokyo from its course of aggression in Southeast Asia? By the American military planners' own admission, such a policy would have had little immediate bearing on the situation in China, which the United States was all but powerless to influence in any case. More important, it would have delayed—perhaps postponed indefinitely—a showdown between America and Japan. Delay would have given the Americans more time to arm and more munitions to share with the British and the Russians. Whether under those circumstances a Japanese-American war could have been avoided altogether is among the weightiest of might-have-beens, with implications for the nature and timing of America's struggle against Hit-

92. Feis, *Road to Pearl Harbor*, 302.

ler and for the shape of postwar Europe as well as Asia. But it was not to be.

Just days after the November 5 Imperial Conference, Tokyo dispatched the seasoned diplomatist Saburo Kurusu to assist the hapless Nomura in presenting a final proposal to Washington. On November 20 Nomura and Kurusu described the Japanese offer to Hull: they asked for a free hand in China and an end to American trade restrictions, in return for a Japanese withdrawal from Indochina and a pledge to undertake no further armed advances in Southeast Asia. There was little new here. But given the Joint Board's recent recommendation to acquiesce in events in China and avoid war with Japan, this Japanese approach held some promise, at which Roosevelt momentarily grasped. Though he remained wary of the Japanese, telling Ickes that "he was not sure whether or not Japan had a gun up its sleeve" (to which Ickes replied that he was sure that before long "Japan would be at our throats"), he drafted notes for a conciliatory reply to this latest Japanese proposal. He envisioned a 6-month *modus vivendi* with Japan and included a significant concession: he dropped the American insistence on withdrawal from China.[93]

Roosevelt next circulated his draft notes for comment by Churchill, Chiang, and his own cabinet members. Morgenthau, Ickes, and Stimson were outraged. So was Chiang, who predicted the utter demoralization and certain surrender of China if American opposition to Japan's role there were relaxed. Churchill concurred with Chiang and spelled out the strategic implications of China's possible downfall: "What about Chiang Kai-shek? Is he not having a very thin diet? Our anxiety is about China. If they collapse our joint dangers would enormously increase."[94] Despite the Joint Board's recommendation that China be cut adrift, China, Roosevelt now saw, had taken on more significance, not less, after the German invasion of Russia. If Chiang were not sustained in the war, Japan would be free to attack the Soviet Union, perhaps precipitating a Soviet collapse and thus nullifying the great gift that Barbarossa had bestowed upon American and British strategists. In any case, prospects for Japanese acceptance of the proposal looked slim. Reports were already coming in to Washington of Japanese troop transports heading south past Formosa, toward Southeast Asia. Roosevelt discarded the

93. Ickes Diary 3:649.
94. C&R 1:277–78.

modus vivendi. The last flimsy hope of avoiding, or even delaying, war with Japan thus evaporated.

At a White House meeting on November 25, administration officials agreed that little room for negotiation remained. War, in some form, seemed inevitable. "The question," Stimson thought, "was how we should maneuver them into the position of firing the first shot without allowing too much danger to ourselves."[95] The second part of Stimson's observation was at least as important as the first. Despite decades of investigation, no credible evidence has ever been adduced to support the charge that Roosevelt deliberately exposed the fleet at Pearl Harbor to attack in order to precipitate war. Risking the entire Pacific Fleet to create a *casus belli* surely constituted far "too much danger to ourselves," especially in light of Roosevelt's repeated efforts to avoid war in the Pacific, his unwavering emphasis on the priority of the Atlantic, and his studied refusal even there to leverage the several naval incidents of 1941 into a request for a declaration of war against Germany.

On November 26 Hull handed Nomura and Kurusu a ten-point statement of the American position. It essentially reiterated the principles to which American diplomacy had clung for the preceding two years: insistence on Japanese withdrawal from China and abandonment of the Southeast Asian adventure.

On December 6 Roosevelt tried one last gambit. He sent a personal message to the Emperor, going so far as to revive some of the promises contained in the recently discarded *modus vivendi*. He had little hope of success. "Well," he joked to a dinner guest, "this son of man has just sent his final message to the Son of God." Later that evening, a navy courier brought to Roosevelt in his White House study the Magic decrypts of the Japanese reply to Hull's November 26 ten-point statement. They offered no hope of any further diplomatic discussion. Roosevelt glanced at them, then turned to Harry Hopkins and said simply: "This means war."[96]

95. Stimson Diary, November 25, 1941.
96. Sherwood, *Roosevelt and Hopkins*, 426.

3

War in the Pacific

The closest squeak and the greatest victory.
> —George C. Marshall Jr. on the Battle of Midway

During the first days of December 1941, Admiral Isoroku Yamamoto, commander-in-chief of Japan's Combined Fleet, fretted in his headquarters aboard the battleship *Nagato* in Hiroshima Bay. On November 26 he had directed a powerful task force under Vice-Admiral Chuichi Nagumo to sortie from Hitokappu Bay in the Kurile Islands, under orders to attack the U.S. Pacific Fleet base at Pearl Harbor, Hawaii. Though Yamamoto had provided that "in the event an agreement is reached in the negotiations with the United States, the Task Force will immediately return to Japan," the negotiations had by now irretrievably collapsed. There would be no turning back.[1]

Other Japanese naval forces were at the same time initiating the massive Southern Operation, slicing southward from Japan to land invasion troops in the Philippines, Malaya, and the great oil-rich prize of the Dutch East Indies. The Hawaii expedition was the pivot of this complex scheme. On the outcome at Pearl Harbor turned the fate of the Southern Operation, which could not imaginably succeed if its eastern flank remained exposed to the firepower of the U.S. Pacific Fleet. Because of the very power of that fleet, concentrated in the midocean anchorage of Hawaii, Nagumo's mission was also the most perilous of the several huge military operations Japan now had under way.

Preparations for the assault on Pearl Harbor had been exhaustive, including repeated mock attacks on a model of the Hawaiian base set

1. Gordon W. Prange, *At Dawn We Slept: The Untold Story of Pearl Harbor* (New York: Penguin, 1982), 387.

91

up in Japan's Saeki Bay. Sailors and airmen had analyzed knotty problems of resupplying ships at sea, navigating the attack convoy without radio communication, and coordinating the waves of high-level horizontal bombers, dive-bombers, torpedo bombers, and fighter planes that would deliver the blow.[2]

Yet so much could go wrong. The strike force, designated First Air Fleet, had been organized only eight months earlier and had never fought a concerted action. With the six aircraft carriers that composed its fighting core, it embodied the experimental concept of naval air power, long advocated by visionaries like the American Billy Mitchell and First Air Fleet's own air staff officer, Commander Minoru Genda, but still virtually untested in the unforgiving crucible of battle. The very length of the attack route — thirty-five hundred miles, well beyond the Japanese navy's traditional radius of action — necessitated tricky refueling at sea and amplified the chances for detection.

Surprise would enormously enhance the prospect of success, just as surprise had favored Japan when it launched its other great war against a Caucasian power by besieging the Russian fleet at Port Arthur in 1904. So Nagumo's ships plowed methodically eastward from Hitokappu Bay in strict radio silence, enveloping themselves as well in the cloud and mist of an eastering weather front. Yamamoto could trace their putative movements on his charts but would know nothing for certain until radio silence was broken.

Short, deep-chested, swift and sarcastic in argument, bold and ingenious in battle, born in 1884 in the great flowering of the Meiji Restoration, Yamamoto was at the summit of his distinguished naval career in 1941. He had firsthand knowledge of his adversary. He had studied English at Harvard in the 1920s and later served as naval attaché in Washington, where he had earned a reputation as a shrewd poker player. He had also acquired a sober respect for the warmaking potential of the United States. He knew that its vast industrial base and large population would make it a formidable foe if it ever mustered the political will to fight, and probably an invincible foe if the conflict were protracted. Through the tense debates since 1937 about Japan's foreign policies, Yamamoto's had been a voice of moderation. He did not fully trust

2. Ironically, a successful British aerial-torpedo attack on the Italian fleet at Taranto in November 1940 gave the Japanese planners confidence that they could adopt shallow-water torpedo tactics for the assault on Pearl Harbor.

WAR IN THE PACIFIC   93

Japan's Axis allies and repeatedly pleaded for alternatives to war with the United States. Yet to Yamamoto had fallen the task of devising the battle plan for that war. A devoted patriot and loyal warrior, Yamamoto had done his duty faithfully—and brilliantly.

The attack on Pearl Harbor fitted Yamamoto's gambler's temperament. It entailed gigantic risks but also held out the promise of extravagant rewards. If fully successful, it might cow the isolationist Americans into acquiescing in Japan's dominance over China and the Pacific. At a minimum, crippling the U.S. Pacific Fleet would buy precious time for the Southern Operation to go forward unmolested and for Japan so to consolidate its hold on Southeast Asia that it could not easily be dislodged.

What was more, success at Pearl Harbor would vindicate the Japanese navy, so long denied a role in the land war in China, yet fiercely proud of the part it had played in the Russo-Japanese War of 1904–5, especially its legendary conquest of the Russian fleet at the Battle of Tsushima Strait in 1905. For the Japanese people, and especially for seamen like Yamamoto, Tsushima represented not only a glorious naval victory but a confirmation and font of racial pride. Tsushima had demonstrated the vulnerability of the haughty Western powers in the face of Japan's rising industrial might and abiding moral superiority. Yamamoto himself had been blooded at Tsushima. His left hand, missing two fingers lost in that battle, daily reminded him of the near-mythical spell that Tsushima still cast for his service and his nation.

At sea on December 4, silent and undetected several hundred miles northwest of Hawaii, Nagumo's sprawling flotilla of nearly three dozen ships pivoted from its easterly course to a southeasterly bearing. On the morning of December 6 Nagumo completed his final refueling. His oilers angled away to take station at the rendezvous point for the return voyage. Freed of the lumbering tankers, at 11:30 Nagumo ordered speed increased to twenty knots and pointed his ships due south, carving a course that would bring them to the launching sector two hundred miles north of Oahu just before dawn the next day. At 11:40 his flagship, the giant carrier *Akagi*, ran up the very Z flag that Admiral Togo had flown at the Battle of Tsushima Strait thirty-six years before. Flushed with patriotic emotion, Japanese sailors and pilots cheered wildly.

With Togo's historic pennant snapping in the wind, Nagumo's arrowhead-shaped armada plunged through heavy seas, bearing relentlessly down on its target. Destroyers patrolled along its flanks, submarines guarded its rear, and an imposing cordon of battleships and cruisers closely jacketed the precious carriers with their lethal cargos at the arrowhead's heart.

Just before 6:00 A.M., Nagumo wheeled due east again, to launch his planes into the wind. Pilots, each wearing a bandana emblazoned with the word *hissho* (certain victory), scrambled into their aircraft. Within minutes, 183 planes had lifted from the decks of the six carriers and were shaping their triangular formations for the first attack wave. Fifty-one dive-bombers made up the high squadron, with forty-nine level bombers below and forty torpedo planes lower still. High overhead ranged forty-three Mitsubishi A6M fighters—the swift and nimble "Zeros" that would soon terrorize American fighting men all over the Pacific. By the time the second attack wave had been launched about an hour later, some 350 aircraft, led by Commander Mitsuo Fuchida, were droning through the leaden dawn southward toward Oahu.

At the very moment that Nagumo ordered his carriers to point their bows into the wind, shortly before noon Washington time, George C. Marshall was returning from a Sunday-morning horseback ride to his War Department office in Washington. There aides presented him with a translation of a freshly decrypted message from Tokyo. It contained a lengthy and final reply to the ten-point American position that Hull had presented to Ambassador Nomura on November 26 and instructed Nomura once and for all to break off negotiations. As Marshall scanned the sterile diplomatic prose, he reached its alarming codicil, ordering Nomura to submit the reply "at 1:00 P.M. on the 7th, your time." To Marshall the highly unusual specification of a precise time, and on a Sunday at that, was ominous. One P.M. was scarcely an hour away. Marshall immediately drafted a message to be sent to army commands in the Philippines, Panama, Hawaii, and San Francisco: "Japanese are presenting at one pm eastern standard time today what amounts to an ultimatum. . . . Just what significance the hour set may have we do not know but be on the alert accordingly. Inform naval authorities of this communication." Within minutes the message was encoded and dispatched by radio to all destinations—except Hawaii. Atmospheric conditions were creating heavy static that temporarily blocked the wireless channel to Honolulu. The War Department signal officer chose the next-fastest communication route: a commercial Western Union teletype. The message left Washington on the Western Union wire at 12:17 P.M. and was relayed by the RCA (Radio Corporation of America) installation near San Francisco to Hawaii. It reached Honolulu sixteen minutes later—7:33 A.M., Hawaii time. A messenger picked up the telegram at RCA's Honolulu office, mounted his motorcycle, and roared away to deliver it to General Walter C. Short at Fort Shafter, several miles away. Fuchida's planes were then twenty minutes north of Oahu. Still en route when the attack commenced, the messenger reached Fort Shafter only several hours after Fuchida's planes had wreaked their destruction.[3]

That communications delay was not the only missed opportunity to spoil the Japanese surprise. As Fuchida's attackers formed up over their carriers, just before 7:00 A.M., an American destroyer patrolling outside Pearl Harbor's mouth sighted and depth-bombed a Japanese midget submarine trying to slip into the anchorage. But the destroyer's report of this contact was discounted as another in a series of frustratingly unconfirmed submarine sightings and set aside for further verification.

Minutes after the submarine contact, an army radar operator on northern Oahu reported an unusually large flight of incoming aircraft. They were, in fact, Fuchida's first wave, still nearly an hour away, but the operator's superior officer irresponsibly intuited that the blips on the screen represented a flight of B-17 Flying Fortresses being ferried in from California to Hickam Field for eventual posting to the Philippines. The officer was brought to this tragic miscalculation at least in part by his recollection that radio station KGMB had been broadcasting all night—a programming schedule that almost invariably meant B-17s were arriving from the mainland, their navigators using the station's beam as a homing signal. In one of the many ironies on this day when irony was in abundant and cruel supply, Fuchida's pilot was meanwhile using that same beam, carrying saccharine Hawaiian tunes, to guide him to Oahu.

When Fuchida sighted land from his lead bomber about 7:30, he gave the order to assume attack positions. Below the warplanes the American ships and aircraft lay serenely unsuspecting and virtually undefended, exactly as described by the espionage reports from Japan's Honolulu consulate. Now certain beyond doubt that complete surprise had been achieved, Fuchida at 7:53 at last broke radio silence and shouted into his mouthpiece, *"Tora! Tora! Tora!"* (Tiger! Tiger! Tiger!)—the coded announcement that Yamamoto's high-stakes gamble was about to pay off in frightful devastation.

For more than an hour, bombs and bullets pelted down on the unmaneuverable American battleships, mostly moored in pairs in

3. Prange, *At Dawn We Slept*, 486, 494–95.

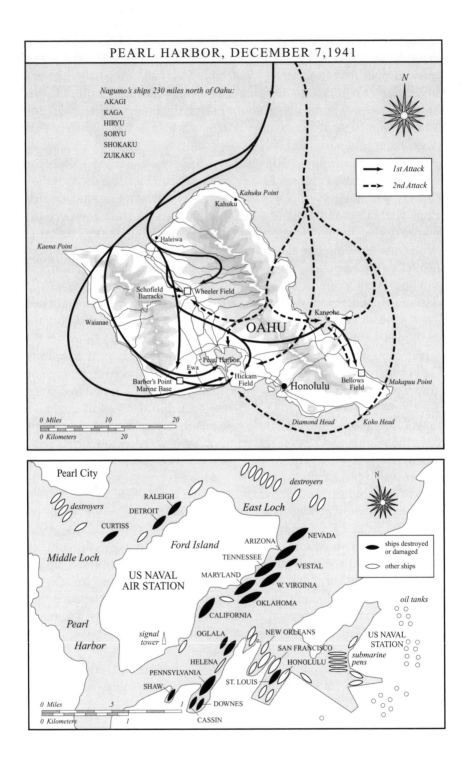

PEARL HARBOR, DECEMBER 7, 1941

Nagumo's ships 230 miles north of Oahu:
AKAGI
KAGA
HIRYU
SORYU
SHOKAKU
ZUIKAKU

N

→ 1st Attack
⇢ 2nd Attack

Kahuku Point
Kahuku
Haleiwa
Kaena Point
Schofield
Barracks
Wheeler Field
Kaneohe
OAHU
Waianae
Pearl Harbor
Ewa
Hickam
Field
Bellows
Field
Makapuu Point
Barber's Point
Marine Base
Honolulu
Diamond Head
Koko Head

0 Miles   10   20
0 Kilometers   20

Pearl City

destroyers

RALEIGH
DETROIT
CURTISS
East Loch
destroyers

Ford Island

Middle Loch

ARIZONA   NEVADA
TENNESSEE   VESTAL
MARYLAND   W. VIRGINIA
OKLAHOMA

US NAVAL
AIR STATION

CALIFORNIA

Pearl

Harbor

signal
tower

OGLALA

NEW ORLEANS

SAN FRANCISCO

HELENA
PENNSYLVANIA
SHAW
ST. LOUIS
DOWNES
CASSIN

HONOLULU

oil tanks

US NAVAL
STATION

submarine
pens

● ships destroyed
   or damaged
○ other ships

N

0 Miles   .5   1
0 Kilometers   1

"Battleship Row" off Ford Island, and on the unflyable American airplanes, parked wingtip-to-wingtip at Bellows, Wheeler, and Hickam
fields so they could be guarded against land-based sabotage. When the
last Japanese plane winged away about 10:00 A.M., eighteen U.S. naval
vessels, including eight battleships, had been sunk or heavily damaged.
More than 180 aircraft were destroyed, and another 120 crippled. Two
thousand four hundred and three men were dead — 1,103 of them en-
tombed in the battleship *Arizona*, which sank almost instantaneously
when a bomb exploded in its forward magazine. Another 1,178 men
were wounded. Columns of smoke obscured Fuchida's final reconnaissance as he departed for the *Akagi*, but he knew beyond question that
his airmen had triumphantly accomplished their mission.

OR HAD THEY? Fuchida's fliers had seen to it that not a single
battleship remained in action in the U.S. Pacific Fleet. But battleships
were the capital weapons of the last war. In the war that was now so
bloodily begun, aircraft carriers would be trumps, and no U.S. Pacific
Fleet carriers had been at Pearl Harbor on December 7. *Yorktown* had
been detached in April for duty in the Atlantic. *Saratoga* was stateside
for repairs. *Enterprise* and *Lexington* were at sea near Wake and Midway
islands respectively. Fuchida's raiders had also failed to damage Pearl
Harbor's repair shops. More important still, they had left intact the enormous fuel-oil tank farm. Loss of that fuel supply, every drop of it laboriously hauled from the American mainland, would probably have
forced the U.S. Navy to retreat to its bases on the West Coast, at a stroke
sweeping the western Pacific of American ships more cleanly than any
other imaginable action. But Nagumo rejected suggestions that he undertake a second strike against the repair and fuel facilities or linger in
the area to search for the missing carriers. He seemed paralyzed by the
very ease of his victory. He had lost but twenty-nine aircraft, and his
fleet remained unsighted. In Gordon Prange's apt phrase, he must have
felt "as if he had rushed forward to break down a door just as someone
opened it."[4] For Nagumo, what he had achieved on the morning of
December 7 was victory enough. Yet his failure to return for the final,
definitive kill risked eventual defeat.

Nor were the political consequences of Pearl Harbor unambiguously
favorable for Japan. Among the fragile hopes that Yamamoto had
harbored as relations with the United States deteriorated was that a

4. Prange, *At Dawn We Slept*, 544.

knockout blow at the war's outset would set the stage for a negotiated settlement with the Americans. But he had never fully answered, perhaps not even in his own mind, the counterargument that such an attack was by its very nature so provocative as to preclude the possibility of subsequent negotiation. The force of that argument seemed confirmed when the U.S. Congress declared war on Japan on December 8 with but a single dissenting vote, amid ferocious and wrathful outcries for a vengeful war without mercy against the treacherous "Japs." The attack stepped up the voltage of a long-running current of American racial hatred toward the Japanese and threatened to make the Pacific war a singularly bitter clash of cultures, as well as armies.[5]

Even the strategic benefit to Japan of the Pearl Harbor attack was questionable. Yamamoto himself was reported to be deeply depressed in the days after December 7, faced at last with the reality of a war that Japan had such slight prospect of winning. In Chungking, Chiang Kaishek "was so happy he sang an old opera aria and played Ave Maria all day. . . . Now China's strategic importance would grow even more. American money and equipment would flow in."[6] Winston Churchill remembered thinking: "So we had won after all . . . ! Hitler's fate was sealed. Mussolini's fate was sealed. As for the Japanese, they would be ground to powder. . . . [T]here was no more doubt about the end. . . . Being saturated and satiated with emotion and sensation, I went to bed and slept the sleep of the saved and thankful." Memory may have distorted Churchill's account. In fact, his first reaction to the news of Pearl Harbor was to make plans for an immediate departure for Washington, to ensure that the clamor for vengeance against Japan did not threaten American supplies for Britain. Britain must be careful, Churchill advised King George, "that our share of munitions and other aid which we are receiving form the United States does not suffer more than is, I fear, inevitable."[7]

5. Fifty representatives and six senators, by contrast, had voted against the resolution taking the United States into World War I in 1917. Jeannette Rankin of Montana, the first woman elected to Congress, has the distinction of being the only person who voted against both war resolutions.

6. Michael Schaller, *The U.S. Crusade in China, 1938–1945* (New York: Columbia University Press, 1979), 88.

7. Churchill, 3:606–8; Martin Gilbert, *Churchill: A Life* (New York: Henry Holt, 1991), 711. If the news of Pearl Harbor worried Churchill, in other ways it emboldened him. When an aide on December 8 urged that at this delicate moment caution was

As for Adolf Hitler, he reportedly exclaimed to his generals: "Now it is impossible for us to lose the war: we now have an ally who has never been vanquished in three thousand years."[8] Though the strict terms of their alliance with Japan did not require it, since Japan had been the attacker, not the attacked, Hitler and Mussolini on December 11 somewhat impetuously declared war on the United States, which then recognized a state of war with Germany and Italy.

Hitler here missed an opportunity to work incalculable mischief with the American commitment to give precedence to the European war. If Hitler had not now obligingly declared war on the United States, Roosevelt, given the apparent willingness of both sides to acquiesce in protracted and undeclared naval war in the Atlantic, would have had undoubted difficulty finding a politically useable occasion for declaring war against Germany. In the absence of such a legal declaration, Roosevelt might well have found it impossible to resist demands to place the maximum American effort in the Pacific, against the formally recognized Japanese enemy, rather than in the Atlantic, in a nondeclared war against the Germans. This was precisely Churchill's worry, and it was not easily laid to rest. Well after the German declaration of war, Roosevelt came under stubborn pressure to give priority to the fight against Japan. Pressure came from the navy, which always took the Pacific war to be its special province, and from public opinion, infected by a legacy of racial animosity toward the Japanese and inflamed by the humiliation of the Pearl Harbor attack.

It was no doubt that same sense of humiliation and wounded racial pride that fueled an almost interminable search for scapegoats for the Pearl Harbor disaster. Conspiracy theories proliferated, as they often do in the face of the improbable. Many Americans instinctively believed that an inferior power like Japan could not possibly have inflicted such damage on the United States unless some individual had failed in his duty, perhaps even behaved treasonably. The most extreme accusations have indicted Roosevelt himself for deliberately putting the Pacific Fleet at risk in order to bait Japan to the attack and thus bring the United States into the war—a thesis that simply will not bear close examination

---

required in dealing with the United States, Churchill replied: "Oh, that is the way we talked to her while we were wooing her; now that she is in the harem, we talk to her differently!" See James MacGregor Burns, *Roosevelt: The Soldier of Freedom* (New York: Harcourt Brace, 1970), 172.

8. John Keegan, *The Second World War* (New York: Viking, 1989), 240.

in light of the president's unwavering insistence on the priority of the Atlantic and European theaters and the unambiguous conviction of his naval and military advisers that not Japan but Germany was the truly dangerous adversary. They all understood that an open conflict with Japan was a distraction, not a back door to war. From that perspective, the question is not who was responsible for Pearl Harbor but who should bear responsibility for failing to pursue a diplomatic settlement with Japan that would have left the United States free to apply its undivided military strength against Hitler. Roosevelt's deepest failure, it might be argued, was his inattentiveness to Asian matters and his unwillingness to be seen as "appeasing" Japan, when in fact a little appeasement — another name for diplomacy — might have yielded rich rewards.

More plausible, but in the end no more convincing, accusations have been leveled at the various military, naval, and civilian intelligence services for failing to predict the Pearl Harbor attack. Exhaustive investigations have turned up numerous "signals" that allegedly should have alerted the authorities to the approach of Nagumo's strike force, including especially an encoded message supposedly intercepted in the early days of December and containing the phrase "east wind rain," code for the announcement of a breakdown in U.S.-Japanese relations. Yet the chief of naval operations had in fact notified all Pacific theater commands on November 27 that "[t]his dispatch is to be considered a war warning" and ordered "appropriate defensive deployment." The War Department sent a similar message the following day, instructing army commanders in the Pacific that "hostile action [is] possible at any moment." It added that "the United States desires that Japan commit the first overt act," while emphasizing the significant qualifier that "this policy should not repeat not be construed as restricting you to a course of action that might jeopardize your defense."[9]

So American forces throughout the Pacific were already on highest alert by the end of November. But Pearl Harbor was only one among many possible places where the first blow might fall, and arguably the least likely. Months, even years, of speculation about Japan's military intentions had focused on China, Soviet Siberia, Malaya, Singapore, Hong Kong, the Dutch East Indies, Thailand, Indochina, and the Philippines as possible Japanese targets — but rarely, if ever, Hawaii. The navy's warning of November 27, for example, plausibly named "the Phil-

9. Roberta Wohlstetter, Pearl Harbor: Warning and Decision (Stanford: University Press, 1962), 44–47.

ippines, Thai or Kra (Malay) Peninsula, or possibly Borneo," as sites for impending hostilities. In the welter of "noise" about the impending showdown with Japan that filled the air in the days before Pearl Harbor, scattered and ambiguous warnings about the possibility of action against Hawaii — so distant from Japan, so apparently impregnable — were easy to discount. The American "failure" at Pearl Harbor, if such there was, was not a thing of the moment or of the Hawaiian locale. It was systematic, pervasive, and cumulative, embedded in a tangle of only partially thought-out strategic assumptions and priorities and colored by smug attitudes of racial superiority that had now been violently challenged.

THE SIMPLE FACT is that Pearl Harbor was a masterful, though incomplete, tactical achievement by the Japanese. It would also prove in time to have been a strategic blunder and a political and psychological catastrophe. So much depended on what use Japan would make of its advantage in the immediate aftermath of the Hawaiian attack. Like a judo fighter, Yamamoto had now knocked his larger American opponent off balance. Could he next bring down his foe before the United States shrugged off its post–Pearl Harbor daze and brought all of its prodigious industrial strength to bear? Swift and sharp follow-up jabs were now essential. In a prolonged conflict, Japan would eventually be smothered under an awesome outpouring of metal and flame that would spew from American arsenals. No one knew better than Yamamoto that time was Japan's worst enemy.

That prospect had long haunted him. "If I am told to fight regardless of the consequences," Yamamoto had warned then–prime minister Konoye in September 1940, "I shall run wild for the first six months or a year, but I have utterly no confidence for the second or third year. . . . I hope," he added, that "you will endeavor to avoid a Japanese-American war." But the war had now come. How would Japan use those crucial six months?[10]

At first Yamamoto's slender hope for victory seemed about to be realized. Japanese forces did indeed "run wild" along a gigantic arc that swept from the Aleutians in the north Pacific to Ceylon (Sri Lanka) in the Indian Ocean. Carrier-borne Japanese aircraft sank the British battleships *Repulse* and *Prince of Wales* off the coast of Malaya on December 10. Hong Kong, Guam, and Wake Island all fell to the Japanese

10. *Reports of General MacArthur: Japanese Operations in the Southwest Pacific Area* 2, pt. 1 (Washington: USGPO, 1966), 33 n. 14.

within days of Pearl Harbor. In lightning moves, Japanese forces struck from Indochina into Thailand and British Malaya and by mid-January of 1942 were advancing almost unopposed into Burma. The crack Japanese Fifth Division, recently retrained for the unfamiliar task of jungle warfare, brilliantly employed flanking attacks and the terrifying tactics of night-fighting ("The night is one million reinforcements," ran a training slogan) as it made its way down the Malay peninsula toward Singapore. On February 15 that British stronghold, the supposedly unconquerable "Gibraltar of the Pacific," surrendered its garrison of eighty-five thousand troops to a Japanese force half that size, in what is usually regarded as the worst defeat in the history of British arms.

Twelve days later, in the Battle of the Java Sea, a hastily assembled American-British-Dutch-Australian fleet pathetically failed to halt the major Japanese invasion of the Dutch East Indies, whose oil fields constituted the main target and the consuming economic logic of the entire Southern Operation. On March 12 the Allies gave up the East Indies. As happened elsewhere in Asia, though by no means uniformly, the Japanese were welcomed by many Indonesians as liberators who had thrown out the hated Dutch colonials and begun at last to make good on the promise of "Asia for the Asians."

Admiral Nagumo next steamed through the now secure Strait of Malacca and for a week raided at will throughout the Indian Ocean, sinking nearly a hundred thousand tons of British shipping and bombing British bases in Ceylon. The remnants of the British Far Eastern fleet withdrew to East Africa. The Royal Australian Navy retired to its home ports. The U.S. Pacific Fleet had not a single surviving battleship. Yet Japan's armada of eleven battleships, six large and four small carriers, and thirty-eight heavy and light cruisers had not been scratched. From the Bay of Bengal to the Bering Sea, a vast quadrant of the world ocean had become a Japanese lake.

Victory took only a bit longer in the American colony of the Philippines. At his Manila headquarters Douglas MacArthur, commanding general of U.S. forces in the Far East, learned early in the morning of December 8 that Pearl Harbor had been attacked. Incredibly, and unforgivably, he made no use of the next ten hours to mount a counterattack against Japanese positions on Formosa (Taiwan), as his air commander urged, or even to launch or disperse his own aircraft. They were caught bunched on the ground — "On the ground! On the ground!" President Roosevelt exclaimed incredulously — when Japanese bombers and fighters appeared overhead shortly after noon. Within minutes Mac-

THE SOUTHWEST PACIFIC, 1941-1942

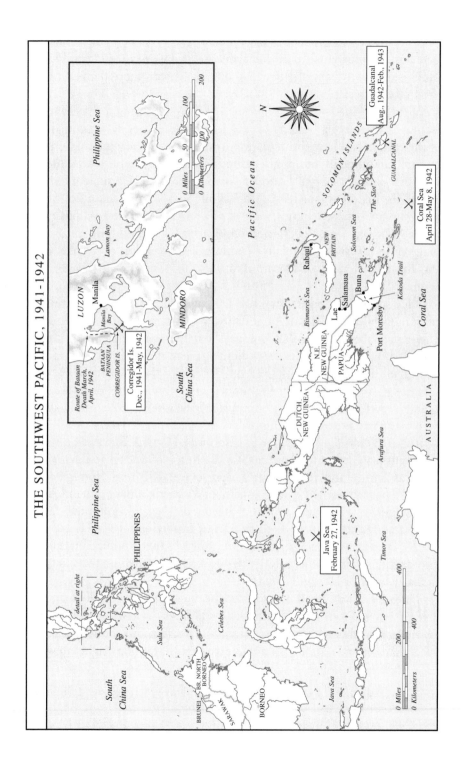

Philippine Sea

Luzon
Manila
Lamon Bay
Manila Bay
BATAAN PENINSULA
CORREGIDOR IS.

0 Miles   50   100   200
0 Kilometers   100   200

Corregidor Is.
Dec., 1941-May, 1942

Route of Bataan
Death March,
April, 1942

MINDORO

South
China Sea

N

Guadalcanal
Aug., 1942-Feb., 1943

SOLOMON ISLANDS

GUADALCANAL

"The Slot"

Coral Sea
April 28-May 8, 1942

Pacific Ocean

Rabaul
NEW BRITAIN
Bismarck Sea
Solomon Sea
Salamaua
Lae
Buna
Kokoda Trail
N.E. NEW GUINEA
PAPUA
Port Moresby

Coral Sea

DUTCH NEW GUINEA

Arafura Sea

AUSTRALIA

South
China Sea

Philippine Sea

PHILIPPINES

detail at right

Sulu Sea

Celebes Sea

BRUNEI
BR. NORTH
BORNEO
SARAWAK

BORNEO

Java Sea

Java Sea
February 27, 1942

Timor Sea

0 Miles   200   400
0 Kilometers   400

Arthur's entire force of some three dozen B-17 bombers, on which he had obstreperously premised his claim to be able to defend the Philippines indefinitely, was utterly wiped out, along with more than two hundred other aircraft.[11]

When the Japanese began landing troops on the principal Philippine island of Luzon on December 22, MacArthur speedily jettisoned his always dubious scheme to repel the invader on the beaches and on the central Luzon plain and began gathering men and supplies for a retreat into the Bataan peninsula and the island fortress of Corregidor, where he set up his command post. MacArthur, sometimes accused of being a legend in his own mind, soon earned himself the derogatory nickname "Dugout Doug," bestowed on him by his suffering troops on Bataan while he sat in the relative comfort of Corregidor, only once making the brief torpedo-boat run across to the peninsula to hearten his men.

They sorely needed heartening. The swift retreat into the peninsula of some eighty thousand American and Filipino troops and another twenty-five thousand civilian refugees left them all wretchedly undersupplied. Lacking fresh food, medicines, clean drinking water, and sanitary facilities, thousands fell victim to scurvy, beriberi, malaria, and dysentery. The Japanese force, unprepared for a long siege, was in scarcely better condition—a circumstance whose hideous implications were soon to be revealed.

Knowing that the Philippine garrison was doomed, Roosevelt ordered MacArthur to depart for Australia. On the night of March 12 the general and his family and personal staff were evacuated from Corregidor in four PT boats, leaving General Jonathan Wainwright in command. With characteristic self-regard and uncharacteristic lack of orotundity, Mac-Arthur announced: "I shall return." As a face-saving measure—and as a prophylaxis against backlash from the general's many political friends—the president simultaneously conferred upon MacArthur the Congressional Medal of Honor.[12]

The medal was small comfort for the masses of sick soldiers and civilians left behind in the Philippines. Though MacArthur fulminated by radio from his new base in Australia that his troops should break out of Bataan and take to the mountains as guerrillas, Wainwright knew the

11. Eric Larrabee, *Commander in Chief: Franklin Delano Roosevelt, His Lieutenants, and Their War* (New York: Harper and Row, 1987), 316.
12. Burns, *Roosevelt: The Soldier of Freedom*, 209.

notion was fatuous. The Bataan contingent surrendered on April 9, and on May 6 an emaciated Wainwright, hopelessly holed up in Corregidor's putrescent Malinta Tunnel, tortured by the resonant moaning of thousands of ill and wounded men crammed into the dank 826–foot shaft, finally capitulated. In his diary, Dwight Eisenhower took note of these events: "Corregidor surrendered last night. Poor Wainwright! He did the fighting . . . [MacArthur] got such glory as the public could find. . . . MacArthur's tirades, to which TJ [MacArthur's aide, T. J. Davis] and I so often listened in Manila, would now sound as silly to the public as they then did to us. But he's a hero! Yah."[13]

In a war that would grotesquely add to history's already extensive annals of cruelty, one of the cruelest episodes now ensued. The world would learn of it more than a year later, after three American survivors escaped from a prisoner-of-war camp on Mindanao, made their way to Australia, and told the story. There were some extenuating circumstances, but scarcely sufficient to exonerate the Japanese from the indictment that they behaved with wanton barbarity. The Japanese had planned on bagging some forty thousand prisoners of war in the Philippines sometime in the summer of 1942. Instead, they found themselves with nearly seventy thousand captives on their hands in April and May, ten thousand of them Americans, all of them suffering from months of siege and illness, as were the Japanese themselves. These logistical and medical problems only exacerbated a more fundamental clash of cultures.

Japanese military leaders had adopted the ancient samurai ethos of Bushido to develop a military code that engendered what two scholars have described as "a range of mental attitudes that bordered on psychopathy," including the notion of "surrender as the ultimate dishonor, a belief whose corollary was total contempt for the captive."[14] That contempt the Japanese troops now vented savagely on the American and Filipino captives they herded along the route of the "Bataan Death March," a grisly eighty-mile forced trek to crude prisoner-of-war camps near the base of the Bataan peninsula. Japanese guards, along with the already roughly used colonial Korean troops often employed for guard duty, denied water to parched prisoners, clubbed and bayoneted stragglers and subjected all the captives to countless humiliations and petty

13. Robert J. Ferrell, ed., *The Eisenhower Diaries* (New York: Norton, 1981), 54.
14. Meirion Harries and Susie Harries, *Soldiers of the Sun: The Rise and Fall of the Imperial Japanese Army* (New York: Random House, 1991), 481.

but excruciating agonies. Some six hundred Americans and as many as ten thousand Filipinos died along the route of the march. Thousands more perished in the filthy camps. This harrowing episode presaged the pitiless inhumanity that came to possess both sides in the ensuing three and a half years of war in the Pacific.

WITH WAINWRIGHT'S SURRENDER in the Philippines in May, Japan had triumphantly concluded the first phase of the Southern Operation, which envisioned the occupation of territories from Burma through the Dutch East Indies and the subsequent exploitation of their critical natural resources. The second phase called for securing a defensive perimeter, strung like a ribbon from island to atoll across thousands of miles of ocean, against the all but inevitable American counterblow.

Lying vast and menacing on the southernmost rim of that defensive perimeter was Australia. Though the Australians lacked the manpower and material resources effectively to challenge the Japanese, and most of Australia's small but tough fighting forces were in any case at that moment helping to defend the British empire on the sands of North Africa, Australia could serve as a staging area for the expected American counterattack. By establishing bases off Australia's northern coast, Japan could pinch off the supply lines from America, isolating and effectively neutralizing the island continent. Accordingly, Vice-Admiral Shigeyoshi Inoue's South Seas Force had seized Rabaul, on New Britain, in January 1942. He proceeded to transform its magnificent caldera-formed harbor into a major naval and air base, designed to anchor the southern end of Japan's defensive perimeter. Almost immediately, however, Japanese military planners determined to use Rabaul to support the further advance of the ribbon defense into the South Pacific, to Papua, the Solomon Islands, Fiji, New Caledonia, and Samoa—a giddily ambitious extension of the original plan that betrayed the symptoms of overreach and imprudence induced by what came to be called "victory disease."

From Rabaul, Inoue in early May dispatched two invasion forces. One was bound for Port Moresby, facing Australia on the south coast of Papua, on whose northern coast the Japanese had already established beachheads at the villages of Lae and Salamaua. He sent the other force to Tulagi, at the southern end of the Solomon Island chain. Disaster awaited the Port Moresby force, as American intelligence had decrypted the principal Japanese naval code, JN-25, thus knew Inoue's destination, and rushed a task force to intercept the invaders. At the Battle of the Coral Sea, a complex action stretching across hundreds of sea miles and five days, from May 3 to 8, 1942, the two sides made naval history, as all the fighting was conducted by carrier-based aircraft. Separated by 175 miles of ocean, the warships neither directly fired upon nor even actually sighted one another. Indicative of the perils and confusion that attended the still unfamiliar tactics of aerial warfare at sea, six Japanese planes tried to land on the U.S. carrier *Yorktown*, mistaking her for one of their own. Japanese pilots also reported sinking two American carriers, *Yorktown* as well as *Saratoga*, but they were less than half right. What they took to be *Saratoga* was in fact *Lexington*, though she had been so badly hit that she was scuttled on May 8. *Yorktown*, nearly mortally damaged, survived to fight another day.[15]

When the Japanese withdrew on May 8, they took the Port Moresby landing forces with them back to Rabaul, never to return. The struggle for Port Moresby would now be waged not on the landing beaches but on the green-draped ridges of the towering Owen Stanley Range, where Australian troops doggedly held out against the Japanese advance from Lae and Salamaua along the steep, fetid, root-choked Kokoda Trail, until relieved by a reborn Douglas MacArthur some six months later. In this sense, Coral Sea represented an allied victory. But it was dearly bought with the loss of *Lexington* and, as events were to prove, with the success of the unopposed Japanese landing on Tulagi, just a few miles across Savo Sound from the jungle-shrouded island of Guadalcanal.

On the flooding tide of Japanese success in early 1942, Coral Sea was at worst a minor back-eddy, a transient nuisance without apparent strategic moment. Its chaotic inconsequentiality underscored the pitiful weakness of the U.S. position in the Pacific, constricted both by the "Germany first" logic of ABC-1 and by the crippling blow received at Pearl Harbor. With its carrier fleet intact, Japan still held all the high cards and all the power of initiative. The Americans seemed reduced to nothing but reactive spoiling tactics like Coral Sea and to harassing but ineffectual air raids, such as had been conducted against some Japanese-held Central Pacific islands in February. But on April 18 one such raid, on the face of it a hare-brained grandstand stunt, set in motion a chain of events with momentous implications.

THE STRING of relatively costless Japanese victories in the first four months of the war provoked a heated debate among Japanese mil-

---

15. Ship misidentification and false claims of sinkings were common on both sides, particularly by pilots who mistook the huge waterspouts thrown up by their near-miss bombs for explosions onboard their targets.

itary planners about what their next step should be. The success and momentum of the Southern Operation seemed to dictate one answer: consolidation and buildup of the bases tenuously established in New Guinea and the Solomons, followed by further advances into New Caledonia, Fiji, and Samoa, perhaps eventually into Australia itself. But Yamamoto put the full weight of his authority behind a contrary plan. Finish the job begun at Pearl Harbor, he urged, by seizing Midway Island, some eleven hundred miles west of Hawaii. Politically, Midway in Japanese hands would menace Hawaii with the threat of invasion, providing a potent bargaining chip with which to force the Americans to a negotiated settlement. Militarily, a Japanese presence on Midway would lure forth the remaining elements of the U.S. Pacific Fleet for the "decisive battle." Toward the waging of that battle all of Yamamoto's career and all the training and preparation of the entire Imperial Japanese Navy had long been consecrated.

The doctrine of decisive battle was distilled from decades of Japanese planning about how to wage war against the United States in the Pacific. That planning derived in turn, ironically enough, from the theories of the American naval strategist Alfred Thayer Mahan. A U.S. naval officer and president of Newport War College (later the Naval War College), Mahan argued in his influential work of 1890, *The Influence of Sea Power upon History*, that command of the sea was the key to success in war and that the way to secure the sea was to engage the enemy's main force in overwhelming strength and destroy it. As Japanese planners adopted this thinking for possible war against the United States, they envisioned the swift capture of the Philippines and Guam, thus forcing the U.S. fleet to battle. As the American navy transited the broad Pacific, Japanese submarines would harass it in the eastern Pacific, and land-based aircraft would strike as it passed through the Marshall and Gilbert islands. When the weakened U.S. fleet approached the Marianas or the Carolines, or perhaps the Philippines, it would confront a fresh, overpowering Japanese naval force and be decisively defeated.

To this basic doctrine the Japanese had by 1941 added some formidable refinements. Like the army, the Imperial Navy was highly trained for night battle, relying on superior optics, special communications systems, distinctive ship markings, and endless drills to turn the cloak of darkness to cunning advantage. In addition, its submarines and surface ships alike were armed with the devastating "Long Lance" torpedo, capable of speeds up to forty-nine knots and with a range of up to twenty-four miles. Nothing comparable existed in the American arsenal. Nor could the Americans in 1942 match the investment the Japanese had made in naval air power. With six large carriers, Japan boasted the largest naval air force in the world. It embarked some five hundred high-performance aircraft flown by magnificently trained pilots and operated as a single, awesomely concentrated strike force in First Air Fleet.

Most important, Yamamoto had argued in 1941 that rather than lie in waiting for the American fleet in the western Pacific, the Japanese navy should employ First Air Fleet to go after it directly in midocean, at its base in Pearl Harbor. That task Japan had only partly accomplished on December 7, Yamamoto insisted. Now was the time to hit the Americans again at a place they would be compelled to defend with their full strength—Midway—and destroy the U.S. Pacific Fleet once and for all. With the Pacific cleansed of American ships, Japan would have an unchallenged defensive perimeter, stretching from the North Pacific through midocean to the South Pacific. The Southern Operation would be impregnably secure. Within its perimeter, Japan would hold Guam and the Philippines as hostages, perhaps Hawaii and Australia as well. Safe behind this barrier, Japan could easily sustain a strategically defensive posture, and sue for a negotiated peace on terms it dictated. These were heady notions. In May 1942 they intoxicated even such a calculating pragmatist as Yamamoto. The faint prospect of victory that had earlier swum mistily at the outermost rim of his imagination, writes John Keegan, now "seemed to lie only one battle away."[16]

American strategic doctrine for war against Japan was virtually the mirror image of this Japanese thinking. Code-named the Orange Plan, it had first been formulated early in the century and also reflected the influence of Mahan. The Orange Plan assumed early Japanese capture of the Philippines and made relief of the Philippines the main American objective. The American garrison there was supposed to hold out for three or four months while the U.S. fleet crossed the Pacific, engaged the main body of the Japanese fleet, destroyed it, and thereby ended the war. Always unrealistic, the plan was revised in 1934 to provide for the capture of the Marshall and Caroline islands as staging areas for the main engagement with the Japanese fleet—a tacit admission that the war would last years, not months, and an admission as well of the cynicism that had always underlain expectations about the sacrificial role of the Philippine garrison. Yet whatever its flaws, the Orange Plan constituted the foundation of the United States' Pacific war strategy in 1942

16. Keegan, *Second World War*, 267.

and would in many ways remain so right down to 1945. In the two interwar decades, war games were fought at the Naval War College on these assumptions no fewer than 127 times, deeply planting the Orange Plan premises into the American strategic mind.

In early 1942, however, the United States could not possibly muster a naval force that would even begin to make Orange operational. The only event that had conformed to the plan's predictions was the loss of the Philippines, and it would take not three months but more than three years to retrieve them. As partial and weak substitute for the great fleet action envisioned by Orange, small strike forces engaged in hit-and-run raids on scattered Japanese island outposts.

By far the most daring and consequential of these raids struck not against outlying military stations in the far Pacific but against the Japanese home islands themselves. Probing carefully westward past Midway Island to within 650 miles of Tokyo, USS *Hornet* on April 18 launched sixteen cumbersome B-25 bombers never designed to be flown from a carrier deck. Wobbling up over the violently churning sea, the planes sidled into formation behind their leader, Lieutenant Colonel James H. Doolittle, bombed Tokyo and a handful of other Japanese cities, then, at the extreme limit of their flying range, crash-landed in China. Japanese occupation troops captured some of the airmen. One died in prison and three were executed after facing charges at a show trial that they had bombed civilian buildings and machine-gunned a school. Not incidentally, these events further fed the appetites of both combatants for a war of vengeance.

The Doolittle raid did little material damage. The Japanese government made no official acknowledgment of the attack, even to its own citizens, to whom the scattered and mostly harmless explosions of April 18 remained somewhat mysterious. But Doolittle's B-25s packed a momentous psychological wallop. They vividly demonstrated to Japanese military leaders the vulnerability of their home islands through the Midway slot in Japan's defensive perimeter. To all of Yamamoto's already weighty arguments about the attractions of an attack on Midway, the necessity of sealing that slot was now added. Debate ceased in the Japanese high command about the relative priority of the South or Central Pacific. Both operations would now go forward, straining to the utmost the already tautly stretched resources of the Imperial Navy.

Summoning Nagumo, hero of Pearl Harbor, Yamamoto began to fit First Air Fleet for an offensive operation against Midway Island. Nagumo's orders this time were to land an occupation force on Midway and begin its outfitting as a forward base that would lure the Americans to the decisive battle and might serve in time as a launching ground for the invasion of Hawaii. It was Yamamoto's most ambitious plan ever, overshadowing even the audacity of the December 7 attack, and it demonstrated that even this prudent planner was not immune to the incautious recklessness induced by victory disease.

Nagumo, buoyed by the magnitude of his success at Pearl Harbor, by the effortlessness of his marauding cruise around the Indian Ocean, and by what he understood to be the results of the Battle of the Coral Sea, had reason to be confident. He commanded at that moment the most advanced naval force in the world. At Pearl Harbor he had disabled the entire American Pacific battleship force, whereas his own unscathed battleships were still capable of screening his carriers from enemy attack and of supporting an amphibious landing. He believed that his failure to find the American carriers in port on December 7 had been handsomely redressed at Coral Sea, where Inoue's pilots had (erroneously) reported sinking two American carriers. Though two of his own fleet carriers, *Shokaku* and *Zuikaku*, were sufficiently damaged at Coral Sea that they could not take part in the assault on Midway, First Air Fleet retained *Akagi*, *Kaga*, *Hiryu*, and *Soryu*, a still potent quartet of fleet-class carriers that embarked more than 270 warplanes.

Nagumo trusted, too, in the complicated battle plan for the Midway operation. It called for a diversionary raid on Alaska's Aleutian Island chain, to draw off American naval strength. Nagumo's First Air Fleet and the invasion transports would also be backstopped by a powerful battleship group, with Yamamoto himself in command aboard *Yamato*, the largest battleship afloat. Yamamoto's battlewagons would lurk in Nagumo's rear, ready to pounce, preferably at night, on any American force that might challenge Nagumo's vanguard. And of course Yamamoto and Nagumo both took comfort as well from the reflection that they held again, as they had so triumphantly at Pearl Harbor, the hole card of secrecy. Anticipating the decisive battle that would crown his career and seal his nation's dream of empire, amid lavish pomp and ceremony on May 27, the anniversary of the Battle of Tsushima Strait, Nagumo sortied First Air Fleet through Bungo Strait from Japan's Inland Sea — and into the jaws of a trap.

While Yamamoto and Nagumo gathered the nearly two hundred ships of the Midway strike force from over the far horizons that bounded

Japan's immense area of conquest, American cryptanalysts feverishly studied their transcripts of the swelling volume of encoded Japanese radio traffic, trying to determine where Japan would strike next. The collective effort to crack the Japanese codes was known as "Magic," and in the upcoming Battle of Midway, Magic would demonstrate its military value as well as the aptness of its name.

Working without sleep amid spine-cracking tension in a windowless basement room at Pearl Harbor, Commander Joseph Rochefort, chief of the Combat Intelligence Office colloquially known as "Station Hypo," pored repeatedly over the maddeningly fragmentary intercepts piled atop his makeshift worktable of planks and sawhorses. Rochefort had adapted to his mole-like existence in his cellar office by working in slippers and a red smoking jacket. In the spit-and-polish navy, he and his equally unkempt colleagues were regarded as eccentric, even downright weird. But their knowledge of the Japanese language, in a navy that only had about forty officers competent in Japanese, was indispensable. Even more indispensable was their mastery of the arcane mysteries of crypt-analysis—the sorcerer's art of deciphering the enemy's most carefully guarded secret communications codes.

Station Hypo's nemesis and obsession was the Japanese naval code, JN-25. It was an immensely complex cipher, and Rochefort and his colleagues could make sense of only 10 to 15 percent of most intercepts. But in the welter of communications traffic that Hypo was monitoring in the spring of 1942, one term recurred with unsettling frequency: "AF," obviously the name of the next major Japanese target. But where or what was "AF"?

Rochefort had a hunch, and he played it shrewdly. Guessing that "AF" designated Midway, in early May he baited a trap by arranging for the small marine and army air force garrison at Midway to radio in clear that their distillation plant had malfunctioned and they were running short of fresh water. The ruse worked. Within two days, Station Hypo received confirmation of a coded Japanese message signaling that "AF" was low on water. Jackpot! Midway it was, then, and Hypo had proved it. The U.S. Navy would be there, ready and waiting.

Admiral Chester Nimitz wasted no time using Rochefort's information, which proved to be the single most valuable intelligence contribution to the entire Pacific war. A descendant of German colonists who had settled the Texas Hill Country's Pedernales Valley early in the nineteenth century, Nimitz was a quiet, scholarly man, fluent in his ancestral German tongue. He sought relaxation by firing his pistol on a target range. He had arrived in Hawaii to take up the position of CINCPAC (commander-in-chief, Pacific Fleet) on Christmas morning 1941. The whaleboat ferrying him from his seaplane to shore had passed the devastated hulks along Battleship Row and threaded through small craft still retrieving surfacing bodies from the sunken ships. As much as any man in the navy, Nimitz burned to retaliate for December 7. But in what his naval academy class book described as his "calm and steady Dutch way," he was determined to do it methodically, with a minimum of risk and more than a fair chance of success. Rochefort's cryptanlysts had now handed this careful, deliberate man a priceless opportunity.[17]

Nimitz reinforced Midway with planes, troops, and antiaircraft batteries. He ordered Task Force 16, comprising the carriers *Enterprise* and *Hornet*, back to Pearl Harbor from the South Pacific. He issued similar orders to Rear Admiral Frank Jack Fletcher's Task Force 17, left now with only the wounded *Yorktown*, which limped into Pearl Harbor on May 27, trailing a long, glistening oil slick as she nosed into a giant drydock. A hipbooted Nimitz was sloshing about at her keel even before the drydock had fully drained, inspecting the damage. Told that repairs would take weeks, a reasonable estimate, Nimitz curtly announced that he must have the ship made seaworthy in three days. The drydock instantly became a human anthill. Hundreds of workers swarmed over the *Yorktown*, amid showers of sparks and clouds of smoke from the acetylene torches cutting away and replacing her damaged hull-plates. As the ship's band incongruously played "California Here I Come," *Yorktown* refloated on May 29. Accompanied by her support ships in Task Force 17, she headed toward the rendezvous point—hopefully dubbed "Point Luck"—with Task Force 16, commanded by Rear Admiral Raymond A. Spruance. Fletcher, aboard *Yorktown*, was in overall command of the task forces.[18]

While the three American carriers stealthily moved to their stations northeast of Midway, Nagumo approached from the northwest. The Japanese commander had good reason to assume that only *Enterprise* and *Hornet* remained afloat in the U.S. Pacific Fleet, and he believed them still to be in the South Pacific, where they had been spotted on May 15. (To abet this misapprehension, Nimitz ordered a cruiser in the South Pacific to transmit on frequencies usually employed by air

17. Larrabee, *Commander in Chief*, 355.
18. Walter Lord, *Incredible Victory: The Battle of Midway* (New York: Harper and Row, 1967), 33–39, provides a colorful account of *Yorktown*'s refitting.

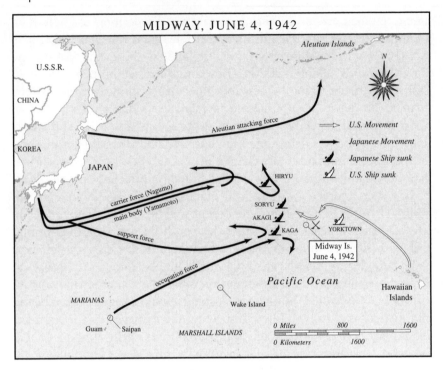

MIDWAY, JUNE 4, 1942

Aleutian Islands

U.S.S.R.

CHINA

Aleutian attacking force

⟹ U.S. Movement

━▶ Japanese Movement

⚓ Japanese Ship sunk

⚓ U.S. Ship sunk

KOREA

JAPAN

HIRYU

carrier force (Nagumo)

main body (Yamamoto)

SORYU

AKAGI

support force

KAGA   YORKTOWN

Midway Is.
June 4, 1942

occupation force

Pacific Ocean

MARIANAS

Wake Island

Hawaiian
Islands

Guam   Saipan   MARSHALL ISLANDS

N

0 Miles   800   1600

0 Kilometers   1600

groups.) As dawn approached on June 4 Nagumo had no inkling that Fletcher and Spruance awaited him over the eastern horizon. All his attention focused on Midway, from which B-17s and Catalina flying boats had ineffectually bombed his troop transports during the preceding afternoon and night.

At 4:30 A.M. on June 4 Nagumo flew off several squadrons of bombers to attack Midway, preparatory to the troop landings. They dropped their ordnance, high-explosive fragmentation bombs designed for ground targets, according to plan. But the strike force commander asked for a second attack to finish the reduction of Midway's defenses. His message arrived just as Nagumo's carriers were coming under attack from Midway-based aircraft. Not a single American bomb touched his ships, but the very appearance of the American planes was enough to convince Nagumo to accede to the request for a second strike on Midway. On *Akagi* and *Kaga*, Nagumo had been holding some ninety-three aircraft armed with armor-piercing antiship ordnance, against the possibility that he might engage elements of the American fleet. But at 7:15, increasingly confident that he had little to fear from American ships, he gave the order to rearm those aircraft with fragmentation bombs for a second assault against Midway. The refitting operation would take about an hour.

Even as Nagumo's perspiring sailors set about their task, Spruance was ordering full deck-loads of bombers and torpedo planes to lift off from *Enterprise* and *Hornet* to strike the Japanese carriers. Nagumo still remained unaware of the presence of the American fleet. His seamen toiled about the decks of his giant carriers, shuffling bomb racks and hurriedly stacking torpedoes. Then, in the midst of the complicated rearmament operation, the Japanese cruiser *Tone*'s scout plane reported at 7:28 that ten enemy ships were in sight. Their position was within range of carrier-based aircraft, but the initial report did not identify the types of ships. Nagumo nevertheless decided as a precaution to halt the rearmament process. Meanwhile he desperately implored the reconnaissance plane to ascertain the ship types.

Nagumo's skull must have throbbed with the agonies of decision and command. He was still under attack from Midway-based aircraft, his own returning assault planes were beginning to appear overhead, his decks were stacked with bombs of all types, and an unexpected American fleet had now been spotted. Ominously, the *Tone*'s patrol plane next radioed that the enemy flotilla was turning into the wind, the position from which carriers launch their aircraft. Apprehension gripped the surprised Japanese, only to be allayed moments later by a report that the enemy flotilla consisted of five cruisers and five destroyers—and then to be revivified yet again by a message minutes afterward that the rising dawn's light had revealed a carrier in the rear of the American formation.

This news was alarming but not catastrophic. Nagumo still believed himself to possess a force far superior in numbers, technology, and skill to anything the Americans could throw against him. Indeed, even while anxiously awaiting word from the *Tone* scout plane, First Air Fleet's ships and fighters had badly mauled the Midway-based attackers, not one of whom had yet managed to score a hit. Mitsuo Fuchida, the Pearl Harbor veteran serving now as *Akagi*'s flight leader, later wrote: "We had by this time undergone every kind of attack by shore-based planes—torpedo, level bombing, dive-bombing—but were still unscathed. Frankly, it is my judgment that the enemy fliers were not displaying a very high level of ability."[19]

19. Mitsuo Fuchida and Masatake Okumiya, *Midway: The Battle That Doomed Japan* (Annapolis: U.S. Naval Institute Press, 1955), 163.

Emboldened by such thoughts, the Japanese now saw the American carrier less as a threat and more as an opportunity for inflicting additional punishment on the inept Americans. The battle thus far had emphatically confirmed Japanese combat superiority. Apprehension gave way to resolve—and to a fatal relaxation of the sense of urgency. Nagumo, confident he still held the upper hand, calmly waited to recover all his Midway bombers and fighters before magisterially turning to meet the American flotilla, still believing that only a single carrier confronted him. Meanwhile, he reversed his earlier rearmament order and directed his planes to be fitted with antiship weapons once again, adding to the confusion and the piles of explosive ordnance strewn about his flight decks.

Shortly after 9:00 A.M., Nagumo executed his change of course to close with the American fleet, perhaps even to force the "decisive battle" that was the stuff of the Japanese navy's dreams. What followed was decisive, all right, but for Japan and the Imperial Navy it was no dream but a nightmare.

Nagumo's several armament changes and his delay in seizing the initiative contributed powerfully to his undoing, but for the moment his change of course proved advantageous. Many of the American planes launched from *Hornet* and *Enterprise*, as well as those from *Yorktown*, which had put its airmen aloft about 8:30, never found him. Flying at the limits of their operational range, they arrived at the sector where the Japanese were supposed to be, only to look out over empty seas. Many wandering American aircraft fell from the sky for want of fuel. Those who did locate the Japanese fleet tried in vain to penetrate the curtain of antiaircraft fire and the swarming Zeros to reach the Japanese carriers. Shortly after 10:00 A.M. a clutch of Zeros almost completely annihilated a torpedo-bombing squadron from *Yorktown* as it came in low to launch its weapons. By 10:24 A.M. Nagumo appeared to have beaten off the last of the attacks. His proud fleet was still unscratched and was poised to loft a massive counterattack against the Americans. For a brief, breathless moment Japan seemed to have won the Battle of Midway, and perhaps the war.

One American flier scanning the scene from above was on the verge of coming to just that conclusion when suddenly he saw "a beautiful silver waterfall" of Dauntless dive-bombers cascading down on the Japanese carriers.[20] Navigating by guess and by God, Lieutenant Commander Wade McCluskey from *Enterprise* and Lieutenant Commander

20. Spector, 174.

Maxwell Leslie from *Yorktown* had managed to arrive over the Japanese fleet at the precise moment its combat air patrol of Zeros had been drawn down to the deck to repel the *Yorktown's* torpedo bombers, and at the moment of First Air Fleet's maximum vulnerability. With the dread Zeros too low to be effective, the Dauntlesses poured down through the miraculously open sky to unload their bombs on the nakedly exposed Japanese carriers, their flight decks cluttered with confused ranks of recovered and warming-up aircraft, snaking fuel hoses, and stacks of munitions from the various rearmament operations.

In five minutes the dive-bombers, no less miraculously scoring the first American hits of the day, mortally wounded three Japanese carriers. Roaring, gasoline-fed fires raged through all three ships. *Kaga* and *Soryu* sank before sunset. *Akagi* was scuttled during the night. Of First Air Fleet's magnificent flotilla of carriers, only *Hiryu* remained to strike a counterblow against Fletcher's flagship, the battered *Yorktown*, which the sea enveloped at last at dawn on June 7. *Hiryu* herself was overtaken by American fliers in the afternoon of June 4 and sank the next morning. Nagumo had lost four of the six carriers with which he had attacked Pearl Harbor just half a year earlier. Spruance wisely refrained from pursuing the remaining Japanese vessels that were retreating to the west, where he would have collided with Yamamoto's battleships — swift, powerful, night-trained, and thirsty for vengeance — just as darkness fell.

At Midway the Americans turned the trick of surprise back upon the Japanese and at least partially avenged Pearl Harbor. In time it became apparent that they had done much more than that. They had demonstrated the inefficacy of high-level bombing against moving ships. The vaunted B-17 Flying Fortresses had a flawless record of misses at Midway, against carriers, battleships, cruisers, destroyers, and transports alike. Midway also definitively heralded the new age of naval warfare, in which aircraft carriers, not battleships, were the decisive elements. As at Coral Sea, the opposing surface ships had not come within sight or gun range of one another. The carriers had shown that they could project firepower further over the horizon than any previous device in the history of sea battles and that naval air power, when properly applied, was lethal in attacks on other ships. Midway also confirmed the value of those oddly attired intelligence officers, though the cryptanalysts would never again play so a dramatic a role as they had in this crucial engagement.[21]

---

21. The priceless asset of Magic was almost lost on June 7, when the *Chicago Tribune* ran a story under the headline NAVY HAD WORD OF JAP PLAN TO STRIKE AT SEA,

When the chaos of combat had subsided, the essential truth of Midway stood revealed: in just five minutes of incredible, gratuitous favor from the gods of battle, McCluskey's and Leslie's dive-bombers had done nothing less than turn the tide of the Pacific war. Before Midway the Japanese had six large fleet-class carriers afloat in the Pacific, and the Americans three (four with *Saratoga*, which was returning from repairs on the West Coast at the time of the battle at Midway). With the loss of just one American and four Japanese carriers, including their complements of aircraft and many of their superbly trained fliers, Midway precisely inverted the carrier ratio and put the Imperial Japanese Navy at a disadvantage from which it never recovered.

As a bonus, the Japanese landings on Attu and Kiska in the Aleutians, though successful, yielded a virtually intact crash-landed Zero fighter on Akutan Island. Analyzed thoroughly by Grumman Aircraft's aeronautical engineers, it helped inspire the F6F Hellcat, a carrier-based fighter plane specifically designed to outperform the Zero. The Hellcat climbed faster and higher, flew and dove more swiftly, maneuvered more agilely, and carried heavier armament than its Japanese opponent. By 1943 Hellcats poured forth in profusion from American aircraft plants and helped to establish American air supremacy over the Pacific.

The Hellcat fighter was but one example that the stage was now set for Yamamoto's worst nightmare. His hopes for a short war vanished at Midway, to be replaced by the prolonged agony of a battle of production between the behemoth American economy and the much tinier Japanese industrial plant. Other examples proliferated. In the two years following Midway, Japanese shipyards managed to splash only six additional fleet carriers. The United States in the same period added seventeen, as well as ten medium carriers and eighty-six escort carriers. Those kinds of numbers, to be repeated in myriad categories of war materiel, spelled certain doom for Japan, though it was a doom still a long and harrowing distance in the future.[22]

---

followed by a remarkably detailed account of Japanese naval dispositions. The author was correspondent Stanley Johnston, to whom a naval officer had indiscreetly shown a copy of a dispatch from Nimitz revealing this information. The navy urged that Johnston be prosecuted for espionage, but the case was eventually dropped. Meanwhile, an irate but slow-witted congressman, Elmer J. Holland, denounced the *Tribune* from the floor of the House, declaring in part that "the Navy had secured and broken the secret code of the Japanese Navy." Incredibly, the Japanese apparently failed to get wind of either of these egregious security breaches. A good brief account of these episodes is in Spector, 451–52.

22. Edmund L. Castillo, *Flat-tops: The Story of Aircraft Carriers* (New York: Random House, 1969), 86.

THE BATTLE OF MIDWAY nudged both Japan and the United States into strategic transition, though neither side fully realized it at the time. Japan was passing onto the defensive after its string of initial victories, fulfilling almost to the day Yamamoto's prophecy about running wild for six months. The United States, for its part, began groping for a place to begin an offensive. The Americans settled finally on the remote, virtually unheard-of southern Pacific island of Guadalcanal, in the Solomon archipelago.

Midway had dramatically turned back the Japanese advance in the Central Pacific, but Japan was still moving forward in the South Pacific. The Battle of the Coral Sea had failed to prevent Japanese landings on Tulagi, in the Solomons. On June 8, just hours after the clash at Midway, the first elements of Japanese construction battalions sailed across Savo Sound from Tulagi, debarked on the Lunga Plain of Guadalcanal Island, and began building an airstrip. Through Magic intercepts and reports from Australian coastwatchers (clandestine observers scattered through the South Pacific atolls with powerful radio sets), Nimitz and his Washington boss, Commander-in-Chief of the U.S. Fleet (COMINCH) Ernest J. King, learned that the Japanese had landed at Guadalcanal. King was determined to evict them.

King, sixty-three years old in 1942, was as gruff a man as Nimitz was a serene one. Hard-drinking and legendarily ill-tempered, he once confessed that he had not actually uttered the self-descriptive epithet "when they get in trouble they send for the sonsabitches" but that he would have if he had thought of it.[23] Yet King's choleric manner masked an incisive strategic intelligence, possessed of qualities that perfectly fitted him for senior command: the ability to anticipate, the capacity for penetrating analysis of his adversary's predicaments, an unerring grasp of the reach and limits of his own forces, and a pit bull's determination to seize the initiative and attack, attack, attack.

King had grown up alone with his father in an Ohio household from which his chronically ailing mother had been removed. He was ever after a loner, a brusque man who fathered seven children but seemed to love only the navy. After graduation from Annapolis near the top of his class in 1901, he had been posted to the Asiatic Squadron and served as a naval observer during the Russian-Japanese War. He had experience in both surface ships and submarines and at the age of forty-eight, in 1927, had qualified as a naval aviator. Roosevelt had appointed King COMINCH in December 1941, and three months later King also

23. Larrabee, *Commander in Chief,* 153.

assumed Harold Stark's functions as chief of naval operations (CNO). Reflecting his single-minded devotion to duty, he took up residence for the duration of the war aboard the yacht *Dauntless*, moored in the Washington Navy Yard, so that he might work at any hour with a secure communication system at hand.

King had long chafed at the restraints imposed on the navy by Plan Dog, Stark's November 1940 memorandum recommending offensive operations in the Atlantic and a defensive posture in the Pacific. To King, Plan Dog and ABC-1 ignominiously consigned the Pacific, the navy's principal arena, to the status of a subordinate theater. Moreover, as a faithful student of Mahan, King gagged on the idea of defensive naval warfare. The "nation that would rule upon the sea," Mahan had preached, "must attack."[24]

Roosevelt found King's headstrong belligerence attractive, though King's implacable insistence on more resources in the Pacific occasionally threatened to play hob with the grand Hitler-first strategy on which the entire American military effort turned. Indeed, even while King pressed for a license to pursue the navy's post-Midway advantage in the Pacific, preparations were grinding ahead in the summer of 1942 for joint British-American landings in North Africa in the autumn, an operation that grand strategy dictated should have priority. Yet King, invoking the offense-minded logic of the venerable Orange Plan, skillfully wrung from his navy-oriented president a concession. The North African campaign would continue to have first claim on all American resources, but Roosevelt's beloved navy, if it could muster the means, would be allowed to undertake its own, smaller offensive in the Pacific.

Just as the Solomons had not figured in Japanese prewar planning, so did they form no part of the traditional Orange Plan's war-gaming. The U.S. Navy even lacked adequate charts of the region. But the news that Japan was constructing an airstrip on Guadalcanal clinched that island's fate as the target of the American initiative. With air power based at Guadalcanal, the Japanese could control the skies over the crucial shipping lanes to Australia and could support a further military advance to the southeast. Yet in American hands, Guadalcanal and its precious airstrip could provide the essential toehold for a step-by-step advance upon Rabaul, the heavily fortified hub of all Japanese operations in the southwestern Pacific.

24. Alfred Thayer Mahan, *The Influence of Sea Power upon History* (New York: Hill and Wang, 1957), 68.

On these premises, King launched the Solomons campaign on a shoe-string and in a hurry. It was attended by none of the stately planning and meticulously analyzed game-board exercises that had informed the Orange Plan and been the principal occupation of the peacetime navy. From the outset, it was characterized by makeshift and make-do, even at the level of command structure, which was already distorted by the thespian presence of Douglas MacArthur in the Pacific.

MacArthur was, by any measure, a character to be reckoned with. Born in 1880 into a distinguished military family, he followed in his father's footsteps and beyond. After graduating first in his class at West Point, he was posted to the Philippines, where his father commanded the American military forces. He served later as President Theodore Roosevelt's military aide, as superintendent at West Point, and as army chief of staff under Herbert Hoover, whose orders he had exceeded when he had cleared the Bonus Army from Washington's Anacostia Flats. President Manuel Quezon named him field marshal of the Phil-ippine army in 1936. He retired from the U.S. Army in 1937, only to be recalled to active duty in 1941 as war approached. By age and experi-ence he was by that time senior to virtually every American officer in all services. He was also the military personality best known to the American public, a position he had carefully cultivated, even turning his question-able behavior in the Philippines in late 1941 and early 1942 to his advan-tage. His crushed hat, aviator glasses, aquiline profile, and corncob pipe all designedly contributed to the image of the gentlemanly general, the squire at war, the scholarly soldier, perhaps the soldier as political savior.

By theatrical gesture and brassy rodomontade, MacArthur, writes Ron-ald Spector, had by this time manufactured a public persona as "a hero of towering stature, a man who had to be employed in some task com-mensurate with his supposed greatness."[25] To propitiate the vainglorious MacArthur and placate his legions of admirers, Roosevelt named him commander-in-chief, Southwest Pacific Area, chiefly comprising Austra-lia, the Philippines, New Guinea, and Papua. As supreme *Allied* com-mander for the Southwest Pacific, MacArthur also controlled the Australian forces in the area, to their frequent dismay. The navy's Nimitz was assigned command of the blue vastness called Pacific Ocean Areas, arcing from the Solomons in the tropical southwestern ocean to the Aleutians in the frigid northeast and subdivided into North, Central, and South Pacific sectors. Nimitz in Hawaii retained direct command

25. Spector, 144.

of the former two and assigned the third, southernmost sector — and the Guadalcanal campaign — to Admiral Robert F. Ghormley, stationed at Noumea in New Caledonia.

The stresses inherent in this bizarre command apparatus, divided both by geography and service, and bereft of an overall theater commander to carry the war against Japan, appeared vividly in the planning for the Solomons campaign. MacArthur at first proposed a direct assault on Rabaul, but the navy refused to relinquish to an army general — especially *this* general — the two-carrier task force that MacArthur demanded to support his landing operations. With only four carriers available in the Pacific after Midway (*Wasp* had now joined the Pacific Fleet), the navy was understandably determined to husband them as carefully as possible, and that meant keeping them out of the confined waters of the Solomon Sea, within range of Japanese airfields. Far better, urged the navy, to proceed methodically and sequentially, first securing airfields for American use before undertaking the final strike at Rabaul.

As finally agreed, the American South Pacific offensive, code-named Watchtower, envisioned three phases: first, the capture of Guadalcanal and the southernmost Solomons; second, the expulsion of the Japanese from Papua and an advance up the Solomon chain toward Rabaul; third, amphibious landings from Papua and the northern Solomons onto New Britain, and the final extinction of Rabaul. The first job fell to the navy. The second and third tasks were to be MacArthur's responsibilities. Like so many war plans, this one bore only a tenuous relation to the eventual reality.

The Japanese had already dislodged, captured, or scattered into the moldy jungle the five hundred or so Europeans who ran the Solomon Islands' few shabby coconut plantations, hacked laboriously by native workers out of the vine-choked tropical rain forest. The Solomons were annually drenched by some of the planet's heaviest rainfalls. The fetid atmosphere buzzed with insects. The damp jungle floor slithered with rodents and reptiles. Above it soared giant hardwood trees with forty-foot-diameter trunks arising from splayed, fin-like bases 150 feet into the virtually opaque canopy. The nearly one hundred thousand Melanesians who had inhabited the islands since time immemorial had already had a taste of Western ways when in 1893 they came under the rule of the British Solomon Islands Protectorate with its rustic and sleepy colonial capital at Tulagi. Now their verdant islands and blue lagoons were about to be convulsed by a spectacle so violently improbable, so murderously fantastic, that their horror and wonder could only be guessed by imagining the citizens of Los Angeles awaking one morning to find flotillas of Eskimos and Mayans, somehow armed with weapons destructive beyond reckoning, descending massively upon the coast of California, there to wage colossal battle.

The improvised character of the Solomons campaign blighted it from the outset, when elements of the First Marine Division, commanded by Major General Archer Vandegrift, steamed into Wellington, New Zealand, in mid-June 1942. Vandegrift had been sent to the South Pacific in what the navy considered an "administrative" move, a preemptive forward positioning of just a part of his division, to await further eventualities. Mostly young recruits who had enlisted in the post–Pearl Harbor rush, Vandegrift's marines were understrength, undertrained, and ill equipped (with WWI-vintage bolt-action rifles). When Vandegrift had sailed from Norfolk in late May, he had no expectation of taking his eager but grass-green troops into combat before 1943. Accordingly, their support ships arrived at Wellington without being "combat loaded"—that is, without their cargo arranged for expeditious unloading in the order necessary to support an amphibious landing. Consequently, when they received their combat orders in New Zealand in late June, and the local longshore unions refused to bend their rules to accelerate the work, the marines' first assignment was to serve as stevedores on the Wellington docks, reloading their own ships. To speed up the task, they downsized everything. They reduced supply stocks from the regulation ninety days to sixty and squeezed personal belongings to a minimum. They cut ammunition to a ten-day reserve.

Escorted by three carrier groups under the command of Frank Jack Fletcher, the transports bearing this skeletally equipped, untested force glided into Savo Sound before dawn on August 7. Under covering fire from naval guns, the marines poured onto the beaches at first light. Despite indescribable snarls and bottlenecks in unloading their supplies, the Guadalcanal landing parties, facing light opposition from construction troops, quickly established their beachhead and seized the nearly completed Japanese airstrip—soon christened Henderson Field in honor of a marine flier killed at Midway. Across Savo Sound on Tulagi, however, where the main Japanese force was well dug in, the marines received their first taste of the Japanese army's tenacious defensive tactics. To the astonishment of the Americans, Japanese defenders in caves and dugouts refused to surrender, even when they witnessed their shrieking comrades being incinerated by gasoline drums lowered into cave mouths on ropes and ignited. Of Tulagi's 350 Japanese defenders, only

3 survived. On the nearby islets of Gavutu and Tanambogo, another five hundred Japanese perished, while only twenty surrendered. One hundred fifteen Americans died during this landing phase, in a curdling preview of the loss ratios of nearly ten to one, Japanese to American, that would characterize the entire Pacific war.

Alerted by the garrison at Tulagi, Vice-Admiral Gunichi Mikawa sortied from Rabaul with a group of five heavy and two light cruisers, plus one destroyer. He intended to race down the "Slot" of the Solomon chain, attack the American transports in Savo Sound, and thereby break up the landings. Given the presence of the American carriers, Mikawa's plan to attack with only a handful of surface ships displayed audacity that verged on bravery. It also benefited, as events soon proved, from American ineptitude that verged on cowardice.

Admiral Fletcher, in command of the carrier escort force comprising *Enterprise*, *Wasp*, and *Saratoga*, had declared during the planning for the Guadalcanal operation that he would hold his carriers on station to cover the landings for only three days. Vandegrift countered that it would take five days to put all his marines ashore and complete the unloading of their already precariously reduced supplies. Fletcher remained adamant. Three days it would be and no more; on August 9 he would withdraw. This was bad news for Vandegrift, but it got worse. On the afternoon of August 8, while the offloading of the transports was proceeding with only slightly diminished confusion, Fletcher received word of Japanese torpedo planes in the area. He peremptorily announced that he was leaving immediately, a day earlier than promised and three days sooner than Vandegrift had wanted. At 6:30 that same evening Fletcher's three carriers commenced their withdrawal to the southeast and out of harm's way.

Fletcher was understandably skittish. *Lexington* had been lost under his command at the Battle of the Coral Sea three months earlier to the day, and *Yorktown* had been virtually blown out from under him at Midway just two months before. The three carriers that he now held off the Solomons represented fully 75 percent of the Pacific carrier fleet. To risk losing them would be to risk reversing the gains of Midway, not to mention clinching Fletcher's reputation as the man who could not keep his capital ships afloat. But whatever allowance he might be granted, the fact remains that Fletcher displayed highly questionable judgment and a conspicuous want of courage. Believing the preservation of the carriers to be more important than protecting the landings, he withdrew the marines' air cover and left Rear Admiral Richmond Kelly Turner with a few surface ships to guard the vulnerable beachhead.

Turner considered Fletcher's withdrawal tantamount to desertion. It compelled him to make a tough decision of his own. Late on the muggy night of August 8, Turner called a conference on his flagship to discuss whether Fletcher's departure dictated withdrawing the transports that same night, now that their air cover was gone. Rear Admiral Victor Crutchley, a British officer in the Australian service who commanded the force screening the northern entrances to Savo Sound, pulled his heavy cruiser *Australia* out of the picket line of patrolling ships and steamed twenty miles south to rendezvous with Turner. Crutchley left his American colleague Captain Howard D. Bode, aboard the heavy cruiser *Chicago*, in command of the screening force. Its ships continued their leisurely, box-shaped patrols in the two channels flanking the dimly silhouetted cone of Savo Island. Downsound, off Tulagi and Lunga Point, the American transports undulated at anchor, their holds still crammed with supplies for the marines ashore.

Mikawa, meanwhile, was just miles away, plunging furiously southward across the glassy sea toward Savo Island. The moonless, overcast sky provided ideal cover for the night-fighting at which his sailors excelled. At almost the precise moment that Crutchley stepped aboard Turner's flagship, Mikawa catapulted four float planes for reconnaissance and flare illumination once the battle was joined. Minutes later he changed course and cut speed slightly to dampen wakes that might alert the outermost American picket ship, the destroyer *Blue*, spotted by his sharp-eyed lookouts as it progressed obliviously across the very path of his oncoming ships.

Leaving *Blue* unaware in his rear, Mikawa resumed attack speed, rounded Savo Island, and lunged toward the first group of Allied cruisers, steaming serenely in the west channel. Signaling his ships with hooded blinkers visible only in his own column, he commenced the action at 1:30 by loosing a volley of Long Lance torpedoes at the still unsuspecting Allied vessels. As the torpedoes hissed toward their targets, Mikawa unleashed his gunners. In a devastating demonstration of their prowess, his sailors firing from five separate ships sent twenty-four shells smashing into the Australian cruiser *Canberra* in the space of one minute. Still untouched, Mikawa's force split in two and curled to port, toward the second group of cruisers in the eastern channel.

The sea south of Savo suddenly lit up with aerial flares, searchlights,

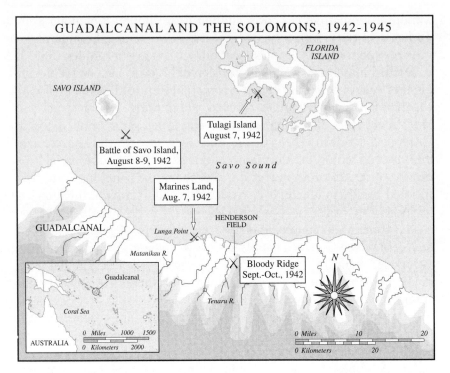

GUADALCANAL AND THE SOLOMONS, 1942-1945

FLORIDA ISLAND

SAVO ISLAND

Tulagi Island
August 7, 1942

Battle of Savo Island,
August 8-9, 1942

Savo Sound

Marines Land,
Aug. 7, 1942

HENDERSON FIELD

GUADALCANAL

Lunga Point

Matanikau R.

Bloody Ridge
Sept.-Oct., 1942

N

Guadalcanal

Tenaru R.

Coral Sea

0 Miles   1000   1500

AUSTRALIA   0 Kilometers   2000

0 Miles   10   20

0 Kilometers   20

muzzle blasts, and flames from the doomed *Canberra*. Aboard the Allied ships all was bedlam. A torpedo slamming into *Chicago* awakened Captain Bode, the officer in tactical command in Crutchley's absence. Bode was so rattled by the lightning assault that he neglected to inform his ships in the far channel that they were about to come under attack. He then limped off in futile pursuit of Mikawa's lone destroyer, leaving the much more destructive Japanese cruiser force unscathed as it executed its high-speed turn and bore down on the remaining American vessels.

Harassed but undeflected by groping gunfire from American destroyers, at 1:50 Mikawa's cruisers locked their searchlights on the heavy cruisers *Quincy*, *Astoria*, and *Vincennes* and began firing. Though the battle had now raged for nearly a quarter of an hour, all three American captains were asleep and caught utterly by surprise. Japanese torpedo and gun crews expertly poured salvo after salvo down their light-beams into the U.S. ships. *Quincy* was the first to succumb. Shuddering violently from countless hits, she rolled over and sank within minutes, taking nearly four hundred sailors with her to the bottom of what soon became known as Ironbottom Sound. *Astoria* went down minutes later, with a loss of more than three hundred men. *Vincennes* survived the night, only to slip beneath the water shortly after noon the next day.

Scarcely thirty minutes after he had launched his first torpedoes, Mikawa completed his U-shaped swing around Savo Island, slapped a half-dozen shells into an outlying American destroyer, and steamed away up the Slot. He had inflicted what the official naval historian calls the worst defeat ever suffered on the high seas by the U.S. Navy.[26] His own ships received only trifling damage, while he had demolished one Australian and three U.S. cruisers. Against his own casualty list of about two hundred could be counted nearly two thousand American killed and wounded—a singular reversal of the loss ratios incurred during the landings some forty-eight hours earlier. While Mikawa sped jauntily back to Rabaul, huge human rafts of dazed American seamen, awaiting dawn and rescue, bobbed about amidst the flaming wreckage and the predatory sharks south of Savo Island.

Recriminations soon followed. Much criticism fell upon Fletcher, whose withdrawal had precipitated Turner's conference, removing Crutchley from command and his heavy cruiser from the battle line at a crucial moment. Moreover, Fletcher, fleeing south to safety during the night, was out of range to pursue Mikawa's force up the Slot the next day. Fletcher would fight one more battle, but his controversial departure on the evening of August 8 shadowed his reputation, and by the end of the month he was relieved of command. As for Captain Bode, his despondency over his sorry role on that devastating night may well have contributed to his later decision to take his own life.

Yet for all the ruination that Mikawa's tornado had visited upon the U.S. Navy, he had in fact failed to reach his objective: the still-unloaded transports lying off Guadalcanal and Tulagi. Like Nagumo at Pearl Harbor, his own special case of victory disease inclined him to clasp the prize of his effortless triumph without gathering the final fruits of victory by smashing the supply ships and thus breaking the back of the American invasion.

On the mournful dawn of August 9, as rescue ships plowed about Savo Sound gathering bodies and traumatized survivors, Admiral Turner took stock of his situation. He decided to continue unloading the transports for one more day. But at sunset, unwilling to tarry any longer without air cover, he sailed for Ghormley's South Pacific base at Noumea, nearly a thousand miles south of Guadalcanal. He took with him

26. Morison, 167.

some eighteen hundred marines who had not managed to get ashore and left the six thousand marines on Tulagi and the eleven thousand on Guadalcanal to their own devices. He also took with him nearly half their supplies, already scaled back by the haste of the reloading operation at Wellington.

Under these less than auspicious circumstances the siege of Guadalcanal began. It would constitute one of the longest and most complicated American campaigns of the war, including six separate naval battles and three major clashes on the island of Guadalcanal itself. On its outcome came to depend not only the military balance in the Pacific but the war-morale of the American public. It was, as much as any single engagement could be, a decisive battle. Yet in the annals of the Pacific war it was also an odd, untypical engagement in many ways. In a strange inversion of much of what was to follow, the Americans were defending an island and the Japanese were trying to dislodge them. Nor did the Americans enjoy, at least at the beginning, the overwhelming logistical advantages that prevailed through much of the subsequent war. When Turner's convoy slipped over the horizon, the marines on Guadalcanal were left on a two-meals-per-day regimen and had only four days of ammunition reserves. Soon they were plundering the meager stocks of food and equipment left behind by the fleeing Japanese construction crews and ripping up cattle fencing to jury-rig a defensive perimeter around Henderson Field.

The airfield constituted not only their objective but their greatest tactical asset. Within two weeks of the landings, it was ready to receive its first aircraft, a handful of Dauntless dive-bombers and Wildcat fighters. More planes followed, as the Americans slowly built up the "Cactus Air Force," titled after the code name for Guadalcanal.

The Japanese, meanwhile, badly failed to grasp American intentions at Guadalcanal. Even after the humiliation of Midway, they believed the Americans incapable of a major military initiative until 1943. They had not reckoned with King's impatient bellicosity. Nor did they correctly estimate the American strength on the island. Misjudging the implications of the Battle of Savo and the hasty withdrawal of the American transports, the Japanese concluded that a maximum of ten thousand Americans had been landed, probably even fewer, and that they were in any case demoralized, undersupplied, and abandoned—much as the recently vanquished Philippine garrison had been.

On the basis of those faulty estimates, Colonel Kiyoano Ichiki recklessly landed on Guadalcanal with 917 men on the night of August 18–

19 and began slogging across the several watercourses that separated him from the American perimeter. In the predawn darkness of August 21 he collided with a much larger than anticipated marine force, equipped with machine guns and a few light tanks, at the mouth of Alligator Creek, which became the scene of appalling slaughter. Waves of Japanese troops mounting foolhardy frontal attacks fell to marine bullets and mortars or were ground to death under the tank treads. At dawn Ichiki committed ritual suicide, while marines shot his remaining troops as they swam away from the blood-reddened lagoon. When some Japanese wounded tried to kill the approaching American medics, the marines systematically massacred all Japanese survivors. Nearly eight hundred Japanese died. One surrendered. The rest disappeared into the jungle or the sea.

At this moment neither the American nor the Japanese high command seemed to have a clear understanding of Guadalcanal's military worth, nor even of the ultimate purpose of the Solomons campaign that was just aborning. The persistent inability of both the Americans and the Japanese to place a precise value on Guadalcanal engendered hesitation and a constant shifting of priorities, at all levels of command of both countries' forces.

On the American side, that pattern had been dimly evident in the haste and niggardliness of Vandegrift's preparations for the landing and darkly foreshadowed in Fletcher's retreat on the night of August 8. Admiral Ghormley, in overall command in the South Pacific Area, shuttered in humid isolation aboard his command ship at Noumea, rarely going ashore or taking recreation of any kind, vacillated between defensive and offensive conceptions of his assignment in the Solomons. Was his mission to protect the sea lanes to Australia, in which case he had merely to deny the use of Guadalcanal and its airfield to the Japanese? Or was he expected to prepare Guadalcanal as a base from which to carry the war northward to Rabaul, a much more demanding task? Ghormley appeared to be incapable of sorting these questions out and slipped ever more deeply into gloom and despondency. And overshadowing the entire operation was the simultaneous and much larger enterprise in North Africa, which severely constrained Admiral King's ability to reinforce Guadalcanal, especially with critical air power.

Analogous ambiguities and conflicting claims plagued the Japanese. The impetuosity of Ichiki's calamitous raid suggested that Guadalcanal at this stage was but a daub on the palette of Japan's strategic drawing board. Japan's main goal in the southeastern Pacific remained the thrust to Port Moresby in Papua. Beyond that, the Imperial Japanese Army was busily consolidating its grip on occupied Malaya, Indochina, the East Indies, and the Philippines. Japan also had a major initiative under way in Burma, not to mention its enormous continuing commitment in China, always the principal focus of all Japanese strategy. As for the Imperial Navy, it still bled from Midway but had by no means given up the doctrine of decisive battle. Yamamoto in particular could not rid himself of the temptation to see the Solomons not as an objective in their own right but simply as the place where that battle might be made to happen at last.

That prospect tantalizingly presented itself in the Battle of the Eastern Solomons on August 24, the war's third great carrier battle. It pitted one light and two Japanese heavy carriers, commanded by the redoubtable Nagumo, against Fletcher's trio of *Enterprise*, *Wasp*, and *Saratoga*. In an ironic reprise of Fletcher's predicament some two weeks earlier, Nagumo, ostensibly providing air cover for a troop convoy transporting the hapless Ichiki's reinforcements, effectively abandoned the transports in order to give battle to the American carrier force. Once again the resolving climax of the decisive battle eluded him. Nagumo lost his light carrier while damaging *Enterprise* enough to send her back to Pearl Harbor for repairs. His unshielded transports, meanwhile, never did reach their destination.

Slowly, incrementally, tentatively, both sides now began a months-long process of upping their stakes in Guadalcanal. High-speed Japanese destroyer convoys—dubbed the "Tokyo Express" by the marines—nightly ran contingents of troops down the Slot, depositing them ashore at the far ends of Guadalcanal, miles from the tiny marine foothold at Lunga Point. By early September the jungle rustled with some six thousand Japanese soldiers. Vandegrift meanwhile shifted units across from Tulagi in anticipation of another Japanese ground offensive, this time in strength. His marines, plagued by heat, bugs, poor diet, jaundice, dermatitis, and gnawing apprehension, tensed for action. Many of them already verged on being unnerved by jungle warfare. Some began to show signs of "going Asiatic"—the marines' term for symptoms of battle psychosis. The Japanese were "full of tricks," one marine told war correspondent John Hersey. "They hide up in the trees like wildcats. Sometimes when they attack, they scream like a bunch of terrified cattle in a slaughter house. Other times they come so quiet they wouldn't scare a snake. One of their favorite tricks is to fire their machine guns off to one side. That starts you shooting. Then they start their main fire under the noise of your own shooting. Sometimes they use firecrackers as a diversion. Other times they jabber to cover the noise of their men cutting through the underbrush with machetes. You've probably heard about their using white surrender flags to suck us into traps. We're onto that one now."[27]

After an exhausting march through diabolically braided jungle, on the night of September 13 a Japanese force crawled up to the base of a low, knobby ridge that bounded the Lunga River drainage to the south of Henderson Field. Atop the ridge, elite marine raider and parachute battalions, commanded by Lieutenant Colonel Merritt Edson, awaited them. Bolstered by the charismatic and fearless Edson, who roamed up and down the firing line murmuring profane encouragement, the marines repelled repeated charges by screaming Japanese soldiers. In the respites between the enemy lunges they rolled grenades down the grassy slope. Daybreak revealed a ghastly mat of some five hundred Japanese corpses carpeting the ridge's shoulder. The marines were shaken and badly blooded but still held what soon became known as "Bloody Ridge" or "Edson's Ridge."

The clash on Bloody Ridge spurred both sides to accelerate their reinforcements. Four thousand more marines arrived on September 18. Four weeks later the 164th Infantry regiment landed, its three thousand former Dakota National Guardsmen looking like old geezers to the nearly adolescent marines. But the soldiers of the 164th toted the army's standard-issue Garrand M-1 semiautomatic rifles, which provided considerably more firepower than the marines' aged weapons. By October some twenty-seven thousand Americans of all services were ashore on Guadalcanal and Tulagi.

The Cactus Air Force, however, grew only haltingly, as the army air force's General Hap Arnold refused to reassign planes from the North African theater. In any case, the American aircraft available at this point in the war suffered from technological deficiencies relative to their opponents that made them of limited value. The B-17s had by now conclusively demonstrated their inability to inflict damage on ships at sea, and the Wildcat fighters, which furnished the principal air defense for Guadalcanal, could only barely claw up to combat altitude if radar and coastwatchers gave them maximum warning time—thirty-five or forty minutes—of approaching Japanese bombers. In any event, the Zeros

27. John Hersey, *Into the Valley: A Skirmish of the Marines* (New York: Knopf, 1943), 20.

that accompanied the bombers still easily outclassed the Wildcats in speed and maneuverability and routinely shooed the marine fliers from the sky.

The Americans undertook a kind of psychological reinforcement as well, aimed at shoring up the home front as much as bracing the fighting line on Guadalcanal. They brought war correspondents like Hanson Baldwin, Richard Tregaskis, and John Hersey to the island. Baldwin's series of articles in the *New York Times* in late September was among the first frontline reports from any theater to reach the home-front public. Americans now began to invest Guadalcanal, the first land action in which the United States had a fighting chance against Japan, with a psychological value no less weighty than its purely military importance. "The shadows of a great conflict lie heavily over the Solomons," the *New York Herald Tribune* editorialized on October 16, reflecting the growing American sense that in this remote and exotic corner of the South Pacific men and machines were gathering for a historic showdown.[28] A fresh sense of resolve gripped President Roosevelt too. He instructed the Joint Chiefs on October 24 to "make sure that every possible weapon gets into that area to hold Guadalcanal"—though not at the expense of the about-to-be-launched North African invasion.[29]

All this was too much for Admiral Ghormley. Stewing at Noumea in the face of these mounting expectations, he wrote to Nimitz on October 15: "My forces [are] totally inadequate to meet [the] situation." Three days later, Nimitz replaced Ghormley with Vice-Admiral William F. "Bull" Halsey, a commander of proved aggressivity who did not suffer from the defeatism that had ground down the bewildered and cloistered Ghormley.

While building up their own ground forces on Guadalcanal, the Japanese continued daily bombing raids on Henderson Field, though the distance from their airbase at Rabaul confined them to brief and predictable appearances at midday. More threatening to the Americans, and deeply injurious to morale, were the almost nightly naval bombardments that accompanied runs of the Tokyo Express. One of the most intensive bombardments occurred on October 13, the night of the 164th Infantry's

28. Richard B. Frank, *Guadalcanal: The Definitive Account of the Landmark Battle* (New York: Random House, 1990), 332. My account draws liberally from Frank's thorough—indeed, "definitive"—study.
29. Frank, *Guadalcanal*, 405.

arrival. It covered the landings of an unusually large Japanese troop contingent, preparatory to a major Japanese offensive.

Three days later some twenty thousand Japanese troops started hacking into the barely penetrable jungle curtain to mount the Imperial Army's third assault on Henderson Field. Each soldier shouldered twelve days of rations, a full ammunition pack, and one artillery shell for the thirty-mile trek across the trackless island to the American perimeter at Lunga. Terrain, temperature, vegetation, insects, and fear punished them every step of the way. Vandegrift had in fact counted upon his jungle "ally" in arranging his defensive dispositions. The shrewdness of his calculation was proved when the first Japanese column arrived exhausted and tattered on the western American perimeter along the Matanikau River and was virtually annihilated by devastating marine artillery fire. A second Japanese column was scheduled to attack simultaneously from the south, but its tortuous progression through the jungle brought it to the base of Bloody Ridge in an equally sorry state and a full day late, permitting the marines to shift their forces from the Matanikau. Once again Bloody Ridge confirmed the fitness of its name. Japanese troops, many of them ignorant rural recruits cowed by the Imperial Army's brutal military indoctrination, were on this as on so many occasions badly and profligately used by their commanders. They spent themselves in waves of useless assaults, their screams of "*banzai*" striking terror into the Seventh Marines and 164th Infantrymen on the ridge top, but falling nonetheless under the disciplined fire of the Americans. Perhaps thirty-five hundred Imperial soldiers died in this second battle of Bloody Ridge, which also proved to be Japan's last ground assault against Henderson Field.

Vandegrift spent the next two months enlarging his defense perimeter and stalking the scattered Japanese detachments in the jungle, until his battered First Marine Division was relieved in early December, when he turned over his command to the Army's Lieutenant General Alexander M. Patch. In four months of grueling siege warfare and frenzied jungle fighting, he had lost 650 dead and another thirteen hundred wounded. The jungle, sometimes his military ally but always his medical nemesis, no less than it was for the Japanese, left fully half of his command carrying away from Guadalcanal one or another tropical disease, chiefly malaria.

The battle for Guadalcanal was now turning into a grisly demonstration of the awful logic of American numbers that Yamamoto had feared. With sure and relentless momentum, the Americans steadily built up their ground and air forces on Guadalcanal. They counted some sixty thousand personnel ashore by year's end. But the Japanese succeeded in landing only a few thousand more troops after the big convoy and the disastrous offensive of October, and they were soon outnumbered nearly two to one. Growing American naval power in the region also hampered efforts to supply the Japanese troops already ashore. The Imperial Navy was eventually reduced to shoving drumloads of rice or barley overboard from high-speed destroyers, to be pulled to the beaches by shore parties. Strafing American pilots and PT-boat gunners soon grew adept at sinking the drums before they made it to shore.

Before long frontline Japanese troops were on one-sixth rations. Rear-echelon personnel made do with one-tenth. Of six thousand men in one Japanese division, only 250 were judged fit for combat by mid-December. One Japanese officer calculated a grim formula for predicting the mortality of his troops:

> Those who can stand — 30 days
> Those who can sit up — 3 weeks
> Those who cannot sit up — 1 week
> Those who urinate lying down — 3 days
> Those who have stopped speaking — 2 days
> Those who have stopped blinking — tomorrow

Shortly thereafter a report reached Yamamoto with a description of soldiers so ravaged by undernourishment and dysentery that their hair and nails had stopped growing. Their buttocks had wasted away to an extent that completely exposed their anuses.[30]

Still, the hope lingered in Yamamoto's mind that Guadalcanal might yet prove the bait to draw the Americans to the decisive battle. He moved his command headquarters to Truk to be in closer touch with the southern Pacific campaigns. Confident that one last blow would dislodge the Americans and provide a chance to exterminate the remainder of the U.S. Pacific Fleet, Yamamoto decided to mount another major offensive in early November, with a large convoy of reinforcements and supplies for Guadalcanal to be covered by a powerful battleship and cruiser escort.

Magic, however, again tipped the scales in favor of the Americans. Knowing the Japanese plans in advance, Halsey countered with a strong battleship force of his own and issued emergency orders for *Enterprise*

30. Frank, *Guadalcanal*, 527, 588.

to dash from the Pearl Harbor repair yards to the Solomons. The ensuing battle raged over four days and nights from November 12 to November 15. Despite their forewarning, American ships fared badly in the first encounters, losing among other ships the ill-starred cruiser *Juneau*. Its spectacular explosion claimed 683 lives, including five Sullivan brothers whose family tragedy formed one of the war's most poignant tales. As the battle raged on around them, *Juneau*'s unrescued seamen drifted for days under the tropical sun without food or water. About them circled an ever more aggressive pod of sharks that chewed off terrified survivors clinging to the nets on the sides of the life rafts.

Despite these agonies, at battle's end the Americans had won a conclusive victory. With *Enterprise*'s timely arrival they destroyed two Japanese battleships, along with sundry other vessels, and almost completely interdicted the Guadalcanal-bound transports, the last of which desperately ran themselves aground on the island's beaches. American pilots and antiaircraft gunners also took a fearsome toll of Japanese fliers, further eroding Japan's already tenuous air superiority.

This so-called Naval Battle of Guadalcanal clinched a decision that had been slowly gathering momentum in Japanese headquarters. In one of the few retreats executed by the Imperial Army in all the war, it evacuated its forces from Guadalcanal in the first weeks of 1943. Probing into the Japanese encampment in early February, Patch's troops found it deserted. On February 9 Patch radioed to Halsey: "Tokyo Express no longer has terminus on Guadalcanal."[31]

If King had launched the Guadalcanal campaign on a shoestring and somehow bootstrapped it to success, the Japanese operation from the outset had dangled from a slender thread that eventually frayed to the breaking point. The remorseless tipping of the military balance in favor of the Americans at Guadalcanal illustrated in microcosm the central logic of the Pacific war. Given time and a fair opportunity, the weight of growing American manpower and munitions inevitably crushed the steadily wasting Japanese reserves of men and materiel. To be sure, the Japanese had abetted their own defeat at Guadalcanal by violating basic military axioms and throwing themselves piecemeal at their foe, when a single, massed assault, delivered at the right time and place, might conceivably have brought them victory. Contempt for their enemy's fighting prowess, ignorance of American intentions, and confusion about their own conception of Guadalcanal's importance all contributed to

31. Morison, 214.

the fragmentation and eventual inefficacy of the Japanese campaign. But more than anything else Guadalcanal demonstrated vividly the ravaging implications of victory disease. For Japan, Guadalcanal was an island too far, a prize beyond reasonable reach given the competing claims of so many simultaneous operations. The repeated Japanese deflection of resources to Guadalcanal from the parallel campaign in Papua proved the point—but too late to salvage Guadalcanal from the Americans.

For their part, the victors at Guadalcanal had learned much about the fiendish arts of jungle fighting and about the three-dimensional geometry of naval aerial warfare. Yet because the Americans had fought a tactically defensive battle on Guadalcanal, they still had much to learn about amphibious fighting as they took to the offensive in the war of a hundred islands that lay ahead.

WITH THE MILITARY EDUCATION of the Americans came, perhaps inevitably, moral coarsening as well. Atrocities on both sides would grow in wretchedness as the war progressed, but for the Americans at least, Guadalcanal provided an early lesson in the wanton barbarism of warfare between two peoples separated so distantly by culture, religion, and race. "I wish we were fighting against Germans," said one marine on Guadalcanal. "They are human beings, like us. . . . But the Japanese are like animals."[32] Of the inhumanity of the Japanese-American war, however, the American public as yet knew little. The news that reached home from Guadalcanal presented a different image entirely. "[Y]ou felt sorry for the boys," correspondent John Hersey wrote. "The uniforms, the bravado, the air of wearing a knife in the teeth — these were just camouflage. The truth was all over their faces. These were just American boys. They did not want that valley or any part of its jungle. They were ex–grocery clerks, ex–highway laborers, ex–bank clerks, ex–schoolboys, boys with a clean record and maybe a little extra restlessness, but not killers. . . . [T]hey had joined the Marines to see the world, or to get away from a guilt, or most likely to escape the draft, not knowingly to kill or be killed." There was truth in that picture, but the makings of a myth as well.[33]

WITH GUADALCANAL SECURE , it was the Americans' turn to attempt a two-pronged offensive, in the Solomons as well as on Papua. MacArthur had assembled sufficient troops and aircraft by October 1942

32. Hersey, *Into the Valley*, 56.
33. Hersey, *Into the Valley*, 43.

to come to the aid of the Australians defending Papua. He made few friends among the Australians, however, when he described their more than six hundred dead along the Kokoda Trail as "extremely light casualties" indicating "no serious effort."[34] MacArthur was no less abusive to his own subordinates. When his troops stalled in front of the heavily fortified Japanese bastion of Buna on Papua's north coast, MacArthur dispatched two senior officers, Robert Eichelberger and Clovis Byers, to assume command in front of Buna. He admonished Eichelberger: "If you don't take Buna I want to hear that you and Byers are buried there."[35] By such hectoring and reckless wastage of his troops, hurled against strong Japanese defenses without adequate air, artillery, or armored support, MacArthur's combined American and Australian force took Buna and the nearby Japanese stronghold of Gona by December 1942, ending the threat to Australia.

Both sides now briefly marked time, preparing for the next round. The Japanese slipped troops surreptitiously to the northwest along the Papuan "tail" of the New Guinea "bird" to strengthen their positions at Lae and Salamaua. They also rushed ahead with construction of new airfields along the Solomon chain, at Buin and other sites on Bougainville and in the New Georgia group at Munda. There Japanese engineers cunningly but unavailingly tried to cloak their work under the jungle canopy, held in place by wires as the giant trees were felled beneath it. The Americans meanwhile reaffirmed the basic goals of Operation Watchtower. They agreed that MacArthur should continue to advance up the Papuan coast, take Lae and Salamaua, and then make the jump across to New Britain. Halsey in the meantime would climb up the Solomon ladder to Bougainville. They would then proceed to close the pincers on Rabaul in a final, coordinated attack. They rechristened their joint undertaking "Operation Cartwheel."

MacArthur forged ahead along the northern New Guinea shore, aided by innovative air tactics devised by General George Kenney, his new air chief. Kenney once and for all put an end to futile high-level bombing of ships by B-17s. Instead he trained his pilots in low-level sweeps by medium bombers carrying fragmentation bombs. These methods proved spectacularly successful in the first week of March, 1943 in a hundred-plane assault in the Bismarck Sea against a Japanese convoy bound for

Lae. After Kenney's bombers sank all the transports and four of the escorting destroyers, strafing aircraft and PT boats machine-gunned the Japanese survivors struggling in the water.[36] Given Kenney's triumphantly established air superiority, Japan thereafter could resupply and reinforce Lae only with the utmost difficulty. Lae fell at last to MacArthur in September.

New American aircraft also made their appearance at this time, early tokens of the American production explosion that was about to engulf all the Allied fighting fronts. Especially notable was the P-38 Lightning, a twin-tailed, twin-engined fighter; it could not outmaneuver the Zero in a dogfight, but its greater speed and higher ceiling enabled it to jump enemy air formations from above.

Witnessing the awesome destruction that Kenney's bombers and the new P-38s were wreaking, Yamamoto scraped together every available Japanese aircraft for a series of massive raids on American airfields—particularly Henderson Field—in April 1943. To encourage his fliers, he rashly decided to visit the forward Japanese airbase near Buin on Bougainville on April 18. It was a fatal decision. Nimitz's cryptographers intercepted a message announcing the legendary admiral's arrival and resolved to get him. An ambush might risk revealing the secret of Magic, but Yamamoto was too tempting a target. As his plane and its escort of Zeros approached their landing field on the morning of the eighteenth, a squadron of P-38s dropped from on high like avenging angels, blasting away with 20mm cannon fire. Yamamoto, the survivor of Tsushima, the reluctant foe of America, the dutiful architect of Pearl Harbor, the disappointed mastermind of Midway, the greatest naval strategist in the Imperial Navy, fell to a warrior's death as the flaming wreckage of his plane slammed into the jungle. Perhaps the gods of war had been kind to Yamamoto after all, as death spared him the agony of watching his nation's inexorable, humiliating defeat.

Yamamoto's passing marked but the briefest cadence in the gathering American onslaught rolling up toward Rabaul. While MacArthur pressed toward Lae, Halsey hammered at Munda, where Japanese resistance was fierce. A month of grueling combat finally pried Munda loose from its Japanese defenders in early August, but the Americans absorbed horrendous losses, especially in the poorly prepared Forty-third Infantry Division, mostly composed of New England National Guardsmen. (It was during this engagement, too, that a Japanese destroyer, racing down

36. Morison, 273.

Blackett Strait on the night of August 1, sliced through Lieutenant John F. Kennedy's PT 109.) Sobered by the spectacle of his ravaged troops, Halsey calculated that a steady, island-by-island progression toward Rabaul would prove inexcusably costly, and, by extension, would take years—perhaps a decade—to reach Japan itself. Halsey therefore decided to bypass the next fortified island up the Solomon chain, Kolombangara, and strike his next blow instead against lightly defended Vella Lavella, further up the Solomons ladder. The lifesaving purpose of this "island-hopping" or "leapfrogging" strategy was to avoid Japanese strongholds so far as possible and leave isolated Japanese garrisons to wither on the vine, cut off from communication and supply. This thinking would soon reshape the objectives of Operation Cartwheel and, indeed, deeply color the tactics of the war all over the Pacific.

Vella Lavella fell easily to the Americans and their New Zealand allies in August, and Halsey began to prepare it as a forward base for the assault on the last and largest of the Solomons, Bougainville. At Empress Augusta Bay on November 1, Halsey's invasion force quickly established a beachhead on Bougainville, while his ships beat back a Japanese effort to inflict another Savo-like humiliation on the landing operation. The Bougainville landings also occasioned ferocious air battles that further winnowed the steadily deteriorating pool of first-rate Japanese pilots. The next month MacArthur finally made the leap from New Guinea to Cape Gloucester, on the western tip of New Britain. After fierce fighting, Japanese resistance on Bougainville was overcome in March 1944. From secure airfields at both ends of the American pincers, planes now routinely bombed Rabaul.

Yet the prize fruit of Rabaul, the goal of Watchtower and Cartwheel, now within Halsey's and MacArthur's grasp, was not to be harvested. Just as Kolombangara had been bypassed, so too would Rabaul be left to wither on the vine—punished daily by bombing raids but never invaded. Meanwhile, in early 1944, the submerged dreams of the Orange planners resurfaced and beckoned American attention to the horizonless expanses of the Central Pacific.

4

Unready Ally, Uneasy Alliance

The British are trying to arrange this matter so that the British and the Americans hold the leg for Stalin to kill the deer and I think that will be a dangerous business for us at the end of the war. Stalin won't have much of an opinion of people who have done that and we will not be able to share much of the postwar world with him.
— Secretary of War Henry Stimson, May 17, 1943

America's war against Germany, like its war against Japan, began at sea. The Battle of the Atlantic, already two years old when the United States entered the war, was a contest for supremacy on the ocean highway across which all American supplies and troops must flow to Europe. Everything depended on keeping that highway open. Dwight D. Eisenhower, newly promoted to brigadier general and freshly installed as chief of the army's War Plans Division, submitted a penetrating assessment of the importance of the North Atlantic sea lanes to George Marshall on February 28, 1942. "Maximum safety of these lines of communication is a 'must' in our military effort, no matter what else we attempt to do," Eisenhower emphasized. Shipping, he presciently added, "will remain the bottleneck of our effective effort," a statement that echoed repeated pronouncements by both Churchill and Roosevelt that the struggle with Hitler would be won or lost at sea.[1]

It looked at first more likely to be lost. When he declared war on the United States shortly after the Pearl Harbor attack, Hitler untethered the German submarine service from the restraints against which it had long chafed. Karl Dönitz could now loose his U-boats as far westward as America's Atlantic shoreline, cutting the Allied supply lines at their

1. *PDDE* 1:150.

source and avenging the insults of the destroyer-bases deal and the Lend-Lease Act. He determined "to strike a blow at the American coast with a *Paukenschlag,*" a word usually translated as "drumbeat" but that also, in German, connotes "thunderbolt."[2] German submariners themselves described the campaign against American coastal shipping as the "Happy Time," or even the "American turkey-shoot." By whatever name, the naval *Blitzkrieg* that Dönitz launched in early 1942 threatened to shut down America's war against Hitler almost before it could get started.

As early as mid-January 1942 Dönitz had dispatched five U-boats, each packing between fourteen and twenty-two torpedoes, to the eastern coastal waters of the United States. Up to a dozen additional boats soon followed, their operational range and ability to remain on battle station enhanced by submarine tankers, or *Milchkuhen* (milkcows), that refueled the U-boats at sea. Within just two weeks Dönitz's undersea raiders sank thirty-five ships in the waters between Newfoundland and Bermuda, a loss of more than two hundred thousand tons. The prize targets were tankers lumbering up from Caribbean and Gulf Coast oil ports to northeastern refineries and storage depots. "By attacking the supply traffic — particularly the oil — in the U.S. zone," Dönitz gloated, "I am striking at the root of the evil, for here the sinking of each ship is not only a loss to the enemy but also deals a blow at the source of his shipbuilding and war production. Without shipping the [English] sally-port cannot be used for an attack on Europe."[3]

Still imagining the war to be far away, and fearing to cramp the tourist trade, seaboard cities like New York, Atlantic City, and Miami refused to enforce blackouts. The backdrop of their bright lights, visible up to ten miles from shore, created a neon shooting gallery in which the U-boats nightly lay in wait on the seaward side of the shipping lanes and picked off their sharply silhouetted victims at will. A single U-boat prowling off New York harbor in January sank eight ships, including three tankers, in just twelve hours. On February 28 a German submarine torpedoed and sank the American destroyer *Jacob Jones* in sight of the New Jersey coast. Only 11 of its 136 sailors survived. On the evening of April 10 a surfaced U-boat used its deck gun to scuttle the SS *Gulf-america* off of Jacksonville Beach, Florida. The flaming tanker went down so close to shore that the departing U-boat captain gazed in

2. Dan Van der Vat, *The Atlantic Campaign: World War II's Great Struggle at Sea* (New York: Harper and Row, 1988), 236.
3. Van der Vat, *Atlantic Campaign,* 266.

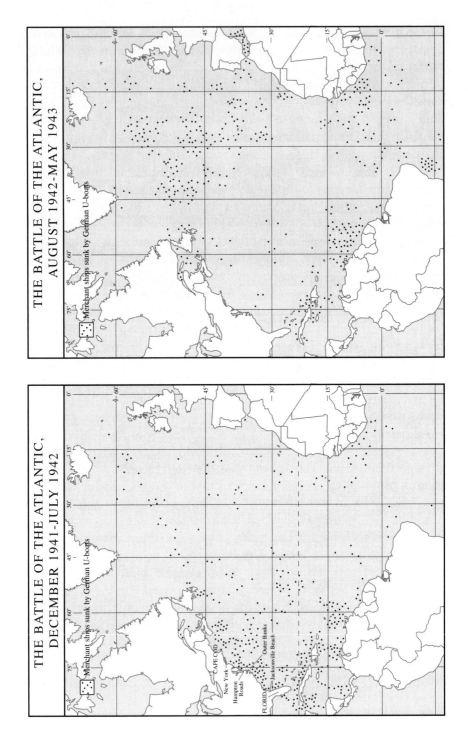

THE BATTLE OF THE ATLANTIC,
AUGUST 1942-MAY 1943

Merchant ships sunk by German U-boats

THE BATTLE OF THE ATLANTIC,
DECEMBER 1941-JULY 1942

Merchant ships sunk by German U-boats

CAPE COD
New York
Hampton Roads
Outer Banks
Jacksonville Beach
FLORIDA

fascination through his binoculars as thousands of tourists, their faces bathed in the red glow of the ship's fire, poured out of their hotels and restaurants to gape at the spectacle. "All the vacationers had seen an impressive special performance at Roosevelt's expense," Commander Reinhard Hardegen gleefully recorded in his log. "A burning tanker, artillery fire, the silhouette of a U-boat—how often had all of that been seen in America?"[4] In broad daylight on June 15 a U-boat torpedoed two American freighters within full view of thousands of horrified vacationers at Virginia Beach, Virginia.

In a still bolder but ultimately less successful venture, one U-boat surfaced near Long Island and another off a Florida beach in June 1942. Each put ashore a party of saboteurs, two four-man squads equipped with explosives, detonators, maps of industrial sites, and thousands of dollars in cash. A lone Coast Guardsman stumbled onto the first group burying their uniforms in a Long Island sand dune and notified his superiors. The FBI quickly captured all members of both groups. The eight infiltrators were swiftly tried before a military tribunal and sentenced to death by electrocution—virtually the only American "victory" to date in the offshore naval war.[5]

Within three months, *Paukenschlag*, or Operation Drumbeat, destroyed 216 vessels, more than half of them tankers. Some 1.25 million tons of shipping capacity, not to mention the valuable cargoes, were forever lost to the Allies. Burning hulks lit American beaches from Cape Cod to Hampton Roads, from the Outer Banks to the Florida Keys. In New York harbor, merchant crews mutinied against sailing into the teeth of such danger. Coastal shipping slowed nearly to a standstill as the navy ordered coastwise vessels to adopt a "bucket brigade" sailing schedule, compelling them to steam only in daylight and to scurry into safe harbors at night. Heady with his success, Dönitz quickened the tempo of Operation Drumbeat in the spring, fanning his refueled U-boats even further afield into the Caribbean. By June 1942 4.7 million tons of Allied

4. Michael Gannon, *Operation Drumbeat: The Dramatic True Story of Germany's First U-Boat Attacks along the American Coast in World War II* (New York: Harper and Row, 1990), 363.

5. Two of the saboteurs testified against their comrades, for which one had his sentence reduced to a life term and the other to thirty years imprisonment. In 1948 President Truman commuted both men's remaining sentences, and they were deported back to Germany. See Francis Biddle, *In Brief Authority* (Garden City, N.Y.: Doubleday, 1962), 325ff, and Kai Bird, *The Chairman* (New York: Simon and Schuster, 1992), 163ff.

shipping had gone to the bottom, the majority in American coastal waters, the operational area the navy called the Eastern Sea Frontier.

"The losses by submarines off our Atlantic seaboard and in the Caribbean now threaten our entire war effort," Marshall warned Admiral King on June 19, 1942. The submarines had sunk one-fifth of the bauxite fleet that hauled precious Jamaican aluminum ore, essential for aircraft manufacture, to North American smelters. Tanker sinkings were consuming 3.5 percent of available oil-carrying capacity every month, a rate of loss so ominous that King had recently confined all tankers to port for two weeks. "I am fearful," Marshall concluded, "that another month or two of this will so cripple our means of transport that we will be unable to bring sufficient men and planes to bear against the enemy in critical theaters to exercise a determining influence on the war."[6]

To counter this menace King could at first do little. In Roosevelt's quaint phrase, there was simply a "lack of naval butter to cover the bread."[7] The U.S. Atlantic Fleet was already hard pressed to shoulder its modest share of the burden of escorting North Atlantic convoys, and the sudden flaring of the Pacific war vacuumed up virtually all new naval construction. The entire antisubmarine force available to the Eastern Sea Frontier command when Operation Drumbeat began consisted of three 110-foot wooden sub-chasers, two 173-foot patrol craft, a handful of World War I–vintage picket ships and Coast Guard cutters, and 103 antiquated, short-range aircraft, almost none of them equipped with submarine-seeking radar. For a time this puny fleet was supplemented by the Coastal Picket Patrol, or "Hooligan's Navy," a motley flotilla organized by private yachtsmen (including a pistol and grenade-toting Ernest Hemingway at the helm of his sport-fishing boat *Pilar*). They formed a swashbuckling but decidedly amateurish patrol line some fifty miles offshore, reporting countless false submarine sightings that caused further dissipation of Eastern Sea Frontier's desperately scant resources.[8]

In an ironic reversal of the Lend-Lease help that America had extended to Britain a year earlier, the Royal Navy transferred ten escort vessels and two dozen antisubmarine trawlers to the Americans for coastal defense, as well as two squadrons of aircraft. In a compound irony, the planes had originally been built in the United States. But even as Eastern Sea Frontier began to accumulate the rudiments of an antisubmarine force, King persisted in deploying it badly. Contrary to

6. Van der Vat, *Atlantic Campaign*, 267.
7. C&R 1:455.
8. Morison, 110; Van der Vat, *Atlantic Campaign*, 244.

all the hard-won lessons of the North Atlantic naval war, King clung to the belief that "inadequately escorted convoys are worse than none, because they made for concentrated targets, only thinly protected."[9] In consequence, merchant ships continued to sail independently, making easy prey for single submarines, while the handful of vessels that Eastern Sea Frontier could muster to protect coastal shipping were dispatched together in futile pursuit of frequently phantom sightings. King's stubbornness infuriated his colleagues. King was "the antithesis of cooperation, a deliberately rude person . . . a mental bully," Eisenhower noted in his diary. "One thing that might help win this war," Eisenhower added, "is to get someone to shoot King."[10]

When King finally relented and in May organized a convoy system along the Atlantic coast, the results were dramatic. Just fourteen ships went down in the Eastern Sea Frontier during that month, a sharp decline from the winter's disastrous loss rates. Dönitz's boats continued to prey upon Caribbean shipping for another two months, but by the summer of 1942 the Interlocking Convoy System protected coastwise sailings from Brazil to Newfoundland. On July 19 Dönitz withdrew his last two U-boats from North American waters. *Paukenschlag* was ended. It had dealt a grievous blow to American shipping and measurably slowed American mobilization, not to mention wounding the pride of the U.S. Navy, but it had been stopped short of catastrophe. Though a few daring marauders continued to mount occasional attacks, the Eastern Sea Frontier was secure.

But if Dönitz had retired from the American coastline, it was merely to concentrate his forces in the midocean zone where the Battle of the Atlantic was now most fiercely joined. After reallocating the last of the U-boats from Operation Drumbeat, Dönitz had well over two hundred submarines available for deployment in the broad Atlantic. German boatyards were adding fifteen new submarines to his fleet every month. Against those growing numbers Dönitz tallied his estimates of Allied carrying capacity and replacement rates. If he could sink seven hundred thousand tons of Allied merchant shipping per month, he calculated, victory would be his: Britain would face starvation, Russia defeat, and America permanent isolation on the far side of the Atlantic. By mid-1942 success seemed to be at hand, as worldwide Allied shipping losses exceeded eight hundred thousand tons per month. Despite frantic, round-the-clock construction in both British and American shipyards,

9. Van der Vat, *Atlantic Campaign*, 242, 247, 239.
10. Robert H. Ferrell, ed., *The Eisenhower Diaries* (New York: Norton, 1981), 50.

new Allied shipbuilding could not offset deficits on that scale. For 1942 as a whole, net U.S. and British shipping tonnage shrank by more than a million tons, a cumulative loss that threatened to rob the Allies of their warmaking power if not soon reversed. "The U-boat attack was our worst evil," Churchill later wrote, "the only thing that ever really frightened me during the war."[11]

The lengthening roster of his U-boat fleet was not Dönitz's only advantage. On February 1, 1942, the German navy switched to the new "Triton" code. Simultaneously, the Germans added a fourth wheel to their Enigma machines, multiplying by a factor of twenty-six the difficulty of deciphering encrypted messages. Those steps instantly blinded the Ultra codebreakers at England's Bletchley Park, and they stayed blind for the remainder of the year. Still worse, just weeks later the German naval intelligence service (*Beobachtungdienst*, "Observation Service," or *B-dienst*) salvaged a British code book from a sinking merchantman off the Norwegian coast, allowing the *B-dienst* to eavesdrop on the convoys' radio traffic. The advantage in the intelligence duel now passed decisively to the Germans. Throughout 1941 Bletchley's painstaking translation of encrypted German radio transmissions had betrayed the wolf packs' whereabouts and allowed many a convoy to be routed out of harm's way. But in 1942, the gray cloak of the Atlantic's surface again drawn securely over them, Dönitz's submariners lurked at points of their own choosing along the vital ocean highway.

Cruising in packs of a dozen or more, guided by *B-dienst* signals that remained opaque to the Allies, the U-boats inflicted increasingly costly damage as 1942 unfolded. The Allied convoys were typically composed of ten columns totaling about sixty vessels, mostly American merchantmen carrying mostly American cargoes. They slogged eastward at eight or nine knots, loosely girdled by as many as a dozen warships, almost all of them British or Canadian, weaving warily around their flanks. (The U.S. Navy provided just 2 percent of the escorts in the North Atlantic.) When aided by aerial reconnaissance, the escorts had a fighting chance of harassing the U-boats away from the convoy's path. But once a submerged wolf pack had closed undetected to torpedo range, it could wreak wholesale destruction on convoy and escorts alike.

The U-boats naturally concentrated, therefore, in those ocean areas out of range of Allied aircraft. There they could steam with impunity on the surface, diving only for the final attack. They especially favored

11. Churchill 4:110, 2:598.

two locations: the Norwegian Sea, the far northern passage to the Russian ports of Murmansk and Archangel; and the "air gap" southeast of Greenland, through which all convoys to both Britain and Russia had to pass. One combined surface, undersea, and air attack on the Russia-bound Convoy PQ17 in the Norwegian Sea in July forced the escorting warships to separate from the convoy, then scattered and sank twenty-three of the thirty-four merchantmen, an especially large loss. Only seventy thousand tons of the original two hundred thousand tons of cargo reached its destination. In August and September U-boats attacked seven convoys in the Greenland air gap and sank forty-three ships. In November total Allied losses again topped eight hundred thousand tons, 729,000 tons of which fell to the U-boats.

Nature added to the Allies' woes in the man- and ship-eating North Atlantic. Blast-force winds, towering green seas, snow squalls, and ice storms claimed nearly one hundred ships during the winter of 1942–43. In March 1943 a screaming gale slammed two convoys together, chaotically scrambling their sailing columns and wreaking wild confusion among their escorts. Dönitz capitalized on the disruption by dispatching elements of four wolf packs to feed on the havoc. At a cost of just one U-boat lost, twenty-two merchantmen were sunk out of the ninety that had set sail from New York a few days earlier, along with one of the escort vessels.

At these rates of loss, the Atlantic lifeline might soon be permanently severed. In fact, the disaster of PQ17 contributed to the Western allies' decision to suspend all North Atlantic convoys to the Russians for the remainder of 1942, triggering bitter complaints from Stalin. (The alternative but much lower capacity supply route to Russia, through the Persian Gulf and overland from Iran, remained open.) As for Britain, the sinkings in the Atlantic had by year's end cut its civilian oil reserves to a three-month supply, and imports of all kinds had withered to two-thirds of prewar levels. The Grand Alliance seemed about to be strangled in its cradle. Dönitz meanwhile added steadily to his undersea fleet, which numbered nearly four hundred boats by the beginning of 1943.

DÖNITZ'S MOUNTING SUCCESSES were menace enough. But in the midst of the shipping emergency the Western allies manufactured a new crisis of their own. It further threatened the North Atlantic supply routes, and it put additional strain on relations with Russia. It also threatened to disrupt all of the American military's best-laid plans for carrying the war to Hitler. American military doctrine had long been Doric in its simplicity: bring overwhelming force to bear against the enemy's main strength and decisively destroy his warmaking capacity. This was "the American way of war," a penchant for swift and total victory that came naturally to a nation rich in materiel and manpower and historically averse to the hair-splitting compromises of diplomacy. It was a tradition rooted in Ulysses Grant's Civil War campaigns and drummed into generations of West Point cadets. It applied axiomatically to the circumstances of 1942: gather a huge, awesomely equipped army in the British Isles and hurl it across the English Channel toward the German economic heartland of the Ruhr. The *Wehrmacht*, obliged to marshal all its resources in defense of Germany's industrial core, would be consumed by that irresistibly superior force. The eventual capture of the Ruhr would tear the heart out of the German economy and shut down Hitler's war machine for good.

To the already formidable logic of that approach the situation of the Soviet Union in 1942 added urgent reinforcement. From the outset of Operation Barbarossa, Stalin had pleaded with the Western powers to open a "second front" that would draw away thirty to forty of the German divisions facing the Red Army in the east. Without such support, Stalin hinted darkly, the USSR might soon collapse, freeing Hitler to loose his full fury on Britain and, eventually, on America. American analysts shared that assessment. *"We should not forget,"* Eisenhower noted with emphasis in July 1942, *"that the prize we seek is to keep 8,000,000 Russians in the war."*[12] That indispensable prize required opening the second front at the earliest possible date.

In April 1942 Roosevelt sent Marshall and Hopkins to London to secure British agreement to a crash program to launch a cross-Channel attack. Russia's needs loomed large in Roosevelt's thinking. "What Harry and Geo. Marshall will tell you," Roosevelt cabled Churchill in advance of their arrival, "has my heart and *mind* in it. Your people and mine demand the establishment of a front to draw off pressure on the Russians, and these peoples are wise enough to see that the Russians are today killing more Germans and destroying more equipment than you and I put together."[13] Meeting with Churchill at 10 Downing Street in the afternoon of April 8, the American envoys presented their proposal. It consisted of three parts. The first, transparently code-named Bolero, envisioned an unrelenting buildup of men and munitions in Britain

12. *PDDE* 1:391; italics in original.
13. *C&R* 1:441.

throughout 1942, swelling in the spring of 1943 to the crescendo of a massive cross-Channel invasion, forty-eight divisions strong, to which the code name Roundup was given. A smaller landing, code-named Sledgehammer, would be launched in 1942 in either of two circumstances, the first more likely than the second: if the Russians were on the point of collapse or if the Germans were about to surrender. In Marshall's shrewd mind, Sledgehammer had another purpose as well. It provided a kind of insurance policy that the pace of Bolero would not slacken. Even if Sledgehammer never happened, preparation for it would seal the Allied commitments to continue waging the Battle of the Atlantic and to concentrate troops and supplies in the British Isles, thus protecting the timetable for Roundup in 1943 and guaranteeing that America's grand strategic design would be realized. As events were to prove, Marshall's preemptive effort to guard Roundup against delay or even derailment was not misplaced.

Late in the evening of April 14, 1942, surrounded by members of his War Cabinet and military chiefs of staff, Churchill solemnly delivered his reply to Hopkins and Marshall: "Our two nations are resolved to march forward into Europe together in a noble brotherhood of arms, in a great crusade for the liberation of the tormented peoples."[14] That statement was as disingenuous as it was melodramatic. Churchill in fact had deep reservations about the entire Bolero-Sledgehammer-Roundup plan, but at this moment he calculated that he dare not risk an open disagreement with Roosevelt. "Anything like a serious difference between you and me would break my heart and surely deeply injure both our countries at the height of this terrible struggle," he cabled to Roosevelt on April 12, while declaring in the same message that "I am in entire agreement in principle with all you propose, as so are the Chiefs of Staff."[15] But Marshall and Hopkins had scarcely departed from London when Churchill revealed just how little he and his chiefs were in agreement with the second-front strategy he had feigned to endorse.

Soviet foreign minister Vaycheslav Molotov arrived in London on May 20, accompanied by unsettling news of a renewed German

---

14. Robert E. Sherwood, *Roosevelt and Hopkins* (New York: Grosset and Dunlap, 1950), 535.

15. *C&R* 1:448–49. Churchill's agreement with the American plan in fact carried one big reservation: that he would not undertake any operation that interfered with British efforts to secure India and the Middle East. But his theatrical display of comradely union was so convincing that Marshall and Hopkins scarcely registered that important qualifier.

offensive that had overrun the Crimean peninsula. A droll joke circu- lated in the British capital that the dour Molotov spoke only four words of English: "yes," "no," and "second front."[16] But Churchill swiftly dis- abused the Russian diplomat of the hope that any such front might soon be opened. In a display of evasion, dissembling, and diversion that soon became familiar, Churchill orated away at the impassive Russian about the shortages of amphibious landing craft necessary to a cross-Channel attack, about the titanic struggle that Britain was waging in North Africa (against eight Italian and three German divisions), and about the fan- tastic prospect of a ten-day air war that "would lead to the virtual de- struction of the enemy's air-power on the Continent"—but conspicu- ously not about the second front that Molotov wanted. The American plan for a second front was vastly premature, Churchill finally told the Russian, reminding his visitor that "wars are not won by unsuccessful operations."[17]

The discouraged Soviet minister went on to Washington. There he got an altogether different reception. Meeting with Roosevelt, Hopkins, Marshall, and King on May 30, Molotov noted bluntly that he had received no positive response in London on the question of a second front. He demanded a straight answer from the Americans. With Mar- shall's assent, the president told Molotov "to inform Mr. Stalin that we expect the formation of a second front this year." Roosevelt repeated that promise the following day. He added the unwelcome news that in order to facilitate the buildup in Britain necessary for opening a second front in 1942, Lend-Lease supplies to Russia must be reduced to 60 percent of the originally agreed amounts. Molotov grew agitated. What would happen if Russia agreed to cut its Lend-Lease requirements and then no second front eventuated? The Soviets could not have their cake and eat it too, Roosevelt blithely replied, and promised for a third time that a second front would be established during the current year. Two days later, the Russians and the Americans agreed to the wording of a joint public communiqué declaring that "full understanding was reached with regard to the urgent tasks of creating a Second Front in Europe in 1942." Privately, Roosevelt wired Churchill: "I have a very strong feeling

16. Mark A. Stoler, *The Politics of the Second Front: American Military Planning and Diplomacy in Coalition Warfare, 1941–1943* (Westport, Conn.: Greenwood, 1977), 43.

17. Churchill 4:298; Leo J. Meyer, "The Decision to Invade North Africa (Torch) (1942)," in Kent Roberts Greenfield, ed., *Command Decisions* (New York: Harcourt, Brace, 1959), 136.

that the Russian position is precarious and may grow steadily worse during the coming weeks. Therefore, I am more than ever anxious that BOLERO proceed to definite action beginning in 1942." In a speech at Madison Square Garden several days later, Harry Hopkins flamboyantly proclaimed that General Marshall was not training his troops "to play tiddlywinks. A second front? Yes," Hopkins declared, "and if necessary a third and a fourth front, to pen the German Army in a ring of our offensive steel."[18]

All this was too much for Churchill. Almost immediately after receiving Roosevelt's message, he hastened to Washington, determined to dissuade the president from keeping his promises to Molotov. Memory and anxiety gnawed at Churchill as he flew westward toward the American capital. In World War I, Britain had departed from its historic policy of avoiding major land war in Europe and landed a large body of troops on the continent. The results had been horrendous, notably at the slaughterhouses of the Somme and Passchendaele, as well as at Gallipoli, the failed amphibious attack on Turkey for which Churchill bore especially heavy responsibility. Those nightmares Churchill was resolved never to see repeated. Better to wait, years if necessary, until the Germans were at the point of exhaustion before attempting a hazardous cross-Channel invasion. In the meantime, Britain should pursue its age-old strategy toward Europe: isolate and weaken its Continental enemies by blockade (and aerial bombing), secure the Mediterranean routes to Asia and the oil fields of the Middle East, incite and support popular uprisings within Nazi-occupied Europe, consolidate a defensive ring around the Continent that would both contain further Axis expansion and serve as the launching area for a series of later, small-scale attacks, and stay alert for opportunities to exploit Nazi vulnerabilities with the time-honored tools of diplomacy.

This "peripheral" strategy entailed huge risks, not least the possibility that Hitler would knock the Soviets out of the war and so tighten his grip on Europe that he would be invulnerable to pinpricks around the Continental littoral. But it was a strategy that suited the character of a traditional maritime power and a seasoned diplomatic actor, especially one badly bloodied in World War I and whose army the *Wehrmacht* had thrice ejected from the Continent in the course of the current war (from Norway and France in 1940, and from Greece in 1941). By the same token, the American way of war reflected the capacities and history

18. Sherwood, *Roosevelt and Hopkins*, 558–79, 588; *C&R* 1:503.

of a well-endowed nation impatient with protracted conflict, unpracticed in diplomacy, and eager to get the war won pronto and be done with it. Could those incompatible strategic visions be reconciled?

Huddled with Roosevelt at Hyde Park on June 19, Churchill began his campaign to block a 1942 cross-Channel attack. He played his hand skillfully, and he held a trump card: because America was so militarily unready, most of the troops in any 1942 operation would necessarily be British. Churchill was not about to commit them to a second front in Europe. The right place to attack, he urged the president, was North Africa, key to the Middle East, where the British had been grappling for two years with the Germans and the Italians in an inconsequential seesaw struggle. Two days later, while seated with Roosevelt in the president's White House study, the prime minister received news that the British stronghold at Tobruk in Libya, the gateway to Egypt and the oil-rich region beyond, had fallen to the Axis. Thirty-three thousand British troops had laid down their arms to half that number of the enemy, a sickening reprise of the capitulation of eighty-five thousand British soldiers to a numerically inferior Japanese force at Singapore in February. "I did not attempt to hide from the President the shock I had received," Churchill remembered. "It was a bitter moment. Defeat is one thing; disgrace is another."[19] The shock of defeat and the sting of disgrace combined to redouble Churchill's effort to deflect the Americans from the Channel attack to a landing in North Africa, where they might help to stem the mortifying British reverses. In an impressive feat of political and psychological legerdemain, the prime minister even strove to convince Roosevelt that a North African landing had been the president's idea to begin with. "This has all along been in harmony with your ideas," he said. "In fact it is your commanding idea. Here is the true second front of 1942."[20]

The American military chiefs disagreed vehemently. In their view North Africa was a marginal, inconsequential theater, far from Germany's vitals and unlikely to provide an opportunity to engage more than a token Axis force. Moreover, the logistical and manpower demands of a North African operation would necessarily dampen the tempo of Bolero and might indefinitely postpone the cross-Channel attack. When on the evening of the Tobruk disaster Churchill in Marshall's presence raised the matter of committing American troops to

19. Churchill 4:344.
20. C&R 1:520.

North Africa, the general turned to Roosevelt and declared that such a plan would be "an overthrow of everything they had been planning for." In a rare loss of temper, Marshall then rose and strode red-faced out of the room, saying he refused to discuss the matter further.[21] But, to the dismay of his military advisers, Roosevelt remained susceptible to Churchill's seductive charm.

As Roosevelt inclined ever further to the North African operation, his military chiefs stiffened their opposition to it. Marshall proposed to the Joint Chiefs of Staff that if the British held out for North Africa and refused to go ahead with Sledgehammer, then the Americans should rewrite the fundamentals of their own highest strategy, abandon the Germany-first principle, and "turn to the Pacific for decisive action against Japan." King emphatically agreed, commenting disgustedly that the British would never invade Europe "except behind a Scotch bagpipe band," in a militarily useless ceremonial finale. On July 14 the two American chiefs formally recommended to Roosevelt that in the event of British insistence on "any other operation rather than forceful, unswerving adherence to full Bolero plans," then "we should turn to the Pacific and strike decisively against Japan; in other words, assume a defensive attitude against Germany . . . and use all available means in the Pacific."[22] Marshall may have been bluffing. King almost certainly was not; just days later, he approved plans for the American assault on Guadalcanal, a sharp break from the earlier concept of fighting only a defensive war in the Pacific. In any case, Roosevelt swiftly squelched any thought of shifting American priorities to the Pacific. The chiefs' suggestion was a "red herring," he told them, akin to "taking up your dishes and going away."[23] Instead, he sent Marshall and King, accompanied by Hopkins, to London for one last effort to salvage Sledgehammer. "I am opposed to an American all-out effort in the Pacific," he instructed his emissaries, because "defeat of Japan does not defeat Germany," while "defeat of Germany means defeat of Japan," adding curiously, "probably without firing a shot or losing a life." If Sledgehammer was definitely impossible, Roosevelt said, "I want you to . . . determine upon another place for U.S. Troops to fight in 1942. . . . It is of the highest importance," the president emphasized, "that U.S. ground troops be brought into action against the enemy in 1942."[24]

21. Stimson Diary, June 22, 1942.
22. Stoler, Politics of the Second Front, 55.
23. Stimson Diary, July 15, 1942.
24. Sherwood, Roosevelt and Hopkins, 605.

Because American production and troop training had still accomplished little, the Americans held a weak hand in London. They encountered a granite wall of opposition to Sledgehammer. On July 22, with little choice and with Roosevelt's blessing, they at last acceded to the British plan for a North African invasion, now code-named Torch. Considerations of domestic morale and politics played no small part in clinching Roosevelt's decision, as did the president's concern to protect the Germany-first strategy. With public opinion howling for vengeance against the Japanese, Roosevelt felt the need to come to grips somewhere with the Germans, if for no other reason than to remind the American public of the United States' strategic priorities. What was more, congressional elections loomed in November, and Roosevelt wanted a victory, or at least a dramatic confrontation with the principal enemy, before his party faced the voters. The tentative date for Torch was October 30. "Please," Roosevelt remarked to Marshall, his hands steepled together prayerfully, "make it before election day."[25]

Only later did Marshall come to appreciate that Roosevelt's militarily dubious decision to invade North Africa did have a defensible political logic. "We failed to see," Marshall reflected, "that the leader in a democracy has to keep the people entertained. . . . The people demand action. We couldn't wait to be completely ready."[26] For the moment, however, Marshall was badly disquieted at the decision for Torch, as were the other members of his delegation. "I feel damn depressed," Hopkins noted, as he contemplated the unraveling of all American strategic planning and the possible cancellation of the cross-Channel attack. Eisenhower wrote that the North African plan was "strategically unsound" and that it "would have no effect on the 1942 campaign in Russia." The day the decision for Torch was made, Eisenhower predicted, would go down as the "blackest day in history," particularly, he added, if Russia were defeated in the meantime, as seemed likely.[27]

If Roosevelt's subordinates were upset, Stalin was livid. The North Atlantic convoys had already been discontinued. As Molotov had feared, the 40 percent shrinkage in Lend-Lease shipments to the Soviets was not to be compensated by a mighty Anglo-American campaign against

25. Forrest C. Pogue, *George C. Marshall: Ordeal and Hope* (New York: Viking, 1966), 402. As it happened, the North African landings came after election day, a quirk of timing that may have contributed to Democratic losses in the 1942 congressional election.

26. Pogue, *George C. Marshall: Ordeal and Hope*, 330.

27. Sherwood, *Roosevelt and Hopkins*, 609; *PDDE* 1:389; Harry C. Butcher, *My Three Years with Eisenhower* (New York: Simon and Schuster, 1946), 29.

Germany's vital organs but only by an insignificant jab at a largely Italian force in the desert wastes of North Africa. The Western allies were apparently not taking the second-front issue seriously, Stalin wrote acidly to Churchill. "I must state in the most emphatic manner," said the Soviet leader, "that the Soviet Government cannot acquiesce in the postponement of a Second Front in Europe until 1943."[28]

Seeking to mollify Stalin, Churchill traveled to Moscow in August. He brooded as he went "on my mission to this sullen, sinister Bolshevik State I had once tried so hard to strangle at its birth." His mission, he thought, was "like carrying a large lump of ice to the North Pole."[29] Stalin received Churchill in his Kremlin rooms with what an American observer described as "bluntness almost amounting to insult." As Churchill summed it up: "Stalin observed that from our long talk it seemed that all we were going to do was no Sledgehammer, no Roundup, and pay our way by bombing Germany," pathetic recompense for the cancellation of the promised second front. "I decided to get the worst over," Churchill later wrote, and "did not therefore try at once to relieve the gloom."[30]

Peering into that Kremlin gloom in August 1942, some historians have discerned the first shadows of the Cold War, that decades-long legacy of distrust and tension that was among the most bitter and ironic fruits of the wartime Grand Alliance. Certainly the Soviets at this point had ample reason to doubt their Western partners. The North African debate might have rent a tear in the fabric of Anglo-American unity, but it threatened to open a gaping chasm separating the Western allies from their Russian comrades-in-arms. Roosevelt meanwhile could do little more than reassure the Soviet leader that "we are coming as quickly and as powerfully as we possibly can."[31]

But the Western allies were coming to Africa, not Europe, and they were coming neither so powerfully nor so quickly. A dense thicket of logistical and political underbrush remained to be cleared before Torch could take place. The decision to throttle back on Bolero and invade North Africa, Eisenhower later wrote, constituted a "violent shift in target, timing, and the circumstances of attack, [which] necessitated a complete reversal in our thinking and drastic revision in our planning and preparation."[32] The elaborately contrived North Atlantic convoy system

28. Churchill 4:242.
29. Churchill 4:248.
30. Churchill 4:432.
31. Sherwood, *Roosevelt and Hopkins*, 622.
32. Dwight D. Eisenhower, *Crusade in Europe* (New York: Doubleday, 1948), 72.

had to be redesigned and redirected toward the Mediterranean. The precious reserves that Bolero had so laboriously built up in Britain, including three U.S. Army divisions, had to be reloaded and reshipped southward. Troops preparing for a battle in northwest Europe had to be retrained and reoutfitted for desert warfare. Not least, the sudden shift in Allied focus from Europe to Africa plunged the United States into a devil's tangle of utterly unanticipated political challenges.

Torch's strategic architecture was simple enough. A combined Anglo-American force, sixty-five thousand strong, would push the Axis armies from the west, while Bernard Montgomery's British Eighth Army squeezed them from the east. There simplicity ended, as military planning encountered political reality. The zones for the Anglo-American landings lay in French Morocco and Algeria, still under the administrative control of Marshal Henri Phillipe Pétain's collaborationist but nominally independent French government at Vichy. Unlike the British, the Americans had held their noses and maintained diplomatic relations with the Vichy regime. Now Roosevelt hoped to cash in on that unsavory political gamble by persuading Pétain to instruct his troops not to resist the Allied landings in North Africa. In the intricate diplomatic dance that ensued, the Americans stumbled repeatedly.

The first step was to convince the French, still embittered toward the British after the melee at Dunkirk and the Royal Navy's attack at Mers el Kebir, that Torch was primarily an American operation. Though the British contributed nearly half the troops and virtually all the naval strength, not to mention the fact that they had fathered the very concept of a North African operation, an American, Eisenhower, was designated the commander. Americans were to hit the beaches first, followed only at a decent interval by British soldiers, thus protecting British troops from vengeful French reprisals. Despite these concessions, direct appeals to the haughty Pétain to suppress resistance in the Moroccan and Algerian landing areas availed little. Eisenhower then looked for an alternative French leader who might command sufficient respect among the French North African garrisons that he could induce them not to oppose the Allied landings. He quickly ruled out Charles DeGaulle, the favorite of the British. As self-proclaimed leader of the "Free French," DeGaulle had been branded a traitor by the Vichy government and condemned to death in absentia, credentials unlikely to recommend him to the French North African commanders who had thrown in their lot with Pétain. For a time Eisenhower tried to recruit General Henri Giraud, whose recent escape from Nazi imprisonment and studied refusal to break completely with Vichy made him an apparently plausible candi-

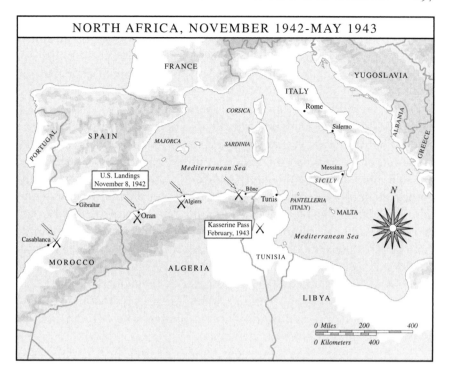

NORTH AFRICA, NOVEMBER 1942-MAY 1943

date. But Giraud insisted on taking over from Eisenhower as supreme commander, an impossible demand, and dithered in Vichy until the landings had already commenced. When the first green American troops went ashore on November 8, to be greeted not with French bouquets but French bullets, Eisenhower cast about desperately for a credible figure who could impose a cease-fire on the French forces. The person he found was Admiral Jean François Darlan, a Nazi sympathizer who had supported the French surrender in 1940 and been rewarded with appointment as commander-in-chief of Vichy's armed forces and anointment as Pétain's designated successor. After forty-eight hours of tense negotiations in Algiers, while hundreds of American soldiers were dying in the landing zones, Darlan at last arranged for a general cease-fire to take effect on November 10, in exchange for Allied recognition of himself as high commissioner for French North Africa.

The "Darlan Deal" saved American lives in North Africa, but it ignited an uproar in the United States. Critics denounced Eisenhower's embrace of the odious Darlan as "sordid" and "squalid," a loathsome repudiation of all that America professed to be fighting for. "If we will make a deal with a Darlan in French territory, then presumably we will make one with a Goering in Germany or with a Matsuoka in Japan," declared one newspaper. Churchill worried that the Allies would suffer "serious political injury . . . throughout Europe, by the feeling that we are ready to make terms with local Quislings [so named after the notorious Nazi collaborator in Norway]."[33] An embittered DeGaulle never forgave Roosevelt for the political and personal affront of being snubbed while the traitorous Darlan was exalted. For his part, Roosevelt concluded that the wrangling among DeGaulle, Giraud, and Darlan foreshadowed chaos, maybe even civil war, in postwar France, a perception that clinched his determination to avoid aligning himself with any French faction for the remainder of the war. Nor did the reverberations from the Darlan Deal stop there. Ignoring Pétain's protests that Darlan had acted without authorization from Vichy, Hitler ordered the immediate occupation of the remainder of France. Italy meanwhile occupied the French Mediterranean island of Corsica. Vichy broke diplomatic relations with the United States and, under extreme duress from Hitler, invited German forces into Tunisia. As for Darlan, a traitor thrice over — to France, to Pétain, and to his German masters — he fell to a French assassin's bullet on Christmas Eve 1942.

The thousands of German troops rapidly pouring into Tunisia were soon joined by hundreds of thousands of German and Italian soldiers streaming westward across Libya after Montgomery's signal victory at El Alamein in early November. Commanded by Erwin Rommel, the Axis forces took up strong defensive positions in the Tunisian mountain ranges and prepared to offer Dwight Eisenhower, a lifelong professional soldier who had never before North Africa heard a shot fired in anger, his first taste of battle. Eisenhower's rickety binational command structure and his unblooded, ill-prepared American troops at first proved no match for Rommel's seasoned staff and battle-hardened veterans. In a series of poorly conceived tank-to-tank duels, the humiliated Americans quickly learned that their vaunted Sherman tanks were easily outgunned by their massively armored and skillfully deployed German adversaries. Tank crews soon dubbed the vulnerable Shermans "Purple Heart Boxes," named for the medal awarded to the wounded.[34] A despondent

33. Dallek, 364. As for Stalin, he observed that "the Americans used Darlan not badly" and that "military diplomacy must be able to use for military purposes" not only Darlan but "even the Devil himself and his grandma" — a chill reminder of the cynical calculus with which the wily Soviet leader gauged the ethics of war and diplomacy. C&R 2:51.

34. George F. Howe, *Northwest Africa: Seizing the Initiative in the West* (Washington: Department of the Army, 1957), 480.

Eisenhower wrote to a confidante that "the best way to describe our operations to date is that they have violated every recognized principle of war, are in conflict with all operational and logistic methods laid down in text-books, and will be condemned, in their entirety, by all Leavenworth and War College classes for the next twenty-five years."[35] At Kasserine Pass in late February, muddle in General Lloyd Fredendall's headquarters contributed to a disorganized American rout before the guns of a powerful German panzer division. Eisenhower soon replaced Fredendall with a new commander already fabled for his aggressive instincts, though not yet for his military accomplishments, George Patton.

Slowly the tide of logistics began to turn the battle in the Allies' favor. By the time an ailing Rommel was invalided back to Germany in March, the 157,000 German and 193,000 Italian troops in North Africa no longer enjoyed air superiority. The tourniquet of the British naval blockade interdicted fresh supplies of munitions and gasoline. Before long the Germans had only seventy-six operational tanks and were reduced to running them with fuel distilled from wine. Patton launched a probing attack against the Axis lines on March 7. It did not succeed, but it provided sufficient distraction that Montgomery effected a breakthrough that ended with the surrender of a quarter of a million Axis troops, 125,000 of them Germans, on May 13. In Russia, meanwhile, the Red Army still confronted more than two hundred Axis divisions, even after destroying twenty German divisions and killing some two hundred thousand Germans in the single, epic battle of Stalingrad.

THE SOVIET VICTORY at Stalingrad in February 1943 rewrote the Grand Alliance's fundamental strategic equation. Russia's survival was now all but guaranteed. What was more, the Red Army now passed irreversibly onto the offensive. With painful slowness at first but then with gathering, inexorable momentum, it began to roll the *Wehrmacht* back across the Russian steppes. If the Western allies had worried through 1942 about Russia's staying power, they began to fret in 1943 about the implications of Russia's fighting power. A new anxiety crept into American assessments of the political geometry of the Grand Alliance triangle. As the moment approached for another full-dress conference between Churchill and Roosevelt, attended by their senior military and naval advisers, that anxiety grew acute. "A defeated and prostrate

35. *PDDE* 2:811.

Germany leaving a strong and triumphant Russia dominating Europe," the U.S. Army's Joint Strategic Survey Committee advised Marshall in the first week of the new year, was not in accord with Britain's historic foreign policy of sustaining a balance of power on the Continent. "It would be in strict accord with that policy, however, to delay Germany's defeat until military attrition and civilian famine had materially reduced Russia's potential toward dominance in Europe." Russia's growing military muscle, in short, might give Britain new reasons to postpone the second front and fresh incentives to temporize with further peripheral operations, probably in the Mediterranean. Such a strategy would prolong the war between Germany and the Soviet Union and leave neither power able to command the Continent. But Britain's policy must not be America's, the army planners warned Marshall. The United States "should forego indirect and eccentric concepts and strike hard and straight at Germany."[36]

Those thoughts were much on Marshall's mind at a White House meeting on January 7, 1943, convened to advise the president about his upcoming conference with Churchill in the Moroccan city of Casablanca. There the issue would be sharply joined: did Mediterranean operations represent a temporary diversion or a way of life? Marshall, as usual, set his face sternly against further "periphery-pecking." Continuing to fight in the distant Mediterranean, he warned, would dissipate Anglo-American strength and risk intolerable shipping losses while achieving no significant strategic purpose. Though Marshall acknowledged that a cross-Channel attack would take a heavy toll in human casualties, he chose to underscore instead what was still the greatest single constraint on all American actions. "To state it cruelly," he said, "we could replace troops whereas a heavy loss in shipping . . . might completely destroy any opportunity for successful operations against the enemy in the near future."[37]

Two days later, Roosevelt departed Washington by train for Florida, where he boarded an aircraft for the lengthy transatlantic flight to North Africa — his first presidential foray outside the Americas. Roosevelt relished the occasion. He would be the first president since Lincoln to visit American troops in the field. Like his former chief, Woodrow Wilson, he fancied himself heading abroad to dispose of the destinies of

36. Stoler, *Politics of the Second Front*, 73.
37. Forrest C. Pogue, *George C. Marshall: Organizer of Victory, 1943–1945* (New York: Viking Press, 1973), 15.

nations. Even grander historical comparisons swam in his head. "I prefer a comfortable oasis to the raft at Tilsit," he mused about the upcoming seance in Casablanca's winter sunshine. That was a telling allusion to the legendary encounter between the Emperor Napoleon and Czar Alexander I in 1807, when the two potentates had met in a Baltic riverport after defeating another German state (Prussia) and redrawn the map of Europe.[38]

But Casablanca was to be no Tilsit. Parlaying among the palms and bougainvilleas in Morocco, two statesmen still militarily on the defensive, Churchill and Roosevelt commanded only a fraction of the power that the pair of supremely self-assured despots afloat on the Neman River had wielded more than a century earlier. And Roosevelt at this moment perhaps resembled Woodrow Wilson more than he appreciated. Like the hapless Wilson vainly urging a liberal peace settlement on the implacable Georges Clemenceau and David Lloyd George at Paris in 1919, Roosevelt still lacked the means to bend Churchill to his will in the ongoing inter-Allied struggle over the second front. Though British foreign minister Anthony Eden described Roosevelt at this time as the "head of a mighty country which was coming out into the arena," the characterization was not yet quite apt.[39] In early 1943 Churchill remained the senior partner in the Anglo-American alliance. More time must pass before American might had been sufficiently amassed to allow Roosevelt to dominate the strategic debate with Churchill, and more time still before the American leader could aspire to be a geopolitical arbiter on an imperial scale.

Churchill arrived in Casablanca attended by a huge retinue, dozens of military and naval advisers and their staffs, all of them supported by a sophisticated communications ship that kept them in touch with even larger staffs in London. The American delegation was small and, as the British had observed on earlier occasions, neither well prepared by staff work nor fully agreed on its own priorities. Marshall clung to the idea of the cross-Channel attack. King continued to demand more resources for the Pacific. The American air chiefs were beginning to insist that air power alone might bring the *Reich* to its knees, without the need for a costly land invasion. Facing those divided ranks and confidently holding the lion's share of disposable military assets, the British easily prevailed. "We lost our shirts," the U.S. Army planner General Albert

---

38. Pogue, *Marshall: Organizer of Victory*, 5.
39. Anthony Eden, *The Reckoning* (Boston: Houghton Mifflin, 1965), 430.

Wedemeyer complained. "One might say we came, we listened, and we were conquered."[40]

The joint communiqué issued by the Casablanca conferees on January 23 announced a bundle of decisions. Taken together, they reflected some compromises between the competing priorities of the two nations and the various service arms, but they also unmistakably signified that Churchill's deepest purposes had in the end been faithfully served. The two allies committed themselves anew to overcoming the U-boat menace in the Atlantic. They promised to fulfill their Lend-Lease commitments to the Russians. And they announced a Combined Bomber Offensive that was to inflict round-the-clock punishment on Germany from the air. In a significant concession to King, they also agreed to allocate 30 percent of their war effort to the Pacific theater, almost double the amount envisioned in earlier Anglo-American plans and a margin that allowed King to remain on the offensive against Japan. Most important, and most galling to the American military chiefs, not to mention the Russians, Churchill and Roosevelt declared that upon termination of the North African campaign they would not immediately undertake the cross-Channel invasion but instead press ahead in the Mediterranean, probably with an invasion of Sicily. Marshall's worst fears were being realized. He warned that the Mediterranean was becoming a "suction pump" that would lead to "interminable" dissipation of effort in that inappropriate theater. Stalin, Churchill predicted, would be "disappointed and furious."[41]

He was. While the British and the Americans had been pretending that North Africa constituted an authentic second front, Germany had transferred thirty-six fresh divisions to the eastern front, six of them armored. An invasion of Sicily, Stalin wrote to Roosevelt, "can by no means replace a Second Front in France. . . . I consider it my duty to state that the early opening of a second front in France is the most important thing. . . . I must give a most emphatic warning . . . of the grave danger with which further delay in opening a second front is fraught."[42]

It is in light of those sentiments that the most notorious fruit of the Casablanca Conference must be understood. Roosevelt made one ad-

40. Stoler, *Politics of the Second Front*, 77.
41. Dallek, 371–72; Stoler, *Politics of the Second Front*, 85.
42. Ministry of Foreign Affairs of the USSR, comp. *Stalin's Correspondence with Roosevelt and Truman, 1941–1945* (New York: Capricorn, 1965), 59.

ditional pronouncement before departing Morocco, not as part of the officially printed joint communiqué but orally, in a press conference on January 24. In an apparently spontaneous but almost certainly well-considered statement, the president called for nothing less than the "unconditional surrender" of Germany, Italy, and Japan. Ostensibly a declaration of bellicose resolve, the unconditional-surrender formula in fact reflected continuing American military and political weakness. Still unable to bring meaningful force to bear against Hitler, unable even to persuade the British to join in delivering on the promise of a cross-Channel attack, fearful that the Darlan affair might nourish Soviet suspicions of his willingness to cut a deal with Rome or Berlin, increasingly worried about Stalin's ultimate intentions in eastern Europe, Roosevelt at this date had little other means with which to reassure his long-suffering Soviet ally. Without the leverage to prise specific agreements about the postwar world out of either the British or the Russians, Roosevelt also seized upon the unconditional-surrender doctrine as a way to defer tough political bargaining until the war's end. When unconditional surrender was announced it was the policy of a militarily unprepared nation with little scope for maneuver. It would survive into an era when America wielded unimaginable power and when the supple Roosevelt was no longer alive to temper its application. By then the unconditional-surrender doctrine would have taken on a life of its own, with consequences not visible in January 1943.[43]

THE TWO WESTERN STATESMEN had received a spectacular reminder of the importance and vulnerability of the Atlantic lifeline even as they had greeted one another in balmy Casablanca. Only days earlier, U-boats off the West African coast had attacked a special convoy ferrying precious oil from Trinidad to support the North African campaign. Just as the Casablanca Conference opened, the convoy's few survivors reached Gibraltar, directly across the mouth of the Mediterranean from Morocco, telling harrowing tales of the shattering losses they had

43. For an excellent account of the background and provenance of Roosevelt's unconditional-surrender pronouncement, see Dallek, 373–76, to which it might be added that, despite Churchill's apparent surprise at Roosevelt's statement, unconditional surrender was also consistent with the policies of no compromise with Hitler enunciated in Neville Chamberlain's last days in office and with such vehemence by Churchill himself in 1940 and 1941, when Britain had few other means of reassuring the Americans, just as Roosevelt in 1943 had few other means of reassuring the Russians.

witnessed: seven of nine tankers sunk, fifty-five thousand tons of shipping and more than a hundred thousand tons of fuel gone, one of the most devastating U-boat attacks of the war. That sorry spectacle surely reinforced Churchill's and Roosevelt's determination to gain the upper hand in the Atlantic.

But though even greater losses lay ahead, in fact the Battle of the Atlantic was already turning in the Allies' favor, and with astonishing swiftness. The scientists at Bletchley had in December 1942 finally broken the Triton cipher and puzzled through the vexations presented by Enigma's fourth wheel. Most important, the arrival from American shipyards of more abundant escort vessels, particularly the new "escort carriers," or "baby flat-tops," each carrying up to two dozen aircraft, at last gave the Allies an insuperable advantage, one that probably weighed more heavily in the scales than did Bletchley's restored electronic eyes and ears.

The U-boats of this era were in fact not true submarines at all but submersible torpedo boats that could dive for brief periods before, during, and after an attack. They were unable to remain submerged for long and were not designed for high-speed running under water. To reach their attack stations, to overtake a prey, and to replenish their air supply, they were obliged to steam on the surface, where they were especially vulnerable to sighting and assault from the air.[44] When Roosevelt in March 1943 compelled King to transfer sixty Very Long Range B-24 Liberator aircraft from the Pacific to the Atlantic, the Allies at last closed the midocean air gap in which Dönitz's submarines had done their worst damage.

After years of terrorizing Allied sailors in the North Atlantic, now it was the German submariners' turn to quail. Aided by aerial reconnaissance as well as by improved shipborne radar and sonar, the naval escorts began to scour the submarines from the sea. Forty-three of the fragile undersea craft died in May 1943 alone, more than twice the rate at which they could be replaced. As Dönitz radioed to one U-boat commander after another, "Report position and situation," he more and more often waited in vain for a reply, while the listeners at Bletchley

44. Later in the war the Germans developed the *Schnorkel* type of U-boat, a true submarine whose diesel engines could breath air through a retractable tube, making the boat fully operational underwater for long periods of time. Had it been available in early 1943 it would have instantly negated almost all the advances in Allied anti–submarine warfare tactics. But the *Schnorkel* boats appeared too late in the war, and in insufficient numbers, to turn the tide in the Battle of the Atlantic.

eavesdropped on the ominous silences. In the "Happy Time" of 1942, a U-boat had enjoyed an operational life of more than a year. Now the average U-boat survived less than three months. Dönitz's orders to sail had become virtual death sentences. Overall the German submarine service lost more than twenty-five thousand crew to death and another five thousand to capture, a 75 percent casualty rate that exceeded the losses of any other service arm in any nation. Faced with such relentless winnowing of his ranks, Dönitz ordered all but a handful of his U-boats out of the North Atlantic on May 24, 1943. "We had lost the Battle of the Atlantic," he later wrote. In the next four months, sixty-two convoys comprising 3,546 merchant vessels crossed the Atlantic, without the loss of a single ship.[45]

Stalin had every reason to expect that victory over the U-boats in the Atlantic would mean full resumption of Lend-Lease shipments to the Soviets, as promised at Casablanca. Four convoys did manage to reach Murmansk in the first few weeks of 1943, paltry recompense, in Stalin's eyes, for the military agonies and the punishing supply famine that the Soviets had been enduring for the preceding six months. "We've lost millions of people, and they want us to crawl on our knees because they send us Spam," one Russian groused about the Americans.[46] But just as Torch had required that shipping be redirected from the North Atlantic to North Africa in mid-1942, now the decision at Casablanca to invade Sicily once again dictated that scarce shipping resources be pulled off the Russian supply routes. Stalin greeted the news curtly: "I understand this unexpected action as a catastrophic diminution of supplies of arms and military raw materials," he wrote to his Western comrades-in-arms. "You realize of course that the circumstances cannot fail to affect the position of the Soviet troops"—a statement sufficiently susceptible to being read as a threat to conclude a separate peace that Churchill felt the need to reassure Roosevelt that it was not. Yet even Churchill shared with Hopkins his anxiety "that in April, May and June, not a single American or British soldier will be killing a single German or Italian soldier while the Russians are chasing 185 divisions around." The Americans meanwhile had moved but eight divisions into the European theater, well short of Bolero's schedule of twenty-seven by this date. Only

45. Van der Vat, *Atlantic Campaign*, 333, 337; John Keegan, *The Second World War* (New York: Viking, 1989), 116–22; Morison, 376.
46. Dennis Dunn, *Caught between Roosevelt and Stalin: America's Ambassadors to Moscow* (Lexington: University Presses of Kentucky, 1998), 180.

one of them was in England, the staging ground for the cross-Channel attack.[47]

In February 1943 Stalin broadcast a message to the Soviet armed forces in which he made no reference to British or American aid and claimed, not without reason, that the Red Army was fighting the war alone. The Soviet armed forces faced four million Axis troops on a two-thousand-mile front, Stalin told Roosevelt's special emissary, Joseph Davies, in May. "The Red Army is fighting on their front alone, and suffering under the occupation of a large part of our territory by a cruel enemy. We are waiting for a real offensive in the west to take some of the load off our backs. We need more fighting planes, more locomotives, more equipment, more rails, more food, more grain."[48]

BUT RATHER THAN UNDERTAKING the "real offensive" that Stalin had in mind—the long-sought invasion of northwest France in overwhelming strength—the Anglo-Americans instead proceeded with their considerably less consequential offensive against the Italian island-province of Sicily. In a remarkable address on the eve of their embarkation from Tunisia, General George S. Patton Jr. sought to embolden his invading troops by playing on all the resonances of American immigrant myths as well as venerable stereotypes about the relation of the New World to the Old:

> When we land, we will meet German and Italian soldiers whom it is our honor and privilege to attack and destroy. Many of you have in your veins German and Italian blood, but remember that these ancestors of yours so loved freedom that they gave up home and country to cross the ocean in search of liberty. The ancestors of the people we shall kill lacked the courage to make such a sacrifice and remained as slaves.[49]

The speech was vintage Patton. He was the grandson of a Confederate colonel who had been killed in action, and war was in his blood. Born in 1885, Patton had grown up in a well-to-do family in then bucolic Pasadena, California, riding his horse through the San Gabriel mountains as a boy, taking no formal schooling until he was twelve years old.

47. C&R 2:179–80; Dallek, 380; Maurice Matloff and Edwin M. Snell, *United States Army in World War II: Strategic Planning for Coalition Warfare, 1941–1942* (Washington: Department of the Army, 1953), 390.
48. Dunn, *Caught between Roosevelt and Stalin*, 186.
49. Harry H. Semmes, *Portrait of Patton* (New York: Paperback Library, 1955), 155.

He arrived at West Point after a year at Virginia Military Institute and immediately established a reputation as a gifted, dedicated athlete, though only a middling student. In 1912 he competed in the military pentathlon in the Stockholm Olympic Games, placing fifth in the event, which comprised a steeplechase, pistol shooting, fencing, swimming, and a five-thousand-meter run. As an aide to John J. Pershing in Mexico in 1916, he had killed three of Pancho Villa's bodyguards in a gunfight, and as a general he toted twin pearl-handled revolvers as a token of his skill with a six-gun. He led a tank brigade at the Meuse-Argonne in 1918 and in the interwar years became a leading proponent of armored warfare. Religious and profane, irascible and sentimental, Patton was one of the most combative and colorful characters in the American or any other army, a man whose swaggering, self-assured manner and edgy pugnacity gave him the aura of having just dismounted from a foam-flecked horse.

On July 10 soldiers from one Canadian, four British, and three American divisions added themselves to the millennia-old roster of armies, from the Phoenicians and the Greeks to the Saracens and the Normans, that had essayed the conquest of polyglot Sicily. British commander Harold Alexander, underwhelmed with the performance of American troops in North Africa, designated his countryman Bernard Montgomery to wield the offensive sword of the attack along Sicily's east coast, with the goal of sealing the island exit across the Strait of Messina to mainland Italy. Patton was given the lesser role of holding a defensive shield to protect Montgomery's left flank on the west. A notable breakdown in the ramshackle Allied communications system caused several of the invasion fleet's antiaircraft crews to open fire on their own transport aircraft, which were towing gliders filled with American paratroopers. Nearly half the gliders were shot down or crash-landed into the sea in the ensuing confusion, drowning hundreds of paratroopers. Only 12 of the 147 gliders launched managed to land on their assigned landing zones.[50]

On the beaches, however, the war's largest amphibious operation to date unfolded fairly smoothly. A wild ruse had helped achieve a measure of surprise. Three months earlier, British agents had planted a corpse, dressed in the uniform of a Royal Marine officer, on a Spanish beach. Falsified papers in a despatch case chained to the body's waist were intended to convince the Axis that the next Allied blow would fall on

50. Carlo D'Este, *Bitter Victory: The Battle for Sicily, 1943* (New York: Dutton, 1988), 227–37.

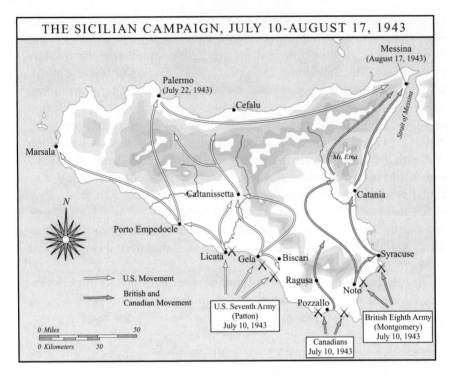

THE SICILIAN CAMPAIGN, JULY 10–AUGUST 17, 1943

Sardinia. The Germans and Italians took the bait and concentrated most of their defensive effort in the large island to Sicily's north.

Though the Americans encountered stiff resistance near Gela, on Sicily's southern coast, in other areas the landings were virtually unopposed. Some Sicilians even helped unload the invaders' landing craft. Inland, Montgomery met two German divisions that notably slowed his progress toward Messina. Patton thereupon seized the initiative. Declaring that "if I succeed Attila will have to take a back seat," he mounted a memorable demonstration of the mobility and aggression soon recognized as his trademarks. Slicing rapidly through weak Italian opposition across western Sicily, he entered Palermo on July 22 while huge crowds cheered, "Down with Mussolini!" and "Long Live America!"[51] Scarcely pausing for breath, Patton's troops then plunged along the island's north coast to Messina. By this circuitous route Patton beat Montgomery to the shores of Messina Strait on August 17. Both generals arrived too late, however, to prevent the successful evacuation of sixty-

51. D'Este, *Bitter Victory*, 412, 423.

two thousand Italian and forty thousand German troops, who survived to fight another day. Patton's performance had been characteristically flamboyant and fast-moving. It had also been costly for his inexperienced and profligately deployed troops, one in eight of whom was a casualty.[52]

The campaign proved personally costly for Patton too. In two separate incidents, soldiers under his command massacred seventy-three unarmed Italian and three German prisoners of war near the airfield at Biscari. Patton tried to cover the matter up—"it would make a stink in the press and also would make the civilians mad," he told a subordinate—but the facts came out, and a sergeant and a captain were charged with murder. Both pleaded that they believed themselves to be following Patton's orders in an inflammatory preinvasion speech, when he admonished his men to beware of enemy troops who might be feigning surrender in order to bait a trap. In case of doubt, Patton had said, "Kill the s.o.b.'s." The captain was acquitted, but the sergeant was sentenced to life imprisonment, later commuted.

In two further incidents, Patton verbally abused and physically struck two soldiers recovering from "battle fatigue" in field hospitals. Patton thought the men were malingerers. "You yellow son of a bitch," he yelled at one of them, brandishing one of his twin pearl-handled revolvers. "I won't have these brave men here who have been shot seeing a yellow bastard sitting here crying. . . . You ought to be lined up against a wall and shot. In fact, I ought to shoot you myself right now, God damn you!" Patton then slapped the man repeatedly. For these actions Eisenhower ordered Patton to apologize publicly to his troops and temporarily removed Patton from command.[53]

In the midst of the whirlwind battle for Sicily, Italy's King Victor Emmanuel III summoned Benito Mussolini to the royal palace, forced his resignation as prime minister, and ordered the humbled dictator arrested and imprisoned. Mussolini's successor was Marshal Pietro Badoglio, former chief of the Italian Supreme General Staff and a longtime Fascist. Though not as unpalatable a specimen as the malodorous Darlan, Badoglio soon proved to have comparably elastic loyalties. While

52. George F. Botjer, *Sideshow War: The Italian Campaign, 1943–1945* (College Station: Texas A&M University Press, 1996), 25–26.
53. D'Este, *Bitter Victory*, 317–29, 483–96. By one accounting, if Patton had been held to the standard applied after the war to the German perpetrators of the Malmédy massacre of American soldiers in December 1944, he would have received a sentence of life imprisonment for the murders at Biscari. See I.C.B. Dear, ed., *The Oxford Companion to the Second World War* (New York: Oxford University Press, 1995), 132.

earnestly reassuring Hitler that Italy would continue to fight by his side, Badoglio opened secret negotiations with Allied representatives to arrange a surrender. Roosevelt responded with his own display of diplomatic dexterity. He declared in a Fireside Chat on July 28 that "our terms to Italy are still the same as our terms to Germany and Japan — 'unconditional surrender.' We will have no truck with Fascism in any way, in any shape, or manner. We will permit no vestige of Fascism to remain." At the same time, he conceded to Churchill that he would settle merely for coming "as close as possible to unconditional surrender" in Italy, opening the possibility that the dubious Badoglio might be allowed to retain power.[54] Separating Italy from its Axis partner had been a goal of British diplomacy for nearly a decade. As the Hoare-Laval deal in 1935 had notoriously illustrated, London had long since shown its willingness to bend principle to that end. After aggravatingly lengthy negotiations with the Italians, Eisenhower was eventually instructed to accept a complicated surrender formula. It not only allowed Badoglio to stay in office but also recognized Italy as a co-belligerent in the war against Hitler. In its first test, the unconditional-surrender doctrine had hardly proved to be the terrible swift sword brandished so belligerently at Casablanca. Nor had the terms of the Italian surrender, entailing the embrace of a barely fumigated Fascist as a comrade-in-arms, done much to reassure the Soviets. "To date it has been like this," Stalin wrote to Roosevelt: "the U.S.A. and Britain reach agreement between themselves while the U.S.S.R. is informed of the agreement between the two Powers as a third party looking passively on. I must say that this situation cannot be tolerated any longer."[55]

The prospect of Italy's capitulation had opened another round in the still-smoldering Allied debate over strategy. At Casablanca the reluctant Americans had agreed only to the Sicilian invasion, hoping that would write finis to the Mediterranean chapter of the war. But at a follow-up Anglo-American planning conference in Washington in May 1943 (code-named Trident), Churchill urged pressing on to the Italian mainland. Knocking Italy out of the war was now the "great prize" to be gained in the Mediterranean, Churchill declaimed. Italy's loss would "cause a chill of loneliness over the German people, and might be the beginning of their doom."[56] That extravagant claim did not much im-

54. PPA (1943), 327; FRUS (1943) 2:332.
55. Stalin's Correspondence with Roosevelt and Truman, 84.
56. Stoler, Politics of the Second Front, 92.

press the Americans, but another of Churchill's arguments did. The repeated slowing of Bolero to date had now compelled the postponement of the cross-Channel attack to the spring of 1944, a conclusion to which the Americans were grudgingly driven at the Trident Conference. Thus the only force-in-being capable of taking action in the European theater for the next twelve months was Eisenhower's Mediterranean command. Eisenhower's troops "could not possibly stand idle" for a year, Churchill insisted. "So long a period of inaction," he said, "would have a serious effect on relations with Russia, who was bearing such a disproportionate weight."[57] Roosevelt was forced to agree, but with qualifications. He first insisted on a British commitment to May 1, 1944, as the target date for the cross-Channel invasion. That agreement signaled the beginning of Roosevelt's ascendance over Churchill in the scales of geopolitical influence and cheered the president's advisers. At long last, Hopkins believed, his boss could "be safely left alone with the Prime Minister."[58] To ensure that Churchill did not again disrupt Bolero with still more Mediterranean distractions, Roosevelt further insisted that Eisenhower should proceed to the Italian mainland with only "the resources already available." All fresh troops and new equipment coming from America would be directed toward the buildup in Britain.[59]

The Italian campaign thus began with weighty liabilities. It had formed no part of earlier planning exercises, was decided on short notice and for opportunistic reasons, and was required to go forward with severely restricted resources. Most important, it had no compelling strategic goal. Its thin rationale of keeping at least some Western forces engaged against the enemy through the remainder of 1943 seemed plausible so long as the Italian surrender negotiations gave promise of an easy victory. But while the two-faced Badoglio was haggling over surrender terms, Hitler poured sixteen divisions into the boot-shaped peninsula. Overnight, Italy went from German ally to German-occupied country. Now it was about to become a battleground in a grinding war of attrition whose costs were justified by no defensible military or political purpose.

On September 8, 1943, three British and four American divisions commanded by the American General Mark Clark glided shoreward in their landing craft across the glassy predawn waters of the Gulf of

57. Dallek, 394.
58. Stoler, *Politics of the Second Front*, 93.
59. Morison, 349.

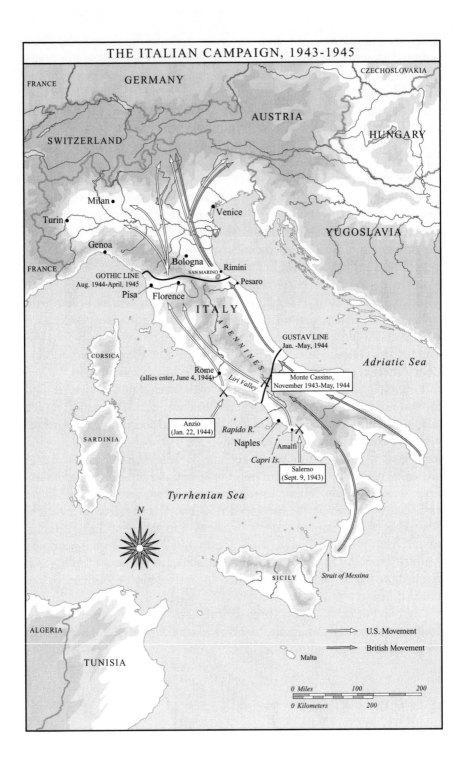

THE ITALIAN CAMPAIGN, 1943-1945

FRANCE

GERMANY

CZECHOSLOVAKIA

AUSTRIA

HUNGARY

SWITZERLAND

Milan

Venice

YUGOSLAVIA

Turin

Genoa

FRANCE

Bologna

Rimini

GOTHIC LINE
Aug. 1944-April, 1945

SAN MARINO

Pesaro

Pisa

Florence

ITALY

CORSICA

A P E N N I N E S

GUSTAV LINE
Jan.-May, 1944

Adriatic Sea

Rome
(allies enter, June 4, 1944)

Liri Valley

Monte Cassino,
November 1943-May, 1944

Anzio
(Jan. 22, 1944)

Rapido R.

SARDINIA

Naples

Amalfi

Capri Is.

Salerno
(Sept. 9, 1943)

Tyrrhenian Sea

N

SICILY

Strait of Messina

ALGERIA

⇒ U.S. Movement

➡ British Movement

TUNISIA

Malta

0 Miles   100   200

0 Kilometers   200

Salerno. As the boats churned ahead, the huddled American troops pointed out to one another the jagged silhouette of the Isle of Capri to their north, in the mouth of Naples harbor, from which many of their forebears had sailed to the United States. They could see the gently bobbing lights of fishing boats beneath the terraced cliffs of the Amalfi coast. They knew that Montgomery had landed unopposed on the toe of the Italian boot just days earlier. Adding to their sense of complacency, at first light Eisenhower's voice came over the radio, announcing a preliminary Italian armistice.

If the landing forces expected that a tourist idyll awaited them on the beaches of Salerno, they were soon disillusioned. Ignoring all the lessons that the Pacific war was teaching about amphibious attack, Clark, a vainglorious third-generation professional soldier and one of the few American senior officers who had seen combat in World War I, chose to forego preliminary bombardment in the hope of achieving tactical surprise. But it was Clark who got the surprise. Awaiting him ashore were some of the same Germans who had recently eluded Patton and Montgomery in Sicily. They counterattacked with such force that Clark prepared to evacuate the beachhead and accept defeat on September 12. He was saved only by aggressive, close-in naval fire support, poured ashore from ships that ran their keels to within inches of the sand.

The near disaster at Salerno was but the prelude to a year-and-a-half-long ordeal in the elongated Italian cul-de-sac. German field marshal Albert Kesselring took ingenious advantage of the Italian peninsula's mountainous spine, seamed by rivers and wrinkled by narrow defiles, to bottle up the Allies without having to transfer additional German troops from other fronts. After effecting an orderly withdrawal from the narrow plain behind Salerno, Kesselring fortified a line (the "Gustav Line") that stretched from the Tyrrhenian Sea to the Adriatic just north of Naples. Its western end was anchored on the Appenine peak of Monte Cassino, overlooking the confluence of the Rapido and Liri rivers and crowned by a magnificent monastery founded by Benedict in the sixth century, one of the jewels of European piety, learning, and art. Repeatedly destroyed by invading Lombards and Arabs, restored most recently in the seventeenth century, Monte Cassino now once again attracted the wrath of the gods of war, who cared little for the Christian god of peace to whom the monastery's gentle monks chanted their nightly vespers. Monte Cassino dominated the entrance to the valley of the Liri, one of the few north-south watersheds in the Appenine range, and for that reason an ancient route to Rome and a coveted military objective.

Repeated attempts by a multinational Allied force to get past Cassino into the Liri Valley all broke against the obstacles of rock, rivers, and German doggedness, abetted by atrocious weather that buried vehicles in axle-deep mud and frequently closed the skies to aircraft. The U.S. Thirty-sixth Division, a National Guard outfit from Texas, suffered especially appalling losses in an abortive attempt to cross the swollen and frigid Rapido River in January. In one of the war's most lamentably destructive actions, Allied bombers pounded the ancient monastery to rubble in February 1944, only to learn that it had held no German troops but that its ruins made for superior defensive emplacements.

Desperate for an exit from the wintry deadlock at Monte Cassino, Churchill championed the bold move of a "cat's-claw" or "end-run"— a second amphibious landing, this time behind the enemy line at Anzio, just south of Rome. Predictably, the Americans took scant interest in this suggestion of a fresh initiative in what they had from the outset regarded as a secondary theater. They had already begun in late 1943 to transfer men and materiel to England preparatory to the cross-Channel attack. "Here the American clear-cut, logical, large-scale, mass production style of thought was formidable," said Churchill, marking his frustration with the increasingly evident fact of American dominance in Allied councils, a dominance symbolized by the accumulating stock-piles of American economic output.[60] But at last, in a direct appeal to Roosevelt, the prime minister succeeded in persuading the president to order a delay in the transfer of landing craft to England from the Mediterranean, in order that the amphibious assault on Anzio, code-named Shingle, might be launched. Marshall had his usual misgivings. "I was furious," he said, that at this late date the Prime Minister still "wanted to push us further in the Mediterranean."[61] The American commander ordered to undertake the Anzio landing, General John P. Lucas, shared Marshall's apprehension. Lucas gave vent to feelings that might have been thinkable but surely inexpressible at Casablanca a year earlier. In a stormy meeting with his British superior, he likened Shingle to Churchill's disastrous World War I brainchild, Gallipoli, acerbically adding, "with the same amateur on the coach's bench."[62]

On January 22, 1944, amphibious trucks, driven by black troops rel-

60. Churchill 5:377.
61. Pogue, *Marshall: Organizer of Victory*, 331.
62. Lucas quoted in David Eisenhower, *Eisenhower at War, 1943–1945* (New York: Vintage, 1987), 124.

egated to noncombat service, began ferrying an Anglo-American force, fifty thousand strong, to the Anzio beaches. The assault troops splashed ashore against mercifully light resistance. But in yet another violation of the principles of amphibious warfare, Lucas failed to exploit his good fortune on the beaches by advancing swiftly inland. He contented himself instead with stabilizing and securing his landing zone. Hitler soon ordered a powerful counterattack, determined to demonstrate that he still had the capacity to hurl an amphibious landing into the sea. As at Salerno, he nearly succeeded. He did seal Lucas's troops inside their besieged beachhead, where they huddled, paralyzed and despondent, for the next four months. One soldier captured the agony of Anzio in verse:

> Praise be to God for this captured sod that rich with blood does seep;
> With yours and mine, like butchered swine's; and hell is six feet deep.
> That death awaits there's no debate; no triumph will we reap.
> The crosses grow on Anzio, where hell is six feet deep.[63]

Landed to rescue the deadlocked force at Monte Cassino, the men on the beaches of Anzio now cowered under the Alban Hills and awaited their own rescue until French Moroccan and Polish divisions finally cracked the Monte Cassino defenses in May and broke through into the Liri Valley. Even then, Clark muffed the opportunity to bag Kesselring's retreating forces. Instead of cinching the noose around them by joining with the British army heading northward from Monte Cassino, he directed his troops to strike for the political prize of Rome, a histrionic gesture that availed little. The Germans swiftly abandoned the city and retreated further to the north. As they passed through the great Renaissance city of Florence, they blew up all the bridges across the River Arno save the famed Ponte Vecchio, deemed too fragile to bear the weight of tanks and hence of little military value. Just north of Florence, Kesselring set up a new defensive line (the "Gothic Line") along the Appenine crest between Pisa and Rimini. His troops held there, unbudgeable, until virtually the last weeks of the war.

The Italian campaign was a needlessly costly sideshow. It wantonly inflicted 188,000 American casualties, as well as 123,000 British, while Kesselring held the peninsula to the end with fewer than twenty divisions, virtually none of them transferred from the eastern front. There in the east, even as Eisenhower had been dickering with Badoglio and

63. Audie Murphy, *To Hell and Back* (New York: Henry Holt, 1949), 125.

while Clark's seven divisions had been preparing to go ashore at Salerno in the summer of 1943, the Red Army had conclusively extinguished the *Wehrmacht's* offensive capability in the cataclysmic battle of Kursk, a colossal clash of four thousand aircraft, six thousand tanks, and two million men.

Stalin's aggravation with his dilatory Western partners was growing ever more pronounced. Roosevelt and Churchill wrestled for days at the Trident Conference over the language of a message that would inform their Soviet ally of their decision to go ahead in Italy and delay the cross-Channel attack until 1944. Stalin responded with cold fury. "Your decision creates exceptional difficulties for the Soviet Union," Stalin wrote to Roosevelt. This latest delay, he said, "leaves the Soviet Army, which is fighting not only for its country, but also for its Allies, to do the job alone, almost single-handed." When, he wondered, would the promised second front ever materialize? "Need I speak of the disheart-eningly negative impression that this fresh postponement of the second front and the withholding from our Army, which has sacrificed so much, of the anticipated substantial support by the Anglo-American armies, will produce in the Soviet Union—both among the people and in the Army?"[64]

NORTH AFRICA had been no kind of second front adequate to Stalin's needs. Neither was the brief expedition into Sicily, and surely not the deliberately limited campaign that ground to such a frustrating stalemate in Italy. But at Casablanca the Western allies had also con-jured the prospect of another kind of second front altogether—in the air. The Combined Bomber Offensive that Churchill and Roosevelt announced in Morocco was invested with extravagant hopes. Its archi-tects nursed the dream that the novel technology of flying machines had at last brought within their grasp the military equivalent of the Holy Grail: an ultimate weapon, one that would not only win this war but revolutionize the nature of warfare itself.

"Generals always fight the last war," the old adage has it, but the infatuation with air power in World War II gave the lie to that conven-tional wisdom. The pursuit of winged victory stemmed above all from a conscious determination *not* to refight World War I, a nightmarish, static war of attrition that had annihilated men by the millions. The fascination with air power infected virtually every nation that had been

---

64. *Stalin's Correspondence with Roosevelt and Truman,* 70–71.

sucked into that earlier conflict. It was driven everywhere by the desperate quest for some means to restore the power of the offensive and foreshorten war's duration. The same quest had propelled innovators in ground combat like Guderian in Germany, Liddell Hart in Britain, DeGaulle in France, and Patton in America to emphasize a mechanized, armored war of mobility, or *Blitzkrieg*. But aerial warfare in particular peculiarly suited the distinctive political, strategic, and economic circumstances of the United States. An unwarlike people living at a great distance from the major theaters of conflict and commanding awesome productive potential took naturally to the idea of a weapon that could be deployed far from American shores, put relatively few Americans in harm's way, and make maximum use of American industrial might and technological know-how.

The principal theorist of war in the air was the Italian Giulio Douhet. His 1921 treatise, *The Command of the Air*, was to the emerging science of combat aloft what Alfred Thayer Mahan's works had been to naval doctrine a generation earlier. Douhet argued that the deadlock on the Italian-Austrian front in World War I could have been broken most efficiently not by applying more force at the points of contact between the two armies along the Isonzo and Piave rivers but by destroying with air attacks the enemy's sources of supply—the arms factories deep inside the Czech provinces of the Austro-Hungarian Empire. Douhet endorsed without scruple the concept that modern warfare was not merely a conflict between uniformed combatants but a total war between entire peoples, in which "the woman loading shells in a factory, the farmer growing wheat, the scientist experimenting in his laboratory" were targets just as legitimate as "the soldier carrying his gun." Douhet envisioned that aerial warfare could be directed against something more than just the physical destruction of the enemy's economic assets. It would prove far easier, he argued, for air power to shatter the morale of civilians at home than of trained troops in the field. Douhet thus helped foster the concept of a "home front," a telling neologism that testifies to the totalizing, all-engulfing implications of warfare in the modern era. "How could a country go on living and working," he asked, "oppressed by the nightmare of imminent destruction and death?"[65]

65. Giulio Douhet, *The Command of the Air*, trans. Dino Ferrari (New York: Coward-McCann, 1942), 196, 22. Douhet more than hinted that the "soldier carrying his gun" was an even *less* legitimate target than civilians. Compared to "a few women and children killed in an air raid," he wrote, "a soldier, a robust young man, should

At the U.S. Army's Air Corps Tactical School in the post–World War I years, Douhet's texts had been required reading. So were the writings of his American counterpart, General Billy Mitchell, whose *Our Air Force* appeared in the same year as *The Command of the Air*. The American air enthusiasts evolved their own version of the doctrine of aerial warfare. Like Douhet, they called for the establishment of an independent air arm, and they championed the idea that air power alone offered the key to military success. In a significant revision of Douhet's thinking, however, they resisted the idea of wholesale assaults on civilian populations, emphasizing instead precision attacks on high-value economic targets like transportation networks, electric power plants, oil supplies, and arms factories. Yet from the outset Douhet's thoughts about the intimidating effects of air attacks on civilian morale shadowed American thinking about aerial war. A 1926 training manual spoke of air power as "a method of imposing will by terrorizing the whole population." A 1930 manual acknowledged the importance of attacks "on civilian populations in the back areas of the hostile country," though it cautioned that such strikes had to be weighed against "the effect upon public opinion," a large consideration in light of the airmen's aspiration to win the public and political approval necessary to establishment as an independent service arm.[66]

Those two very different conceptions of the targeting choices of aerial warfare — economic assets or civilian populations — continued to reside uncomfortably together in AWPD-1, drafted in the context of the Victory Program discussions in late 1941. AWPD-1, the founding document that guided America's air war, declared that the air arm's first objective was the German economy. But "as German morale begins to crack," the document allowed, terror raids on civilians might speed the final collapse. Specifically, AWPD-1 urged that it might be "highly profitable to deliver a large-scale, all-out attack on the civil population of Berlin."[67]

In 1933 the U.S. Army, of which the air arm was then and would through the war be a part, sponsored a design competition to develop the technological means by which the airmen's large ambitions might be realized. The winner was Boeing Model 299. By 1937 Boeing's plane was in production as the B-17, the United States' first weapon designed

---

be considered to have the maximum individual value in the general economy of humanity" (195). The discussion that follows is heavily indebted to Ronald Schaffer's superb study, *Wings of Judgment* (New York: Oxford University Press, 1985).

66. Schaffer, *Wings of Judgment*, 27–28.
67. Schaffer, *Wings of Judgment*, 32–33.

to accomplish a "strategic" mission. Popularly known as the "Flying Fortress," the B-17 lived up to its nickname. Designed to be self-defending, it was heavily armed and armored. The models being produced by the time the United States entered the war bristled with thirteen machine guns. They were intended to be flown in tight formations of a hundred aircraft and more, whose combined firepower could spew out up to thirty tons of .50-caliber machine gun slugs per minute. That deadly curtain of defensive fire was thought sufficient to ward off fighter attacks, while heavy steel plating and bulletproof Plexiglas windows would supposedly protect against antiaircraft fire from the ground. Though the B-17s sacrificed bomb-carrying space to all that defensive capacity, the United States Army Air Forces (USAAF) counted on the "Forts" to penetrate deep into enemy territory, precisely lay down their destructive loads, and fight their way home to bomb again another day.

By the time the Americans entered the war, rough experience had already taught the British that "precision bombing" was extraordinarily difficult and intolerably costly to accomplish. Heavy losses early in the war drove the Royal Air Force to bomb only under the cape of darkness, which badly compromised accuracy. A study in the summer of 1941 concluded that just one in three British bombers managed to get within five miles of its target; in the heavily defended Ruhr, only one in ten. In February 1942, therefore, the Imperial Air Staff directed that British Bomber Command should henceforth focus on destroying "the morale of the enemy civil population and in particular of the industrial workers." The British euphemistically called this new practice "area bombing," but the bald truth was that terror bombing, not precision targeting, was now Britain's official policy.

When the first elements of the USAAF appeared in Britain in the spring of 1942, they shunned the British approach, less for moral reasons than for military and political ones. They believed that scarce resources were best used against high-value targets and that in any case "area bombing" would have a disastrous impact on American public opinion, crippling the airmen's campaign to be recognized as an independent service. USAAF head General Hap Arnold therefore welcomed the Casablanca commitment to "round-the-clock" aerial attacks, with the British continuing area bombing by night and the Americans precision bombing by day. Casablanca was "a major victory," said Arnold, "for we would bomb in accordance with American principles using methods for which our planes were designed."[68]

68. Schaffer, *Wings of Judgment*, 38.

Organized as the Eighth Air Force under General Ira C. Eaker, American heavy bombers flew their first mission of the European war in August 1942.[69] A dozen B-17s, shielded by a swarm of RAF Spitfire fighters, took off from England, bombed railroad marshaling yards near Rouen in France, and returned to base without the loss of a single Fortress. For the remainder of 1942, the handful of American bombers available to Eaker hit targets in France and the Low Countries, rarely venturing beyond the 175-mile combat radius of the protecting Spitfires. By the time of the Casablanca Conference in January 1943, not a single USAAF bomber had yet penetrated German airspace. But by then Eaker had five hundred planes in England. He was eager to carry the attack directly to the *Reich* and to demonstrate that the "self-defending" Flying Fortresses could do the job they were designed to do. On January 27, 1943, just days after the conferees had departed from the subtropical warmth of Casablanca, ninety B-17s lifted off their airfields in the south of England to strike their first blow against Germany. Their target was the submarine construction yards in Vegesack, on the Weser River near Bremen. Bad weather, however, forced their diversion to the less important objective of the North Sea port of Wilhelmshaven. Only fifty-five planes managed to find it. Three did not return. It was scarcely an auspicious beginning.

The theorists of air war had reckoned little with the human factor in their strategic equations. They had also underestimated the cunning of their adversaries. Men went aloft in bulky flying suits that poorly insulated them from temperatures that could fall to fifty below zero at cruising altitudes. Fliers frequently suffered from frostbite and went woozy or even passed out from hypoxia when moisture froze in the tubes of their oxygen masks or when airsickness or fear caused them to vomit into their mouthpieces. Crews often returned with uniforms befouled from long missions that precluded any chance to urinate or defecate. Fear was the aircrew's companion from the moment of takeoff. The difficulty of flying off hundreds of aircraft within minutes of one another, then assembling them in the sky into their huge formations—high, middle, and low squadrons of up to sixteen planes each, endless streams of fully laden bombers laboriously circling upward for nearly three-quarters of an hour to operational altitude—resulted in frequent midair collisions

69. The first American air action in Europe was a joint USAAF-RAF raid on July 4, 1942, against enemy airfields in Holland. The six American crews flew only light bombers, however, and only two of them managed to drop their bombs on the target. The Rouen raid was the first *heavy* bomber attack by the Americans. See Craven and Cate 1:658.

even before the big sky convoys headed across the Channel. Accidents claimed nearly as many airmen's lives (approximately thirty-six thousand) as did combat (approximately forty-nine thousand).[70]

Despite the B-17's legendary defensive power, the Fortresses proved highly vulnerable once they flew beyond the range of fighter escort. Though the sturdy bombers could absorb up to twenty hits from 20mm cannon fire and still keep flying, they were not indestructible. German interceptors soon learned that the bombers' forward turret guns could not be depressed to an angle that adequately covered a head-on attack. Luftwaffe pilots adopted the harrowing tactic of flying a parallel course to the bomber stream, in sight of the traumatized B-17 crews but out of range of their guns. At a point about two miles ahead of the lead planes, the fighters U-turned into the path of the bombers and opened fire at a closing rate of up to six hundred miles per hour. The planes that survived the fighter attacks had ultimately to fly through a preset "box barrage," a flak-saturated section of sky athwart the final approach to the target. The Eighth Air Force in 1943 lost on average 5 percent of its aircraft per mission to accident, destruction in combat, or irreparable damage. Two-thirds of all American airmen in that year did not finish their required tour of twenty-five missions.

In March 1943, pursuant to the dictates of prewar strategic doctrine, USAAF drew up a list of precisely sixty specific targets. Their destruction, the airmen claimed, would "gravely impair and might paralyze the Western Axis war effort."[71] These "strategic" objectives, the supposed Douhetian vital points in the German production machine, conspicuously included oil refineries and ball-bearing plants. To knock them out, USAAF estimated, would require a force of 2,702 heavy bombers and 800 medium bombers. USAAF at the time disposed of fewer than half that many aircraft, but Hap Arnold was determined to get started. Here was the opportunity to deliver on the second-front promise, and not incidentally to vindicate the war-winning claims of the air barons.

In the recently recaptured Libyan desert, squadrons of the Ninth USAAF's B-24 Liberator bombers, the B-17s' longer-range but more balky and less technologically sophisticated teammates, began in the summer

70. *United States Strategic Bombing Survey: Over-All Report, European War* (Washington: USGPO, 1945); Michael Clodfelter, *Warfare and Armed Conflicts: A Statistical Reference to Casualty and Other Figures, 1618–1991* (Jefferson, N.C.: McFarland, 1992), 960.

71. Alan J. Levine, *The Strategic Bombing of Germany, 1940–1945* (Westport, Conn.: Praeger, 1992), 85.

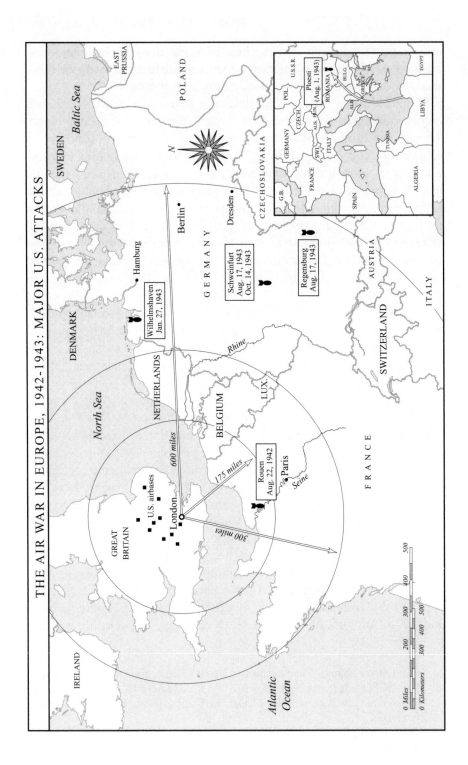

THE AIR WAR IN EUROPE, 1942–1943: MAJOR U.S. ATTACKS

GREAT BRITAIN

U.S. airbases

London

IRELAND

Atlantic Ocean

North Sea

Baltic Sea

SWEDEN

EAST PRUSSIA

POLAND

DENMARK

Hamburg

NETHERLANDS

Wilhelmshaven
Jan. 27, 1943

Rhine

Berlin

Dresden

G E R M A N Y

Schweinfurt
Aug. 17, 1943
Oct. 14, 1943

Regensburg
Aug. 17, 1943

CZECHOSLOVAKIA

BELGIUM

LUX.

Rouen
Aug. 22, 1942

Paris

Seine

F R A N C E

SWITZERLAND

AUSTRIA

ITALY

600 miles

175 miles

300 miles

N

0 Miles   200   300   400   500
0 Kilometers   300   400   500

Ploesti
(Aug. 1, 1943)

U.S.S.R.

POL.

CZECH.

GERMANY

AUS. HUN.

SWI.

ITALY

ROMANIA

BULG.

GREECE

ALB.

TUR.

EGYPT

LIBYA

TUNISIA

ALGERIA

SPAIN

FRANCE

G.B.

of 1942 to practice low-level attacks on a mock-up of the great Rumanian refinery complex at Ploesti, which processed a quarter of Germany's oil supply. On August 1, 1943, 177 bomb-laden B-24s, even trickier than usual to fly because they were overloaded with extra machine guns and auxiliary fuel tanks, took off from Libyan airbases to destroy Ploesti. No fighters could accompany them on the thirteen-hundred-mile run. Surprise and mass would be their best defenses.

Approaching the Albanian coast, the lead plane went out of control and crashed. Dense cloud banks over the Balkans enveloped the remaining aircraft. Under strict orders to maintain radio silence, the five groups in the giant air armada lost contact with one another. The badly disrupted formations finally emerged over Ploesti into a hell-in-the-heavens of confusion, flak, and fighters. Fifty-four B-24s went down, 310 fliers were killed, and another 150 parachuted into captivity. The burning oil installations that the returning bombers left behind slowed Ploesti's production for a few months, but by drawing on reserves and forcing slave workers to make emergency repairs, Germany hardly felt the pinch.

Scarcely two weeks later, Eaker's Eighth Air Force launched a dual raid against two more "strategic" targets: a fighter-aircraft plant in Regensburg and a ball-bearing works at Schweinfurt—both deep inside Germany and well beyond the range of fighter escort. Three hundred seventy-six B-17s droned off the tarmac from various English aerodromes on the morning of August 17. Twenty-four of the planes on the Regensburg run never returned, nor did thirty-six of those that flew to Schweinfurt, a 16 percent loss rate. Some six hundred American aircrew were killed or captured. One flier described the scene after a squadron of the feared Messerschmitt 109s made their usual U-turn and closed on the advancing bomber formation:

> [T]he plane shook with the chatter of our guns. . . . As other planes were hit, we had to fly through their debris. I instinctively ducked as we almost hit an escape hatch from a plane ahead. When a plane blew up, we saw their parts all over the sky. We smashed into some of the pieces. One plane hit a body which tumbled out of a plane ahead. A crewman went out the front hatch of a plane and hit the tail assembly of his own plane. No chute. His body turned over and over like a bean bag tossed into the air. . . . A German pilot came out of his plane, drew his legs into a ball, his head down. Papers flew out of his pockets. He did a triple somersault through our formation. No chute.[72]

72. Harry H. Crosby, A Wing and a Prayer: The "Bloody 100th" Bomb Group of the U.S. Eighth Air Force in Action over Europe in World War II (New York: HarperCollins, 1993), 94–95.

Neither raid had achieved success remotely commensurate with the price paid in machines and men. Surviving crews were demoralized by the losses. When they learned at their morning briefing of October 14 that Eaker was sending them back to Schweinfurt, many were gripped by icy dread. Like Ulysses Grant's troops at Cold Harbor, who advanced to all but certain death with papers pinned to their jackets bearing their names and addresses, some fliers returned to their barracks to scrawl a last letter and to don additional clothing, suitable for surviving capture — or for burial. Others piled aboard so much extra .50-caliber ammunition that officers had to order it offloaded to remain within operational weight limits. Three hundred eighty-three Fortresses and a handful of Liberators took off. Too few B-24s made it into the air to compose a formation, so the remainder flew a diversion over the North Sea. Fright, confusion, and chaos thinned the bomber stream to just 291 Fortresses even before the Channel was reached. Two hundred twenty-eight reached Schweinfurt, where they inflicted only minimal damage. There and back, the Germans unleashed a savagely effective combination of antiaircraft fire and fighter attacks, including time-fused bombs dropped from above on the bomber formations. The B-17s vibrated wildly from the firing of their heavy machine guns and bucked when hit by enemy 20mm cannon fire. Sixty Fortresses never made it back, nor did more than six hundred airmen who were killed or captured. Some men too badly wounded to make it home were shoved out in their parachutes, desperately consigned to the mercies of enemy medical personnel. Several shot-up B-17s lowered their wheels, the sign of surrender, as their pilots struggled to get the disabled planes onto the ground, where the crews, if they were lucky, might hope for internment.

Ploesti, Regensburg, and the two Schweinfurt raids consumed nearly two hundred heavy bombers and well over a thousand airmen in a matter of weeks. Faced with such horrendous losses, Eaker grudgingly accepted that his supposedly self-defending bombers fared little better than slow-flying ducks when they ventured into well-defended enemy airspace without fighter escort. He yielded to the inevitable and suspended further deep-penetration raids. For the time being, the American strategic revolution in the air was grounded. And the second front whose promise it held still lay well over the horizon of the future.

ONLY IN THE PACIFIC could Americans seek some consolation at the close of their second year at war, and chill comfort it was. King had succeeded at Casablanca in securing an agreement to allocate 30 percent of the American war effort to the struggle against Japan. In the ensuing weeks he hurried to launch a new offensive campaign in the Central Pacific, not least, as he explained to Nimitz, "so that the British would not back down on their agreements and commitments. We must be so committed in the Central Pacific," he said, "that the British cannot hedge."[73] King had never counted on much from the campaign in the Southwest Pacific, other than to block Japan's advance while awaiting some opportunity to shape an offensive along the lines of the old Orange plans. But by the end of 1943 the outlines of a plan for the defeat of Japan had begun to emerge. It envisioned a powerful thrust into the Central Pacific area, first cracking the outer ring of Japan's far-flung oceanic defensive perimeter in the Gilbert and Marshall islands, then puncturing the inner ring of the Carolines and Marianas. Meanwhile, MacArthur would continue his drive along the north coast of New Guinea toward the Philippines, a stepping-stone to the Chinese coast and Formosa, from which air attacks on the Japanese home islands could be launched.

The first objectives in the Central Pacific campaign were the tiny atolls of Makin and Tarawa in the Gilbert archipelago, necessary as bases to support further jumps into the Marshalls. Tarawa, a three-square-mile dot on the map, about the size of New York City's Central Park, proved an especially bloody affair. Garrisoned by some five thousand Japanese soldiers, Tarawa was encircled by a coral reef, a hazard that landing craft could clear only at high tide. A twenty-minute interval between an ineffectually brief naval bombardment and the first wave of landing ships allowed the Japanese defenders to man their guns just as the assault craft began to hang up on the reef. At least twenty landing vessels crammed with dead and dying marines perched helplessly on the coral outcropping while the gunners ashore raked them with deadly accurate fire. Photographs of dead marines floating in the tide and half-buried in the beaches shocked the American public. But at a cost of some one thousand dead and two thousand wounded, Tarawa was taken, as was Makin. King was at last positioned to push his advance through the Pacific island chains toward Japan: to Kwajelein and Eniwetok in the Marshalls, Truk in the Carolines, then on to the great prize of the Marianas, only two thousand miles from Japan.

Success in the Pacific, however, was small comfort to Stalin. He pointedly reminded Roosevelt that "in the Far East . . . the U.S.S.R. is not in a state of war."[74] In a bitter tirade addressed to Churchill in

73. Spector, 260.
74. *Stalin's Correspondence with Roosevelt and Truman*, 50.

mid-1943, Stalin gave full vent to his accumulated frustrations. Even the woodenness of Soviet diplomatic prose could not mask the old Bolshevik's anger. From the war's outset, he complained, he had been given nothing but a beggar's diet of broken pledges. He rehearsed in detail the long and lamentable record: the empty assurances to Molotov of a second front in 1942; the repeatedly canceled North Atlantic convoys; the several diversions into North Africa, then Sicily, then Italy; Casablanca's hollow promise of a second front in the air; the persistent infatuation of the British with the Mediterranean; and the unceasing attraction of the Americans to their own version of the Mediterranean, in the Pacific. "The point here," Stalin concluded, "is the preservation of [Soviet] confidence in its Allies, a confidence which is being subject to severe stress." The Red Army had sustained millions of casualties, Stalin reminded Churchill, "compared with which the sacrifices of the Anglo-American armies are insignificant." Churchill found the message "very unpleasant" and replied in kind.[75] He worried that the acerbic exchange might terminate his relation with Stalin.

Roosevelt, meanwhile, was casting about on his own for some means to retain what was left of Stalin's rapidly waning confidence. A way had to be found, Secretary of State Cordell Hull said, "to talk Mr. Stalin out of his shell, so to speak, away from his aloofness, secretiveness, and suspiciousness."[76] Roosevelt characteristically sought a face-to-face meeting, a setting in which he could work his legendary charm, man to man. In May 1943 he entrusted his former ambassador to the Soviet Union, Joseph E. Davies, with a personal message to be hand-delivered to Stalin in the Kremlin. It proposed "an informal and completely simple visit for a few days between you and me." No staff should attend, Roosevelt suggested; he would bring only Harry Hopkins, already known to Stalin, as well as an interpreter and a single stenographer. Where to meet? Iceland was approximately equidistant from Moscow and Washington, but Roosevelt wanted to see Stalin alone, and meeting in Iceland "would make it, quite frankly, difficult not to invite Prime Minister Churchill at the same time." One or another side of the Bering Strait seemed the best solution, the president concluded, repeating his hope "that you and I would talk very informally and get what we call "a meeting of the minds.""[77]

Churchill was understandably nervous when he got wind of a possible

75. *Stalin's Correspondence with Roosevelt and Truman*, 74–76; *C&R* 2:285.
76. Cordell Hull, *The Memoirs of Cordell Hull* (New York: Macmillan 1948), 2:1248.
77. *Stalin's Correspondence with Roosevelt and Truman*, 63.

Roosevelt-Stalin meeting from which he would be excluded. Roosevelt awkwardly tried to reassure him with the outright lie that such a meeting had been "Uncle Joe's" idea. Stalin meanwhile refused to travel so far as the Bering Sea. Eventually all three leaders agreed to meet in December in Teheran, the Iranian capital, just beyond the Soviet Union's southern frontier. A preliminary October meeting of foreign ministers in Moscow would help prepare the agenda.

As preparations for the historic encounter at Teheran went forward in the last weeks of 1943, the stresses in the Grand Alliance grew more, not less, pronounced. At another full-dress joint Anglo-American staff conference in Quebec in August 1943, the British nominally reaffirmed their promise to open a second front in France in 1944, but the Americans still had reason to doubt the firmness of Churchill's commitment. On the eve of the Quebec Conference, Henry Stimson had an angry exchange with Churchill in which the prime minister conjured a "Channel full of corpses" if the invasion plans went ahead. Even after Quebec, Harry Hopkins worried out loud to the prime minister's physician and confidante, Lord Moran, about Churchill's steadfastness: "I don't believe he is really converted," Hopkins opined.[78] On the eve of Teheran, at a preliminary British-American gathering in Cairo, Churchill justified Hopkins's skepticism when he once again proposed a still further operation in the Mediterranean, this time to dislodge the Germans from the island of Rhodes. "His Majesty's Government can't have its troops standing idle," Churchill said. "Muskets must flame." An exasperated George Marshall could take no more: "Not one American soldier is going to die on [that] goddamned beach," he replied, with apparent finality. But as events soon revealed, Churchill was not yet done with the Mediterranean.

Even larger anxieties proliferated about Soviet intentions. In midsummer Stalin had withdrawn his ambassadors from both London and Washington. In September came rumors that the Germans had extended a peace feeler to Moscow through Japan, stimulating anew the fear of a separate settlement in eastern Europe before a second front had even opened in the west. One observer detected "an atmosphere alarmingly reminiscent of that which had preceded the Molotov-Ribbentrop Pact of August, 1939."[79] Then, at the Moscow foreign

78. Stimson Diary, August 4, 1943; Lord Moran, *Churchill: Taken from the Diaries of Lord Moran: The Struggle for Survival, 1940–1965* (Boston: Houghton Mifflin, 1966), 117.
79. *FRUS* (1943) 3:697; Sherwood, *Roosevelt and Hopkins*, 734.

ministers' meeting in October, the Russians baffled and worried the American delegates with their own endorsement of possible further action in the Mediterranean theater, directed at a heavier investment in Italy, or maybe even the Balkans. In early November the U.S. military attaché at the Moscow embassy sent a message to the War Department that Stimson described as "throwing disquiet into our ranks by suggesting that the Russians were not quite so keen about Overlord [the new code name for the cross-Channel attack] as they had been."[80] Perhaps Stalin had at last arrived at the point that many American analysts had anticipated and dreaded, where he no longer needed Western help and in fact preferred that the British and the Americans stay out of Europe altogether. "If Germany collapses before the democracies have been able to make an important military contribution on the continent of Europe," a State Department assessment had warned, "the peoples of Europe will with reason believe that the war was won by the Russians alone. Under such conditions the prestige of the Soviet Union will be so great that it will be difficult for Great Britain and the United States to oppose successfully any line of policy which the Kremlin may choose to adopt."[81]

What might that line of policy be? Unknown to his Allies, Stalin confided something of his intentions to the Yugoslav Communist Josip Broz Tito: "This war is not as in the past," Stalin said. "Whoever occupies a territory also imposes his own social system. Everyone imposes his own system as far as his army can reach. It cannot be otherwise."[82] Successful at Stalingrad and victorious at Kursk, as 1943 ended Stalin's Red Army was about to evict the *Wehrmacht* from the Soviet Union once and for all and was poised to cross the Soviet frontier and enter Europe. William Bullitt had warned Roosevelt some months earlier that Stalin intended to reach "as far west as the Rhine, perhaps even beyond."[83] America's unreadiness, the halting pace of mobilization in the United States, Roosevelt's repeated submission to Churchill's importunings to delay the second front, the distractions of the Mediterranean and the Pacific — all might in the end mean that much of Europe would be lost to the Soviets even before the British and the Americans had a fighting chance to win it back from the Germans.

80. Stimson Diary, November 11, 1943.
81. Stoler, *Politics of the Second Front*, 88.
82. Milovan Djilas, *Conversations with Stalin* (New York: Harcourt, Brace and World, 1962), 114.
83. Stoler, *Politics of the Second Front*, 88.

At Teheran, Roosevelt would at last have his chance to take the measure of the man who seemed on the verge of locking all of Europe within his grasp. Even before America had fully entered the war, the American president would have to begin the process of preparing for the postwar world that was already aborning.

5

The War of Machines

> *The most important things in this war are machines. . . . The United States . . . is a country of machines.*
>
> — Josef Stalin, Teheran Conference, 1943

"I don't see much future for the Americans," Adolf Hitler crowed to his cronies in the aftermath of the Pearl Harbor attack. "It's a decayed country. And they have their racial problem, and the problem of social inequalities. . . . American society [is] half Judaized, and the other half Negrified. How can one expect a State like that to hold together—a country where everything is built on the dollar." Hitler's foreign minister, Joachim von Ribbentrop, took a more sober view of the possible consequences of American belligerency. He warned Hitler in December 1941: "We have just one year to cut off Russia from her American supplies. . . . If we don't succeed and the munitions potential of the United States joins up with the manpower potential of the Russians, the war will enter a phase in which we shall only be able to win it with difficulty." More than a year earlier Admiral Yamamoto had made the same point to Fumimaro Konoye when he had predicted that Japanese forces would run wild for six months but that he had "utterly no confidence for the second or third year."[1]

Between them, Ribbentrop and Yamamoto illuminated the three fundamental determinants of the war's eventual outcome and hinted at their complex interaction: time, men, and materiel. Time was the Axis pow-

---

1. William L. Shirer, *The Rise and Fall of the Third Reich* (New York: Simon and Schuster, 1960), 895n.; David Irving, *Hitler's War* (New York: Viking, 1977), 354; *Reports of General MacArthur: Japanese Operations in the Southwest Pacific Area* 2, pt. 1 (Washington: USGPO, 1966), 33, n. 14.

ers' most threatening enemy. By the same token, time was the fourth and most potent partner in the Grand Alliance. Germany and Japan alike pinned their hopes for victory on a short war. Both powers had formulated their strategies and composed their force structures on that premise. Hitler built the *Wehrmacht's* highly mechanized but relatively small panzer force for *Blitzkrieg* warfare, a concept whose essential logic was to rob the enemy of time, to win quick victories before his adversaries could marshal their resources, before they could force the painful burdens of full economic mobilization upon Germany and turn the war into the kind of prolonged battle of attrition that had ground down the kaiser's regime in 1918. Japan, because it was far less well economically endowed than Germany, had for similar but even more compelling reasons starved its other services in the 1930s to assemble a sophisticated naval air spearhead that it counted upon to deliver a one-punch knockout blow, as it had tried to do at Pearl Harbor. If that first strike failed to fell the Americans in the war's opening round, disaster loomed. Japan was even less prepared than Germany to endure sustained counterpunching from an enemy with practically boundless industrial potential.

Hence the crucial role of men—especially Russians, the hard-used masses of Soviet soldiery that stopped the *Wehrmacht* in front of Moscow in late 1941 and snuffed out the German offensive at the cruel pivot of Stalingrad a year later. The staggering Soviet sacrifices of men—more than three million lost to wounds, death, or capture in 1941 alone— bought in turn the precious, crucial asset of time, time for the Americans to amass the arms and machines that could clinch Allied victory. With the Russians battered but still holding the field, Allied hopes now squarely rested, said Britain's Lord Beaverbrook, on "the immense possibilities of American industry."[2] Yet as 1942 opened, those possibilities were not yet realities. Could the Americans grasp the opportunity that the Russians had given them? And could they do it in time to make a difference?

Even in its weakened Depression state, the American economy was a fearsome, if slumbering, behemoth. In 1938, the last full peacetime year and a year in which the pinch of the Roosevelt Recession especially dampened American production, national income in the United States was nevertheless nearly double the combined national incomes of Germany, Japan, and Italy. In that same Depression year, American steel

2. Richard Polenberg, *War and Society: The United States, 1941–1945* (Philadelphia: Lippincott, 1972), 221.

output dwarfed Germany's, and American coal miners hauled up out of the earth almost twice the tonnage of their German counterparts. Automobile manufacturing, the characteristic twentieth-century high-mass-production industry and a crucial contributor to military success in the age of mechanized warfare, spectacularly illustrated the wildly asymmetric advantage in economic resources that America wielded. American carmakers turned out 4.8 million automobiles in 1937; in the same year Germany produced 331,000 cars; Japan, just 26,000.[3]

America enjoyed other advantages too. Somewhat paradoxically, the Great Depression itself was one of them, as comparison with the First World War suggests. The United States had entered that earlier war in 1917 with a fully employed civilian economy. Raising an army from the ranks of already employed workers and converting factories and forges from civilian to military production were consequently slow and tortured processes that never did come to complete fruition. The United States mustered only a two-million-man American Expeditionary Force and managed to field it in France only at the very end of 1918; the British and the French meanwhile supplied the great bulk of the its ships, planes, and artillery. But in 1940, after more than a decade of depression, the situation was different. Nearly nine million workers were out of work at the time of the fall of France, and even as late as the Pearl Harbor attack three million were still unemployed. Vast reservoirs of physical productive capacity also lay unused, including factories, heavy construction equipment, machine-tool stocks, electrical generating plants, trucks, locomotives, and railcars. Average plant utilization was about forty hours a week. As much as 50 percent of capacity stood idle in automobile manufacturing plants alone. As the war crisis now snapped the drooping American economy to attention, all those dormant resources could be swiftly directed to martial purposes with minimal disruption to the fabric of peacetime life. In that sense, not only did the war rescue the American economy from the Depression; no less significant, the Depression had in turn poised the economy for phenomenally rapid conversion to war production. What was more, the United States commanded a virtually self-sufficient continental economy, and the huge American industrial heartland rested safely distant from the threat

3. Harold G. Vatter, The U.S. Economy in World War II (New York: Columbia University Press, 1985), 15; Alan S. Milward, War, Economy, and Society, 1939–1945 (Berkeley: University of California Press, 1979), 49; Richard Overy, Why the Allies Won (New York: Norton, 1995), 224.

of invasion or bombing. Alone among the belligerent states, the United States was an abundantly endowed and uniquely privileged sanctuary where economic mobilization could proceed free from most supply problems, safe from enemy harassment, and therefore with maximum efficiency. The country where Hitler thought everything was built on the dollar was thus capable, at least in theory, of an astonishing demonstration of just how many weapons the dollar could build, and how swiftly. Could the Americans pull it off?

"It will not be sufficient for us and the other United Nations to produce a slightly superior supply of munitions to that of Germany, Japan, Italy," Roosevelt told Congress in January 1942. "The superiority of the United Nations in munitions and ships must be overwhelming . . . a crushing superiority of equipment in any theater of the world war." Roosevelt went on to set breathtakingly ambitious production goals: 60,000 aircraft in 1942 and 125,000 more in 1943; 120,000 tanks in the same period; 55,000 antiaircraft guns; 16 million deadweight tons of merchant shipping. At the same time, he warned that at some point civilian consumption might have to yield to the need for military production. That moment might be closer than many people realized. "I was a bit appalled," he told reporters as 1942 opened, to learn "that so much of our production was still going into civilian use."[4]

Donald Nelson, head of one of the principal mobilization agencies, was not the only person who was "startled and alarmed" when he heard Roosevelt's numbers. "He staggered us," Nelson recalled. "None of our production people thought that this volume was possible. . . . We thought that the goals set by the President were out of the question." Nelson was especially anxious about the threat the military program posed to civilian standards of living. Yet there was a deep strategic logic in what Nelson thought were Roosevelt's "awesome" plans for military production. Part of that logic lay in the realm of psychological warfare. "I believe these figures will tell our enemies what they are up against," Roosevelt said. The Germans and the Japanese would be intimidated by a truly monstrous vision of the nightmarish war of economies that they most feared. Just for that reason, the president explained to a skeptical Nelson, "I want to make the figures public."[5]

4. *PPA* (1942), 7, 36–37, 22. I have combined remarks from Roosevelt's annual budget message of January 5, his State of the Union address on the following day, and his press conference of the same date.

5. Donald M. Nelson, *Arsenal of Democracy: The Story of American War Production* (New York: Harcourt, Brace, 1946), 185–87.

The president's call for "crushing superiority of equipment" had a deeper rationale still, one that stemmed from a shrewd calculation of America's comparative advantage in modern warfare and of the political dangers and economic opportunities that American belligerency posed on the home front. Thanks to the dispensations of timing and geography, the United States could choose to fight a war of machines rather than men. Substituting material production and technology for manpower had been the essence of the "arsenal of democracy" or short-of-war strategy during the neutrality period. That same strategic doctrine continued to resonate vibrantly in American planning even after Pearl Harbor. Expending motors and metal rather than flesh and blood was the least-cost pathway that the Americans could take toward victory. It was the route that would claim the smallest toll in American lives, by leaving most of the battlefield fighting to others while Americans toiled on the production lines. It would run the lowest risk of alienating public commitment to the war effort. It was a pathway that opened naturally in front of a president who had struggled for years to convince a skeptical public of its stake in the international order and who worried even now that if he asked his countrymen to bear too great a burden of sacrifice he might trigger a sharp isolationist backlash. The strategy of "overwhelming" material superiority also opened a road that led beyond military victory to other especially alluring destinations: an end to the Depression, the revitalization of the American economy, and the positioning of the United States for the exercise of unprecedented international economic power at the war's conclusion. That vision may not have been fully formed in Roosevelt's mind in early 1942, but it was consistent with his policies in the neutrality period, and its possibilities were latent both in the military strategy he adopted and in the mobilization program he outlined. In time the full implications of this peculiarly American way of war would be much more clearly visible. Nineteen forty-two was thus a year that swung like a gate to the future. The choices made then would deeply affect the course of the fighting, the shape of American society both during and after the war, and the fate of the wider postwar world.

JUST AS THE NEW DEAL had to invent the apparatus of the modern American state in the midst of the Depression crisis, so Roosevelt now had to cobble a war administration out of the patchwork mobilization machinery slapped together during the period of American neutrality. The pathetic inadequacy of the Office of Production Management for orchestrating the kind of robust military economy that Roosevelt envisioned was vividly illustrated on January 5, 1942, when OPM head William Knudsen gathered a roomful of businessmen, recited a list of needed military items, and asked for volunteers to produce them.[6] Yet even now the daunting logistical complexities of mobilizing a multibillion-dollar economy, the ticklish political difficulties of reconciling all the interested parties, and Roosevelt's penchant for administrative profligacy all contributed to the creation of a notably ramshackle, poorly articulated array of mobilization agencies with overlapping and sometimes conflicting missions. Mimicking the administrative proliferation of the New Deal, a bewildering host of new war bureaucracies sprang into being. The National War Labor Board (NWLB), with power to impose binding arbitration and even to request federal seizure of struck plants, replaced the National Defense Mediation Board in January 1942. The War Manpower Commission appeared in April 1942, a new agency charged with allocating workers between civilian and military demands but effectively denied any voice either in labor relations, the province of the NWLB, or in occupational deferments, whose assignment remained the prerogative of the semiautonomous Selective Service System. The Supply Priorities and Allocation Board, as well as the hapless Office of Production Management, disappeared into the War Production Board (WPB), created in January 1942 and headed by former Sears, Roebuck executive Donald Nelson.

Nelson was amiable, slow-moving, and conciliatory. He had worked at Sears for thirty years, rising to the chairmanship of the giant retailer's executive committee. He liked to brag to reporters that in his day he had edited the largest-circulation publication in America—the Sears, Roebuck catalogue. He was also a dedicated public servant and a favorite of the New Dealers, "the one leading businessman," said the journalist I. F. Stone, "prepared to uphold the rights of labor . . . bargaining as firmly in buying for his country as he would have in buying for his company."[7]

In theory the WPB was to be a commanding superagency, loosely modeled on the War Industries Board of World War I. But in practice Nelson's powers were far less formidable than they appeared on paper (as had in fact been the case with the WIB in the earlier war). His

6. Alan Clive, *State of War: Michigan in World War II* (Ann Arbor: University of Michigan Press, 1979), 25.
7. David Brinkley, *Washington Goes to War* (New York: Knopf, 1988), 68.

mandate did not extend to labor and manpower issues. The Office of Price Administration (OPA) retained authority over prices. Most telling, the old military and naval purchasing bureaus — the Army Service Forces, the Army Air Forces, the U.S. Maritime Commission (which contracted for cargo ships), and several navy agencies under the Office of Procurement and Material — refused to relinquish the power to place contracts.

These jerry-built arrangements had far-reaching consequences. The WPB was supposedly a civilian agency, and Nelson fancied himself the civilians' advocate, a friend of the consumers he had long served at Sears and a patron of both labor and small business. But the retention of final contracting authority by the army and navy naturally left preponderant power in the hands of the military. The mild-mannered Nelson proved no match for the single-minded warriors devoted to brassing through the military's production program. Army Undersecretary Robert Patterson sported a belt stripped from the body of a German soldier he had killed in 1918. He took his leisure on a seventy-acre farm directly across the Hudson River from West Point, where he was a frequent and reverential visitor. Patterson was not the sort of man who was likely to knuckle under to the pipe-smoking, pencil-pushing, former mail-order salesman at the WPB. Lieutenant General Brehon B. Somervell, the no-nonsense, spit-and-polish professional soldier who ran the Army Service Forces, was cut from the same cloth as Patterson. A decorated hero of the Battle of the Meuse-Argonne in 1918, he was a man in whom organizational genius and Olympian arrogance were mixed in equal measure. In Somervell's view, all the civilian war agencies amounted to nothing more nor less than an effort by "Henry Wallace and the leftists to take over the country."[8]

Military procurement officers understandably preferred to deal with familiar, reliable large manufacturers. A pattern quickly emerged whereby the very largest corporations, including Ford, U.S. Steel, General Electric, and DuPont, garnered the lion's share of military contracts. General Motors alone supplied one-tenth of all American war production. More than two-thirds of prime military contracts went to just one hundred firms. The thirty-three largest corporations accounted for half of all military contracting.[9] In June 1942 Congress tried to buck that trend by establishing the Small War Plants Corporation (SWPC) to pro-

8. Polenberg, *War and Society*, 220.
9. R. Elberton Smith, *The Army and Economic Mobilization* (Washington: Department of the Army, 1959), passim; see also Vatter, *U.S. Economy in World War II*, 60, and Polenberg, *War and Society*, 219.

vide working capital to small businesses and otherwise facilitate their efforts to land military contracts. But the SWPC made little headway in the face of Somervell's adamant insistence that "all the small plants of the country could not turn out one day's requirements of ammunition." The war thus made the nation's biggest corporations bigger, and considerably richer as well. The pattern of military contracting intensified the tendency toward oligopoly in large sectors of American industry. Firms with fewer than one hundred employees accounted for 26 percent of total manufacturing employment in 1939 but only 19 percent by the war's end. After-tax corporate profits fattened—from $6.4 billion in 1940 to nearly $11 billion in 1944. None of this troubled the military authorities. "If you are going to try to go to war, or to prepare for war, in a capitalist country," Henry Stimson reflected, "you have got to let business make money out of the process or business won't work." Robert Patterson brushed aside criticism of the War Department's pro–big business policies with the bland statement that "we had to take industrial America as we found it." The historian Richard Polenberg wryly observes that "he might have added that they by no means left industrial America as they found it." At war's end, when some $17 billion of government-financed plant and equipment was sold at distress prices, two-thirds of it ended up in the hands of just eighty-seven companies.[10]

After months of trial and error, by the end of 1942 the government had hammered out a set of policies to lever the economy onto a war footing. There were elements of command and coercion in the methods used, and occasional examples of outright government fiat, but for the most part the administration tried when it could to brandish the carrot, not the stick—to rely on voluntary methods, on tax inducements, financial enticements, and market mechanisms rather than on the naked fist of government power. When that fist had to be bared, it was usually as far "upstream" in the production process as possible—by creating incentives in the tax codes and setting raw materials allocations and transportation priorities, for example, rather than commandeering shops or railroads. On occasion the government did resort to outright seizure of industrial and transportation facilities, but always temporarily and only when driven by extreme emergencies. In this, war mobilization resembled the New Deal itself, which despite its occasional *diktats* preferred whenever possible to work by indirection and by artful tinkering, by

10. Vatter, *U.S. Economy in World War II*, 59, 61, 65; Stimson Diary, August 26, 1940; Polenberg, *War and Society*, 13, 219.

ingenious commingling of the private and public realms rather than by roughly closing the hand of state power over the free market.

There was, however, one enormous difference between the economic policies of the New Deal and those of the war administration. The highest objectives of the former had been economic security and social equity—stability, not expansion. The overriding goals of the latter were production and more production—expansion, not stability. The result was far more direct government intrusion in the marketplace in wartime than the New Deal had ever attempted, but also the creation of a business-friendly economic climate unimaginable in the confrontational days of the 1930s. To many veteran New Dealers, such as Harold Ickes, Leon Henderson, and Eleanor Roosevelt, it seemed that the Depression decade's reform spirit was among the first casualties of the war.

Tax legislation passed in 1940, for example, began to fuel the engines of the war economy and provided a kind of template for wartime policies by relying on incentives, not compulsion, to nudge the nation's industries onto a war basis. The law aimed to stimulate industrial retooling for military production by allowing the full amortization of investment in war-related plant and equipment over just five years, a provision that sheltered otherwise taxable profits. To some observers that simple but powerful device seemed unconscionably generous to business. "This is abandoning advanced New Deal ground with a vengeance," Harold Ickes railed to his diary. "It seems to me intolerable to allow private people to use public capital in order to make a guaranteed profit for themselves."[11] If the new tax law offended New Deal sensibilities, worse was yet to come. When tax-advantaged private capital was not forthcoming, the Reconstruction Finance Corporation stood ready to provide government loans for needed plant expansion. As a further emolument, Roosevelt ordered the Justice Department to relax antitrust prosecutions. In perhaps the sweetest deal of all, military procurement agencies let contracts on a cost-plus basis, providing iron-clad guarantees of profits beyond the most avaricious monopolist's dreams.

Money for defense was no problem. If anything, the government's principal worry in wartime was not too little money but too much. Fighting inflation, not finding funds, became the principal task. One obvious way to close the so-called inflationary gap in World War II was to ration certain commodities and to impose a legal limit on both wage and price

11. Ickes Diary 3:295, 210.

increases, but that was predictably a messy business, fraught with political and administrative difficulties. Another and much simpler method, though not without its own political liabilities, was to confiscate excess personal income through taxation or to sterilize it for the duration of the war through a forced-saving program. The Roosevelt administration employed a mix of all those methods, but it adopted voluntary means when possible and tried to the extent it could to take the sting out of those unavoidably coercive measures that it was compelled to adopt, such as stiffer taxation policies.

The Revenue Act of 1942 provided for some $7 billion in new individual income taxes, a near doubling of the federal tax burden. The act filled the treasury's vaults and soaked up at least some potentially inflationary purchasing power. It also permanently revolutionized the American tax system. Up to the eve of the war no more than four million Americans had been required to file tax returns. All those with incomes below the basic exemption level of fifteen hundred dollars (a heavy majority of wage-earners, as median wage income was only $1,231 in 1939) had paid nothing. Depending on marital and family status, those with incomes up to four thousand dollars (some 70 percent of all households fell below that level in the 1930s) had been liable to federal income taxation, but at a rate no higher than 4 percent. Despite the alleged fiscal promiscuity of the New Deal, to all but a plutocratic few Americans the prewar federal tax system was an utter irrelevancy, or at most a decidedly minor nuisance. All that now changed, forever. By lowering the personal exemption to $624, the 1942 law immediately brought thirteen million new taxpayers into the system. Mushrooming employment rolls and rising incomes soon caught millions more in the tax net. By war's end, 42.6 million Americans paid personal income taxes, at rates ranging from 6 to 94 percent. In the aggregate, individuals for the first time now paid more in income taxes than did corporations, a pattern that held and even deepened in the postwar years. And as of 1943 they paid at work, thanks to a new withholding system whereby employers became tax collectors and deducted taxes from paychecks—another feature of the wartime tax regime that became a permanent part of America's remarkably compliant "taxpayer culture."[12]

12. The discussion of the Revenue Act of 1942 is based primarily on W. Elliot Brownlee, "Tax Regimes, National Crisis, and State-building in America," and Carolyn C. Jones,

The administration took several steps to ease the pain of these un-accustomed levies. To avoid a double tax bite when the new withholding system went into effect in 1943, it forgave most taxes due for 1942.[13] It appealed to patriotism with a specially commissioned Irving Berlin jin-gle, "I Paid My Income Tax Today," broadcast endlessly from hundreds of radio stations:

> You see those bombers in the sky
> Rockefeller helped build them and so did I
> I paid my income tax today.[14]

Despite such patriotic emotion, and despite the unimpeachable soundness of the principle of paying for as much of the war as possible out of current taxation, the country stoutly resisted any further tax in-creases. When Roosevelt sought $10.5 billion in additional tax revenues in 1943, Congress presented him with legislation that raised only $2 billion. The Revenue Act of 1943 also contained so many benefits tar-geted on special interests that Roosevelt issued a stinging veto. He con-demned the bill as "not a tax bill but a tax relief bill, providing relief not for the needy but for the greedy."[15] Congress passed the bill over the president's veto—the first time in American history that a revenue law was enacted without presidential approval, and one of several times in the war that Congress overrode the president's will.

In the end, the United States covered about 45 percent of the $304

"Mass-Based Income Taxation: Creating a Taxpayer Culture, 1940–1952," both in Brownlee, ed., *Funding the Modern American State* (New York: Woodrow Wilson Center and Cambridge University Press, 1996), 37–104 and 107–147 respectively; on Sidney Ratner, *Taxation and Democracy in America*, rev. ed. (New York: Science Edi-tions, 1967); John R. Craf, *A Survey of the American Economy, 1940–1946* (New York: North River, 1947); and on *HSUS*, 303, 1107.

13. The new withholding system created a problem; through 1942 the handful of federal taxpayers were always one year in arrears in their tax obligation—paying in 1942, for example, the taxes due on their 1941 incomes. Withholding would keep tax payments current and smooth the flow of revenues into the treasury, but it meant that when the new payroll-deduction system was first implemented in 1943 taxpayers would be simultaneously liable for their new and higher 1943 taxes as well as their 1942 obligation. The solution was a onetime forgiveness of all 1942 taxes under fifty dollars and of 75 percent of any amount over that. That ingenious scheme's prin-cipal architect, New York financier Beardsley Ruml, said that his plan would simply move the tax clock forward, with no fiscal consequence "until the day of Judgment, and at that date no one will give a damn." Polenberg, *War and Society*, 28.

14. Jones, "Mass-Based Income Taxation," 122.

15. *PPA* (1944–45), 80.

billion cost of the war out of current taxation. That was a far higher percentage than in either the Civil War or World War I but markedly lower than the comparable figures in England (53 percent), Canada (55 percent), or Germany (48 percent).[16] Borrowing paid the remainder of the war bill. Some government officials, remembering the hysteria and intimidation that accompanied World War I–era bond sales campaigns, favored a forced-saving plan through compulsory bond purchases, but Roosevelt and Treasury Secretary Morgenthau characteristically preferred a voluntary program. Morgenthau especially favored small-denomination Series E bonds, registered in the bearer's name and therefore replaceable if lost (an important feature in the frantically mobile society that was wartime America). Like taxes, bond sales both provided the treasury with revenue and soaked up purchasing power, helping to keep inflation in check. Morgenthau saw still further virtues in bonds. There were to be "no quotas . . . no hysteria . . . no appeal to hate or fear," Morgenthau directed, but he nevertheless insisted that selling bonds could be used "to sell the war, rather than vice-versa." He envisioned mass bond-sales campaigns as "the spearhead for getting people interested in the war," occasions for patriotic displays that would stamp out isolationist indifference and "make the country war-minded." Artists and entertainers from the concert violinist Yehudi Menuhin to the movie star Betty Grable pitched in to peddle bonds and in the process peddle the war. From a strictly financial point of view, the results were mixed. Wartime government borrowing added up to nearly $200 billion, but only about a quarter of that came out of the pockets of individual bond buyers. The rest came from the vaults of banks and other financial institutions, which held billions of dollars' worth of monetizable government paper at war's end, helping to set the stage for an explosive postwar increase in the money supply. Commercial banks alone increased their holdings of Treasuries from less than $1 billion in 1941 to more than $24 billion in 1945.[17]

AS MONEY BEGAN to pour into the treasury, contracts began to flood out of the military purchasing bureaus — over $100 billion worth in the first six months of 1942, a stupefying sum that exceeded the value

16. Milward, *War, Economy, and Society*, 107.
17. John Morton Blum, *V Was for Victory: Politics and American Culture during World War II* (New York: Harcourt Brace Jovanovich, 1976), 16–21; Vatter, *U.S. Economy in World War II*, 107–9.

of the entire nation's output in 1941. Straining to meet the ambitious goals the president had set, procurement officers loosed their imaginations, abandoned any vestige of managerial discipline, and lost all sight of the larger context within which they were operating. Military purchase orders became hunting licenses, unleashing a jostling frenzy of competition for materials and labor in the jungle of the marketplace. Contractors ran riot in a cutthroat scramble for scarce resources. Makers of cargo vessels gobbled up steel supplies, snarling the construction of warships. Naval purchasing agents robbed aircraft assembly plants of aluminum. Locomotive foundries converted to tank production when locomotives were far more urgently needed. When construction was not stalled outright, it could end up uselessly squandered. A manufacturer who contracted to make a hundred thousand trucks, for example, might be able to deliver twenty-five thousand completed vehicles, but because aircraft and tank plants expropriated tires and spark plugs, the remaining seventy-five thousand trucks sat unfinished and unuseable, having meanwhile wastefully consumed and criminally idled millions of tons of steel that could have built dozens of cargo ships or made billions of bullets. At the same time, troops in training were throwing rocks in the grenade course and using firecrackers to simulate the scarce live ammunition that had to be carefully husbanded for the battlefield.[18]

Economists working under Simon Kuznets at the WPB labored over the summer of 1942 to breathe some realism into the helter-skelter armament program. Kuznets's 140-page report, recommending significant cutbacks and slowdowns in military purchases, landed on General Somervell's desk late on the Saturday afternoon of September 8, 1942, igniting the so-called Feasibility Dispute. His predictable wrath no doubt exacerbated by the hour and day of the report's arrival, Somervell erupted in rage. In a handwritten response to the WPB, he sneered that the economists' analysis was nothing but "an inchoate mass of words" that should be "carefully hidden from the eyes of thoughtful men." Kuznets fired back that Somervell was "adopting an ostrich-like attitude when goals are established that are above probability of achievement." Portions of Kuznets's letter became public when the columnist Drew Pearson began to bruit the confrontation as a fight to the finish between

18. John E. Brigante, *The Feasibility Dispute: Determination of War Production Objectives for 1942 and 1943* (Washington: Committee on Public Administration Cases, 1950), 35. See also Bureau of the Budget, *The United States at War* (Washington: USGPO, 1946), 113–14, and Eliot Janeway, *The Struggle for Survival* (New Haven: Yale University Press, 1951), 308–9.

civilian and military officials. There was no denying the menace that a runaway military procurement program posed to civilian standards of living. The army alone was placing orders for a quarter-billion pairs of trousers, 250 million pairs of underwear, and half a billion socks. By one estimate, fulfilling all the army and navy orders would cut civilian consumption to 60 percent of its level in 1932, the darkest year of the Depression. Vice-President Henry Wallace was not alone in wondering if "the public could be brought to accept such a reduction."[19]

The showdown came in Nelson's office on October 6, 1942. Wallace and OPA chief Leon Henderson squared off for the civilians against Patterson and Somervell for the military. Tempers flared and bitter words flew. "If we can't wage war on 90 billions," Henderson snapped, "we ought to get rid of our present Joint Chiefs, and find some who can." In the end, it was Henderson who got the sack. He resigned in December, to the acute distress of the New Deal faithful, the victim both of his clash with the generals and of the inevitable unpopularity he accrued as director of the price-control program. I. F. Stone lamented that Henderson's departure marked "the second phase of the New Deal retreat, as the alliance with big business in May 1940 marked the first."[20] But if the WPB civilians lost one of their paladins, they nevertheless won some kind of victory. At the end of 1942 the Joint Chiefs agreed to shrink their purchasing program by $13 billion and to extend production schedules for many items. The ground forces bore most of the reduction. Their projected numbers were cut by three hundred thousand, and their scheduled shift to full live-ammunition training was delayed.[21]

The Feasibility Dispute defined a major turning point in the war mobilization program. Eventually, it also helped to underwrite a redefinition of American military strategy. The controversy had forced recognition of the fact that even the enormous American economy was not exempt from the laws of scarcity and the iron necessity of choice. The dispute's resolution fostered a new mechanism for allotting scarce raw materials: the Controlled Materials Plan, announced in November 1942. Instead of allowing each individual contractor to shop willy-nilly for critical materials, bidding up prices and creating production logjams, the new plan gave the major government contracting agencies the power

19. Brigante, *Feasibility Dispute*, 83–86; Polenberg, *War and Society*, 223.
20. Doris Kearns Goodwin, *No Ordinary Time: Franklin and Eleanor Roosevelt: The Home Front in World War II* (New York: Simon and Schuster, 1994), 395.
21. Brigante, *Feasibility Dispute*, 83–86, 105; Smith, *Army and Economic Mobilization*, 156.

to allocate the key metals of copper, aluminum, and steel to their suppliers. The WPB itself was to arbitrate competing claims among those major purchasing agencies. This new scheme brought a measure of order to economic mobilization. It also further advantaged the largest contractors, the favorites of the military and naval bureaus, by making it more difficult than ever for small producers to gain access to needed materials in the open market. The Controlled Materials Plan also concentrated the tough questions about trade-offs at the highest political level, where they could be dealt with more expeditiously and efficiently, though scarcely less urgently, than in the hugger-mugger of the marketplace. Just for that reason, the WPB found itself under excruciating pressure as the cockpit where all the controversies between the various services, between the services and the civilians, and between competing economic sectors, were bitterly contested.

Roosevelt characteristically reacted to the rising pressure on the WPB in October 1942 by creating yet another mobilization body, the Office of Economic Stabilization, which officially metamorphosed into the Office of War Mobilization (OWM) in May 1943. Each was headed in its turn by former South Carolina senator and Supreme Court justice James Byrnes. In a blunt demonstration of the president's sometimes callous administrative techniques, Nelson learned of Byrnes's initial appointment from the news ticker in his WPB office and assumed he was being fired. Nelson in fact lingered on at the WPB until the summer of 1944, when he went down at last in yet another confrontation with the generals, this time over the scheduling of reconversion to civilian production.

With the appointment of Byrnes, Roosevelt openly acknowledged the political dimension of economic mobilization. The crooked timber of humanity, not scarce critical materials, was now recognized as the principal obstacle to efficient production. Byrnes was no businessman. He had neither executive experience nor technical expertise. But he was a consummate political operator. He had begun his long Washington career as a protégé of Pitchfork Ben Tillman, South Carolina's infamously racist baron, and he enjoyed the lavish patronage of his sometime fellow South Carolinian, Bernard Baruch, the Democratic Party's multimillionaire gray eminence. Elected to the House in 1910 and the Senate in 1930, Byrnes had fully mastered the ways of the capital by the time of Roosevelt's assumption of the presidency and had made himself into an indispensable lieutenant for Roosevelt's New Deal. A man of slight build and cool blue-gray eyes, he dominated other men with his hypnotically penetrating gaze. Cocking his head birdlike to one side when he spoke, he had for nearly a decade worked the corridors and offices of the Senate on Roosevelt's behalf, skillfully ringmastering his skeptical southern colleagues in support of the president's reform program. His reward was appointment to the Supreme Court in 1941, but after little more than a year in what the restless Byrnes regarded as the "marble mausoleum" atop Capitol Hill he now left the bench and set up shop as the supreme war mobilizer in the new east wing of the White House. The location of his office served as a potent reminder, in the words of a biographer, "that he was in the presidential, rather than the bureau-cratic, business." "Your decision is my decision," Roosevelt told him. "[T]here is no appeal. For all practical purposes you will be assistant president" — a soubriquet by which Byrnes was soon familiarly known.[22] Though the WPB endured, its influence waned as Byrnes turned his east-wing office into the real command center of the mobilization effort. By mid-1943 Byrnes had his hands securely on the big levers of eco-nomic and political power. Nearly four years after the German invasion of Poland, and a year and a half after Pearl Harbor, America's mobili-zation machinery was at last complete.

The Feasibility Dispute that brought Byrnes to the pinnacle of power along the Potomac converged with two other developments in late 1942, one along the Seine in northern France and the other on the frozen banks of the Volga, deep within the Soviet Union. Together these events changed the very nature of the mobilization program over which "assis-tant president" Byrnes now presided. On August 17, 1942, the U.S. Army's Eighth Air Force carried out its first heavy bomber raid on con-tinental Europe. A squadron of a dozen B-17s attacked railroad mar-shaling yards near Rouen on the lower Seine River. Their bombs caused minimal damage, but the very appearance of American planes in the air over Nazi-held Europe further fed the already ravening ambitions of the advocates of aerial warfare. The second development, far more im-mediately consequential, was the Battle of Stalingrad, a savage four-month ordeal that slaughtered tens of thousands of German and Soviet troops before the exhausted Germans surrendered at last in February 1943. As much as any single battle could be, Stalingrad was the turning point of Hitler's war. It broke the back of the *Wehrmacht's* eighteen-month-old Russian offensive and allowed the Soviets to seize the initia-tive. Stalingrad did not allay all anxieties about Russia's ultimate military and political goals, but it forever laid to rest doubts about Russia's ability

22. David Robertson, *Sly and Able: A Political Biography of James F. Byrnes* (New York: Norton, 1994), 323.

to survive. In the highest reaches of the American government, Stalin-grad also helped to clinch a crucial strategic decision.

Driving the maniacal frenzy of the first year's mobilization effort were the assumptions of the Victory Program of 1941. It had envisioned a Russian collapse and the consequent need to build a mammoth American ground force of 215 divisions. The practical limits on American production that the Feasibility Dispute laid bare, combined with Rouen's fragile promise of a successful air war and Stalingrad's convincing demonstration of Russian staying power, now prompted a thorough rethinking of the Victory Program's premises. Army planners in late 1942 began to scale back their estimates of future troop needs—first to one hundred divisions, then to ninety, a number that by the summer of 1943 was firmly ratified as the uppermost limit of the army's needs. "The strategic basis for this conclusion," writes official army historian Maurice Matloff, "was in part the demonstration by the Soviet armies of their ability to check the German advance. Another significant factor brightening the strategic picture was the improving prospect of gaining air superiority over the Continent. These developments finally made obsolete the initial Victory Program estimates of 1941." The economic basis for that conclusion was the sense of economic limits that the Feasibility Dispute had imposed. With the so-called Ninety-Division Gamble the logic of Roosevelt's "arsenal of democracy" strategy had fully matured. American military planners now irrevocably embraced the concept of a war of machines rather than men. As Matloff writes, the Ninety-Division Gamble cemented into place the core American strategic principle that until the end of 1942 had been hopefully but still somewhat tentatively held: "that the single greatest tangible asset the United States brought to the coalition in World War II was the productive capacity of its industry." The United States now aimed not to field a numerically overwhelming land force but a relatively small one. That force would count for its battle weight not on masses of manpower but on maximum possible mechanization and mobility. Building a smaller army would be compensated by the construction of a gigantic, heavy-fisted air arm: bombers in fantastic numbers that would ultimately carry bombs of unimaginable destructive power.[23]

THE NINETY-DIVISION DECISION, though it settled the key question of the size of the military establishment the nation was building,

23. Maurice Matloff, "The 90-Division Gamble," in Kent Roberts Greenfield, ed., *Command Decisions* (Washington: Department of the Army, 1960), 373.

brought only partial resolution to the conundrum of manpower policy. The gods of war demanded men — but exactly which ones were most needed where and when, in precisely what numbers and, most puzzling of all, whether in uniform or overalls, toting a rifle or tending a machine tool, were questions that had defied easy answers in the war's first year. So, too, and for even longer, did the related question of the degree to which womanpower might take the place of manpower, either in the armed forces or on the factory floor. The riddle of manpower mirrored the perplexities of materials allocation, but a solution like the Controlled Materials Plan was not as easily imposed on human beings as it was on critical metals. The division of responsibilities between the War Manpower Commission (WMC) and the Selective Service System further complicated matters.

The original Selective Service Act of 1940 had registered some sixteen million men between the ages of twenty-one and thirty-six. Amendments in the following two years extended the age limits from eighteen to sixty-five, yielding some forty-three million registrants by the end of 1942. That was by any standard a huge manpower pool, rivaled among the major belligerents only by the Russians. But the military wanted no men over forty-five and strongly preferred to take only those under the age of twenty-six. Those considerations instantly shrank the pool of military eligibles to fewer than thirty million, a number that contracted still further when the needs of the civilian work force, family status, and physical, mental, and educational disqualifications were taken into account. Confusion and compromise beset all efforts to sort out those competing demands in the war's early months. The programs for both military induction and industrial employment were conspicuously deficient in coordination, efficiency, and, most telling, in fairness.

The Selective Service System established guidelines for classifying registrants: Category I for those judged fit for military service, II for those exempted by reason of critical occupation, III for those deferred because they had dependents, and IV for men deemed physically or mentally unqualified. Effective authority over classification and deferment decisions rested with the 6,443 local draft boards. As in World War I, this system was deliberately designed to sustain the illusion of local control and democratic participation and, not least, to diffuse accountability. In case of controversy, Selective Service director Lewis B. Hershey explained, "6,443 local centers absorb the shock."[24]

24. George Q. Flynn, *Lewis B. Hershey, Mr. Selective Service* (Chapel Hill: University of North Carolina Press, 1985), 77.

There was controversy aplenty. Local volunteers composed the boards, prominent men of substance and standing, often veterans of World War I, who were supposed to embody their community's standards of deference and hierarchy and thus legitimate the boards' authority. They could also reflect their community's prejudices: just three southern states, for example (Virginia, North Carolina, and Kentucky), allowed blacks to sit on local boards, and only 250 blacks served nationwide.[25]

A local board's most important and ticklish function was to grant deferments from military service. Contrary to much later mythology, the nation's young men did not step forward in unison to answer the trumpet's call, neither before nor after Pearl Harbor. Deferments were coveted, and their distribution traced a rough profile of the patterns of political power, racial prejudice, and cultural values in wartime America.

No deferments proved more controversial than those claimed by conscientious objectors. In World War I only members of the traditional peace churches (Quakers, Brethren, and Mennonites) had been exempted for military service by reason of conscience. The Selective Service Act of 1940 defined considerably broader grounds for exemption; it released from the obligation to serve any person "who, by reason of religious training and belief, is conscientiously opposed to participation in war in any form." Hershey, who came from Mennonite stock but was not a practicing churchgoer, defined permissive guidelines for conscientious objection: the applicant need not prove membership in a traditional peace church, only that his objection was based on "religious training and belief." More than seventy-thousand young men so described themselves. The Selective Service System honored more than half of those claims and consigned about twenty-five thousand to noncombat military duty and another twelve thousand to "alternative service" in CCC-like Public Service Camps, where they worked without pay on forestry projects, on road building, and in mental hospitals. Jehovah's Witnesses, whose theology led them to oppose this particular war but not violence in general, posed particularly thorny problems for Hershey's boards, and some five thousand Witnesses ended up in jail.[26]

25. Flynn, *Lewis B. Hershey*, 121.
26. *Selective Service System: Conscientious Objection: Special Monograph No. 11* (Washington: USGPO, 1950), 327–28; Mulford Q. Sibley and Philip E. Jacob, *Conscription of Conscience: The American State and the Conscientious Objector, 1940–1947* (Ithaca: Cornell University Press, 1952), 83–84.

Congress imposed the most egregious of the blanket deferments when it succumbed to pressure from the still potent Farm Bloc and passed the Tydings Amendment in November 1942, effectively exempting all agricultural workers from the draft. Nearly two million farm laborers thus hoed and shoveled beyond General Hershey's reach. They made up three times the proportion of the under-twenty-six-year-olds who were deferred for industrial work, though as the sheltering power of occupational exemption became clear, over four million men of all ages sought and received industrial occupational deferments. "Essential occupation lists mushroomed," one authority concludes, with thirty-four "essential" occupations listed in the repair and trade services alone.[27]

The situation of black Americans posed compound problems of equity. At the insistence of black leaders, the Selective Service Act stipulated that "there shall be no discrimination against any person on account of race or color." But because the army remained committed to segregated units, Hershey issued draft calls on a racial basis, reaching into the black community only when it was necessary to bring an all-black outfit up to strength. That practice stretched the outermost boundaries of the law. Furthermore, because the army also remained skeptical about sending blacks into combat, relatively few black units were formed in the first place. (The marines at first refused all black enlistments; the navy took only a few as messmen.) The result was that though blacks represented 10.6 percent of the population, they constituted less than 6 percent of the armed forces at the beginning of 1943. While some three hundred thousand single black men in the prime eligibility pool, I-A, went undrafted, many southern draft boards were eventually compelled to send up married white men for induction, a disparity that provoked bitter resentment in southern black and white communities alike. In his state, Mississippi senator Theodore Bilbo complained to Hershey in the fall of 1942, "with a population of one half Negro and one half white . . . the system that you are now using has resulted in taking all the whites to meet the quota and leaving the great majority of Negroes at home."[28]

Married men had enjoyed exemption from the first draft calls—a provision that by one estimate prompted 40 percent of the twenty-one-year-olds caught in the first registration in late 1940 to marry within six weeks. Hershey declared in February 1942 that he would act on "the

27. Flynn, Lewis B. Hershey, 108.
28. Flynn, Lewis B. Hershey, 119–26; Paula S. Fass, Outside In: Minorities and the Transformation of American Education (New York: Oxford University Press, 1989), 144.

presumption that most of the recent marriages . . . might have been for the purpose of evading the draft." Fathers proved even more untouchable, especially those with children born before Pearl Harbor. Down to early 1944 only 161,000 pre–Pearl Harbor fathers were conscripted. A story circulated about a young couple who named their baby "Weatherstrip" because he kept his father out of the draft. Only late in the war did Hershey finally abolish the exemption for fathers, and in 1944 and 1945 nearly a million fathers were drafted. By war's end one out of every five fathers between the ages of eighteen and thirty-seven was on active duty.[29]

Many youngsters — flushed with patriotic fervor or driven by youthful passion for adventure, or simply motivated by the wish to "choose while you can," as the navy's recruitment slogan put it — did indeed volunteer (the navy and marine corps relied exclusively on volunteers until the end of 1942). But they stepped forward in such unpredictable numbers and in such haphazard patterns that volunteering raised hob with the concept of efficient manpower utilization. Army and navy recruiters pulled in men from all walks of life and sometimes "parked" them in cadet training programs, as a reserve against an uncertain future. The army's Special Training Program absorbed 140,000 young men at its height. The navy's V-12 program signed up seventeen-year-olds and sent them to college for as long as two years, rendering them draftproof when they reached eligibility on their eighteenth birthday. The air corps cadet program by war's end held some two hundred thousand young men who never left home. Those practices indiscriminately depleted the industrial labor pool, complicated military staffing, and raised rankling questions about fairness. One Selective Service official recalled the tense situation in his New England community "when fathers in their middle thirties were being inducted from their stores, garages, and other businesses. The presence of several hundred able-bodied students in uniform in that community created a situation difficult to describe."[30]

All these chronic inefficiencies and inequities were begging for remediation by the end of 1942. In the wake of the Feasibility Dispute and

29. Flynn, *Lewis B. Hershey*, 108; William M. Tuttle Jr., *Daddy's Gone to War: The Second World War in the Lives of America's Children* (New York: Oxford University Press, 1993), 20, 31; Lee Kennett, *G.I.: The American Soldier in World War II* (New York: Charles Scribner's Sons, 1987), 5.
30. Kennett, *G.I.*, 21–22.

in the context of firming up the ninety-division decision, Roosevelt ordered an end to all voluntary enlistments and repealed the marital exemption. On December 5 he placed the Selective Service System under the direct control of Paul McNutt's War Manpower Commission, an obvious step toward a single, coordinated civil-military manpower policy, but one that alarmed Hershey and the military authorities. By delivering both the carrot of deferment and the stick of induction into one pair of hands, Roosevelt hoped to enable McNutt to channel manpower where it could best be utilized. To that end McNutt in early 1943 announced a draconian "work-or-fight" order. Most startling, he ended blanket deferments for fathers. He invoked the quite defensible rationale that occupational status should be a stronger determinant of manpower disposition than family status.

But McNutt's sweeping directive staked out a policy position well beyond the boundaries of what organized labor, General Hershey, or the Congress would tolerate. His work-or-fight order was virtually dead on arrival. Hershey administered the coup de grace. McNutt's order had set the stage for a confrontation between the WMC and the Selective Service System that paralleled the clash between the military and the WPB. Hershey, a career army officer who affected the manner of a village rustic, was in fact an exceptionally wily political infighter. In wartime Washington he first displayed the skills that would sustain him as director of the Selective Service System for three decades, well into the Vietnam era — a tenure in office by a senior political appointee probably exceeded only by J. Edgar Hoover's forty-eight-year stint as director of the FBI, and one that surely touched far more lives. Hershey now flexed his bureaucratic muscle to frustrate McNutt's effort to elevate the WMC over the military's own Selective Service System. He flatly informed McNutt that "I will not transmit any order from you for classification," thus nullifying the WMC's fathers-must-fight announcement. Though he himself had earlier proposed drafting fathers, and would eventually take a million of them, Hershey cunningly lent his support to a congressional bill, passed in December 1943, explicitly protecting them from military service, because the bill also contained provisions preserving Hershey's paramount authority over the military draft. Hershey had fought McNutt to a messy draw. Manpower policy remained divided between civil and military authorities.

Hershey proceeded in 1943 to draft men in accord with the lesser levels and the recomposed configurations targeted in the ninety-division scheme: 7,700,000 for the army, of whom 2 million were now slated for the army air forces; 3,600,000 for the navy, almost 500,000 of them marines. Before 1943 was out he was nearly there: 7,500,000 in the army, 2,800,000 in the navy and marines. Almost one family in five — 18.1 percent — contributed at least one member to the armed forces. All told, more than 16 million men and women served in uniform during the war. A revision to the Selective Service law passed in the week after Pearl Harbor made them liable to service for "the duration of the war," and they served, on average, for nearly three years. For many of them, those war years were the pivot of their lives, a defining moment whose importance advancing age could not diminish, nor whose details could memory dim.[31]

Yet even at those levels, the U.S. Army, especially as a fraction of the U.S. manpower pool, would scarcely be a mighty host: somewhat larger than the Japanese army (5.5 million at war's end), somewhat smaller than the *Wehrmacht* (6.1 million), and less than half the size of the Red Army (which the Germans estimated at more than 12 million by 1945).[32]

WHILE HERSHEY was imposing at least a measure of order on the military side of the manpower equation, something approaching chaos continued to reign on the civilian side. As the remaining pools of unemployed workers swiftly evaporated in 1942, labor markets tightened severely. Competitive bidding for increasingly scarce labor sucked women from their homes and farmers from the countryside into the roaring maw of the booming industrial economy. Labor shortages drove workers from plant to plant, from city to city, even from region to region, in search of fatter paychecks. Their restless mobility wreaked havoc with production schedules, and their giddily levitating wages threatened to kick off a cyclonic inflationary spiral. The administration consequently groped for ways both to reduce labor turnover and to control wages as well as prices.

McNutt's abortive work-or-fight order in 1943 had given brief public display to one scheme for regulating labor that had lurked beneath the surface ever since Pearl Harbor: a comprehensive national service policy

---

31. *HSUS*, 1140; Tuttle, *Daddy's Gone to War*, 31; Flynn, *Lewis B. Hershey*, 85, 100.
32. John Ellis, *World War II: A Statistical Survey* (New York: Facts on File, 1993), 227–28; I.C.B. Dear, ed., *The Oxford Companion to the Second World War* (New York: Oxford University Press, 1995), 1235.

that would lay the government's hand upon all citizens and push them into whatever employment was deemed necessary. Other countries adopted such forced-labor drafts in wartime, and the United States itself had experimented with a feeble version of such a policy in World War I. But coercing labor cut deeply against the American grain, and in any case the Depression years had helped the organized union movement to acquire the kind of political clout that made such a drastic measure difficult to impose. Union leaders and the Roosevelt administration alike strongly preferred less heavy-handed techniques. The West Coast Manpower Plan, devised in the fall of 1943 and generalized elsewhere, brought some reduction in turnover rates by letting contracts only where labor was certified to be available and by regulating job-shifting through a central employment referral service. But the problems of wages and prices, and the exceptionally thorny issues of union prerogatives and union integrity, eluded tidy solution.

All the major union leaders dutifully announced "no-strike" pledges in the days after the Pearl Harbor attack, evincing their desire to play statesmanlike roles in the war crisis, as well as their wariness about their own members' attitudes and their fear of a government clamp-down if they did not put their own house in order. Labor was restless on the eve of the war. Just as in 1937, when the first flush of genuine economic recovery had triggered the massive organizing campaigns in steel and autos, so in 1941 war-borne prosperity had sparked campaigns to complete the union movement's unfinished business. Some two million workers staged more than four thousand strikes in 1941, many of them over organizational issues. Ford recognized the UAW at last in April; the steelworkers unionized Bethlehem Steel; International Harvester, Weyerhauser, and Allis-Chalmers all capitulated to the CIO in the course of that last peacetime year.

Several of those industrial actions in 1941 gave warning about the dangers that lay ahead. Workers walked out of the Allis-Chalmers plant in Milwaukee in the winter of 1940–41 just as the company was gearing up to fulfill a $40 million contract to build turbines for navy destroyers—a chilling display of the capacity of labor disturbances to cripple the rearmament program. Equally ominous, and even more dramatic in its outcome, was a strike in June against North American Aviation's plant in Inglewood, California. The situation at North American was tangled, a jumble of jurisdictional disputes between CIO and AFL organizers trying to come to terms with the thousands of new workers streaming into the aviation industry, with wage and workplace grievances, and with

Communist intrigue.[33] But a work stoppage that threatened to shut down 25 percent of all fighter aircraft production was intolerable to the government, whatever the grounds. At the urging of Secretary Stimson, the administration made an example of the North American strikers. Hershey canceled their occupational deferments and threatened them with immediate induction into the armed services. On June 9, 1941, twenty-five hundred soldiers with fixed bayonets seized the North American plant. The cowed workers soon returned to their lathes and drill presses. But the prospect of having repeatedly to crush labor under the army's mailed fist was not pleasant to contemplate. Neither were the renewed antics of John L. Lewis. He demonstrated his continuing capacity for mischief in 1941 when he called his United Mine Workers out on a nationwide strike to secure the union shop in the so-called captive mines, owned by the steel companies and excluded from the coal settlements of the 1930s. After a long, acrimonious standoff, amid mounting wintertime coal shortages and bitter denunciations of Lewis as a traitor and saboteur, the miners finally went back to work—on December 7, 1941.

Labor had two great fears in wartime: that prices would rise while workers' ability to negotiate wage increases would be curtailed; and that the great industrial unions born in the 1930s would decompose under the triple burden of management pressure, public hostility, and worker indifference. The isolationism of many union leaders, including conspicuously Lewis, was due in large part to their memories of labor's setbacks in the World War I era, when inflation more than ate up all of workers' wage gains and a mood of hyperpatriotism helped management to crush the AFL's great membership drives, notably in steel.

The CIO in particular was an immature, unstable institution in 1941. The very rapidity of its growth left it an organizational hollow shell. Its headquarters had but the thinnest apparatus for managing a far-flung and now highly mobile membership, and in many localities it could field only a skeletal staff. How could this young, untried union cope with the vast demographic surges that were washing over the nation's wartime workplaces? CIO leaders were rightly apprehensive that the

33. The Communist Party USA still toed the official Moscow line that Germany was a Soviet ally and should be protected from British and American imperialist harassment; ironically, the Germans invaded Russia virtually in the midst of the North American strike, prompting an instantaneous reversal of Moscow's position. Thereafter the CPUSA became among the most impassioned advocates of peaceable labor relations and maximum production.

millions of new workers crowding through the factory gates into the throbbing war plants lacked the kind of commitment to unionism that had made possible the historic gains of the 1930s. North American Aviation employed so many green, first-time industrial workers at its troubled Inglewood, California, plant that shift change was said to resemble a high school dismissal. To the teenagers, women, blacks, Dust Bowl refugees, and other rural migrants who now thronged into their first-ever industrial jobs, the concepts of worker solidarity, wage guarantees, seniority rules, pay differentials, collective bargaining, jurisdictional boundaries, shop stewards, grievance procedures, and union-consciousness—the very stuff of trade union life and the union movement's reasons for being—were alien and irrelevant. In the let-'er-rip, booming, steady-work, high-wage environment in which these new workers found themselves, who needed a union?

Against this backdrop the administration took three significant policy steps affecting labor in the first months of 1942. Faced with evidence of mounting price inflation, Leon Henderson's OPA announced its General Maximum Price Regulation in April, soon ubiquitously though not always fondly referred to as "General Max." It capped prices as of March. In a companion initiative, the National War Labor Board in July settled a wage dispute with the lesser steelmakers—Bethlehem, Republic, Youngstown, and Inland—by imposing a settlement limiting wage increases to the rise in the cost of living between January 1941 and May 1942: about 15 percent, a number soon generalized to all wage settlements. The intended effect of these twin measures, General Max and the Little Steel Formula, was to preserve workers' standards of living for the duration of the conflict. Whether that preservation was better described as a "freeze" or as "stabilization" was a matter of dispute. However it was described, the administration's wage-and-price control policies represented a significant departure from the mildly redistributive thrust of the New Deal, which had sought to redress imbalances among various social and economic sectors, not hold their economic relationships constant.

These wage-and-price policies soon ran afoul of the usual difficulties, including hard-to-monitor evasions and political interference, that beset all command economies. Though General Max put a fairly effective lid on some commodity prices, it was easily frustrated in many product lines by model changes or relabeling. Congress dealt pricing policy one of its first and most damaging blows when it once again truckled to the Farm Bloc in early 1942 and legislated ceilings on farm prices that had no relation to the General Max directive. Taking the farmers' exceptionally prosperous years 1910–14 as the baseline for defining the parity ratio between agricultural and industrial prices, the legislators mandated crop price ceilings at 110 percent of parity. Only extensive government subsidies kept something of a damper on food bills in neighborhood markets, as the administration bought crops at parity prices and sold them to retailers at a loss. Consumers thus paid less at the grocer's but more in taxes, while farmers waxed fat. As for wages, job reclassification, premium pay for specified shifts, and overtime payments were all ways to end-run the nominal wage freeze.

Seeking to contain these various evasive maneuvers, Roosevelt tried to bring the farmers to heel and stiffen the spines of his price and wage regulators with a "hold-the-line" wage-and-price order in April 1943. Yet by war's end farm prices had risen nearly 50 percent. The overall inflation rate was 28 percent, a much better performance than World War I's 100 percent rate, but still well short of the regulators' ambitions. Average weekly earnings, thanks more to overtime than to wage gains, went up 65 percent; adjusted for inflation, manufacturing workers enjoyed about 27 percent more real income in 1945 than they had in 1940. Corporate profits, meanwhile, nearly doubled.[34]

With the no-strike pledge, unions had denied themselves their historically most powerful weapon. With the Little Steel Formula, the government had sharply confined their power to influence wages, the item that most interested their members. CIO chief Philip Murray damned the Little Steel agreement less because of its strictly economic restrictions than because it threatened to enfeeble the unions by leaving them no legitimate role to play. Wage controls, he warned, conjuring the unsettling prospect that John L. Lewis's fallen star might rise again, "would decrease the prestige of those labor leaders who have supported the President," and would "leave the field wide open for the isolationists in the union movement and result in chaotic labor conditions."[35]

But in June 1942 the labor movement received a notable consolation prize for these debilitating restrictions. In the third and most cunning of the government's major labor policy pronouncements, the National War Labor Board promulgated its supremely important "maintenance-of-membership" rule. That regulation provided that in any place of em-

---

34. *HSUS*, 210–11; Nelson Lichtenstein, *Labor's War at Home: The CIO in World War II* (Cambridge: Cambridge University Press, 1982), 111.

35. Lichtenstein, *Labor's War at Home*, 77.

ployment already covered by a union contract, all new employees would be automatically enrolled in the union unless they explicitly requested otherwise in the first fifteen days on the job. The maintenance-of-membership ruling was a fabulous boon for organized labor. Employers had long hated the concept of mandatory union membership—the so-called closed shop. Now the NWLB required not only that employers live with the closed shop but that they play the role of enforcers, collecting union dues and firing workers who fell behind in their payments. At a stroke, the government's maintenance-of-membership rule not only provided powerful protections against union disintegration; it also allowed the unions easily to capture all those new workers freshly recruited for war production. At the same time, maintenance-of-membership became the principal mechanism by which labor was kept in line. What government gave, government could take away. Fear of losing the maintenance-of-membership guarantee worked powerfully to restrain the militancy of labor leaders.

The Roosevelt administration offered labor dramatically impressive evidence that it would honor the maintenance-of-membership rule when the Montgomery Ward Company tried to repudiate its provisions. Leading a contingent of steel-helmeted U.S. soldiers, Attorney General Francis Biddle personally entered the Chicago office of Montgomery Ward president Sewell L. Avery on April 27, 1944. He ordered the troops to eject Avery and seized control of the company in the name of the government. "To hell with the government," the fuming Avery shouted as he was being toted out the door of his office. Glaring at Biddle, he summoned the most contemptuous words he could think of: "You— New Dealer!" he spat. A widely published photograph of the slight, elderly Avery being carted away by uniformed troops brought down a torrent of abuse on Biddle from conservatives. The *Chicago Tribune* caricatured him as a black-capped executioner. But Biddle's flamboyant assertion of federal supremacy had potently demonstrated to labor the indispensable importance of its wartime partnership with government.[36] Under the WLB's benign patronage, union membership vaulted upward, from fewer than ten million to nearly fifteen million over the course of the war.

For all of its efficacy in calming labor and promoting union growth, the maintenance-of-membership rule was a devil's bargain, and labor leaders knew it. The unions gave up effective power in wartime in

36. Francis Biddle, *In Brief Authority* (Garden City, N.Y.: Doubleday, 1962), 314–18.

exchange for mushrooming membership rolls and the prospect of enhanced influence later. As historian Alan Brinkley concludes, "the labor movement had become, in effect, a ward of the state."[37] One labor leader, John L. Lewis, would have none of it. Lewis's United Mine Workers in fact reaped no benefit from the rule, since they already enjoyed the privilege of a closed shop. Unconstrained by the fear of being stripped of the government guarantee, Lewis had little to lose. In 1943, openly scorning both the Little Steel Formula and the hold-the-line order, he demanded a two-dollar-a-day wage increase for his coal miners. He sought as much to loosen the NWLB's stranglehold over labor relations as to put more money in miners' pockets. When the coal operators refused to cave in, he hurled defiance in their face, and in the NWLB's too. Lewis ordered his half-million UMW members out of the pits. The government seized the mines and blustered about drafting the miners. As coal stocks dwindled, steel mills banked their blast furnaces and railroads cut back their schedules. Newspapers condemned the miners as traitors and heaped vilification on Lewis. An air force pilot reportedly said: "I'd just as soon shoot down one of those strikers as shoot down Japs—they're doing just as much to lose the war for us." *Stars and Stripes*, the army's official newspaper, editorialized: "John L. Lewis, damn your coal-black soul."[38] Some members of Congress demanded his indictment for treason. Polls confirmed that he was the most unpopular man in America. (Eighty-seven percent of respondents had an "unfavorable opinion" of him in June 1943.)[39] In the end, after a messy struggle that dragged on into 1944, Lewis won the wage concessions for his miners. But it was a Pyrrhic victory; the losses in public confidence and political support for labor were immeasurable. When Lewis's defiant example helped to trigger more labor disturbances, including a railroad strike that led to federal seizure of the roads in December 1943, President Roosevelt despaired of his self-absorbed countrymen's commitment to the war effort. "One of the best things that could happen," he remarked darkly to his presumably

37. Alan Brinkley, *The End of Reform: New Deal Liberalism in Depression and War* (New York: Knopf, 1995), 200.
38. William L. O'Neill, *A Democracy at War: America's Fight at Home and Abroad in World War II* (New York: Free Press, 1993), 210–11. Harry S. Truman later opined that "Lewis ought to have been shot in 1942, but Franklin didn't have the guts to do it" (213).
39. Cantril, 397.

astonished cabinet, "would be to have a few German bombs fall here to wake us up."[40]

By mid-1943 the country had had a bellyful of John L. Lewis. Egged on by the rising tide of public anger over the coal strike, a wrathful Congress passed the Smith-Connally War Labor Disputes Act in June. Ostensibly a war measure, it actually dealt the labor movement a blow that conservatives had been itching to land since the passage of the Wagner Act in 1935. Capitalizing on Lewis's plummeting reputation, they took their revenge for nearly a decade's worth of labor gains. The Act broadened presidential authority to seize struck war plants, imposed a thirty-day "cooling-off" period for strikes, established criminal penalties for strike leaders, required majority approval of a union's membership before a strike, and, for good measure, forbade union contributions to political campaigns in wartime. Not least because of that last provision, a transparent effort to slap at Roosevelt and stem the growth in labor's political influence that the New Deal had fostered, the president vetoed the bill. Congress speedily repassed it, in another pointed reminder of Roosevelt's loss of control over the Congress and the antilabor swing in public sentiment since the reforming heyday of the Depression years. "I think," Roosevelt remarked glumly to Eleanor, "the country has forgotten we ever lived through the 1930s."[41]

FOR MANY AMERICANS on the home front, the Depression years did seem but a distant, if painful, memory. The war did not merely banish the decade-long scourge of unemployment. It also provided jobs for the 3.25 million new job-seekers who reached employable age during the conflict, as well as to another 7.3 million workers, half of them women, who would not normally have sought work even in a full-employment peacetime economy. Thanks to the government's cost-plus contracting practices and the ubiquitous availability of overtime, wartime jobs paid fabulously well, especially for Americans who had suffered through the cramped years of the 1930s. Even more than the purpose-built programs of the New Deal, this economic sea-change bestowed an unprecedented sense of security on men and women who had long made do without it. "Going to work in the navy yard," one

40. Frank Freidel, *Franklin D. Roosevelt: Rendezvous with Destiny* (Boston: Little, Brown, 1990), 496.
41. Goodwin, *No Ordinary Time*, 443.

shipyard laborer in Portsmouth, Virginia, recalled, "I felt like something had come down from heaven. I went from forty cents an hour to a dollar an hour. . . . At the end of the war I was making two seventy-five an hour. . . . I couldn't believe my good fortune. . . . I was able to buy some working clothes for a change, buy a suit. . . . It just made a different man out of me. . . . After all the hardships of the Depression, the war completely turned my life around." Another man, recollecting his wartime boyhood in Portland, Oregon, remembered that "for the first time we began to have money. . . . You started to think you could do things. We used to go out to a restaurant now and then, where we would never do that before the war. We hardly ever went to picture shows during the Depression; now I did all the time. . . . My mother saved enough money to buy a modest home. That was the first home we ever bought."[42]

Rationing curbed the purchase of a few items—notably meat, butter, coffee, tires, and gasoline—forcing some changes in menus and life habits. Regulations aimed at conserving scarce materials also wrought some conspicuous changes in fashion. To save scarce fabrics, the War Production Board banned double-breasted suits, vests, trouser cuffs, and patch pockets for men; pleated skirts disappeared, hemlines went up, and women's bathing costumes got skimpier, promoting the widespread adoption of the previously rare two-piece swimming suit. Some items disappeared altogether. The WPB sharply restricted new private home construction in 1942 and prohibited the manufacture of automobiles for private use. Autoworkers organized little ceremonies as the last motorcar chassis moved down the assembly lines on February 10, 1942, then proceeded to rip out the old dies and stamping presses and prepare for weapons production.

Even with a handful of such restrictions, the war created a glittering consumer's paradise. Though Roosevelt had warned that the nation could not afford to build a war economy on top of a consumer economy, in fact the United States managed to do exactly that—mounting a robustly expanding military production machine atop a steadily rising curve of civilian output. Three developments underwrote the war's fantastic explosion of goods: full resource utilization, including both un-

42. Mark Jonathan Harris et al., *The Homefront: America during World War II* (New York: G. P. Putnam's Sons, 1984), William Pefley interview, 39–40, 241; James Covert interview, 240.

employed workers and idle plants; the diversion of resources, especially underutilized agricultural labor, from lower- to higher-productivity employments; and notable gains in productivity, fueled by burgeoning investment in more efficient plant and equipment, increased reliance on electrical power, and technological improvements. By one estimate American output per worker hour was double that in Germany, five times that in Japan.

Despite the occasionally bitter tension between the administrators who oversaw them, the civilian and the military sectors alike benefited from these economic improvements, even if disproportionately. War spending skyrocketed from $3.6 billion in 1940, about 2 percent of national product, to a peak of $93.4 billion in 1944, by which date roughly half of the nation's productive energy was flowing to military uses. Yet in that same span of time, civilian purchases of goods and services managed to grow by 12 percent.[43] Most Americans had never had it so good. They started half a million new businesses. They went to movies and restaurants with unhabitual frequency. They bought books, recordings, cosmetics, pharmaceuticals, jewelry, and liquor in record volumes. Racing fans wagered two and a half times more on the horses in 1944 than they had in 1940. Housewives shopped at well-stocked supermarkets, eleven thousand of them newly built during the war. The war even narrowed the gap between rural and urban living standards that had been widening for nearly half a century. "As farm prices got better and better," a young woman from Idaho remembered, "the farmers suddenly became the wealth of the community. . . . Farm times became good times. . . . We and most other farmers went from a tarpaper shack to a new frame house with indoor plumbing. Now we had an electric stove instead of a woodburning one, and running water at the sink where we could do the dishes; and a hot water heater; and nice linoleum. . . . We bought a vacuum cleaner too. . . . [It] had a little gadget with a jar on it that sprayed floor wax, and, oh, God that was really wonderful. It was

43. Bureau of the Budget, *The United States at War* (Washington: USGPO, 1946); Mark Harrison, "Resource Mobilization for World War II: The U.S.A., U.K., U.S.S.R., and Germany," *Economic History Review* 2d ser. 16 (1988): 171–92; Milward, *War, Economy, and Society*, especially 63ff.; and Smith, *Army and Economic Mobilization*. The WPB estimated that labor productivity in the United States increased by 25 percent during the four war years, a remarkable gain, accounting for a third of the total increase in output; see Milward, 230.

just so modern we couldn't stand it."[44] Retail sales ascended to a record high in 1943 and then went higher still in 1944. On a poignantly symbolic date, December 7, 1944, the third anniversary of Pearl Harbor, the thousands of cash registers in the Macy's department store chain rang up the highest volume of sales in the giant retailer's history.[45]

That civilian consumption increased at all in the United States was a singularly American achievement. In Britain personal consumption shrank by 22 percent. In the Soviet Union, the third Grand Alliance partner, the home-front experience was nearly the opposite of that in the United States—massive invasion, followed by a crash mobilization program characterized by harshly regulated scarcity rather than the Americans' loosely supervised abundance. While the Americans fought the war from an ever-expanding economic base, the Russians were the only people forced to fight the war on a steadily diminishing one, a circumstance that inflicted large and punishing transfers from the civilian to the military sector. As German armies advanced over the Soviet agricultural heartland, Russian food output fell by two-thirds. Even in areas the *Wehrmacht* did not reach, Russians by the millions slid into agonies of squalor and deprivation; many starved.[46] In Germany and Japan as well the demands of war production, not to mention Allied bombers and submarines, inevitably encroached upon civilian production, sharply degrading standards of living. Both the Axis powers devoted well over half of their productive capacity to the war effort by war's end. Over the course of the war, civilian consumption fell by nearly 20 percent in Germany and 26 percent in Japan.[47] Only in America was it different. The United States, alone among all the combatant societies, enjoyed guns and butter too—and both of them in unrivaled quantities.

NATIONAL ECONOMIES, like people, have their own distinctive personalities. America's singular economic character in World War II was defined first of all by its matchless plenty, by the prodigious quantity of resources it could command and the avalanche of goods it could pour out. From that central fact flowed the credibility of Roosevelt's strategy of "overwhelming" superiority in the implements of war, as well as the unique achievement of expanding both the civilian and military

44. Harris et al., *Homefront*, Laura Briggs interview, 164.
45. Blum, *V Was for Victory*, 98.
46. Richard Overy, *Why the Allies Won* (New York: Norton, 1995), 206; Milward, *War, Economy, and Society*, 92ff.
47. Bureau of the Budget, *United States at War*, 509.

sectors in wartime. So plentiful were American resources that what the American economy lacked in physical materials it simply created. Entirely new industries came into being, notably synthetic rubber. When Japan seized Malaya and the Dutch East Indies, cutting the United States off from virtually all its usual sources of natural rubber, the government invested some $700 million in fifty-one spanking-new synthetic plants, enough to replace the annual harvest from millions upon millions of rubber trees. The Farm Bloc managed to compromise the efficiency of the synthetic rubber program by insisting that some portion of the essential ingredient of butadiene be derived from alcohol rather than the more sensible chemical base of petroleum. Even with that politically imposed encumbrance, American rubber companies more than made up for the lost imports. By 1944 they were producing some eight hundred thousand tons of the synthetic material; one sprawling, seventy-seven-acre West Virginia facility alone accounted for more than 10 percent of the total.

But the American "production miracle" owed to more than just a plethora of resources. Precisely how those resources were used made a difference too. The German armaments minister, Albert Speer, shrewdly assessed the peculiar nature of the American economy in a memorandum to Hitler in 1944. The war, he said, was a "contest between two systems of organization." The Americans, he insisted, "knew how to act with organizationally simple methods and therefore achieved greater results, whereas we were hampered by superannuated forms of organization and therefore could not match the others' feats. . . . If we did not arrive at a different system of organization . . . it would be evident to posterity that our outmoded, tradition-bound, and arthritic organizational system had lost the struggle."[48]

Speer took accurate measure of his adversary's economic system, as well as of his own. It was universally understood, as the economic historian Alan Milward has explained, "that the gain in output was far greater than 10 percent if an armament was produced to only 90 percent rather than to 100 percent, of the specifications."[49] In the inescapable trade-off between quality and quantity, the Germans characteristically chose the former, the Americans the latter. The *Wehrmacht* counted for its margin of victory on "qualitative superiority," on precision-made, flawlessly performing, high-standard weapons. It encouraged special

48. Albert Speer, *Inside the Third Reich* (New York: Macmillan, 1970), 213.
49. Milward, *War, Economy, and Society*, 186.

ordering and custom designing that frustrated long production runs and thereby prevented optimal resource utilization. Until Speer brought a modicum of efficiency to the German production effort late in the war, the Germans were making 425 different kinds of aircraft, 151 types of trucks, and 150 different motorcycles.[50] The Americans, in contrast, consciously eschewed variety and willingly sacrificed some measure of quality in order to achieve higher production numbers: "quantitative superiority." Given their national "style" of production, the Germans typically excelled at performance-enhancing improvements in machine-tool technology and metallurgy. Though the Americans also ultimately proved capable of some epochal scientific and technical breakthroughs, they innovated most characteristically and most tellingly in plant layout, production organization, economies of scale, and process engineering. If Germany aimed at the perfection of many things, America aspired to the commodification of virtually everything.

In part, the Americans made a virtue of necessity. Their wartime preference for generic, high-volume output over specially engineered, high-performance armaments flowed in significant measure from the historical nature of the American work force, disproportionately composed of ill-educated immigrants with scant industrial skills. From the dawn of the industrial revolution in the United States, the characteristics of America's working class had placed a premium on organizing production around simple repetitive tasks that did not demand technical adeptness or extensive training. Henry Ford's clattering automobile assembly line, tended by gangs of often unlettered Polish and Italian immigrants, Appalachian whites, and transplanted southern black sharecroppers, was the archetypal example of America's peculiar industrial style. From its introduction in 1908 through the 1920s, Ford's Model T ascended to a near-mythological status as the characteristic American product. Ford manufactured some fifteen million Model T's and made the United States into the most motorized society in the world by perfecting his assembly-line methods, steadily lowering his production costs and his selling price, and putting his simple car within the average workingman's financial reach. Frederick Winslow Taylor and other "efficiency experts" had tried to give Ford's production practices a systematic rationale and mantle them with the dignity of management theory. Fordism was in many ways a dehumanizing, impersonal production method, long vilified in books like Aldous Huxley's *Brave New World*, caricatured in films

50. Overy, *Why the Allies Won*, 201.

like Charlie Chaplin's *Modern Times* — and bitterly contested by the craft unions affiliated with the American Federation of Labor. But for better or worse, it was a system that had taken deeper root in America than in any other industrialized country, and it had proved its capacity to deliver the goods. Now, in the heat of war, the distinctive national genius for that way of working, already an American signature, spectacularly blossomed.

No wartime product better exemplified the American talent for mass production than the Liberty Ship. In a perfectly apt tribute, Donald Nelson called it "the Model T of the seas." Others, including naval aficionado Franklin Roosevelt, called it an ugly duckling. By whatever name, the Liberty Ship was the workhorse of both the British and the American merchant fleets: a 440-foot-long vessel that could steam at a sluggish ten knots and into whose five holds a skilled cargo master could pack 300 freight cars, 2,840 jeeps, 440 tanks, 230 million rounds of rifle ammunition, or 3.4 million servings of C-rations. Swinging the traditional bottle of champagne, Mrs. Henry A. Wallace, wife of the vice-president, christened the first Liberty Ship, appropriately named the *Patrick Henry*, in Baltimore's Bethlehem-Fairfield shipyard on December 30, 1941. It was one of sixty vessels ordered by Britain to make up for losses in the Battle of the Atlantic. To assemble its 3,425-ton steel hull, 2,725 tons of plate, and 50,000 castings, the many men and the handful of women who made the *Patrick Henry* had toiled for 355 days.

Just six months later, in mid-1942, shipyard gangs could take a Liberty Ship from keel-laying to launch in less than a third of that time, 105 days. By 1943 construction crews were splashing Liberty Ships from scratch in forty-one days. In November 1942 workers in Henry Kaiser's mammoth Richmond, California, shipyard put together one ship, the *Robert E. Peary*, complete with life jackets and coat hangers aboard, in exactly four days, fifteen hours, and twenty-six minutes. The *Peary* was a publicity stunt, but it augured a further reduction in average construction time at the extraordinarily productive Richmond yard to just seventeen days.[51]

Admirers dubbed Kaiser "Sir Launchalot" for his prodigies of ship construction, and in many ways Kaiser was the very model of the modern manufacturer, a quintessentially American big-time operator for whom the era of the Depression and the war — and the emergence of

51. Marilynn S. Johnson, *The Second Gold Rush: Oakland and the East Bay in World War II* (Berkeley: University of California Press, 1993), 66.

big government—opened dazzling opportunities. Kaiser became a war-time symbol of entrepreneurial energy and the glories of the free enter-prise system, but he was also a creature of government, the living em-bodiment of what later came to be known as the military-industrial complex. Well before Pearl Harbor triggered the flood of government war orders, Kaiser had erected a business empire on government con-tracts. His was one of the fabled Six Companies that built Boulder (later Hoover) Dam, the biggest public works project to date in American history and a venture that yielded Kaiser some $10 million in after-tax profits. In the New Deal years, government paid Kaiser and the Six Companies more millions to build Bonneville and Grand Coulee dams on the Columbia River, Shasta Dam on the Sacramento, and the great bridges across San Francisco Bay. From his suite in Washington's Shore-ham Hotel, Kaiser built bridges of his own to the federal officers who signed the big contracts. When the war came, few businessmen were better placed than Kaiser to exploit its rich possibilities for gain. With astonishing speed and with the government's money, he threw up sprawling shipyards at Portland and Vancouver along the Columbia and at Richmond on San Francisco Bay. An RFC loan helped him to erect a gigantic new steel mill at Fontana, in southern California, to keep the yards supplied with steel.

The Richmond shipyard was a monument to Kaiser's all-American production techniques, and Richmond itself became a prototypical ex-ample of the boom towns that pulsed to life in the months after Pearl Harbor. Abandoning the traditional method of building a ship from the keel upward, rib by rib, plate by plate, and rivet by rivet, Kaiser adopted techniques developed in his prewar dam-construction ventures, espe-cially prefabrication. He laid out the huge Richmond facility on the grid pattern distinctive to American cities, especially those in the West, with numbered and lettered streets. Behind the several shipyards at the water's edge, streets and rail lines rayed back as far as a mile from shore to great assembly sheds. There the huge superstructures of several ships at a time inched forward along assembly lines, parts and components fed into the sheds by overhead conveyors from still more subassembly plants beyond. Giant cranes eventually lifted completed superstructure sections and bulkheads, already plumbed, wired, and finished, onto the hull, which was not riveted together but welded—a highly innovative technique whose merits were hotly contested by many naval architects. The enor-mous Richmond complex crawled with tens of thousands of workers, many of them first-time industrial employees—men as well as women, young and old, black and white, including the Oakies, Arkies, and Texies who had drifted into California in the Depression years or rushed to the coast in search of wartime jobs. A woman shipyard worker from Iowa described the Richmond yard as "such a huge place, something I had never been in. People from all walks of life, all coming and going and working, and the noise. The whole atmosphere was overwhelming to me."[52]

The history of the Kaiser shipyard at Richmond recapitulated in the compressed compass of the war's several months the saga of mass industrial production, with all its possibilities and problems, that had taken decades to unfold at Ford. Assembly-line prefabrication fractured the ancient art of shipbuilding into a series of discrete processes. An individual worker performed only a few basic tasks, a construction method that deskilled many occupations but optimally used the novice workers who thronged into the shipyard's employment office. Seasoned journeyman electricians, for example, might once have strung together an entire vessel's wiring system. Now neophyte workers were given brief electrical training courses and assigned to a single specific job, like cabin lighting or control panels. Replacing riveting with the much less technically demanding technique of welding opened up a whole new category of employment for women, who constituted 40 percent of the welders at Richmond.

Predictably, the American Federation of Labor's affiliated unions resented Kaiser shipyards' wholesale assault on traditional craft specializations, just as the International Association of Machinists (IAM) had at North American Aviation. As the IAM had done at North American, the Boilermakers Union at Kaiser took advantage of the maintenance-of-membership rule and enrolled all those thousands of new workers. But at Richmond as at Inglewood, the AFL affiliates stuck those new members, particularly if they were female or black, into auxiliaries where they had little voice in the union's affairs. Their membership dues amounted to little more than a fee they paid for the right to work. Kaiser, meanwhile, tried to dampen labor turnover by extending unprecedented benefits to his workers, especially health care — the origins of the postwar era's most noted health maintenance organization, a war-born creation destined to outlive Kaiser's industrial empire, the Kaiser Permanente Health Plan. The combined effect of the AFL's hostility and Kaiser's paternalistic solicitude toward workers, as historian Marilynn Johnson concludes, heightened workers' distrust of unions and encouraged many

---

52. Johnson, *Second Gold Rush*, 63.

employees, especially if they were blacks or women, "to see employers — rather than unions — as the true guardians of their interests." Those attitudes did not bode well for organized labor in the postwar era, but they did open the door to a "benefits revolution," a new era of corporate welfare in which perquisites like Kaiser's health plan became standard employment practices — and something in the gift of employers, not of unions, nor of the government.[53]

Kaiser's shipbuilding techniques did not always make for seaworthy ships; at least one foundered at the pier before sailing, and seamen lived in dread that the welded hulls would split open in heavy seas, as some tragically did. But what they lacked in artful design and elegant construction the Liberty Ships more than made up in the poetry of numbers. Some twenty-seven hundred Liberty Ships slipped down the ways in the four years after Mrs. Wallace wetted the bow of the *Patrick Henry*, almost a third of them from Kaiser's yards. They carried guns to the marines in the Pacific, planes and medical supplies to the army in Europe, trucks to the Russians, food and tanks to the British. Some were pressed into service as hospital ships and freshwater distilling plants. Other shipyards, adopting their own versions of the techniques that Kaiser had perfected and employing nearly two million workers by war's end, turned out another three thousand ships of all types, including no fewer than 1,556 naval vessels.

Not to be outdone by the upstart Kaiser, Henry Ford himself, seventy-eight years old as the war began and a crusty icon of industrialized America, erected a gargantuan war installation of his own some thirty-five miles southwest of Detroit along a meandering creek named Willow Run. Like Richmond, "The Run" was an instant facility. The foundations of its L-shaped sixty-seven-acre main building sprouted almost overnight out of bucolic Washtenaw County's prairie farmland in March 1941. Eight months later, the first of the plant's eighty-five hundred B-24 bombers rolled off the end of the mile-long assembly line. Like Richmond, too, The Run was huge, a monument to American mass, muscle, and know-how. Its surreal scale inspired countless wartime ovations to the American production miracle. One awed visitor found it "impossible in words to convey the feel and smell and tension of Willow Run under full headway. . . . The roar of the machinery, the special din of the riveting gun absolutely deafening nearby, the throbbing crash of the giant

53. Johnson, *Second Gold Rush*, 82.

metal presses . . . the far-reaching line of half-born skyships growing wings under swarms of workers, and the restless cranes swooping overhead." Novelist Glendon Swarthout evoked The Run's "immensity, insane, overpowering immensity." Famed aviator Charles Lindbergh called it "a sort of Grand Canyon of the mechanized world." "Bring the Germans and Japs in to see it," boasted Ford's production chief, Charles Sorenson. "Hell, they'll blow their brains out."[54]

The Run vacuumed up workers from the midwestern industrial heartland and from the gutted hollows of Appalachia, though Ford's indifference to providing amenities like adequate housing badly exacerbated problems of labor turnover and kept production runs beneath predictions. Ford put them to work making airplanes the way he made cars and the way Kaiser made ships, by dividing and subdividing the manufacturing and assembly processes into hundreds of repetitive tasks. At peak operation more than forty thousand men and women toiled at The Run, including midgets specially recruited to work in the cramped wing spaces. By 1944 Willow Run's crews were rolling a B-24 through the main assembly shed's gaping exit and out on to the airfield every sixty-three minutes.

What the Liberty Ship was to the sea, the B-24 was to the air. Produced in greater quantity than any other American aircraft, it was the main battlewagon of the army air forces' bomber fleet. And like the Liberty Ship, the B-24 traded numbers for performance. Charles Lindbergh labeled an early production model "the worst piece of metal aircraft construction I have ever seen."[55] With a combat range of three thousand miles and an operational ceiling above thirty-five thousand feet, the B-24's specifications ostensibly exceeded those of its stablemate, the B-17. But though it could supposedly fly higher and further, it lacked the armament and handling characteristics of the Flying Fortress, which most American pilots preferred to fly.

All told, American war plants delivered some 18,000 B-24s, almost half of them from Willow Run, while building 12,692 B-17s and 3,763 B-29s, which went into production only late in the war. The soaring demands of the air war, especially after the decision at Casablanca to mount the round-the-clock Combined Bomber Offensive, drew more

54. Clive, *State of War*, 30–31; Goodwin, *No Ordinary Time*, 363.
55. *The Wartime Journals of Charles A. Lindbergh* (New York: Harcourt Brace Jovanovich, 1970), 645.

than two million workers into the aircraft industry. At plants in Seattle, San Diego, and Wichita, as well as at Willow Run, they produced 299,293 airplanes between 1940 and 1945, at a cost of some $45 billion dollars, nearly a quarter of the war's $183 billion munitions bill. At maximum output in 1944, the 96,318 military and naval aircraft that poured out of American factories exceeded the combined production in that year of Germany and Japan, as well as Britain.[56]

American armaments output surged passed that of Britain in the summer of 1942. By 1944 it was six times greater. The United States was then producing 60 percent of the Allies' munitions and 40 percent of all the world's arms. More than a quarter of all Britain's implements of war were coming from the United States. By war's end the Americans supplied as much as 10 percent of Russia's military needs, including 1,966 locomotives, 7,669 miles of track, 350,000 trucks, 77,900 jeeps, and 956,000 miles of telephone cable.[57]

By 1943 the United States had completed its administrative apparatus for managing economic mobilization, revised its strategic plan and estimates of force requirements, stabilized its manpower and labor problems, and erected the factories and recruited the workers necessary to pour out the greatest arsenal of weaponry the world had ever seen. The military production machine was running in such high gear by mid-1943 that Donald Nelson tried to slow it down. He began to plan for "reconversion," the transition back to a peacetime economy. Military authorities resisted vigorously. Brehon Somervell contemptuously dismissed the civilians who in his eyes were prematurely dreaming of peace. "They have never been bombed," Somervell said, accurately enough. "They have little appreciation of the horrors of war and only in a small percentage of instances do they have enough hate."[58] In the face of sentiments like those, stoutly seconded by Henry Stimson and all the military and naval chiefs, Nelson's tentative effort to begin reconversion flopped. The engines of the military economy roared on, pounding out by the war's end a fantastic statistical litany: 5,777 merchant ships, 1,556 naval vessels, 299,293 aircraft, 634,569 jeeps, 88,410 tanks, 11,000 chain saws, 2,383,311 trucks, 6.5 million rifles, 40 billion bullets. By comparison, Germany made 44,857 tanks and 111,767 air-

56. Craven and Cate 6:331, 350.
57. Milward, War, Economy, and Society, 67–74.
58. Polenberg, War and Society, 229–30.

craft; Japan a handful of tanks and 69,910 planes; Britain, over the much longer period of 1934 to 1945, just 123,819 military aircraft.[59]

IN ALL THAT STUPENDOUS NIAGARA of numbers, the figure that in the end weighed most heavily in the scales of war and still leaps dramatically from the pages of history's ledger book is, simply, two—the two atomic bombs that brought the fighting to its awful crescendo at Hiroshima and Nagasaki in August 1945. The bombs were the singular achievement of the age. It was no accident that they were made in America, and only in America. Indeed, the tale of the bombs' making braids together into one plot so many strands of the era's history that it might be taken as the greatest war story of them all, the single most instructive summary account of how and perhaps even why the conflict was fought and the way the Americans won it.[60]

With the discovery in the 1890s of radioactivity—the spontaneous decay of the nuclei of certain elements by the emission of particles— scientists had begun to speculate on the powerful forces locked within the atom. They wondered if man might somehow accelerate the schedule of nuclear disintegration, forcing the atom to pump out in mighty bursts the energy that niggardly nature took millions of years to release in infinitesimal emanations. The quantity of energy involved was clearly enormous. One physicist, applying Albert Einstein's famous equation defining the equivalence of mass and energy ($E = mc^2$), estimated that changing the hydrogen atoms in a single glass of water into helium "would release enough energy to drive the 'Queen Mary' across the Atlantic and back at full speed."[61] As the twentieth century opened, the

59. Smith, *Army and Economic Mobilization*, 9–22; Craven and Cate 6:352; Frederic C. Lane, *Ships for Victory: A History of Shipbuilding under the U.S. Maritime Commission in World War II* (Baltimore: Johns Hopkins University Press, 1951), 4; F. G. Fassett Jr., *The Shipbuilding Business in the United States of America* (New York: Society of Naval Architects and Marine Engineers, 1948), 120; Milward, *War, Economy, and Society*, 74.

60. The story has been magnificently well told by Richard Rhodes in *The Making of the Atomic Bomb* (New York: Simon and Schuster, 1986), a superb book on which the account here liberally draws, as it does also on Richard B. Hewlett and Oscar E. Anderson Jr., *The New World, 1939–1946* (University Park: Pennsylvania State University Press, 1962), vol. 1 of *A History of the United States Atomic Energy Commission*, and on David Holloway, *Stalin and the Bomb: The Soviet Union and Atomic Energy, 1939–1946* (New Haven: Yale University Press, 1994).

61. Rhodes, *Making of the Atomic Bomb*, 140.

quest to understand the nature of the atom and tap into nature's atomic powerhouse drove one of the most feverish inquiries in the history of science. The possibility of a military application of the atom's awesome power stalked that inquiry from the start. As early as 1904 the British physicist Frederick Soddy warned that "the man who put his hand on the lever by which a parsimonious nature regulates so jealously the output of this store of energy would possess a weapon by which he could destroy the earth if he chose."[62]

When James Chadwick discovered the neutron in 1932, the scientists' knowledge-fever spiked. Breakthroughs in understanding came at an accelerating pace, heralding a golden age for physics. Neutrons had mass but no electrical charge. They could thus pass through the electrical barrier of the nucleus and probe the astonishingly strong forces that somehow bound its particles together. Neutron bombardment could force the nucleus to give up its secrets—and possibly some of its power.

Thinking about neutrons while waiting for a London traffic light in late 1933, the peripatetic physicist Leo Szilard had a key insight. Neutron penetration might so perturb the atomic nucleus, Szilard reasoned, that more energy would be released than the neutron itself supplied. "As the light changed to green and I crossed the street," he recalled, "it . . . suddenly occurred to me that if we could find an element which is split by neutrons and which would emit *two* neutrons when it absorbs *one* neutron, such an element, if assembled in sufficiently large mass, could sustain a nuclear chain reaction. . . . If the [mass] is larger than the critical value," he concluded, "I can produce an explosion."[63]

Szilard was an intense, eccentric Hungarian who had studied physics with Einstein in the 1920s and taken up an academic career at the University of Berlin. He was also a Jew, which is why in 1933 he found himself in London, not Berlin. When the Nazis promulgated their first anti-Jewish ordinance on April 7, 1933, forcing the retirement of all "non-Aryan" civil servants, Szilard and hundreds of other Jewish university professors lost their jobs, including a quarter of all the physicists in Germany, eleven of whom were already or would become Nobel Prize winners. Like Szilard, many emigrated. Einstein himself, long harassed for the compound crime of being both a Jew and a pacifist, had already departed for the new Institute for Advanced Study in Princeton, New Jersey (which he found to be "a quaint and ceremonious village

62. Rhodes, *Making of the Atomic Bomb*, 44.
63. Rhodes, *Making of the Atomic Bomb*, 28, 214.

of puny demi-gods on stilts"). So had Einstein's fellow physicist and eventual Nobel Prize winner Eugene Wigner and the distinguished mathematician John von Neumann.[64] Helped by Columbia University philosopher John Dewey, scores of other scholars fled their German university posts for America. Their ranks included Hans Bethe, who moved from Tübingen to Cornell, and Edward Teller, who left Göttingen for George Washington University, both of them destined to win the Nobel Prize. Szilard himself eventually moved on to America from England. Scientist-refugees came from Italy, too, following Benito Mussolini's announcement in July 1938 that "Jews do not belong to the Italian race" and the commencement of Rome's own anti-Semitic campaign. Future Nobelist Emilio Segrè left Palermo for the University of California at Berkeley. Listening to his radio in Rome, Enrico Fermi heard the announcement of his own Nobel Prize during the same news broadcast, on November 10, 1938, that reported the horrors of *Kristallnacht*, the murderous pogrom that had swept Germany the night before. Fermi used his Nobel Prize money to emigrate to New York, evading Italian financial restrictions on emigrants and sheltering his Jewish wife from Mussolini's clutches. Thirty Jewish scientists and other scholars came to America from Europe in 1933, thirty-two in 1934, nearly one hundred physicists over the course of the decade. They came not to make war but to seek refuge. They came for the same reasons that had propelled so many of their immigrant predecessors across the Atlantic. "America," wrote Segrè, "looked like the land of the future, separated by an ocean from the misfortunes, follies, and crimes of Europe"—a sentiment that isolationist Americans broadly shared in the 1930s.[65] But by the time the European war erupted and engulfed America too, Hitler's and Mussolini's racialist policies had bestowed a priceless intellectual endowment on the United States.

While other Germans were smashing glass in Jewish stores and synagogues, two German scientists, Otto Hahn and Fritz Strassmann, were trying to smash atoms at Berlin's Kaiser Wilhelm Institute for Chemistry. In the month after *Kristallnacht* they succeeded, splitting uranium into two other elements and releasing an astonishing two hundred million electron volts of energy. In the first week of the year that would bring the war, they published their results in *Die Naturwissenschaften*. A new word flashed into the scientific lexicon: fission. News of the

64. Rhodes, *Making of the Atomic Bomb*, 196.
65. Rhodes, *Making of the Atomic Bomb*, 241.

Hahn-Strassmann experiment raced like lightning through the international physics community. Within a year scientists in several countries published more than one hundred papers on fission. The basic understanding of what it would take to build an atomic weapon was swiftly and widely diffused. In his office overlooking San Francisco Bay at the University of California at Berkeley, the physicist Robert Oppenheimer was chalking a crude diagram of a bomb on his blackboard within a week of hearing of the Hahn-Strassmann results. In Germany a young physicist described to the War Office in April "the newest development in nuclear physics, which . . . will probably make it possible to produce an explosive many orders of magnitude more powerful than the conventional ones. . . . That country which first makes use of it has an unsurpassable advantage over the others." At a secret conference in Berlin on April 29, 1939, it was agreed to pursue research on a possible nuclear weapon. The War Office took over the Kaiser Wilhelm Institute. German agents hurried to the synthetic ammonia plant at Vermork, Norway, to buy its tiny but precious stocks of deuterium oxide ("heavy water"), a by-product of ammonia manufacture and one of the few known neutron moderators that might make a chain reaction possible. All exports of uranium from the Joachimsthal mines in Nazi-controlled Czechoslovakia, one of the world's few sources of the newly precious metal, were banned. Other governments stirred themselves as well. Nuclear weapons research commenced in Britain in the summer of 1940. The Japanese Imperial Army Air Force authorized an atomic bomb project in April 1941. Stalin launched a Russian research program a year later.[66]

Fittingly, it was the refugees who alerted the American government to the menace of nuclear weaponry. Fermi was the first to try. On March 17, 1939, he went to the Navy Department to brief officers from the army's Bureau of Ordnance and the Naval Research Laboratory on the recent developments in atomic physics. He carried a letter of introduction from a Columbia University colleague, who noted "the possibility that uranium might be used as an explosive. . . . My own feeling," the colleague added, "is that the probabilities are against this." Introduced with such skepticism, Fermi hit a wall of ignorance and doubt at the Navy Building. "There's a wop outside," Fermi heard the receptionist say by way of announcing him, rudely foreshadowing the puzzled indifference of the officers he addressed. A few months later, the refugee

66. Rhodes, *Making of the Atomic Bomb*, 296, 346; Holloway, *Stalin and the Bomb*, 84.

scientists tried again. Szilard, Wigner, and Teller—the so-called Hungarian Conspiracy—visited Einstein at his vacation home on Long Island in the summer of 1939. Together they drafted a letter for Einstein's signature. Alexander Sachs, an economist with access to the White House, agreed to carry Einstein's message to Franklin Roosevelt.

On October 11 Sachs finally got his appointment with the president. Reminding Roosevelt that Napoleon had muffed the chance to exploit the greatest technological marvel of his day when he foolishly rejected the young Robert Fulton's offer to build a fleet of steamships, Sachs tendered Einstein's letter and proceeded to explain the military potentialities of nuclear energy. Einstein had closed his appeal to the president with a warning that the *Reich* had stopped the sale of uranium from the Czech mines, a sure tipoff that the Germans were already at work on a nuclear weapon. The president quickly grasped the point. "Alex," he said, "what you are after is to see that the Nazis don't blow us up." The president called in an aide. "This requires action," he said. Thus was born the Advisory Committee on Uranium, which met for the first time at the Bureau of Standards on October 21 to explore an American nuclear weapons program. The committee continued to meet sporadically for more than two years, but the scientific novelty of nuclear physics and the daunting engineering challenges of actually fabricating a bomb made it difficult to arrive at firm recommendations.[67]

The scientific principles that pointed to the ultimate promise of a nuclear weapon were clear enough. Far less clear was the technical feasibility of constructing a deliverable weapon in time to be useful. Three questions overshadowed all others. How could a sufficient amount of radioactive material be collected? What quantity of such material might constitute the critical mass that would sustain a chain reaction? And how could the material be assembled rapidly enough so that it exploded, rather than simply fizzled like a pile of gunpowder?

The near-maniacal nuclear research frenzy of 1939 established that the energy Hahn and Strassmann had released came from the relatively rare isotope U-235, which occurred in natural uranium, U-238, in the ratio of one part in 140. Plutonium, a man-made radioactive element first created from uranium in experiments at Berkeley in 1940, soon emerged as a second possible energy source. But isolating enough U-235 or fabricating enough plutonium to make a weapon struck many

67. Hewlett and Anderson, *New World*, 16–20; Rhodes, *Making of the Atomic Bomb*, 304–15.

scientists as next to impossible. "It would take the entire efforts of a country to make a bomb," said the eminent Danish physicist Niels Bohr. "[I]t can never be done unless you turn the United States into one huge factory."[68] What was more, early estimates of the critical mass necessary to sustain a nuclear chain reaction ran to many tons, far too big and unwieldy a radioactive lump for a practical, deliverable weapon, with the possible but highly implausible exception of a device that could be carried into an enemy port aboard a ship.

Roosevelt's Uranium Committee shared those doubts. The expense of isotope separation and the uncertainty about whether a controlled chain reaction was even possible seemed like insurmountable obstacles. Assessing those difficulties, the committee easily fell into a mind-set that was much more interested in proving that no one, the Germans in particular, could build a bomb than in committing the United States to a bomb-making program. "This uranium business is a headache!" wrote Vannevar Bush, director of the Office of Scientific Research and Development, in mid-1941.

Bush, an engineer trained at Harvard and MIT, enjoyed a reputation as an innovator. He was a pioneer in the emerging field of electronic calculating who had helped build a hundred-ton analog computer that could solve differential equations with up to eighteen variables. In the ferment following the German scientists' achievement of nuclear fission in 1939, Bush, then head of the Carnegie Institution in Washington, pushed for the creation of the National Defense Research Council (NDRC), a body of scientists committed to lending their expertise to war work. In May 1941 the Roosevelt administration subsumed the NDRC in the newly created Office of Scientific Research and Development (OSRD), which it named Bush to head. Under his leadership, the government began to move weapons research out of government-run arsenals and into corporations and, significantly, into universities. The OSRD forged a lasting relationship between government-funded scientific research and American higher education that was institutionalized after the war with the creation of the National Science Foundation in 1950.

Yet for the moment even a man as temperamentally inclined to innovation as Bush remained skeptical about the prospects for a nuclear weapon. "Even if the physicists get all that they expect," he wrote, "I believe that there is a very long period of engineering work of the most

68. Holloway, *Stalin and the Bomb*, 51; Rhodes, *Making of the Atomic Bomb*, 294.

difficult nature before anything practical can come out of the matter, unless there is an explosive involved, which I very much doubt."[69] Then, in the summer of 1941, British scientists produced credible estimates that only a few kilograms of U-235 might be enough to manufacture a highly explosive weapon, a key conclusion that began to bring the prospect of a deliverable weapon into the circle of the possible. This so-called Maud Committee report made a believer of Bush. The fact of American belligerency made a gambler out of Roosevelt. Armed with the Maud Committee's findings, Bush recommended a full-scale American effort to the White House. It would be a serious and costly undertaking, Bush warned. Seeking to impress upon the president the scale of the effort required, Bush opined that "a vast industrial plant costing many times as much as a major oil refinery would be necessary to separate the U235"—an estimate that proved orders of magnitude too modest. On January 19, 1942, Roosevelt penned a terse reply: "O.K.—returned—I think you had best keep this in your own safe."[70]

Roosevelt's simple "OK" proved galvanic. In Washington, the president created a Top Policy Group to oversee the bomb program. It consisted of Vice-President Wallace, Secretary of War Stimson, Army Chief of Staff Marshall, Bush, and James Bryant Conant, Harvard president and, for the duration, head of the National Defense Research Council. In Chicago, where Fermi had moved after burying some cash in the coal bin of his New Jersey house as a precaution against the prospect that as an "enemy alien" his assets would be confiscated, the Italian scientist began to put together a "pile" of radioactive materials. It "went critical"—attained a sustained chain reaction—in December 1942, a crucial breakthrough that established the reality of what had theretofore been only a theoretical prospect. Fermi celebrated with a straw-covered fiasco of Chianti. In Berkeley, Robert Oppenheimer gathered a group of physicists to work on bomb design. For security reasons they and others would soon remove to a remote mesa at Los Alamos, in the New Mexican desert.

At Los Alamos, behind a high steel fence topped with a triple course of barbed wire, Oppenheimer's scientists grappled with the myriad scientific and ordnance problems of bomb design. "The object of the project," the scientists heard on arrival, "is to produce a practical military weapon in the form of a bomb in which the energy is released by a fast

69. Rhodes, *Making of the Atomic Bomb*, 362, 366.
70. Rhodes, *Making of the Atomic Bomb*, 377, 388.

neutron chain reaction in one or more of the materials known to show nuclear fission."[71] The question of assembly posed an especially stubborn puzzle. A difference of just a few microseconds in pushing subcritical quantities of fissile material together into a "critical mass" made the difference between a spectacular but militarily useless radioactive splutter or a large-scale explosion. A gun-type mechanism, in which a cannon fired a subcritical slug into a subcritical core, eventually proved a useable design for a bomb made from U-235. But neutron flux in plutonium happened at such a rate and in such quantities that even a cannon-fired assembly was too slow. The plutonium-based bomb required the devilishly tricky design of an assembly mechanism that would symmetrically implode a plutonium sphere in upon itself, instantaneously assembling a critical mass.

Over such matters as these the scientists labored. Their ranks included refugees and native-born Americans alike, an assemblage of scientific brains and intellectual prima donnas the likes of which had never been gathered before. Yet among their remarkable characteristics was the fact that for all their density of numbers and ability, they represented only a fraction of wartime America's scientific talent. Hundreds of other scientists continued to work on other projects, including radar and aircraft design. Some chose to work elsewhere for moral reasons. The physicist I. I. Rabi, for example, turned down Oppenheimer's invitation to be the associate director at Los Alamos because he could not stomach the idea that making a weapon of mass destruction represented "the culmination of three centuries of physics."[72]

Oppenheimer, a cadaverously thin theorist widely acknowledged to have a preternaturally swift and absorptive mind, occasionally shared some of Rabi's moral anxieties. Oppenheimer would in later years come to symbolize the dilemmas of an era when the growth of scientific knowledge seemed to have outraced the evolution of moral wisdom. A second-generation German-Jewish American, he had been raised in privilege on New York's Upper West Side, graduated summa cum laude from Harvard in just three years, went off to study physics in Europe, and returned to a notable scholarly career—and a flirtation with left-

71. Rhodes, *Making of the Atomic Bomb*, 460–61.
72. Rhodes, *Making of the Atomic Bomb*, 452. In yet another indication of the surplus of scientific talent in wartime America, even some of the scientists at Los Alamos, notably Edward Teller, did not work exclusively on the atomic bomb project but also found time to explore the even more distant possibility of a "super" or hydrogen bomb based on fusion.

wing politics—in Depression-era California. As a young man he had hiked through the Joachimsthal Valley. As a graduate student in Germany in the 1920s he had made the acquaintance of many of the scientists who were now working on Hitler's atomic project.

Besides the Top Policy Committee in Washington and the scientists at Los Alamos, few others shared in the deep secret of the bomb project. One who did was General Leslie Groves. In September 1942 Groves took charge of the bomb project, now placed under the War Department's control and code-named the Manhattan Engineering District. Groves was then a forty-six-year-old second-generation career army officer. He had grown up as an itinerant service brat in Cuba, the Philippines, and the western United States. Following in his father's footsteps, he had attended West Point, where he placed fourth in his class. He took graduate degrees in engineering and joined the Army Corps of Engineers. In 1942 he had just finished building the Pentagon, then the world's largest office building. He was big, bluff, all-army and can-do, an overstuffed man with a brusque front and no apologies. "I hated his guts," his chief aide once remarked, "and so did everybody else." In one of his first meetings with the scientists who were now nominally his underlings, Groves noticed an equation that had been improperly copied and thought the learned professors were trying to trick him. He pointed out the error and put them on notice that his engineering work was worth two of their Ph.D.'s. "They didn't fool me," he later reflected. "There were a few Nobel Prizewinners among them. But I showed them. . . . They never forgave me for that."[73]

It is easy to see Professor Oppenheimer and General Groves as foils for one another—the gaunt, soul-tortured scientist, melancholic child of the Jewish diaspora, sensitive reader of Sanskrit epics and T. S. Eliot's poetry, the brooding genius who orchestrated all the exotic savants gathered at Los Alamos, playing the tragic hero opposite Grove's corpulent Rotarian Babbitt, West Point engineer, career soldier, gruff maker of buildings and bombs and a man without scruple, delicacy, or conscience. But if Oppenheimer and his scientists at Los Alamos constituted a crucial American asset in the race to build the bomb, Groves also embodied a kind of genius—the peculiarly American genius for organization and management and for thinking in terms of stunningly vast enterprises.

73. *Dictionary of American Biography* (New York: Charles Scribner's Sons, supp. 8, 1988), 231, 229.

Oppenheimer managed mathematical formulae and the art of orchestrating the often idiosyncratic men who generated them. Groves managed the much more prosaic but no less indispensable arithmetic of budgets and the engineer's arts of sheer prodigiousness. Confronted with choices among five different methods of isotope separation and seven different techniques for plutonium extraction, for example, Groves's Manhattan Project went to work on all of them. "This Napoleonic approach," Conant thought, "would require the commitment of perhaps $500,000,000 and quite a mess of machinery."[74] That proved an understatement. Before it was over, the Manhattan Project consumed more than $2 billion, employed 150,000 people, and required a mess of machinery, plant, and other resources that were available nowhere but in America. In places, the bomb project changed the very face of the continent. On a fifty-nine-thousand-acre site near Oak Ridge, Tennessee, squarely in the midst of the vast power grid that the TVA had been building for nearly a decade, twenty thousand construction workers laid down fifty miles of railroad and three hundred miles of paved roads and streets and built several gaseous diffusion and electromagnetic installations for the extraction of U-235. The precious isotope offered itself in minuscule quantities at first. Yields were so low from the tons of ore being processed that workers plucked mere specks from their overalls with tweezers.

Along the banks of the Columbia River, whose pristine waters Lewis and Clark had paddled a century and a half before, thousands of other workers erected a brand-new town at Hanford, the site of an old ferry crossing in the nearly vacant interior of Washington State. The Hanford plant used the river's water for coolant and the river's energy — transformed into electricity by the New Deal's Bonneville and Grand Coulee dams — to drive its three atomic piles and four chemical separation plants. In those gargantuan facilities rising improbably from the sere tableland of the Columbia bench, workers tortuously squeezed out plutonium from grudging nature, a dime-size radioactive pellet from every two tons of uranium.

At both plants, forbidding technical problems repeatedly threatened to sink or fatally delay the project. Groves coped imperiously with them all. When boron contamination in graphite control rods threatened the operation of Fermi's uranium piles, he badgered manufacturers to make graphite to standards of purity once considered impossible. Building the

74. Rhodes, *Making of the Atomic Bomb*, 407.

Oak Ridge gaseous-diffusion plant was in itself a herculean assignment, even for a man who had erected the Pentagon. When completed, at a cost of $100 million, it was a forty-two-acre building housing thousands of diffusion tanks and flanked by a 2.9-million-square-foot machine shop and other buildings covering some fifty additional acres. When copper shortages threatened to scuttle Oak Ridge's electromagnetic separation facility, Groves contracted for more than thirteen thousand tons of silver from the federal depository at West Point with which to wind the separator's two thousand giant magnets. When some of the magnets proved defective, Groves ordered Allis-Chalmers to remake them. When output at Oak Ridge proved too slow, Groves directed an engineering firm to build an additional twenty-one-hundred-column diffusion plant to enrich the ore being fed to the electromagnetic separators, and he ordered it to be done in ninety days or less, a schedule that was met.

Under these engineering hammer-blows, nature began at last to yield useable quantities of fissionable material. By early 1945 Oak Ridge was giving up some seven ounces a day of 80 percent enriched U-235, enough to make one bomb by midyear and a bomb every six weeks thereafter. Hanford's giant piles went reliably critical in December 1944, prompting Groves to predict to George Marshall that he could have about eighteen five-kilogram plutonium bombs ready by the second half of 1945. In the space of three years, Groves had erected out of nothing a vast industrial complex, as large in scale as the entire prewar automobile industry. "You see," said Bohr on a later visit to the United States, "I told you it couldn't be done without turning the whole country into a factory. You have done just that."[75]

Fear of Germany had spurred the American atomic project. "We may be engaged in a race toward realization," Bush advised Roosevelt in early 1942. Conant worried about the same time that "there are still plenty of competent scientists left in Germany. They may be ahead of us by as much as a year."[76] Ironically, at virtually the same time the Americans were expressing these anxieties, and unbeknownst to them, the Germans were canceling their own bomb project. The reasons are instructive. In June 1942 German armaments minister Albert Speer summoned German scientists, including Otto Hahn and the brilliant Werner Heisenberg, to brief him about the possibilities of nuclear weapons. Heisenberg answered vaguely. It would take at least two years, he said, and

75. Rhodes, *Making of the Atomic Bomb*, 500.
76. Rhodes, *Making of the Atomic Bomb*, 405–6.

would require enormous and unstinting economic and technological support. Speer considered the matter carefully, discussed it with Hitler, and made his decision. By the autumn of 1942, he later wrote, "[we] scuttled the project to develop an atom bomb. . . . Perhaps," Speer reflected in his memoirs, "it would have proved possible to have the atom bomb ready for employment in 1945. But it would have meant mobilizing all our technical and financial resources to that end, as well as our scientific talent. It would have meant giving up all other projects. . . . [I]t would have been impossible — given the strain on our economic resources — to have provided the materials, priorities, and technical workers corresponding to such an investment." Finally, Speer added, "our failure to pursue the possibilities of atomic warfare can be partly traced to ideological reasons. . . . To his table companions Hitler occasionally referred to nuclear physics as 'Jewish physics.' "[77]

Similarly, Japanese officials estimated in 1942 that U-235 separation would consume one-tenth of Japan's electrical capacity as well as half its copper output and would in any case take ten years to produce results, a prospective schedule that ruled out any serious commitment to atomic weapons development. Japanese scientists further advised their government that neither the Germans nor the Americans could possibly deflect enough of their productive resources to a bomb project to have a weapon useable in the current war — a judgment in which they were half right. Some atomic work went ahead in wartime Japan, but the results were exceedingly sparse. By the summer of 1944 Japan had manufactured a total of 170 grams of uranium hexafluoride, a crucial element in the isotope-separation process. The American plants by then measured their production of uranium hexafluoride in tons. A fire raid on Tokyo in April 1945 definitively ended Japan's feeble atomic effort when it burned Japan's one tiny nuclear research laboratory to the ground. Britain, under the shadow of the Luftwaffe and unable to keep up even in conventional armaments without American aid, had long since abandoned its own atomic project. Most British nuclear scientists had transferred to the United States and been folded into the American project. As for the Russians, they lurched ahead with atomic research during the war, fed periodic and incomplete espionage reports on the American effort by a wary Stalin but making little progress.[78]

77. Speer, *Inside the Third Reich*, 225–29. Einstein later commented, "If I had known that the Germans would not succeed in constructing the atom bomb, I would never have lifted a finger." Quoted in Michael Walzer, *Just and Unjust Wars* (New York: Basic, 1977), 263.

78. Rhodes, *Making of the Atomic Bomb*, 458, 581.

World enough and time, the poet sang, and when it came to atomic weapons development the United States was the one country that enjoyed amplitudes of both. The United States had a world of resources, physical as well as intellectual, a pool of things and talent so vast and deep that the Americans could build the first atom bombs while simultaneously pursuing advanced scientific research on other wizardly war technologies, including sonar, radar, the proximity fuse, the bazooka, amphibious vehicles, and steady improvements in the range, speed, and performance of combat aircraft, culminating in the B-29 "Superfortresses" that eventually delivered the two atomic bombs. Thanks to the pugnacity of the British in 1940 and the tenacity of the Russians since 1941, the United States had been granted the time to do all those things, and more. The Manhattan Project thus stands as the single best illustration of the American way of war—not so much for the technological novelty of the bombs, or the moral issues they inevitably raised, but because only the Americans had the margins of money, material, and manpower, as well as the undisturbed space and time, to bring an enterprise on the scale of the Manhattan Project to successful completion. They did it while making good on the promise that they would build an arsenal of democracy with a crushing superiority in munitions. And they did it while equipping their allies abroad, lifting civilian living standards at home, and raising, training, and equipping a triphibious force of their own that was the best equipped and most mechanized in the world.

By the end of 1943 the Americans had stockpiled an arsenal that would give them a three-to-one munitions advantage over their foes when they finally took the field in force. In the Pacific the disparities were especially dramatic. Every American combatant in the last year and a half of war in the Pacific islands could draw on four tons of supplies; his Japanese opponent, just two pounds. So far, American forces had fought only scratch actions in the Mediterranean, mounted a few foolhardy forays in the skies over Europe, and struggled to some brave but still inconclusive victories in the Pacific. But as 1943 drew toward its close, the Americans and their overwhelming array of machines were nearly ready to swing into action, with all the energy of an exuberant economy and all the craft of modern science breathing power unimaginable behind them. After years of indifference, muddle, and make-do, the United States was at last prepared to fight its kind of war. It remained actually to fight it.

6

The Struggle for a Second Front

The year 1944 is loaded with danger.
— Winston Churchill to Franklin Roosevelt, October 27, 1943

Late on the evening of Armistice Day, November 11, 1943, Roosevelt and a handful of aides stole away from the White House and boarded the presidential yacht *Potomac*. At dawn the president's little craft lay alongside the massive battleship *Iowa*, anchored in Chesapeake Bay. A special rig hoisted the commander-in-chief up onto the *Iowa's* main deck. The dreadnought weighed anchor and headed out to the open sea. Eight days later the presidential party disembarked at Oran, in French North Africa. Roosevelt transferred to a specially fitted Army Air Corps Douglas C-54 transport plane, whimsically named "the Sacred Cow." His ultimate destination was Teheran and his first-ever meeting with Stalin. But the Sacred Cow first touched down at Cairo. It was not a stop that the president had originally wanted, and not one he anticipated with relish.

Just weeks earlier Churchill had warned Roosevelt that in the new phase of the war then emerging, when American might was at last beginning to weigh heavily in the scales, "[g]reat differences may develop between us." The first such difference had been over whether Roosevelt should meet Stalin alone, as the president wished. Churchill had muscled in and claimed a chair at the Teheran conference table. The prime minister then went further and insisted on a preliminary meeting between the two Western allies at Cairo before they confronted the Soviets at Teheran. Roosevelt had countered by suggesting that Soviet representatives as well as Chinese generalissimo Chiang Kai-shek should attend the preparatory talks. But the Soviets, still at peace with Japan, refused to parley with Chiang for fear of provoking Tokyo. Thus it was just

Churchill, Roosevelt, and Chiang who sat down for dinner at Ambassador Alexander C. Kirk's Nile-delta villa on the evening of November 22 to initiate the Cairo Conference.[1]

Perhaps to repay his annoyance with Churchill, Roosevelt spent most of his time over the next four days with Chiang, and the president saw to it that whatever discussion there was among all three leaders focused principally on the war in Asia. In that theater the differences between Churchill and Roosevelt were especially great and potentially explosive. Unlike the conflict in Europe, the war in Asia was in no small part a war about colonies. Britain was determined to hold on to India and to reclaim its other Asian possessions, lost to Japan in the first weeks of the war. France and the Netherlands, though for the moment under the Nazi heel, had similar plans to recapture their Japanese-occupied Asian colonies as soon as the war was over. The Americans, on the other hand, had long since pledged themselves to grant independence to the Philippines, and Roosevelt frequently badgered Churchill to do the same for India, Burma, Malaya, and Hong Kong.

In Roosevelt's mind, China would serve as a counterweight to Britain and the other European powers in postwar Asia, thus helping to secure permanent decolonization. A strong China would also help protect against a resurgent Japan and would check Soviet ambitions in the region as well. Churchill considered Roosevelt's concept of China as an eventual great power nothing less than ludicrous. "To the President, China means four hundred million people who are going to count in the world of tomorrow," Churchill's physician noted in his diary. "But Winston thinks only of the colour of their skin; it is when he talks of India or China that you remember he is a Victorian." At Cairo, Churchill tried in vain to send the irrelevant and pestiferous Chiang off sightseeing to the Pyramids. Instead, Churchill recalled drily, "the talks of the British and American staffs were sadly distracted by the Chinese story, which was lengthy, complicated, and minor."[2]

America's part in the Chinese story began well before Pearl Harbor. Indeed, it was America's stubborn commitment to China that had set the stage for Pearl Harbor. Early in 1941 the retired U.S. Army Air Corps colonel Claire Chennault had begun recruiting American pilots to fly under Chinese command in the American Volunteer Group, which

1. C&R 2:565.
2. Lord Moran, *Churchill: Taken from the Diaries of Lord Moran: The Struggle for Survival, 1940–1965* (Boston: Houghton Mifflin, 1966), 140; Churchill 5:289

journalists soon inappropriately labeled the "Flying Tigers" because of the sharks' teeth painted on the noses of their aircraft. Chennault entertained extravagant dreams of bringing Japan to its knees by flying from Chinese airbases to interdict Japanese merchant shipping and to inflict incendiary raids on Japanese cities. All he needed to accomplish this, he said, were thirty medium and twelve heavy bombers!

Few people, least of all George Marshall, took Chennault's wild claims seriously. Marshall instead looked for ways to help Chiang wage a more effective ground war against the one million Japanese troops in China and Southeast Asia. In early 1942 he sent Lieutenant General Joseph W. Stilwell to Chunking. Stilwell wore many hats in Chiang's capital: commander of all the American forces in China, Burma, and India (designated the CBI theater); Roosevelt's personal military representative to Chiang; Lend-Lease administrator for China; and, at least nominally, Chiang's chief of staff. Stilwell was a peppery, profane combat veteran of World War I and a seasoned infantry commander. He had done four tours of duty in China in the interwar years and spoke fluent Chinese. On paper, he seemed a perfect choice for the assignment.

But Stilwell's troubles began as soon as he arrived in Chunking in March 1942. At that moment Japanese forces were driving the remnants of the British army from Burma. Stilwell took personal command of a Chinese force and raced to Burma to prop up the British. Instead, the British-Chinese lines collapsed, and Stilwell had to execute a 140-mile retreat through rugged mountains to India. The Japanese victory closed the last overland supply route to China, the "Burma Road," a sinuous track that ran from the Irrawaddy River north of the Burmese port of Rangoon easterly into China's Yunan province. All Lend-Lease supplies for China now had to be laboriously airlifted from India over a series of towering Himalayan ranges known as "the Hump." Stilwell began immediately to plan a campaign to retake Burma and meanwhile started construction on the Ledo Road, a gargantuan engineering undertaking to build a new land route from Ledo in India, across northern Burma to Myitkyina, and thence into China. His inaugural defeat stung. "We got a hell of a beating," Stilwell told reporters. "We got run out of Burma and it's humiliating as hell."[3]

It was more than humiliating. Stilwell discovered during the brief and disastrous Burma campaign that the Chinese officers allegedly under his command were in fact taking their instructions from Chiang, who fre-

3. Spector, 332.

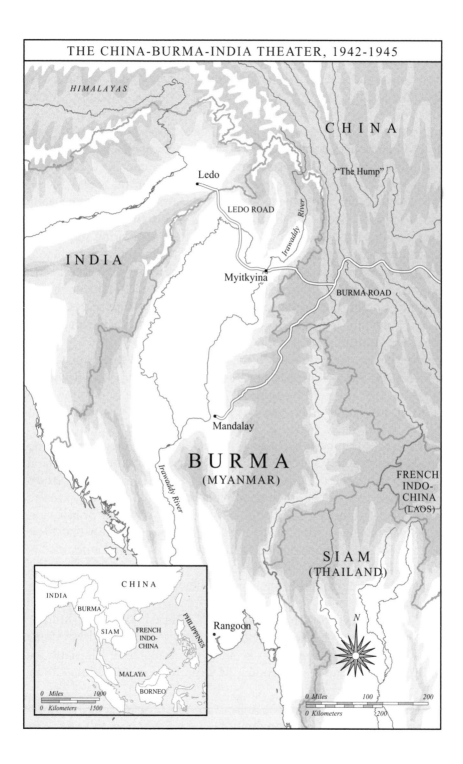

THE CHINA-BURMA-INDIA THEATER, 1942-1945

HIMALAYAS

CHINA

Ledo

"The Hump"

LEDO ROAD

Irrawaddy River

INDIA

Myitkyina

BURMA ROAD

Mandalay

BURMA
(MYANMAR)

FRENCH
INDO-
CHINA
(LAOS)

Irrawaddy River

SIAM
(THAILAND)

N

CHINA

INDIA

BURMA

SIAM

FRENCH
INDO-
CHINA

PHILIPPINES

Rangoon

MALAYA

BORNEO

0 Miles   1000
0 Kilometers   1500

0 Miles   100   200
0 Kilometers   200

quently countermanded Stilwell's orders. The Burma episode sowed the seed of Stilwell's frustration with the evasive, scheming Chiang. Stilwell soon concluded that the Chinese leader was content to leave the job of defeating Japan to the Americans in the Pacific, while in China Chiang intended to wait out the war, accumulate reserves of American money and materiel, and prepare for an eventual showdown with Mao Tse-tung's Communists, against whom he had been waging a civil war since 1927. The Japanese, Chiang reportedly said, were merely "a disease of the skin," while the Communists were a "disease of the heart." By the time of the Cairo Conference, Stilwell had been struggling for nearly two years with the several Sisyphean tasks of reconciling Chiang and Mao, forging the corrupt and undisciplined Chinese army into an effective fighting force, and inducing it to fight. Stilwell's cantankerous temperament had earned him the nickname "Vinegar Joe" even before he arrived in China. Trying to grapple with the mercurial Chiang soured him still further. His aggravation with Chiang grew into scarcely concealed contempt. He took to calling Chiang, a compact man with a clean-shaven head, "the peanut."[4]

The peanut now sat across the table from FDR, while Vinegar Joe stewed in the wings at Ambassador Kirk's suburban Cairo villa. Roosevelt began to take his own measure of the generalissimo and found him grasping, weak, and indecisive. Nevertheless, wanting to keep China in the war and to retain Chinese friendship, Roosevelt gave Chiang several assurances: continued backing for Chennault's airmen; stepped-up Lend-Lease supplies over the Hump; resources for a simultaneous land offensive in northern Burma and an amphibious assault on the Andaman Islands, off the Burmese coast; and support for the newly created inter-Allied Southeast Asia Command (SEAC) under the British vice-admiral Lord Louis Mountbatten. Stilwell objected in vain that these several piecemeal efforts dissipated his scant resources and amounted to no strategy at all. His staff cracked that "SEAC" stood for "Save England's Asiatic Colonies." The several thousand mostly air and engineering troops under Stilwell's command in Ledo meanwhile quipped that "CBI" described them all too well: "Confused Bastards in India."

In fact, developments in late 1943 and 1944 were rapidly diminishing China's military significance. Stilwell would eventually reach Myitkyina in August 1944 and begin pushing the Ledo Road eastward into China.

4. Michael Schaller, The U.S. Crusade in China, 1939–1945 (New York: Columbia University Press, 1979), 39

But the Japanese Ichi-go offensive at the same time captured all the Chinese airbases from which the bombing of Japan was to be conducted. And even while the statesmen were talking in Cairo, U.S. marines were taking the Gilbert Island atoll of Tarawa, opening the door for an American advance into the Central Pacific and the even more useful airfields of the Mariana Islands, just two thousand miles south of Japan. Chiang at last forced Stilwell's removal in October 1944, though he had the grace to rename the Ledo Road in Stilwells' honor on its completion in January 1945. By that time, China was a hopeless mess of renewed civil war and had ironically become all but irrelevant to the defeat of Japan.

THE "CHINESE BUSINESS occupied first instead of last place at Cairo," Churchill fumed. He and Roosevelt alike itched to put first things first at Teheran — above all, Overlord. As the sun touched the tops of the Giza pyramids on November 27, 1943, the Sacred Cow lifted off from Cairo West airport, bearing Roosevelt toward his long-anticipated encounter with Josef Stalin. The president's plane winged over Suez, swooped low for sight-seeing over the Holy Land, droned on across the Syrian desert to the green valleys of the Tigris and Euphrates, and finally topped the mountainous shoulder of western Iran. Looking out his window at the landscape passing below, Admiral William Leahy, Roosevelt's chief of staff, reflected on this flight "over territory rich in history that dated back to the earliest days of our civilization." The meeting of the "Big Three" that lay ahead in Teheran, representing what Churchill called "the greatest concentration of worldly power that had ever been seen in the history of mankind," promised to take its own prominent place in this ancient tapestry of historical significance.[5]

Roosevelt's continuing anxiety about Soviet intentions had been exacerbated not three weeks earlier when Major General John R. Deane, chief of the American military mission in Moscow, had cabled to Washington his alarming impression that now, as the Red Army rolled toward the Polish frontier, the Russians might be losing interest in Overlord. In the upcoming meetings at Teheran, Deane warned, the Soviets might well present demands for increased pressure in Italy and the Balkans, coupled with a request that Overlord be postponed. Whether long-term

5. William D. Leahy, *I Was There: The Personal Story of the Chief of Staff to Presidents Roosevelt and Truman Based on His Notes and Diaries Made at the Time* (New York: McGraw-Hill, 1950), 202–3; Churchill 5:290, 307.

political considerations—a desire to keep the Anglo-Americans out of the European heartland, or possibly even a plan to negotiate a separate peace with Germany—underlay this Russian line of thinking was impossible to say. But the prospect that Stalin, for whatever reason, might at Teheran buttress Churchill's familiar reservations about Overlord deeply disturbed American planners. For them, the cross-Channel invasion remained the supreme and jealously guarded foundation stone of anti-German strategy.

In midafternoon on the twenty-seventh, the presidential aircraft slipped through a pass in the mountains and descended into the horseshoe-shaped valley that cradled Teheran, a picturesque city surrounded by earthen ramparts and a moat, its historic center reached by twelve arched gates. To mollify Stalin and facilitate their exchanges, Roosevelt agreed to stay in the Russian compound. Stalin offered to call on the president the following day.

The man Roosevelt had flown halfway around the earth to meet remained an enigma, a shadowy figure even after nearly two decades at the pinnacle of power in the world's only Communist state. The menacing persona that constituted his image in the West reflected his own brooding, furtive temperament and testified as well to the character of the suspicion-saturated society over which he presided. Churchill had dreaded his own first encounter with the leader of the "sullen, sinister Bolshevik State I had once tried so hard to strangle at its birth." But at their initial meeting, in Moscow in August 1942, the prime minister had found Stalin to be remarkably astute, with a startling capacity for "swift and complete mastery of a problem hitherto novel to him."[6] Less generously, Lord Moran, Churchill's physician and confidant, called Stalin a "hard-boiled Asiatic."[7] Averell Harriman, the American ambassador to Moscow since October 1943, considered Stalin "the most inscrutable and contradictory character I have ever known," a baffling man of "high intelligence [and] fantastic grasp of detail," possessed of both "shrewdness" and "surprising human sensitivity." In Harriman's judgment, Stalin was "better informed than Roosevelt, more realistic than Churchill, in some ways the most effective of the war leaders. At the same time he was, of course, a murderous tyrant."[8] George Marshall

6. Churchill 4:428, 434
7. Moran, Churchill, 146.
8. W. Averell Harriman and Elie Abel, Special Envoy to Churchill and Stalin, 1941–1946 (New York: Random House, 1975), 536.

thought Stalin simply "a rough SOB who made his way by murder."[9] Admiral Leahy, who observed Stalin closely throughout the meetings that were about to begin, came to Teheran expecting to meet "a bandit leader who had pushed himself up to the top of his government" but later confessed that "that impression was wrong. . . . [W]e were dealing with a highly intelligent man who spoke well . . . quietly, without gestures."[10] Hopkins, Roosevelt's personal emissary to Moscow in 1942, had reported that in his conversations with Stalin "not once did he repeat himself. . . . There was no waste of word, gesture, nor mannerism. It was like talking to a perfectly co-ordinated machine, an intelligent machine. . . . What he says is all the accent and inflection his words need."[11]

Into Roosevelt's quarters in the Soviet compound Stalin strode self-confidently at 3:15 on the twenty-eighth. This was the moment Roosevelt had so long awaited, when his personal charm and political skill could be directed full force at the taciturn Russian. Roosevelt had "come to Teheran determined . . . to come to terms with Stalin," Harry Hopkins told Lord Moran, "and he is not going to allow anything to interfere with that purpose. . . . After all," Hopkins said, "he had spent his life managing men, and Stalin at bottom could not be so very different from other people."[12]

"I am glad to see you," Roosevelt began ingratiatingly. "I have tried for a long time to bring this about." Stalin, his chunky frame draped in a simple khaki tunic, extended his hand. He accepted the blame for the delay in this meeting—and pointedly added that "he had been very preoccupied because of military matters."[13]

Seeing an opening, Roosevelt inquired as to the situation on the eastern front. Stalin said that while his forces held the initiative around Kiev, the Germans were still able to bring in reinforcements from the west and were counterattacking. Roosevelt replied that he had, of course, come to Teheran to discuss the Anglo-American plan to draw off thirty to forty German divisions from the eastern front. Stalin responded tersely that this would be "of great value." Roosevelt then tendered the

9. Forrest C. Pogue, *George C. Marshall: Organizer of Victory, 1943–1945* (New York: Viking Press, 1973), 313.

10. Leahy, *I Was There,* 205, 204.

11. Robert E. Sherwood, *Roosevelt and Hopkins: An Intimate History* (New York: Grosset and Dunlap, 1948, 1950), 343–44.

12. Moran, *Churchill,* 143.

13. *FRUS: The Conferences at Cairo and Teheran, 1943,* 483.

surprisingly generous suggestion that after the war British and American merchant ships might be turned over to the Soviets. This too, Stalin said laconically, would be "of great value." The conversation turned briefly to the Asian theater. Stalin declared that "the Chinese have fought very badly." He went on to speak scornfully about the shameful collaboration of the French with their Nazi masters and the need to punish France after the war, including stripping her of her colonies in Indochina. Roosevelt said he was "100% in agreement." After forty-five minutes of talk, much of it consumed by the awkward business of translation, the two leaders adjourned to join Churchill and the senior military planners for the first plenary session of the conference.[14]

Roosevelt, the master charmer, felt frustrated. "I couldn't get any personal connection with Stalin," he later reflected. "He was correct, stiff, solemn, not smiling, nothing human to get ahold of. . . . I had come there to accommodate Stalin. I felt pretty discouraged because I thought I was making no personal headway. . . . I had to cut through this icy surface."[15]

In a large Soviet Embassy conference room, seated at a round table with a green baize cover, the Big Three opened the first formal session of the Teheran Conference. Roosevelt and Churchill began with introductory badinage. Stalin sat silently through these ceremonial preliminaries, then simply announced: "Now let us get down to business."[16]

There was much business at hand. For four days discussion among the heads of state and their military advisers ranged over the globe and reached out toward the uncertain future of the war's next stages and the even more unknowable contours of the postwar world. The three leaders probed the sensitive issue of Poland's postwar boundaries. They opened the volatile subject of what to do with defeated Germany. They talked about the war in Asia. They sketched a tentative accord on a successor organization to the League of Nations, without defining its exact structure. Most important, they talked about Overlord.

With respect to Poland, Roosevelt acquiesced in Stalin's proposal to move the entire Polish state westward by setting the eastern Polish frontier at the World War I–era "Curzon Line" and the western frontier at the Oder River. In a remarkable one-on-one session with Stalin, Roo-

14. The Roosevelt-Stalin exchange is described in *FRUS: Cairo and Teheran*, 483–86. The same volume is the principal source of the account that follows.
15. Frances Perkins, *The Roosevelt I Knew* (New York: Viking Press, 1946), 83–84.
16. Moran, *Churchill*, 145. Other accounts of this meeting are in *FRUS: Cairo and Teheran*, 487ff.; Pogue, *Marshall: Organizer of Victory*, 310ff.; and Dallek, 431ff.

sevelt spoke frankly as one politician to another. He explained "that there were in the United States from six to seven million Americans of Polish extraction, and, as a practical man, he did not wish to lose their vote." (Roosevelt here foreshadowed his intention to run for a fourth term in 1944.) He hoped, therefore, that Stalin would understand that "he could not publicly take part in any such arrangement [to redefine Poland's frontiers] at the present time." By the same token, Roosevelt "went on to say that there were a number of persons of Lithuanian, Latvian, and Estonian origin" in the United States. He joked that "when the Soviet armies re-occupied these areas, he did not intend to go to war with the Soviet Union on this point," but pointed out to Stalin that he could use some political cover with the American electorate. "[I]t would be helpful for him personally," the president pleaded, "if some public declaration in regard to . . . future elections [in eastern Europe] could be made."[17]

Stalin would thus leave Teheran confident that the Western allies had no stomach for interfering with his intention to close the hand of Soviet power over eastern Europe. Roosevelt had conceded as much even before leaving for Teheran. To an American Catholic prelate, New York's Archbishop Francis Spellman, he had confided that eastern Poland, the Baltic States, Bessarabia, and Finland were already lost to the Soviets. "So better give them gracefully," he told Spellman. "What can we do about it?" Roosevelt rhetorically questioned the Polish ambassador in Washington: "[Do] you expect us and Great Britain to declare war on Joe Stalin if they cross your previous frontier? Even if we wanted to, Russia can still field an army twice our combined strength, and we would just have no say in the matter at all."[18]

Though Roosevelt remained diffident about publicly acknowledging such distasteful realities, they were the inevitable precipitate of the war's military chemistry. Soviet power would stand supreme in the east, in all those territories overrun by the Red Army. The Western allies would dominate such areas as they could manage to liberate from Axis control—Italy, for example, and whatever other zones the eventual second front might allow them to penetrate. Stalin himself had said as much when he told the Yugoslav Communist Josef Tito that "whoever occupies a territory also imposes his own social system. Everyone imposes his own system as far as his army can reach. It cannot be otherwise."

17. *FRUS: Cairo and Teheran*, 594–95.
18. Frank Freidel, *Franklin D. Roosevelt: A Rendezvous with Destiny* (Boston: Little, Brown, 1990), 479; Dallek, 436.

Here was darkly foreshadowed the division of Europe in the half-century-long Cold War.[19]

As for Germany, Stalin made it clear that he intended to deal harshly, even cruelly, with his Nazi foes. He spoke bitterly about the political docility and submissiveness of the German people. He recalled an old story about a band of several hundred German workers who failed to reach a political rally in Leipzig because they meekly declined to leave a railway station at which there was no controller to punch their tickets. Time and again he insisted that Germany must be reduced to several smaller states, else it would recover within a generation and once again plunge the world into the maelstrom. At dinner on the twenty-ninth Stalin proposed that fifty thousand German officers be "physically liquidated." The statement brought Churchill indignantly to his feet, saying: "I will not be a party to any butchery in cold blood. . . . I would rather be taken out now and shot than so disgrace my country." Roosevelt, ever eager to play the conciliator, interjected: "I have a compromise to propose. Not fifty thousand, but only forty-nine thousand should be shot."[20] The discussion ended with general but unspecified agreement on the postwar dismemberment of Germany, which, Roosevelt remarked, "had been less dangerous to civilization when in 107 provinces," before Bismarck's day.[21]

Yet the president, mindful as ever of the hesitant and unreliable commitment of his countrymen to international involvement, stopped well short of accepting Stalin's suggestion that American ground forces participate in the long-term occupation of a splintered Germany. By way of explaining to Churchill and Stalin the persistent strength of American isolationism, Roosevelt observed that "if the Japanese had not attacked the United States he doubted very much if it would have been possible to send any American forces to Europe."[22]

Roosevelt's repeated references to the tenuousness of American internationalism cannot have failed to make a deep impression on Stalin's calculations about the correlation of forces that would shape the postwar international order. The Americans, Stalin had every reason to conclude, would in all likelihood retire from the international scene at war's end, just as they had after World War I. Whatever the ambitions of

19. Milovan Djilas, *Conversations with Stalin* (New York: Harcourt, Brace and World, 1962), 114–15.
20. Moran, *Churchill*, 152. Another account is in *FRUS: Cairo and Teheran*, 553–54.
21. *FRUS: Cairo and Teheran*, 603.
22. *FRUS: Cairo and Teheran*, 531.

American leaders, including the obviously internationalist Roosevelt, public opinion would compel a return to the historic American policy of isolation. Churchill, indeed, never wasted an opportunity to sermonize his American audiences about the dangers of such a regression, as he had in a speech at Harvard the preceding September. ("There was no use saying . . . 'our forebears left Europe to avoid those quarrels; we have founded a new world which has no contact with the old,'" Churchill had preached. "The price of greatness is responsibility. . . . The people of the United States cannot escape world responsibility.")[23] But Churchill's nightmare was Stalin's dream. With Germany broken, Britain enfeebled, and America withdrawn across the sea, Europe at war's end would lie prostrate and helpless before Soviet power.

Even as these contrasting visions of the postwar world swam in the heads of Churchill, Roosevelt, and Stalin at Teheran, more immediate questions clamored for answers. None was more urgent than Overlord. "The second front decision," Admiral Leahy wrote, "overshadowed all other accomplishments of the Teheran meeting."[24] In the first plenary session, Roosevelt forthrightly opened the subject. Stalin sat inscrutable and silent, his eyes downcast. He chain-smoked mechanically and doodled wolf heads with a red pencil. For more than a year, Roosevelt explained, the British and American military staffs had been addressing the question of relieving German pressure on the Soviet front. At Quebec the previous August the decision had been taken to launch Overlord, an attack across the English Channel onto the French coast, at the earliest feasible date. Because the Channel was such "a disagreeable body of water," Roosevelt went on, the invasion could not begin before May 1944. (The British, Churchill interjected, had much reason to be thankful for the disagreeableness of the Channel.)

Then, to the astonishment of his entire entourage, Roosevelt veered away from the Channel altogether. Before Overlord could be launched in the spring of 1944, he mused, what use might be made of the British and American forces already deployed in the Mediterranean? At the risk of delaying Overlord by as much as three months, he said, those forces could be employed to intensify the offensive in Italy, or perhaps to undertake new offensives in the Adriatic or Aegean Sea. What did Stalin think?

23. "The Ceremonies in Honor of the Right Honorable Winston Spencer Churchill" (Cambridge: Harvard University, September 6, 1943), 11.
24. Leahy, I Was There, 209.

It was a tense moment. These various Mediterranean schemes, Roosevelt knew, were anathema to his own military chiefs. Marshall later remarked that he was "always fearful that Roosevelt might lightly commit them to operations in the Balkans. 'When President Roosevelt began waving his cigarette holder,'" Marshall told an interviewer, "'you never knew where you were going'"[25] Yet these same Mediterranean strategies were dear to Churchill, and General Deane had warned just days earlier that Stalin seemed to be favoring them. So just what, Roosevelt now asked, was Stalin's opinion?

Stalin replied in barely audible Russian. No hint of animation or emphasis gave his Anglophone listeners any clue to the drift of his remarks. Roosevelt, Churchill, and their military chiefs impatiently waited for the interpreter. At last they heard that Stalin was confirming the Soviet Union's commitment to enter the war against Japan after Germany was finally defeated. This was a matter of no small consequence. The war in Asia showed little prospect at this date of being won soon or easily. Chinese forces, corrupt, divided, and inefficient, proved hopelessly unable to inflict serious damage on the Imperial Japanese Army on the mainland. In the broad Pacific, American ground forces were still only inching forward against stiff Japanese resistance in the Solomons and New Guinea. The navy's Central Pacific thrust was just beginning to crack the outermost shell of Japan's many-layered defensive perimeter in the Gilbert Islands. To reach Japan from the Gilberts, the Americans still had to cross more than four thousand miles of an ocean studded with fortified islands. It seemed axiomatic at this point in the war—and for a long time thereafter—that to avoid a protracted bloodbath in the fight against Japan, Russian help was desperately needed. The Russian's pledge to declare war on Japan had still further strategic implications: it drastically reduced the importance of China as a base from which to attack Japan, and it reduced the threat that the Soviets would expand beyond the agreed armistice lines at the end of the fighting in Europe while the British and Americans were busy finishing the war in Asia.

Following this brief but important statement about Asia, Stalin addressed himself directly to Roosevelt's question about Europe. He reminded his allies that 210 German and fifty satellite divisions were now battling the Soviet armies in the scorched and devastated Russian heartland. Italy, effectively sealed off from the rest of Europe by the Alps, he

25. Pogue, Marshall: Organizer of Victory, 641, n. 35.

said, was hardly a proper place from which to attack the Germans. Like-wise, he continued, the Balkans were far from the heart of Germany. Northern France, he declared unequivocally, was still the best place to open the second front.

Churchill conceded that the North African and Italian offensives had never amounted to the kind of second front that the Soviets had been promised since 1942. Overlord, he said, continued to have the highest claim on British and American resources. But he then plunged into an exposition of the advantages to be gained by continued operations in the Mediterranean theater.

Roosevelt, perhaps intending to placate Churchill, whom he had been snubbing since Cairo, interjected with a suggestion of a drive from Italy across the Adriatic into the Balkans. The other Americans present were flabbergasted. "Who's promoting that Adriatic business?" a startled Harry Hopkins scribbled to Admiral King, who was as mystified and worried as Hopkins.[26] Stalin, however, peremptorily discounted Chur-chill's assurance that continued Italian operations would not compro-mise the buildup for Overlord. He declared that scattering Allied forces in uncoordinated attacks was unwise. Overlord must be the priority, Stalin repeated. Along with a closely coordinated attack from the south of France, Overlord would enclose the German armies in the west within the arms of a giant pincer movement.

Churchill, upset that "the President was in private contact with Mar-shal Stalin and dwelling at the Soviet Embassy, and that he had avoided ever seeing me alone since we left Cairo," returned to the subject at the next day's plenary session.[27] Roosevelt's musings on the preceding day seemed to offer him an opening. Now the prime minister, according to Hopkins's biographer, "employed all the debater's arts, the brilliant lo-cutions and circumlocutions of which he was a master."[28] He again went on at length about Italy, Yugoslavia, Turkey, the island of Rhodes. Stalin at last, fed up with "all the dodges and feints of his practiced adversary," said that he wished to ask an "indiscreet question": "[D]o the British really believe in Overlord or are they only saying so to reassure the Russians?"[29]

Churchill countered with a proposal for further study of the political

26. Sherwood, *Roosevelt and Hopkins*, 780.
27. Churchill 5:331.
28. Sherwood, *Roosevelt and Hopkins*, 789.
29. Sherwood, *Roosevelt and Hopkins*, 789; *FRUS: Cairo and Teheran*, 539.

implications of his Mediterranean proposals. "Why do that?" Stalin exploded in a rare burst of animation. "We are the chiefs of government. We know what we want to do. Why turn the matter over to some subordinates to advise us?"[30] The Mediterranean proposals were nothing more than "diversions," said Stalin. He had no interest in them. "Who will command Overlord?" he demanded. Told that the matter of command was not yet decided, he growled: "Then nothing will come out of these operations." He insisted on knowing the precise date of the invasion. "If we are here to discuss military matters," Stalin declared summarily, "then Russia is only interested in Overlord."[31]

Roosevelt now said, finally and firmly, that the target date ("D-Day") for Overlord was May 1, 1944. Nothing, he added emphatically, would be allowed to alter that date. "[T]here was no God-damn alternative left," Hopkins gloated later to Lord Moran. Stalin looked triumphantly at Churchill, according to Hopkins, as if to say, "Well, what about that?"[32] Then, in his conciliatory way, the president observed "that in an hour a very good dinner would be awaiting," and the session adjourned.[33]

The following day all three leaders formally approved the Overlord plan. It called for a massive attack across the Channel in May 1944, supported by landings in the south of France and coordinated with a Russian offensive in the east. They further agreed to implement a "cover plan" to mystify and deceive the enemy as to the site and timing of the invasion. "The truth," said Churchill in one of his inimitable flourishes, "deserves a bodyguard of lies."[34]

"I thank the Lord Stalin was there," said Stimson upon hearing the reports of the Teheran Conference. "[H]e saved the day. He was direct and strong and he brushed away the diversionary attempts of the Prime Minister with a vigor which rejoiced my soul."[35] The prime minister meanwhile moped, gripped by what his physician called a "black depression." His ability to guide Roosevelt had clearly waned. No longer was Britain the dominant partner in the Anglo-American alliance, as it had been at least through the Casablanca Conference at the beginning of 1943. Indeed, Churchill's dogged insistence on his Mediterranean

30. Leahy, I Was There, 207.
31. Moran, Churchill, 147.
32. Moran, Churchill, 147.
33. FRUS: Cairo and Teheran, 552.
34. FRUS: Cairo and Teheran, 578.
35. Stimson Diary, December 5, 1943.

proposals may have stemmed in part from what British historian Michael Howard calls his "sheer chauvinism," his "chagrin at the increasing preponderance of American forces in the European war," and his "desire to form a purely British theater where the laurels would be all ours."[36]

"I could have gained Stalin," Churchill later reflected, "but the President was oppressed by the prejudices of his military advisers and drifted to and fro in the argument. . . . I regard the failure to use otherwise unemployable forces to bring Turkey into the war and dominate the Aegean as an error in war direction which cannot be excused by the fact that in spite of it victory was won."[37] Stalin, Churchill brooded, "will be able to do as he pleases. Will he become a menace to the free world, another Hitler?" Roosevelt had behaved ineptly, in Churchill's view; he "was asked a lot of questions and gave the wrong answers. . . . Stupendous issues are unfolding before our eyes," Churchill told Lord Moran, warming grandiloquently to his subject, "and we are only specks of dust, that have settled in the night on the map of the world. . . . We've got to do something with these bloody Russians."[38]

Roosevelt's translator at Teheran, Foreign Service officer Charles E. Bohlen, shared many of Churchill's forebodings. The Big Three had left "all political questions, except for the British-Soviet accord on Poland's eastern border . . . , completely up in the air," Bohlen reflected. Germany was apparently to be broken up, France stripped of her colonies, and Poland relocated to the west, but, he noted, "these ideas were so inchoate and informal that they did not constitute decisions. . . . Viewed in retrospect, there were many forerunners of Yalta [the second and endlessly controversial meeting of the Big Three, in February 1945] at Teheran." It seemed to Bohlen entirely possible that at war's end "the

36. Michael Howard, *The Mediterranean Strategy in the Second World War* (New York: Praeger, 1968), 57.
37. Churchill 5:305–6.
38. Moran, *Churchill*, 149–55. Churchill's despondency was due ostensibly to his anxiety about Russian expansion into eastern Europe, the Balkans, and the eastern Mediterranean. But Churchill's memoirs record an intriguing private conversation that he held with Stalin on the morning of November 30 at Teheran, in which Stalin raised the specter of another kind of danger in the east — Russian withdrawal from the war. "Stalin said he must warn me," Churchill wrote, "that the Red Army was depending on the success of our invasion of Northern France. If there were no operations in May 1944 then the Red Army would think that there would be no operations at all that year. . . . If there was no big change in the European war in 1944 it would be very difficult for the Russians to carry on. They were war-weary." Churchill 5:335.

Soviet Union would be the only important military and political force on the continent of Europe. The rest of Europe would be reduced to military and political impotence." The only definite consequence of the Teheran meeting, Bohlen concluded, was "that we had reached a solid military agreement."[39]

Roosevelt, too, left Teheran harboring some doubts about Russian intentions. Would Stalin actually deliver on his promise to declare war on Japan? Would the Russians in fact join a postwar international league? These questions worried the president in private. In public, concerned as ever to wean his countrymen from their isolationist ways, he insisted that the Teheran Conference had cemented the basis for great-power cooperation and established a close personal relationship between himself and Stalin. The Soviet premier was a "realist," he told a journalist, "something like me." "I got along fine with Marshal Stalin," he reported in a Christmas Eve Fireside Chat to the American people. "I believe that we are going to get along very well with him and the Russian people — very well indeed."[40] There was some dissembling in those remarks, though as in so much of Roosevelt's prewar struggle against isolationist opinion, it was a dissembling born of necessity and hope — the necessity now of nurturing the Soviet alliance and the hope that American influence might be brought to bear in the postwar world.

Yet Roosevelt the realist remained capable of more dissembling still. Despite his eagerness to win Stalin's confidence, he had conspicuously declined at Teheran to share with the Soviet leader the secret of Ultra and the infinitely more consequential secret of the Manhattan Project. As for the political commitments he had signaled at Teheran, Roosevelt disingenuously replied to an inquiring congressman in March 1944 that "there were no secret commitments made by me at Teheran. . . . This, of course, does not include military plans which, however, had nothing to do with Poland."[41] Left unmentioned was Roosevelt's effective acquiescence in a Soviet sphere of influence in Poland and the Baltic States. With these silences, the president laid up trouble for the future — trouble with his wartime ally and trouble with his own people, who would one day have to divest themselves of the idealistic illusions spun by their calculating leader and try to face the world the war was making with as much realism of their own as they could muster.

39. Charles E. Bohlen, *Witness to History, 1929–1969* (New York: Norton, 1973), 153.
40. Dallek, 439.
41. *FRUS: Cairo and Teheran*, 877

"WHO WILL COMMAND OVERLORD?" Stalin had demanded at Teheran. Stopping again in North Africa on his way home, Roosevelt gave Stalin his answer, though it was not one easily arrived at. At Quebec in August 1943 Churchill had conceded that the command of Overlord should go to an American, since the Americans would contribute the bulk of the materiel and the manpower. It had been widely assumed that the American would be George Marshall. In anticipation of her husband's new assignment, Mrs. Marshall had even begun to move the family belongings out of the chief of staff's residence at Fort Myer, in northern Virginia. Marshall, it was thought, was the only American with sufficient prestige and resolve to pull off Overlord in the face of all kinds of British blandishments to engage in delay and "scatterization." "[T]he one prayer I make for the Commander-in-Chief is steadfastness," Stimson wrote on the eve of the Teheran meetings. "Marshall's command of Overlord is imperative for its success," Stimson continued. "Marshall's presence in London will strongly tend to prevent any interference with Overlord."[42]

The prospect of Marshall's appointment provoked a controversy that festered through the autumn of 1943 and was not yet resolved when Roosevelt arrived at the conference table in Teheran. In his usual fashion, the president listened to many voices and kept his own counsel. When World War I icon General John J. Pershing protested to Roosevelt that Marshall's value as chairman of the Combined Chiefs of Staff far outweighed his possible contribution as a field commander, the president had disarmingly replied: "I think it is only a fair thing to give George a chance in the field.... I want George to be the Pershing of the Second World War—and he cannot be that if we keep him here."[43] On his way to the Cairo and Teheran meetings, the president had expanded on this theme in a conversation with General Eisenhower—the most frequently mentioned alternative to Marshall as Overlord commander. "Ike," said Roosevelt, "you and I know who was the Chief of Staff during the last years of the Civil War [it was Major General Henry W. Halleck, a feckless gossip deservedly swallowed by obscurity] but practically no one else knows, although the names of the field generals—Grant, of course, and Lee, and Jackson, Sherman, Sheridan and the others—every schoolboy knows them. I hate to think that 50 years from now practically nobody will know who George Marshall was. That

42. Sherwood, *Roosevelt and Hopkins*, 766.
43. Sherwood, *Roosevelt and Hopkins*, 770.

is one of the reasons I want George to have the big command—he is entitled to his place in history as a great General."[44] Hopkins and Stimson, Roosevelt knew, strongly supported this reasoning. So too, he had every reason to believe, did Churchill and Stalin.

Yet the president's military advisers voiced powerful reservations. Admiral Leahy, along with Marshall's colleagues on the Chiefs of Staff, Admiral King and General Arnold, agreed with Pershing. They wanted Marshall to remain in Washington. There his towering intelligence and monumental integrity made him a uniquely effective leader in the ceaseless clamor of argument over the competing claims of different services, widely separated theaters of war, and fractious allies. Marshall himself scrupulously determined not to embarrass the president by expressing his own preference, though surely, his biographer notes, command of Overlord was "the climax to which all his career had been directed."[45]

Roosevelt in the end acceded to the arguments of his military advisers. He may have been influenced as well by the consideration that, with Stalin's strong advocacy of Overlord now assured, there was less need for a figure of Marshall's stature to stand up to the British in London. On December 5 Roosevelt summoned Marshall to his villa in Cairo and told him, "I didn't feel I could sleep at ease if you were out of Washington."[46] Betraying no sign of disappointment, Marshall graciously drafted for the president's signature a note informing Stalin that "the immediate appointment of General Eisenhower to Command of Overlord operation has been decided upon." If Stalin harbored any thought that the appointment of Eisenhower rather than Marshall signaled some downgrading of the Overlord operation, the record does not reveal it.

The president then flew on to Tunis. Eisenhower, a balding, middle-aged man of average height, his open face brightened by a luminous grin, a warm, popular, plain-spoken officer known affectionately to his associates as "Ike," awaited him at the airport. Roosevelt "was scarcely seated in the automobile," Eisenhower later recalled, when he said, "Well, Ike, you are going to command Overlord." It was December 7, 1943, two years to the day since the Pearl Harbor attack.[47]

So it would not be Marshall but Eisenhower whose name, like

44. Sherwood, Roosevelt and Hopkins, 770.
45. Pogue, Marshall: Organizer of Victory, 320.
46. Pogue, Marshall: Organizer of Victory, 321.
47. Dwight D. Eisenhower, Crusade in Europe (New York: Doubleday, 1948), 207–8.

The Nazi juggernaut. Hitler seemed unstoppable as he swallowed up Austria and part of Czechoslovakia in 1938. The other European countries looked on helplessly, while the isolationist Americans remained aloof and unarmed. (FITZPATRICK COLLECTION, STATE HISTORICAL SOCIETY OF MISSOURI, COLUMBIA)

"Expecting us to untie 'em again?" Sour memories of America's apparently futile sacrifices in World War I power-fully reinforced isolationist sentiment in the 1930s—particularly in the pages of the stridently anti-internationalist *Chicago Tribune,* which regularly pub-lished opinions like this cartoon from February 28, 1940. (© COPYRIGHTED CHICAGO TRIBUNE COMPANY)

The Four Freedoms. Popular artist Norman Rockwell here rendered artistically a notable passage from Franklin Roosevelt's address of January 6, 1941, when he spoke of the "four freedoms" that were threatened by German and Japanese aggression. (NATIONAL ARCHIVES 208-PMP-43, 208-PMP-44, 208-PMP-45, 208-PMP-46)

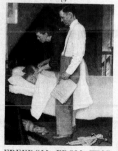

War in the Pacific

The USS Arizona at Pearl Harbor, December 10, 1941. More than 1100 sailors went down with the battleship on December 7, 1941, when a Japanese bomb exploded in its forward magazine. (NATIONAL ARCHIVES PACIFIC REGION, SAN FRANCISCO, NRHS-181-GENCORFC-L[11]1[BB3]2-8)

War at sea. This Japanese hit on the flight deck of the USS Enterprise in August 1942 killed the photographer who took the picture. (NATIONAL ARCHIVES W&C 976)

The jungle war. The Pacific War was a war of islands, involving dangerous amphibious landings like this one on Cebu Island, in the Philippines, in 1945. (LIBRARY OF CONGRESS LC-USZ62-99499)

Tarawa, November 1943. As yet unskilled in amphibious warfare, American forces suffered heavy casualties at Tarawa. The War and Navy Departments did not at first allow photographs like this to be shown to the American public. (NATIONAL ARCHIVES W&C 1342)

The face of battle. This marine's face reflects the stress and horror of the campaign for Peleliu, in the Palau Islands, in late 1944. (NATIONAL ARCHIVES W&C 1182)

War without mercy. A flamethrower, one of the war's most hideous weapons, in action on Kwajelien, February 1944. (NATIONAL ARCHIVES W&C1187)

The Grand Alliance

Roosevelt and Churchill at Casablanca, January 1943. At this fateful meeting, the two western leaders declared the "unconditional surrender" formula. They also announced the Combined Bomber Offensive, a coordinated plan of Anglo-American night-and-day bombing of Germany. Both measures were designed in part to compensate the Soviets for the western allies' failure to open a second front in 1943. (NATIONAL ARCHIVES [AMERICAN IMAGE 158])

Peril in the air. This U.S. bomber over Germany has apparently just had its rear horizontal stabilizer sheared off by bombs falling from above. Yet another bomb appears to be about to hit the fuselage. (FRANKLIN D. ROOSEVELT LIBRARY 74201301)

Teheran, November 1943. Roosevelt and Stalin meet at last, the first of two occasions (the second would be at Yalta in February 1945). The President tried to win the confidence of the Soviet dictator, with mixed results. Tensions in the alliance persisted to the end of the war, laying the groundwork for the half-century of Cold War that followed. (LIBRARY OF CONGRESS LC-USZ62-122309)

The Production Miracle

"The Run." The American economy rebounded from the greatest depression in memory to unprecedented outputs of war materiel. Here B-24 bombers pour off the assembly line at Ford's Willow Run plant, which at its peak produced one aircraft every sixty-three minutes. (FRANKLIN D. ROOSEVELT LIBRARY 66129 [31])

The war of motors. Men and women alike assembled these Dauntless dive bomber engines at the Douglas Aircraft plant in El Segundo, California. (NATIONAL ARCHIVES RG 80G-412712)

The night shift. Wartime factories and shipyards worked round the clock to make up for a decade of unpreparedness and to field a fighting force in time to win the war. Even with this crash effort, it took more than two years after the attack on Pearl Harbor to open a second front that engaged major elements of the German army in western Europe. (NATIONAL ARCHIVES RG 208 PP-252-2, BOX 23)

Women at war. The government mounted a vigorous propaganda campaign to lure women into the wartime work force. Contrary to legend, most chose to stay at home. (NATIONAL ARCHIVES W&C 823)

D-Day: A Second Front at Last

The fruits of production. By mid-1944, crammed equipment parks like this one were to be found throughout southern England, in preparation for the long-awaited cross-Channel attack. (FRANKLIN D. ROOSEVELT LIBRARY 65592[28])

A final briefing. Supreme Allied Commander General Dwight D. Eisenhower talks to paratroopers on June 5, 1944, the eve of the D-Day invasion. The encounter weighed heavily on Eisenhower, who feared that he was sending most of these men to their deaths. (NATIONAL ARCHIVES W&C 1040)

D-day, June 6, 1944. History's largest naval armada disgorged an enormous weight of men, materiel, and firepower onto the Normandy beaches, beginning the Battle for Northwest Europe. (NATIONAL ARCHIVES RG26-G-2517, BOX 37)

The price of victory. The landing craft carrying these men ashore on D-Day was sunk before it reached the beach. They were lucky to have survived. (NATIONAL ARCHIVES W&C 1042)

The Battle of the Bulge. In a last desperate lunge, Hitler threw much of his remaining army at the Allies in the Ardennes Forest in December, 1944, pushing a large "bulge" into the Anglo-American line. The advancing Germans had stripped these dead G.I.s of much of their equipment, including their shoes. (NATIONAL ARCHIVES W&C 1339)

Confronting the Holocaust. Kentucky Senator Alben Barkley at the Nazi death-camp of Buchenwald, April 24, 1945. The enormity of the Holocaust struck much of the world as simply incomprehensible. (NATIONAL ARCHIVES RG-111-SC-204745, BOX 63)

Evacuation of Japanese and Japanese-Americans from the West Coast. In March 1942, the U.S. Army's Western Defense Command ordered the forced evacuation of all Japanese living on the Pacific Coast, including American-born citizens. Most spent much of the remainder of the war in "relocation centers" in the western interior. A divided U.S. Supreme Court eventually upheld the constitutionality of the deportations, in a case that has remained controversial ever since. (LIBRARY OF CONGRESS LC-USF34-72313-2)

The war of cultures. The Japanese-American war was to an unusual degree a race war, characterized by racial stereotyping, the demonization of the adversary, hatred, and atrocities—on both sides. (NATIONAL ARCHIVES NWDNS-208-COM-132)

Women welders, New Britain, Connecticut, 1943. Employment opportunities in defense industries drew millions of African-Americans out of the South in wartime, changing America's racial demography and opening the door to the civil rights revolution of the post-war era. (LIBRARY OF CONGRESS LCUSW3-34282-C)

Waging Total War

Tokyo, August 1945. Firebomb raids on Tokyo and other Japanese cities killed far more people than the two atomic blasts at Hiroshima and Nagasaki. A single attack on Tokyo on the night of March 9, 1945, killed 90,000 Japanese and left another million homeless. (NATIONAL ARCHIVES 80-G-490421)

J. Robert Oppenheimer and Leslie Groves. The scientist and the administrator who brought the Manhattan Project to completion in time to help end the war against Japan. They are pictured here at the Alamogordo, New Mexico, test site where the first device was exploded. (ENERGY TECHNOLOGY VISUALS COLLECTION, U.S. DEPARTMENT OF ENERGY)

"Little Boy." The dark herald of the nuclear age: the uranium-fueled atomic bomb dropped on Hiroshima on August 6, 1945. The plutonium-fueled bomb dropped on Nagasaki 3 days later was code-named "Fat Man." (NATIONAL ARCHIVES RG-77-BT-115)

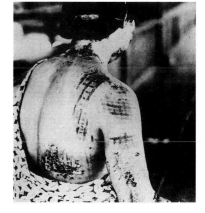

Atomic wounds. The pattern of this Hiroshima survivor's kimono was burned into her skin by the nuclear explosion. (NATIONAL ARCHIVES W&C 1244)

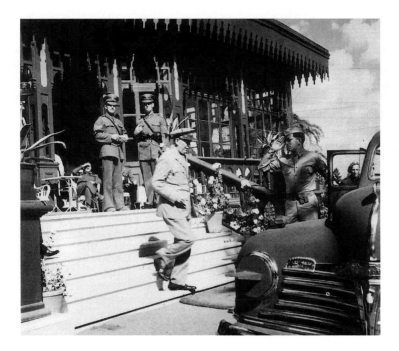

General George C. Marshall, "the organizer of victory." Pictured at the Cairo Conference in 1943, en route to the fateful meeting of the Big Three at Teheran. (NATIONAL ARCHIVES RG-306-NT-320D-2)

General George S. Patton Jr. in Sicily in 1943. He was among the most able and controversial of all the American military leaders. (NATIONAL ARCHIVES W&C 1024)

Pacific War Conference, Hawaii, July 1944. From the left, General Douglas MacArthur, Roosevelt, Admiral William D. Leahy, and Admiral Chester Nimitz. Roosevelt summoned the conference largely for political purposes related to his 1944 presidential re-election campaign. When the President refused to choose between MacArthur's Southwest Pacific drive and Nimitz's Central Pacific campaign, both campaigns went forward, possibly delaying the final assault on the Japanese home islands. (NATIONAL ARCHIVES W&C 749)

"I have returned." Douglas MacArthur returns to the Philippines at Leyte, October 20, 1944. With characteristic self-dramatization, he announced: "People of the Philippines…. The hour of your redemption is here…. Rally to me." (NATIONAL ARCHIVES W&C 1207)

Victory

The victors. Churchill, Truman, and Stalin at Potsdam, July 25, 1945. Roosevelt had been dead since April; an election replaced Churchill before the Potsdam Conference ended. Of the great Allied wartime leaders, Stalin alone remained. At Potsdam unresolved issues about the nature of the post-war world boiled menacingly to the surface. The new American president soon had to grapple with a new kind of conflict, the Cold War. (NATIONAL ARCHIVES CENTRAL PLAINS REGION NRE-338-FTL[EF]-7215[5])

Grant's, would be inscribed in the schoolbooks as the man who held the "big command." Like Grant, too, another renownless midwestern career military officer plucked from obscurity by the caprice of war, Eisenhower would later ascend to the presidency—the first professional soldier since Grant, to be so honored. The prospect that command of Overlord might well clear a pathway to the White House cannot have escaped Roosevelt and had doubtless contributed to his anguish over withholding the prize from Marshall.

Dwight David Eisenhower, like nearly all the senior American commanders in the war, was a man of the nineteenth century. Born in Texas in 1890 and reared in Abilene, Kansas, he was an army "lifer," approaching twenty-five years of service when World War II broke out. He had scant hope, before the war changed everything, for promotion beyond the rank of colonel, which he attained only in March 1941. In common with many officers in the interwar army, he had never seen combat. He had spent World War I training tank troops in a stateside camp and had languished through the postwar years in a series of humdrum assignments, including service in France writing a guidebook to American battlefields. Though only a middling student at West Point, he shone during a stint at the army's Command and General Staff School at Fort Leavenworth in 1926, placing first in his class of 275 officers. He had served on Douglas MacArthur's staff in Washington in 1933 and accompanied MacArthur to the Philippines in 1935. MacArthur called him "the best officer in the Army. When the next war comes," MacArthur advised, "he should go right to the top."[48]

He did. Marshall summoned him to Washington in December 1941 to head the Pacific and Far Eastern Section of the War Department's War Plans Division. Amidst the chaos of war-girding Washington, Marshall needed assistants who would shoulder heavy responsibilities and act decisively without coming to him for consultation. Eisenhower did not disappoint. He quickly distinguished himself for the thoroughness of his analyses and the lucidity of his reports. Literally within hours of his arrival in Washington, Eisenhower had drafted a plan to use Australia as a base of operations against the beleaguered Philippines. Sounding what would become a characteristic note, he justified his proposal for swift and heavy military effort with an appeal to considerations of morale: "The people of China, of the Philippines, of the Dutch East Indies

48. Stephen E. Ambrose, *Eisenhower: Soldier, General of the Army, President-Elect, 1890–1952* (New York: Simon and Schuster, 1983), 93.

will be watching us. They may excuse failure but they will not excuse abandonment."[49] Marshall was impressed. He selected Eisenhower in June 1942 over 366 senior officers to command all American forces in the European theater. Promoted to lieutenant general the following month, Eisenhower then assumed command of the Allied armies that cleared North Africa and invaded Italy.

A careful student of war, Eisenhower was a still more careful student of human psychology—especially of those elements that made up the mysterious compound of effective leadership. "The one quality that can be developed by studious reflection and practice is the leadership of men," he wrote to his son in 1943. "The idea is to get people working together . . . because they instinctively want to do it for you. . . . [E]ssentially, you must be devoted to duty, sincere, fair and cheerful."[50] Conspicuously absent from this list of a military leader's qualities was any mention of the need for aggression or for the bravura posturing associated with the likes of Douglas MacArthur or George Patton. Eisenhower, clearly, was no ordinary soldier.

As the head of the combined-service, inter-Allied forces in the North African and Italian campaigns, Eisenhower had amply demonstrated his capacity for leadership in the uniquely collaborative circumstances of the Anglo-American military partnership. "The seeds for discord between ourselves and our British allies were sown," he wrote to Marshall in April 1943, "as far back as when we read our little red history school books. My method is to drag all those matters squarely into the open, discuss them frankly, and insist upon positive rather than negative action in furthering the purpose of Allied unity."[51] Unity in allied command, he advised Lord Louis Mountbatten, "involves the human equation. . . . Patience, tolerance, frankness, absolute honesty in all dealings, particularly with all persons of the opposite nationality, and firmness, are absolutely essential."[52]

In the Mediterranean campaigns Eisenhower had proved his ability to fathom and manipulate "the human equation." He had established his reputation as a sunny personality, fair and upstanding in his dealings with all, unflappable in crisis. Yet even Eisenhower's geniality contained elements of his purposeful artifice. No matter how wearing his duties or how grim the military outlook, Eisenhower by act of will "firmly

49. Stephen E. Ambrose, *The Supreme Commander: The War Years of General Dwight D. Eisenhower* (Garden City, N.Y.: Doubleday, 1970), 6.
50. *PDDE* 2:1198.
51. *PDDE* 2:1071.
52. *PDDE* 3:1420–23.

determined that my mannerisms and speech in public would always reflect the cheerful certainty of victory."[53] This stratagem worked, to marvelous effect. Even his sometimes bitter critic Bernard Montgomery conceded that Ike's "real strength lies in his human qualities. . . . He has the power of drawing the hearts of men towards him as a magnet attracts the bits of metal. He merely has to smile at you, and you trust him at once. He is the very incarnation of sincerity." His colleague General Omar Bradley said simply that Ike's smile was worth twenty divisions.[54]

Eisenhower's studied geniality found an appreciative admirer in Franklin Roosevelt, himself an adept scholar of the human psyche and a virtuoso practitioner of the recondite craft of leadership. Now, flying from Tunis to Sicily for an inspection tour of American troops, Roosevelt the accomplished master instructed Eisenhower the sedulous apprentice in the arts that he must summon and hone in his new assignment. Huddling in a seat alongside the general as their aircraft droned over the Mediterranean, the president dwelt on the teeming difficulties that awaited Eisenhower in London. There he would confront head-on, day in and day out, the full majesty of the British Government and the seductive personality of Winston Churchill. Churchill still believed, Roosevelt warned, that a failed Channel attack could cost the Allies the war—and that the risk of failure was large. Despite his assurances at Quebec and his submission at Teheran, Churchill had not laid to rest his gnawing anxieties about Overlord. It would take all of Eisenhower's skill and resolution, Roosevelt advised, to keep Overlord on schedule.

Eisenhower listened carefully. Occasionally he gazed pensively at the blue waters beneath as the aircraft approached the Sicilian coast. To him now fell not only the task of managing the inevitable tensions that beset the British-American alliance. He also faced the colossal responsibilities of organizing a vast command that embraced land, sea, and air arms, orchestrating the tendentious wills of countless admirals, generals, and statesmen, and meshing the million upon million gears, the prodigious material tonnage and the precious human flesh, that would constitute the largest, most complex military operation in history.

PLANNING FOR OVERLORD had already begun—on both sides. Even as the final preparations for the Teheran Conference were being

---

53. Unpublished introduction to Eisenhower's *Crusade in Europe*, quoted in Fred I. Greenstein, *The Hidden-Hand Presidency: Eisenhower as Leader* (New York: Basic, 1982), 37.
54. Ambrose, *Supreme Commander*, 325; Omar N. Bradley and Clay Blair, *A General's Life* (New York: Simon and Schuster, 1983), 240–41.

made, Hitler had issued Führer Directive 51 on November 3, 1943. "The threat from the East remains," Hitler proclaimed,

> but an even greater danger looms in the West: the Anglo-American landing! In the East, the vastness of space will, as a last resort, permit a loss of territory even on a major scale, without suffering a mortal blow to Germany's chance for survival.
>
> Not so in the West! If the enemy here succeeds in penetrating our defenses on a wide front, consequences of staggering proportions will follow within a short time. All signs point to an offensive against the Western Front of Europe no later than spring, and perhaps earlier.... I have therefore decided to strengthen the defenses in the West, particularly at places from which we shall launch our long-range war against England. [Hitler here referred to the pilotless V-1 flying bombs and the later V-2 rocket bombs then under development in the Baltic village of Peenemunde.] For those are the very points at which the enemy must and will attack; there — unless all indications are misleading — will be fought the decisive invasion battle.[55]

Hitler had much to worry about. Where would the eventual blow fall? The "West" as Führer Directive 51 defined it stretched from the Bay of Biscay to Denmark, even to Norway, where *der Führer* insisted on keeping eleven divisions in readiness to repel an invasion. To the urgent task of fortifying that vast perimeter, a task that necessarily implied guessing at the most likely landing zone, Hitler assigned one of his most senior commanders, the seasoned "Desert Fox" of the North African campaigns, Field Marshal Erwin Rommel. His nominal superior but effective co-equal in command was Field Marshal Gerd von Rundstedt, an elderly, aristocratic veteran who had distinguished himself in Poland, the Low Countries, and Russia in the early phases of the war before reaching retirement age in late 1941. Rundstedt had been called back to active duty in July 1942 and appointed commander-in-chief for the west, responsible for anti-invasion preparations. Two field marshals, Rommel and Rundstedt, now essentially held the same assignment, with telling consequences for the inefficiency of the German command structure in the west.

After a brief inspection of defensive preparations in Denmark, Rommel arrived in December 1943 in France. Its northern coast, he rightly calculated, was the overwhelmingly probable site of the anticipated in-

55. Gordon A. Harrison, *Cross-Channel Attack* (Washington: Department of the Army, 1951), 455.

vasion. But without knowing precisely where his enemy would strike on that still expansive terrain, Rommel still faced a daunting challenge.

Even as Eisenhower was heading toward his new headquarters in England, directly across the English Channel Rommel was commandeering his own command post on the upper reaches of the Seine River, in the Château La Roche-Guyon, where Thomas Jefferson had once been a guest. Before Rommel's arrival, France had been a kind of convalescent hospital for German troops recovering from the ghastly slaughter in the east. From his sumptuous headquarters in the Hotel George V in Paris, Rundstedt presided serenely over his mercifully placid sector. Far from battle, members of an occupying army to be sure, but one rarely put on its mettle by the mostly subdued French population, Rundstedt's soldiers ate well, idled much, slept soundly, gave thanks for their agreeable billeting, and prayed that their good fortune would last.

Rommel changed all that. Within weeks of his arrival, toiling at obsessive pace under his swinging field marshal's baton, the Germans cobbled together an "Atlantic Wall" along the northern French coast, designed with desperate cunning to repel the Allied invasion before it ever got off the tidal flats. They beavered up half a million bristling steel and concrete antitank obstacles on the beaches from Brest to Calais, emplaced and registered gun batteries, built and armed pillboxes, laid four million mines, flooded lowlands, and planted countless inland fields with "Rommel's asparagus," cruel spikes rising eight to twelve feet out of the earth, festooned with barbed wire and booby traps and intended to impale descending parachutists or blow up landing aircraft. By early May Rommel would survey his work with satisfaction. "If the British give us just two more weeks," he said on May 5, "I won't have any more doubt of it."[56]

On their side, the British and the Americans had set the ponderous machinery of planning in motion in the spring of 1943, even before the Teheran Conference. An Anglo-American team working in London under British General Frederick Morgan, designated COSSAC (chief of staff to the supreme Allied commander, who was of course not yet named), had first wrestled with the same question that confounded the Germans: where, exactly, should the blow be struck? Because the planners deemed air superiority over the landing zone to be essential, the

---

56. Rommel quoted in John Keegan, *The Second World War* (New York: Viking, 1990), 372.

site must necessarily lie within an arc defined by the 175-mile radius of action of the British Spitfire—still, as planning began in 1943, the principal fighter aircraft in the Allied arsenal. That simple calculus immediately eliminated Denmark and Norway, as well as Brittany, a sentimental favorite with the Americans, who had landed the American Expeditionary Force through the Breton ports of Brest and St. Nazaire in the First World War. From their bases in the south of England, Spitfires could cover a zone stretching from Holland in the north to France's Cotentin peninsula in the south. The Netherlands' watery lowlands lacked sufficiently hard beaches or solid interior plains across which to transport large numbers of men and machines. The Cotentin peninsula could be easily sealed at its base, marooning an invasion force.

By process of elimination, therefore, the choice reduced to two sites: the Pas de Calais, a short hop across the English Channel from Dover; or the bucolic region to the west of the Seine's mouth, Normandy's Calvados Coast, so called from the apple-based drink typical of the region. Calais had conspicuous attractions, especially the shortness of the sea voyage from Dover and its proximity to the great German industrial plexus of the Ruhr—the Allies' ultimate and highest strategic objective. But the very conspicuousness of those considerations meant that the Germans would expect an attack there and mount a fierce defense.

Normandy was farther from Germany, and from England, too, for that matter, but it had irresistible advantages. Its broad, hard beaches could accommodate the hundreds of thousands of troops and the tens of thousands of vehicles that must come ashore, until such time as proper ports—at Cherbourg, Brest, and eventually Antwerp—could be secured and fitted to supply the expeditionary force. In the meantime, two artificial harbors, known as "Mulberries," would be towed across the Channel to the Normandy shore.

Normandy had a further and invaluable advantage, one that compounded the returns on the deception scheme agreed upon at Teheran. Code-named Fortitude, that scheme enfolded the secret of secrets—the location of the Overlord landing—deep within the fraudulent embrace of Churchill's "bodyguard of lies." Fortitude constituted perhaps the war's most extravagant demonstration of the wonderful wages of untruth. The lie that Fortitude fed to the Germans was simple enough: that the cross-Channel invasion would be aimed at Calais (or even, possibly, at Norway).[57] To render this already plausible fiction credible, a real gen-

57. "Fortitude" actually consisted of two lies—one that the invasion would fall at Calais (Fortitude South) and the other that it would fall on Norway (Fortitude North).

eral, George Patton, was named to command a wholly imaginary body, First U.S. Army Group. The illusion of First U.S. Army Group's existence, some fifty fictive divisions strong, was sustained by generating radio traffic, sure to be overheard on the Continent, among Patton's notional units and by sprinkling the countryside and waterways of Kent and Sussex, opposite Calais, with dummy aircraft, tanks, trucks, and landing craft, all to fool aerial reconnaissance. Perhaps most consequentially, the shadowy "Twenty Committee," cryptically taking its name from the Latin signification of the "double cross" (XX), cashed in on the elaborately cultivated plot by means of which it had turned every single German informant in England into an Allied agent. Through these sources word passed to German headquarters that Patton's army was real and that Calais was almost certainly the place.

Diverting German attention to Calais held out the prospect of rich rewards. Achieving surprise, to be sure, would enormously facilitate the initial landings, but even more important than achieving surprise at the battle's outset was inducing lingering indecision once the battle was joined. Establishing the beachhead was the relatively easy part of Overlord, Morgan's planners reasoned. The race of the buildup, which would wager the Allies' capacity to reinforce against the enemy's ability to counterattack, would ultimately determine the success or failure of Overlord.[58] Thus the Germans might at first consider the Normandy landings a feint—something they would never presume in the case of a direct assault on Calais—and so hesitate to commit the full force of their mobile reserves. He who hesitates is lost, the old maxim goes, and the hope of producing a fatal tentativeness in the German response to the cross-Channel attack was the greatest prize for which Fortitude aimed.

As it happened, the confusion that Fortitude sought to sow exacerbated one of the knottiest problems that the Germans faced as they attempted to implement Führer Directive 51: what mix of static and mobile forces, deployed in what dispositions, offered the best possibility of repelling the Allied invaders? From the moment that Rommel had arrived in France, he and Rundstedt had disagreed over this issue. Rundstedt, despairing of adequately defending his entire coastal sector and

---

Fortitude South, however, was far the more elaborate and consequential deception. See Charles Cruickshank, *Deception in World War II* (New York: Oxford University Press, 1979); and J. C. Masterman, *The Double-Cross System in the War of 1939 to 1945* (New Haven: Yale University Press, 1972).

58. As Churchill had told Stalin at Teheran: "I was not afraid of going on shore, but of what would happen on the thirtieth, fortieth, or fiftieth day." Churchill 5:335.

wary of a feint, proposed to let the invaders come ashore and then massively counterattack. Once the main enemy force was clearly identified, he would choose his own battleground and unleash armored panzer divisions held in reserve well behind the beaches. Rommel, on the other hand, like Yamamoto in the Pacific, feared "the numerical and material superiority of the enemy striking-forces" and wanted to give his enemy no opportunity to put ashore in France even a part of the stupendous weight of flesh and firepower he knew to be accumulating in England. More immediately, unlike Rundstedt, who had never fought a major battle in which the enemy enjoyed air superiority, Rommel in Africa had firsthand experience of the difficulty of shifting even fast-moving mechanized formations under the wrathful eye of Allied air power. "British and American superiority in the air alone has again and again been so effective," he wrote, "that all movement of major formations has been rendered completely impossible, both at the front and behind it, by day and by night." From this analysis it followed axiomatically, in Rommel's view, that the *Wehrmacht* must be committed to "beat off the enemy landing *on the coast* and to fight the battle in the more or less strongly fortified coastal strip."[59] Rommel proposed, therefore, to pre-position the panzer divisions as near to the beaches as possible. As his old desert foe Montgomery worriedly described it on the eve of D-Day:

> Rommel is an energetic and determined commander; he has made a world of difference since he took over. He is best at the spoiling attack; his forte is disruption; he is too impulsive for the set-piece battle. He will do his level best to "Dunkirk" us — not to fight the armoured battle on ground of his own choosing but to avoid it altogether and prevent our tanks landing by using his own tanks well forward.[60]

Yet for all that he worried Montgomery, Rommel could never adequately answer Rundstedt's practical objections to his theoretically sound doctrine: well forward *where*, near to *which* beaches, exactly, in Normandy or the Pas de Calais? The result was a compromise by which some panzer divisions were assigned to Rommel and some to Rundstedt, with Hitler himself thickening the viscosity of this already awkwardly divided command by retaining final authority over release of the reserve

59. Rommel quoted in Carlo D'Este, *Decision in Normandy* (New York: HarperCollins, 1994), 116–17; emphasis added.
60. Montgomery quoted in Keegan, *Second World War*, 374, and more fully in D'Este, *Decision in Normandy*, 85.

units. This poorly resolved dispute over defensive doctrine — aggravated by the poorly articulated German command structure in the west — Fortitude had helped to foster and would artfully exploit.

Despite the problems that plagued the German defense, Rundstedt and Rommel still had a formidable fighting machine at their disposal. To be sure, the principal theater of war was still in the east, where 165 German divisions continued to bleed before the relentless advance of the Red Army. But through the winter of 1944 Germany deployed some sixty German divisions, eleven of them panzers, all superbly equipped and many of them combat-hardened, in France and the Low Countries. Most of that force was gathered north of the Loire River. The Seventh Army stood in Normandy, the Fifteenth Army at Calais; the panzer reserves waited near Paris. All knew that with the spring the war would come to the west. As the days lengthened, they drilled and dug, watched and prayed.

Across the Channel, meanwhile, Eisenhower struggled to assemble his invasion force. His command structure reflected the combined-arms, inter-Allied complexities of Overlord. Eisenhower's deputy supreme commander, Air Marshal Sir Arthur Tedder, and all three subordinate commanders, were British: Sir Trafford Leigh-Mallory for air, Sir Bertram Ramsey for sea, and Sir Bernard Montgomery for land. In the first phase of the battle, Montgomery's Twenty-first Army Group would include both British and American ground forces, the latter under the command of General Omar N. Bradley. When American troop strength had built to sufficient size — it would eventually greatly outnumber the British — Bradley would assume command of Twelfth U.S. Army Group and report thereafter directly to Eisenhower. At a later stage of the battle, Eisenhower himself would move his headquarters to the Continent and assume direct control of the land battle.

Eisenhower had much confidence in Tedder, and affection for him as well. Ramsey and Leigh-Mallory, on the other hand, especially the latter, he regarded as "ritualistic" in outlook. And in Montgomery, Eisenhower found himself again at close quarters, as he had been in Africa and Italy, with one of the most colorful and controversial personalities of the war. A compact man, jittery in public, solitary and reclusive by nature, Montgomery was in demeanor and temperament the gregarious Eisenhower's opposite. At El Alamein, Montgomery had stopped the German advance in North Africa, giving Britain its first major victory of the war and earning a hero's laurels for himself. But the victory he wanted most was not in Africa, or even in Italy, but in France.

Montgomery seethed to avenge the humiliation of Dunkirk, where he had been evacuated along with the rest of the British army in 1940.

Grievously wounded and taken for dead in the First World War, "Monty" bore with him for the rest of his life not only the battle scars on his body but a deep horror of the futile, homicidal wastage of troops he had witnessed in trench warfare. This dread Churchill shared, as indeed did all the British leaders. With methodical application, Montgomery devoted himself to sustaining the morale of troops under his command. He cultivated eccentricities, including his trademark beret, in order to facilitate his recognition by his men and their identification with him; his beret, he once said, was worth two divisions in bolstered morale. Montgomery also laboriously trained his troops to a knife-edge sharpness and committed them to action only after the most careful deliberation. As with General George McClellan in the American Civil War, these characteristics made him fabulously popular with his soldiers. But his notorious reluctance to move until his army was prepared to the last button also frequently aggravated his allies and even his own superiors. Montgomery's caution on the Normandy battlefield would cause Eisenhower and Churchill alike many headaches. Yet in defense of Montgomery's record in Overlord, it might be added that no one knew better than he that the British forces he led were a wasting asset. Unlike the Americans, with their huge potential reserves of manpower, the British army by 1944 had been severely winnowed by battle. The army Britain fielded in Normandy would be the last force it could throw into the war. Its losses could not be made good by reinforcements. It must, therefore, be used wisely and sparingly.

Omar Bradley, on the other hand, would assume a command position in Overlord whose growing responsibilities would reflect the growing preponderance of American strength on the ground, just as Montgomery's role would shrink in proportion to the relative role of the British army. A steady, self-effacing Missourian, Bradley was as loyal a subordinate as Montgomery was an aggravating one. Like his West Point classmate Eisenhower, Bradley had never seen combat until he arrived in North Africa in 1942. But he had by 1944 already acquired a reputation, nourished by the worshipful dispatches of war correspondent Ernie Pyle, as "the GI's general"—a persona reflected in the title of his postwar memoir, A *Soldier's Story*.

BY THE EVE OF D-DAY southern England teemed with twenty American divisions, fourteen British, three Canadian, one Polish, and one French. Those numbers did not add up to the three-to-two attacker-to-defender ratio that conventional military wisdom held to be minimally necessary for a successful offensive, but the Allied plan hoped to improve upon that classical arithmetic with deception, air power, and time. Deception would divide and delay the enemy's forces, reducing his effective strength at the point of attack. Air power would isolate the battlefield, interdicting Rommel's and Rundstedt's ability to reinforce and resupply. If the initial landing could thus buy sufficient time, a lodgement area would be secured into which an additional million Allied troops, most of them American, could eventually be poured. Then the full logic of what Rommel called the Americans' "numerical and material superiority" would play itself out in a relentless war of attrition, pitting the exhausted Germans against wave after wave of fresh manpower and the lavish output of American factories. This, reduced to its bare essentials, was the Overlord plan.

Yet there were limits even upon the Americans' apparently prodigious supplies of men and machines — especially machines. When he first saw the COSSAC plan in October 1943, even before his appointment to head the Supreme Headquarters Allied Expeditionary Forces (SHAEF), Eisenhower instantly concluded that it projected too puny a force for the initial landing. Among his first decisions as supreme Allied commander was to increase the D-Day assault from three attacking infantry divisions to five, with additional divisions to land by the end of the first day. That decision raised anew a maddeningly familiar problem: Where would the landing craft come from to carry the additional divisions across the Channel on D-Day? The debate over this issue, tortuously protracted and inordinately wearing on Eisenhower, illustrated once again the shaping role of industrial production on military strategy, as well as the bitter competition among various theaters for the inevitably finite material resources on which modern warfare depended.

Those lessons had been borne in upon President Roosevelt within hours of parting from Stalin at Teheran. On his return to Cairo after the Big Three meeting, Roosevelt reneged on his promise to Chiang Kai-shek, scarcely a week old, to support an amphibious operation in connection with Stilwell's offensive in northern Burma. Roosevelt explained his reasoning to Chiang, pleading the finitude of American resources but avoiding any mention of China's diminished strategic importance now that Stalin had agreed to enter the war against Japan. The commitment made to Stalin to launch the cross-Channel attack in May, said Roosevelt, imposed "so large a requirement of heavy landing craft as to make it impracticable to devote a sufficient number to the amphibious operation in the Bay of Bengal." Chiang received a consolation prize of sorts in the form of the Cairo Declaration, reiterating the unconditional-surrender formula and applying it to Japan in particular.[61]

Now Eisenhower had complicated the logistical equation still further by doubling the projected size of the D-Day landing force. The practical result of that decision soon became apparent. The specific items required, their numbers starkly modest yet irreducible in their concreteness, were 72 LCIs, 47 LSTs, and 144 LCTs.[62] "The destinies of two great empires," Churchill grumbled, "seem to be tied up in some God-damned things called LSTs."[63] Eisenhower determined that half of this added "lift" necessary to an expanded Normandy assault would be found by scaling back the projected simultaneous landing in southern France, code-named Anvil, and transferring some of its ships to Overlord. The remaining vessels would be provided by postponing D-Day to a new target date of June 5, in order to secure an additional month of factory production.

Thus, almost from the moment of assuming command, Eisenhower had been compelled to take decisions that delayed Overlord and reduced and reconfigured the Anvil supporting operation. Those developments directly contradicted assurances that Roosevelt had made to Stalin about both the timing and the shape of the second front. By the same token, delay of the cross-Channel attack and deemphasis on southern France suited the British just fine.

Back in Washington, Marshall watched these developments with mounting concern. Anvil in fact was destined to persist as an item of contention between the British and Americans for the next eight months. It was in the end as much a test of wills among the Allied leaders as it was a military or strategic issue. The British had never wanted Anvil. Churchill repeatedly insisted that Anvil and Overlord bore no strategic relation to one another, given the huge distance (some five hundred miles) between them. He also, no doubt, resented Anvil because it oriented Allied resources in the Mediterranean northwestward,

61. Sherwood, *Roosevelt and Hopkins*, 802.
62. Respectively, Landing Craft, Infantry; Landing Ship, Tank; and Landing Craft, Tank.
63. Harrison, *Cross-Channel Attack*, 64. Churchill also wrote to George Marshall on April 16, 1944: "How it is that the plans of two great empires like Britain and the United States should be so much hamstrung and limited by a hundred or two of these particular vessels will never be understood by history." Churchill 5:454.

out of Italy and the east, the regions of his own nearly obsessive strategic preoccupation. The Americans, on the other hand, Marshall in particular, saw Anvil and Overlord as parts of a single operation, not in competition with one another but mutually supportive. Besides, the Americans had promised Stalin at Teheran that they would undertake Anvil as an integral part of the Overlord plan.

Behind Marshall's thinking lay both military and political considerations. Marshall the soldier worried that a diminished Anvil would preclude the envelopment of the German forces in France in the pincer movement Stalin had touted at Teheran, require the Allies to secure a long, vulnerable flank along the Loire River to forestall the Germans from shifting troops from southern France to the Normandy front, and delay the Allied acquisition of desperately needed port facilities at Marseilles.

Marshall the statesman worried, as did Roosevelt, that a smaller Anvil would break faith with Stalin. Equally worrisome, marooning in Italy a sizeable body of troops previously intended for Anvil threatened to reopen the eternally vexed Mediterranean question. For the Americans, Anvil was a prophylaxis against further British "periphery-pecking" in Italy and to the east. It would supplant the dead-end Italian campaign and in the process ensure that whatever Allied effort was to be made in the Mediterranean would be oriented northwestward, toward Germany, away from the Adriatic and the Balkans, a region the Americans regarded with a blend of ignorance and dread. Eisenhower's retreat from Anvil put all those benefits at risk. It seemed to return the Anglo-American strategic dialogue to its unresolved status of pre-Teheran days. In the words of Marshall's biographer: "All the Churchillian predilections for an overall strategy of bleeding Hitler's Reich to death by a lengthy nibbling at the fringes rather than risking dwindling British manpower in a now-or-never assault, apparently buried at Teheran, now were resuscitated."[64] Marshall fretted that Eisenhower was perhaps showing insufficient spine, succumbing to the very Churchillian blandishments about which Roosevelt had cautioned him at the time of his appointment to SHAEF. In a pointed warning, Marshall admonished Eisenhower in early February "to be certain that localitis is not developing and that pressures on you have not warped your judgment."[65]

Events in Italy reinforced Churchill's anxieties and compounded Eisenhower's difficulties. The Anzio landing, undertaken in January 1944,

---

64. Pogue, *Marshall: Organizer of Victory*, 337–38.
65. Pogue, *Marshall: Organizer of Victory*, 331, 335.

was still stalled as winter passed into spring. If the Anzio beachhead were not to be written off as a failure, it might have to be reinforced with a second amphibious attack. Did a similar—or a worse—fate await the landings in Normandy, where the enemy was prepared and watchful? The Italian stalemate stirred Churchill's darkest memories of the First World War. "I was not convinced," Churchill later reflected, that "a direct assault across the Channel on the German sea-front in France . . . was the only way of winning the war, and I knew that it would be a very heavy and hazardous adventure. The fearful price we had had to pay in human life and blood for the great offensives of the First World War was graven in my mind. Memories of the Somme and Passchendaele and many lesser frontal attacks upon the Germans were not to be blotted out by time and reflection."[66]

The difficulties at Anzio quickened long-standing British fears and had a more immediate consequence as well: not merely the reduction of Anvil, but its postponement. Landing craft scheduled for release from Italy to the Anvil landing must now be held in reserve for further possible operations to break the Italian deadlock. Consequently, Eisenhower noted in his diary on February 7, 1944: "It looks like Anvil is doomed. . . . I hate this."[67] In the weeks that followed, Eisenhower formally agreed to postpone Anvil—until August, as it eventually turned out. Though the Allies did proceed to transfer troops from Italy to England, the fighting in the Mediterranean peninsula ground on, to D-Day and beyond. Bit by bit, the promises made at Teheran to quit the Mediterranean and give unassailable priority to Overlord were being eroded.

THE ITALIAN FIASCO, with its claim to retention of landing-craft in the Mediterranean, threatened Anvil-Overlord from the sea. Another no less formidable threat loomed in the air. Eisenhower was nominally the supreme Allied commander, yet his apparently sweeping authority did not at first extend to the air forces. Though SHAEF did control something called the Allied Expeditionary Air Force (AEAF), ostensibly committed to tactical support for Overlord, AEAF remained an undernourished organization, headed by the widely distrusted British officer Leigh-Mallory. The huge "strategic" air arms—British Bomber Command under the single-minded Arthur Harris, and the United States

66. Churchill 5:514.
67. Robert H. Ferrell, ed., *The Eisenhower Diaries* (New York: Norton, 1981), 110–11.

Strategic Air Forces in Europe (USSTAF), now commanded by the calculating Carl Spaatz, who in January 1944 had become commander-in-chief of the U.S. strategic air arm in Europe—remained anomalously beyond the reach of Eisenhower's authority. Bringing their fearful power to bear on the success of Overlord proved to be one of Eisenhower's most daunting challenges.

The big bombers had been shouldering the main burden of the Allied war effort against Germany for years—since 1940 in the British case and 1942 in the American. Whatever their national differences, the airmen, British and American alike, nursed a passionate ambition to demonstrate once and for all the truth of the Douhetian doctrine that strategic bombing was the ultimate war-winning weapon. They resisted any surrender of the independent role necessary to clinching their alluring—and self-justifying—thesis. They resisted with special obduracy now, in the early months of 1944, when the promise of air power's singular capacity to change the very nature of warfare seemed to hover tantalizingly within their reach.

After the disastrous raids on Schweinfurt and Regensburg in 1943, the Americans had been forced to curtail the deep-penetration missions that held the promise of extinguishing German industrial production and thus starving the *Wehrmacht* into submission. But as he arrived in Europe to assume command of the air arm in early 1944, Spaatz believed a new weapon had brought America's bomber force to the brink of success at last, to the exciting edge of nothing less than a strategic revolution. The development that invigorated Spaatz was the advent of a new aircraft, the P-51 Mustang fighter. Able to stay aloft for more than seven hours, with a range of eight hundred miles and beyond, faster, nimbler, and with a higher operational ceiling than its German counterparts, the P-51 could now protect bomber streams flying to the farthest reaches of the *Reich*. Like the F6F Hellcat in the Pacific, the Mustang dramatically altered the combat equation in the skies over Europe. The Luftwaffe acknowledged as much when it rewrote the rules of engagement for its own Me109s and Focke-Wulf 190s in early 1944. Henceforward, German fighters were instructed to continue attacking P-38s anywhere, to engage P-47s below twenty thousand feet, but to break off and dive away on contact with P-51s.[68]

68. Stephen L. McFarland and Wesley Phillips Newton, *To Command the Sky: The Battle for Air Superiority over Germany, 1942–1944* (Washington: Smithsonian Institution, 1991), 56.

Exulting in the promise of this new weapon, and sensing the imminent vindication of the airmen's cherished strategic doctrine, Spaatz, joined by Harris, returned with a vengeance in February 1944 to the implementation of one of the Combined Bomber Offensive's priority missions: suppression of the Luftwaffe by destroying German aircraft production facilities. During "Big Week," February 19–26, 1944, British and American bombers flew more than six thousand sorties and dropped some eighteen thousand tons of bombs on German airframe and ball-bearing factories. As Midway had avenged Pearl Harbor, Big Week avenged the Schweinfurt debacles of August and October 1943. American bomber losses for Big Week were less than 6 percent. Even more telling, fighter losses were only 1 percent. The Luftwaffe, on the other hand, lost over one-third of its strength in that single week. Through dispersal and improvisation, Germany managed to resume and even increase aircraft production for another several months, but the German pilots who had plummeted from the heavens during the murderous raids of Big Week proved irreplaceable.

Big Week was a pivot, and the airmen knew it. While the Luftwaffe shriveled as a fighting force, spanking new P-51s and fresh, well-trained American pilots poured in swelling numbers into the British airdromes. With even more dramatic suddenness than the turnaround in the Atlantic sea battle in the spring of 1943, Big Week decisively marked the Allies' ascendancy in the European air war.

Confident of his new superiority, Spaatz shifted tactics at the end of February. The new objective would be not simply to crush the Luftwaffe on the ground, by pouring bombs on airfields and factories, but to capitalize on the technical and numerical superiority of the P-51s by engaging and destroying enemy aircraft in the sky. The new mission was graphically defined when the head of the Eighth Air Force Fighter Command changed the sign on his office wall. It had previously read: "The first duty of the Eighth Air Force fighters is to bring the bombers back alive." Now it stated: "The first duty of the Eighth Air Force fighters is to destroy German fighters."[69] The "little friends" in their sleek new P-51s were to be freed of the bomber formations, encouraged to pursue enemy interceptors and leave the lumbering "big friends" to fend for themselves. The chilling realization dawned on the bomber crews that the amply discredited notion of the B-17s as self-defending Flying Fortresses was being resurrected — ironically enough, just at the moment

69. McFarland and Newton, *To Command the Sky*, 160.

when the arrival of the P-51s had promised a new level of safety for the bomber formations. One B-17 pilot recollected bitterly that "morale was declining" as the realization sank in that "we were expendable . . . we were bait."[70]

In the first week of March, Spaatz aggressively implemented this new approach of baiting the Germans to the attack. The strategy required selecting a target so precious that German fighters would be obliged to rise in swarms to defend it. That thinking led directly to Berlin. British Bomber Command had been targeting Berlin heavily since November and imploring Spaatz to join in the attack. Now Spaatz agreed. In the process he edged uncomfortably close to mimicking Harris's practice of bombing "area targets."[71] In a directive explaining that pre-D-Day bombing targets in France had been selected with an eye to minimizing civilian casualties, Spaatz added: "This consideration does not apply in Germany."[72] Huge airfleets of Fortresses and Liberators began dumping their deadly tonnage on Berlin, their crews less concerned now about the accuracy of their bomb drops than about their ability to attract and annihilate Luftwaffe fighters.

Spaatz and the American airmen had now narrowed the moral ground that they had proudly insisted separated them from the indiscriminate terror tactics of the British Bomber Command. To be sure, Harris and Spaatz had different motives—the former to "dehouse" workers and break the back of civilian morale, the latter to lure the Luftwaffe into the sky—but to the dying civilians on the ground below that was a distinction without a difference. The British pacifist Vera Brittain made just that point when she published a stinging condemnation of area bombing in a religious journal in March 1944. She sparked an intense but brief flurry of commentary in the United States, where the destruction by bombing of Monte Cassino had already provoked a similar controversy. These scattered protests registered the first faint stirrings of the American conscience about the ghastly havoc that Yankee technological ingenuity was now able to wreak on civilians as well as soldiers.

Aglow with renewed ambition in the wake of their triumphs of February and March, both Spaatz and Harris were emboldened to assert the classic Douhetian dogma with new vigor. More loudly than ever

70. McFarland and Newton, *To Command the Sky*, 163–64, 215.
71. Spaatz used the phrase in a memo to his chief, General H. H. Arnold, on January 23, 1944, quoted in McFarland and Newton, *To Command the Sky*, 194.
72. Ronald Schaffer, *Wings of Judgment: American Bombing in World War II* (New York: Oxford University Press, 1985), 68.

they claimed that air power alone could win the war. Overlord, they trumpeted, with its huge risks and inevitable carnage, was unnecessary. Harris had already claimed that if he were allowed to continue full force with his saturation bombing of German cities he could achieve "a state of devastation in which surrender is inevitable" by April 1, 1944.[73] April came and that claim proved to be inflated, as had so many of the airmen's promises. Yet Spaatz could still declare in that same month that "it is of paramount importance the Combined Bomber Offensive continue without interruption. . . . If this were done, the highly dangerous Overlord operation could be eliminated."[74]

Churchill predictably seized upon these enthusiasms as providing yet another possible alternative to the dreaded cross-Channel attack. In a meeting with Eisenhower that dragged late into the night of February 28, he heatedly refused to release Bomber Command to the supreme commander's control. The huge Lancasters, he said, were like the historic British "Home Fleet," indispensable symbols of British prestige and independence. Eisenhower replied that without full control of all the air arms of both nations he might "have to pack and go home."[75]

Against this backbeat of renewed confidence among the airmen and renewed intransigence on Churchill's part, Eisenhower convened a tense meeting at his suburban London headquarters on March 25. "If a satisfactory answer is not reached," Eisenhower wrote in his diary on the eve of the meeting, "I will request relief from this command."[76] At issue were Spaatz's proposal to accelerate the momentum of recent air-war successes by attacking German oil refineries and a competing scheme to employ the heavy bombers against French transportation facilities in the Normandy hinterland in order to isolate the invasion beachhead and allow the buildup to go forward with minimum disruption. Both plans had their advocates.

Oil was the lifeblood of German industry, Spaatz argued, and, not incidentally, of the feared panzer divisions as well. Deprive Germany of oil, and its economy and army alike would grind to a halt. As a bonus, Spaatz added, the Luftwaffe would have no choice but to raise whatever fighter strength it had left in defense of the refineries, thus bringing to a triumphant climax the ongoing elimination of the German air arm as

73. Hastings, *Overlord*, 48.
74. Hastings, *Overlord*, 49.
75. Accounts of the Churchill-Eisenhower meeting on February 28 are found in David Eisenhower, *Eisenhower*, 152, and in *PDDE* 3:1755–60.
76. Ferrell, *Eisenhower Diaries*, 115.

an effective fighting force. Whatever its promised benefits, the "oil plan" was also, Eisenhower recognized, a scheme to maintain the independence of the bomber forces so that they might continue to pursue the elusive dream of winning the war through air power alone. It would also leave the Normandy beaches dangerously exposed to the threat of German counterattack.

Eisenhower's deputy supreme commander, Air Chief Marshal Sir Arthur Tedder, presented the alternative "transportation plan." It was premised on the assumption that the ground invasion — Overlord — not the air war, had the highest priority. Accordingly, it envisioned using air power primarily to isolate the Normandy battlefield by knocking out bridges along the Seine River and creating a "railway desert" in the French interior through concerted and repeated attacks on carefully selected marshaling yards and switching points. To achieve those goals, Tedder argued, Bomber Command and USSTAF must come under SHAEF's direction.

Eisenhower weighed these arguments carefully. The oil plan had merit, he knew, but it also had a formidable defect: it would take time to work its effects. "[N]o one who does not have to bear the specific and direct responsibility of making the final decision . . . can understand the intensity of these burdens," he complained to his diary a few weeks later. "The supreme commander, much more than any of his subordinates," he reflected, must assess "the political issues involved, particularly," he emphasized, "the anticipated effect of delay upon the Russians."[77] Adopting the oil plan almost certainly implied another delay in Overlord. Eisenhower therefore declared in favor of the transportation plan. That should have settled things. But the issue was not yet resolved.

Churchill fought a further delaying action to avoid implementing the March 25 decision. Showing a solicitude for French civilian casualties that formed no part of his thinking when it came to Germans, he appealed to Roosevelt in May to reconsider whether the transportation plan was "the best way to use our Air Forces," particularly in view of the "French slaughters" that it entailed. In yet another reminder of who was now the senior partner in the alliance, Roosevelt brusquely replied that the decision had been Eisenhower's and he would not second-guess it.[78]

Spaatz succeeded in retaining sufficient independence to continue bombing at least some of his oil targets, but Eisenhower had won his

77. Ferrell, *Eisenhower Diaries*, 119–20.
78. *C&R* 3:122–23, 127.

own "air war" against the strategic bombing enthusiasts. On April 14 the strategic air wings passed under Eisenhower's control. They were to remain there until such time as the invasion force was considered to be safely ashore. Systematic attacks now began against the Seine crossings and the railways of northern France—attacks deliberately spread over a considerably wider area than the intended landing zone, for purposes of sustaining the Fortitude deception.

Having won these battles to secure Overlord against threats from sea and air, Eisenhower in the spring of 1944 fought a final battle for Overlord on the ground—or, rather, a battle over who would control the ground of France once it was liberated. This one he lost. Two considerations drove the supreme commander's thinking. First, he wanted the cooperation of the French resistance forces, modest though they were in scale and influence, during the landings and thereafter. Second, and far more important, he wanted a civil authority to govern liberated France, freeing the Allies of the burden of deploying an occupying army for administrative purposes.

The obvious candidate to constitute such a civil authority was Charles DeGaulle. His French Committee of National Liberation (FCNL) had joined hands with the Allies in North Africa, had fighting divisions to offer (especially General Jacques Phillipe LeClerc's Second Armored Division), and had clearly positioned itself as a government-in-exile, awaiting only liberation to establish its legitimate rule over France. To Eisenhower all this seemed self-evident. He had in fact as early as December 1943 assured DeGaulle at a meeting in Algiers that his forces would play a role in Overlord, including the liberation of Paris. But the supreme commander here ran afoul of his own president, whose obstinacy on the question of DeGaulle rivaled or exceeded Churchill's tenacity on all matters touching on the Mediterranean.

Roosevelt's policy toward France was a tangled skein of contradictions, shot through with an unreasoning disdain for DeGaulle whose ultimate sources are not easily located. Washington had made an uneasy and unholy peace with Vichy and had cut a controversial deal with Admiral Darlan to facilitate the invasion of North Africa. Yet Roosevelt had uttered no dissent from Stalin's vindictive tirade against the French at Teheran, nor had he shown the slightest interest in supporting DeGaulle, transparently the chief challenger to Vichy's authority and the towering symbol of French resistance to Nazi rule. Roosevelt insisted, rather, that embracing DeGaulle would amount to foisting an unwanted ruler on the French by force of arms and would likely precipitate a civil war. To DeGaulle, Roosevelt's attitude "seemed to me on the same order as Alice's Adventures in Wonderland," a judgment from which it is frankly difficult to dissent. Eisenhower patiently explained to his president that "there exists in France today only two major groups, of which one is the Vichy gang, and the other characterized by unreasoning admiration for DeGaulle." But Roosevelt would not relent. He refused to recognize the FCNL as the legitimate or even provisional government of France, and he would not extend the hand of friendship to DeGaulle. Under those circumstances, the haughty DeGaulle flatly refused to make an invasion-eve broadcast in support of Overlord. "To hell with him," said Eisenhower, "if he doesn't come through we'll deal with someone else." It was a hollow threat, as there was no someone else.[79] DeGaulle would have the last word. He gave his own broadcast on D-Day itself, unapologetically claiming for the FCNL the title of "the French government." And when Paris was liberated, he, and LeClerc, would be there.

79. This account relies heavily on Ambrose, *Supreme Commander*, 377–91.

7

The Battle for Northwest Europe

Almighty God: Our sons, pride of our Nation, this day have set upon a mighty endeavor. . . . These men are lately drawn from the ways of peace. . . . They yearn but for the end of battle, for their return to the haven of home.

— Franklin Roosevelt, D-Day prayer, June 6, 1944

As spring began to unroll its green carpet across the south of England in 1944, American GIs drilled on the softly undulating fields, staged mock attacks on the shingle beaches and in the leafing copses, rumbled in trucks and tanks along stone-hedged roads, snickered at the quaint ways of the tea- and warm-beer-drinking British, and oiled and sighted their gleaming new weapons. Occasionally they relieved their boredom by setting fire to haystacks with tracer bullets. The teeming Yanks, arriving at a rate of 150,000 per month since late 1943, were "overpaid, oversexed, and over here," the British quipped. (To which the Yanks replied that their British comrades-in-arms were underpaid, undersexed, and under Eisenhower.) Yanks and Britons alike joked that only the thousands of barrage balloons tethered to southern England kept the island afloat under the stupendous weight of materiel stockpiled for the invasion: some five million tons of munitions and supplies, including more than a hundred thousand vehicles. Offshore, an armada of more than six thousand ships was assembling to move that horde of apprehensive men and those mountains of weapons, food, and equipment across the Channel.

The nearly two million American ground troops and the almost equal number of U.S. Army Air Forces personnel in Britain represented the bulk of the more than seven million men the U.S. Army then had under arms. That huge force, mass-produced in short order like so much else

284

in the American arsenal, had mushroomed from the skeletal prewar regular army of fewer than two hundred thousand men in 1940. Over the course of the war, almost sixteen million men, most of them conscripted, as well as half a million women, all of them volunteers, would serve in the U.S. armed forces. Young men had begun pouring into the Selective Service System's induction centers for physical and psychological examinations in the last weeks of 1940. Eventually nearly eighteen million were examined, and their records provided a remarkable composite portrait of a generation's physical and mental makeup. Most were judged fit for service, though almost two million men were rejected for neuropsychiatric reasons (conspicuously including homosexuality, though many homosexuals in fact served in all service arms), and four million more for various medical and educational deficiencies, such as rotten teeth, poor eyesight, and illiteracy. To meet its manpower needs, the army eventually undertook remedial work with draftees. Some twenty-five thousand army dentists pulled fifteen million teeth and fitted 2.5 million sets of dentures; army optometrists fitted 2.25 million pairs of eyeglasses; and special army schools bestowed the gift of literacy on almost a million recruits.

The average GI was nearly twenty-six years old in 1944, born in the year the war to end wars had ended (sailors and marines were somewhat younger). He stood five feet eight inches and weighed 144 pounds, an inch taller and eight pounds heavier than the typical recruit in World War I. Four out of ten white but fewer than two out of ten black draftees had finished high school. Almost a third of the whites and more than half the black recruits had no education beyond grade school. Overall, the statistically average GI had completed one year of high school — three full years more education than the average "Doughboy" of 1917.[1]

Those judged fit to serve at the induction center were fingerprinted and then given a perfunctory interview in which they could indicate

1. Lee Kennett, *G.I.: The American Soldier in World War II* (New York: Charles Scribner's Sons, 1987), passim. Much of the following discussion relies on Kennett's work and on Geoffrey Perrett, *There's a War to Be Won: The United States Army in World War II* (New York: Random House, 1991). See also Samuel A. Stouffer's classic study, *The American Soldier* (Princeton: Princeton University Press, 1949); and the relevant volumes in the official *U.S. Army in World War II* series: *The Organization of Ground Combat Troops, The Procurement and Training of Ground Combat Troops,* and *The Employment of Negro Troops* (Washington: Department of the Army, 1947, 1948, 1966, respectively); and *Selective Service and Victory: The 4th Report of the Director of Selective Service* (Washington: USGPO, 1948).

their choice of service. Until the end of 1942, the period when most men were inducted and when the navy and marines took only volunteers, draftees had just three choices: the Army Ground Forces, the Army Services of Supply, or the Army Air Forces. The last was the most popular, but individual choice yielded to the army's estimation of its own needs. The air forces skimmed off the best performers on the Army General Classification Test, a 150-question, forty-minute aptitude test administered to every recruit. (Sample question: "Mike had 12 cigars. He bought 3 more and then smoked 6. How many did he have left?") A disproportionate share of low-scorers on the AGCT ended up in the infantry. Interestingly, the typical combat infantryman was also shorter and weighed less than his counterparts in the Services of Supply or the air forces. The infantry's fighting echelons were almost entirely white. Ignoring the performance of Negro troops in the Civil War, the World War II army considered blacks unfit for combat duty and consigned the great majority of them to service units.

During 1941 and 1942 millions of draftees flowed into the hastily erected training camps, 242 of them in all, concentrated in the South, where the requirements for camp siting were most easily met. A divisional training camp ideally needed at least forty thousand acres of varied terrain for weapons practice and maneuvers, a reliable water source, adequate roads, access to rail transport, proximity to an urban center for recreation and supply, and good weather. Fort Lewis in Washington State was among the few large training facilities outside the South that fitted those specifications. Among the biggest camps were Fort Benning, Georgia, which could handle almost one hundred thousand trainees; Fort Shelby, Mississippi (eighty-six thousand); Fort Bragg, North Carolina (seventy-six thousand); and Fort Jackson, South Carolina (sixty-five thousand).

Reveille woke the inductees at 6:05 A.M. They ate breakfast, cleaned their barracks, trained from 8:00 to 5:30, took evening mess, were back in barracks at 7:00, and observed "lights out" at 9:45. They passed first through "basic" or "branch-immaterial" training, including close-order drill, military protocol, and physical conditioning. They also underwent seven hours of indoctrination about their country's war aims, much of it conveyed in a series of films, *Why We Fight*, made by the renowned Hollywood director Frank Capra. They then passed to a second phase of instruction in small-arms firing and weapons maintenance and proceeded to specialized training in skills such as radio communications and heavy weapons deployment. Next came combined-arms training, in which infantry, armor, artillery, and tactical air units worked together, forty-four weeks in all, followed by eight weeks of exercises and maneuvers at divisional strength, and capped by a twenty-five-mile road march with full thirty-pound pack. At all levels of training, the army's basic instructional technique was the same: demonstration, explanation, performance.

A handful of National Guard divisions retained a regional identity, and blacks were rigidly segregated both in the camps and in the field, but the army tossed the remaining millions of men into the mother and father of all melting pots. The dozens of conscript divisions were all-American mixtures recruited from north, south, east, and west. They jumbled together farm boys and factory hands, old-stock Yankees and new immigrants, rich as well as poor, Protestants, Catholics, and Jews. Many young men who had never left their rural county or urban neighborhood confronted in the army more social, ethnic, and religious diversity than they had ever encountered, perhaps ever imagined. In the year that it took to train a division, and in the months of service that followed—most men remained in uniform "for the duration," usually a term of thirty-three months, half of it overseas—human barriers were often breached and long-lived bonds between men created. Old stereotypes withered and once-improbable friendships flowered. Because no new divisions were formed after the ninety-division program was completed in late 1943, individuals were trained thereafter as replacements in cycles of eight to seventeen weeks. They were destined to be slotted into the line as needed and had less chance to form close ties with their comrades-in-arms than the original trainees did.

For millions of men born during and just after the Great War of 1914–18, their experience as GIs defined their generational identity as nothing else could, not even their long boyhood agony during the Great Depression. World War II took them away from home, taught them lessons both dreadful and useful, formed their friendships, and, if it did not end them, shaped the arc of their lives ever after. For those who survived, the war laid up a store of memories that time could not corrode —indeed, memories often embroidered by time's indulgent hand. Benjamin Bradlee, later the editor of the *Washington Post*, spoke for many veterans when he remembered the war as "more exciting, more meaningful than anything I'd ever done. This is why I had such a wonderful time in the war. I just plain loved it. Loved the excitement, even loved being a little bit scared. Loved the sense of achievement, even if it was only getting from Point A to Point B; loved the camaraderie . . . the responsibility. . . . The first time a man goes into battle," Bradlee added, "is strangely like the first time a man makes love to a woman. The anticipation is overpowering; the ignorance is obstructive; the fear of disgrace is consuming; and survival is triumphant." And if the war made its mark on these men, they left their mark too — not only on the women they wooed and in the battles they fought but also on every flat surface from Fort Benning to Normandy and Okinawa, their own ubiquitous inscription, probably the single most famous sentence of the war: "Kilroy was here."[2]

The army improved the standard of living of many recruits. Not only did they receive proper medical attention, some for the first time in their lives, but at the garrison food ration of 4,300 calories per day, many ate better than they ever had before. Even the standard field provender, the C-ration and the K-ration, contained about 3,400 calories, as well as a stick of chewing gum and four cigarettes. Training typically expanded a man's chest measurement by an inch and added six pounds to his weight. Privates, many ladled from the vast pool of the unemployed, earned fifty dollars a month after mid-1942, and every soldier was covered by a ten-thousand-dollar life insurance policy.

The American bases in wartime England were oases of abundance that were the wonder and envy of the British. Liberty Ships disgorged tons of commodities that had all but disappeared from British civilian life. Hungry Britons, whose standard of living declined by more than 20 percent after the war's outbreak, counted themselves lucky to befriend American servicemen. Then they might feast on the cocoa, canned meat ("Spam"), orange juice, tinned and even fresh fruit, soft drinks, candy bars, chewing gum, and tobacco that GIs obligingly liberated from their overstuffed military warehouses. The Americans had more of everything: more men, more food, more trucks, more guns — even more toilet paper. The allotment in the British army's bathrooms was 3 sheets per man per day; the American ration was 22.5 sheets.[3]

The U.S. Army's tail-to-teeth ratio, the relation of its service to its combat arms, was the highest of any army in the war. In the *Wehrmacht's* order of battle, one noncombatant provided for every two frontline soldiers. The Americans reversed the ratio: two service personnel

2. Ben Bradlee, A *Good Life: Newspapering and Other Adventures* (New York: Simon and Schuster, 1995), 76, 65; Samuel Hynes, "So Many Men, So Many Wars: 50 years of Remembering World War II," *New York Times Book Review*, April 30, 1995, 12.

3. Kennett, *G.I.*, 96.

stood behind every combatant in the field. Every GI landed in Europe would be supported with forty-five pounds per day of supplies, a quarter of it petroleum and petroleum products, contrasted with twenty pounds for a British soldier and a German quota that sometimes fell to four pounds. Much of that fabulous wealth of material, especially the fuel, was necessary for the war of movement that the Americans had come to fight. But some British observers grumbled that the shipping shortages that had bedeviled the planning for Overlord might have been avoided if the Americans were less committed to maintaining troops in training and even in combat at the standard of living to which they were accustomed in civilian life.[4]

The GIs' army was designed by George Marshall. Well before the war began, Marshall had led an effort to replace the old four-regiment "square" divisions that had fought in France in World War I with a new three-regiment "triangular" formation. The triangular structure informed the army's table of organization from top to bottom. Three twelve-man squads, led by noncommissioned officers, made up a platoon. Three platoons, each led by a lieutenant, composed a company. Three companies, each commanded by a captain, made a battalion. Three battalions, each under a major or lieutenant colonel, formed a regiment. Three regiments, each commanded by a colonel, made up a division, which was led by a general. The battalion was the smallest unit to have a staff, or headquarters company. It also comprised a heavy weapons company, wielding antitank guns, mortars, and .50-caliber machine guns. Under divisional command was a two-thousand-man field artillery unit, equipped with 75mm, 105mm, and 155mm howitzers. Division also controlled a medical detachment, five hundred strong, as well as another two thousand men in various service and auxiliary units, such as engineers and military police. Marshall also organized several independent tank battalions that could be assigned as needed, as well as five airborne and sixteen armored divisions, the latter composed of two tank regiments with a total of 375 tanks, an armored infantry regiment mounted on half-tracks, and an attached self-propelled artillery regiment. The infantryman's standard weapon was the .30-caliber M-1 Garrand rifle, which could be field-stripped and reassembled using only a

4. Richard Overy, *Why the Allies Won* (New York: Norton, 1995), 319; Max Hastings, *Overlord: D-Day and the Battle for Normandy, 1944* (London: Pan, 1985), 234; Richard M. Leighton and Robert W. Coakley, *United States Army in World War II: Global Logistics and Strategy, 1940–1943* (Washington: Department of the Army, 1955), 723.

bullet's nose and firing rim as a tool. An average rifleman could fire forty rounds per minute, an expert up to one hundred. All told, the fifteen-thousand-man triangular division packed twice the firepower of the twenty-four-thousand-man square division of World War I.

The U.S. Army had also modernized in other ways since that earlier conflict, though in some cases belatedly. Only in 1940 did West Point abandon the genteel requirement that cadets devote six hours a week to horsemanship, to be replaced by the same basic training that the millions of conscripts were receiving. But at the army's Command and General Staff School at Fort Leavenworth, Kansas, senior officers had for almost two decades before 1941 passed through a challenging curriculum of 124 map problems and terrain exercises. The program at Leavenworth emphasized speed and skill in deploying mobile formations. It was there that future generals learned how to handle multidivisional corps, armies, and army groups. And it was there that they came to appreciate the value of a war of movement and the fluid genius of the triangular scheme, which put a premium on swift decisiveness at the highest levels of command.

The triangular organizational device was meant above all to maximize mobility. Movement was everything in American military planning: movement in amphibious vehicles onto the landing beaches, movement of men and guns on the ground, movement by tank and half-track and truck, and movement in the air as well. All American divisions were motorized, and the armored divisions' half-track troop transport and supply vehicles meant that they were not confined to the road. By some estimates, the GIs' army could move ten times faster and farther than the American Expeditionary Force in World War I. Mobility was the Americans' trump card on the battlefield, at all levels of engagement. The operational doctrine for the triangular force, whatever its size, was the "holding attack": one unit, whether platoon, battalion, or regiment, engaged the enemy's front; a second tried to turn his flank; a third was held in reserve, ready to move swiftly to the point of maximum advantage. George Patton, perhaps the premier tactician of mobile warfare, reportedly summarized the logic of the holding attack as "grab the enemy by the nose, then kick him in the seat of the pants." The ultimate application of the holding attack, at divisional level and above, was the "wide envelopment," in which a nose-held enemy would be encircled by a lightning run to his rear. In the battle that was about to be joined, the wide envelopment of the German forces in Normandy by Patton's high-speed armored divisions would hold the key to victory.

These were the men, and this was the army, whose job it now was to turn the pronouncements of the statesmen and the diagrams of the planners into reality. One disaster marred the preinvasion training exercises in Britain: German torpedo boats chanced upon troop-laden landing craft rehearsing an amphibious landing at Slapton Sands near the Devonshire village of Dartmouth on April 28, 1944, drowning some seven hundred Americans. But to a remarkable degree, the assemblage and training of the Overlord invasion force went forward methodically. Steadily the British equipment parks filled with rank upon rank of jeeps, Dodge trucks, Sherman tanks, half-tracks, howitzers, self-propelled guns, ambulances, bulldozers, towering stacks of artillery shells, cartons of grenades, cartridges, bazookas, K-rations, C-rations — and medical supplies.

Of the 5.4 million Americans who would eventually fight in the Battle for Northwest Europe, 135,576 GIs and airmen would die. In all theaters, and in all service arms, 291,557 Americans were killed in action, another 113,842 succumbed to accident or disease, and nearly a million more were wounded. Wounded American servicemen benefited from dramatic advances in medical science, especially whole-blood transfusions and penicillin, the first effective antibiotic, developed in England in 1941 and available in significant quantities by late 1944, just as the major American offensives began. Only 4.5 percent of wounds proved mortal in the army and 3.2 percent in the navy, where a stricken sailor could swiftly reach onboard hospital facilities. An American's chance of dying in battle in World War II was about one in one hundred, one-third the rate of World War I and one-tenth the rate of the Civil War.[5]

In the last days of May endless columns of troops, trucks, and tanks began to snake down the narrow roads of southern England, squeezing into the "sausages," the assembly areas that bulged on the planners' maps behind the loading ports from Cornwall to Dorset. After months of argument and planning, of agonies political, psychological, and logistical, "the mighty host," wrote Eisenhower, "was tense as a coiled spring . . . coiled for the moment when its energy should be released and it would vault the English Channel in the greatest amphibious assault ever attempted."[6]

5. Kennett, G.I., 173–78; HSUS, 1140; Charles B. MacDonald, United States Army in World War II: The European Theater of Operations, the Last Offensive (Washington: Department of the Army, 1973), 478; Michael Clodfelter, Warfare and Armed Conflicts: A Statistical Reference to Casualty and Other Figures, 1618–1991 (Jefferson, N.C.: McFarland, 1992), 962–63.
6. Dwight D. Eisenhower, Crusade in Europe (New York: Doubleday, 1948), 249.

At SHAEF's new forward headquarters at Southwick House in Portsmouth, one last ordeal tortured Eisenhower: the weather. The success of the amphibious attack depended on a peculiar constellation of moon, sun, and tide. The airborne troops to be dropped before dawn on D-Day needed at least a half-moon to illuminate their landing zones. The engineers needed a low tide at first light to expose Rommel's beach obstacles and allow maximum time for demolition. The necessary conjunction of tide and light occurred on only three days in early June—the fifth, sixth, and seventh. The next available date was June 19, a fortnight that might as well have been an eternity when the effects on troop morale, logistical revision, and Russian impatience were taken into account.[7]

By June 3 all troops were aboard their ships along the coast of southern England. Some elements of the American fleet, harbored in more distant ports in the Bristol Channel and beyond, had already put to sea, in order to arrive off the Normandy beaches on schedule on the morning of June 5. Then, early in the morning of June 4, Eisenhower received word from his meteorologists that a rising Atlantic storm headed for the Channel spelled disaster. Blanketing cloud layers, heavy rain, and heaving seas would deprive the assault forces of air cover, jeopardize small craft, and rob supporting naval gunfire of accuracy. Eisenhower recalled the ships already at sea and ordered a twenty-four-hour postponement, to June 6.

At 3:30 the next morning, June 5, Eisenhower awoke to violent confirmation of his meteorologists' forecast. A gale-force wind keened through the steel cables anchoring the barrage balloons to the ships in Portsmouth harbor. Rain pelted in sheets against the windshield of Eisenhower's car as he made his way through the glowering darkness to the elegant white Georgian mansion of Southwick House. In theory, he still had the option of postponing one more day, to June 7. In fact, the difficulty of refueling the convoys already once recalled meant that any further postponement must be to June 19—a prospect whose consequences, Eisenhower recalled, "were almost too bitter to contemplate."[8]

7. Unforeseeable at this time was the fact that June 19 would also witness the most severe summer storm in the Channel in forty years. The storm destroyed the American "Mulberry" artificial harbor off Omaha Beach and rendered any Channel crossing of the invasion force on that date impossible. Thus a postponement beyond June 6 would, as events turned out, have delayed the invasion by at least another month.

8. Eisenhower, *Crusade in Europe*, 250.

Far to the east in Moscow, General Deane suffered similar agonies at the American military mission. "Each time I announced a postponement," he recalled, "my stock reached a new low. The [Russian] General Staff had never been convinced that the May date agreed upon in Teheran was not part of a deception plan that the western powers were using against their Russian ally."[9]

At Southwick House in the predawn gloom of June 5, Eisenhower and his military chieftains sipped coffee around the fireplace in the high-ceilinged conference room, awaiting the latest weather reports. The weather officer arrived. "I think we have found a gleam of hope for you, sir," he said. A break in the storm front was developing. A thirty-six-hour window of relatively clear weather would open on the morning of June 6. When it closed again the following day it might wreak havoc on the follow-up forces scheduled to land after the initial waves had gone ashore. But at least it was an opening. Eisenhower asked for the opinions of his assembled colleagues. "I would say—Go!" Montgomery replied. The others agreed. Eisenhower sat on a sofa in silence, weighing his choices. The rain wept at the windows. Finally he looked up and said: "Well, we'll go."[10]

ON THE FAR NORMANDY SHORE, the same storm convinced the Germans that no landing was imminent. Rommel took advantage of the respite provided by the ugly weather to motor to his hometown of Ulm for a family visit. In the early hours of June 6, Rundstedt slept in the suburbs of Paris. Hitler, in his Bavarian mountain stronghold at Berchtesgaden,

9. John R. Deane, *The Strange Alliance: The Story of Our Efforts at Wartime Cooperation with Russia* (New York: Viking, 1947), 150.

10. Montgomery quoted in Gordon A. Harrison, *Cross-Channel Attack* (Washington: Department of the Army, 1951), 274. Eisenhower quoted in Walter Bedell Smith, *Eisenhower's Six Great Decisions* (New York: Longman's, 1956), 55. Different accounts of this meeting place slightly different words in Eisenhower's mouth. See Stephen E. Ambrose, *The Supreme Commander: The War Years of General Dwight D. Eisenhower* (Garden City, N.Y.: Doubleday, 1970), 417n. In Eisenhower's pocket as he made this decision was a handwritten note that he had prepared in the event the landings failed: "Our landings in the Cherbourg-Havre area have failed to gain a satisfactory foothold and I have withdrawn the troops. [In his first draft Eisenhower had written: "and the troops have been withdrawn."] My decision to attack at this time and place [the first draft read "This particular operation"] was based upon the best information available. The troops, the air and the Navy did all that bravery and devotion to duty could do. If any blame or fault attaches to the attempt it is mine alone." See *PDDE* 3:1908.

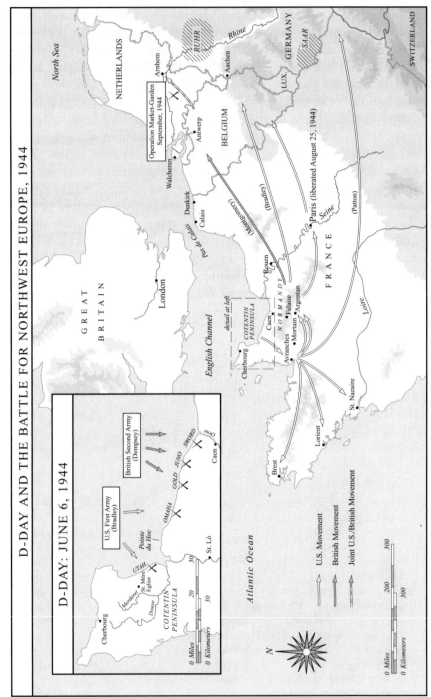

D-DAY AND THE BATTLE FOR NORTHWEST EUROPE, 1944

D-DAY: JUNE 6, 1944

U.S. First Army
(Bradley)

British Second Army
(Dempsey)

COTENTIN
PENINSULA

Cherbourg

Merderet
St. Mère
Eglise
Douve
UTAH
Pointe
du Hoc
OMAHA
GOLD
JUNO
SWORD
Orne
Caen
St. Lô

0 Miles   20   30
0 Kilometers   30

Atlantic Ocean

N

U.S. Movement

British Movement

Joint U.S./British Movement

0 Miles   200   300
0 Kilometers   300

North Sea

NETHERLANDS

Arnhem

RUHR

Rhine

Aachen

GERMANY

SAAR

LUX.

SWITZERLAND

Operation Market-Garden
September, 1944

Walcheren

Antwerp

BELGIUM

Dunkirk

Calais

Pas de Calais

London

GREAT
BRITAIN

English Channel

(Montgomery)

(Bradley)

Rouen

Seine

Paris (liberated August 25, 1944)

(Patton)

FRANCE

Loire

NORMANDY

Caen
Falaise
Argentan

COTENTIN
PENINSULA

detail at left

Cherbourg

Avranches
Mortain

St. Nazaire

Lorient

Brest

prepared to take his nightly sleeping draft. His staff were under strict orders not to disturb his few hours of fretful, drug-induced repose.

Parachutes, meanwhile, began soughing down out of the night sky over Normandy. The British 6th Airborne Division dropped onto the east flank of the landing area, to secure the bridges over the Orne River. The U.S. 82nd and 101st Airborne divisions descended into the valleys of the Merderet and Douve rivers, to hold the west flank and impede enemy reinforcement of the Cotentin peninsula. Many of the green C-47 transport pilots, spooked by flak, flew too fast and too high. Men had to jump into the darkness at airspeeds that ripped equipment from their bodies and jolted them into unconsciousness from the too-rapid deceleration when their static lines tore the cover from their chutes. The pilots scattered their "sticks" of eighteen paratroopers per plane across the neck of the Cotentin. Many C-47s overshot the narrow peninsula altogether and jettisoned their heavily laden paratroopers to swift deaths in the inky Channel waters. Others drowned, still snarled in their harnesses, in the swampy valleys of the Cotentin, which German defensive flooding had turned into vast shallow lakes. At the village of Ste. Mere Eglise, paratroopers dropped into the midst of a German garrison already aroused by a fire in the town square, and many were shot in their chutes even as they descended. Once on the ground the dispersed and decimated sticks struggled to assemble, signaling one another from concealment with double clicks from the "cricket" toys they had been issued for that purpose.

Ironically, the chaotic dispersal of the airborne troops, abetted by the drop of thousands of dummies, worked to the invaders' advantage by amplifying confusion among the German defenders. The liabilities of the Germans' fragmented command structure and the value of the Fortitude deception plan were now dramatically demonstrated. The first jumbled reports of Allied paratroopers prompted pleas from frontline German commanders for release of the reserve panzer divisions, but that decision lay in the hands of a man tossing in narcotized slumber in faraway Berchtesgaden. Hitler would not even be informed of the attack until noon. In the meantime, the German general staff was paralyzed by indecision: was this *the* invasion or simply *an* invasion, perhaps the first and fainter blow of a two-pronged attack, such as the Allies had just successfully pulled off in Italy? Logic — and Fortitude — still dictated that the main blow would land at the Pas de Calais. And so, for fateful hours, while the Allies poured soldiers and weapons ashore, the panzer reserves did not move.

In the Channel, still furrowed by foam-rows from the unspent storm, the colossal armada of 6,483 vessels churned toward the Normandy coast in the gray dawn. Overhead swarms of aircraft roared southward to bomb and strafe German installations. So thoroughly had the earlier air war suppressed the Luftwaffe that the Germans could mount only 319 in-effective sorties on D-Day, against some fifteen thousand by the Allies. Warships, some of them running in as close as eight hundred yards from the shore, blasted the coastal defenses with their big guns. In the buck-eting assault boats, frightened men huddled together, cold and seasick, bent by their sixty-eight-pound battle packs, as the boats yawed and slewed through the choppy water toward the beaches.

In the eastern landing zones, code-named Sword, Juno, and Gold, one Canadian and two British divisions splashed ashore against mod-erate resistance and linked up with the airborne troops on the Orne. By late afternoon they awaited only the arrival of their inexplicably delayed armored brigades to push inland toward their immediate objective, the old Norman capital of Caen, some eight miles inland up the Orne. Safely ensconced on the beaches, their purgatory was soon to come.

To the westward, the U.S. 4th Division, though pushed by an erratic current some two thousand yards south of its targeted landing zone, code-named Utah, otherwise enjoyed almost unimaginable good for-tune. It overwhelmed the poor-quality German 709th Division waiting in the low dunes behind the waterline, quickly secured several exits from the beach lodgement, and joined hands with the airborne units raggedly reassembling inland. With casualties of only 197 out of some twenty-three thousand put ashore, the 4th was the most lightly scarred of all the invasion forces.

The veteran 1st Division at Omaha Beach was less lucky. It con-fronted the excellent 352nd German Division, well dug into the brow of towering cliffs from which their precisely registered gun batteries raked the shoreline with deadly artillery and machine-gun fire. Invasion planners had hoped that "swimming" Sherman tanks, fitted with duplex-drive propellers and waterproof canvas skirts, would shoot their way ashore in the first wave, providing a screen for the infantry to follow. At Omaha those hopes sank along with the tanks themselves, many of which foundered in deep water far from the beaches. Unprotected in-fantrymen, clothes and equipment crusted with salt, throats clogged with terror and vomit, emerged dazed and unprotected from the pitching landing craft into a fearsome curtain of fire. Those that survived the first murderous seconds cringed for shelter behind the beach obstacles, hampering the engineers' efforts to destroy them. When the follow-up wave of troops from the 29th Division landed on the day's second low tide later in the afternoon, they stumbled across a shoreline awash in a chaos of floating bodies, beached ships, and wrecked equipment. So appalling was the slaughter that the Allied commanders offshore briefly considered abandoning Omaha and directing all further landings eastward, to the British beaches. At day's end Omaha claimed more than two thousand casualties, the highest of any of the landing beaches and a number that, had it been matched elsewhere, would have confirmed Churchill's most sanguinary nightmares of the costs of the cross-Channel attack. Yet somehow the sheer weight of newly arriving troops seemed to push the soldiers already on the beach out of their cowering paralysis. To this "thin wet line of khaki that dragged itself ashore," Bradley reflected, the battle now belonged.[11]

Among the first units to move inland were the specialized Ranger companies assigned to scale the promontory of Pointe du Hoc and to spike its 155mm guns dominating Omaha Beach. With grappling irons and climbing ropes, suffering horrendous losses, the Rangers emerged on the bomb-cratered clifftop only to find the gun emplacements empty. On a day that tested men's courage and sported war's caprice like no other, theirs was among the most brave—and futile—of acts.

By nightfall the three airborne and five assault infantry divisions, plus elements of the follow-up 29th Division, were ashore—more than a hundred thousand men in all. D-Day, the long-awaited mother of battles and perhaps history's most prolific womb of war stories, was over. But the real test—the battle of the buildup and breakout—was to come. The catastrophe at Anzio had shown the danger of allowing an amphibious attack to "congeal" or "stabilize" on the beachhead. "We must blast our way ashore and get a good lodgement before the enemy can bring sufficient reserves up to turn us out," Montgomery had said at the last high-level preinvasion briefing. "Armoured columns must penetrate deep inland, and quickly on D-Day. . . . We must gain space rapidly and peg out claims well inland."[12]

The most important of those claims was the city of Caen, a road and rail hub and the gateway to the open country to the south, toward Falaise. There tanks could be brought to bear and the American tactics of mobile warfare fully employed. The master plan for Overlord called for

11. Omar N. Bradley, A Soldier's Story (New York: Henry Holt, 1951), 219.
12. Carlo D'Este, Decision in Normandy (New York: HarperCollins, 1994), 86.

Montgomery to reach Caen on D-Day itself, June 6, and Falaise just days later. The bulk of the British and American force would then "break out" of the beachhead and execute a great left wheel eastward to the line of the Seine River, where the Germans could be expected to take up a strong defensive position. Closest to the pivot of Caen, the British armies would break out first, swinging the inner hub of the wheel toward the lower Seine. The Americans would form the wheel's outer rim— the classic wide envelopment—by sweeping far southward and then up the Loire River to the upper Seine. In the meantime, a portion of the American forces was to veer westward to secure vital ports, necessary to supply the buildup of the invasion force: first Cherbourg on the Cotentin, then the Brittany ports at Brest, Lorient, and St. Nazaire.

By the afternoon of June 6, as Rommel was racing by motorcar back from Germany to take direct command of the battle, his troops were already wreaking havoc on this tidy Allied plan. At 4:30 P.M. 21st Panzer Division, the German armored unit positioned closest to the beaches, launched a savage counterattack, with orders to throw the British into the sea. In that it failed, but 21st Panzer, soon joined by 12th SS Panzer, succeeded spectacularly in checking the British advance on Caen—not just on June 6, but for a full month to follow. Repeatedly Montgomery tried to take Caen, and repeatedly he failed. The British front congealed much as the beachhead at Anzio had done, much as the assault on Gallipoli had done, with colossal traffic jams on the beaches and no room to maneuver in the straitened strip of the lodgement. Churchill hounded Montgomery to move. The prime minister murmured darkly to Eisenhower about his fears of another Anzio.[13] By early July, Omar Bradley later wrote, "we faced a real danger of a World War I–type stalemate in Normandy."[14]

At the American end of the front, the battle at first went little better. A great Channel storm on June 19 demolished the American artificial Mulberry harbor at Omaha Beach, seriously constricting the flow of supplies to the American beachhead and delaying Bradley's advance on Cherbourg—whose port facilities were now all the more urgently needed. When at last the Americans entered Cherbourg on June 27, they found its harbor so systematically devastated by the Germans as to be useless for at least another month.

By the end of June the Americans had secured the entire Cotentin

13. D'Este, *Decision in Normandy*, 302.
14. Omar N. Bradley, *A General's Life* (New York: Simon and Schuster, 1983), 272.

peninsula to the west of the landing beaches, but they proved scarcely more able than the British to advance southward, through the marshy hinterland behind Utah and the unexpectedly treacherous terrain of the *bocage* country that belted the Norman interior. Over the centuries the methodical Norman farmers had turned their land into a quilt of pastures and meadows, their boundaries demarcated by densely planted berms called hedgerows. Seamed and cross-hatched by those ancient barriers — up to five feet high and ten feet wide, the earth thickly braided with the roots of trees planted over innumerable generations — the *bocage* was a countryside as ill suited to offensive warfare as it was picturesque to the eye. Every field became a tiny natural fortress bounded by hedgerows that served as deadly tank obstacles and provided superb concealment for machine guns whose fire swept every line of approach at ground level. The hedgerows, Eisenhower later wrote, afforded "almost the ultimate in battle-field protection and natural camouflage." The tremendous advantage that this terrain offered to the defense was one item that had escaped even COSSAC's meticulous planners. "Although there had been some talk in the U.K. before D-Day about the hedgerows," one American general wrote, "none of us had really appreciated how difficult they would turn out to be."[15]

On June 17 Hitler came to Soissons, fifty miles northeast of Paris and as close as he ever got to the Normandy battlefield, to confer with Rundstedt and Rommel. Still expecting that the main attack was yet to come across the Strait of Dover, Hitler continued to reject all suggestions that the German Fifteenth Army at Calais be released for action in Normandy. Hitler's reasoning proceeded in part from the fact that the Calais area harbored the launching sites for the *Vergeltungswaffe* (reprisal weapons), the pilotless flying bombs or V-1s. They were Hitler's response to Bomber Command's terror attacks, devices that conjured for him, as the manned bombers did for Arthur Harris, the dream of an ultimate war-winning weapon. On June 13 the first V-1s, powered by crude jet engines and carrying thousand-pound bombs, had begun to rain upon London. Hitler calculated that their fearful effect would compel the Allies to throw the main weight of their invasion force against the

---

15. Eisenhower, *Crusade in Europe*, 268. The American general was James M. Gavin, in his *On to Berlin: Battles of an Airborne Commander, 1943–1946* (New York: Viking Press, 1978), 121. Eventually an American sergeant, Curtis G. Culin, devised a "hedgehog" for fitting on the front of tanks. It consisted of a two-bladed steel prow that sliced through the hedgerows and helped to restore mobility to the American advance.

launching sites, where Fifteenth Army waited to crush the attackers. At Soissons *der Führer* also heard and rejected his generals' proposal to execute a limited withdrawal in Normandy and mass their armored forces for a concerted counterattack. "[T]here must be no withdrawal— You must stay where you are," Hitler ordered. Rundstedt demurred, and was soon relieved of command, to be replaced by Field Marshal Gunther Hans von Kluge, a weathered veteran of the eastern front. "What shall we do?" the retiring Rundstedt's military superiors asked him. "End the war!" he replied. "What else can you do?"[16]

Hitler's refusal to countenance either significant reinforcement or withdrawal—not to mention peace—condemned Rommel's Seventh Army to fight a piecemeal battle of delay. For the next several weeks, Normandy became the stage for a patternless series of small-unit clashes, savage encounters among men rendered steadily more callous by the dehumanizing slaughter of face-to-face combat. Yet even without Hitler's interference, Rommel would have had enormous difficulty mounting an organized counterattack in force. Allied aircraft, roaming by the thousands at will over northern France, had already snarled his transportation system and harassed every movement of his troops and tanks in daylight. But *der Führer*'s obstinacy sealed Seventh Army's fate.

Despite the handicaps imposed on them by Hitler's rigidity and Allied air supremacy, Rommel's troops sustained a remarkably effective defense. To the advantages of terrain they added the astonishing ferocity of their own fighting spirit and the undisputed superiority of their weaponry, especially their tanks. Nothing in the Allied armory could match the solidity and the slugging power of the German heavy tanks, the Mark V Panther and the still more formidable Mark VI Tiger. A fifty-six-ton behemoth, the Tiger had only to rumble onto the battlefield to strike terror into the hearts of its opponents. It outweighed the American Sherman tank by twenty-three tons and mounted a tank-adapted version of the infamously deadly 88mm gun. Against the Panthers, and especially against the ponderous Tigers, the vulnerable and undergunned Shermans had scant chance. The Shermans were designed for speed and mobility, for infantry support, pursuit, and exploitation, but not for tank-to-tank duels. Dubbed "Ronsons" after the ubiquitous GI cigarette lighters because of their propensity to burn when hit—or "brew up," as the tankers said—the Shermans could not throw a shell from any range that

16. B. H. Liddell Hart, *The German Generals Talk* (1948; New York: Quill, 1979), 244–45.

would pierce the Tiger's hundred-millimeter-thick frontal armor. The Tigers, in contrast, could penetrate the thin skin of the Shermans at a range of four thousand yards. But the Shermans did have, in addition to their speed and simplicity of operation, the advantage of numbers. Some eighty-eight thousand Shermans rolled out of American factories by the end of 1944, against some twenty-five thousand tanks produced by the Germans—another example of the fabulous industrial preponderance that constituted the key element in the American way of war. The sheer abundance of the Shermans could in some cases make up for their individual deficiencies. Under certain conditions, attacking in a pack from front and sides, the Shermans could stand up to their German foes. The rule of thumb was that it took five Shermans to knock out one Panther. The Tigers usually took more.

Stalled before Caen and in the *bocage*, the Allied armies came under growing pressure to advance, and Montgomery bore the brunt of the criticism. American newspapers began to draw stinging contrasts between the slowdown in Normandy and the spectacularly successful Russian offensive that began on June 22 (the third anniversary of Barbarossa). In keeping with his promise at Teheran, Stalin launched a broad frontal assault on German Army Group Center north of the Pripet Marshes. It crunched forward hundreds of miles in weeks, with a bag of 350,000 *Wehrmacht* troops killed, wounded, or captured. Churchill, his anxieties about stalemate in Normandy exacerbated by the V-1s falling upon London, grew increasingly impatient for movement. Eisenhower griped to Montgomery that American journalists were asking why British casualties were so much lower than American. The supreme commander made the same point to Churchill, imploring the prime minister "to persuade Monty to get on his bicycle and start moving."[17]

Montgomery responded in early July by pushing his troops forward along a "carpet" of destruction prepared by the heavy bombers—one of the first uses of the "heavies" in direct tactical support of a ground action. He took Caen at last on July 10, more than a month behind schedule. But in Operation Goodwood, a follow-up action several days later, again preceded by heavy bombing, Montgomery failed once more to reach the open ground of the Falaise plain. Eisenhower worried that Goodwood had gained only seven miles at a cost of seven thousand tons

17. Arthur Bryant, *Triumph in the West, 1943–1946: Based on the Diaries and Autobiographical Notes of Field Marshal the Viscount Alanbrooke* (London: Collins, 1959), 241, 243.

of bombs and wondered if even the Allies' well-stocked arsenal could afford a thousand tons of bombs per mile of advance.[18]

Yet Goodwood had in fact served a crucial purpose. It drew several panzer divisions to the British front just as the Americans were about to uncoil their own offensive, code-named Cobra, near St. Lô, a key cross-roads village they had taken on July 18. Allied strategy now shifted. The British sector, instead of being the first-turning inner hub of the great wheel envisioned in Overlord planning, was to become a solid, stationary anvil against which Montgomery held the bulk of the panzer divisions while the heavy American hammer smashed through on the western end of the front.

Operation Cobra opened on the night of July 24–25 with another mammoth carpet bombing of the German positions facing the Americans west of St. Lô. Waves of fighter-bombers, fifty at a time, laid high explosives and incendiaries along the German line. Next came four hundred medium bombers with five-hundred-pound fragmentation bombs, followed by fifteen hundred heavy bombers and then three hundred additional fighters with more high explosives and incendiaries. The bombardment annihilated half the German defenders. "Short" bomb drops also fell into the American lines, killing hundreds of GIs as well as Lieutenant General Lesley J. McNair. (The GIs dubbed the inexperienced U.S. tactical air units "the American Luftwaffe.") Despite these tragedies, the overwhelming weight of the American bombing succeeded at last in cracking the defensive ring that the Germans had so desperately tightened around the Normandy beachhead. In a manner unforeseen, with consequences unanticipated, the breakout had finally happened. It soon developed into a virtually all-American show.

Once unleashed, the Americans moved with astonishing speed. Within five days they were at Avranches, at the far southwestern extremity of Normandy. General Patton, the master of mobile warfare and the phantom of the Fortitude deception, arrived to take command of a very real U.S. Third Army. Patton's infantry and armor poured through the narrow Avranches corridor, turned the corner into Brittany, and spilled out toward the Atlantic ports. Patton's mechanized columns plunged exuberantly through a region that had been virtually denuded of German troops for the defense of Normandy. In what has variously been

18. Harry C. Butcher, *Three Years with Eisenhower* (New York: Simon and Schuster, 1946), 617.

called an "armored parade" and a "road march," Third Army raced virtually unopposed across Brittany to the west and toward the Loire to the south. They reached Brest by August 7, though it remained in German hands until September and then was so thoroughly demolished as to be useless. At Lorient and St. Nazaire the German garrisons held out until the end of the war. This denial of the French Atlantic ports to the Allies, along with the stubborn German defense of the Channel ports at Le Havre, Boulogne, Calais, and Dunkirk, with all the complications thus entailed for Allied supply operations, had telling consequences later in the war.

Gasping at the speed of the American breakout and stupefied by the fantastic "wealth of material" that the Anglo-Americans brought to the battlefield, Kluge concluded that "whether the enemy can still be stopped at this point is questionable. The enemy air superiority is terrific, and smothers almost every one of our movements. . . . Losses in men and equipment are extraordinary." His superiors on the German general staff agreed. They advised Hitler that the *Wehrmacht* should execute an orderly withdrawal from France. The recommendation rested upon sound military logic. But logic proved a weak instrument in the face of *der Führer*'s wrath.[19]

In one among the abundant ironies of war, all the horrendous tonnage of the bombs dropped in Normandy counted for less in shaping the next phase of the battle than did a single explosion in East Prussia on July 20. Shortly after noon on that day, Colonel Claus von Stauffenberg, a handsome, debonair German officer, his gait stiffened by wounds suffered in North Africa, walked into Hitler's headquarters and placed a bomb under the conference table. He reached down and broke a tiny vial of acid that would disintegrate a wire restraining the firing pin, then excused himself. Ten minutes later the acid had done its work, releasing a blast that killed four men in the room. Hitler, protected by the heavy tabletop over which he was leaning, was not one of them.

The attempt on his life invested Hitler's chronic suspicion of his generals with a ghastly and diabolical fury. Stauffenberg was summarily shot in Berlin. Other conspirators were hanged in front of movie cameras, so that Hitler might watch the filmed record of their death throes. The fear of further bloody reprisals swept through the German officer corps like an Arctic wind, withering whatever faint will remained to stand up

19. D'Este, *Decision in Normandy*, 459; Hastings, *Overlord*, 325.

to *der Führer's* increasingly deranged military dicta. Unquestioning obedience to Hitler's orders, without demurral or commentary, was now the test of loyalty, and perhaps the price of life itself.

To Kluge Hitler now issued the command to counterattack. The blow was to be aimed at the village of Mortain at the narrow neck of the Avranches corridor, in the hope of severing the American columns that had already passed through Avranches from their sources of supply. It was a hopeless scheme. The divisions still left to Kluge in Normandy had been mercilessly shredded in two months of constant bombing and grinding battles of attrition. What was more, Hitler was choosing to make battle at the farthest end of the Normandy battlefield. Kluge's weakened forces would have to stretch westward between the enlarging Allied beachhead to their north, anchored on the firm British shoulder at Caen, and the growing strength of Patton's Third Army to the south, already building along the Loire in anticipation of executing a wide envelopment of the German forces west of the Seine. The Mortain counteroffensive, in short, was launched into the jaws of an immense trap. Kluge recognized the hollow futility of what he was about to do but after the events of July 20 was powerless to resist *der Führer's* command. "If, as I foresee, this plan does not succeed," Kluge noted with resignation, "catastrophe is inevitable."[20]

Ultra helped spring the trap. Bradley received word from the codebreakers on the night of August 6 that the Germans would strike in the morning. Deprived even of the advantage of surprise, the four tattered panzer divisions that Kluge was able to cobble together were decisively checked at Mortain. Now a matchless opportunity presented itself. Instead of the long envelopment for which Patton was positioning his troops, a short envelopment, enclosing virtually all the remaining German forces in Normandy, might be executed by drawing the noose taut between Falaise and Argentan at the eastern edge of the elongated Normandy battlefield. All that was needed was more time for Patton to swing around the enemy's flank. "This is an opportunity that comes to a commander not more than once in a century," Bradley exulted to visiting Treasury Secretary Henry Morgenthau on August 9. "If the other fellow will only press his attack here at Mortain for another 48 hours, he'll give us time to close at Argentan and there completely destroy him. And when he loses his Seventh Army in this bag," Bradley tantalizingly

20. D'Este, *Decision in Normandy*, 415.

predicted, "he'll have nothing left with which to oppose us. We'll go all the way from here to the German border."[21]

Kluge obligingly pressed his attack for more than the requisite forty-eight hours before ordering a full-scale retreat on August 16. It was the last order he ever gave. Pinned down in a ditch by Allied aircraft on August 15, Kluge lost contact with his forces for nearly twelve hours, nourishing Hitler's suspicion that his incommunicado commander was trying to arrange a surrender to the Western allies. Kluge was relieved of command on the seventeenth, to be replaced by Field Marshal Walter Model. Ordered back to Germany for an accounting, including an explanation of rumors linking him to the July 20 assassination attempt, Kluge swallowed a capsule of poison. Under a similar cloud of suspicion, Erwin Rommel joined Kluge in suicide some two months later.

By the evening of August 12 the first elements of Patton's armored units were nosing into Argentan. To cinch the noose around Seventh Army, it only remained to close the "Falaise Gap" that separated the Americans entering Argentan from the British and Canadians, stalled some fifteen miles northward at Falaise. Ravening to plunge ahead, scornful as ever of Montgomery's alleged timidity, Patton hectored Bradley for permission to push on: "Let me go on to Falaise and we'll drive the British back into the sea for another Dunkirk," Patton blustered. But at this crucial juncture Bradley, in one of the campaign's most controversial decisions, held back. "Nothing doing," he told Patton. Nineteen German divisions were now stampeding eastward to escape the trap sprung at Mortain, Bradley reasoned. Their headlong retreat might easily smash through the thin line Patton was then able to stretch across the Falaise Gap. Better to pound the Germans in their shrinking pocket than attempt to draw it shut altogether, Bradley prudently concluded. As he said later: "I much preferred a solid shoulder at Argentan to the possibility of a broken neck at Falaise."[22]

The Allies hesitated just long enough over the prospect of the short envelopment at Falaise to frustrate the full achievement of the long envelopment at the Seine. But it scarcely mattered. While 12th SS Panzer Division fought tenaciously to hold the narrow neck of the Falaise pocket open, some twenty thousand Germans braved the gauntlet of Allied artillery and aircraft fire to escape across the Seine, taking with

21. Bradley, Soldier's Story, 304.
22. Bradley, Soldier's Story, 304–5.

them thousands of trucks but only a few dozen tanks and artillery pieces. Left behind on the hellish escape corridor around Falaise were piles of wrecked guns and charred tanks, as well as fifty thousand prisoners and ten thousand dead, putrefying in the summer sun. The sheer weight of American ordnance and firepower had simply overwhelmed the Germans. "If I did not see it with my own eyes," one German commander wrote of the American onslaught, "I would say it is impossible to give this kind of support to front-line troops so far from their bases." American resources seemed inexhaustible. "I cannot understand these Americans," wrote another overawed German officer. "Each night we know that we have cut them to pieces, inflicted heavy casualties, mowed down their transport. But—in the morning, we are suddenly faced with fresh battalions, with complete replacements of men, machines, food, tools, and weapons. This happens day after day."[23] Eisenhower wrote:

> The battlefield at Falaise was unquestionably one of the greatest "killing grounds" of any of the war areas. Roads, highways, and fields were so choked with destroyed equipment and with dead men and animals that passage through the area was extremely difficult. Forty-eight hours after the closing of the gap I was conducted through it on foot, to encounter scenes that could be described only by Dante. It was literally possible to walk for hundreds of yards at a time, stepping on nothing but dead and decaying flesh.[24]

Falaise marked the ghoulish finale of the battle for Normandy. In the meantime, finally fulfilling the Anvil plan—now renamed Dragoon in peevish recognition of Churchill's continuing resistance to it—additional Allied forces had landed in the south of France on August 15. They rushed virtually unopposed up the Rhone Valley. By the end of August the "thin wet line of khaki" that had stumbled ashore on June 6 had swelled to twenty American divisions, twelve British, three Canadian, one French, and one Polish, and was still growing.[25] And while Allied strength in France grew, Germany's collapsed. The *Wehrmacht* had sacrificed nearly 450,000 men in Normandy, half of them killed or wounded, the rest taken prisoner. Fifteen hundred tanks and over twenty thousand other vehicles were destroyed. More than forty German divisions had been utterly annihilated. The gaunt men who escaped were

23. Overy, *Why the Allies Won*, 227, 319.
24. Eisenhower, *Crusade in Europe*, 279.
25. Eisenhower, *Crusade in Europe*, 289.

reduced to scattered and fugitive remnants, shorn of both weapons and elan. Their pell-mell retreat carried them beyond the Seine to a hastily organized defensive line along the Meuse and Scheldt rivers in eastern France and Belgium.

Scarcely pausing for breath, the Allied forces harried the Germans across the north of France at breakneck speed. Paris, which Eisenhower originally intended to bypass lest his already stretched supply operation be saddled with the requirement of provisioning two million Parisians, was liberated on August 25. The surging throngs that flanked the Champs Elyseés to greet Charles DeGaulle on August 26 gave the lie to Roosevelt's dogged refusal to recognize the legitimacy of DeGaulle's leadership.

Within another week the British raced past Paris and entered the valley of the Somme. The Americans rolled up to the banks of the Meuse. These were the old battlegrounds of the First World War, when movement had been measured in yards, not the scores of miles that these modern mechanized armies gobbled daily.

The dizzying pace of the pursuit, perhaps accelerated by refreshed memories of the earlier war's stalemate, induced a kind of euphoria in the pursuers. It affected their superiors at home as well. From the Combined Allied Intelligence Committee in London came the prediction that "organized resistance . . . is unlikely to continue beyond December 1, 1944, and . . . may end even sooner."[26] On August 26 the SHAEF intelligence summary exulted that "two and a half months of bitter fighting, culminating for the Germans in a blood-bath big enough even for their extravagant tastes, have brought the end of the war in Europe within sight, almost within reach. The strength of the German Armies in the West has been shattered, Paris belongs to France again, and the Allied Armies are streaming towards the frontiers of the Reich."[27] Less than three weeks later George Marshall notified his senior commanders that redeployment of American forces from the European to the Pacific theater was imminent. "[C]essation of hostilities in the war against Germany may occur at any time," Marshall explained, predicting that the end would come "between September 1 and November 1, 1944."[28]

Eisenhower was more cautious. He wrote to Marshall on September

26. Cornelius Ryan, A Bridge Too Far (New York: Fawcett Popular Library, 1975), 67.
27. Chester Wilmot, The Struggle for Europe (London: Collins, 1952), 458.
28. PDDE 4:2117.

4: "We have advanced so rapidly that further movement in large parts of the front even against very weak opposition is almost impossible."[29] Yet even the supreme commander was not immune to the familiar virus of victory disease, the infectious military malady that deluded even prudent commanders, in their heady moments of triumph, into believing that anything was possible. Though abundant evidence indicated otherwise, Eisenhower could not entirely divest himself of the delusion that with just one more push the reeling *Reich* would finally collapse.

That alluring prospect soon confronted some hard realities as the thrill of the chase gave way to the mundane arithmetic of logistics. The original Overlord plan had envisioned an offensive consolidation along the line of the Seine, a manageable distance from the Allies' principal supply points in Normandy, about ninety days after June 6 (D+90). But the dash eastward had carried the Anglo-Americans a hundred miles and more beyond the Seine by D+90 (September 4) and had added the provisionment of Paris to the Allied logistical burden. A week later, D+98, Allied soldiers were crowding up against the frontiers of Germany, defended by the "Siegfried Line" (also known as the "West Wall"), a chain of fortifications hastily refurbished to halt the Allied advance. The Overlord forecasters had assumed that line would be reached at D+350. The British and the Americans had outdone themselves; they were some eight months ahead of schedule. Those numbers registered the sweet fruits of military success. They also contained the seeds of a logistical nightmare.

An American division in active combat consumed six to seven hundred tons of supplies every day. With some forty divisions in France by early September, and more arriving weekly, the Allies required that at least twenty thousand tons of materiel move to the front daily from the Channel beaches and their solitary functioning port at Cherbourg. The difficulty lay not with the availability of goods. Stocks were still piled high in England, and American farms and factories continued to pour out a deluge of food, guns, and munitions. The problem, rather, was transport. Despite monuments of engineering ingenuity like the sole surviving Mulberry and eventually an ingenious cross-Channel oil delivery pipeline (PLUTO—Pipe Line Under the Ocean), many supplies still had to be cumbersomely manhandled across the beaches. Worse, given the havoc wreaked by the transportation plan on the French rail system, the bulk of those goods, including all the army's precious gas-

29. *PDDE* 4:2118.

oline, then had to be hauled across northern France by truck. The Red Ball Express, a jury-rigged road transport system patched together with herculean effort and named for the railroaders' expression for a fast freight, began on August 25 to shuttle its trucks between the Calvados coast and the fighting front. But relentlessly, as the Allied divisions accelerated eastward, the thinning stream of supplies that reached them raised the old question that had bedeviled planners earlier in the war. Though for a brief season in 1944 it had seemed possible to do this *and* that, now Eisenhower was confronted with the hard choice between this *or* that.

Eisenhower's dilemma consisted in the "this" of Montgomery's clamor to be unleashed with full force toward the Ruhr on the northern end of the eastering front and the "that" of Patton's demand to be allowed to penetrate the Saar region — Germany's other great industrial center — on the southern end. The iron constraints of the supply famine and the gasoline drought that beset the Allied armies at the end of August precluded doing both. Eisenhower compromised. He insisted that both allies should advance shoulder by shoulder on a broad front, as fuel and other supplies permitted. In this the supreme commander was doubtless influenced by political considerations of national prestige as much as by logistical limits and military logic. Neither ally, he reasoned, should be allowed to claim all the glory for the eventual defeat of Germany. Even more compellingly, Eisenhower knew that the American people, not to mention his own American military subordinates, would never tolerate idling the U.S. Army and leaving the triumphal endgame to Montgomery, as the British commander repeatedly demanded.

Yet Montgomery's insistence that his army should have priority made much sense. On his front, along the Channel coast, lay the great port of Antwerp, Europe's largest, sorely needed to relieve the logistics bottleneck by shortening the Allies' lines of supply. Near Antwerp, too, were the remaining V-weapon sites, from which, after September 8, V-2s as well as V-1s were soaring against London.[30] The northern route was also the shortest to the Ruhr, the industrial heart of Germany that had always been Overlord's prime objective. For all these reasons, though he

---

30. The V-2 was a far more sophisticated weapon than the V-1, a true rocket powered by a liquid-oxygen-fueled jet engine that lofted the missile to an altitude of sixty miles and aimed it earthward in a free-fall of twenty-two hundred miles per hour. The V-2 outran its own sound waves, exploding without any warning of its arrival. At that speed, it was incapable of interception by antiaircraft or fighter interceptors.

continued to insist on the "broad front" advance, Eisenhower leaned toward Montgomery and the north.

On September 4 Montgomery formally proposed to Eisenhower that he be given all the resources he needed to launch "a powerful and full blooded thrust toward Berlin" that would end the German war.[31] Patton, meanwhile, thundered that "if Ike stops holding Monty's hand and gives me the supplies, I'll go through the Siegfried Line like shit through a goose."[32] Eisenhower again temporized. He told Montgomery on September 5 that both the Saar and Ruhr, as well as the port of Antwerp, remained his principal objectives and pointedly reminded Montgomery that "no re-allocation of our present resources would be adequate to sustain a thrust to Berlin."[33] Montgomery exploded, haranguing Eisenhower so relentlessly at a meeting aboard the supreme commander's aircraft at Brussels airport on September 10 that Eisenhower put his hand on Montgomery's knee and said: "Steady Monty! You can't speak to me like that. I'm your boss."[34]

But Eisenhower at last relented, at least in part. While Patton continued to badger forward as he could, capturing and cadging gasoline from any available source, Montgomery secured Eisenhower's approval for a major thrust on the northern end of the front. Code-named Market-Garden, it was an uncharacteristically bold plan for the methodical Montgomery. "Had the pious and teetotaling Montgomery wobbled into SHAEF with a hangover," Omar Bradley later wrote, "I could not have been more astonished than I was by the daring adventure he proposed."[35]

Hardly a "full-blooded thrust toward Berlin," Market-Garden was nevertheless to be mounted on such a scale as to preclude, for a brief but crucial period, virtually all other initiatives. Constrained by the continuing supply famine, Eisenhower dismounted three freshly arrived American divisions in Normandy, stripping them of all their vehicles in order to feed Montgomery's demand for forty-seven hundred aircraft, thirty-five thousand airborne troops, and a massive concentration of armor. Market-Garden envisioned a two-phase assault. "Market" called for three airborne divisions, two American and one British, to secure the river crossings along a sixty-mile-long corridor stretching from the Belgian-Dutch border to Arnhem, a river port on the lower Rhine and a gateway

31. *PDDE* 4:2120.
32. Ryan, *Bridge Too Far*, 71n.
33. *PDDE* 4:2120.
34. Ambrose, *Supreme Commander*, 515.
35. Bradley, *Soldier's Story*, 335.

into the Ruhr. "Garden" would send British armored units dashing up the corridor to consolidate the paratroopers' "air-heads" and to clear the path for a massive follow-up invasion of the German industrial heartland, home to fully half of the enemy's coal and steel production. Deprived of those critical materials, the *Wehrmacht* would be left essentially weaponless and immobilized in the field and must sue for peace. The bridges were the key. Success depended, said one British officer, on "threading seven needles with one piece of cotton and we only have to miss one to be in trouble."[36]

Market-Garden, launched on September 17, 1944, was a breathless gamble, embraced by men intoxicated by the bloodshed at Falaise and the swiftness of the race to the German frontier. As it actually unfolded, it was, in a sense, the anticlimactic coda following the crescendo of victory in Normandy, featuring many of the same players, and recalling many of the earlier battle's scenarios. It marked the end of Overlord, not with a bang but with a whimper.

Normandy veterans of the 101st Airborne Division failed to secure one of their assigned bridges at Eindhoven. That unthreaded needle delayed the advance of the ground forces. The armored units were in any case forced to move up narrow roads single file, in "one-tank fronts," through tightly jacketed valleys that were easily defended. Further up the road, paratroopers in the 82nd Airborne Division, mindful of the slaughter of their comrades descending onto the Cotentin on the night of June 5–6, jumped over Nijmegen shouting, "Remember Ste. Mere Eglise," and with guns blazing. But at the far end of the invasion corridor, the British 1st Airborne Division played out the most ironic reprise of the battle for Normandy. The British found the Arnhem bridges defended by elements of their old foes, 9th and 10th SS Panzer divisions, licking their wounds from Normandy but still packing enough firepower to contain an outgunned and underarmored airborne unit. After a desperate and costly week of trying to take the "bridge too far," the 1st Airborne Division received orders to withdraw, and Operation Market-Garden was declared a failure. With its collapse, the momentum of Overlord sputtered out and dreams of a German surrender in 1944 began to fade.

THE PRICE FOR MARKET-GARDEN was to be reckoned not only in lost lives but in the lost opportunity to relieve the supply famine by

36. Ryan, *Bridge Too Far*, 142.

quickly securing the immense port of Antwerp. "If we can only get to using Antwerp," Eisenhower told Marshall, "it will have the effect of a blood transfusion."[37] The British had taken the port itself, with its long-shore facilities intact, on September 4, but Montgomery's impatience to penetrate the Ruhr deflected the Allies away from the port at a critical moment. Even Montgomery's customary champion, chief of the British Imperial General Staff General Alan Brooke, felt that "Monty's strategy for once is at fault. Instead of carrying out the advance on Arnhem he ought to have made certain of Antwerp in the first place. . . . Ike nobly took all blame on himself as he had approved Monty's suggestion to operate on Arnhem."[38]

The distraction of Market-Garden allowed the Germans to consolidate their hold on the approaches to Antwerp along the fifty-four miles of the Scheldt River estuary that separated the city from the open North Sea, notably on Walcheren Island at the Scheldt's mouth. Efforts to dislodge the Germans commenced on October 2 and took more than a month to complete. The first supply ship finally steamed up the Scheldt only on November 28. In the meantime, the first U.S. Army infantry units nosed into the *Reich*. On October 21 they captured Aachen, a German city west of the Rhine. But they proved unable to breach the West Wall, which ran just to the south of the city, much less to cross the Rhine itself, Germany's last line of defense in the west. The regrouped Germans demonstrated their still formidable capacity for destruction in the Battle of Huertgen Forest near Aachen, where they inflicted some twenty thousand casualties on the Americans and held their ground for more than two months. Hitler meanwhile continued to stuff the Siegfried Line with whatever reserves he could scrape together. Incredibly, he even began to lay plans for one last offensive in the west, through the Ardennes Forest.

In a bravura gesture reflecting the victory disease that still infected many men on the Allied front, some of Bradley's subordinates sent him on September 28 a captured bronze bust of Hitler and boasted: "With seven units of fire [i.e., seven days' supply of ammunition] and one additional division, First U.S. Army will deliver the original in thirty days." But before that thirty-day period ended, Bradley ruefully recol-

37. PDDE 4:2168.
38. Byrant, *Triumph in the West*, 291.

lected, "Hitler had briefed his senior commanders on plans for the Ardennes counterattack."[39]

In the weeks that followed Arnhem, Eisenhower despaired that "German morale on this front shows no sign of cracking." He suggested to Marshall that the unconditional-surrender formula might be revised as a way to induce the Germans to lay down their arms.[40] Roosevelt explored the idea with Churchill, who seized the opportunity to remind the president that "I remain set where you put me on unconditional surrender." Political considerations weighed heavily in Churchill's mind. He explained to Roosevelt that "we can, it seems to me, speak no words of which the Russians, who are still holding on their front double the number of divisions opposite us, are not parties." To drive his point home, Churchill cited a bit of American history: "I do not see any alternative," he said, "to the General Grant attitude 'To fight it out on this line, if it takes all summer.' "[41]

The summer was still a long way off, and a winter of savage fighting remained in front of the West Wall. An even more wretched season loomed in the east. As the Western allies were sprinting across France, the Red Army had been grinding steadily into Poland. In August it reached the suburbs of Warsaw. The ragtag Polish Home Army then did its best to match DeGaulle's achievement in liberating his national capital by mounting an uprising, but the hapless Poles got no help from Stalin. The German occupiers brutally suppressed the Warsaw rising, even while the Red Army idled within earshot, cynically content to let its hated adversary exterminate any threat to Soviet hegemony in postwar Poland. Here were starkly revealed the chilling implications of the free hand in eastern Europe that Roosevelt had conceded to Stalin at Teheran. "Good God," exclaimed Churchill, "the Russians are spreading across Europe like a tide."[42] Yet the Anglo-Americans were still trying to

39. Bradley, *Soldier's Story*, 343.
40. *PDDE* 4:2312.
41. *C&R* 3:409. Churchill was referring to a famous communiqué that Grant issued on May 11, 1864, during the Battle of Spotsylvania: "I intend to fight it out on this line if it takes all summer."
42. Lord Moran, *Churchill: Taken from the Diaries of Lord Moran: The Struggle for Survival, 1940–1965* (Boston: Houghton Mifflin, 1966), 173. "Winston never talks of Hitler these days," Moran recorded on August 21. "[H]e is always harping on the dangers of Communism. He dreams of the Red Army spreading like a cancer from one country to another. It has become an obsession, and he seems to think of little else" (185).

placate their Russian ally. As winter began to settle over the western front, the British and the Americans continued to chip at the Germans as best they could, for political reasons as well as military. Any other course of action, Bradley observed, "would surely have precipitated an angry protest from our allies in the Kremlin."[43]

George C. Marshall, accompanied by War Mobilization director James Byrnes, landed at Verdun on October 7 for an inspection tour of the American front. Roosevelt had loaned them the Sacred Cow, the same plane that had borne the president to Cairo and Teheran almost a year earlier. As Bradley recalled, "It was apparent from the Chief of Staff's opening conversations that the chill which had caused us to revise our rosy September estimates on the end of the war had not yet filtered through to Washington and the War Department. While we were now resigned to a bitter-end campaign, he spoke with the cheery optimism we had discarded three weeks before."[44] But after a week at the front, Marshall was fully divested of his illusions. When the Sacred Cow lifted off from Paris on the evening of October 13, the day's last light was just evaporating from the top of the Eiffel Tower. The sun was setting, too, on hopes for an end to the war in 1944.

Hitler, meanwhile, was gathering what strength he could for a last desperate roll of the dice. Antwerp, already under constant V-2 bombardment, was the prize. With the great port again in German hands, the Allied supply famine would starve the Allies to a halt in the west. A full-scale V-weapon blitz could then be loosed against England, and the Anglo-Americans might yet be forced into a negotiated peace, freeing the *Wehrmacht* for a last-ditch defense against the relentlessly oncoming Russians. It was a mad scheme, but reason by now held small purchase in Hitler's mind.

Winter was to be the *Wehrmacht*'s cloak and comrade. The lowering weather would provide respite from the merciless air bombardment that Harris and Spaatz had resumed with a fury after the Normandy breakout. The shortening days would shroud the panzers moving into attack position in the Eiffel Mountains opposite the Ardennes Forest along the Belgian-German frontier. "Fog, night and snow," Hitler told his skeptical but submissive generals, would give them their "great opportunity."[45] In the snowy woods of the Eiffel, the *Wehrmacht* gathered itself up for one final battle.

43. Bradley, *Soldier's Story*, 350.
44. Bradley, *Soldier's Story*, 345.
45. Wilmot, *Struggle for Europe*, 478.

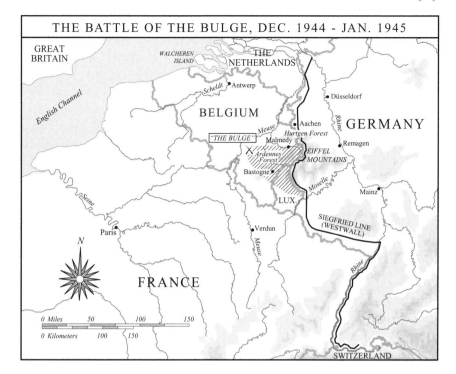

THE BATTLE OF THE BULGE, DEC. 1944 - JAN. 1945

GREAT BRITAIN

WALCHEREN ISLAND

THE NETHERLANDS

Scheldt • Antwerp

English Channel

BELGIUM

Düsseldorf •

Meuse

"THE BULGE"

Aachen

Hurtgen Forest

Rhine

GERMANY

Malmedy

Remagen

Ardennes Forest

EIFFEL MOUNTAINS

Bastogne •

Moselle

Mainz •

Seine

LUX.

N

Paris

Verdun •

SIEGFRIED LINE (WESTWALL)

Meuse

Rhine

FRANCE

0 Miles   50   100   150
0 Kilometers   100   150

SWITZERLAND

Eisenhower had deployed his ever-growing army in two great concentrations—the British to the north and the Americans to the south, trying to slug their ways respectively into the Ruhr and the Saar. At the hinge between the British and American armies spread the heavily timbered and hilly Ardennes Forest, launching site for Hitler's great *Blitzkrieg* attack on France in 1940. As if he had forgotten that history, Eisenhower decided the Ardennes was too thickly wooded and confined for a massive Allied attack—or for a German counterattack. He therefore placed just four U.S. divisions to hold his front facing the Ardennes.

At 5:30 A.M. on December 16, just as German forces had done in 1940, one *Panzergrenadier* and eight panzer divisions roared out of the Ardennes, their way forward through the bitterly cold morning air illuminated by searchlight beams reflecting off low-hanging clouds. They had achieved complete tactical surprise. Many American units, totaling some ten thousand men, surrendered almost immediately—a number exceeded in the army's history only by the disaster in the Philippines in 1942. Panic coursed through the Allied ranks, fed by rumors of German infiltrators in American uniforms and reports that near the Belgian village of Malmédy German troops had massacred nearly a hundred unarmed American prisoners of war, as well as a number of civilians. Soon the spearhead of the German attack was approaching the banks of the Meuse. In the southern sector of the salient the attackers surrounded the American garrison in the village of Bastogne, key to a vital road network. Presented with a demand to surrender his troops or risk their annihilation and Bastogne's, Brigadier General Anthony C. McAuliffe gave a reply destined to be celebrated in American folklore: "Nuts!" When the English-speaking German lieutenant who received McCauliffe's reply allowed as how he did not understand the term, McAuliffe's aide explained that "in plain English it is the same thing as 'Go to Hell!' "[46]

Eisenhower meanwhile pondered the Germans' strategic intentions. Was this merely a local spoiling attack? A feint? An attempt to drive a wedge between the British and American ground forces? A thrust to recapture Antwerp? As the battle lengthened and more German units swarmed into the swelling "bulge" in the Allied line — the configuration that gave the battle its name — it became clear that the Germans had somehow mustered the wherewithal for a major counterattack and that Antwerp was the objective.

Eisenhower rushed from his headquarters to a meeting at Verdun with his senior commanders on the morning of December 19. Characteristically, he announced that "there will be only cheerful faces at this conference table." The Germans, Ike said, had forsaken their fixed defenses to make battle in the open, presenting the Allies with an "opportunity," not a "disaster." With characteristic bombast, Patton proposed "to let the sons of bitches go all the way to Paris. Then we'll really cut 'em off and chew 'em up." More soberly, Eisenhower asked Patton if he could take three of his divisions facing eastward along the Moselle and pivot them northward to drive into the flank of the German salient. Patton was prepared for the question. Yes, he replied, and what was more, he could do it within forty-eight hours — an astonishing feat of logistical and tactical reorientation.[47]

Patton was as good as his word. In an impressive demonstration of his own genius for war and of the American capacity for battlefield mobility, he swung his columns ninety degrees and relieved the garrison at Bas-

---

46. Trevor N. Dupuy et al., *Hitler's Last Gamble: The Battle of the Bulge, December 1944–January 1945* (New York: HarperCollins, 1994), 194.
47. Eisenhower, *Crusade in Europe*, 350.

togne. On December 22 the skies cleared, and Allied air power once again came into play. The Russians meanwhile bestirred themselves from the banks of the Vistula and mounted a massive assault that carried them by the end of January to the banks of the Oder, within miles of Berlin. Hitler at last allowed his tattered forces left in the now-shrinking Ardennes pocket to withdraw. By the second week in January, the Battle of the Bulge was over. It had claimed more than seventy thousand Allied casualties and more than a hundred thousand German. Measured by the numbers of dead and wounded, it was the single most costly American battle of the war. It had also eaten up Hitler's last reserves of men, armor, and aircraft.

AFTER THE NORMANDY BEACHHEAD had been secured, General Carl Spaatz's U.S. Strategic Air Forces, along with British Bomber Command, had recommenced the air war against Germany in earnest and with a vengeance. With the huge airfleets now at their command, the Eighth and Fifteenth U.S. Air Forces, based respectively in Britain and in the Mediterranean, dropped the majority of their bombs in the eleven months of war after D-Day (72 percent in the case of Eighth Air Force). Most of them fell on the oil and transportation targets whose destruction had always held the promise of a "strategic" constriction of the German economy. By the end of 1944 the bombers had wreaked immense devastation. German synthetic oil production fell to less than 7 percent of pre-D-Day levels, and aviation gasoline output to less than 3 percent. Though German aircraft fabrication actually increased through July 1944, the Luftwaffe's planes sat on the ground for want of fuel to fly them. With the skies thus cleansed of German aircraft, Spaatz's bombers ranged freely over the *Reich*. They cut the traffic on Germany's rail, road, and water transport systems by more than 50 percent, effectively dismembering the German economy into several isolated regions that survived only by consuming their accumulated stores of food and fuel. Some 4.5 million workers, 20 percent of the industrial labor force, had to be committed to debris removal and the production and manning of antiaircraft weapons. For 1944 as a whole, bombing deprived Germany of 35 percent of its anticipated tank production and 31 percent of its expected output of aircraft. Overall economic output fell by 10 percent and munitions production by 15 percent. In January 1945, while Eisenhower's armies were still stalled west of the Rhine, German munitions minister Albert Speer notified Hitler that "the war was over in the area of heavy industry and armaments." On March 15, when coal and steel production, electrical generation, and freight-car loadings had all been reduced to about 15 percent of normal, Speer reported that "the German economy is heading for an inevitable collapse within 4–8 weeks."[48]

Beneath the economy-strangling logic of "strategic" aerial warfare, another idea about the role of bombing had long slumbered in the minds of some American air strategists. In the war's final weeks it stirred uneasily to life: that bombardment might not only inflict physical damage but could break the enemy's spirit as well, by so terrorizing civilian populations that they would compel their governments to beg for peace. Though the Americans had somewhat sanctimoniously distanced themselves from the Royal Air Force's "area" attacks on civilian targets, terror bombing had intrigued the American air planners from the outset. AWPD/1, the Army Air Forces' original planning document drafted as part of the Victory Program in 1941, had qualified its acceptance of the tactic but hardly repudiated it outright. "Timeliness of attack is most important in the conduct of air operations directly against civilian morale," it noted. "If the morale of the people is already low because of sustained suffering and deprivation . . . then heavy and sustained bombing of cities may crush that morale entirely. . . . As German morale begins to crack," the document concluded, it might be "highly profitable to deliver a large-scale, all-out attack on the civil population of Berlin." At the Casablanca Conference in 1943, the Allied leaders had affirmed that though the primary objective of the Combined Bomber Offensive was "destruction and dislocation of the German military, industrial, and economic system," a secondary mission was "the undermining of the morale of the German people to a point where their capacity for armed resistance is fatally weakened." Doctrine aside, many American bomber groups regularly took to the air when weather conditions made "precision" bombing next to impossible. The air crews referred to such missions as "women's and children's days."[49]

In the summer of 1944, the British brought to the Americans a pro-

48. Overy, *Why the Allies Won*, 125–33; *United States Strategic Bombing Survey Summary Report* (Washington: USGPO, 1945); Albert Speer, *Inside the Third Reich* (New York: Macmillan, 1970), 424.
49. Conrad Crane, *Bombs, Cities, and Civilians: American Airpower Strategy in World War II* (Lawrence: University Press of Kansas, 1993), 93; Ronald Schaffer, *Wings of Judgment: American Bombing in World War II* (New York: Oxford University Press, 1985), 33; *United States Strategic Bombing Survey Summary Report*, 2; Alan J. Levine, *The Strategic Bombing of Germany, 1940–1945* (Westport, Conn.: Praeger, 1992), 103.

posal aimed explicitly at shattering German civilian morale. Code-named Thunderclap, it envisioned a combined Anglo-American attack on Berlin in overpowering strength, enough to kill or seriously injure some 275,000 people. Many of the American airmen recoiled. One senior officer called it another of the British "baby killing schemes," and he warned that "this would be a blot on the history of the Air forces and of the U.S. . . . It gives full reign [sic] to the baser elements of our people." Spaatz advised Eisenhower that Thunderclap was an attempt by the RAF "to have the U.S. tarred with the morale bombing aftermath which we feel will be terrific." Eisenhower's reply was alarming. He had consistently favored precision bombing, said the supreme Allied commander, but "I am always prepared to take part in anything that gives real promise to ending the war quickly."[50]

The result was an Anglo-American attack on Berlin on February 3 that killed twenty-five thousand civilians. A second combined assault on Dresden ten days later ignited a firestorm that killed thirty-five thousand people by both flames and suffocation—a horror described by Kurt Vonnegut Jr., an American POW in Dresden, in his postwar novel *Slaughterhouse-Five*. Though the Americans maintained that their role in these raids was to strike at military targets only, both attacks, especially that on Dresden, became instantly notorious as confirming proof that the USSTAF had now slid across the same moral threshold that the RAF had crossed in 1942. As the *St. Louis Post-Dispatch* described it: "Allied air bosses have made the long-awaited decision to adopt deliberate terror bombing of the great German population centers as a ruthless expedient to hasten Hitler's doom."[51]

In the wake of the invading American ground armies, teams of economists and psychologists swarmed into Germany to analyze the effects of the bombing and to assess the air strategists' claims that air power was decisive in Germany's defeat—lessons that could then be applied in Japan. In its 208 separate studies, the United States Strategic Bombing Survey concluded that bombing had contributed significantly to Allied victory but had not by itself been decisive. German economic output had actually trebled between 1941 and 1944, despite heavy bombing. Only when air attacks were concentrated on oil and transportation did they produce dramatic results, and because that targeting scheme was introduced only late in the war, its effects were difficult to separate from

50. Schaffer, *Wings of Judgment*, 83–84; Crane, *Bombs, Cities, and Civilians*, 106.
51. Schaffer, *Wings of Judgment*, 99.

the impact of ground invasion. As for morale, the USSBS psychologists reached even more qualified conclusions. Bombing surely depressed *morale*, they found, but had markedly less effect on *behavior*. Personal habits, police-state discipline, and propaganda all kept workers on their jobs and protected the Nazi regime from overthrow even under the cruelest bombardment.

For the airmen, the USSBS results in Germany were disappointing. Their claim that air power was not simply one weapon among many but was *the* decisive war-winning weapon remained unproved. They would have one more chance to make their case in the war against Japan. "It seems to me we ought to be shot if we don't have more [air power] than we can deploy in the Pacific," Assistant Secretary of War Robert Lovett wrote to Spaatz in November 1944. The war against Japan held out "the possibility of exerting such overwhelming air power on the enemy as to give us a chance to find out whether air power can bring a nation to its knees or not. I don't see how we can make a bear rug until we have killed the bear."[52]

Eisenhower meanwhile restored his front in mid-January and continued to claw at the West Wall. Pummeled on the ground and from the air, the Germans began slowly to withdraw to the eastward. They executed an orderly retreat, demolishing the Rhine River bridges as they crossed over them into the heartland of the *Reich*. But on March 7 advance units of the U.S. 9th Armored Division probing as far as the Rhine found a railway bridge at Remagen miraculously intact. Bradley poured troops across it into central Germany. Patton meanwhile crossed the upper river near Mainz, and Montgomery leapt the lower Rhine below Düsseldorf. By the first of April the Allies had overrun the Saar and encircled the Ruhr. On April 11 the first American units reached the banks of the Elbe River, the already agreed boundary between the Soviet and Western zones of occupation. There Eisenhower stopped, while the Red Army proceeded to take Berlin in ferocious street fighting that claimed tens of thousands of lives. The Battle for Northwest Europe was all but over. The climactic battle against Japan remained to be fought. The battle for advantage in the postwar world was just beginning.

52. Lovett quoted in Crane, *Bombs, Cities, and Civilians*, 119. For a comprehensive discussion of the USSBS results, see Bernard Brodie, "Strategic Bombing in World War II," chap. 4 in his *Strategy in the Missile Age* (Princeton: Princeton University Press, 1959).

8

The Cauldron of the Home Front

The Second World War is bound to change all trends. . . . [N]ot since Reconstruction has there been more reason to anticipate fundamental changes in American race relations, changes that will involve a development toward the American ideals.
—Gunnar Myrdal, An American Dilemma, 1944

On September 9, 1942, shortly before the sun peeped over the North American continent's western edge and drove the night from the sea, Japanese submarine I-25 porpoised to the surface of the Pacific Ocean a few miles off the Oregon coast. Moving with practiced efficiency in the darkness, its crew assembled a fragile, single-engine float plane on the boat's deck, slung two 168-pound incendiary bombs under its wings, and pitched it skyward with a catapult. Guided by the beam from the Cape Blanco lighthouse, Warrant Officer Nobuo Fujita piloted his little aircraft over the coastal cliffs and into American airspace. As dawn was breaking, he released his two bombs into the dense pine and fir woods near the logging town of Brookings, wheeled oceanward again, and rendezvoused with his mother ship. Submarine, pilot, and airplane, swiftly restowed with folded wings into the boat's minuscule cargo hold, dove to safety.

Three weeks later, Fujita flew an almost identical mission, dropping two more incendiary devices into the coastal-range evergreen forest. With Fujita's second sortie, Japan's bombing campaign against the continental United States ended. His four bombs were the only ones ever to fall from an enemy aircraft onto any of the forty-eight American states in World War II. None did any serious damage.[1]

1. *New York Times*, October 3, 1997, C20.

321

The puny impact of Fujita's raids, quixotically intended to ignite vast forest fires and compel the diversion of American resources from the Pacific war to firefighting and coastal defense, underscored a fundamental fact about America's unique situation in the war. Despite Franklin Roosevelt's repeated insistence that the ocean barriers no longer shielded the United States from enemy assault, in reality they did. Alone among all the belligerent peoples, Americans went about their daily wartime lives in a mercifully unscarred homeland that lay safely beyond the enemy's reach.

But if Americans were spared from the threat of attack, they were not exempt from the upheavals that the waging of total war everywhere inflicted. Indeed, America's very distance from the battlefields in some ways opened opportunities for more quarrelsome political clashes and perhaps even for more consequential social changes than occurred elsewhere. Most other wartime governments, including Winston Churchill's, suspended elections for the duration of the war, but in the United States the constitutionally mandated rhythms of the political cycle beat on unperturbed. Congressional elections pitted Democrats against Republicans on schedule in 1942. Two years later, the quadrennial presidential campaign unfolded even as the fighting in Europe and the Pacific was reaching a crescendo. Those familiarly contentious rituals reminded Americans that in the political realm, in war as in peace, much in their lives remained the same. Yet in countless other domains of wartime American life things changed, often dramatically. The winds of war lifted up a people dazed and inert after a decade of paralyzingly hard times. As a thunder squall ionizes the sultry summer air, World War II left the American people energized, freshened, and invigorated. Depression America had been a place of resignation, fear, and torpor. America at war was quickened by confidence, hope, and above all by movement.

Not since the great surge of pioneers across the Appalachian crest in the early years of the Republic had so many Americans been on the move. Fifteen million men and several hundred thousand women — one in nine Americans — left home for military training camps. Three-quarters of them eventually ended up overseas, six times the number that had gone to France with the American Expeditionary Force in 1917–18. Another fifteen million persons — one out of every eight civilians — changed their county of residence in the three and a half years after Pearl Harbor. By war's end, one in every five Americans had been swept up in the great wartime migration. Eight million of them moved permanently to different states, half of those to different regions. One great migratory stream carried people from south to north. A second and larger stream flowed from east to west. As if the entire continent had been tilted westward, people spilled out of the South and the Great Plains into the Pacific coastal states, especially California. The populations of Washington, Oregon, and California mushroomed by more than one-third between 1941 and 1945. As the momentum of the wartime migration continued even after the war's end, California was home to 72 percent more people in 1950 than it had been in 1940. Endless rivers of workers poured into the great metropolitan centers of defense production—Detroit, Pittsburgh, Chicago, San Diego, Los Angeles, Oakland, Portland, and Seattle. In a harbinger of postwar social geography they settled disproportionately not in the central cities but in the newly burgeoning suburbs, which grew at nearly three times the rate of the traditional urban cores. By the end of the war decade, the long-depressed farmlands of the South and the Midwest held fewer souls than they had in 1940, while some eight million Americans had lifted their heels for the Pacific Coast. In the long history of the westward movement, this was its most dramatic chapter.[2]

NOT ALL OF THE MOVEMENT in this churning demographic cauldron was voluntary, especially in the case of Warrant Officer Fujita's kinsmen resident in the United States. Some two hundred thousand Japanese immigrants and Japanese-Americans lived in the Territory of Hawaii in 1941. Another 120,000 resided on the American mainland, mostly in the Pacific Coast states, California in particular. For them, geography was destiny.

Following the attack on Pearl Harbor, Hawaii passed under martial law, the writ of habeas corpus was suspended, and the military police took several hundred suspected spies and saboteurs of Japanese extraction into custody. But the very size of the Japanese community in Hawaii (nearly half the territory's population), and its vital importance to the islands' economy, foreclosed any thought of wholesale evacuation. The mainland community, however, was proportionately much smaller (in

---

2. Henry S. Shryock Jr. and Hope Tisdale Eldridge, "Internal Migration in Peace and War," *American Sociological Review* 12, no. 1 (February 1947): 27–39; Shryock, "Redistribution of Population," *Journal of the American Statistical Association* 46, no. 256 (December 1951), 417–37; Richard White, *It's Your Misfortune and None of My Own: A New History of the American West* (Norman: University of Oklahoma Press, 1991), 496–504.

California, barely 1 percent of the population), more economically marginal and socially isolated, and long buffeted by racist pressures. The
mainland Japanese for the most part kept warily to themselves, many of
them toiling with exemplary efficiency on their family fruit and vegetable farms. Insular and quiescent, they were also internally riven by age
and legal status. Their elders, the forty thousand first-generation immigrant Japanese, or Issei, were generally over the age of fifty and debarred
from citizenship by the Immigration Restriction Act of 1924, a statutory
impediment that perversely exposed them to the accusation that as non-
citizens they were poorly assimilated into American society. A majority
of their children, the eighty thousand second-generation Nisei, were
under the age of eighteen. Born in the United States, they were also
citizens. Alien and citizen alike, the peculiarly vulnerable Pacific Coast
Japanese community was about to feel the full wrath of war-fueled hysteria.

Curiously, no clamor for wholesale reprisals against the mainland Japanese arose in the immediate aftermath of the Pearl Harbor attack. The
Los Angeles Times soberly editorialized on December 8 that most of the
Japanese on the Coast were "good Americans, born and educated as
such," and serenely foresaw that there would be "no riots, no mob law."
General John L. DeWitt, chief of the army's Western Defense Command, at first dismissed loose talk of mass evacuations as "damned nonsense." He condemned any broadside assaults on the rights of the
American-born Nisei. "An American citizen, after all, is an American
citizen," he declared.[3] Individual arrests were another matter. Government surveillance, ongoing since 1935, had identified some two thousand potentially subversive persons in the Japanese community. Along
with fourteen thousand German and Italian security risks nationwide,
they were quietly rounded up in the last days of 1941. But those individual detentions stopped well short of wholesale incarcerations. "I was
determined," Attorney General Francis Biddle wrote, "to avoid mass
internment, and the persecution of aliens that had characterized the
First World War."[4]

---

3. Peter Irons, *Justice at War: The Story of the Japanese Internment Cases* (Berkeley:
University of California Press, 1983), 6, 30; Francis Biddle, *In Brief Authority* (Garden
City, N.Y.: Doubleday, 1962), 215.

4. Biddle, *In Brief Authority*, 207. Biddle also took heed from the embarrassing example
of Britain, where a panicky government in 1940 had briefly impounded some seventy-
four thousand enemy aliens, only to realize that most of them were German and
Austrian Jewish refugees, hardly fifth columnists for the *Reich*. In the United States

In fact, the immigrants whose loyalty had been questioned during World War I had then been freshly arrived and seemed to many observers unarguably alien. But by 1941 those older European groups were settled communities, well assimilated, their patriotism as well as their political loyalty actively cultivated by Roosevelt's New Deal. Though a surprising six hundred thousand Italians—more than 10 percent of the entire Italian-American community—remained Italian citizens and were automatically labeled "enemy aliens" after Mussolini's declaration of war, Roosevelt instructed Biddle to cancel that designation in a joyfully received announcement at Carnegie Hall, shrewdly delivered on Columbus Day 1942, just weeks before the congressional elections.

The Japanese were not so fortunate. As war rumors took wing in the weeks following Pearl Harbor, sobriety gave way to anxiety, then to a rising cry for draconian action against the Japanese on the West Coast. Inflammatory and invariably false reports of Japanese attacks on the American mainland flashed through coastal communities.[5] Eleanor Roosevelt's airplane, en route to Los Angeles on the evening of the Pearl Harbor attack, was grounded in the Midwest while the first lady telephoned Washington to check a radio message that San Francisco was under bombardment. Painters at Stanford University blacked out the skylight of the library's main reading room so that it could not serve as a beacon to enemy pilots. Carpenters hammered up dummy aircraft plants in Los Angeles to decoy Japanese bombers away from the real factories. Athletic officials moved the traditional New Year's Day football classic from the Rose Bowl in Pasadena, California; the game was played instead in North Carolina, presumably safe from Japanese attack. Japan's astonishing string of victories in the Pacific further unsettled American public opinion. Hong Kong fell on December 2, Manila on January 2, Singapore on January 25.

The release at the end of January of a government investigation of

---

in World War II some five thousand Germans and Italians, both citizens and "enemy aliens," were eventually interned, principally in camps at Bismarck, North Dakota, and Missoula, Montana. See Biddle, 204–11; and Rose Schierini, "Executive Order 9066 and Italian Americans: The San Francisco Story," *California History* 70, no. 4 (Winter 1991–92): 367–77.

5. The only authenticated Japanese attacks on the American mainland, other than Fujita's two raids, were the shelling of an oil refinery near Santa Barbara on February 23, 1942, which damaged a pump-house, and of the Oregon coast near Fort Stevens on June 21, which damaged a baseball-diamond backstop. Both incidents involved ineffective fire from a submarine's deck gun, and both happened *after* the presidential evacuation order was signed on February 19.

the Pearl Harbor attack proved the decisive blow. The report, prepared by Supreme Court Justice Owen J. Roberts, alleged without documentation that Hawaii-based espionage agents, including Japanese-American citizens, had abetted Nagumo's strike force. Two days later, DeWitt reported "a tremendous volume of public opinion now developing against the Japanese of all classes, that is aliens and non-aliens." DeWitt himself, described by Biddle as having a "tendency to reflect the views of the last man to whom he talked," soon succumbed to Rumor's siren. He wildly declared to an incredulous Justice Department official that every ship sailing out of the Columbia had been attacked by submarines guided by clandestine radio operators near the river's mouth. When evidence of actual attacks failed to materialize, DeWitt invoked the tortured logic that the very absence of any sabotage activity on the West Coast proved the existence of an organized, disciplined conspiracy in the Japanese community, cunningly withholding its blow until it could be struck with lethal effect. In February the respected columnist Walter Lippmann alleged that military authorities had evidence of radio communications between "the enemy at sea and enemy agents on land" — a charge that FBI director J. Edgar Hoover had already advised Biddle was utterly without foundation. A radio technician from the Federal Communications Commission reviewed DeWitt's "evidence" of electronic signals and declared it hogwash. All 760 of DeWitt's suspicious radio transmissions could be accounted for, and not one involved espionage. "Frankly," the technician concluded, "I have never seen an organization [the U.S. Army's Western Defense Command] that was so hopeless to cope with radio intelligence requirements. The personnel is unskilled and untrained. Most are privates who can read only ten words a minute. . . . It's pathetic to say the least."

But by this time facts were no protection against the building gale of fear and prejudice. "Nobody's constitutional rights," Lippmann magisterially intoned, "include the right to reside and do business on a battlefield." Lippmann's colleague Westbrook Pegler echoed him less elegantly a few days later: "The Japanese in California should be under armed guard to the last man and woman right now," Pegler wrote in his widely read column, "and to hell with habeas corpus until the danger is over." Unapologetically racist voices also joined the chorus. "We're charged with wanting to get rid of the Japs for selfish reasons," a leader of California's Grower-Shipper Vegetable Association declared. "We might as well be honest. We do. It's a question of whether the white man lives on the Pacific Coast or the brown man." Prodded by such sentiments, in early February 1942 DeWitt officially requested authority to remove all Japanese from the West Coast. It was impossible, he claimed, to distinguish the loyal from the disloyal in the peculiarly alien and inscrutable Japanese community. The only remedy was wholesale evacuation. The same man who had said a month earlier, "An American citizen, after all, is an American citizen," now announced, "A Jap's a Jap. . . . It makes no difference whether he is an American citizen or not. . . . I don't want any of them."[6]

At the Justice Department several officials, including conspicuously Edward J. Ennis, director of the Alien Enemy Control Unit, as well as Biddle's assistant James H. Rowe, struggled to quell this irrationally mounting fury. Rowe denounced Lippmann and Pegler as "Armchair Strategists and Junior G-Men" whose reckless charges came "close to shouting FIRE! in the theater; and if race riots occur, these writers will bear a heavy responsibility." Attorney General Biddle informed Secretary of War Stimson "that the Department of Justice would not under any circumstances evacuate American citizens." But at a fateful meeting in the living room of the attorney general's Washington home on the evening of February 17, the gentle and scholarly Biddle buckled. Facing off against Assistant Secretary of War John J. McCloy and two army officers, Ennis and Rowe argued heatedly that DeWitt's request for evacuation orders should be denied. Unknown to his two subordinates, however, Biddle, new to the cabinet, unsure of his standing with Roosevelt, and overawed by the Olympian figure of Stimson, had told the secretary of war by telephone earlier in the day that he would not oppose DeWitt's recommendation. When this became clear, Rowe remembered, "I was so mad that I could not speak. . . . Ennis almost wept." Even Stimson had grave misgivings. "The second generation Japanese can only be evacuated," he wrote in his diary, "either as part of a total evacuation, giving access to the areas only by permits, or by frankly trying to put them out on the ground that their racial characteristics are such that we cannot understand or even trust the citizen Japanese. This latter is the fact but I am afraid it will make a tremendous hole in our constitutional system to apply it." Despite his own reservations and the sputtering opposition of the Justice Department officials, Stimson advised

6. Eleanor Roosevelt, *This I Remember* (New York: Harper and Brothers, 1949), 236; John Morton Blum, *V Was for Victory: Politics and American Culture during World War II* (New York: Harcourt Brace Jovanovich, 1976), 159; Biddle, *In Brief Authority*, 215; Irons, *Justice at War*, 39–40, 41, 60–61, 283.

the president that DeWitt should be authorized to proceed. The cabinet devoted only a desultory discussion to the matter. On February 19 Roosevelt signed Executive Order 9066. It directed the War Department to "prescribe military areas . . . from which any and all persons may be excluded." No explicit reference to the Japanese was necessary. When Biddle feebly objected that the order was "ill-advised, unnecessary, and unnecessarily cruel," Roosevelt silenced him with the rejoinder: "[T]his must be a military decision."[7]

The original order neither prescribed what should happen to the evacuees nor precluded voluntary withdrawal. Some fifteen thousand Japanese took it upon themselves to leave the prohibited Pacific coastal zone in February and early March 1942, moving in with relatives or friends in the Midwest or East. (Japanese residing outside the Western Defense Command were never subject to detention.) To facilitate this kind of voluntary resettlement, Roosevelt created the War Relocation Authority and named Milton S. Eisenhower, brother of Dwight D. Eisenhower, its director. But many states in the nation's interior made it clear that Japanese migration eastward spelled trouble. "There would be Japs hanging from every pine tree," the governor of Wyoming predicted, if his state became their destination. "We want to keep this a white man's country," said the attorney general of Idaho, urging that "all Japanese should be put in concentration camps."[8]

On March 27 DeWitt put a stop to voluntary withdrawal. He issued a "freeze order," prohibiting the remaining Japanese from leaving the Pacific Coast military zone without permission. Further orders soon followed to report to "assembly centers," makeshift facilities that included southern California's Santa Anita racetrack, where detainees were jammed into hastily converted horse stalls until they could be transferred to permanent "relocation centers." Yamato Ichihashi, a sixty-four-year-old Japanese-born Stanford professor of history swept up in the forced evacuation, described Santa Anita as "mentally and morally depressive," a place where "thousands are housed in stables which retain smells of animals. A stable which housed a horse now houses 5 to 6 humans. . . . There is no privacy of any kind. In short the general conditions are bad

---

7. Irons, *Justice at War*, 61–62; Biddle, *In Brief Authority* 213, 218, 219; Stimson Diary, February 10, 1942; Kai Bird, *The Chairman: John J. McCloy and the Making of the American Establishment* (New York: Simon and Schuster, 1992), 153–54.
8. Irons, *Justice at War*, 72

without any exaggeration; we are fast being converted into veritable Okies."[9]

Like the itinerant Okies, the Japanese were soon on the move again, headed for ten relocation camps, one in Arkansas and the others scattered through the arid western interior. Deeply troubled by this turn of events, Eisenhower resigned as director of the War Relocation Authority. He advised his successor, Dillon S. Meyer, to take the job only if his conscience would allow him to sleep at night. His own, Eisenhower explained, did not. Within weeks, more than a hundred thousand Japanese were uprooted from their homes and livelihoods. In the haste of departure, scant provision could be made for protecting houses, farms, businesses, and other assets. The evacuees' property losses alone would eventually total in the millions of dollars, to say nothing of spiritual stagnation and lost wages as they languished in the camps, odd oases of enforced idleness in the midst of the wartime boom.

The camp at Manzanar, on the barren flats of a dried-up lake bed in California's Inyo County, received the first evacuees in June 1942. Though an improvement on the transient assembly centers, Manzanar, like all the other camps, greeted the new arrivals with stark reminders of their predicament. Barbed wire fencing girdled the six-thousand-acre site. A second range of fence further enclosed the 560-acre residential area. Guard towers, searchlights, and machine-gun installations punctuated the compound's perimeter at regular intervals. The summer's heat made the twenty-by-twenty-foot uninsulated cabins virtually uninhabitable, and the winter's wind drove desert sand into everything. Still, as Ichihashi reported, the sanitary facilities were adequate and the food was good, at least compared with Santa Anita.

The camps soon became little cities, complete with the kinds of tensions endemic to real cities. A riot at Manzanar in late 1942, precipitated by anger over the government's use of "stool pigeons" to keep tabs on dissidents, left two internees dead and eight seriously wounded. "You can't imagine how close we came to machine-gunning the whole bunch of them," one official told a San Francisco reporter. "The only thing that stopped us, I guess, were the effects such a shooting would have had on the Japs holding our boys in Manila and China."[10] But for the

---

9. Gordon Chang, ed., *Morning Glory, Evening Shadow: Yamato Ichihashi and His Internment Writings, 1942–1945* (Stanford: Stanford University Press, 1997), 104, 108.
10. Bird, *Chairman*, 683, n. 99.

most part, the residents tried to establish as normal a life as they could. They organized newspapers, markets, schools, and police and fire departments. Farmers daily passed through gates in the first fence to tend their plots. Inmates willing to submit to a humiliating process of interrogation to establish their loyalty to the United States could be furloughed for work beyond the second fence.

When Meyer in early 1943 made the loyalty-interrogation process compulsory for all internees, many of them bristled. Asked if they would foreswear allegiance to the Japanese emperor and if they were willing to serve in the armed forces of the United States, several thousand camp inmates, offended at the implication that their presumptive loyalty was to Japan and suspicious that they were being recruited for suicide missions, answered no to both questions. The eighty-five hundred internees in this "No-No" group, mostly Nisei young men, were then labeled disloyal and dispatched to a camp at Tule Lake, California. Among those whose loyalty was confirmed, some three thousand were recruited into the 442nd Regimental Combat Team, an all-Japanese (segregated) unit that distinguished itself fighting in Italy. Slowly, other certifiably loyal internees began to be released. By mid-1944 as many as twenty-five thousand had departed the camps.[11]

The policy of segregating the loyal from the allegedly disloyal Japanese detainees highlighted some of the most painful contradictions in the entire relocation scheme and exposed it to especially potent legal challenge. "When the segregation is effected," Ichihashi shrewdly queried a Stanford colleague in mid-1943, "how could the American government continue to justify the present policy of keeping the loyal citizens and aliens in the relocation centers? It conflicts with the fundamental reason given for the wholesale evacuation."[12]

Ichihashi's question already hung heavily over the minds of many in Washington. Biddle's unquiet conscience continued to trouble him, and he pressed for accelerated releases from the camps. Anything else, he told Roosevelt at the end of 1943, "is dangerous and repugnant to the principles of our government." Secretary of the Interior Harold Ickes advised the president in June 1944 that "the continued retention of these innocent people in the relocation centers would be a blot upon the

11. Jacobus tenBroeck et al., *Prejudice, War, and the Constitution* (Berkeley and Los Angeles: University of California Press, 1970), 150–51; U.S. Department of Interior, War Location Authority, *Impounded People: Japanese Americans in the Relocation Centers* (Washington: USGPO, 1946), 112–33.
12. Chang, *Morning Glory*, 244.

history of this country." Even Stimson favored "freeing those who had been screened and found loyal," but in a significant qualification Stimson added that he "doubted the wisdom of doing it . . . before the [1944 presidential] election." Roosevelt agreed. He feared the ruckus that the returning Japanese might stir up, especially in electorally weighty California. For the time being, releases would continue only at a deliberately controlled snail's pace.[13]

War Department officials watched anxiously as several lawsuits challenging the constitutionality of the relocation scheme made their way through the courts. On June 21, 1943, the Supreme Court ruled unanimously in the government's favor in the first two cases, though both turned on technicalities that allowed the Court to evade a decision on the central issues of coerced evacuation and compulsory internment. In one of those cases, *Hirabayashi v. United States*, Justice Frank Murphy's concurring opinion sounded an ominous warning. The relocation program, he admonished, ventured perilously close "to the very brink of constitutional power." For the first time in history, Murphy wrote, the Court had "sustained a substantial restriction of the personal liberty of citizens of the United States based upon the accident of race or ancestry." The government's policy, he darkly concluded, bore "a melancholy resemblance to the treatment accorded to members of the Jewish race in Germany and in other parts of Europe."[14]

Of the remaining suits, Fred Korematsu's held the greatest threat to the constitutionality of the relocation program. Korematsu was an unlikely paragon of his sorely abused people. A twenty-three-year-old American-born Nisei living in the San Francisco Bay area in the spring of 1942, he had a good welding job and an Italian-American fiancée, and no wish to leave either. When DeWitt issued his evacuation order, Korematsu forged his identity papers, underwent plastic surgery to change his facial appearance, and prepared to wait out the war as a "Spanish-Hawaiian" named "Clyde Sarah." The subterfuge came to an inglorious end on the afternoon of May 30, 1942, when police acting on a tip arrested Korematsu as he was strolling down a street with his girlfriend in San Leandro, California. An American Civil Liberties Union lawyer read of the arrest in the newspaper, visited Korematsu in jail, and asked if he would allow his case to be used as a test of the evacuation decree. Somewhat surprisingly, Korematsu agreed.

13. Irons, *Justice at War*, 271–73.
14. *Hirabayashi v. United States*, 320 U.S. 81 (1943), 62–63.

While Korematsu's case began its slow journey through the legal system, DeWitt's deputy Colonel Karl R. Bendetsen was drafting a document for DeWitt's signature entitled *Final Report, Japanese Evacuation from the West Coast, 1942*. Ten months in preparation, 618 pages long, it offered DeWitt's official explanation for what he had done: "military necessity." Justice Department lawyers first saw the report in January 1944, as they were preparing their briefs in the Korematsu case. What they read stunned them. The *Final Report* ignited an uproar that raged for eight months, a donnybrook between the Justice and War departments that ended with a pathetic but constitutionally fateful whimper in a last-ditch skirmish over a three-sentence footnote.

To buttress the argument that forced evacuation was a matter of military necessity, Bendetsen had laced the *Final Report* with hundreds of examples of subversive activities on the West Coast in the winter and spring of 1942. That evidence was the indispensable basis for the government's claim that its relocation program lay within constitutional bounds. But the Justice Department lawyers quickly saw that Bendetsen had cooked his facts. His statement that an FBI raid had turned up "more than 60,000 rounds of ammunition and many rifles, shotguns and maps," for example, failed to mention that those items had come from a sporting-goods store. Worse, when Biddle asked the FBI and the Federal Communications Commission (FCC) to review the report's charges, the responses were unequivocal. Hoover replied that "there is no information in the possession of this Bureau" that supported Bendetsen's claims about espionage. The FCC's response was even more damning. Citing its own 1942 study that had shown DeWitt's claims about supposedly illicit radio transmissions to be false, the FCC expressed its outrage that the allegations had resurfaced in the report. "There wasn't a single illicit station and DeWitt knew it," an FCC technician said.[15]

Armed with these findings, Justice Department attorneys determined to disavow the *Final Report* in their presentation of the *Korematsu* case. Excluding the evidence in the report—in legal language, instructing the Court to take no judicial notice of it—would fatally undermine the factual basis for the argument that military necessity justified the violation of Fred Korematsu's constitutional right to live where he pleased. To that end, the department's drafting team carefully tamped a high-explosive footnote into its brief:

15. Biddle, *In Brief Authority*, 221; Irons, *Justice at War*, 281, 284.

The Final Report of General DeWitt is relied on in this brief for statistics and other details concerning the actual evacuation and the events that took place subsequent thereto. The recital of the circumstances justifying the evacuation as a matter of military necessity, however, is in several respects, particularly with reference to the use of illegal radio transmitters and to shore-to-ship signaling by persons of Japanese ancestry, in conflict with information in the possession of the Department of Justice. In view of the contrariety of the reports on this matter we do not ask the Court to take judicial notice of the recital of those facts contained in the Report.

Privately, the lawyers used less measured language. The report's allegations of espionage, sabotage, and treason, they said, were "lies." Propagating these intentional falsehoods was "highly unfair to this racial minority." Left uncorrected, the report would mean that "the whole historical record of this matter will be as the military choose to state it."[16]

The footnote detonated in Assistant Secretary of War McCloy's hands when he read a draft of the Justice Department's brief on Saturday morning, September 30, 1944. McCloy reflexively understood that its effect would be to explode the shaky consensus the Court had patched together in the *Hirabayashi* case, and probably to induce a judgment that the entire relocation program was unconstitutional. He insisted that the damning footnote be amended. After two days of frantic argument, the top officials at the Justice Department once again buckled under McCloy's pressure and deleted the offending footnote. Ignorant of this dispute, the Supreme Court justices proceeded to deliberate on the *Korematsu* case deprived of a basis on which to challenge the factual assertions of the *Final Report*.

Even so, the Court was clearly queasy about the *Korematsu* case. Justice Hugo Black's majority opinion upheld Fred Korematsu's original conviction for violating the evacuation decree while carefully avoiding any pronouncement on the legality of his subsequent internment. "All legal restrictions which curtail the civil rights of a single racial group are immediately suspect," Black cautioned, and must be subjected to the strictest scrutiny. But military necessity, Black concluded, provided sufficient grounds to believe that the government's actions passed the strict scrutiny test in Korematsu's case. Justices Roberts, Murphy, and Jackson dissented. Jackson objected that the Court had "validated the

16. Irons, *Justice at War*, 286, 288.

principle of racial discrimination." If McCloy had not succeeded in expunging the footnote that called DeWitt's *Final Report* into question, a majority of the Court would quite possibly have found in Korematsu's favor. As it was, though no racially restrictive law has ever since passed the strict scrutiny test, the *Korematsu* precedent, in Jackson's phrase, "lies about like a loaded weapon ready for the hand of any authority that can bring forward a plausible claim to an urgent need."[17]

When the Court pronounced on the *Korematsu* case on December 18, 1944, safely after the November presidential election, the camps had already begun to empty. Just the day before the Court's decision was announced, the government had declared that the period of "military necessity" was ended. West Coast military authorities rescinded DeWitt's original evacuation order and restored to the remaining camp residents "their full rights to enter and remain in the military areas of the Western Defense Command."[18]

The sorry history of Korematsu's bowdlerized brief condemns the Court's ruling as a judicial travesty. For the Japanese internees, the entire episode had been a cruel torment. By one estimate they suffered some $400 million in property losses as a result of evacuation. Congress in 1948 provided a paltry $37 million in reparations. In another spasm of conscience forty years later, Congress awarded $20,000 to each surviving detainee. President Bill Clinton rendered further atonement in 1998 when he bestowed the nation's highest civilian honor, the Presidential Medal of Freedom, on that implausible paladin, Fred Korematsu.[19]

Yet for the Nisei generation, the ordeal of the camps yielded at least some inadvertently compensatory fruit. The detention experience cracked the thick cake of custom that had encrusted the prewar Japanese community. It undermined the cultural authority of the elderly Issei, liberated their children from hidebound tradition and cultural isolation, and dramatically catalyzed the Nisei's assimilation into the larger society. However painful and unintentional the process, internment allowed younger Japanese-Americans to break out of their defensive ethnic enclaves during the war and rapidly ascend the ladder of social mobility thereafter. Within three decades of the war's end, the Nisei were among

17. *Korematsu v. United States*, 323 U.S. 214 (1944), 216, 245–46.
18. Irons, *Justice at War*, 276.
19. In 1984 a federal court voided Korematsu's 1944 conviction on a writ of coram nobis—a judicial ruling that the original verdict had been tainted by official misconduct. See *Korematsu v. U.S.*, 584 F. Supp. 1406 (N.D. Cal. 1984).

the best-educated Americans and enjoyed incomes more than a third above the national average (ranking second among American ethnic groups only to Jews). Their improbable destiny mirrored the experience of millions of other Americans whose lives were touched by the war.[20]

THE JAPANESE INTERNMENT affronted American ideals of justice. Yet in a sense the harsh treatment of the Japanese may have been no less an anomaly than Fujita's two bombing raids, and the Nisei's eventual fate might be taken as more typical of the war's impact on many Americans. The chronic discomfort of government officials with their own policy, and the obvious caution and even distaste with which the Supreme Court handled the evacuation cases, bore witness to the singular awkwardness with which American culture tried to come to terms with the internment episode. What happened to the Japanese was especially disquieting in wartime America precisely because it so loudly mocked the nation's best image of itself as a tolerantly inclusive, fair-minded, "melting pot" society—an image long nurtured in national mythology, and one powerfully reinforced by the conspicuously racialized conflict that was World War II.

The deliberate burnishing of that image had begun well before Pearl Harbor. Citing the contrasting example of Hitler's campaign against the Jews, Franklin Roosevelt throughout the 1930s had purposely invoked religious toleration as a distinguishing American trait, one that spelled the difference between Americans and their adversaries and defined the very essence of the American character. He struck that note with special eloquence when he listed "the freedom of every person to worship God in his own way" as one of the "essential human freedoms" in his famous "Four Freedoms" address in January 1941. He expanded upon that theme time and again in the weeks after Pearl Harbor. "Remember the Nazi technique: 'Pit race against race, religion against religion, prejudice against prejudice. Divide and conquer!' We must not let that happen here," he declared in January 1942. In his State of the Union address in the same month he warned: "We must be particularly vigilant against racial discrimination in any of its ugly forms. Hitler will try again to breed mistrust and suspicion between one individual and another, one group and another, one race and another."[21]

Those sentiments were not simply the ritual incantations of a prag-

20. Thomas Sowell, *Ethnic America* (New York: Basic 1981), 5, 171–79.
21. PPA (1940), 672; (1942), 6, 39.

matic wartime leader presiding over a notoriously plural people. Count-less Americans shared them, and many made a point of saying so pub-licly. Several interfaith and interracial groups sprang up in wartime. In June 1940 more than one hundred prominent social scientists formed the Committee for National Morale to promote the idea, as the historian Henry Steele Commager said, "that the American people is a nation." Visitors to the New York World's Fair in 1940 flocked to "the American Common," a pavilion vacated by the Soviet Union after the Nazi-Soviet Pact and reoutfitted to display what a press release called the "mingled traditions" of the American folk, a modern idiom for an old idea: *e pluribus unum.* The ubiquity of that sentiment on the eve of the war was illustrated by the saga of "Ballad for Americans," a sentimentally patriotic eleven-minute cantata originally composed for a leftish Federal Theater Project revue in 1937 and eventually used to open the Repub-lican presidential nominating convention in 1940.

"Am I an American?" the song asked.

> I'm just an Irish, Negro, Jewish, Italian, French and English, Spanish, Russian, Chinese, Polish, Scotch, Hungarian, Litvak, Swedish, Finnish, Canadian, Greek and Turk, and Czech and double Czech American.
> And that ain't all, I was baptized Baptist, Methodist, Congregationalist, Lutheran, Atheist, Roman Catholic, Orthodox Jewish, Presbyterian, Seventh Day Adventist, Mormon, Quaker, Christian Scientist and lots more.

When the great Negro bass-baritone Paul Robeson sang the "Ballad" on the radio in 1939, the CBS studio audience stamped, shouted, and bra-voed for nearly twenty minutes. Appreciative callers jammed the net-work's switchboard for two hours.

Hollywood, encouraged by the Office of War Information's Bureau of Motion Pictures, gave wartime Americans countless film portraits of themselves as a people both diverse and unified — a message that became a cliché in the image of the legendary World War II infantry rifle squad, invariably portrayed as the cheery nursery of comradely gusto, its roll call announcing an outlandishly diverse roster of exotic ethnic surnames.[22]

Nothing better demonstrated the peculiar wartime intensity of those

22. *New York Times Magazine,* November 10, 1940, 3; Robert W. Rydell, *World of Fairs: The Century-of-Progress Expositions* (Chicago: University of Chicago Press, 1993), 185; *Time,* November 20, 1939, 58–59; "Ballad for Americans," Robbins Music Cor-poration, copyright 1940. I am indebted to Wendy Wall for these references.

inclusionary sentiments than the publication of a remarkable book in the very year that the *Korematsu* case was decided: Gunnar Myrdal's *An American Dilemma: The Negro Problem and Modern Democracy*. Myrdal was a brilliant young Swedish economist commissioned by the Carnegie Corporation to undertake a comprehensive study of the status of American Negroes. He had begun his researches in 1938 by motoring through the South in a big Buick with his black American colleague, Ralph Bunche. (To avoid trouble, Bunche posed as Myrdal's chauffeur.) The onset of war had slowed but not stopped his investigation. More impressive, neither Myrdal nor the Carnegie Corporation flinched from publication when the project was completed while the fighting still raged in 1944. The book's release in that year reflected their confidence that even in the midst of a global war, perhaps precisely *because* of the war, the American people were prepared to hear a probing report about their country's most enduringly painful social issue: race. "[T]he book was published during the most anxious months of the war. I know of no other country where such a thing could have happened," Myrdal recalled. *An American Dilemma* swiftly became a best-seller, confirming Myrdal's and his sponsors' intuitions.[23]

Myrdal's book was in essence a secular sermon. He spared few details in his two-volume, fifteen-hundred-page description of the regime of segregation that still held the majority of black Americans in its malevolent grip. He aimed not only to make his white American readers see the enormity of their racial system but also to prompt them to change it, and he assumed that by accomplishing the first objective he would automatically realize the second. Here, despite his foreignness, Myrdal adopted a strategy with roots in American political culture that reached back to Abraham Lincoln and beyond: it consisted in the simple belief that a factual appeal to the better angels of their nature would induce Americans to do the right thing.

All Americans, Myrdal asserted, "even a poor and uneducated white person in some isolated and backward rural region in the Deep South," carried within them a commitment to what he called "the American Creed," a set of values embracing "liberty, equality, justice, and fair opportunity for everybody." But unreasoning prejudice, he argued, had corrupted the white mind, making a mockery of those ideals. The resulting tension between good values and bad behavior constituted "the

---

23. Gunnar Myrdal, *An American Dilemma: The Negro Problem and Modern Democracy* (1944; New York: Harper and Row, Twentieth Anniversary Edition, 1962), xxv.

American dilemma." Myrdal believed that such tension was inherently unstable and must inevitably be resolved as Americans brought their attitudes and practices into conformity with the praiseworthy tenets of the American Creed. *An American Dilemma* held out the prospect of a virtually painless exit from the nation's racist history. The book thus complimented and comforted Americans even as it criticized them. In the patriotic glow of wartime, blacks and whites alike greeted Myrdal's message with extravagant hosannas of praise, hymned gratefully by a nation more flattered than shamed by his exposé and obviously hungry for the counsels of hope about race.[24]

In Myrdal's view discrimination by whites was the single most powerful determinant of the baleful condition of American blacks. The mechanism of oppression worked according to what he called the "principle of cumulation": discrimination forced blacks into lowly social positions, which, in turn, confirmed the bigoted belief in black inferiority and thereby reinforced the barriers to change. But this self-reinforcing cycle of perception, behavior, and discrimination could work two ways, he argued: an objective improvement in the social standing of blacks would diminish white prejudice, opening opportunities for further gain. The trick was to find a way to crack open ancient habits of behavior and belief, black as well as white. In the cauldron of war, the principle of cumulation was about to be reforged into a powerful tool for black advancement.

One black leader had already eagerly grasped that instrument. Asa Philip Randolph was the head of the Brotherhood of Sleeping Car Porters, an all-black union of railroad workers. Randolph was a courtly man whose early training as a Shakespearean actor endowed him with a deep, resonant voice. He had come to New York from his native Florida when the Harlem Renaissance was flourishing. The city's intellectual and social ferment nourished him. He became a skilled street-corner orator, writer, editor, and associate of the black nationalist Marcus Garvey. In 1917 Randolph helped to found the *Messenger*, which took outspoken stands against racial discrimination as well as against American participation in World War I. His opposition to that war got him arrested, though the charges were eventually dropped. Attorney General A. Mitchell Palmer had called him "the most dangerous Negro in America." In 1925 he accepted an invitation from a group of Pullman Company porters to lead the new Brotherhood of Sleeping Car Porters; be-

24. Myrdal, *American Dilemma*, lxxii.

cause he was not a porter himself, the Pullman Company could not fire him. Significantly, the Brotherhood was one of the few Negro organizations of any type with a solid foothold in the national industrial economy, and Randolph was one of the rare black leaders with a constituency and a vision that extended beyond Dixie. He also had a remarkable talent for shaping and wielding public opinion, which he called "the most powerful weapon in America."[25]

As Congress was passing the Burke-Wadsworth Selective Service Act in mid-September 1940, the Brotherhood met in its annual convention at the Harlem YMCA. At Randolph's urging, the delegates passed a resolution urging the government to avoid discrimination against blacks in the armed forces. Among the guest speakers at the gathering was Eleanor Roosevelt, here as so often serving as her husband's ambassador to black America. With her help, Randolph arranged a meeting to present the Brotherhood's resolution to the president in person.

Two weeks later, Randolph and a delegation of African-American leaders, including Walter White, executive secretary of the National Association for the Advancement of Colored People (NAACP), arrived at the White House. Randolph and White were veterans of many such Oval Office meetings, in which deferential Negro spokesmen reenacted a tableau from slavery days by humbly supplicating the Boss-man in the Big House for whatever favors he might see fit to dispense. Randolph had been present at one unforgettable encounter in 1925, when Calvin Coolidge sat stonily through a speech by William Monroe Trotter on the evils of lynching, then impassively bade his visitors good day, whereupon Trotter and the other Negroes meekly departed. Franklin Roosevelt was more cordial than the notoriously taciturn Coolidge, but in fact in his first two terms he had done little to change the essential character of these hollow ceremonies, and precious little indeed to improve the lot of black Americans. Though Eleanor had reached out to black America, and though prominent New Dealers like Harold Ickes and Harry Hopkins had made gestures toward racial equality, Roosevelt, like all presidents since Reconstruction, had not meaningfully bestirred himself on behalf of blacks.

Most African-Americans on the eve of World War II lived lives scarcely different from those to which their freedmen forebears had been consigned after the Civil War. In an urban age, black Americans

25. Kenneth T. Jackson, ed., *Dictionary of American Biography* (New York: Charles Scribner's Sons, 1995), Supp. 10, 658–61.

remained a rural people. Three of every four Negroes still dwelled in the South, the poorest inhabitants of the nation's poorest region. Jim Crow bound them to make their way warily through the shabby interstices of southern white society, well out of America's mainstream. Three-quarters of adult blacks had not finished high school. One in ten had no schooling whatever, and many more were functionally illiterate. Blacks led shorter and unhealthier lives than whites and worked at tougher and far less lucrative jobs. They earned, on the average, 39 percent of what whites made. Almost nine of ten black families eked out a living on incomes below the federal poverty threshold. Most employed black men were marooned in unskilled occupations. One-third were sharecroppers or tenant farmers. A far higher percentage of black women than white worked for wages, a majority as domestic servants or farmhands. Negroes were politically voiceless throughout the South; fewer than 5 percent of eligible blacks in the states of the old Confederacy could exercise democracy's most fundamental right, the right to vote.[26]

The continued isolation of black Americans was made achingly obvious as war mobilization began to lift the pall of the Depression. Management and labor joined arms to exclude black workers from the benefits of the war boom. "We will not employ Negroes," the president of North American Aviation flatly declared. "It is against company policy." Kansas City's Standard Steel Corporation announced: "We have not had a Negro worker in twenty-five years, and do not plan to start now." In Seattle the district organizer of the International Association of Machinists put the Boeing Aircraft Company on notice that "labor has been asked to make many sacrifices in this war," but the "sacrifice" of allowing blacks into union membership "is too great." As for the armed forces, the army deliberately replicated the patterns of civilian society by confining black troops to segregated units and assigning the bulk of them to noncombat service and construction duty. The regular army in 1940 had just five black officers, three of them chaplains. The navy accepted blacks only as messmen, cooks, and stewards; not one black man had ever attended lily-white Annapolis. The elite services of the air corps and the marines refused any black enlistments whatsoever.[27]

26. Gerald David Jaynes and Robin M. Williams Jr., A Common Destiny: Blacks and American Society (Washington: National Academy Press, 1989), 35–42, 271–73.
27. Jervis Anderson, A. Philip Randolph: A Biographical Portrait (New York: Harcourt Brace Jovanovich, 1973), 241–42.

When Randolph and his colleagues rehearsed these matters for the president at their meeting on September 27, the president worked his customary charm, and the little delegation departed aglow with a sense of satisfaction. But just two weeks later a Roosevelt aide announced that "the policy of the War Department is not to intermingle colored and white enlisted personnel in the same regimental organizations."[28]

Randolph was stunned. It was expressly to put an end to segregation in the military that he had gone to the White House, and he thought Roosevelt had given him a sympathetic hearing. Betrayed and angry, Randolph made a historic decision. "[C]alling on the President and holding those conferences are not going to get us anywhere," he told an associate. Instead, it was time to take the campaign for Negro rights into the streets. The goal would be not simply desegregation in the military but now, even more important, jobs in defense industries. "I think we ought to get 10,000 Negroes to march on Washington in protest, march down Pennsylvania Avenue," he told an aide. This was an incendiary suggestion. Randolph was proposing to have done with the tactics of entreaty and petition and to force the government's hand with a massive public display of Negro strength. He was less concerned with formal legal rights in the South, the traditional agenda of black leaders, than with opportunities for employment in the reviving industrial economy. What was more, Randolph envisioned an all-black demonstration. "We shall not call upon our white friends to march with us," he announced. "There are some things Negroes must do alone." Randolph's strategy and objectives foreshadowed as well as inspired the civil rights movement of the postwar era, but the rich promise of that future was still veiled in 1941, and the brazen novelty of Randolph's idea rattled other Negro leaders. "It scared everybody to death," one recalled. The *Pittsburgh Courier*, the largest-circulation Negro newspaper, branded it "a crackpot proposal." White's NAACP gave only lukewarm support. But Randolph pushed on, and thousands of black men and women responded with enthusiasm. As the idea of the march caught fire in the black community, Randolph raised his sights. By the end of May his March on Washington Movement was summoning a hundred thousand Negroes to descend on the capital on July 1. "I call on Negroes everywhere," he proclaimed, "to gird for an epoch-making march."[29]

28. Ulysses Lee, *United States Army in World War II Special Studies: The Employment of Negro Troops* (Washington: Department of the Army, 1963), 76.
29. Anderson, *Randolph*, 247–53.

The prospect of one hundred thousand Negroes in the streets of the capital rattled Franklin Roosevelt as well. He induced Eleanor to write a letter warning Randolph that "your group is making a very grave mistake." On June 13 the president called in National Youth Administration chief Aubrey Williams, a liberal southerner with good ties to the black community, and told him to "go to New York and try to talk Randolph and White out of this march. Get the missus and Fiorello [La Guardia, mayor of New York] and Anna [Rosenberg, a member of the Social Security Board], and get it stopped." Williams failed in his mission, but out of it came another meeting between Randolph and the president at the White House on June 18. Less than two weeks remained before the marchers were scheduled to throng Pennsylvania Avenue.[30]

Roosevelt opened the session with his customary persiflage, irrelevantly inquiring which Harvard class Randolph was in. "I never went to Harvard, Mr. President," Randolph coolly replied. "Well, Phil, what do you want me to do?" Roosevelt asked at last. Issue an executive order prohibiting discrimination in the defense plants, answered Randolph. "You know I can't do that," said Roosevelt. "In any event, I couldn't do anything unless you called off this march of yours. Questions like this can't be settled with a sledge hammer." He was sorry, said Randolph, but without an executive order the march would take place as scheduled. It was not the policy of the president of the United States to be ruled with a gun at his head, Roosevelt declared. "Call it off," he said curtly, "and we'll talk again." But Randolph was no Trotter, and he calmly stood his ground. Fiorello La Guardia finally broke the impasse. "Gentlemen," he said, "it is clear that Mr. Randolph is not going to call off the march, and I suggest we all begin to seek a formula."[31]

The formula took the shape of Executive Order 8802, issued on June 25, 1941. "There shall be no discrimination in the employment of workers in defense industries or government because of race, creed, color, or national origin," it declared, adding that both employers and labor unions had a positive duty "to provide for the full and equitable participation of all workers in defense industries." A newly established Fair Employment Practices Committee (FEPC) was empowered to investigate complaints and take remedial action. Ironically, there was no mention of segregation in the armed forces, the issue that had been Randolph's original concern. Yet the order represented a spectacular victory

30. Anderson, *Randolph*, 255.
31. Anderson, *Randolph*, 257–58.

for Randolph and defined a crucial pivot in the history of African-Americans. As one Negro newspaper noted, it "demonstrated to the Doubting Thomases among us that only mass action can pry open the doors that have been erected against America's black minority." A rising mood of militancy took hold in the black community. The former Doubting Thomases at the *Pittsburgh Courier* now called for a "Double V" campaign—"victory over our enemies at home and victory over our enemies on the battlefields abroad." The war crisis presented a matchless opportunity, said the *Courier*, "to persuade, embarrass, compel and shame our government and our nation . . . into a more enlightened attitude toward a tenth of its people." The NAACP grew nearly tenfold during the war, to some half a million members. The more militant Committee (later Congress) of Racial Equality (CORE) began in 1942 to mount interracial demonstrations to force the desegregation of restaurants, theaters, and municipal bus lines. Tellingly, picketers outside a Washington, D.C., restaurant in 1944 carried placards that read: "Are you for Hitler's Way or the American Way?" and "We Die Together. Let's Eat Together."[32]

It would be too much to say that Executive Order 8802 was a second Emancipation Proclamation. Yet, however grudgingly, Franklin Roosevelt had set the nation back on the freedom road that Abraham Lincoln had opened in the midst of another war three-quarters of a century earlier. For seven decades it had remained the road not taken. Now, for the first time since Reconstruction, the federal government had openly committed itself to making good on at least some of the promises of American life for black citizens. Coming at a moment that was kindled with opportunities for economic betterment and social mobility, Executive Order 8802 fanned the rising flame of black militancy and initiated a chain of events that would eventually end segregation once and for all and open a new era for African-Americans.

The lure of defense-industry jobs and the assurance of at least a measure of federal protection triggered an enormous black exodus from the South, one that eventually rivaled in size the huge European migrations earlier in the century. Some seven hundred thousand black civilians left the region during the war years. In every month of 1943 ten thousand Negroes, mostly from Texas and Louisiana, streamed into Los Angeles alone. Millions more abandoned the South in the two postwar decades,

32. Anderson, *Randolph*, 259, 260; Blum, *V Was for Victory*, 208, 217–18; Jaynes and Williams, *Common Destiny*, 63.

free at last from the stifling grip of King Cotton and keen to participate in the industrial economy. Within three decades of Pearl Harbor, a majority of blacks lived outside the states of the old Confederacy, and they no longer worked in the agricultural and domestic service sectors.[33]

The war gave Myrdal's principle of cumulation a wide new field on which to work its positive effects. The experience of Sybil Lewis was typical. When defense production began to gear up, Lewis left her position as a $3.50-per-week housemaid in Sapulpa, Oklahoma, and headed for Los Angeles, where she found employment as a $48-per-week riveter at Lockheed Aircraft. "When I got my first paycheck, I'd never seen that much money before," she remembered, "not even in the bank, because I'd never been in a bank too much." On the Lockheed assembly floor she was teamed with a "big strong white girl from a cotton farm in Arkansas." Like many of the white women in the plant, for her workmate "to say 'nigger' was just a way of life. Many of them had never been near, let alone touched a Negro." But shared work meant that "both of us [had] to relate to each other in ways that we never experienced before. Although we had our differences we both learned to work together and talk together." Repeated in thousands upon thousands of wartime workplaces, mundane encounters like Sybil Lewis's with her Arkansas co-worker began to sand away the stereotypes that had ossified under segregation. "We learned that despite our hostilities and resentments we could open up to each other and get along. . . . She learned that Negroes were people, too, and I saw her as a person also, and we both gained from it." Looking back years later, Lewis also recalled that she "saw in California that black women were working in many jobs that I had never seen in the South. . . . I saw black people accepted in the school system and accepted in other kinds of jobs that they had not been accepted in before. . . . Had it not been for the war I don't think blacks would be in the position they are in now," she concluded. "[S]ome people would never have left the South. They would have had nothing to move for." Lewis went on to college, became a civil servant, and entered the middle class. "The war," she said, "changed my life."[34]

Not every story ended as happily as Lewis's. The great black hegira, commingling with the wartime flood of white migrants, sometimes ex-

---

33. The postwar advent of the mechanical cotton picker, which could do the work of fifty field hands, accelerated the displacement of southern blacks.

34. Mark Jonathan Harris et al., *The Home Front: America during World War II* (New York: G. P. Putnam's Sons, 1984), 37–39, 118–21, 251–52.

ploded into violent turbulence. In the roaring, overcrowded war-production centers, petty frictions between people who had little more in common than their shared status as war-borne nomads could erupt into ugly confrontations. Competition for scarce housing in Detroit in 1942 led a white mob, brandishing stones and clubs, to prevent three black families from moving into the Sojourner Truth Homes—a tense rehearsal for a far bloodier confrontation in Detroit a year later. "Hate strikes" were common in the defense plants, as when white women employees shut down a Western Electric factory in Baltimore rather than share a rest room with their black co-workers. In Mobile, Alabama, swollen by an influx of some forty-five thousand war-job seekers, white ship-yard workers rioted in 1943 over the promotion of black welders, seriously injuring eleven Negroes. In Beaumont, Texas, plagued by shortages of housing and schools, whites rampaged through the black neighborhoods, murdering two Negroes and wounding dozens of others. Not all such outbursts were directed at blacks. Gangs of soldiers and sailors roamed the streets of Los Angeles in June 1943 attacking Mexican-American youths wearing the outsize outfits known as "zoot suits."

By the summer of 1943 Detroit thundered with war production and throbbed with racial tensions. In the preceding three years, more than fifty thousand blacks had moved into the Detroit metropolitan area, along with some two hundred thousand whites, many of them Appalachian "hillbillies" who brought their undiluted racial prejudices with them. On Sunday, June 20, more than one hundred thousand people, most of them black, sought refuge from the cauterizing summer heat on Belle Isle, a riverfront municipal park. Scuffles broke out between black and white teenagers. By late evening a rumor pulsed through the black neighborhoods that whites had killed three Negroes. Blacks swarmed into the streets, pulled white passengers from streetcars, and beat them savagely. White mobs soon counterattacked, and wide-open racial warfare raged through the night. By the time federal troops quelled the riot at midday on the twenty-first, twenty-five blacks and nine whites were dead, including a milkman murdered while making his rounds and a doctor beaten to death on his way to a house call. Just weeks later, New York's Harlem also exploded in a riot that claimed six black lives. The carnage in Detroit even echoed in faraway England, helping to spark a vicious racial brawl among American troops encamped at Bamber Bridge, in Lancashire.[35]

35. Alan Clive, *State of War: Michigan in World War II* (Ann Arbor: University of Michigan Press, 1979), 94, 133, 156–62.

Some of the worst racial clashes took place in army and navy training centers, where even military discipline could not always keep taut young black and white men from each other's throats. Racial fights and even lynchings occurred at several camps, as well as overseas; one squabble on Guam between Negro seamen and white marines ended in fatalities. At the army's request, the famed director Frank Capra put together a sensitively crafted film, *The Negro Soldier*, intended to alleviate racial tensions in the camps by educating blacks and whites alike about the Negro's military role, but it would take more than Capra's art to overcome racial problems in the military. Northern blacks especially resented their first encounters with formal segregation in the South. All blacks chafed at the gratuitous humiliations that military life inflicted on them—from lack of access to recreational facilities to segregated blood plasma supplies to the galling spectacle of German prisoners of war seated at southern lunch counters that refused to serve Negro soldiers. Worst of all, the army persisted in ghettoizing Negro recruits in all-black outfits and assigning them almost exclusively to noncombat roles.

Negro leaders hammered at the War and Navy departments to end segregation and train blacks for combat, but military authorities took only a few halting steps to mollify them. In 1940 Stimson appointed William Hastie, dean of Howard University's law school, as his civilian aide on Negro affairs and promoted the army's senior black officer, Colonel Benjamin O. Davis, to brigadier general. But when Hastie urged in late 1941 that a start be made toward banishing Jim Crow from the armed forces, General Marshall turned him down cold. Hastie was proposing, said Marshall, that the U.S. Army should solve "a social problem that has perplexed the American people throughout the history of this nation. . . . The Army is not a sociological laboratory."[36]

The army may not have been a sociological laboratory, but it soon generated sociological data that starkly exposed the wretched plight of black America. The Selective Service System rejected 46 percent of black registrants as unfit for service, compared with a 30.3 percent rejection rate for whites. Fully one-quarter of black inductees were infected with syphilis, a disqualification for service that ultimately was removed after treatment with sulfa drugs. Less easily remediable were educational deficiencies. In some units a third or more of black troops were illiterate. Ill-educated southern blacks scored especially poorly on the Army General Classification Test. The AGCT, often misunderstood

36. Lee, *Employment of Negro Troops*, 140–41.

as a general intelligence test, was instead an aptitude test designed to sort recruits into categories according to their suitability for different kinds of duty. As the army's chief psychologist carefully explained, the AGCT "reflects very definitely the educational opportunities the individual has had." Recruits who placed in Grades I, II, and III were tracked to become airmen, officers, specialists, and technicians. Those scoring in Grades IV or V were thought fit mainly for infantry duty or for common pick-and-shovel or dishwashing labor. In a disheartening demonstration of the deficiencies of the South's segregated educational system, 84 percent of blacks scored in the bottom two categories, compared to one-third of whites; almost half of blacks fell into the lowest category, Grade V, six times the rate for whites. Despite Marshall's determination not to turn the military into a social reform agency, the army was soon obliged to offer remedial instruction. By war's end it had taught more than 150,000 black recruits to read and had trained others in valuable work skills.[37]

The poor qualifications of so many black soldiers reinforced the army's already considerable reluctance to send them into combat. Only two black divisions were combat-rated, and the army considered neither fully reliable. The 93rd Division faced enemy fire in the Pacific theater, but mostly in rearguard and "mopping up" operations. The ill-starred 92nd Division, its black bison insignia proudly evoking memories of the Negro "buffalo soldiers" of Indian warfare days, had been removed from the line in disgrace in World War I and continued to suffer from deep distrust between its resentful black troops and condescending white officers. In one incident, enlisted men stoned a car in which white officers were riding. Wracked by such tensions, the 92nd turned in another mixed performance in Italy. It was ultimately reconfigured to include one black and one white regiment, as well as the Japanese-American 442nd Regimental Combat Team — a dubious concession to the principle of desegregation, and one that blacks protested. A handful of other black units saw combat, including the 761st Tank Battalion, sent into battle in Normandy by George Patton with the admonition: "I don't care what color you are, so long as you go up there and kill those Kraut sonsabitches."[38]

37. Lee Kennett, G.I.: The American Soldier in World War II (New York: Charles Scribner's Sons), 34–35: Lee, Employment of Negro Troops, 242–44; Stephan Thernstrom and Abigail Thernstrom, America in Black and White (New York: Simon and Schuster, 1997), 74. See also Samuel Stouffer et al., The American Soldier (Princeton: Princeton University Press, 1949); and Paula S. Fass, Outside In: Minorities and the Transformation of American Education (New York: Oxford University Press, 1989).
38. Lee, Employment of Negro Troops, 661.

Only in the acute manpower crisis of the Battle of the Bulge at the end of 1944 did the army form several dozen black rifle platoons to serve alongside white soldiers in integrated companies. For the most part, the two thousand black service troops who volunteered for this reassignment to combat duty performed admirably, earning the respect and gratitude of their white comrades. In 1948 President Truman at last ordered full desegregation of the armed forces.

The Army Air Corps eventually consented to take a handful of black fliers, including the 99th Pursuit Squadron, trained at the famed Tuskegee Institute founded by Booker T. Washington and known colloquially as the Tuskegee Airmen. When Eleanor Roosevelt visited the trainees in 1941 and went for a flight with Chief Alfred Anderson in a Piper Cub, the photographs were a sensation, in both the white and black press. The 99th distinguished itself in North Africa and Italy and later over Germany, though in 1943 Hastie resigned in protest over the isolation of the "Lonely Eagles" in an all-black, segregated unit. The Marine Corps began training men for its first all-Negro battalion in the summer of 1942, but they would not serve under black officers. The first Negro marine lieutenant was commissioned only after the end of the war.

As for the navy, manpower needs prompted it to step up black inductions in 1943. Most black sailors were indifferently trained and destined for unglamorous and backbreaking shore duty. The navy assigned several gangs of black stevedores to loading ammunition at its sprawling munitions depot at Port Chicago, California. Like all naval facilities, Port Chicago was rigidly segregated. Black sailors waited for white sailors to finish eating before entering the mess hall. Only black crews did the nerve-grating work of wrestling grease-slathered bombs down planks into the holds of the Liberty Ships. They were given no safety manuals or training in the handling of high explosives. "We were just shown a boxcar full of ammunition, wire nets spread out on the docks and the hold in the ship and told to load," one black winch operator remembered. White officers wagered on which crew could load the most tonnage on a shift, a practice known as "racing."

On July 17, 1944, black sailors raced through the afternoon and into the night to finish packing some forty-six hundred tons of explosives into the E.A. Bryan, and to rig its sister ship, the Quinalt Victory, to begin loading the next day. At 10:18 in the evening, a terrific blast obliterated both vessels, hurling debris thousands of feet into the air and shattering windows in San Francisco, thirty-five miles to the west. It was the worst war-related disaster in the continental United States. Flying glass and metal killed 320 men and maimed hundreds more. Of the dead, 202 were black. When the unnerved Negro survivors were ordered back to work three weeks later, fifty refused; they were court-martialed and sentenced to fifteen years hard labor and dishonorable discharge. Thurgood Marshall, chief counsel for the NAACP, declared: "This is not 50 men on trial for mutiny. This is the Navy on trial for its whole vicious policy toward Negroes. Negroes in the Navy don't mind loading ammunition. They just want to know why they are the only ones doing the loading! They want to know why they are segregated; why they don't get promoted, [and] why the Navy disregarded official warnings by the San Francisco waterfront unions . . . that an explosion was inevitable if they persisted in using untrained seamen in the loading of ammunition."

Partly as a result of the Port Chicago catastrophe, the navy tiptoed toward integration in August 1944. It assigned some five hundred black seamen to twenty-five auxiliary vessels. Negroes were not allowed to compose more than 10 percent of a ship's crew—roughly their percentage in the general population—and the experiment went forward without incident. In December 1945 the navy ended segregation altogether, and in 1949 the first black officer graduated from the Naval Academy at Annapolis.[39]

From much of this turmoil Franklin Roosevelt remained studiously aloof. Despite his wife's evident sympathies, and whatever might have been his personal predilections, political considerations continued to stay his hand from bold racial initiatives, as they had in the New Deal years. In 1942 Eugene "Bull" Connor, the commissioner of public safety in Birmingham, Alabama, and a man destined to play a violently repressive role in the civil rights struggles two decades later, presciently warned the president that further federal pressure on the South's segregationist regime would lead to "the Annihilation of the Democratic Party in this section of the Nation." When the Supreme Court ruled in *Smith v. Allwright* in 1944 that the Democratic Party's all-white primary in Texas was unconstitutional, Attorney General Biddle wanted to go forward with a similar suit in Alabama. But an aide who sounded out southern opinion cautioned the President that Biddle's proposal "would

39. John Boudreau, "Blown Away," *Washington Post*, July 17, 1994, sec. F, 1; Robert L. Allen, *The Port Chicago Mutiny* (New York: Warner 1989), 119–20. In 1946 the Port Chicago sailors were quietly released from prison and given less than dishonorable discharges.

translate impotent rumblings against the New Deal into an actual revolt at the polls. I am sure that any such action would be a very dangerous mistake." Even Eleanor Roosevelt shared her husband's wariness about the political volatility of racial issues. Responding to a young black woman's complaint that Wendell Willkie professed more advanced racial views than did the president, Eleanor wrote that Willkie enjoyed the luxury of not having to govern. "If he were to be elected President," Eleanor explained, "on that day, he would have to take into consideration the people who are heads of important committees in Congress . . . people on whom he must depend to pass vital legislation for the nation as a whole." Most of those people were southerners, and for them segregation was still a sacrosanct way of life.[40]

But however politically straitjacketed, the president found some room for maneuver on race. When it became apparent that some employers were violating the spirit of Executive Order 8802 by employing blacks only in the most menial jobs and denying them access to the kinds of training necessary for advancement, the president significantly strengthened the FEPC. In 1943 he increased its budget to half a million dollars. He replaced its part-time appointees working out of make-shift Washington quarters with a professional staff distributed through a dozen regional offices. When he learned that unions were shunting blacks into powerless "auxiliaries," he encouraged the National Labor Relations Board to decertify unions that practiced discrimination. He sent in federal troops to break a strike on the Philadelphia transit system in 1944, compelling the hiring of black trolley drivers. By war's end, blacks held some 8 percent of defense-industry jobs, a proportion that approached their presence in the population, and a major advance from the 3 percent they held in 1942. The number of African-American civilians in the federal employ more than tripled, to two hundred thousand. Among whites, meanwhile, the principle of cumulation was slowly working its effects. In 1942 three-fifths of whites told pollsters that they imagined blacks were contented with their lot. Two years later, only a quarter of whites thought that blacks were being treated fairly.[41]

The NAACP's Walter White returned from a tour of the fighting fronts at the war's end to publish a prophetic book: A Rising Wind.

---

40. Blum, V Was for Victory, 193, 212; Doris Kearns Goodwin, No Ordinary Time: Franklin and Eleanor Roosevelt: The Homefront in World War II (New York: Simon and Schuster, 1994), 353.
41. Cantril, 988–89.

Echoing Myrdal, he wrote: "World War II has immeasurably magnified the Negro's awareness of the disparity between the American profession and practice of democracy." Black soldiers and sailors, he predicted, "will return home convinced that whatever betterment of their lot is achieved must come largely from their own efforts. They will return determined to use those efforts to the utmost." Jim Crow was far from dead in 1945, but he was beginning to weaken.[42]

IF THE WAR HAD BEGUN to usher Jim Crow off the stage of American history, it was ushering another mythical character onto it: Rosie the Riveter. Unlike Jim Crow, born in antebellum Dixie and destined to survive for more than a century, Rosie was a war baby with an uncertain future. She owed her very name not to spontaneous folk usage but to War Manpower Commission propaganda campaigns to entice women to work in war plants. "Rosie's got a boyfriend, Charlie; Charlie, he's a marine," ran a wartime jingle:

> Rosie is protecting Charlie
> Working overtime on the riveting machine.[43]

Like Jim Crow, Rosie was a fictional symbol for a complex social reality that eluded tidy description. Rosie's denim-clad, tool-wielding, can-do figure was meant to personify the nearly nineteen million women who worked for wages at one time or another during the war. In fact, she typified very few of them. She was certainly an imperfect emblem for the 350,000 women who donned uniforms in the Women's Auxiliary Army Corps (WAACs — or WACs after the "Auxiliary" was dropped in 1943), the navy's Women Accepted for Voluntary Emergency Service (WAVES), the air corps' Women's Auxiliary Service Pilots (WASPS), the Coast Guard's SPARS (from the service's Latin motto, *Semper Paratus*), or the singularly unnicknamed women's branch of the marines. Nor did Rosie make a very good poster girl for the many millions of women who worked not for wages but as volunteers in war-related programs — packing Red Cross surgical dressings, entertaining troops at reception centers, or serving as OPA price monitors. Even for the decided minority of American women who received paychecks in the wartime civilian

42. Walter White, *A Rising Wind* (Garden City, N.Y.: Doubleday, Doran, 1945), 142, 144.
43. Alice Kessler-Harris, *Out to Work: A History of Wage-Earning Women in the United States* (New York: Oxford University Press, 1982), 276.

economy, Rosie was a misleading symbol, though one whose heroically iconic stature powerfully molded memories of the war.

Nearly twelve million women had been employed on the eve of Pearl Harbor, most of them the victims — or beneficiaries — of traditional occupational segregation along gender and racial lines. Ninety percent of all women workers in 1940 fell into just ten employment categories. If they were black or Hispanic, they were probably domestic servants, living threadbare lives in a spare back room, precariously beholden to the goodwill of their employer. White women who worked were likely to hold jobs in teaching, nursing, social work, and the civil service — largely Depression-proof occupations that had afforded an unusual measure of job security in the 1930s. Minority or white, these prewar women workers were usually single. Following customs unchanged since the nineteenth century, young women typically worked for a few years, then left their jobs when they married, as most eventually did. Almost half of all single women were gainfully employed in 1940, but only 15 percent of the much larger number of married women, and a scant 9 percent of mothers with children under the age of six. Those numbers measured some surprisingly stubborn conceptions of sexual roles that the war crisis only slightly dislodged.

As early as 1942 it became obvious that even the scaled-back draft calls of the ninety-division mobilization would leave the industrial economy short of labor. New workers had to be found. Some came from beyond the nation's borders. In July the United States and Mexico reached an accord, patterned on a similar World War I arrangement. It took its name from the Spanish word for manual laborer, *bracero*. The bracero program licensed over two hundred thousand Mexicans as temporary contract laborers. They maintained railroad tracks in the Southwest and harvested potatoes in Idaho; fruit, sugar beets, tomatoes, and lettuce in California; and apples and wheat in Washington. (Sour memories of the mistreatment of Mexican workers in World War I produced the "Texas Proviso," which for a time excluded Texas from the bracero program.)

But immigrant workers were only a partial solution. Idle pools of domestic labor also had to be tapped. "In some communities," the president said in his 1942 Columbus Day Fireside Chat, "employers dislike to employ women. In others they are reluctant to hire Negroes. . . . We can no longer afford to indulge such prejudices or practices." He might have added that many women themselves, especially married women, apparently disliked to be employed. Fully three-quarters of all women of working age were "at home" as the war began. The overwhelming majority of them were still there when the war ended. In both Britain and the Soviet Union, by contrast, those proportions were almost precisely reversed. There more than 70 percent of women toiled outside their homes during the war, many of them involuntarily drafted into the work force.[44]

Many voices, including that of *Fortune* magazine, advocated conscripting stay-at-home American women into industrial service. But here, as in so many areas of wartime life, America was spared such coercive measures. Instead, government and industry orchestrated advertising campaigns, invoking Rosie's strapping but stylish image, to persuade women willingly to leave kitchen and sewing table for the factory floor. More than six million women responded. By war's end almost nineteen million women were working, more than at any previous time in American history. Yet even that surge looks less dramatic on close inspection. About half of those six million new entrants were young women school-leavers who would have entered the labor force in any case. The number who answered the trumpet's call and entered the war economy over and above the "normal" increase attributable to population growth and maturation has been estimated between 2.7 and 3.5 million.[45]

Nearly two million women—never more than 10 percent of female workers in wartime—did indeed labor in defense plants. Almost half a million worked in the aircraft industry. In some West Coast airframe factories they made up nearly 50 percent of the labor force. Another 225,000 worked in shipbuilding. Following the patriotic example of famously long-locked film star Veronica Lake, women bobbed their hair to keep it out of the machinery, swapped their dresses for slacks, toted their lunches in paper bags (tin lunch pails were deemed unfeminine), ran cranes and tractors, blushed and seethed at their male co-workers' catcalls and wolf whistles—and helped build thousands of ships, tanks, and airplanes. Few, however, drilled rivets, a relatively high-skill task for which employers were unwilling to train workers whom they considered

44. PPA (1942), 422. Seven out of eight women in the "at home" category in 1941 remained "at home" in 1944. See D'Ann Campbell, *Women at War with America: Private Lives in a Patriotic Era* (Cambridge: Harvard University Press, 1984), 77. See also Claudia D. Goldin, "The Role of World War II in the Rise of Women's Employment," *American Economic Review* 81, no. 4 (September 1991): 741–56.
45. See the slightly divergent estimates in Campbell, *Women at War with America*, 73, and Kessler-Harris, *Out to Work*, 276–77.

as transient, short-term employees. Instead, defense plant supervisors usually employed women as American management had traditionally used unseasoned laborers—by "Taylorizing" production routines into separate and repetitive functions that required little skill and minimum training. That practice was notorious in the shipyards, where low-skill welding became the typical woman's job. Faced with such work conditions, it was small wonder that a majority of women in a 1943 poll said they would not take a job in a war plant, or that turnover and absenteeism among female defense workers occurred at twice the rate for men. Women held just 4.4 percent of war jobs classified as skilled and a far smaller percentage of management positions. A solitary woman engineer at Lockheed Aircraft remembered her difficulty in winning her male colleagues' respect. "If I say we ought to do it this way, they don't hear me." Only "if I say 'God damn . . . ' then they pay attention."[46]

Rosie the Riveter might therefore have been more appropriately named Wendy the Welder, or more appropriately still Sally the Secretary, or even, as events were to prove, Molly the Mom. Despite the surge of women into heavy industry, markedly larger numbers of new women entrants into the wartime work force took up clerical and service jobs, in line with historical trends, and there women's gains proved far more durable. The number of women factory operatives plummeted at war's end. Shipbuilding effectively ceased, laying off hundreds of thousands of women (as well as blacks, cruelly cutting short their first foray into the industrial workplace). Women left the aircraft and automobile industries in droves. One in four autoworkers was a woman in wartime; only one in twelve in 1946. By 1947 the proportion of working women in blue-collar occupations was actually smaller than it had been at the war's outset—24.6 percent as against 26.2 percent in 1940. The future of women's work lay not in the wartime heavy industries, destined to fade in relative importance in the postwar economy, but in the burgeoning service occupations, which within a decade of the war's conclusion eclipsed factory work as the nation's principal source of employment. Banking, for example, an all-male bastion before the war, employed more women than men by 1950, including most tellers and 15 percent of middle managers.[47]

Women's labor-force participation rate, slowly rising through the cen-

46. Cantril, 1046; Rosalind Rosenberg, Divided Lives: American Women in the Twentieth Century (New York: Hill and Wang, 1992), 132; Campbell, Women at War with America, 116.
47. Campbell, Women at War with America, 239, 111.

tury to 26 percent in 1940, spiked to 36 percent in 1944, then swiftly receded to 28 percent in 1947, back in line with longtime historical trends. In a significant harbinger of what the future held, by 1944 married women for the first time made up a majority of female workers. Typically they were women over the age of thirty-five who had already discharged their child-rearing responsibilities. Many women wanted to continue working at the war's end, and some did. But many were also fired, pressured by employers and unions to cede their place at the workbench to returning veterans. Strikingly, a far larger number quit voluntarily, and their reasons proved instructive about the nation's wartime and postwar mood. Among former women war workers polled in a Census Bureau survey in 1951, half cited "family responsibilities" as their principal motive for leaving the work force. In-depth interviews with a sample of women who gave birth in 1946 were even more revealing. Only 8 percent considered it a sacrifice to give up their war jobs; 16 percent had mixed feelings; but an overwhelming 76 percent positively welcomed the transition from employment to motherhood.

Those kinds of attitudes had manifested themselves in wartime as well. Recruitment drives emphasized that women were being hired only "for the duration." Wartime polls repeatedly showed that majorities of women as well as men disapproved of working wives and even more heavily censured working mothers. Alarmists claimed that hordes of "latchkey" children, left to their own devices by employed mothers, were growing up psychologically stunted and even criminally inclined. But talk of wartime juvenile delinquency, and even, as it turned out, of long-term characterological damage to the children of working mothers, was greatly exaggerated—not least because relatively few mothers of young children worked at all during the war. In a striking demonstration of the persistence of traditional cultural norms, the percentage of working mothers with children under the age of six barely inched up in wartime, from 9 percent in 1940 to 12 percent in 1944. The thirty-one hundred day-care centers that the government built to accommodate working mothers operated at one-quarter capacity, serving only 130,000 children. As for the long-term psychological effects on Rosie's children, one postwar study concluded that there was "no evidence that maternal employment affected the personality development of children in unfortunate ways."[48]

48. Campbell, *Women at War with America*, 86–87, 82; Susan M. Hartmann, *The Home Front and Beyond: American Women in the 1940s* (Boston: Twayne, 1982), 84; Kessler-Harris, *Out to Work*, 294. William M. Tuttle Jr., *Daddy's Gone to War: The Second World War in the Lives of America's Children* (New York: Oxford University

"Did deep societal values change [in World War II]?" historian D'Ann Campbell asks. So far as women are concerned, she gives an ironic but unimpeachable answer. "Yes. Americans emphasized more strongly the primacy of family and children in their lives than in previous eras." As the *Ladies' Home Journal* proclaimed in 1944, "Motherhood's Back in Style." The marriage rate, which had dipped in the Depression years, rose rapidly in the war decade. In 1942 it reached the highest level since 1920. By war's end a higher proportion of American women were married than at any time in the century, and women's median age at marriage had dipped to a historic low. Births shot up as well. In 1943 more babies were born than in any previous year in the century, marking the highest birth rate (babies per thousand women of child-bearing age) since the pre-Depression year of 1927. In the immediate postwar years, the average number of children per household climbed from two to three, as Rosie and her sisters abandoned war work to become the mothers of the fabled baby-boom generation, whose statistical origin actually dates from 1940. Ironically, a vigorous resurgence of natalism and what Betty Friedan was later to call the feminine mystique of domesticity and motherhood were the war's immediate legacies to American women.[49]

Jim Crow's days were numbered by 1945 because the war threw into high relief the contradiction between America's professed values and its actual behavior. In contrast, Rosie's day still lay in the future at war's end because her wartime behavior was not yet sanctioned by a shift in social values—and values proved far less mutable than behavior. Yet Rosie had given birth to a mystique of her own. Her strong, capable, tool-toting image lingered in the nation's collective memory. It helped inspire a later generation of women to challenge sexual stereotypes and to demand what Rosie never had: economic freedom as well as family security, a child *and* a paycheck, a place of work and place to call home, too, not one or the other. Rosie thus went on doing her cultural work well after she laid down her rivet gun. The reverberations that she set off in American culture provided but one example among many of how the war's echoes would ring down the years long after the shooting stopped.

Press, 1993), 89. The Lanham Act centers were poorly administered; some private centers, notably those at the Kaiser shipyards, were much more heavily utilized. See Susan E. Riley, "Caring for Rosie's Children: Federal Child Care Policies in the World War II Era," *Polity* 26, no. 4 (Summer 1994): 655–75.

49. Campbell, *Women at War with America*, 99–100; Tuttle, *Daddy's Gone to War*, 27; HSUS, 49, 64.

ON ELECTION DAY, November 3, 1942, the fighting on distant Guadalcanal was locked in stalemate. The transports bearing American troops to North Africa were still at sea. At home, all was bustle and confusion, the inevitable effects of a crash mobilization program that had uprooted millions of people but had so far produced more aggravation and griping than tanks and bullets. Frustration and mobility conspired to keep many voters away from the polls. Only twenty-eight million cast their ballots, seven million fewer than in the last off-year election in 1938 and twenty-two million fewer than in 1940. Democrats took a shellacking. Republicans gained forty-seven seats in the House and seven in the Senate, as well as the governorships of several key states, including the electoral colossus of New York, where the youthful Thomas E. Dewey emerged victorious. Post-election analysis attributed the GOP's gains to the low turnout, as well as to smoldering resentment — resentment of mushrooming government bureaucracy, particularly the nettlesome Office of Price Administration, and especially bitter resentment of Uncle Sam's continuing inability to land a glove on his enemies. If "the African campaign had preceded rather than followed the elections," the secretary of the Democratic National Committee opined, "the results would have been different."[50]

The election yielded the most conservative Congress in a decade, filled with what *Fortune* magazine called "normalcy men." Old-guard southern Democrats joined with Republicans to form a substantial majority that was anti-Roosevelt, anti–New Deal, and unreliably internationalist. Of 115 identifiable isolationists, all but five were reelected. Some southerners were reported to be privately hoping for a Democratic defeat in 1944, because it would give them four years to purge the New Dealers once and for all from the party. *Time* magazine saw a parallel with the election of 1918, which had seated the anti-Wilson Congress that thwarted America's entry into the League of Nations. "It is by no means certain," said the *Economist*, that at war's end the Americans would not once again "return to Hardingism."[51]

The New Deal had been a walking corpse since at least 1938, a political casualty well before it became a casualty of war. The new Seventy-eighth Congress moved swiftly to lay the New Deal finally in its

50. Blum, *V Was for Victory*, 233.
51. Blum, *V Was for Victory*, 232; Frank Freidel, *Franklin D. Roosevelt: A Rendezvous with Destiny* (Boston: Little, Brown, 1990), 494; *Time*, November 16, 1942, 16; *Economist*, November 7, 1942, 572.

grave, and then to drive a stake through its heart. By the end of 1943 congressional conservatives had extinguished many of the signature New Deal agencies. The Civilian Conservation Corps, the Works Progress Administration, and the National Youth Administration—deemed unnecessary in the full-employment wartime economy—were all gone. The National Resources Planning Board, a planning body much favored by the president and headed by his uncle Frederic Delano, was legislated out of existence in the same year. The Farm Security Administration and the Rural Electrification Administration, which had done so much to change the face of the American countryside, were defunded down to skeletal operations. For good measure, Congress also terminated the domestic arm of the Office of War Information, which it accused of being a liberal propaganda organ and Roosevelt's private political tool. Yet significantly, conservatives raised no hand against the New Deal's core achievements: Social Security, farm price supports, child labor and minimum wage legislation, and banking and securities regulation. Those reforms were already firmly in place as untouchable pillars of the new social and economic order that Roosevelt had wrought out of the Depression crisis.

Roosevelt, freshly returned from Teheran and his mind fastened on diplomacy, not domestic reform, appeared to deliver his own ungainly requiem for the New Deal at a rambling press conference on December 28, 1943. "How did the New Deal come into existence?" he asked. "It was because there was an awfully sick patient called the United States of America, and it was suffering from a grave internal disorder.... And they sent for the doctor." "Dr. New Deal" had saved the banks and rescued farmers, cleaned up the securities markets, put the idle back to work, built dams and bridges, and prescribed old-age and unemployment insurance. But now, said the president, "[w]e have done nearly all of that," and it was time for "Dr. Win-the-War" to take over.

Roosevelt summoned Dr. Win-the-War into being partly to refocus the nation's evidently flagging attention on the great martial enterprise that had not yet reached its climax. America's major battles against Germany and Japan remained unfought at the end of 1943, yet strikes continued to interrupt military production. He felt "let down" on his return from Teheran, Roosevelt confessed, as he saw so many of his countrymen "laboring under the delusion that the time is past when we must make prodigious sacrifices—that the war is already won and we can begin to slacken off." Some voices were already calling for "reconversion" of war industries to satisfy consumer demand. In a further effort to concentrate the country's energies, the president would soon ask, in vain, for a national service law to "make available for war production . . . every able-bodied adult in this Nation." But if conservatives imagined that Roosevelt had abandoned Dr. New Deal altogether, he quickly proved them mistaken.[52]

In 1935 Roosevelt had briefly placated the right with promises of a "breathing spell," only to launch an exceptionally combative presidential campaign the following year. This time Roosevelt had scarcely dismissed Dr. New Deal before he tried to reinstate him less than two weeks later. The occasion was his annual State of the Union address. Too ill to make his customary personal appearance before Congress, he broadcast his speech over the air from his White House office. As millions of Americans gathered around their radios on the evening of January 11, 1944, they heard the president call for "a second Bill of Rights . . . an economic bill of rights" that would guarantee every citizen a job, a living wage, decent housing, adequate medical care, education, and "protection from the economic fears of old age, sickness, accident, and unemployment." Roosevelt concluded with a ringing reaffirmation of the New Deal's animating philosophy. "All of these rights," he said, "spell security." The speech has been called the most radical of his life, and so it was if advocacy of government-sponsored social provision was the test of radicalism. In 1944, however, much of the country was in no mood to hear it. The president's remarks, notes one biographer, "fell with a dull thud into the half-empty chambers of the United States Congress."[53]

Roosevelt's proposals had their origin in two reports that his uncle's National Resource Planning Board (NRPB) had submitted before its demise: *Post-War Planning* and *Security, Work, and Relief Policies*. Their provenance from a defunct agency offered a clue to the political reception they received. More telling, the clash of the reports' dreary Depression-era premises with the lusty realities of wartime America revealed just how obsolete much of the New Deal was becoming.

"The need for socially provided income," said the authors of *Security, Work, and Relief Policies*, in language as lifeless as the ideas it expressed, "is in large measure a consequence of the imperfections in the operation

---

52. *PPA* (1943), 569–75; (1944), 34, 36, 37.

53. *PPA* (1944), 32–42. On the radicalism of Roosevelt's speech, and its reception, see James MacGregor Burns, *Roosevelt: The Soldier of Freedom, 1940–1945* (New York: Harcourt Brace Jovanovich, 1970), 424–26.

our economy. . . . [F]ull employment of all our resources, including labor, is a condition which cannot as yet be regarded as a normal characteristic of our economy." The problem "antedates the depression" and
would continue into the indefinite future: "[I]t is problematical whether
private demand for investment will be sufficient, upon termination of
the war." Therefore, the planners concluded, "even if spending for war
should raise the level of national income to its practical maximum . . .
the public-aid problem is likely to be both large and persistent for some
time to come." Elsewhere, the planners specified $100 billion as the
target "practical maximum" of national income that policy should try to
achieve, just $14 billion more than in the less populous America of
1929. "Our recommendation," they concluded, "envisages the attribu-
tion to government of a more active role in the economic life of the
country."[54]

Those assumptions, fixed on the inadequacy of the economy rather
than its promise, lay at the foundations of the reform edifice that the
New Dealers had erected in the Depression decade. But in 1942, the
year the planners published their reports, national income had already
reached $137 billion. In 1944, the year of Roosevelt's "radical" speech,
it topped $180 billion. Contrary to the expectations of the NRPB plan-
ers, national income did not drop at war's end but ascended to $241
billion in 1950. In the following two fabulously prosperous decades it
more than tripled again, to $800 billion in 1970.[55]

No one could have imagined such economic growth in the 1930s,
and only a few even remotely sensed its possibility in wartime. The
Great Depression had seemed to many to demonstrate that the American economy had "matured," that the age of economic expansion had
ended and "secular stagnation" had irrevocably set in. That premise,
echoing Frederick Jackson Turner's fin-de-siècle threnody for the closing
of the frontier era in 1890, had informed Franklin Roosevelt's thinking
from the time of his first presidential campaign in 1932. It was the
intellectual bedrock on which the great New Deal reforms had been
built. It had animated John Maynard Keynes's insistence that compensatory public spending was permanently required to stabilize modern
economies at high levels of employment, a new policy gospel embraced

54. National Resources Planning Board, *Security, Work, and Relief Policies* (Washington: USGPO, 1942), 445, 487, 490, and *Post-War Planning* (n.p., n.d. [September
1942]), 1, 25.
55. *HSUS*, 224.

by a rising generation of economists in the 1930s. The most influential American Keynesian, Harvard's Alvin H. Hansen, had argued in his 1938 tract, *Full Recovery or Stagnation*, that only massive government deficits could maintain full employment. The war, however, was shattering the economists' theories of secular stagnation. Hansen saw the implications of the economy's wartime performance more clearly than many others. He still clung to a preference for public spending over private, but he could not help but be impressed at the economic vitality the war had stimulated. "We know now," he wrote in 1944, "as a result of the war experience, that we have reached a stage in technique and productivity which a few years ago no one believed possible. All of us had our sights too low. . . . We have suddenly realized this enormous advance in productive capacity. We did not know we had it in 1940."[56]

Ordinary Americans shared Hansen's sense of amazement. They had never had it so good, and they wanted it better. Corporate advertisers, with little to sell in wartime but keen to build a reservoir of pent-up demand that could be released later, fed the public's dreams of affluence with seductive images of the consumers' paradise that waited at the war's end. The war was thus opening the window to a future in which building structural reforms would give way to fueling the engines of economic growth, when the politics of equality would yield to the politics of expansion. If the New Deal had stabilized America, the war energized the country in ways inconceivable just years earlier. The goal of the New Deal had been to achieve a measure of security for all Americans in a presumably static economy. The goal, even the obsession, of Americans in the postwar years would be the pursuit of individual prosperity in the midst of apparently endless economic growth.

In those circumstances, the only result of Roosevelt's call for a universal bill of economic rights was another bill of rights altogether, one much more limited in scope but packing powerful implications for those whose lives it touched. Prodded by the American Legion and prompted in part by lingering worries about the postwar economy's ability to absorb demobilized soldiers, Congress unanimously passed the famed GI Bill of Rights, and Roosevelt signed it in June 1944. The bill aimed to regulate the flow of returning veterans into the job market by offering them vocational training and higher education, as well as housing and medical benefits while in school and low-interest loans thereafter for buying homes and starting businesses. Ironically, the only significant opposition

56. Alvin H. Hansen, "Planning Full Employment," *Nation*, October 21, 1944, 492.

to the bill came from educators. "Education is not a device for coping with mass unemployment," University of Chicago president Robert Maynard Hutchins warned, adding snootily that "colleges and universities will find themselves converted into educational hobo jungles. And veterans . . . will find themselves educational hobos."[57]

Events proved Hutchins spectacularly wrong. More than a million eager veterans attended the nation's universities at Uncle Sam's expense in the immediate postwar years. Within a decade some eight million had taken advantage of the bill's educational programs. They were hardly hobos. On the contrary, they were highly motivated students who helped to transform American universities from sleepy citadels of privilege into vibrant educational centers. Fewer than 10 percent of young people attended college in the prewar years; almost 15 percent did in 1948, and double that proportion, nearly a third of young Americans, just two decades later.[58] GI Bill beneficiaries changed the face of higher education, dramatically raised the educational level and hence the productivity of the work force, and in the process unimaginably altered their own lives. The GI Bill thus stood out as the most emblematic of all World War II–era political accomplishments. It aimed not at restructuring the economy but at empowering individuals. It roared on after 1945 as a kind of afterburner to the engines of social change and upward mobility that the war had ignited, propelling an entire generation along an ascending curve of achievement and affluence that their parents could not have dreamed.

Roosevelt's 1944 State of the Union address had been an effort to ring one last hurrah out of the old New Deal record. Congress greeted all its proposals as dead on arrival, as Roosevelt knew they would, but he calculated that impossible policies would make for good politics in an election year. Looking ahead to November, Roosevelt also wooed the soldier vote in 1944, not only with his warm endorsement of the GI Bill but also with his support for the so-called federal ballot. Regretting the low turnout of 1942 and remembering the crucial margin that Union soldiers had provided for Lincoln over McClellan in 1864, Roosevelt proposed that the federal government should issue special absentee ballots to the eleven million servicemen and women away from home in 1944. Traditional states'-rights advocates, already nervous at federal court

57. Keith Olson, The G.I. Bill, the Veterans, and the Colleges (Lexington: University of Kentucky Press, 1974), 25.
58. HSUS, 383.

encroachments on the white primary, were apoplectic at the prospect of this further intrusion of federal power into the political process. "Who is behind this bill?" Mississippi's John Rankin rhetorically asked on the House floor. The Communists, he viciously responded, and he extended his indictment to include the radio broadcaster Walter Winchell, "the little kike . . . who called this body the 'House of Reprehensibles'" (because it had opposed virtually every reform measure Roosevelt had proposed in wartime). In the end, Congress so emasculated the soldier-vote bill that only 112,000 federal ballots were issued.[59]

Unlike in 1940, Roosevelt made no secret of his intentions to run for reelection in 1944. The real question was who would be his running mate, a matter of more than usual gravity because Roosevelt was not a well man. A secretary remarked that Roosevelt now routinely replied "rotten" or "like hell" when asked how he was. A physical examination in March 1944 disclosed high blood pressure and serious heart disease. Even after a full month's rest at Bernard Baruch's South Carolina estate in April, his associates thought he looked ghastly. He had dark patches under his eyes, his hands noticeably trembled, and his shirt collar hung loosely around his neck. One close friend thought "that he would never survive his term." Should that occur, Vice-President Henry Wallace would become president. That prospect struck fear and loathing into the breasts of the Democratic Party bosses. Roosevelt had shoved the unapologetically liberal and unpredictably loony Wallace down the throat of his party in 1940; the Democratic barons had been gagging on him ever since. Whatever else happened in 1944, they were determined to get Wallace off the ticket.[60]

The Republicans unceremoniously repudiated their 1940 candidate, Wendell Willkie (who as it turned out was dead of a heart attack before election day). Some conservatives, including Robert McCormick of the *Chicago Tribune*, beseeched General MacArthur to run, promising that this time they could stage a victorious replay of General McClellan's unsuccessful challenge to Lincoln in the midst of the Civil War. But when publication of the general's impolitic letters to a supporter revealed him to be vain and possibly insubordinate, MacArthur's candidacy ignominiously collapsed.

Meanwhile, the star of Thomas E. Dewey steadily rose. A former hard-

59. Burns, *Soldier of Freedom*, 431; Polenberg, *War and Society*, 197.
60. Freidel, *Franklin D. Roosevelt*, 507; Edward J. Flynn, *You're the Boss* (New York: Viking, 1947), 179.

hitting Manhattan prosecutor, the forty-year-old Dewey had felt cheated out of the 1940 nomination by the surprising Willkie boom. In the Republican resurgence of 1942 he was elected governor of the traditionally Democratic stronghold of New York. Like Willkie, he was an internationalist. Unlike Willkie, he was methodical and dapper. He was also the kind of man who would say to a friend with a hangover, "I told you so." From a thermos on his desk he poured himself ice water at regular intervals. Some thought it flowed in his veins. His critics mocked him as a comically prim figure who was capable of strutting while sitting down. Dewey was so stiff, wrote one journalist, that when he took the stage to speak, "he comes out like a man who has been mounted on casters and given a tremendous shove from behind." Dewey enjoyed the advantages of a strong political base in Roosevelt's own home state, rich in votes and money. But neither he nor any other Republican could hope to mount much of a challenge to a war-winning president whose popularity had been enhanced by war-borne prosperity. Dewey showed himself a man of principle when he chose to remain silent about the potentially explosive information, suggested to him by Republican congressmen and confirmed in strictest confidence by George Marshall, that the government had broken Japanese codes before the Pearl Harbor attack. But in the end Dewey was reduced to campaigning on just two issues: Roosevelt's health and the alleged influence of Communists in the Roosevelt administration.[61]

All the preelection drama revolved around the Democratic vice-presidential nomination. Roosevelt at various times tendered his support to Wallace as well as to Office of War Mobilization chief James Byrnes, though Byrnes was as objectionable to liberals as Wallace was to conservatives. As a lapsed and twice-married Catholic, Byrnes also carried big liabilities with many of the ethnic constituencies that were the heart of the New Deal coalition. The attempt to put either Wallace or Byrnes on the ticket would ignite a raucous political donnybrook and might even fracture the Democratic coalition so painstakingly put together in the New Deal years. Seeking some acceptable middle ground, the party's political operatives pressed Roosevelt to embrace the candidacy of Missouri senator Harry S. Truman.

Truman was surely a man of the middle. He was a son of the Middle Border, blunt-spoken, plain-living, and proud of his ordinariness. Standing five feet, eight inches tall, he had the taut little body of a jockey and

---

61. Richard Norton Smith, *Thomas E. Dewey and His Times* (New York: Simon and Schuster, 1982), 509.

the manner of a country boy who had made good but never forgot his origins. He was as straightforward as a sentence without commas. He had spent his earliest boyhood on a six-hundred-acre farm near Grandview in Jackson County, Missouri. When Harry was six his family moved to the town of Independence. He graduated from high school there in 1901, and that was the end of his formal education. In any case, "[i]t was on the farm that Harry got his common sense," his mother once said. "He didn't get it in town." He was employed briefly as a bank clerk in Kansas City, then returned to Grandview to work the family farm for a time, without much success. World War I offered him an exit. He joined a Missouri National Guard unit, and his comrades, many of them Catholics from Kansas City, elected him a first lieutenant. He commanded an artillery battery at the Battle of the Meuse-Argonne in 1918 and ended the war as a captain. Many of his troops regarded their no-nonsense, bespectacled captain with respect and even affection. Eventually, they became the nucleus of his own modest political machine.

Captain Truman came home in 1919, started a men's clothing store in Kansas City, and went broke in the recession of 1921. Having flopped as a farmer and failed as a haberdasher, he went into politics. He got help from a wartime acquaintance who was a nephew of Thomas J. Pendergast, boss of the Kansas City Democratic machine. Pendergast endorsed Truman for the position of "county judge"—the local description for a county supervisor. With the support of Pendergast and his fellow veterans, he was elected in 1922 and held the position for the next twelve years, punctuated only when he lost an election in 1924 and spent two years selling memberships in a Kansas City automobile club. Pendergast held power by engaging in every known form of political corruption. He eventually fattened on New Deal relief money and construction projects, some of which Judge Truman supervised. "Boss Tom" was convicted in 1939 of tax evasion and served time in federal prison. Through all this Truman kept his hands clean. "Looks like everybody got rich in Jackson County but me," Truman commented to his wife when Pendergast was indicted.[62]

In 1934 the Pendergast machine ran Judge Truman for the U.S. Senate, and he won easily. His colleagues at first dismissed him as the "senator from Pendergast," but in fact Truman had not shared in Pendergast's spoils. His own financial circumstances were so modest that Senator Truman took the bus to work on Capitol Hill and had his teeth

62. David McCullough, *Truman* (New York: Simon and Schuster, 1992), 240.

fixed by a public health dentist. He became known in the Senate as "go-along, get-along Harry," a well-liked and decent legislator who could be counted on to make no waves. He voted the straight New Deal line, breaking ranks only to override FDR's veto of the bonus-bill payments to his World War I comrades-in-arms in 1936. He privately opposed Roosevelt's Court-packing plan but kept mum in public.[63]

Truman won reelection to the Senate in 1940, notwithstanding the fact that Pendergast's fall from grace in the previous year had led to the removal of some fifty thousand "ghost voters" from the Missouri election rolls. In his second term, perhaps because he was now fully free of Pendergast's leading-strings, Truman began to forge a political identity of his own. In February 1941, after checking with Roosevelt, he called for the creation of a Special Senate Committee to Investigate the National Defense Program. Truman and FDR alike feared that Congress might move to replicate the Joint Committee on the Conduct of the War that had so bedeviled Abraham Lincoln. General Brehon B. Somerville, head of the Services of Supply, sneered that Truman's proposal was "formed in iniquity for political purposes." But Roosevelt appreciated that a committee headed by the safe and reliable Truman would preempt the creation of a more troublesome body. The president therefore gave the senator, whom he scarcely knew, his blessing.

The Truman Committee proceeded to expose profiteering and mismanagement in the construction of army camps, abuses of cost-plus contracting, and the delivery of substandard materials to the armed forces — notably the faulty steel plating that caused at least one Liberty Ship to crack in two. In the process, Truman burnished his reputation for honesty and square-dealing. By one estimate, his investigations saved the taxpayers as much as $15 billion. And by tempering his criticisms of the administration and thereby avoiding the kind of wholesale congressional onslaught that Lincoln had been forced to endure, he also earned Roosevelt's gratitude — though not Roosevelt's full confidence. In common with all but a handful of legislators, Truman remained uninformed about the greatest military secret of them all, the Manhattan Project.[64]

Over dinner at the White House on July 11, Roosevelt therefore agreed to take Truman. The senator was the man who would hurt the ticket the least. Truman, one of them recalled, "just dropped into the

63. McCullough, *Truman*, 220.
64. McCullough, *Truman*, 262, 288–91.

slot," a one-man "Missouri Compromise" who might not add much but was unobjectionable to Roosevelt and would do no political harm.

It remained to convince Truman, who had recently remarked to a friend that "the Vice President simply presides over the Senate and sits around hoping for a funeral. . . . I don't have any ambition to hold an office like that." Truman himself favored Byrnes and agreed to put the South Carolinian's name in nomination at the Chicago convention. But on July 19 Roosevelt telephoned Truman in his room in Chicago's Blackstone hotel. An aide took the call. The president's voice was so loud that Truman could hear every word. "Have you got that fellow lined up yet?" Roosevelt asked. No, said the aide, "he is the contrariest goddamn mule from Missouri I ever dealt with." "Well you tell the Senator that if he wants to break up the Democratic party in the middle of the war, that's his responsibility." A faithful party soldier, Truman reluctantly accepted the nomination.

The following day, as the convention formally ratified the ticket, Roosevelt had a seizure in San Diego while preparing to watch a marine amphibious-landing exercise at Camp Pendleton. No one outside the president's inner circle was told. Roosevelt recovered, delivered his acceptance speech over the radio, and boarded a navy vessel for a rendezvous with MacArthur and Nimitz in Hawaii to discuss the endgame strategy of the Pacific war. When Truman joined his running mate for lunch on the White House south lawn a month later, he noticed that Roosevelt's hand shook so badly he could not pour cream into his coffee. But in a rollicking speech on September 23, the old master campaigner roused a nationwide radio audience with a spirited defense of the New Deal and a good-humored rebuttal of Republican charges that he had left his dog, Fala, on an Aleutian island and dispatched a navy destroyer to retrieve him. Fala, said the president, was a Scottie, and "his Scotch soul was furious" at such baseless Republican calumnies. "He has not been the same dog since," said Roosevelt with mock seriousness. "I am accustomed to hearing malicious falsehoods about myself," he said. "But I think I have right to resent, to object to libelous statements about my dog." With that deft stroke Roosevelt suppressed much of the whispering campaign that he had lost his physical and mental vigor and his political touch.[65]

65. Arthur M. Schlesinger Jr., *The History of American Presidential Elections* (New York: McGraw-Hill, 1971), 4:3025; McCullough, *Truman*, 298–99, 314, 323–27; *PPA* (1944–45), 290.

In November, for the third time in history, an American presidential election took place in wartime. As in 1812 and again in 1864, the voters reelected the commander-in-chief, though Roosevelt's victory margin was his smallest ever, 25.6 million votes to Dewey's 22 million, 432 to 99 in the Electoral College. The Democrats gained just twenty seats in the House and maintained their 56–38 majority in the Senate. To Roosevelt's delight, several isolationists went down to defeat, including his own congressman, Hamilton Fish. Yet domestic issues had dominated the campaign. Roosevelt won because he convincingly conjured the prosperous future that the war had licensed Americans to covet, a future full of jobs and houses and cars and all the other fruits of affluence. "He promised what wartime advertising had displayed," writes historian John Morton Blum. "He promised what the polls said the people wanted. He promised the kind of society to which the GIs wanted to return."

Stretched out on a bed in a Kansas City hotel room, Truman listened to the election returns, thought of the future, and confided in a friend. "He knew," the friend recalled, "that he was going to be President of the United States, and I think it just scared the very devil out of him."[66]

THE ROOSEVELT-TRUMAN TICKET had clearly profited from wartime prosperity. It had also been the beneficiary of favorable news from the fighting fronts. Shortly before election day, the navy defeated the Japanese in the war's last great sea duel at Leyte Gulf, MacArthur histrionically waded ashore in the Philippines, and the first U.S. troops entered Germany. Americans prayed for their sons and sweethearts and took pride in their victories, but distance and censorship had conspired to shield Americans on the home front from ever having to stare into the face of battle. The navy had waited a year to release photographs of the destruction at Pearl Harbor, and the pictures showed only smoking wreckage, not human carnage. Not until September 1943, when it was worried about waning civilian war-spirit, did the War Department permit *Life*, the most popular American photo-essay magazine, to run the first photographs of dead GIs. "Here lie three Americans," read the caption alongside a striking image of the dead, strewn limply on the sand of Buna beach in New Guinea.[67]

66. Blum, V Was for Victory, 298–99; McCullough, Truman, 332.
67. Life, September 20, 1943, 34.

But for the most part Americans at home saw photos and films of the GIs as jaunty heroes or gaunt but unbowed warriors. They read in the dispatches of war correspondents like Ernie Pyle, John Steinbeck, or John Hersey about young men who were wholesome, all-American boys, soft-hearted suckers for needy kids, summer soldiers who wanted nothing more than to come home, as one of them famously told Hersey, "for a piece of blueberry pie." But the truth could be quite different. "It is in the things not mentioned," Steinbeck later reflected, "that the untruth lies."[68] "What kind of war do civilians suppose we fought, anyway?" asked one correspondent after the war. "We shot prisoners in cold blood, wiped out hospitals, strafed lifeboats, killed or mistreated enemy civilians, finished off the enemy wounded, tossed the dying into a hole with the dead, and in the Pacific boiled the flesh off enemy skulls to make table ornaments for sweethearts, or carved their bones into letter openers."[69]

Of the war's single greatest horror, Hitler's campaign of genocide against Europe's Jews, Americans also comprehended little. They knew some facts, but facts did not necessarily mean understanding, especially for a people so mercifully sheltered from the war's harshest suffering. In August 1942 Gerhart Riegner, a representative of the World Jewish Congress, informed American officials in Switzerland that Germany had begun mass exterminations of Jews in the areas under Nazi control. The Americans were skeptical, remembering the atrocity stories that British propagandists had manufactured in World War I. They nevertheless forwarded Riegner's report to Washington, with the notation that it had the "earmarks of a war rumor inspired by fear." But further evidence soon came in, and on December 8, 1942, Roosevelt summoned American Jewish leaders to the White House and somberly informed them that the government now had "proof that confirms the horrors discussed by you." No one as yet grasped the degree to which the killing was going on systematically in purpose-built death camps. But it was now clear that the question facing Washington was not a matter of providing asylum to refugees but of rescuing prisoners trapped in a death-machine. How to effect a rescue? For a country that had not yet landed a single soldier on the continent of Europe, the options were few. Roosevelt did induce Churchill and Stalin to join him in a declaration on December

68. John Hersey, *Into the Valley: A Skirmish of the Marines* (New York: Knopf, 1943), 137; John Steinbeck, *Once There Was a War* (New York: Viking, 1958), xiii.
69. Edgar Jones, "One War Is Enough," *Atlantic Monthly*, February 1946, 49.

17, 1942, that the allies intended to try "war criminals" in formal courts of law when the war was over—the origins of the postwar tribunals that convened at Nuremberg and Tokyo.[70]

American Jewish groups publicized what they knew, and the mainstream press reported what scant news of the Holocaust it had. The government meanwhile cast about for an effective policy. Roosevelt called for a Conference on Refugees to meet in Bermuda in April 1943, but it foundered on Britain's refusal even to discuss Palestine as a destination for whatever Jews might somehow be liberated from the Nazis' grasp. A few months later, the uneasy German satellite of Romania tentatively revived a scheme to allow some seventy thousand Romanian Jews to be ransomed, but because their presumed destination would be Palestine, the State Department deferred to British wishes and quietly buried the Romanian proposal. When treasury officials learned at last of the State Department's apparently willful obstruction, they drafted a report for their chief, the cabinet's only Jew, Henry Morgenthau. Its title screamed its outrage: "Report to the Secretary on the Acquiescence by This Government in the Murder of the Jews." It was dated January 10, 1944. By then millions of European Jews had already perished.

At Morgenthau's insistence, Roosevelt established the War Refugee Board (WRB) on January 22, with instructions to do what it could but little hope that it could do much. Eight months later, the board brought 982 refugees, most of them Jews who had managed to make their way into occupied Italy, to a refugee camp near Oswego, New York. The journalist I. F. Stone called it "a kind of token payment to decency, a bargain-counter flourish in humanitarianism."[71]

Opportunities for bigger flourishes soon presented themselves. In March 1944 Hitler occupied Hungary, another satellite growing restless as the tide of war turned against its German ally, and home to the largest intact Jewish community in Europe, some 750,000 souls. SS Obersturmbannführer Adolf Eichmann soon arrived in Budapest to impose the Final Solution on Hungary's Jews. As Eichmann ordered mass deportations to Auschwitz to begin, the WRB sent Raoul Wallenberg to Hungary under Swedish diplomatic cover. With bribery and bravura, he saved thousands of Jews. The WRB also arranged for air-leaflet drops renewing the threat of war-crime prosecutions against Eichmann and

---

70. David S. Wyman, *The Abandonment of the Jews: America and the Holocaust, 1941–1945* (New York: Pantheon, 1984), 42, 72.
71. Wyman, *Abandonment of the Jews*, 187, 266.

his accomplices and induced New York's Francis Cardinal Spellman to record a radio broadcast reminding Catholic Hungarians that persecution of the Jews was "in direct contradiction" to Church doctrine. Eichmann offered to halt the deportations and exchange up to one hundred thousand Jews for ten thousand trucks that he promised would be used only on the eastern front. The Soviets suspected, probably correctly, that this was an eleventh-hour ploy to split the Grand Alliance and prepare the way for a separate peace in the west. The deal collapsed, but in all, the WRB's initiatives in Hungary may have spared some two hundred thousand Jews from the gas chambers.

In the midst of the Hungarian deportations, two inmates miraculously escaped from Auschwitz and brought to the west one of the first accounts revealing the stupefying scale and cold-blooded efficiency of the Holocaust. Even with this evidence, its dimensions defied belief. The WRB nevertheless submitted a recommendation to Assistant Secretary of War McCloy that the Auschwitz death camp should be bombed out of commission, even if the bombs would kill some of the Jewish inmates. McCloy rejected the idea. An attack on Auschwitz, he told the WRB, "could be executed only by the diversion of considerable air support essential to the success of our forces now engaged in decisive operations elsewhere." In a later message McCloy misleadingly added that "the target is beyond the maximum range of medium bombardment, dive bombers and fighter bombers located in UK, France or Italy. Use of heavy bombardment from UK bases would necessitate a round trip flight unescorted of approximately 2000 miles over enemy territory."[72]

In fact, American heavy bombers, escorted by long-range P-51 Mustangs, had already attacked several times in the vicinity of Auschwitz. Two considerations may help to explain McCloy's apparently callous decision. First, the WRB request arrived just as the breakout at Normandy was holding out the alluring prospect that the war would be over in months, perhaps weeks. McCloy may well have concluded that rescue through victory was more likely than rescue through a singular action deep inside Poland.

But a second factor may have figured just as large: McCloy's inability, shared by many of his comfortable countrymen, to imagine the full enormity of the Holocaust. In December 1944 McCloy said to A. Leon Kobowitzki, a World Jewish Congress official, "We are alone. Tell me the truth. Do you really believe that all those horrible things happened?"

72. Wyman, *Abandonment of the Jews*, 296–97.

Even then, Kobowitzki recalled, "he could not grasp the terrible destruction."[73]

Nor could others. In the summer of 1943 Supreme Court Justice Felix Frankfurter, probably the most eminent American Jew and a devoted Zionist, went to the Polish embassy in Washington to meet the Polish socialist Jan Karski, another death-camp escapee. When Karski finished describing what he had seen at Belzec, Frankfurter paced in somber silence for ten minutes. "I am unable to believe you," he said to Karski at last. "Felix, you cannot tell this man to his face that he is lying," the Polish ambassador interjected. "I did not say that this young man is lying," Frankfurter replied. "I said that I am unable to believe him. There is a difference." Frankfurter extended both arms and waved his hands. "No, no," he said, and walked out.[74]

Americans had been fortunate in the war, singularly fortunate in a world that inflicted unspeakable punishments on so many millions of others. But good fortune could be the father of innocence, and the world the war was making would be no place for the innocent, no matter how very much of it they seemed poised to inherit.

73. Bird, *Chairman*, 206.
74. Bird, *Chairman*, 206.

9

Endgame

I . . . have concluded that continuing the war can only mean destruction for the nation.

—Japanese emperor Hirohito, August 9, 1945

On the morning of January 20, 1945, Franklin Roosevelt fitted his wasted legs into his heavy steel braces for the first time in four months. He was wheeled to the south portico of the White House, rose laboriously from his chair with the help of his son James, and gripped a lectern to deliver his fourth inaugural address, the briefest in American history, just 573 words. "We have learned that we must live as men and not as ostriches," he said. "We can gain no lasting peace if we approach it with suspicion and mistrust—or with fear." The perfunctory ceremony was over in minutes. As the president withdrew, observers murmured about his pallor and gauntness. He had lost almost twenty-five pounds since the preceding summer. James told him frankly that he looked like hell. When the presidential party went back inside the White House, FDR sat his son down to talk about his will and about the funeral instructions he had deposited in the White House safe. He did not disclose that ten months earlier the cardiologist Howard G. Bruenn had diagnosed him with hypertension, hypertensive heart disease, and failure of the left ventricular chamber. In plain language, Bruenn described the president's health as "God-awful." But as he had done for years with his paralysis, Roosevelt did his best willfully to ignore his cardiovascular illness. Though Bruenn prevailed upon him to cut his working day back to just a few hours, the president concealed the severity of his condition from others, asked no questions of his physician, and tried to carry on in public as if nothing in his life had changed.[1]

1. PPA (1944–45), 524; Howard G. Bruenn, M.D., "Clinical Notes on the Illness and Death of President Franklin D. Roosevelt," *Annals of Internal Medicine* 75: 579–91

Two days after the inauguration, Roosevelt went to the basement of the Bureau of Engraving and Printing, just a few blocks from the White House. On an underground spur line, built to allow the bureau to ship newly printed money in secret, waited the president's specially fitted railroad car, the *Ferdinand Magellan*, a 140-ton armor-plated Pullman coach, equipped with three-inch bulletproof-glass windows, watertight doors, and three emergency escape hatches adapted from submarines. The *Ferdinand Magellan* rumbled away, bearing the president to Norfolk, Virginia. There he boarded the heavy cruiser *USS Quincy* and made course for the Mediterranean island of Malta, where he rendezvoused with Churchill on February 2. The two leaders still faced a seven-hour flight to Yalta, in the Soviet Crimea, where Stalin awaited them. He had slept ten hours a night on the sea voyage, Roosevelt said, but still did not feel rested.

Malta was no Cairo, which had been a full-dress Anglo-American staging ground for the historic three-power meeting that followed at Teheran. Roosevelt remained on the island for less than twenty-four hours, did some sight-seeing, and spent little time with Churchill. The lack of preparation for the upcoming meeting with Stalin made British foreign secretary Anthony Eden uneasy. "[W]e are going into a decisive conference," he complained to Harry Hopkins at Malta, "and had so far neither agreed what we would discuss nor how to handle matters with a Bear who would certainly know his own mind."[2]

On February 2, escorted by fighter planes, the same "Sacred Cow" that had carried the president to Teheran bore FDR from Malta to the airfield at Saki, in the Black Sea's Crimean peninsula. Under three tents at the edge of the landing area the Russians had laid out a welcoming luncheon of hot tea, smoked sturgeon, caviar, and black bread. Roosevelt transferred to an automobile; five hours and eighty miles of wretched road later, he finally reached the moldering czarist resort of Livadia Palace, near the city of Yalta, for the second, and last, wartime meeting of the Big Three Grand Alliance partners. Lord Moran, Churchill's phy-

---

(1970); Robert H. Ferrell, *The Dying President: Franklin D. Roosevelt, 1944–1945* (Columbia: University of Missouri Press, 1998), 101–2, 37. After Dr. Bruenn's diagnosis in March 1944, Roosevelt did alter some of his dietary habits, cut back on his use of both alcohol and tobacco, and take medications. But he apparently never entertained the idea that his health might impede his performance as president or considered not running for a fourth term.

2. Anthony Eden, *The Reckoning: The Memoirs of Anthony Eden* (Boston: Houghton Mifflin, 1965), 592.

sician, was observing Roosevelt keenly. "To a doctor's eye," Moran noted, "the President appears a very sick man. . . . I give him only a few months to live."[3]

Four issues dominated the agenda at Yalta: the voting procedures and membership rules for the United Nations Organization, a new international body approved in outline form at Dumbarton Oaks, in Washington, D.C., in the fall of 1944; the fate of eastern Europe, Poland in particular; the treatment of defeated Germany; and Soviet participation in the war against Japan. The Big Three had touched on all of these matters at Teheran, scarcely more than a year earlier. Then the discussion had been mostly about military matters. At Yalta, with the partial exception of Soviet entry into the Asian war, the discussion would be mainly about political issues. If Teheran was in many ways a rehearsal for Yalta, then Yalta in turn set the stage for the dawning international regime that came to be known as the Cold War.

Roosevelt began at Yalta as he had at Teheran, meeting with Stalin for a private conversation before the conference's first plenary session on February 4. Still hoping to win Stalin's confidence and coax the Soviet Union into playing a cooperative role in the postwar world, he once again strained to be ingratiating to the Soviet dictator. As on the earlier occasion, that gambit prompted the president to say some astonishing things; yet it proved insufficient motive for him to speak about some other things, notably the Manhattan Project.

During the drive from the airfield at Saki, Roosevelt remarked, he had been struck by the devastation the Germans had wrought in the Crimea. Seeing that destruction had made him "more bloodthirsty in regard to the Germans than he had been a year ago," Roosevelt announced. He "hoped that Marshal Stalin would again propose a toast to the execution of 50,000 officers of the German Army."[4] Stalin replied that the ruination in the Ukraine was even worse. There followed, as there had at Teheran, an exchange about the fecklessness of the French and the self-aggrandizing delusions of DeGaulle. Roosevelt gratuitously added a few jibes at the British — "a peculiar people," he called them. Then it was time to proceed to the main conference room. Roosevelt had not mentioned the atomic bomb project to Stalin, nor would he ever.

3. Lord Moran, *Churchill: Taken from the Diaries of Lord Moran: The Struggle for Survival, 1940–1965* (Boston: Houghton Mifflin, 1966), 242.
4. *FRUS: The Conferences at Malta and Yalta, 1945*, 571.

Stalin immediately set the tone for the week's discussions. He was self-confident, assertive, demanding, sarcastic. Sometimes he paced impatiently behind his chair as he talked. As for Roosevelt, Eden found him "vague and loose and ineffective."[5] Militarily, Stalin held all the high cards. The Red Army had overrun Romania, Bulgaria, Hungary, Poland, and East Prussia and had battled to within miles of Berlin. The Western allies, meanwhile, had not yet crossed the Rhine. They had barely recovered from the Ardennes counterattack—and only with the help, Stalin noted pointedly, of an accelerated Soviet winter offensive that prevented Hitler from reinforcing his troops in the "Bulge."

Stalin now moved to translate his hard-won military advantage into permanent political gains. Here, as throughout the war, Bernard Montgomery later reflected, "Stalin made almost no mistakes; he had a clearcut political strategy and he pursued it relentlessly."[6]

The subject of the United Nations was the least difficult of the topics on the table at Yalta, though not without its vexations. Stalin held out for a single-power veto in the United Nations Security Council, a reasonable demand, and for two extra Soviet votes in the General Assembly, for the Soviet republics of Ukraine and White Russia, respectively—a transparently unreasonable attempt to pack the assembly in favor of the USSR. Eager to please, Roosevelt acceded readily to the first Soviet request, though only grudgingly to the second.

About Poland Stalin was adamant. At Teheran Roosevelt had indicated that he had no objection to shifting the Polish state westward by ceding much of eastern Poland to the Soviet Union and moving Poland's western frontier to the line of the Oder and Neisse rivers. But now Stalin wanted more—not more territory but more iron-fisted political control over the postwar Polish government. For the Russians, Stalin said, Poland "was a question of both honor and security," even "one of life and death."

Since the summer of 1944, the Russians had sponsored a provisional Polish government dominated by Communists and temporarily seated in the eastern Polish city of Lublin. The "Lublin Poles" contended for recognition as the legitimate government of liberated Poland against the "London Poles," a rival government-in-exile resident in the British capital and favored, even if lukewarmly, by the British and the Americans.

5. Eden, *Reckoning*, 593.
6. Bernard Montgomery, *A History of Warfare* (Cleveland: World Publishing, 1968), 544.

It was to extinguish elements aligned with the London Poles that Stalin in 1940 had ordered the massacre of thousands of captured Polish army officers in the Soviet-occupied Katyn Forest near Smolensk, and then in 1944 had instructed the Red Army to stall on the banks of the Vistula so that the Germans might bloodily suppress the Warsaw Rising. Now the Lublin Poles, said Stalin, were sustaining an orderly civil government in Poland, while the London Poles fomented armed resistance to the Red Army. Partisans backed by the London Poles, he charged, had murdered more than two hundred Soviet soldiers. "We want tranquility in our rear," Stalin said. "We will support the government which gives us peace in the rear. . . . When I compare what the agents of the Lublin government have done and what the agents of the London government have done I see the first are good and the second bad."[7]

As at Teheran, Roosevelt had neither the will nor the means to challenge Soviet hegemony in eastern Europe, but he needed political cover for his acquiescence in the Soviet fait accompli. The United States was "farther away from Poland than anyone else here," FDR said. Nevertheless, Roosevelt went on, the Poles were "quarrelsome people" wherever they might be, and therefore he "felt it was very important for him in the United States that there be some gesture made for the six million Poles there indicating that the United States was in some way involved with the question of freedom of elections" to determine the permanent government of Poland. He emphasized, however, "that it was only a matter of words and details." In a personal note he assured Stalin that "the United States will never lend its support in any way to any provisional government in Poland that would be inimical to your interests." The result was the Declaration on Liberated Europe. It pledged the signatories "to arrange and conduct free elections" in liberated countries looking to the creation of governments that were "broadly representative of all democratic elements." These were hollow words, as Roosevelt well knew. "Mr. President, this is so elastic that the Russians can stretch it all the way from Yalta to Washington without ever technically breaking it," said Roosevelt's chief of staff, Admiral William Leahy, when he saw the draft of the declaration. "I know, Bill—I know it," said FDR. "But it's the best I can do for Poland at this time." And it was— unless Roosevelt was prepared to order Eisenhower to fight his way across the breadth of Germany, take on the Red Army, and drive it out

---

7. *FRUS: Malta and Yalta*, 669–70.

of Poland at gunpoint. At this stage of the war in Europe, political decisions could do little more than ratify military realities. On this point in particular, Yalta was only a postscript to Teheran.[8]

The Big Three next turned to the question of Germany. Stalin wanted to know "whether the President or Prime Minister still adhered to the principle of dismemberment," as they had indicated at Teheran. He also wished to discuss reparations. Unknown to Stalin, these matters had for months been the subject of contentious and unresolved debate within Roosevelt's government and between the British and the Americans.

In September 1944 Treasury Secretary Morgenthau had brought to the Anglo-American conference at Quebec a radical plan to deindustrialize the Ruhr and the Saar and partition Germany into two or more pastoral states. Secretary of State Hull was aghast at this "plan of blind vengeance." Wrecking the German economy, Hull believed, would ruin the economy of all Europe. He considered the Morgenthau Plan "cataclysmic," "a tragedy for all concerned," precisely the kind of Carthaginian peace that had ravaged the interwar international economy and bred the German lust for revenge that Hitler had exploited. Henry Stimson warned Roosevelt, "It is not within the realm of possibility that a whole nation of seventy million people . . . can by force be required to abandon all their previous methods of life, be reduced to a peasant level with virtually complete control of industry and science left to other peoples." Churchill at first agreed with that assessment. When Morgenthau unveiled his plan at Quebec, Churchill unleashed "the full flood of his rhetoric, sarcasm, and violence." An economically moribund Germany would drag down all of Europe, he said. He had not come to Quebec, Churchill declaimed, to discuss chaining England to the body of a dead German. But over Anthony Eden's strenuous objections, the prime minister relented, perhaps mollified by the treasury secretary's intimations that only British agreement to the Morgenthau Plan would secure the treasury's approval of postwar credits for Britain. On September 15, seated at a table in the Citadel in Quebec, Roosevelt and Churchill put their initials to an agreement "for eliminating the war-making industries in the Ruhr and in the Saar" and "converting Germany into a country primarily agricultural and pastoral in its character."

8. *FRUS: Malta and Yalta*, 727, 846–48, 861; William D. Leahy, *I Was There: The Personal Story of the Chief of Staff to Presidents Roosevelt and Truman Based on His Notes and Diaries Made at the Time* (New York: Whittlesey House, 1950), 315–16.

Back in Washington after the Quebec conference, however, Hull and Stimson refused to accept the Morgenthau Plan as settled policy. They bombarded Roosevelt with dissenting memoranda. Hull soon concluded that Roosevelt "had not realized the extent to which . . . he had committed himself at Quebec." When Stimson carefully read the Quebec agreement aloud to the president at lunch on October 3, Roosevelt "was frankly staggered by this and said he had no idea how he could have initialed this; that he had evidently done it without much thought." The president thereupon backed away from the Morgenthau Plan. He now declared, "I dislike making detailed plans for a country which we do not yet occupy." He thus arrived at Yalta with no American plan to present.[9]

Stalin suffered from no such divided counsel, confusion, or apparent mental distraction. The Germans would recover, he said, unless drastic action was taken to contain them. "Give them twelve to fifteen years and they'll be on their feet again," he had predicted to Marshal Tito. Accordingly, Stalin wanted not only to dismember Germany but also to exact heavy reparations from the conquered *Reich*. He proposed to strip Germany of at least $10 billion worth of industrial equipment for shipment to the Soviet Union, with a like amount to be allotted to other victims of Nazi aggression. The Western allies demurred. Churchill called the Soviet demands unrealistic. Though Roosevelt "thought the division of Germany into five states or seven states was a good idea," he tried to deflect the conversation to the topic of zones of occupation, a matter well short of permanent partition. At times he tried to deflect the conversation further still, at one point telling a rambling and perplexing story about a Jew and an Italian who were members of the Ku Klux Klan in a small southern town but "were considered all right since everyone in the community knew them." In the end, these tactics buried the topic of permanent partition. As for reparations, though the Americans agreed in principle to the Soviet proposal for $10 billion in industrial transfers, the fact remained that it would be the British and the Americans who would control the industrial heartland of western Germany and could later grant or withhold reparations as they pleased. Stalin emphasized "the unsatisfactory nature of the reparations question at the conference," but for the time being there the matter rested. Roo-

---

9. *FRUS: Malta and Yalta*, 612; Cordell Hull, *The Memoirs of Cordell Hull* (New York: Macmillan, 1948), 2:1606, 1611–12, 1619, 1621; *FRUS: The Conference at Quebec, 1944*, 483, 467; Stimson Diary, October 3, 1944.

sevelt did say that "he did not believe that American troops would stay in Europe for much more than two years," encouraging Stalin to believe that he need only bide his time to manage events in postwar Europe as he wished.[10]

The most concrete—and among the most controversial—agreements reached at Yalta concerned Soviet entry into the war against Japan. Roosevelt told Stalin that he "hoped that it would not be necessary actually to invade the Japanese islands." To avoid that bloody business, he needed Soviet help. A Soviet declaration of war against Japan would shock the Japanese into recognizing the hopelessness of their case, enable the Red Army to tie down the large Japanese force in Manchuria, make Siberian bases available to the United States for bombing Japan— and, Roosevelt privately calculated, keep the Russians from working more mischief in Europe while the Americans waged the finish-fight in Asia.

Stalin replied that "it would be difficult for him . . . to explain to the Soviet people why Russia was entering the war against Japan . . . a country with which they had no great trouble." But, he added unctuously, if certain "political conditions were met, the people would understand . . . and it would be very much easier to explain the decision." Specifically, he wanted to annex the Kurile Islands, asked for guarantees that the postwar settlement would not disturb the status of the pro-Soviet Mongolian People's Republic, and demanded restoration of Russia's losses to Japan in the war of 1904—southern Sakhalin Island, the ports of Dairen and Port Arthur, and control over the Chinese-Eastern and South-Manchurian railroads, "on the understanding that China should continue to possess full sovereignty in Manchuria."

These were considerable demands, and they came largely at China's expense. Roosevelt agreed to all, revealing how much he had come to regard China as America's client state. In return for Stalin's promise to declare war on Japan within two or three months of Germany's surrender, Roosevelt undertook to "inform" Chiang of these arrangements at the appropriate time. When that might be was left unresolved. It would not be soon. The promised movement of twenty-five Soviet divisions into eastern Siberia must be undertaken in secret, and "one of the difficulties in speaking to the Chinese," Roosevelt told Stalin, "was that

10. Milovan Djilas, *Conversations with Stalin* (New York: Harcourt, Brace and World, 1962), 114; *FRUS: Malta and Yalta*, 614, 617, 921–22.

anything said to them was known to the whole world in twenty-four hours." Nor did Roosevelt immediately inform Churchill of the terms of this agreement.[11]

Roosevelt left Yalta on February 11. In a fitting postscript to the inconclusive bickering among the Big Three, and a fitting reminder of the global convulsions the war had wrought, Roosevelt returned to the *Quincy*, moored at Great Bitter Lake in the Suez Canal, for brief talks with three kings: Ibn Saud of Saudi Arabia, Farouk of Egypt, and Haile Selassie of Ethiopia. Churchill had been flabbergasted at Roosevelt's surprise announcement on the last day of the Yalta Conference that he was about to insert himself into the complex tangle of Middle Eastern affairs, traditionally a British preserve. In the event, Roosevelt's royal visitations at Suez proved no more conclusive than the talks in the Crimea. The conversation with Ibn Saud, Harry Hopkins recorded, "was short and to the point." Would Ibn Saud allow more Jewish refugees to enter Palestine, Roosevelt asked? "No," Ibn Saud replied, and added that the Arabs would take up arms to prevent further Jewish immigration to Palestine.[12]

On March 1 Roosevelt appeared before a joint session of Congress to report on the Yalta parley. In a highly unusual reference to his disability, he began by asking his listeners' pardon for addressing them from a sitting position. "[I]t makes it a lot easier for me not to have to carry about ten pounds of steel around on the bottom of my legs," the president explained. He then delivered a patchy, inchoate speech laced with ad-lib remarks that one close associate described as "wholly irrelevant, and some of them almost bordered on the ridiculous." He occasionally slurred his words, and his hands trembled. He made much of the prospects for free elections in Poland and of the Declaration on Liberated Europe. He touted the agreements on the United Nations, scheduled to convene for the first time in San Francisco on April 25. He made no reference to his deal with Stalin about Soviet entry into the war against Japan. Nor did he mention his acquiescence in Stalin's demand for the two extra Soviet votes in the U.N. General Assembly. Word of that odd concession nevertheless quickly leaked, lending credibility to the soon-rampant suspicion that Roosevelt had brought back from the Crimea a

11. *FRUS: Malta and Yalta*, 766, 769, 896.
12. Robert E. Sherwood, *Roosevelt and Hopkins* (New York: Grosset and Dunlap, 1950), 872.

Pandora's box full of "Yalta Secrets" that compromised the interests of the United States.[13]

Controversy over the Yalta Conference reverberated well into the postwar years, when it was alleged that Roosevelt, sick and mentally enfeebled, possibly misguided by scheming pro-Communist advisers, had witlessly kowtowed to Stalin, cut backroom deals, betrayed Poland, delivered eastern Europe into Soviet hands, and sold out Chiang Kai-Shek, opening the door to the eventual Communist takeover in China. All of those charges were vastly overdrawn. If Yalta represented an American diplomatic failure, it was attributable not to the frailties of Franklin Roosevelt's mind and body in February 1945, and surely not to the machinations of supposedly subversive aides, but to the pattern of more than five years of war that left the American president with few options. "I didn't say the result was good," Roosevelt conceded to an associate, "I said it was the best I could do."[14]

The president was unquestionably ill at Yalta, but he did little there that he had not signaled his willingness to do at Teheran, when he was in full possession of his faculties, and did little differently than any American leader could have done at this juncture. His concealment about the United Nations votes was regrettable but humanly understandable in view of his embarrassment about the matter, and in any case substantively unimportant. He perhaps misjudged his ability to speak candidly to the American people about Soviet dominance in eastern Europe but surely judged rightly that the United States could not do much about it. With reference to Germany, his obfuscation managed to head off formal partition and deferred the reparations question for discussion on another and presumably more auspicious day. In China, Chiang's regime was already so rotten as to be beyond salvation. Nothing promised at Yalta appreciably contributed to its eventual collapse.

As for Soviet entry into the war against Japan, Roosevelt had two aims in mind. He wanted to tie the Russians' hands in Europe by deflecting at least part of their attention to Asia in the immediate aftermath of the German surrender. With respect to Asia itself, the commander-in-chief followed the best counsel of his senior military advisers, eager for any means to spare American troops from further bloodletting in the

13. PPA (1944–45), 570–86; Samuel I. Rosenman, Working with Roosevelt (New York: Harper and Brothers, 1952), 527.
14. Beatrice Bishop Berle and Travis Beal Jacobs, eds., Navigating the Rapids, 1918–1971: From the Papers of Adolf A. Berle (New York: Harcourt Brace Jovanovich, 1973), 477.

increasingly vicious Pacific war. The Joint Chiefs estimated that the Soviet declaration of war might shorten the fighting by a year or more and thereby preclude the dreaded invasion of Japan itself. The atomic bomb, still untested — still unmade — its possible tactical effects unknowable and its potential strategic impact still conjectural, figured scarcely at all in these calculations.[15]

On March 20 Roosevelt held his last White House press conference. He seemed mentally alert, but to steady his hand sufficiently to light a cigarette, he had to wedge his elbow into a partially closed desk drawer. Visitors in the last days of March noticed that he was repeating himself, unwittingly recounting the same lengthy anecdotes to the same listeners on the same occasion. Dr. Bruenn advised a period of total rest. On March 29 the *Ferdinand Magellan* carried Roosevelt to his retreat at Warm Springs, Georgia. He was deadweight limp when the Secret Service men transferred him to an automobile at the railroad siding in Warm Springs, and observers gasped when the president's head lolled strangely. On April 12 Roosevelt awoke complaining of a headache but proceeded to work at his makeshift desk in the Warm Springs "Little White House." Shortly after one o'clock, he passed his hand jerkily over his forehead and slumped forward, unconscious. At 3:35 P.M., Dr. Bruenn pronounced him dead of a cerebral hemorrhage. By his deathbed was Lucy Mercer, the lover he had promised to forsake twenty-seven years earlier.

Less than four hours later, standing in the White House Cabinet Room under a portrait of Woodrow Wilson, Harry S. Truman put his hand on an inexpensive Gideon Bible and swore the presidential oath. "There have been few men in all history the equal of the man into whose shoes I am stepping," he said the next day. "I pray God I can measure up to the task." In Grandview, Missouri, Truman's mother told reporters: "Harry will get along all right."[16]

15. Groves had informed Marshall on December 30, 1944, that a single U-235 bomb (the type ultimately used against Hiroshima), with a predicted explosive power of ten thousand tons of TNT, "should be ready about August 1, 1945," with a second such weapon available "by the end of the year." The first plutonium bomb (the type dropped on Nagasaki) Groves had expected to be ready in the late spring, but "scientific difficulties" had postponed its development until "sometime in the latter part of July." It was expected to have an explosive yield of about five hundred tons of TNT. *FRUS: Malta and Yalta*, 383–84.

16. Ferrell, *Dying President*, 111–119; Bruenn, "Clinical Notes," 590; David McCullough, *Truman* (New York: Simon and Schuster, 1992), 347–52.

While Americans were mourning their fallen leader, Italian partisans shot Benito Mussolini on April 28 and dumped his body in Piazza Loreto in Milano. After several women had squatted over the dead *Duce* and lifted their skirts to urinate in his face, the mob hanged him by his heels. The next day German forces in Italy surrendered, following secretive negotiations from which the Soviets had been excluded. This had triggered a bitter exchange between Stalin and the dying Roosevelt. "The Germans on the Western front have in fact ceased the war against Britain and America," Stalin had written. "At the same time they continue the war against Russia, the Ally of Britain and the U.S.A." For his part, in what was to be his penultimate communication with Stalin, Roosevelt had replied that he felt "bitter resentment toward your informers, whoever they are, for such vile misrepresentation of my actions" in the Italian surrender negotiations, though he did not offer a convincing explanation for having excluded the Soviets. "It would be one of the great tragedies of history," Roosevelt had concluded, "if at the very moment of victory . . . such lack of faith should prejudice the entire undertaking after the colossal losses of life, material and treasure involved."[17]

Two days after Mussolini's death, in his bunker fifty-five feet below central Berlin, Adolf Hitler pressed a pistol to his head and squeezed the trigger. Red Army troops meanwhile clambered through the charred ruins above, fighting a hellish street-by-street battle for the Nazi capital. Just one week after *der Führer's* suicide, Admiral Karl Dönitz, Hitler's hand-picked successor as head of the thousand-year *Reich*, the wily seaman who had nearly won the Battle of the Atlantic in 1942, tendered Germany's unconditional surrender. On May 7, 1945, Dönitz ordered all German units to cease operations at 11:01 P.M. on the following day. The war in Europe was over.

The war in the Pacific was not.

THE PACIFIC WAR was a parallel war, fought simultaneously with the conflict in Europe but almost never touching it directly. This was as true for the Axis as it was for the Allies. Germany and Japan undertook no joint diplomatic initiatives after 1941, made not the slightest gesture toward economic cooperation, and neither executed nor even discussed

17. Robert Leckie, *Deliver Us from Evil: The Saga of World War II* (New York: Harper and Row, 1987), 835; Ministry of Foreign Affairs of the USSR, Comp., *Stalin's Correspondence with Roosevelt and Truman, 1941–1945* (New York: Capricorn, 1965), 206, 208.

a single combined military or naval operation. On the Allied side the war in the Pacific was almost exclusively an American affair, prosecuted from Washington with scant reference to London or Moscow. And as far as Washington was concerned, its war against Japan was "the other war," one that more artful diplomacy in 1940–41 might have postponed or even avoided and that was always subordinate to the premier objective of defeating Hitler. Prewar American planning had contemplated only defensive action in the Pacific. But the inflammatory insult of the Pearl Harbor attack, followed by fabulous luck at Midway and hard-won success at Guadalcanal, not to mention the prodigious flow of guns and ships from American factories, eventually shaped a pivot on which Admiral King had swung from the anticipated holding action against Japan and gone on the offensive.

The Americans had cracked Japan's outermost defensive shell with the attack on Tarawa in the Gilbert Islands at the end of 1943. They had widened the crack in February 1944 with the capture of Kwajelein and Eniwetok, both in the Marshall Islands, and the destruction by aerial bombardment of the major Japanese base at Truk, in the Carolines. As more machines of war poured off American assembly lines and more men marched out of the training camps, the United States was poised as 1944 began not only to launch Overlord in Europe but at the same time to undertake two distinct offensive operations across the immense reaches of the Pacific.

The Pacific war was a war of distances, distances measured culturally as well as geographically. Each combatant, Japan and the United States alike, saw its adversary through a distorting lens laminated from historically accumulated layers of ignorance, arrogance, prejudice, and loathing. To a degree that had no equivalent in the western European theater, that for the ferocity it spawned compared only with the savage encounter between "Aryans" and Slavs on Hitler's eastern front, the Japanese-American war was a race war, and just for that reason, in the historian John Dower's phrase, a "war without mercy." Japan's desperate gamble at Pearl Harbor had rested on the derisive and fatally erroneous assumption that the supposedly decadent, self-indulgent Americans had no stomach for war's hardship and would be so traumatized by the attack that they would quickly sue for peace. Like so many stereotypes, the Japanese image of the Americans reversed the self-image of the beholder. The Japanese prided themselves on being genetically pure, the "Yamato Race," uncontaminated by immigration, rooted for more than two millennia in their island realm, a single people bound together by blood and history. They were the "One Hundred Million," Japanese propaganda repeatedly reminded them, who lived, worked, and fought as one. They considered the Americans, in contrast, to be a contemptibly polyglot and divided people, historically unanchored, driven by ethnic and racial conflict, labor violence, and political strife, incapable of self-sacrifice or submission to the common weal. Japanese pupils read in their schoolbook *Cardinal Principles of the National Polity* that they were "intrinsically quite different from the so-called citizens of Occidental countries" and that the biggest difference was their immunity to the detestable western virus of individualism.[18]

The Americans reciprocated with depictions of the Japanese as servile automatons devoid of individual identity. Frank Capra strikingly invoked that imagery in an indoctrination film devoted to the Pacific War in his *Why We Fight* series: *Know Your Enemy—Japan.* Viewers saw repeated hammer-blows to a steel bar while the narrator told them that the Japanese were like "photographic prints off the same negative." That dehumanizing motif was reinforced by ideas that had long pedigrees in Western culture. Wartime cartoons and posters routinely depicted the Japanese as murderous savages, immature children, wild beasts, or bucktoothed, bespectacled lunatics. All those images were appropriated from a cultural storehouse built millennia earlier, when the Greeks first distinguished between themselves and "barbarians," and abundantly stocked over the centuries of European expansion into the New World, Africa, and Asia. The long record of Western racialist disdain made it easy to demonize the Japanese. From the war's outset, American officials and the organs of popular culture conspired to breed virulent hatred of the Asian adversary. Admiral William F. "Bull" Halsey notoriously defined his mission as "Kill Japs, kill Japs, kill more Japs" and vowed that at war's end Japanese would be spoken only in hell. Wartime Hollywood films like *The Purple Heart*, about the Doolittle air raid on Tokyo in 1942, depicted Japanese captors torturing downed American fliers, scenes that incited audiences to cold fury. In late 1943, about the time the Tarawa casualty reports were coming in, the War Department released the diary of a Japanese soldier that described the beheading of a captured American airman, and in early 1944, just as the major American offensives in the Pacific were getting under way, the government published grisly accounts of the Bataan Death March. All these were

18. John W. Dower, *War without Mercy: Race and Power in the Pacific War* (New York: Pantheon, 1986), 221. This discussion relies heavily on Dower's excellent study.

calculated to magnify the American public's already ample animosity toward Japan.[19]

On its side, the Imperial Japanese Army indoctrinated its troops according to the code of Bushido—the Way of the Warrior—an ancient samurai ethos that emphasized loyalty, austerity, self-denial, and indifference to pain. "Loyalty is heavier than a mountain, and our life is lighter than a feather," Japanese soldiers were taught. The lesson was rammed home with harsh discipline. All superiors, of whatever rank, regularly kicked, punched, and slapped their subordinates. Brutal treatment made for brutal soldiers and for an ugly war, not only against the Americans in the Pacific but against the Chinese and other Asians as well, as the Rape of Nanking in 1937 and the Bataan Death March in 1942 had grotesquely demonstrated. "If my life was not important," a Japanese soldier recalled, "an enemy's life became inevitably much less important. . . . This philosophy led us to look down on the enemy."[20]

The Japanese army's *Field Service Code*, promulgated by then–war minister Hideki Tojo in 1941, laid out one consequential implication of this severe martial doctrine: "Never give up a position but rather die." The *Field Service Code* contained no instructions on how to surrender, offered no guidance about what to do if captured, made no mention of the Geneva Convention for treatment of prisoners of war. To surrender was to be disgraced. Reciprocally, enemies who surrendered were regarded as craven cowards shorn of dignity and respect. Those few Japanese soldiers who did fall into American hands frequently gave false names (often that of a famous Kabuki actor, Kazuo Hasegawa) or begged that notification of their capture not be sent to their homeland, for fear of reprisals against their families. More immediately, fear of the Americans reinforced Japanese reluctance to raise the white flag. Eighty-four percent of Japanese prisoners interrogated in one study stated that they had expected to be tortured or killed if captured. Rumors circulated among Japanese troops that young Americans qualified for the marine corps by murdering their parents and that raping civilians was standard American military practice.

Those accounts were fanciful, but others were not. American servicemen strafed lifeboats, shot prisoners, mutilated the dead, slashed open

---

19. In another sign of the subordinate status of the Pacific war, *Know Your Enemy—Japan* was the last film to be made in Capra's series. It was released only in August 1945 and was withdrawn after less than three weeks.

20. Iris Chang, *The Rape of Nanking: The Forgotten Holocaust of World War II* (New York: Basic Books, 1997), 58.

the cheeks of the wounded to gouge out gold teeth, made necklaces of severed Japanese ears, decorated vehicles with Japanese skulls, and fashioned letter openers from Japanese bones (one was sent to Franklin Roosevelt, who refused it). The *Baltimore Sun* ran a story in 1943 about a mother whose son had cut off a Japanese ear that she wished to nail to her front door. "It is virtually inconceivable," writes Dower, "that teeth, ears, and skulls could have been collected from German or Italian war dead and publicized in the Anglo-American countries without provoking an uproar; and in this we have yet another inkling of the racial dimensions of the war."[21]

Beginning with the treacherous ambush of some two dozen marines on Guadalcanal by Japanese soldiers purporting to surrender, both sides fell into the practice of taking few prisoners, though it was the outgunned and overwhelmed Japanese who most frequently were driven to fight to the death. Fear of mistreatment at the hands of the enemy inspired American troops to sometimes superhuman efforts to rescue wounded buddies, as Norman Mailer described in one of the most gripping of all World War II novels, *The Naked and the Dead*. Most of the twenty-five thousand Americans taken prisoner in the Pacific had surrendered in the Philippines in 1942. Their captors accorded them no better treatment than they themselves would have expected in such a fallen state. The Japanese frequently consigned guard duty to Formosans or Koreans, themselves cruelly mistreated by their imperial masters and inclined to mistreat their captives in turn. Ninety percent of American prisoners of war in the Pacific reported being beaten. More than a third died. Those who survived spent thirty-eight months in captivity on average and lost sixty-one pounds. In Europe, by contrast, the average American POW spent ten months in captivity and lost thirty-eight pounds. Virtually all the Americans who fell into German hands—99 percent—survived.[22]

There were other differences from Europe. The Pacific was a peculiarly alien place for American servicemen, and an achingly lonely one too. Most of the fighting took place in the tropics, home to exotic diseases like dengue fever and filariasis, a lymphatic infection. Malaria was so endemic throughout the Pacific islands that troops on the ground were put on a compulsory regimen of Atabrine, a drug of dubious efficacy which the men resisted because it jaundiced the skin and was

21. Dower, *War without Mercy*, 26n., 68, 66.
22. Lee Kennett, *G.I.: The American Soldier in World War II* (New York: Charles Scribner's Sons, 1987), 184–87.

rumored to cause insanity and impotence. For the moment, impotence was in any case a small worry, since there were few available women, as evidenced by the fact that servicemen in the Pacific had markedly lower rates of venereal disease, the traditional soldier's scourge, than did those in Europe. AWOL (Absent Without Leave) rates were also lower in the Pacific, because there was no place to go. So was the incidence of death and wounding, since most casualties were inflicted by artillery and mortar shelling, for which the Japanese were not well equipped. The standard Japanese infantry rifle was also of such inferior design that it forced Japanese soldiers into close-quarters fighting, for which they kept their bayonets fixed at all times. Unlike their comrades in Europe, who typically fought long campaigns against modern, mechanized German adversaries, fighting usually at rifle-shot-length and beyond, the American soldiers and marines in the Pacific experienced a war of isolation, boredom, and disease, punctuated by long ocean crossings and brief bursts of combat, much of it in harrowing hand-to-hand struggle with poorly outfitted but ferociously motivated Japanese Imperial soldiers.

THE PACIFIC was also physically vast. More than three thousand miles of ocean separated San Diego from Honolulu; five thousand miles lay between Hawaii and the Philippines; twenty-five hundred between Tarawa and the Marianas; two thousand between the Mariana islet of Tinian and Hiroshima. Those distances dictated Japan's war plan, which was to fight a strategic defense-in-depth behind a series of concentric lines defined by the far-flung island chains that ringed the Japanese homeland: the Gilberts and the Marshalls in midocean Micronesia; the Philippines, Formosa, and the Ryukyus in the China Sea; and the Carolines and Marianas to Japan's south.

To reach and penetrate those widely separated fortifications, the U.S. Navy built a stupendous flotilla, organized around the novel technology of naval air power. Its fighting heart was an immense "Task Force," somewhat confusingly designated Task Force 38, or Third Fleet, when commanded by the impulsive, charismatic Admiral Halsey, and Task Force 58, or Fifth Fleet, when commanded by the methodical, self-effacing Admiral Raymond A. Spruance. The fourteen or more Essex-class carriers at the Task Force's core—888-foot-long floating airfields with three-thousand-man crews—could each embark up to one hundred aircraft. Supported by enormous "fleet trains" of oilers, ammunition ships, tenders, repair vessels, lighters, escort carriers, seagoing tugs, hospital ships, and a screen of battleships, cruisers, and destroyers, Halsey and Spruance could keep their long-legged carriers at sea for indefinite periods and could range over virtually the entire Pacific. From the bridges of their flagships in TF 38/58, they commanded several times the striking power of Nagumo's force that attacked Pearl Harbor.

Not until the end of 1943 was a plan agreed upon for waging offensive war against Japan, and even then it contained elements of opportunism, compromise, and willful indecision. The desire to placate Douglas Mac-Arthur, the political need to appear faithful to the dispossessed American colony of the Philippines, and the investment already somewhat adventitiously made in the Southwest Pacific all conspired to the approval of MacArthur's demand that he be allowed to continue up the northern New Guinea shore, liberate the Philippines, and prepare for a further assault on Formosa and the China Coast. At the same time, the navy would wage a second campaign, thrusting across the Central Pacific, through the Gilberts, Marshalls, Carolines, and Marianas, to converge eventually with MacArthur's anticipated offensive against Formosa and China. Japan would thus be cut off from its sources of supply in South Asia, and China-based American bombers as well as amphibious assault forces would lie within striking range of the Japanese home islands.

Underlying the Central Pacific drive was the navy's old Orange Plan, which had envisioned a "decisive battle" with the Japanese Imperial Navy in the broad waters of the western Pacific. For that reason, the navy tended to favor the Central Pacific advance over MacArthur's effort in the Southwest Pacific, but for the time being the Joint Chiefs assigned no clear priority to either campaign. Before 1944 was out, however, two developments would significantly modify this two-pronged scheme: Japanese successes against Chiang in the Ichi-go Campaign effectively precluded the use of Chinese airbases, robbing Formosa and the China coast of strategic value; and the advent of the new, long-range B-29 Superfortress bomber made it possible to mount aerial attacks on Japan from bases in the Marianas, notably from Tinian.

In June 1944, virtually at the same moment that the huge D-Day armada was churning across the English Channel, Admiral Nimitz launched Spruance and Task Force 58 against the Marianas. After the costly lessons of Tarawa and Anzio, the Americans had refined their techniques of amphibious warfare. They had improved their communication systems, had rehearsed better coordination of naval gunfire and tactical air support for the assault troops, and now defined the landing phase of the attack not as a discrete operation but as part of an "am-

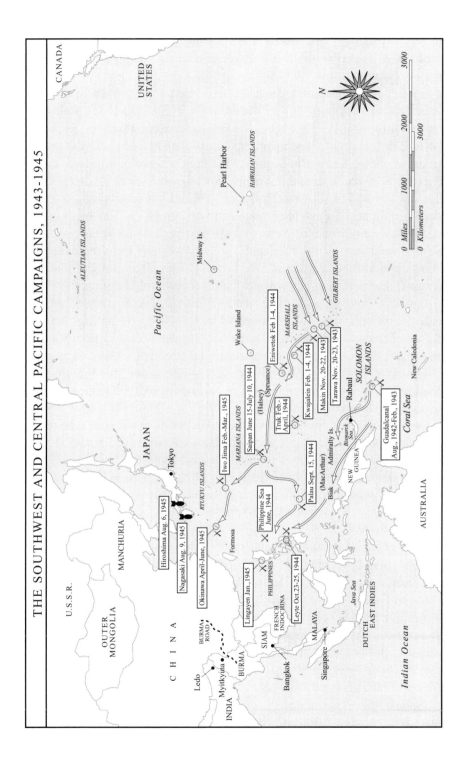

THE SOUTHWEST AND CENTRAL PACIFIC CAMPAIGNS, 1943-1945

CANADA

UNITED STATES

U.S.S.R.

OUTER MONGOLIA

MANCHURIA

JAPAN

Tokyo

C H I N A

BURMA ROAD

Ledo

Myitkyina

INDIA

BURMA

SIAM

FRENCH INDOCHINA

Bangkok

MALAYA

Singapore

DUTCH EAST INDIES

Java Sea

Indian Ocean

AUSTRALIA

New Caledonia

Coral Sea

NEW GUINEA

SOLOMON ISLANDS

Rabaul

Bismarck Sea

Admiralty Is.

Biak

Guadalcanal Aug. 1942-Feb. 1943

Tarawa Nov. 20-23, 1943

Makin Nov. 20-22, 1943

Kwajalein Feb. 1-4, 1944

GILBERT ISLANDS

MARSHALL ISLANDS

Eniwetok Feb 1-4, 1944

(Spruance)

Truk Feb.-April, 1944

Palau Sept. 15, 1944 (MacArthur)

Philippine Sea June, 1944

Leyte Oct.23-25, 1944

PHILIPPINES

Lingayen Jan.,1945

Formosa

Saipan June 15-July 10, 1944 (Halsey)

MARIANA ISLANDS

Iwo Jima Feb.-Mar. 1945

RYUKYU ISLANDS

Okinawa April-June, 1945

Nagasaki Aug. 9, 1945

Hiroshima Aug. 6, 1945

Wake Island

Midway Is.

ALEUTIAN ISLANDS

Pacific Ocean

Pearl Harbor

HAWAIIAN ISLANDS

N

0 Miles   1000   2000   3000
0 Kilometers   3000

phibious blitzkrieg," making maximum use of firepower and motorized transport to sweep across the beaches and as far inland as possible in one continuous thrust.

On June 13 a line of seven battleships began raining shellfire onto Saipan, at the northern end of the Mariana chain. On the morning of the fifteenth, ringed by a huge protective cordon of battleships, cruisers, carriers, and support vessels and covered by air strikes along the green fringe of shore, transports began disgorging armored amphibian craft. Their 75mm cannon and machine guns blasted away at the beach, clearing the way for the assault troops in hundreds of amphibious tractors ("amphtracs"), wave after wave of them, ninety-six abreast in every wave. Each amphtrac carried a dozen terrified young men over the island's coral reef, across the lagoon it enclosed, and onto the beaches. Mortar and artillery shell-bursts pocked the water all around them while shrapnel and machine-gun rounds thudded and rattled against the sides of the little landing craft. The offshore breeze assaulted their nostrils with the stench of night soil–covered fields. Many trembling men in the amphtracs vomited; others fouled themselves. Within twenty minutes eight thousand troops were ashore; by nightfall, twenty thousand; within days, nearly a hundred thousand—one army and two marine divisions, as well as numerous service and construction battalions (CBs, or, more colloquially, Seabees).

Despite the Americans' heavy firepower, swift movement, and concentrated force, the Japanese garrison, thirty-two thousand strong, fought back fiercely. The defenders pushed a large bulge into the center of the American line, held by the Army's 27th Division, a New York National Guard unit whose commander was relieved of his post—by the *marine* general in overall command, igniting an interservice squabble that echoed long thereafter.

With continuing support from naval gunfire, the Americans pressed steadily inland. Segregated Negro units performed especially well. Marine Corps Commandant Archer Vandegrift announced that with the Battle of Saipan, "[t]he Negro Marines are no longer on trial. They are Marines, period."[23] The Japanese made the Americans pay for every yard of advance. On July 7 three thousand desperate Japanese troops, some wielding no weapon other than a knife tied to a bamboo pole, rushed the American line, screaming the Japanese battle cry, "Banzai!" (literally,

23. Spector, 390.

ten thousand years). They inflicted heavy casualties but were themselves annihilated virtually to a man.

Meanwhile, at Marpi Point at Saipan's northern tip, thousands of Japanese civilians, mostly women and children, scuttled frantically to the lip of the two-hundred-foot cliffs at the sea's edge, evidently preferring suicide to capture by the Americans. Interpreters and a few captured Japanese soldiers, shouting through bullhorns from boats below, begged them not to jump, but as many as a thousand people leapt to their deaths on the rocks and in the surf below or blew themselves up with hand grenades. The Americans gaped at the spectacle in horrified astonishment. When one couple hesitated at the cliff's edge, a Japanese sniper shot them both, then walked defiantly out of his hiding place and crumpled under a hail of American bullets. "What did all this self-destruction mean?" asked war correspondent Robert Sherrod in *Time* magazine. "Did it mean that the Japanese on Saipan believed their own propaganda which told them that Americans are beasts and would murder them all . . . ? Do the suicides of Saipan mean that the whole Japanese race will choose death before surrender?" The civilian deaths on Saipan, their numbers exaggerated both in American press accounts and in Japanese propaganda, reinforced the conviction of both adversaries that the finish-fight would be bloodiest of struggles. At battle's end on July 9, the Americans on Saipan had suffered some fourteen thousand casualties, including 3,426 killed. Almost the entire Japanese garrison had perished, along with thousands of civilians. Within another month, American forces secured the neighboring island of Tinian, as well as Guam, the first scrap of conquered American territory retaken from Japan.[24]

As the battle for Saipan was raging on the night of July 15, Spruance received word that a large Japanese naval force was bearing down on the Marianas, with the apparent intention of giving battle to Spruance's Task Force 58—or maybe of disrupting the Saipan landings. The news confronted Spruance with a painful decision: should he continue to protect the landing operation at Saipan, his assigned mission, or break away to intercept and engage the Japanese fleet? His blood raced at the thought that with just a few hours steaming he might at last be in a

24. Robert Sherrod, *On to Westward* (New York: Duell, Sloan and Pearce, 1945), 146; *Time*, August 7, 1944, 27; Haruko Taya Cook, "The Myth of the Saipan Suicides," *MHQ* (Spring 1995): 12–19.

position to fight the Orange Plan's "decisive battle" and achieve the war's ultimate naval victory. He had fifteen carriers on station, embarking nearly a thousand aircraft, a mighty force. He ravened to go. When Nimitz radioed him that "we count on you to make the victory decisive," go he did. Leaving several surface ships behind to screen Saipan, Spruance gathered up his carriers and plunged away from the Marianas into the open waters of the Philippine Sea.

As Spruance probed southwestward in pursuit of his adversary, Vice-Admiral Jisaburo Ozawa pushed his nine carriers northeastward to find Spruance. Despite the greater size of the American fleet, Ozawa held some formidable assets. Japan still possessed numerous island-airfields in the Philippine Sea, from which land-based aircraft could join in the battle and to which his own carrier-based planes could fly in one-way "shuttle" attacks that substantially increased their operational range. The lighter Japanese carrier planes in any case had a greater combat radius than their more heavily armed and armored American counterparts, a difference of some 560 miles to 350 miles. In this oceanic region, too, the easterly tradewinds favored Ozawa with the lee gauge, so that he could launch and recover his aircraft while steaming into the wind and simultaneously closing with his enemy. Spruance, in contrast, had to turn his ships to windward, back toward the Marianas and away from Ozawa, to conduct flight operations. What was more, Spruance could not put out of mind his commitments at Saipan. He well knew what had happened on the night of August 8, 1942, when Frank Jack Fletcher had pulled his carriers away from Savo Sound, contributing to the U.S. Navy's worst-ever defeat at sea and nearly scuttling the Guadalcanal landing. So when he had still not found Ozawa by the night of June 18, Spruance ordered his ships to backtrack toward Saipan, while still flying off search planes to look for the Japanese fleet.

As the two naval forces groped for each other across the waters of the Philippine Sea, both commanders itching for the decisive battle, one of Ozawa's scout planes at last spotted TF 58 on the morning of June 19. Ozawa immediately flew off four waves of attacking aircraft. They had the advantage of surprise, but not for long. Radar operators on the battleship screen to the west of Spruance's carriers picked up Ozawa's lead planes, and within minutes hundreds of aircraft lifted off the decks of the American ships. Deep within the bowels of the carrier *Lexington*, fighter-direction teams made further use of radar to calculate the enemy's direction, level, and speed of approach, environing conditions of cloud cover and sun angles, and relative force sizes and dispositions.

Swiftly computing the mix of these complex variables, they vectored American pilots into optimal positions for attack.

The Americans had yet another telling advantage. U.S. naval aviators had at least two years of flight training and over three hundred hours in the air before facing combat. Battle-tested pilots were rotated home to help school the next generation of aviators, so that the entire American air contingent by 1944 represented an accumulation of training and experience that had no equal among its enemies. Japanese pilots flew until they died. Japan had long since lost most of the highly skilled fliers with whom it started the war and had made poor provision for training replacements. Most of Ozawa's pilots had no more than six months of training, and some as little as two. Fuel shortages had by this time become so acute in Japan that student pilots got much of their instruction on the ground, watching films shot by a boom-mounted camera simulating different approaches to six-foot models of American warships in an artificial lake.

The result on June 19 was an immense aerial slaughter. By the end of the day, American pilots had shot down more than three hundred Japanese planes while losing fewer than thirty of their own. U.S. submarines meanwhile sank two Japanese carriers. In a desperate last pursuit of Ozawa's fleet in the twilight hours of June 20, American pilots operating at and beyond the limits of their flying range sent a third Japanese carrier to the bottom. In the darkness that followed, though U.S. carrier commanders defied caution and lit up their ships to facilitate recovery, dozens of American aircraft were wrecked attempting night landings, or were forced to ditch in the inky sea.

In the typically heedless vernacular of the victors, U.S. aviators called the Battle of the Philippine Sea "the Great Marianas Turkey Shoot." It was, by any standard, an overwhelming victory, the greatest carrier battle of the war and one that effectively extinguished the Japanese navy's capacity to give battle in the air. The Imperial Navy had lost three fleet carriers and some 480 aircraft all told, and its pool of already ill-trained pilots had dwindled to the vanishing point. "It will be extremely difficult," a Japanese admiral wrote, "to recover from this disaster and rise again."[25]

Yet some senior U.S. Navy commanders criticized Spruance for letting Ozawa escape with as many ships as he did. Because he had hung back to protect Saipan and had not more aggressively pursued Ozawa,

25. Thomas J. Cutler, *The Battle of Leyte Gulf* (New York: HarperCollins, 1994), 47.

the Battle of the Philippine Sea did not shape up as the "decisive fleet action" for which both American and Japanese sailors still hungered. The unsated yearning of both navies to fight that battle would have telling consequences just sixteen weeks later, in the next battle to be fought in the Philippine Sea, at Leyte Gulf.

NEWS OF SAIPAN'S LOSS brought down the government of General Hideki Tojo on July 18. A few senior Japanese statesmen thought that the time had come for a civilian premier who might put Japan on the road to liquidating its disastrous military adventure, but their faint voices went unheeded. The generals and the admirals still held the upper hand. Kuniaki Koiso, another general, succeeded Tojo as Japan's premier. The men who started the war were still in power and showed no sign of wanting to end it. Though Japan's defeat was now all but certain, its surrender was not. The conflict seemed to have generated its own momentum, with no stopping point in sight.

There was inertia on the American side too. While Tojo's government was falling in the last days of July 1944, Franklin Roosevelt had traveled to Hawaii to confer with his Pacific commanders, Nimitz and MacArthur, about the next phase of the Pacific war. Now that the Marianas were securely in American hands, their ostensible agenda was to decide whether MacArthur's Southwest Pacific or Nimitz's Central Pacific campaign should have priority. Nimitz and some strategists in Washington were advocating that the Philippines be bypassed in favor of an assault on Formosa or the Ryukyus, or even a direct attack on Japan from the Marianas. MacArthur predictably insisted that he should press on to the liberation of the Philippines. If their Filipino "wards" were left to languish, MacArthur reportedly warned Roosevelt, "I dare say that the American people would be so aroused that they would register most complete resentment against you at the polls this fall" — an astonishingly audacious and thinly veiled political threat, unimaginable from any American commander save MacArthur.

Political considerations may in any case have had more to do with Roosevelt's trip than strategic ones. He and MacArthur struck a deal, at least implicitly: the general could go on to Manila, and the president would profit from MacArthur's favorable news reports about the progress of the Pacific war and from the general's flattering comments about FDR's strategic acuity. After a scant three hours of talk on July 28 in an airy mansion on Honolulu's Waikiki Beach, a parody of a strategic discussion, the conferees reached their mutually beneficial nondecision:

both campaigns, to the Philippines and through the Central Pacific, would continue.[26]

On August 26, 1944, as scheduled, Fifth Fleet passed from Spruance's hands to Halsey's and once again became Third Fleet. In an exceedingly bloody action, Halsey proceeded to seize the Palau Islands, considered necessary to secure the invasion route to the Philippines. He also raided the Japanese airfields on Formosa, destroying more than five hundred of Japan's rapidly disappearing stock of combat aircraft. In the course of air attacks on the Philippines in September, an American flier shot down over Leyte managed to get back to his ship and report that there were virtually no Japanese on the island. That discovery changed the destination for the Philippine invasion and accelerated its timetable. Now the attacking troops would go ashore not on Mindanao, as originally planned, but on the more northerly island of Leyte, in the gulf of the same name on the island's southeastern coast. Halsey's Third Fleet would cover the landings, as Spruance had been charged to do at Saipan. But Nimitz's orders to Halsey contained an unmistakable echo of both men's frustration that Spruance had missed the decisive battle with Ozawa in the Philippine Sea: "In case opportunity for destruction of major portion of the enemy fleet offers or can be created, such destruction becomes the primary task."[27]

On October 20, 1944, the invasion convoys began unloading on the lightly defended beach at Leyte Gulf. In a carefully arranged ritual, MacArthur walked down the ramp of a landing craft and waded ashore through the shallow surf, a moment captured in one of the war's most famous photographs. "People of the Philippines," MacArthur intoned into a waiting microphone, "I have returned. . . . The hour of your redemption is here. . . . Rally to me."[28]

American submarines had by now cut Japan's oil supplies to a trickle. What little there was reached Japan from the Dutch East Indies behind a screen of islands that ran from the Philippines through Formosa and the Ryukyus. Japan had to defend the Philippines or risk seeing its lifeline to the south completely severed.[29]

26. James MacGregor Burns, *Roosevelt: The Soldier of Freedom* (New York: Harcourt Brace Jovanovich, 1970), 489.
27. Cutler, *Battle of Leyte Gulf,* 60.
28. Douglas MacArthur, *Reminiscences* (New York: McGraw-Hill, 1964), 216–17.
29. U.S. submarines largely succeeded in doing to Japan what German submarines had failed to do to Britain: interdicting the island nation's merchant marine and choking off its supplies of food, fuel, and raw materials. Inexplicably, Japan never prepared

To conserve precious fuel, the Imperial Navy had been forced to base nearly half its battle fleet at Lingga Roads, near Singapore and close to the East Indian oil fields. From there, and from two other fleet anchorages, three Japanese naval formations steamed toward Leyte to check the American landing. Vice-Admiral Shoji Nishimura's force left Brunei, and Vice-Admiral Kiyohide Shima's column came down from the Ryukyus. Their plan was to rendezvous in the Mindanao Sea and proceed together through Surigao Strait into Leyte Gulf. Vice-Admiral Takeo Kurita headed from Lingga Roads across the Palawan Passage and the Sibuyan Sea. He was to pass through San Bernardino Strait and descend on Leyte from the north just as the Nishimura-Shima force emerged out of Surigao from the west. To this already dauntingly intricate plan the Japanese added a further complication: Ozawa, his air strength reduced to just a handful of warplanes after the catastrophe in the Philippine Sea and the raids on Formosa, would steam southward from Japan with his remaining aircraft carriers, using the largely planeless ships as sacrificial decoys to lure away at least part of the American force.

The Americans meanwhile brought two fleets of their own to Leyte. Seventh Fleet, under Admiral Thomas C. Kinkaid, was composed of several big gunships and eighteen "escort carriers," small vessels built on merchant hulls, each embarking just two dozen warplanes and designed principally for ferrying aircraft, anti–submarine patrol, and close-in tactical air support for beach assaults. Kinkaid's battle ships and cruisers took up station off the eastern end of Surigao Strait. He deployed his escort carriers in three six-ship squadrons, respectively code-named Taffy 1, 2, and 3, off Samar Island on the east side of Leyte. Halsey's Third Fleet meanwhile held its big carriers off San Bernardino Strait to the north.

Six naval forces, four Japanese and two American, were converging on Leyte Gulf to fight the largest naval battle in history, a titanic clash spread over three days and a hundred thousand square miles of sea, engaging 282 ships and two hundred thousand sailors and airmen.

---

for antisubmarine warfare and deployed its own submarines almost exclusively against enemy warships or in resupply operations to isolated garrisons. American submarines, in contrast, concentrated on the Japanese merchant marine, which by war's end had been reduced to about one-third of its size in 1941 and consisted mostly of small wooden vessels in the Inland Sea. U.S. submarines accounted for 201 of the 686 Japanese warships sunk during the war but sank more than 1,200 Japanese merchantmen, 60 percent of the total destroyed. Morison, 511.

THE BATTLE OF LEYTE GULF, OCT. 23-25, 1944, AND THE PHILIPPINE CAMPAIGN

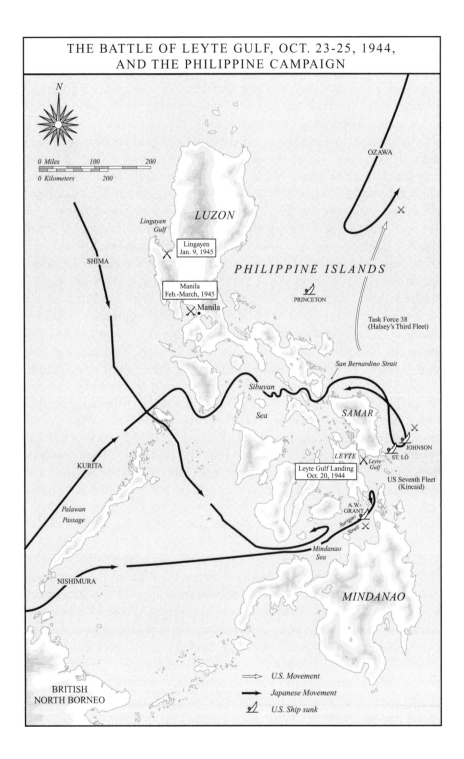

N

0 Miles 100 200
0 Kilometers 200

OZAWA

LUZON

Lingayen
Gulf

Lingayen
Jan. 9, 1945

SHIMA

PHILIPPINE ISLANDS

Manila
Feb.-March, 1945

Manila

PRINCETON

Task Force 38
(Halsey's Third Fleet)

San Bernardino Strait

Sibuyan

Sea

SAMAR

JOHNSON
ST. LÔ

LEYTE

KURITA

Leyte Gulf Landing
Oct. 20, 1944

Leyte
Gulf

US Seventh Fleet
(Kincaid)

Palawan
Passage

A.W.
GRANT

Surigao
Strait

Mindanao
Sea

NISHIMURA

MINDANAO

BRITISH
NORTH BORNEO

⟹   U.S. Movement
→   Japanese Movement
       U.S. Ship sunk

Nishimura's two battleships, one cruiser, and four destroyers arrived in the Mindanao Sea on October 24. Not finding Shima, Nishimura proceeded on his own into Surigao Strait, through waters that Ferdinand Magellan had sailed in 1521. As darkness fell, American PT (patrol torpedo) boats harassed the Japanese column while it plowed eastward, disrupting Nishimura's formation but inflicting little damage. Then five U.S. destroyers, withholding gunfire that would disclose their positions, raced down either side of the strait and loosed several volleys of torpedoes that knocked out one of the battleships and three of the destroyers. There followed a maneuver whose classic naval geometry Magellan himself would have appreciated. Arrayed in a battle line across the neck of the strait were Kinkaid's six battleships, five of them survivors of Pearl Harbor, together with four heavy and four light cruisers. Kinkaid had effortlessly "crossed the T," the dream of every sea commander since the dawn of gun-bearing ships. Perpendicular to Kinkaid's six-, eight-, fourteen-, and sixteen-inch guns, Nishimura's truncated column lay all but naked under round after round of thundering American broadsides. Firing by radar direction from a range of more than twenty miles, the American battle line laid down a fearsome barrage. The Japanese formation disintegrated. The second battleship went down, the cruiser was crippled, and the lone surviving destroyer reversed course and withdrew. When the late-arriving Shima sailed into this chaotic melee and collided with Nashimura's wallowing cruiser, he too decided to withdraw, but pursuing American warships and planes sank three of his ships. All told, the Battle of Surigao Strait cost the Imperial Japanese Navy two battleships, three cruisers, and four destroyers. The Americans lost one PT boat, as well as 39 sailors killed and 114 wounded, most of them on the U.S. destroyer *Albert W. Grant*, which was caught in a murderous crossfire from both Japanese and American guns during the bedlam of the night battle.

In the pewter morning light, U.S. rescue vessels crept into the strait to pick up the thousands of Japanese survivors. Most of the swimmers submerged themselves below the oil-stained surface as the Americans approached, choosing death by drowning over the shame of capture.

To the north, meanwhile, U.S. submarines had intercepted Kurita's formidable group of three battleships, twelve cruisers, and thirteen destroyers as they made their way across Palawan Passage on October 23. Several well-placed torpedo volleys damaged one cruiser and sank two others, including Kurita's flagship. Fished from the sea, Kurita transferred his flag to the *Yamato*. The *Yamato* and its sister ship *Musashi* were the two biggest battleships afloat, mounting eighteen-inch guns that fired one-and-a-half ton projectiles, larger than any gun in the U.S. Navy could throw. Halsey's fliers caught Kurita again in the Sibuyan Sea on the following day and sank another cruiser as well as the supposedly impregnable *Musashi*. Land-based Japanese aircraft meanwhile attacked Third Fleet and sent the carrier *Princeton* to the bottom.

Halsey's airmen reported that Kurita's force had no train or transports, a sure sign that the Japanese flotilla had sortied only to give battle at sea, not to land reinforcements on Leyte. Halsey was spoiling for a fight. He drafted a contingency battle plan, signaling to Nimitz at Pearl Harbor that he intended to detach several ships to form a new "Task Force 34" that would stop Kurita at the mouth of San Bernardino Strait. But there was one thing wrong: Kurita's force was composed entirely of surface gunships. Where were the Japanese carriers, the great prize for which Halsey thirsted?

The answer was that they were to Halsey's north, doing their best to be discovered and tempt Halsey away from San Bernardino. When some of Third Fleet's fliers reported at midday on the twenty-fourth that they had engaged planes with tail-hooks, unmistakably identifying them as carrier-based aircraft, Halsey was off like a greyhound after a hare. Faced with the choice of protection or pursuit, and believing erroneously that he had already inflicted enough damage on Kurita to stop him, Halsey scarcely hesitated. He scrapped the plan to create Task Force 34 and steamed away with his entire fleet to chase the Japanese carriers. Like George Armstrong Custer in search of the Sioux on the high plains in 1876, Halsey worried that the Japanese would cut and run before he could wage the decisive battle, as Ozawa had managed to do to Spruance in the Philippine Sea. Emulating Custer in that perilously exhilarating moment atop Medicine Tail Coulee, now that Halsey had spotted his adversary he lunged reflexively after him. He took Ozawa's bait, leaving the door of San Bernardino Strait wide open for Kurita.

Through San Bernardino Kurita steamed unopposed shortly after midnight on October 25. His badly mauled but still powerful force bore down on the most northerly of Kinkaid's escort-carrier squadrons, Taffy 3. A colossal mismatch ensued — the *Yamato* and several heavy and light cruisers against a handful of destroyers and six escort carriers never designed for full-scale battle at sea. Slow, thinly armored, undergunned, and mostly munitioned with ordnance for tactical air support, the "baby flat-tops" were sitting ducks. Great green, purple, and yellow geysers erupted among them as Japanese shells, with their telltale dye-marked bursts, scattered the surprised American ships. Taffy 3's little carriers made smoke and dove into a rain squall for further concealment, while the U.S. destroyers brazenly charged the larger and more numerous Japanese ships. The destroyer *Johnston* took so many hits from the huge Japanese gun batteries that one crewman compared it to "a puppy being smacked by a truck." Eventually, he said, "we were in a position where all the gallantry and guts in the world could not save us," and Abandon Ship was ordered. A swimming survivor saw a Japanese officer salute as the *Johnston* slipped beneath the surface.[30]

Kinkaid and Nimitz meanwhile were frantically signaling to Halsey for help. At 10:00 A.M. on the twenty-fifth, a signalman handed Halsey a message from Nimitz that was destined to become notorious: "Where is, Repeat, Where is Task Force 34, The World Wonders?" The last phrase, "The World Wonders," was "padding," the kind of verbiage, frequently nonsensical, that was routinely inserted in encrypted messages to foil enemy cryptographers. (Nimitz's full message read: "Turkey Trots to Water RR Where Is Rpt Where Is Task Force Thirty Four RR The World Wonders?," with the double capital letters setting off the real message.) But the decoding officer on Halsey's flagship apparently believed the end-padding in Nimitz's signal was part of the message. He typed it onto the page that was handed to the admiral. The presumed insult unnerved Halsey. He threw his hat to the deck and began to sob. An aide shook him by the shoulders. "What the hell's the matter with you? Pull yourself together!"[31]

Third Fleet's carriers continued to press the attack on Ozawa, all four of whose carriers eventually went down, including *Zuikaku*, the last survivor from the force that had lofted the planes that opened the war at Pearl Harbor. Halsey, however, headed back to Samar with his battleship group. He was too late to relieve Kinkaid, but it scarcely mattered. Kurita, perhaps rattled by his unplanned swim in Palawan Passage, had incredibly concluded that the little scratch force of baby flat-tops desperately trying to evade him off Samar was Halsey's powerful, big-carrier TF 38. Ironically, at about the moment Halsey was reading Nimitz's radiogram, Kurita decided to break off the attack and head back to Lingga Roads.

The epic battle of Leyte Gulf was not quite over. Even as Kurita was withdrawing, the Japanese launched a fearsome new weapon against the

30. Morison, 457–58.
31. Spector, 438; Cutler, *Battle of Leyte Gulf*, 250–51.

Taffy groups: suicide attacks by land-based kamikaze warplanes. *Kamikaze* means "divine wind," a reference to the typhoon that scattered Kublai Khan's invasion fleet headed for Japan in the thirteenth century. Kamikaze pilots prepared for their missions with elaborate ceremonials, including ritual prayer, the composition of farewell poems, and the presentation to each flier of a "thousand-stitch belt," a strip of cloth into which one thousand women had each sewn a stitch, symbolically uniting themselves with the pilot's ultimate sacrifice. Late in the morning of October 25, the first wave of kamikazes lashed out of the sky over Taffy 3. One headed straight for the escort carrier *St. Lô*. Disbelieving antiaircraft gunners tried desperately to knock it down, to no avail. The plane crashed into the *St. Lô*'s flight deck and disgorged a bomb deep into the ship's interior. As sailors on nearby ships watched in horrified fascination, the *St. Lô* exploded, heeled over on her side, and sank with 114 men aboard. It was a grisly demonstration of the kind of resistance Japan was still prepared to offer.

The Battle of Leyte Gulf ended an era, but it did not end the war. The encounters at Surigao and at Samar were the last of their kind. They closed an epoch of ship-to-ship gunnery duels, the standard form of naval warfare for centuries before 1944. No nation would ever again build a battleship; aircraft carriers had proved themselves as the final arbiters of battle at sea. The Imperial Japanese Navy had suffered a crushing defeat, losing four carriers, three battleships, nine cruisers, a dozen destroyers, hundreds of aircraft and thousands of sailors and pilots. But as the kamikaze raids spectacularly illustrated, Japan had not lost its will to fight.

The Japanese army rapidly reinforced Leyte, which MacArthur did not manage to secure until December, when it became the staging area for his next assault on the main Philippine island of Luzon. Renewed and even more deadly kamikaze attacks shredded the American invasion convoys on their way to Luzon's Lingayen Gulf on January 9, 1945. MacArthur landed more than ten divisions at Lingayen, the largest assault force to date in the Pacific war, but General Tomoyuki Yamashita denied it easy victory with a shrewdly executed defensive campaign. Fighting a war of attrition in mountainous, Italian-like terrain that favored the defenders, Yamashita held out for months. Other Japanese units resisted still longer in the outlying Philippine Islands, a few diehards even beyond the formal end of the war. On Palawan Island, the Japanese herded 140 American and Filipino POWs into a trench, doused them with gasoline, and burned them alive. Reports of that and

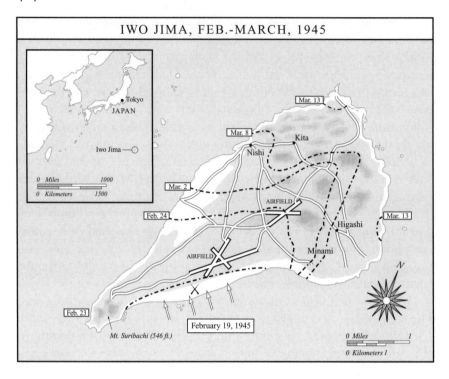

IWO JIMA, FEB.-MARCH, 1945

other atrocities spurred MacArthur to intensify his campaign to liberate Philippine territory, a costly operation that had little direct bearing by this time on Japan's ultimate defeat. The Battle of Manila in February and March, a vicious street-by-street affair that resembled some of the cruelest fighting in Berlin or Warsaw, took the lives of a hundred thousand Filipino civilians and thousands of American soldiers. Yamashita's tactics of delay, his soldiers' willingness to fight to the last breath, and the mounting savagery of combat provided a bitter foretaste of what awaited the Americans to the north, on Iwo Jima and Okinawa.

WITH THE PHILIPPINES substantially secure by the end of March and the Formosa-China objective now definitely ruled out, Nimitz focused all his resources on the Central Pacific and on reaching Japan itself. In November 1944 new long-range B-29 Superfortresses had begun bombing Japanese cities from bases in the Marianas. Midway between Saipan and Tokyo lay Iwo Jima, literally "Sulfur Island," a diabolically forbidding 4.5-mile-long and 2.5-mile-wide chunk of rock reeking of sulfur from the dormant volcano of Mt. Suribachi at its south end and covered by a thick layer of fine black volcanic emissions. Nimitz wanted Iwo because its airfields and radar station forced the B-29s to fly a lengthy dogleg course from the Marianas to Japan. The Japanese were determined to hold it, one of their last outer defenses shielding the home islands.

The twenty-one-thousand-man Japanese garrison had honeycombed Iwo's basaltic ridges and Suribachi's ashen flanks with reinforced concrete-and-steel bunkers and stuffed them with artillery, antiaircraft guns, mortars, and machine guns. They were so well and deeply entrenched that seventy-two days of aerial bombing and three days of naval shelling barely scratched them. At first light on February 19 two divisions of marines, each man carrying up to a hundred pounds of gear, stepped from their amphtracs onto Iwo's beaches and sank to their boot-tops in the powdery mixture of sand and volcanic ash. Vehicles, including tanks and half-tracks, soon bogged down in the quicksand-like topping of pumice and cinder that blanketed the island. From the Japanese bunkers and pillboxes a hellish rain of shells and bullets pelted the beaches, where the marines seemed to be moving in slow motion through the sucking sand.

As they had done in preceding Pacific battles, Navaho "code-talkers" relayed messages among the marine units. The Navaho language, a branch of Athabaskan with no alphabet and highly irregular syntax, was known to fewer than three dozen non-Navahos in the world, none of them Japanese. Many Navahos thus volunteered for duty in the marine signal corps, and their native language was their own very special code. Though Navaho lacked words for many modern military terms, the code-talkers improvised: *chay-da-gahi*, turtle, for example, became their word for tank. Certain that no Japanese eavesdropper could understand them, the code-talkers spoke freely over their radios and walkie-talkies, creating one of the war's most secure communications systems.

On February 22 a Navaho code-talker notified the Pacific high command that the marines had planted an American flag on Mount *'dibeh* (Sheep), *no-dah-ih* (Ute), *gah* (Rabbit), *tkin* (Ice), *shush* (Bear), *wol-la-chee* (Ant), *moasi* (Cat), *lin* (Horse), *yeh-hes* (Itch): S-U-R-I-B-A-C-H-I. Working in a different medium altogether, Associated Press photographer Joe Rosenthal climbed up on some rocks and snapped a photograph of the Suribachi flag-raising that was destined to become one of the most famous images of the war and the inspiration for the Marine Corps monument near Arlington National Cemetery.[32]

Taking Suribachi did not end the fighting on Iwo Jima. The battle

32. *New York Times*, February 1, 1998, 21.

ground on for another month, with unmatched barbarity. Japanese soldiers stubbornly refused to surrender. Many died the most hideous of deaths, incinerated by flamethrowers that jetted burning gasoline into their bunkers. When the fighting ended at last in late March, only a few hundred Japanese, mostly wounded, had allowed themselves to be taken prisoner. More than twenty thousand had perished, along with nearly six thousand U.S. marines. Another seventeen thousand marines had been wounded. Courage in battle, it has been said, consists in the desire to show other men that one has it. On Iwo Jima, many Americans showed courage above and beyond the call of duty. On a single day, five marines in the 5th Marine Division earned the Congressional Medal of Honor. "Among the Americans who served on Iwo Island," Nimitz wrote, "uncommon valor was a common virtue."[33]

More uncommon valor was needed just a month later, on the island of Okinawa, the largest in the Ryukyu chain. Commodore Matthew C. Perry had visited Okinawa in 1853, during the course of his historic voyage that ended two centuries of Japan's studied isolation from the rest of the world. Okinawa had been a Japanese prefecture since 1879. Though its indigenous people were racially distinct from the Japanese, Tokyo considered Okinawa part of its heartland. It lay less than 350 miles south of the home islands. In American hands it could provide close-in airbases for attacks on Japan and could serve as a staging area for the massive amphibious assault on the southern Japanese island of Kyushu that was scheduled for the autumn of 1945.

On the Easter Sunday morning of April 1, 1945, standing on the crest of Mt. Shuri at Okinawa's southern end, Colonel Hiromichi Yahara peered through his binoculars across the island's rolling green hills planted to sweet potatoes and sugarcane. Far below him he could see a thousand American landing craft disembarking two army and two marine divisions. It seemed "as if the sea itself were advancing with a great roar," thought Yahara. Scarcely a single Japanese bullet greeted the invaders. "He who wields power is unperturbed," Yahara serenely reflected. He and the seventy-seven thousand other Japanese defenders of Okinawa, along with twenty thousand Okinawan militiamen, intended to let the Americans advance inland, then wear them down in a prolonged battle of attrition, as Yamashita had done to MacArthur on Luzon. Their power was in their spirit, in their fealty to Bushido and their devotion to the emperor. The Japanese on Okinawa knew that their ultimate

33. Spector, 503.

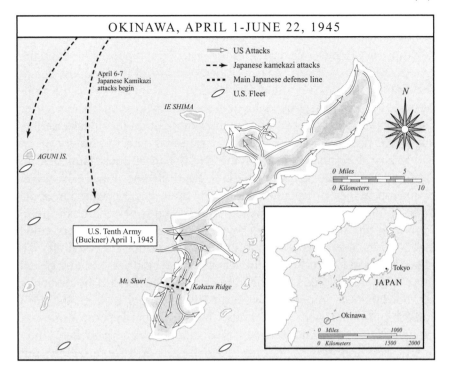

OKINAWA, APRIL 1-JUNE 22, 1945

defeat was inevitable. Their goal was to buy time to prepare the defense of the home islands and to inflict the kind of damage that might even yet induce the United States to sue for a compromise peace. They had built elaborate fortifications into the limestone ridges and rocky escarpments that belted the island's southern end. In that bristling redoubt they would fight to the last cartridge, and then die. They had limited munitions, no hope for reinforcements, and no effective long-range weapons against the Americans' terrifying tank-mounted flamethrowers. But they had volunteers who would serve as human bazookas, strapping twenty-two-pound satchel charges to their bodies and throwing themselves on a tank's hull or under its treads.[34]

As Yahara watched, the Americans kept coming, fifty thousand strong by evening, with nearly three times that number to follow in the succeeding days. General Simon Bolivar Buckner's invasion force rivaled Eisenhower's at Normandy in size. As the American troops felt their way forward and still met no resistance, Admiral Turner radioed to Nimitz:

34. Hiromichi Yahara, *The Battle for Okinawa* (New York: John Wiley and Sons, 1995), xi, xii, 12–13.

"I may be crazy but it looks like the Japanese have quit the war, at least in this sector." Nimitz replied: "Delete all after 'crazy.' "[35]

Nimitz was right. Five days after the virtually unopposed landing, the Americans ran up against Kakazu Ridge, the first of the Japanese defensive lines. As the marines and GIs tried to claw their way up the near-vertical 250-foot-cliffs, the defenders fought back with whatever they had. They dropped buckets of human excrement on the attackers clinging to the rock faces below them and grappled with the Americans in hand-to-hand combat. On the same day, Japanese fliers launched an enormous kamikaze attack on the U.S. fleet offshore. For weeks, waves of suicide planes in squadrons of up to three hundred aircraft, some three thousand sorties in all, defied steel blizzards of antiaircraft fire to zero in on the American ships. They sank 36, damaged 368 others, killed 4,900 sailors, wounded 4,824 more. Aboard the ships anchored off Okinawa, a correspondent wrote, the terror of the kamikaze onslaught "sent some men into hysteria, insanity, breakdown." In an equally desperate act, the Japanese Imperial Navy sortied the pride of its fleet, the great battleship *Yamato*, with only enough fuel in its bunkers for a one-way trip to Okinawa. Its mission was to disrupt the American fleet, then beach itself and employ its huge 18-inch-guns as a shore battery. But the *Yamato* had scarcely exited the Inland Sea when it was chased down by American planes and sunk on April 7.[36]

On April 12 the Japanese garrison on Okinawa briefly rejoiced at the news of Franklin Roosevelt's death. Their celebration was short-lived. The sheer weight of American men and firepower was taking a gruesome toll. The Americans improvised what the Japanese called "horse-mounting" attacks, placing themselves above and astride the mouth of a fortified cave, dropping drums of napalm into the cave entrance, igniting them with grenades or tracer bullets, then shooting all who fled to escape death by fire or suffocation. To avoid those fates, Japanese soldiers by the thousands retreated deep into the limestone caverns and killed themselves with grenades and cyanide injections. Piles of dead bodies putrefied in the dank caves. "Even the demons of the world would mourn at this sight," Yahara wrote.

Japanese staff officers, sometimes standing in waist-high water from underground flooding, took stock of the dwindling stores in their fetid labyrinths with the help of the most ancient of calculators, an abacus.

35. Spector, 534.
36. Spector, 539.

The Americans meanwhile deployed the most modern of technologies and the most abundant of arsenals against them. Radar-directed U.S. naval gunfire and aerial bombardment shook the very mountains, while flamethrowing tanks spewed burning tongues of jellied gasoline into the Japanese fortifications. In early June what was left of the Japanese garrison tried to mount a counterattack. Some six thousand men, armed only with sidearms and bamboo spears, *banzai*ed forward. They encountered "millions of shells from the enemy's formidable fleet, planes, and tanks," Yahara recorded. "All vanished like the morning dew."[37]

Late in June the Japanese commander on Okinawa, General Mitsuru Ushijima, ordered an assistant to behead him after he had thrust the ritual hara-kiri dagger into his own abdomen. Before the general died, one of his staff officers took up a writing brush, dipped it in red ink, and formed the Kanji characters that composed Ushijima's last directive to his few surviving soldiers: "Every man in these fortifications will follow his superior officer's order and fight to the end for the sake of the motherland. . . . Do not suffer the shame of being taken prisoner."[38]

Few did. When the battle officially ended on June 22, only some 7,000 Japanese of the original complement of 77,000 remained alive. The fighting had also killed over 100,000 Okinawan civilians. The Americans suffered 7,613 killed or missing, 31,807 wounded, and 26,211 non-battle casualties on the island, a nearly 35 percent casualty rate, in addition to the nearly 5,000 who died and 4,824 who were wounded at sea. Among the dead were Buckner, his chest sundered by a Japanese shell fragment, as well as the celebrated war correspondent Ernie Pyle, felled by a sniper's bullet. The awful carnage on Okinawa, like that on Iwo Jima, weighed heavily on the minds of American policymakers as they now contemplated the war's endgame.

President Truman met with the Joint Chiefs of Staff on June 18 to discuss the landing on Kyushu scheduled for November, code-named Olympic. Every man in the room expected the Japanese to fight with unyielding ferocity to defend their home islands. Truman pressed the chiefs for an estimate of just how bloody the last battle would be. The record is confused as to precisely what they answered. According to one account, Marshall projected losses that "should not exceed the price we have paid for Luzon"—some 31,000 casualties. Other sources claim that Marshall estimated "more than 63,000." Extrapolating from Okinawa's

37. Yahara, *Battle for Okinawa*, 96, 130, 135.
38. Yahara, *Battle for Okinawa*, 134.

35 percent casualty rate, Leahy figured that as many as 268,000 Americans would end up dead or injured in the projected invasion force of some 766,000. Leahy also expressed his "fear . . . that our insistence on unconditional surrender would result only in making the Japanese desperate and thereby increase our casualty lists. He did not think that this was at all necessary." Assistant Secretary of War John J. McCloy seconded that idea. "We ought to have our heads examined," he said, "if we don't explore some other method by which we can terminate this war than just by another conventional attack and landing." McCloy named two specific "other methods": modifying the unconditional-surrender formula and/or giving the Japanese a warning about the atomic bomb. The military chiefs swiftly scotched the latter proposal, arguing that the bomb was as yet untested. But McCloy had raised some intriguing possibilities: that the bomb, if successful, might make invasion unnecessary; and that a change in the unconditional-surrender doctrine might make the bomb unnecessary. Both ideas remained for the moment ill-defined and unsupported by the critical decision makers. Truman gave his approval to Olympic. But he hoped, said the president, "that there was a possibility of preventing an Okinawa from one end of Japan to the other."[39]

ON OKINAWA, three Japanese divisions had stood up to an American force twice that size for nearly a hundred days. As many as fourteen Japanese divisions waited on Kyushu, more than 350,000 soldiers. Japan had well over two million men under arms throughout its home islands, plus up to four million reservists, and had husbanded more than five thousand kamikaze aircraft for a last-ditch defense. If Olympic came to pass, the butcher's bill would surely be high. The bill for Coronet, the code name for the still larger invasion of the main Japanese island of Honshu contemplated for the spring of 1946, threatened to be higher still. Yet some leaders in Tokyo, like Truman in Washington, were also hoping to avoid an American invasion.

When MacArthur had landed on Luzon in January 1945, the Marquis Koichi Kido, lord keeper of the privy seal, Emperor Hirohito's confidant and a powerful insider in the tensely muted world of Japanese politics, had concluded that Japan's defeat was inevitable. Japan's *sur-*

39. Spector, 543; *FRUS: The Conference of Berlin (The Potsdam Conference), 1945* 1: 903–10; Leahy, *I Was There*, 384; Kai Bird, *The Chairman: John J. McCloy and the Making of the American Establishment* (New York: Simon and Schuster, 1992), 246.

render, however, was another matter. It remained scarcely thinkable and absolutely unutterable. In his pursuit of peace, Kido dared not act openly. Kuniaki Koiso, an army general, was still premier. The war and navy ministers continued to hold any imaginable Japanese cabinet hostage to their oft-proclaimed pledge to fight to the last corpuscle of blood. Kido therefore quietly organized a series of discreet visitations to the Imperial Palace in January and February by several like-minded *jushin*, or senior statesmen, former premiers who served as informal advisers to the emperor. Tentatively, obliquely, clandestinely, they began to explore with Emperor Hirohito the possibility of ending the war by means of negotiation.

The American landings on Okinawa brought down Koiso's government on April 5. That same day, the entire group of *jushin*, including Tojo, "the Razor," convened in the imperial audience chamber to select a new premier, presumably one who would somehow bring the war to a conclusion. But how? By a bloody Armageddon that would extinguish the twenty-six-hundred-year-old Japanese nation in a homicidal finale? By a ferocious finish-fight to wrest some last concessions from the Americans? By submitting to unconditional surrender? The army and navy leaders still wielded formidable power, and they inclined to one or the other of the first two options. Incredibly, Tojo had even exclaimed to the emperor just weeks earlier—after Saipan, after the Battle of the Philippine Sea, after Leyte Gulf and MacArthur's invasion of the Philippines, after Iwo Jima—that "with determination, we can win!" Now he reminded the senior statesmen that the army could still "look the other way," thereby breaking any cabinet it did not control.[40]

The *jushin* finally settled on seventy-seven-year-old Admiral Baron Kantaro Suzuki. He was no stranger to intrigue, nor to the wrath of the militarists. He walked with a limp from the four bullets that ultranationalist army officers had pumped into his body during an attempted coup in 1936. Suzuki selected Shigenori Togo, foreign minister at the war's outbreak, a man who had been skeptical about the Pearl Harbor attack and who had had the courage to resign in protest from Tojo's cabinet, to return to his old post. Kido, Suzuki, and Togo, with the quiet approval of Hirohito (constrained by his status as constitutional monarch from playing an overtly directive role), set out to explore various roads toward peace. The chief obstacle they faced, writes historian Robert J.

40. Robert J. C. Butow, *Japan's Decision to Surrender* (Stanford: Stanford University Press, 1954), 47, 61.

C. Butow, was "the crushing control exerted by the militarists over all forms of national life and thought."[41]

On June 8, while the fighting still raged on Okinawa, the military demonstrated once again their ability to dictate Japan's course. In the presence of the emperor, who characteristically said not a word, senior government officials formally affirmed their "Fundamental Policy": "[W]e shall . . . prosecute the war to the bitter end in order to uphold the national polity (*Kokutai*), protect the imperial land, and accomplish the objectives for which we went to war." This was a decision to commit national suicide, paralleling the mass suicides at Saipan's Marpi Point and in the caves on Okinawa.[42]

On June 22, the day the Okinawa campaign officially ended, Hirohito, at Kido's urging, took the unusual step of summoning his government leaders back to the Imperial Palace. Although the decision of June 8 had committed Japan "to the bitter end," said the diffident monarch, choosing his words carefully, had the government given any thought to other methods of ending the war? Yes, said Togo, there was a possibility that Japan might approach the Soviet Union to use its good offices to negotiate a cease-fire. Togo suggested that Fumimaro Konoye, Japan's last civilian prime minister, the man who had tried in vain to meet with Franklin Roosevelt to work out a *modus vivendi* in late 1941, be sent to Moscow to open negotiations. Togo emphasized that Konoye's instructions would preclude any offer of *unconditional* surrender. Any formula for capitulation must include guarantees that the person and institution of the emperor would be preserved and that the precious, millenia-old *Kokutai* would be left undisturbed. With luck, Japan might hold out for other conditions as well: no military occupation of the homeland, no international trials of alleged war criminals, and retention of some of its conquered territories.

In Washington, Truman was meanwhile preparing for his own discussions with the Russians. Ten days after addressing the closing session of the first United Nations conference in San Francisco's Opera House on June 26, he boarded the cruiser *Augusta*, bound for two weeks of talks with British and Soviet leaders in the miraculously undamaged Berlin suburb of Potsdam. Late in the morning of July 16, Churchill came to Truman's lakeside residence near Potsdam to meet the new president for the first time. "He gave me a lot of hooey about how great

41. Butow, *Japan's Decision*, 80.
42. Butow, *Japan's Decision*, 99–100, n. 69.

my country is and how he loved Roosevelt and how he intended to love me etc. etc.," Truman wrote in his diary. "I am sure we can get along if he doesn't try to give me too much soft soap." The question was soon moot. In the midst of the Potsdam Conference, Churchill received word that the British elections had turned him out of office. On July 28 Clement Atlee took the British prime minister's seat at the conference table.

In the afternoon of July 16, Truman drove by car through Berlin. He had never seen such devastation. The Nazi capital's "absolute ruin" put him in mind of other conquered cities and other conquerors. "I thought of Carthage, Baalbek, Jerusalem, Rome," he noted in his diary, and of "Scipio . . . Sherman, Jenghis Khan, Alexander, Darius the Great." Even as he wrote those words, science was about to bestow upon Truman himself a destructive power that would dwarf all of theirs combined.[43]

Back in his lakeside mansion on the evening of July 16, Truman received a top-secret telegram from Washington: "Operated on this morning. Diagnosis not yet complete but results seem satisfactory and already exceed expectations." The president understood: hours earlier, scientists in the remote Sonoran desert near Alamogordo, New Mexico, had imploded a plutonium sphere the size of an orange and successfully detonated history's first nuclear explosion.[44]

Stimson and General Leslie Groves had given Truman his first extensive briefing about the Manhattan Project just a dozen weeks earlier, on April 25. "Within four months we shall in all probability have completed the most terrifying weapon ever known in human history," Stimson had read from a carefully prepared memorandum, "one bomb of which could destroy a whole city." The conversation lasted just forty-five minutes. None of the three men expressed any doubt that the bomb should be used as soon as it was ready.

In the weeks thereafter, various groups of Washington policymakers and atomic scientists discussed the implications of the Manhattan Project's imminent success. Given the bomb's momentous implications, and in light of all the subsequent controversy about its use, it is striking how few of those men, and virtually none in the inner circle of decision-making, seriously contemplated not dropping it.

Seated amidst the brilliant foliage of a Hyde Park autumn, Roosevelt and Churchill had agreed on September 19, 1944, that the new atomic

43. Robert H. Ferrell, ed., *Off the Record: The Private Papers of Harry S. Truman* (New York: Harper and Row, 1980), 51, 52.
44. *FRUS: Berlin (Potsdam)* 2:1360.

weapon, if available in time, "might perhaps, *after mature consideration*, be used against the Japanese, who should be warned that this bombardment will be repeated until they surrender." (In the same agreement, Churchill and Roosevelt took steps to continue to keep the Manhattan Project a secret from their Soviet ally. There must be "no leakage of information," they ordered, "particularly to the Russians.") But the deliberate mood of that now distant autumn had long since given way to the frantic tempo of the war's last spring. Amidst the gathering clamor to end the bloodshed, and in the chaotic circumstances of Truman's sudden ascension to the presidency, "mature consideration" proved chimerical. History had its own momentum, and it tolerated no delay.[45]

On May 1 Stimson named an Interim Committee of eight civilian officials, supplemented by a four-member Scientific Panel, to advise him about the bomb. Though Stimson later described the Interim Committee as having "carefully considered such alternatives as a detailed advance warning or a demonstration in some uninhabited area," in fact the committee did no such thing during its brief lifetime. To a degree that later generations would find remarkable, the advent of the nuclear age was heralded by little fanfare and even less formal deliberation. Events were in the saddle, and they rode men hard.[46]

Significantly, Truman at first neglected to appoint his own personal representative to the Interim Committee, an assignment that eventually fell, more or less by default, to James F. Byrnes, soon to become secretary of state. Even more telling, Stimson's charge to the Committee asked principally for advice about postwar controls on nuclear weaponry, and in that connection about *how*, but not *whether*, the bomb should be employed against Japan. "It seemed to be a foregone conclusion," one Scientific Panel member later wrote, "that the bomb would be

45. Richard Rhodes, *The Making of the Atomic Bomb* (New York: Simon and Schuster, 1986), 624; *FRUS: Quebec*, 492–93 (emphasis added).
46. Stimson's co-author, McGeorge Bundy, later wrote: "After the war Colonel Stimson, with the fervor of a great advocate and with me as his scribe, wrote an article [Stimson's famous piece, "The Decision to Use the Bomb," in the February 1947 edition of *Harper's*] intended to demonstrate that the bomb was not used without a searching consideration of alternatives. That some effort was made, and that Stimson was its linchpin, is clear. That it was as long or wide or deep as the subject deserved now seems to me most doubtful." Bundy, *Danger and Survival: Choices about the Bomb in the First Fifty Years* (New York: Random House, 1988), 92–93. Indeed, Bundy's account calls into question whether it is even proper to use the word "decision" in explaining the sequence of events that led to Hiroshima and Nagasaki.

used." Only briefly and informally, during a lunch break in the Pentagon dining room at their meeting on May 31, did several members of
the Interim Committee discuss "some striking but harmless demonstration of the bomb's power before using it in a manner that would cause
great loss of life." As the official historians describe it:

> For perhaps ten minutes, the proposition was the subject of general
> discussion. Oppenheimer could think of no demonstration sufficiently
> spectacular to convince the Japanese that further resistance was futile.
> Other objections came to mind. The bomb might be a dud. The
> Japanese might shoot down the delivery plane or bring American pris-
> oners into the test area. If the demonstration failed to bring surrender,
> the chance of administering the maximum surprise shock would be
> lost. Besides, would the bomb cause any greater loss of life than the
> fire raids that had burned out Tokyo?

So much for Stimson's "careful consideration." The following day,
the Interim Committee made its formal recommendation: "that the
bomb should be used against Japan as soon as possible; that it be used
on a war plant surrounded by workers' homes; and that it be used without prior warning."[47]

Some of the scientists at work on the Manhattan Project, particularly
those in Chicago, tried to reopen the question of a demonstration on
June 12. They submitted to Stimson's deputy, George L. Harrison, a
document authored mainly by Leo Szilard but named for the emigré
physicist James Franck. Harrison referred the Franck Report to the Scientific Panel. Truman never saw it. The panel's scientists reported back
four days later that "we can propose no technical demonstration likely
to bring an end to the war; we see no acceptable alternative to direct
military use."[48]

That essentially settled the matter. The "decision" to use the bomb
might better be described as a series of decisions not to disturb the
momentum of a process that was more than three years old by the spring
of 1945 and was rapidly building toward its all but inevitable climax. In
a profound sense, the determination to use the bomb at the earliest
possible date had been implicit in the original decision to build it at

47. Richard G. Hewlett and Oscar E. Anderson Jr., *The New World, 1939–1946* (Uni-
    versity Park: Pennsylvania University Press, 1962), 358; Martin J. Sherwin, *A World
    Destroyed: The Atomic Bomb and the Grand Alliance* (New York: Knopf, 1975), 207,
    209.
48. Sherwin, *World Destroyed*, app. M, 305.

the fastest possible speed. "Let there be no mistake about it," Truman later wrote. "I regarded the bomb as a military weapon and never had any doubt that it should be used." Winston Churchill put it this way: "The historic fact remains, and must be judged in the after-time, that the decision whether or not to use the atomic bomb to compel the surrender of Japan was never even an issue. There was unanimous, automatic, unquestioned agreement around our table; nor did I ever hear the slightest suggestion that we should do otherwise."[49]

As Truman prepared to depart for the Potsdam Conference, two questions remained unresolved: what, if anything, to tell the Russians about the atomic project, and whether there should be any modification of the unconditional-surrender formula with respect to Japan. To the latter question, many American policymakers gave an affirmative answer. Leahy and McCloy had so recommended in the fateful White House meeting of June 18. Former ambassador to Japan Joseph Grew was also urging Truman to offer the Japanese assurances about the future of the emperor. Stimson was edging close to a similar recommendation. He summed up his thinking in a detailed memorandum to Truman on July 2. Contrary to much popular misconception, Stimson argued, "I believe Japan *is* susceptible to reason. . . . Japan is not a nation composed wholly of mad fanatics of an entirely different mentality from ours." The shock of an atomic attack, Stimson reasoned, would "carry convincing proof of our power to destroy the Empire," thereby allowing the "liberal leaders" in Japan to overcome the militarists and bid for peace. The new nuclear weapon thus offered Truman a possible alternative to the dreaded invasion that would confront "a last ditch defense such as has been made on Iwo Jima and Okinawa." And to maximize the possibility that the shock of the bomb might induce the Japanese to surrender, Stimson recommended that "we should add [to the peace terms] that we do not exclude a constitutional monarchy under her present dynasty." Such a guarantee might compromise the unconditional-surrender principle but "would substantially add to the chances of acceptance." Looking to the shape of the postwar world, Stimson also overruled Groves and struck the ancient capital of Kyoto, a shrine of Japanese art and culture, from the roster of proposed targets. The "bitterness which would be caused by such a wanton act might make it impossible during the long postwar period to reconcile the Japanese to

49. Harry S. Truman, *Memoirs: Year of Decisions* (Garden City, N.Y.: Doubleday, 1955), 419; Churchill 6:553.

us in that area rather than to the Russians," Stimson explained. Four other cities—Kokura, Niigata, Hiroshima, and Nagasaki—stayed on the list.[50]

At Potsdam on July 17 Truman met Josef Stalin for the first time. The diminutive president was delighted to discover that the legendary Stalin was just "a little bit of a squirt." For the next several days, discussion among the Big Three rambled tediously, at times rancorously, over issues that had been intractable at Yalta and proved no more tractable now, especially reparations from Germany and the composition of the Polish government. It was the new president's diplomatic baptism. He was understandably edgy, unsure of himself, and not a little frustrated. "I was so scared I didn't know whether things were going according to Hoyle or not," Truman wrote to his wife. "I'm not going to stay around this terrible place all summer just to listen to speeches. I'll go home to the Senate for that," he complained to his diary. Truman wanted to appear resolute, in command, a worthy and credible successor to the fallen Roosevelt. "I don't want just to discuss, I want to decide," he announced at the first plenary session on July 17. "You want something in the bag each day," Churchill responded.[51]

Truman got little decided at Potsdam, even though he had what he called "some dynamite" in his bag—his knowledge of the successful test at Alamogordo. Franklin Roosevelt, diplomatic virtuoso that he was, may have had some fine scheme deep within his mind for laying his nuclear trump card on the table when the moment came for a showdown with Stalin. But as with so much in the life of that enigmatic president, the record does not reveal precisely what his scheme was. He surely never shared it with his last vice-president. As a consequence, Truman at Potsdam appeared uncertain about how to make diplomatic use of America's new atomic asset, or even what precise valuation to put on it. At first he seemed to have scant conception that the bomb might render unnecessary a Soviet declaration of war against Japan—the prize for which Roosevelt had been willing to pay so much, in Chinese coin, at Yalta. When Stalin reiterated to Truman his promise to "be in the Jap War on August 15th," Truman exulted to his diary in the argot he had learned as a Doughboy: "Fini Japs when that comes about." "I've gotten

50. Henry L. Stimson, "The Decision to Drop the Bomb," *Harper's Magazine*, February 1947, 97–107; and Stimson and McGeorge Bundy, *On Active Service in Peace and War* (New York: Harper and Brothers, 1948), 617; Stimson Diary, July 24, 1945.

51. McCullough, *Truman*, 417, 424; Ferrell, *Off the Record*, 54; FRUS: *Berlin (Potsdam)* 2:63.

what I came for," he wrote to his wife; "Stalin goes to war August 15 with no strings on it. . . . [W]e'll end the war a year sooner now, and think of the kids who won't be killed!" Yet the following day he wrote: "Believe Japs will fold up before Russia comes in. I am sure they will when Manhattan appears over their homeland. I shall inform Stalin about it at an opportune time."[52]

The opportune time, such as it was, soon arrived. As another contentious session was ending late in the afternoon of July 24, Truman nonchalantly walked up to Stalin and his interpreter. "I casually mentioned to Stalin that we had a new weapon of unusual destructive force," Truman recalled. "The Russian premier showed no special interest. All he said was that he was glad to hear it and hoped we would make 'good use of it against the Japanese.' " It was a singularly undramatic moment.

52. McCullough, *Truman*, 424; Ferrell, *Off the Record*, 53, 54. Some historians, notably Gar Alperovitz in *The Decision to Use the Atomic Bomb and the Architecture of an American Myth* (New York: Knopf, 1995) have suggested that Truman's swelling confidence about the bomb led him to try to delay or prevent Russian entry into the war. It was this anti-Soviet strategy, so the argument goes, that precluded the consideration of time-consuming alternative methods of ending the war. The evidence does suggest that Byrnes did some thinking along these lines. Churchill recorded at Potsdam: "It is quite clear that the United States do not at the present time desire Russian participation in the war against Japan." *FRUS Berlin (Potsdam)* 2:276. But a loss of American interest in the Soviet declaration of war scarcely amounts to a calculated strategy for using the bomb as an instrument of diplomacy against the Soviets or for accelerating the scheduled drops on Hiroshima and Nagasaki. American policy regarding the relation of the bomb to the Russian presence in Asia remained uncoordinated and episodic. Byrnes himself said that he "had hoped that we could finish up with the Japanese *without* participation by the Russians, but the atmosphere of the conference, and the attitude of the Russians made it *inevitable* that Russia come in." David Robertson, *Sly and Able: A Political Biography of James F. Byrnes* (New York: Norton, 1994), 427, emphasis added. In McGeorge Bundy's trenchant conclusion, "The assertion [that a desire to impress the Russians with the power of the bomb was a major factor in the decision to use it] is false, and the evidence to support it rests on inferences so stretched as to be a discredit both to the judgment of those who have argued in this fashion and the credulity of those who have accepted such arguments . . . assuming conspiracy when the reality is only confusion." Bundy, *Danger and Survival*, 88, 651; see also Barton J. Bernstein, "The Atomic Bomb and American Foreign Policy, 1941–1945: An Historiographical Controversy," *Peace and Change* 2 (Spring 1974): 1–16; and Bernstein, "The Atomic Bomb and American Foreign Policy: The Route to Hiroshima," in Bernstein, ed., *The Atomic Bomb: The Critical Issues* (Boston: Little, Brown, 1976), 94–120.

Neither man gave any sign that he appreciated the potential of the "new weapon" to alter the course of history.[53]

It remained to decide what to say to the Japanese, especially about the role of the emperor, as Stimson and others were urging. The Americans knew that at least some Japanese officials were trying to arrange a cease-fire. Rumors of Japanese peace initiatives had been flying for a month. They had been discussed on the floor of the U.S. Senate and in the pages of American newspapers. Stalin told Truman on July 28 what the American president already knew from intercepted Japanese cables—that Konoye was asking to come to Moscow. (His answer to the Japanese would be negative, Stalin said, and Konoye never did get to Moscow.) But the Japanese feelers thus far were neither unambiguously official nor signs of willingness to submit to unconditional surrender. Konoye was not a member of the Suzuki cabinet. Who could be sure whether he represented the Tokyo government or merely some Japanese political faction? What was more, Byrnes read an intercepted cable concerning the Konoye mission that declared: "With regard to unconditional surrender, we are unable to consent to it under any circumstances whatsoever."

Byrnes, a southerner, understood the difference between defeat and surrender. He knew that almost two years had elapsed between Gettysburg and Appomattox. He may well have remembered the futility of Lincoln's parley with Confederate negotiators at Hampton Roads in February 1865, when armistice negotiations foundered on the Confederacy's demand to be recognized as an independent state. Now was no time to prolong the killing while the diplomats niggled, nor was it a time to appear weak by modifying America's peace terms. Unconditional surrender had been promulgated by Roosevelt at Casablanca in January 1943 and reaffirmed at Cairo almost a year later, with special reference to Japan. The phrase had long since taken on the character of a political shibboleth, a test of toughness and resolve. When Truman had given his first address as president to Congress on April 16, the packed chamber rose thunderously to its feet when he uttered the words "unconditional surrender." The president would be "crucified," said Byrnes, if he backed off from that commitment now. Cordell Hull advised Byrnes that "terrible political repercussions would follow in the U.S." if the unconditional-surrender formula were abandoned at this climactic

53. Truman, *Year of Decision*, 416.

moment. Anything less than unconditional surrender would be branded with that vilest of epithets, "appeasement." Byrnes accordingly repudiated the suggestions of Leahy, McCloy, Grew, and Stimson. He deleted all references to preserving the emperor from the draft of what was soon to be known as the Potsdam Proclamation. Truman offered no dissent. As finally issued on July 26 over the signatures of Truman, Churchill, and Chiang, who wired his concurrence, the proclamation called for "the unconditional surrender of all the Japanese armed forces" and warned: "The alternative for Japan is prompt and utter destruction."

In Tokyo, Suzuki and Togo sought desperately for a response that would reconcile their own inclination to accept the terms of the proclamation and the cry of the militarists to dismiss it out of hand. The compromise term they finally chose was *mokusatsu,* a picturesque word that meant "to ignore" or "to withhold comment" but could also be construed as "kill with contempt." The Americans interpreted *mokusatsu* as outright rejection, tinged with brazen defiance. The nuclear clock now ticked off its last few beats.[54]

THE POTSDAM PROCLAMATION was about to carry the United States across a forbidding military threshold, one that marked the opening of a new chapter in the history of warfare and diplomacy. But by August 1945 the atomic bombs hardly represented a moral novelty. The moral rules that had once stayed men's hands from taking up weapons of mass destruction against noncombatants had long since been violently breached in World War II, first in the aerial attacks on European cities, then even more wantonly in the systematic firebombing of Japan.

On January 7, 1945, Air Force General Curtis LeMay had arrived on Guam to take command of the 21st Bomber Command. He was a gruff, stocky man, one of the youngest generals in the army. He chewed perpetually on a cigar butt to mask his Bell's palsy, a nerve disorder that made the right corner of his mouth droop, the result of flying so many high-altitude bombing missions over Europe in unheated and unpressurized B-17s. LeMay had led the disastrous raid against Regensburg in 1943 but had long since abandoned the idea of "precision" bombing in favor of terror attacks on civilians. "I'll tell you what war is about," he once said, "You've got to kill people, and when you've killed enough they stop fighting." Cheated out of a conclusive demonstration of the

54. Robertson, *Sly and Able,* 431; *FRUS: Berlin (Potsdam),* 2:1267, 1476; Butow, *Japan's Decision,* 147.

war-winning power of aerial bombardment in Europe, LeMay was determined to vindicate his service, and the Douhetian doctrine of "strategic" warfare, in the fight against Japan.[55]

LeMay deployed two intimidating new technologies against Japan's highly flammable cities, where most people lived in wooden houses. The first was a fiendishly efficient six-pound incendiary bomblet developed by Standard Oil chemists—the M-69 projectile, which spewed burning gelatinized gasoline that stuck to its targets and was virtually inextinguishable by conventional means. The second was the B-29 Superfortress, an awesome specimen of American engineering prowess and mass-production techniques. The Boeing Corporation had won the army air force design competition for a long-range, intercontinental bomber in 1940, and the first production model B-29s were flying by 1943. LeMay had some 350 B-29s in the Marianas in January 1945 and more arriving constantly. They were nearly one hundred feet in length, with a 141-foot wingspan and a three-story-high tail section. They were powered by four twenty-two-hundred-horsepower Wright eighteen-cylinder radial air-cooled magnesium alloy engines, each fitted with two General Electric exhaust-driven turbo-superchargers. The B-29 carried a crew of eleven in its pressurized cabin and a bomb load of up to twenty thousand pounds. It had an operational ceiling over thirty-five thousand feet and a combat range of more than four thousand miles. An onboard computerized central control system allowed for remote firing from its five defensive gun turrets.

LeMay set out at once to perfect the 21st Bomber Command's fire-bombing techniques. To enlarge bomb loads, he stripped all but the tail-turret guns from his B-29s. To avoid the recently discovered jet stream, which foiled some of his earliest raids on Japan, he trained his pilots in low-altitude attacks. He experimented with bombing patterns and with mixes of explosive and incendiary bomb loads. His goal was to create firestorms, like the ones that had consumed Hamburg and Dresden—conflagrations so vast and intense that nothing could survive them, not mere fires but thermal hurricanes that killed by suffocation as well as by heat, as the flames sucked all available oxygen out of the surrounding atmosphere.

After practice runs on Kobe and on a section of Tokyo in February, Lemay launched 334 Superfortresses from the Marianas on the night of March 9. A few minutes after midnight, they began to lay their

---

55. Richard Rhodes, "The General and World War II," *New Yorker*, June 19, 1995, 47ff.

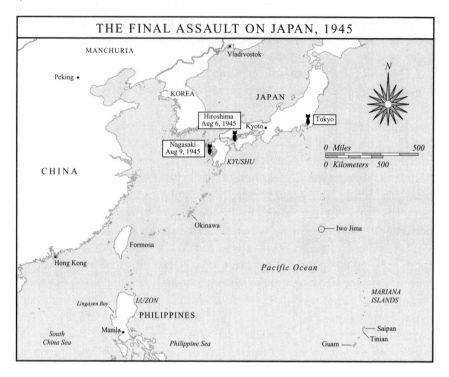

THE FINAL ASSAULT ON JAPAN, 1945

clusters of M-69s over Tokyo, methodically criss-crossing the target zone to create concentric rings of fire that soon merged into a sea of flame. Rising thermal currents buffeted the mile-high B-29s and knocked them about like paper airplanes. When the raiders flew away shortly before 4:00 A.M., they left behind them one million homeless Japanese and nearly ninety thousand dead. The victims died from fire, asphyxiation, and falling buildings. Some boiled to death in super-heated canals and ponds where they had sought refuge from the flames. In the next five months, LeMay's bombers attacked sixty-six of Japan's largest cities, destroying 43 percent of their built-up areas. They dehoused more than 8 million people, killed as many as 900,000, and injured up to 1.3 million more. Hiroshima and Nagasaki survived to be atomic-bombed only because LeMay's superiors removed them from his target list.[56]

Japan meanwhile was attempting fire raids of its own against its Amer-

56. Ronald Schaffer, *Wings of Judgment: American Bombing in World War II* (New York: Oxford University Press, 1985), 128ff.; Craven and Cate 5:614.

ican enemy. Using the same jet stream that had at first frustrated LeMay, Japanese technicians had begun in November 1944 to loft high-altitude balloons designed to carry small incendiary bombs across the broad Pacific and drop them on the western United States. Japanese schoolgirls assembled the balloons in large indoor spaces like sumo wrestling arenas, theaters, and music halls. They painstakingly laminated the four-ply mulberry paper to form the balloons' skin, and sealed the seams of each balloon's six hundred joined panels with a potato-flour paste that many of the hungry children surreptitiously stole and ate. Beneath the balloon's thirty-two-foot-diameter inflated sphere, technicians suspended a small gondola basket containing the incendiary device and ringed by thirty-two sandbags. With the help of a simple altimeter, a battery-powered mechanism released hydrogen from the balloon at thirty-eight thousand feet and detonated a small explosive to jettison two counter-balanced sandbags at thirty thousand feet, keeping the balloon stable within the jet stream's vertical envelope through sixteen precisely calculated transpacific up-and-down cycles. When the last sandbag fell, a demolition charge ignited and detached the incendiary device, presumably over the United States.

While LeMay's B-29s were torching the cities of Japan in the winter of 1945, ninety-three hundred Japanese balloons were drifting mutely eastward in the jet stream's embrace. Those that made it across the Pacific dropped their fiery loads to earth all across North America, from the Yukon Territory to Baja California, though most landed in the northwestern corner of the United States. Some alarmed American officials worried that the balloons might be instruments of germ warfare. But though Japan had once tried such a tactic against Russian troops, and the Imperial Army's infamous Unit 731 conducted sadistic biological warfare experiments at a secret station in Manchuria, these balloons were designed to spread fire, not contagion. They ignited some minor forest fires, many of them promptly extinguished by the "Triple Nickels," the 555th Negro Parachute Infantry Battalion, consigned to duty as smoke-jumpers. A voluntary American news blackout denied the Japanese any confirmation that the balloons had actually completed their journey. As Japan's hydrogen stocks dwindled, the last balloons were launched in April 1945. A month later, on May 5, the Reverend Archie Mitchell and his wife, Elsie, were leading a Sunday school outing in the woods near Bly, Oregon. While Reverend Mitchell was moving his car, Mrs. Mitchell and five children tugged at a strange object they had found in the underbrush. The balloon bomb exploded, killing her and all the children. The six victims were the only mainland American casualties of the war.[57]

The Japanese fire raids were no match for what the Americans could do. While the schoolgirls of Japan had been gluing their balloon panels together in sumo arenas, the women of Omaha, Nebraska, were riveting together the fuselages of B-29s on the assembly line of the Glenn L. Martin aircraft plant. While Japanese technicians were rigging up the first balloon gondolas on Ninety-nine League Beach east of Tokyo, Air Force Colonel Paul Tibbets went to Omaha to handpick B-29 Number 82 off the Martin production line. He soon renamed it after his mother, *Enola Gay*. As the spent Japanese balloons were soughing down into the western American fir forests, Tibbets was leading his specially selected 509th Composite Group in dummy bomb drops onto the dry bed of prehistoric Lake Bonneville at Wendover Field, Utah, practicing an unorthodox 155-degree diving turn after bomb release. Not long after Elsie Mitchell's funeral in Oregon, two sailors at Hunter's Point in San Francisco Bay shouldered a crowbar from which was suspended a lead bucket holding the U-235 bullet for the first combat atomic bomb. They carried it aboard the USS *Indianapolis*, and the heavy cruiser weighed anchor for Tinian, in the Marianas. On August 6, 1945, while thousands of dud balloon-bombs were rotting away harmlessly on the densely wooded slopes of the Oregon and Washington Cascade Range, Tibbets throttled the *Enola Gay* off the runway from Tinian. Its four twenty-two-hundred-horsepower Wright eighteen-cylinder radial air-cooled magnesium alloy engines, each fitted with two General Electric exhaust-driven turbo-superchargers, barely strained under the load of its single bomb.

TRUMAN WAS AT SEA on August 6, returning from Potsdam. When the news from Tinian came over the *Augusta*'s radio, the White House released a prearranged statement: "Sixteen hours ago an American airplane dropped one bomb on Hiroshima. . . . It is an atomic bomb. It is a harnessing of the basic power of the universe." Some Japanese leaders refused to believe what had happened—nearly forty thousand people killed in an instant, a hundred thousand additional dead within days from burns and radiation. Mirroring the astonishment

57. Robert C. Mikesh, *Japan's World War II Balloon Bomb Attacks on North America* (Washington: Smithsonian Institution, 1973); John McPhee, "Balloons of War," *New Yorker*, January 29, 1996, 52–60.

of many Americans at Pearl Harbor, several Japanese scientists thought it was impossible for the United States to have tamed the atom and transported such an unstable explosive all the way across the Pacific. Even if it had, they argued, the Americans could not imaginably have produced enough radioactive material to permit additional atomic bombings, an argument apparently supported by the fact that "conventional" fire raids were meanwhile continuing. Only on August 10, a day after a second nuclear explosion had devastated Nagasaki, eventually killing another seventy thousand people, did Japanese experts agree that their country was under atomic attack and that it might be sustained. By then Suzuki's government had already tendered a surrender offer. It remained to be seen if it would be accepted.[58]

Debate had raged among Japanese officials since the first news reports had come in from Hiroshima. Shortly before midnight on August 8, the Soviet Union declared war on Japan, adding a second shock to the calamity of the atomic bomb. That morning, the Supreme Council for the Direction of the War, the "Big Six," met to discuss the twin crises. They quickly deadlocked. Suzuki, Togo, and the navy minister advocated accepting the Potsdam Declaration, with the sole reservation that the imperial system be maintained. The war minister and the army and navy chiefs of staff held out for three additional conditions: there should be no military occupation of Japan, Japanese armed forces should be allowed to disarm themselves, and any trials of war criminals were to be conducted by Japanese courts. The army chief went so far as to insist that Japan was not yet defeated. "We will be able to destroy the major part of an invading army," he said. The Japanese people would surely fight. Posters were going up all over Tokyo denouncing Kido and the "peace faction" as traitors who should be shot on sight.

As the stalemate continued, word of the Nagasaki bomb arrived. The Big Six adjourned, nothing resolved. The cabinet deadlocked similarly later in the day. Just before midnight, the cabinet and the Supreme Council together entered the air raid shelter under the Imperial Palace grounds for an unprecedented event: a meeting in the emperor's presence at which they were not able to present a unanimous decision. Prime Minister Suzuki apologized to Emperor Hirohito for the embarrassment. The various officials argued their positions. At last Hirohito arose from his chair and spoke: "I swallow my own tears and give my sanction to the

58. *Public Papers of the Presidents of the United States: Harry S. Truman, April 12 to December 31, 1945* (Washington: USGPO, 1961), 93; Butow, *Japan's Decision*, 151.

proposal to accept the Allied proclamation." There would be not four conditions but only one: preservation of the Imperial House.[59]

Palace officials prepared an imperial rescript to announce the decision to the Japanese people. In another unprecedented step, the emperor recorded his surrender announcement for broadcast over the radio. Most Japanese had never heard his voice.

The Japanese surrender offer, relayed through the Swiss government, arrived in Washington on the morning of August 10. Its proviso that "the prerogatives of His Majesty as a Sovereign Ruler" were to remain intact was a sticking point. Byrnes objected that "I cannot understand why now we should go further than we were willing to go at Potsdam when we had no atomic bomb, and Russia was not in the war." Stimson countered that "use of the Emperor must be made in order to save us from a score of bloody Iwo Jimas and Okinawas." A compromise was reached, stating that "the authority of the Emperor and the Japanese Government to rule the state shall be subject to the Supreme Commander of the Allied Powers."[60]

The American response was sufficiently ambiguous that some Japanese officials did not want to accept it. In a second highly unorthodox display of imperial command, Hirohito overruled them on the morning of August 14. That night, some die-hard military officers stormed the Imperial Palace to seize the recording of the surrender announcement, scheduled for broadcast the next day. Others attacked the residences of Suzuki and Kido. All failed. At noon on August 15, the emperor's unfamiliar voice, speaking over the radio in a courtly, archaic Japanese that most of his listeners could scarcely understand, declared Japan's war at an end.

Among the American troops on Okinawa, unconditional jubilation broke out. They fired every available weapon skyward. The subsequent rain of shell fragments killed seven men. Halfway around the world, near Rheims, France, GIs in the 45th Infantry Division, awaiting transfer to the Pacific for the invasion of Honshu, wept with joy. Now they would be going home. "The killing was all going to be over," one of them reflected. "We were going to grow to adulthood after all."[61]

59. Butow, *Japan's Decision*, 163, 176,198–99.
60. Robertson, *Sly and Able*, 434; Stimson Diary, August 10, 1945; Truman, *Year of Decisions*, 429.
61. Kennett, *G.I.*, 225; Paul Fussell, "Thank God for the Atom Bomb," *Guardian*, February 5, 1989, 10.

Epilogue: The World the War Made

We cannot get away from the results of the war.
— Josef Stalin, Potsdam, July 1945

Of the men who had survived the Great War of 1914–18 to lead the major powers into World War II, only one still stood on history's stage by the end of 1945. Roosevelt was dead of natural causes, Hitler and Konoye by their own hands. Churchill had been shunted out of office by a people more weary of sacrifice than warmed by gratitude. Still unsated, Stalin alone remained.[1]

The war with Japan formally concluded on September 2, 1945. Days earlier, the battleship *Missouri* had glided into Tokyo Bay and anchored within cannon-shot of Commodore Matthew C. Perry's moorage of 1853. At dawn on Sunday the second, crewmen set up a table on the *Missouri's* deck and laid out the surrender documents. On a bulkhead above, they displayed the thirty-one-star flag that Perry's flagship, the sidewheeler steam frigate *Mississippi*, had carried into Tokyo Bay nearly a century earlier. High atop the big battleship's flagstaff luffed the forty-eight-star flag that had flown above the Capitol dome in Washington on December 7, 1941.

Shortly before 9:00 A.M., the Japanese delegates arrived, the civilian officials in formal morning clothes, the naval and military officers in dress uniform. A few minutes later General MacArthur and Admirals Nimitz and Halsey stepped onto the deck, dressed simply in open-collar khaki shirts. MacArthur gave a brief speech. He expressed the hope "that from this solemn occasion a better world shall emerge . . . a world founded on faith and understanding." The Japanese officials came

---

1. Rather than face trial as a war criminal, Konoye took cyanide at his Tokyo home on December 16, 1945.

427

forward under the shadow of the *Missouri*'s sixteen-inch guns and put their signatures to the surrender instruments. MacArthur and Nimitz signed for the Americans. One onlooking Japanese diplomat wondered "whether it would have been possible for us, had we been victorious, to embrace the vanquished with a similar magnanimity. Clearly, it would have been different."[2]

America was officially at peace, and so was Japan. Elsewhere in Asia peace remained elusive. The war in that region had been more than a struggle between the United States and Japan, or even between China and Japan. The conflict also marked the penultimate chapter in the history of Western colonialism in Asia that had lasted since the fifteenth century. "It almost seems that the Japs were a necessary evil in order to break down the old colonial system," Franklin Roosevelt had told a journalist in 1942.[3] From that perspective, it might be said that Japan had won the war after all, finishing the work begun with Admiral Togo's victory over the Russians at Tsushima Strait in 1905, a victory that Nagumo had so vividly memorialized when his aircraft carriers descended on Pearl Harbor flying Togo's old battle flag. If a major Japanese war aim had been to evict the Westerners and build "Asia for the Asians," that aim had been accomplished as early as 1942 and was never effectively reversed. The Philippines proceeded on schedule toward independence on July 4, 1946. India wrested its nationhood from Britain in 1947; Ceylon (Sri Lanka) and Burma (Myanmar), in 1948. In other countries, where the old colonial powers tried to reassert their authority, the final chapter of the struggle to rid Asia of Western dominance took longer to write and was often written in blood, but written it was. Rebellion against the reimposition of Dutch rule went on for four years in the East Indies after 1945, until Indonesia established its independence at last in 1949. Malaya slipped the British harness only in 1957. Japan's former colony of Korea remained divided for the remainder of the century, sucking the United States into a second Asian war within half a decade of the ceremony on the *Missouri*'s deck. The French waged a futile struggle to recolonize Indochina until they gave up in 1954, leav-

---

2. Morison, 574–77; Toshikazu Kase, *Journey to the Missouri* (New Haven: Yale University Press, 1950), 13. Halsey's apparent magnanimity was strained. After the ceremony he told reporters that he would "like to have kicked each Jap delegate in the face." James T. Patterson, *Grand Expectations: Postwar America, 1945–1974* (New York: Oxford University Press, 1996), 7.

3. Christopher Thorne, *Allies of a Kind: The United States, Britain, and the War against Japan, 1941–1945* (New York: Oxford University Press, 1978), 728n.

ing a messy legacy that eventually precipitated America's third twentieth-century Asian war in Vietnam.

As for China, whose friendship had been the great goal of American diplomacy before 1941, a friendship deemed so valuable as to set the United States on the collision course with Japan that led to Pearl Harbor, there the results were peculiarly ironic, and not a little bitter. Mao Tse-tung finally defeated Chiang Kai-shek in 1949. The new Communist regime openly declared its hostility to the United States and committed itself to force-marching China into the modern era. Everywhere in Asia it was clear by century's end that World War II had set the stage for the definitive finale of a five-century saga of Western imperial hegemony.

In Europe the end of World War II almost instantly introduced a new era of conflict with a martial name of its own, the Cold War. Of the traditional great European powers, France was humbled, Britain exhausted, Germany demolished and divided. Hitler had brewed a catastrophe so vast that for his own people it seemed to sunder the web of time itself. Germans would call the moment of their surrender on May 8, 1945, *Stunde null* — zero hour, when history's clock must be made to start anew. Stalin closed his fist over eastern Europe and dared the Western powers to break his grip. Counting on the resurgence of traditional American isolationism, he anticipated having a free hand with which to harvest the fruits of victory in the vast domain he had conquered at the price of more than twenty million Soviet dead.

The Americans surprised him, and perhaps themselves, by taking up Stalin's challenge, inaugurating the four and a half decades of Soviet-American confrontation known as the Cold War, the unwanted war baby conceived in the fragile marriage of convenience that was the Grand Alliance. Who could have predicted that the nation that had repudiated the League of Nations in 1920 would emerge as the foremost champion of the United Nations a generation later? That the Congress that had passed five neutrality statutes in the 1930s would vote overwhelmingly to make the United States a charter member of the North Atlantic Treaty Organization in 1949? That the country that had so reluctantly armed itself in 1941 would become a virtual garrison state in the postwar decades? Or that the people who had refused asylum to Europe's Jews in their hour of greatest peril would welcome some seven hundred thousand refugees in the decade and a half after 1945?[4]

---

4. David M. Reimers, *Still the Golden Door: The Third World Comes to America* (New York: Columbia University Press, 1985), 26.

World War II led directly to the Cold War and ended a century and a half of American isolationism. Yet future historians may well conclude that the Cold War that came to an end in 1989 was neither the most surprising nor the most important or durable of the war's legacies for American diplomacy. In the long sweep of time, America's half-century-long ideological, political, and military face-off with the Soviet Union may appear far less consequential than America's leadership in inaugurating an era of global economic interdependence. In this dimension, too, there was much that was surprising. Who could have foretold that the nation that had flintily refused to cancel the Europeans' war debts in the 1920s would establish the World Bank in 1945 and commit $17 billion to the Marshall Plan in 1948? That the country that had embraced the Fordney-McCumber and Smoot-Hawley tariffs would take the lead in establishing the General Agreement on Tariffs and Trade, and later the World Trade Organization? That the government that had torpedoed the London Economic Conference in 1933 would create the International Monetary Fund in 1944? That isolationist America would step forward to midwife the European Union, another war baby whose maturation muted centuries of old-world rivalries and symbolized the international regime that by century's end came to be called "globalization"? And who could deny that globalization — the explosion in world trade, investment, and cultural mingling — was the signature and lasting international achievement of the postwar era, one likely to overshadow the Cold War in its long-term historical consequences?

Americans could not see that future clearly in 1945, but they could look back over the war they had just waged. They might have reflected with some discomfort on how slowly they had awakened to the menace of Hitlerism in the isolationist 1930s; on how callously they had barred the door to those seeking to flee from Hitler's Europe; on how heedlessly they had provoked Japan into a probably avoidable war in a region where few American interests were at stake; on how they had largely fought with America's money and machines and with Russia's men, had fought in Europe only late in the day, against a foe mortally weakened by three years of brutal warfare in the east, had fought in the Pacific with a bestiality they did not care to admit; on how they had profaned their constitution by interning tens of thousands of citizens largely because of their race; on how they had denied most black Americans a chance to fight for their country; on how they had sullied their nation's moral standards with terror bombing in the closing months of the war; on how their leaders' stubborn insistence on unconditional surrender had led to the incineration of hundreds of thousands of already defeated Japanese, first by fire raids, then by nuclear blast; on how poorly Franklin Roosevelt had prepared for the postwar era, how foolishly he had banked on goodwill and personal charm to compose the conflicting interests of nations, how little he had taken his countrymen into his confidence, even misled them, about the nature of the peace that was to come; on how they had abandoned the reforming agenda of the New Deal years to chase in wartime after the sirens of consumerism; on how they alone among warring peoples had prospered, emerging unscathed at home while 405,399 American soldiers, sailors, marines, and airmen had died. Those men were dignified in death by their service, but they represented proportionately fewer military casualties than in any other major belligerent country. Beyond the war's dead and wounded and their families, few Americans had been touched by the staggering sacrifices and unspeakable anguish that the war had visited upon millions of other people around the globe.

That would have been a reasonably accurate account of America's role in World War II, but it did not describe the war that Americans remembered. In the mysterious zone where history mixes with memory to breed national myths, Americans after 1945 enshrined another war altogether. It was the "good war," maybe the last good war, maybe, given the advent of nuclear weapons, the last war that would ever be fought by huge armies and fully mobilized industrial economies in a protracted contest of attrition. The future of warfare, if there was one, lay not on the traditional battlefield but in cities held hostage by weapons of mass destruction that the war had spurred American science to create.

Americans remembered World War II as a just war waged by a peaceful people aroused to anger only after intolerable provocation, a war stoically endured by those at home and fought in far-away places by brave and wholesome young men with dedicated women standing behind them on the production lines, a war whose justice and necessity were clinched by the public revelations of Nazi genocide in 1945, a war fought for democracy and freedom and, let the world beware, fought with unstinting industrial might and unequaled technological prowess — an effort equivalent, one journalist wrote at war's end, to "building two Panama Canals every month, with a fat surplus to boot."[5]

The dimensions of the surpluses that rested in America's hands at war's end were staggering. "The United States," said Winston Churchill

5. Bruce Catton, *The Warlords of Washington* (New York: Harcourt Brace, 1948), 306.

in 1945, "stand at this moment at the summit of the world." Americans commanded fully half of the entire planet's manufacturing capacity and generated more than half of the world's electricity. America owned two-thirds of the world's gold stocks and half of all its monetary reserves. The United States produced two times more petroleum than the rest of the world combined; it had the world's largest merchant fleet, a near monopoly on the emerging growth industries of aerospace and electronics, and, for a season at least, an absolute monopoly on the disquieting new technology of atomic power.[6]

The war had shaken the American people loose and shaken them up, freed them from a decade of economic and social paralysis and flung them around their country into new regions and new ways of life. It was a war that so richly delivered on all the promises of the wartime advertisers and politicians that it nearly banished the memory of the Depression. At the end of the Depression decade, nearly half of all white families and almost 90 percent of black families had still lived in poverty. One in seven workers remained unemployed. By war's end unemployment was negligible. In the ensuing quarter century the American economy would create some twenty million new jobs, more than half of them filled by women. Within less than a generation of the war's end, the middle class, defined as families with annual incomes between three and ten thousand dollars, more than doubled. By 1960 the middle class included almost two-thirds of all Americans, most of whom owned their own homes, unprecedented achievements for any modern society. The birth dearth of the Depression years gave way to the baby boom, as young couples confident about their futures filled the Republic's empty cradles with some fifty million bawling babies in the decade and a half after the war. The social and economic upheavals of wartime laid the groundwork for the civil rights movement as well as for an eventual revolution in women's status.

Small wonder that Americans chose to think of it as the good war. It was a war that had brought them as far as imagination could reach, and beyond, from the ordeal of the Great Depression and had opened apparently infinite vistas to the future. The huge expenditures for weaponry clinched the Keynesian doctrine that government spending could underwrite prosperity and inaugurated a quarter century of the most

6. David Cannadine, ed., *Blood, Toil, Tears and Sweat: The Speeches of Winston Churchill* (Boston: Houghton Mifflin, 1989), 282.

robust economic growth in the nation's history—an era of the very grandest expectations.

The young Americans who went off to war in the twilight years of the New Deal came home to a different country. By 1950, for the first time in history, a majority of Americans were women, thanks to battle deaths, improvements in maternal health care, and the paucity of immigrants in the preceding generation. Because of the birth slump in the prewar decade, the statistically typical thirty-year-old American woman in 1950 was four years older than her statistically abstracted male counterpart on the eve of the Depression. She had been born in the aftermath of the Great War, spent her childhood in the prosperous twenties, and became a teenager in the year Franklin Roosevelt became president. The Depression had blighted her youth, but as she entered adulthood the country was mobilizing for war and she had found a good job, not in a defense plant but in a clerical position that she had left at war's end and intended one day to take up again. She had married a veteran, a young man who had gone to war believing it was just and necessary and came back still believing so. The GI Bill had sent him to college, and he was on his way up. On his income of almost $3,445 a year they were flush beyond their parents' dreams, or their own Depression-era dreams either, for that matter. They bought a freshly built suburban tract home with room enough for their three children. Their parents talked about the days of outhouses and kerosene lanterns, but their place was plumbed and wired and fitted out with every kind of modern appliance: telephone, radio, refrigerator, washing machine, and the newest gadget of all, television.[7]

They had cast their first presidential ballot for Franklin Roosevelt, in 1944, and their second for his scrappy little successor, Harry Truman, in 1948, though they were uneasy that Truman's party was promising at last to secure full civil rights for Negroes. The Russians had just exploded their own atomic bomb, and the Communists had recently taken power in China. Somehow the good war had not settled things to the degree that Roosevelt had promised. They had inherited a new world, and a brave one too. Like all worlds, it held its share of peril as well as promise.

7. This composite portrait is drawn from data in *HSUS*.

Bibliographical Essay

The literature concerning the major subject of this book—World War II—is enormous. What follows is not an exhaustive bibliography, but a highly selective one, intended as a guide for further reading.

World War II was, as Churchill once remarked, perhaps the only war in which the victors eventually gained access to the bulk of their foes' records. Much of that material is available in English, for example, *Documents on German Foreign Policy* (Washington: U.S. Department of State, 1957–), as well as the extensive materials collected for purposes of the Nuremberg and Tokyo war crimes trials: *Trials of War Criminals Before the Nuernberg Military Tribunals* (Washington: USGPO, 1949–1953) and the records of the Military Tribunal for the Far East, for which an extensive index has been compiled by R. John Pritchard, *The Tokyo War Crimes Trial: Index and Guide* (New York: Garland, 1981–1987). See also the extensive United States materials gathered in *Pearl Harbor Attack: Hearings before the Joint Committee on the Investigation of the Pearl Harbor Attack*, 79th Cong., 1st sess. (1946), and in the oddly named but remarkably rich *Reports of General MacArthur: Japanese Operations in the Southwest Pacific Area* (Washington: USGPO, 1966). For U.S. military operations, including planning, logistics, and medical developments, among other topics, the various official histories of the several services are marvelously detailed (for specific titles, see the footnote citations): *The United States Army in World War II* (Washington: Department of the Army, various years); Wesley Frank Craven and James Lee Cate, *The Army Air Forces in World War II* (Chicago: University of Chicago Press, 6 vols., 1953); Samuel Eliot Morison, *History of U.S. Naval Operations in World War II* (Boston: Little, Brown, 15 vols., 1947–1962); *History of Marine Corps Operations in World War II* (Washington: Historical Branch, U.S. Marine Corps., 5 vols., 1958–1971). Also invaluable are Alfred D. Chandler Jr., et al., eds., *The Papers of Dwight David Eisenhower* (Baltimore: The Johns Hopkins University Press, 19 vols., 1970–). See also *Stalin's Correspondence with Roosevelt and Truman, 1941–1945*

435

(New York: Capricorn, 1965); and Milovan Djilas, *Conversations with Stalin* (New York: Harcourt, Brace, and World, 1962).

Among the many general histories of World War II, I have relied especially on three: John Keegan, *The Second World War* (New York: Viking, 1989); Gerhard L. Weinberg, *A World at Arms: A Global History of World War II* (New York: Cambridge University Press, 1994); and A. Russell Buchanan, *The United States in World War II* (New York: Harper and Row, 2 vols., 1964). Also useful is James L. Stokesbury, *A Short History of World War II* (New York: Morrow, 1980), and, among reference books, I. C. B. Dear, ed., *The Oxford Companion to the Second World War* (New York: Oxford University Press, 1995); John Ellis, *World War II: A Statistical Survey* (New York: Facts on File, 1993); and John Keegan, ed., *The Times Atlas to the Second World War* (New York, Harper and Row, 1989).

Among studies of the war's diplomatic dimensions, Gaddis Smith provides a brief introduction in *American Diplomacy During the Second World War* (New York: Wiley, 1965). More detailed are William Hardy McNeil, *America, Britain, and Russia: Their Cooperation and Conflict, 1941–1946* (New York: Oxford University Press, 1953); Mark Stoler, *The Politics of the Second Front* (Westport, Conn.: Greenwood, 1977); and three titles by Herbert Feis: *Churchill, Roosevelt, and Stalin: The War They Waged and the Peace They Sought* (Princeton: Princeton University Press, 1957); *Between War and Peace: The Potsdam Conference* (Princeton: Princeton University Press, 1960); and *The Atomic Bomb and the End of World War II* (Princeton: Princeton University Press, 1961). On specific wartime diplomatic episodes, see Keith Sainsbury on Teheran, *The Turning Point* (New York: Oxford University Press, 1985); Diane Shaver Clements, *Yalta* (New York: Oxford University Press, 1970); and Charles Mee, *Meeting at Potsdam* (New York: Evans, 1975). See also Gabriel Kolko, *The Politics of War: The World and United States Foreign Policy, 1943–1945* (New York: Random House, 1968).

Kent Roberts Greenfield, *American Strategy in World War II* (Baltimore: The Johns Hopkins University Press, 1963), gives a lucid overview. The same author's *Command Decisions* (New York: Harcourt, Brace, 1959) is more selective, but also highly useful for the study of grand strategy, as is Eric Labaree, *Commander in Chief: Franklin Delano Roosevelt, His Lieutenants, and Their War* (New York: Harper and Row, 1987). See also the relevant portions of Russell V. Weigley, *The American Way of War* (New York: Macmillan, 1973), and his *History of the U.S. Army* (Bloomington: Indiana University Press, 1989).

Among the biographies and memoirs of wartime figures, the following are notable: Forest C. Pogue, *George C. Marshall* (New York: Viking, 4 vols., 1963–1987); David Eisenhower, *Eisenhower at War* (New York: Random House, 1986); Stephen Ambrose, *The Supreme Commander: The War Years of General Dwight D. Eisenhower* (Garden City, N.Y.: Doubleday, 1970); Robert H. Ferrell, ed., *The Eisenhower Diaries* (New York: Norton, 1981); Eisenhower's own *Crusade in Europe* (Garden City, N.Y.: Doubleday, 1948); Harry C. Butcher, *My Three Years with Eisenhower* (New York: Simon and Schuster, 1946); Walter Bedell Smith, *Eisenhower's Six Great Decisions* (New York: Longman's, 1956); Russell V. Weigley, *Eisenhower's Lieutenants: The Campaigns of France and Germany* (Bloomington: Indiana University Press, 1989); Clayton James, *The Years of MacArthur* (Boston: Houghton Mifflin, 3 vols., 1970–); MacArthur's own *Reminiscences* (New York: McGraw-Hill, 1964); Martin Blumenson's *Patton* (New York: Morrow, 1985); Omar Bradley, *A Soldier's Story* (New York: Holt, 1951); Bradley and

Clay Blair, *A General's Life* (New York: Simon and Schuster, 1983); Godfrey Hodgson, *The Colonel: The Life and Times of Henry L. Stimson, 1867–1959* (New York: Knopf, 1990); the relevant chapters of Kai Bird, *The Chairman: John J. McCloy and the Making of the American Establishment* (New York: Simon and Schuster, 1992); H. H. Arnold, *Global Mission* (New York: Harper, 1949); Curtis LeMay, *Mission with LeMay* (Garden City, N.Y.: Doubleday, 1965); and Lord Moran, *Churchill: Taken from the Diaries of Lord Moran: The Struggle for Survival, 1940–1965* (Boston: Houghton Mifflin, 1966).

Walter LaFeber, *The Clash: U.S.-Japanese Relations Throughout History* (New York: Norton, 1997), provides valuable background and historical perspective. Gordon W. Prange, *At Dawn We Slept: The Untold Story of Pearl Harbor* (New York: Penguin, 1982) is an exhaustive account. See also Roberta Wohlstetter, *Pearl Harbor: Warning and Decision* (Stanford: Stanford University Press, 1962), which definitively lays to rest accusations that Roosevelt conspired to invite the Pearl Harbor attack. Prange has also written a fine account of the Battle of Midway, *Miracle at Midway* (New York: Penguin, 1982), as has Walter Lord, *Incredible Victory: The Battle of Midway* (New York: Harper and Row, 1967). For a Japanese perspective on that pivotal battle, see Mitsuo Fuchida and Masatake Okumiya, *Midway: The Battle That Doomed Japan* (Annapolis: U.S. Naval Institute Press, 1955).

Ronald Spector, *Eagle Against the Sun: The American War with Japan* (New York: Free Press, 1985), is an excellent overall history of the Pacific War. Unfortunately, no comparable volume exists for the European Theater. Spector's account can be profitably supplemented with Akira Iriye, *Power and Culture: The Japanese-American War, 1941–1945* (Cambridge: Harvard University Press, 1981), and John Dower's fascinating *War Without Mercy: Race and Power in the Pacific War* (New York: Pantheon, 1986), as well as with Christopher Thorne, *Allies of a Kind: The United States, Britain, and the War against Japan* (New York: Oxford University Press, 1978), which is especially informative on the colonial dimension of the Asian conflict. See also Michael Schaller, *The U.S. Crusade in China, 1939–1945* (New York: Columbia University Press, 1979); and Barbara Tuchman, *Stilwell and the American Experience in China* (New York: Macmillan, 1971).

In addition to the accounts in the official service histories, specific actions in the Pacific are covered especially well in Richard B. Frank, *Guadalcanal* (New York: Random House, 1990); Thomas J. Cutler, *The Battle of Leyte Gulf* (New York: Harper-Collins, 1994); and Colonel Hiromichi Yahara, *The Battle for Okinawa* (New York: Wiley, 1995).

The naval war in the Atlantic is the subject of several studies that nicely complement Admiral Morison's somewhat dated account (which, for example, makes no mention of the role of ULTRA, which was not made public until well after Morison had written): Thomas A. Bailey and Paul B. Ryan, *Hitler vs. Roosevelt: The Undeclared Naval War* (New York: Free Press, 1979); Dan Van der Vat, *The Atlantic Campaign* (New York: Harper and Row, 1988); Nathan Miller, *War at Sea: A Naval History of World War II* (New York: Oxford University Press, 1995); and Michael Gannon, *Operation Drumbeat* (New York: Harper and Row, 1990).

The air war has generated a large literature of its own. See especially Richard Overy, *The Air War* (London: Europa, 1980); Michael Sherry, *The Rise of American Air Power* (New Haven: Yale University Press, 1987); Stephen L. McFarland and Wesley Phillips Newton, *To Command the Sky: The Battle for Air Superiority over Germany, 1942–1944*

(Washington: Smithsonian Institution Press, 1991); Alan J. Levine, *The Strategic Bombing of Germany, 1940–1945* (Westport, Conn.: Praeger, 1992); Conrad Crane, *Bombs, Cities, and Civilians: American Airpower Strategy in World War II* (Lawrence: University Press of Kansas, 1993); and Ronald Schaffer's impassioned *Wings of Judgment: American Bombing in World War II* (New York: Oxford University Press, 1985), which discusses both the European and Pacific theaters.

For the Mediterranean and European fighting, worthwhile supplements to the official histories include: Chester Wilmot, *The Struggle for Europe* (London: Collins, 1952), which is highly critical of Roosevelt's strategy, or lack thereof, for dealing with the Soviets; Michael Howard, *The Mediterranean Strategy in the Second World War* (New York: Praeger, 1968); Carlo D'Este, *Bitter Victory: The Battle for Sicily, 1943* (New York: Dutton, 1988), and the same author's *Decision in Normandy* (New York: HarperCollins, 1994); Max Hastings, *Overlord* (London: Pan Books, 1985); Stephen E. Ambrose, *D-Day* (New York: Simon and Schuster, 1994), and his *Citizen Soldiers* (New York: Simon and Schuster, 1997); Cornelius Ryan, *The Longest Day* (New York: Simon and Schuster, 1959), and the same author's account of the failure of Operation Market-Garden, *A Bridge Too Far* (New York: Fawcett, 1975); Trevor N. Dupuy, et al., *Hitler's Last Gamble: The Battle of the Bulge* (New York: HarperCollins, 1994), and Richard Lamb, *War in Italy* (New York: St. Martin's Press, 1993). The controversial surrender of the German troops in Italy is covered in Allen Dulles, *The Secret Surrender* (New York: Harper and Row, 1966).

My own thinking on the economic and social implications of the war for the United States has been deeply shaped by two excellent comparative studies: Alan S. Milward, *War, Economy, and Society, 1939–1945* (Berkeley: University of California Press, 1979); and Richard Overy, *Why the Allies Won* (New York: Norton, 1995). For the American homefront, see Bureau of the Budget, *The United States at War* (Washington: U.S.G.P.O, 1946); Harold G. Vatter, *The U.S. Economy in World War II* (New York: Columbia University Press, 1985); Donald M. Nelson, *Arsenal of Democracy: The Story of American War Production* (New York: Harcourt Brace, 1946); Keith E. Eiler, *Mobilizing America: Robert P. Patterson and the War Effort, 1940–1945* (Ithaca: Cornell University Press, 1997); Bruce Catton's highly critical *The Warlords of Washington* (New York: Harcourt Brace, 1948); Eliot Janeway, *The Struggle for Survival* (New Haven: Yale University Press, 1951); Richard Polenberg, *War and Society: The United States, 1941–1945* (Philadelphia: Lippincott, 1972); John Morton Blum's imaginative *V Was for Victory* (New York: Harcourt Brace Jovanovich, 1976); Doris Kearns Goodwin's lavish biographical account, *No Ordinary Time: Franklin and Eleanor Roosevelt: The Home Front in World War II* (New York: Simon and Schuster, 1994); William L. O'Neill's argumentative *A Democracy at War: America's Fight at Home and Abroad in World War II* (New York: Free Press, 1993); Richard Lingeman's breezy *Don't You Know There's a War On?* (New York: Putnam, 1970); Geoffrey Perrett's *Days of Sadness, Years of Triumph: The American People, 1939–1945* (New York: Coward, McCann and Geoghegan, 1979); and Michael C. C. Adams's revisionist *The Best War Ever* (Baltimore: The Johns Hopkins University Press, 1994). Studs Terkel provides a fascinating oral history in *"The Good War"* (New York: Pantheon, 1984); as do Mark Jonathan Harris, et al., *The Home Front* (New York: G. P. Putnam's Sons, 1984), derived from the excellent documentary film of the same title. H. G. Nicholas, ed., *Washington Despatches, 1941–1945* (New York: Free Press, 1981) presents the incomparably insightful commentaries on wartime Washington of the young British diplomat Isaiah Berlin.

Special studies of interest include: Alan Clive, *State of War: Michigan in World War II* (Ann Arbor: University of Michigan Press, 1979); Marilyn S. Johnson, *The Second Gold Rush: Oakland and the East Bay in World War II* (Berkeley: University of California Press, 1993); John E. Brigante, *The Feasibility Dispute* (Washington: Committee on Public Administration Cases, 1950); Nelson Lichtenstein, *Labor's War at Home: The CIO in World War II* (New York: Cambridge University Press, 1982); Allan M. Winkler, *The Politics of Propaganda: The Office of War Information* (New Haven: Yale University Press, 1978); George Q. Flynn, *Lewis B. Hershey: Mr. Selective Service* (Chapel Hill: University of North Carolina Press, 1985); Mulford Q. Sibley and Philip F. Jacob, *Conscription of Conscience: The American State and the Conscientious Objector, 1941–1947* (Ithaca: Cornell University Prerss, 1952); William M. Tuttle Jr., *Daddy's Gone to War: The Second World War in the Lives of America's Children* (New York: Oxford University Press, 1993); Clayton R. Koppes and Gregory D. Black, *Hollywood Goes to War* (New York: Free Press, 1987); Keith Olson, *The G.I. Bill, the Veterans, and the Colleges* (Lexington: University of Kentucky Press, 1974); and Allan Bérubé, *Coming Out Under Fire: The History of Gay Men and Women in World War II* (New York: Free Press, 1990).

The wartime internment of Japanese immigrants and Japanese-American citizens has spawned several studies, including: Jacobus tenBroek, et al., *Prejudice, War, and the Constitution* (Berkeley and Los Angeles: University of California Press, 1970); and Peter Irons, *Justice at War: The Story of the Japanese Internment Cases* (Berkeley: University of California Press, 1983), which focuses especially on the legal aspects of the internment. Gordon Chang, ed., *Morning Glory, Evening Shadow: Yamato Ichihashi and His Internment Writings, 1942–1945* (Stanford: Stanford University Press, 1997), gives the perspective of one especially insightful internee. Also worth consulting is the relevant chapter in Attorney General Francis Biddle's memoir *In Brief Authority* (Garden City, N.Y.: Doubleday, 1962).

The situation of African-Americans in wartime helped to occasion Gunnar Myrdal's classic, *An American Dilemma: The Negro Problem and Modern Democracy* (New York: Harper and Row, 1944); see also the pertinent portions of Jervis Anderson, *A. Philip Randolph* (New York: Harcourt Brace, 1973); and of Walter White, *A Rising Wind* (Garden City, N.Y.: Doubleday, Doran, 1945), as well as the same author's *A Man Called White* (New York: Viking, 1947). See also Neil Wynn, *The Afro-American and the Second World War* (London: P. Elek, 1976); and Richard M. Dalfiume, *Desegregation of the U.S. Armed Forces* (Columbia: University of Missouri Press, 1969).

The war's impact on women has excited much scholarly controversy, beginning with William Chafe, *The American Woman: Her Changing Political, Economic, and Social Role in the Twentieth Century* (New York: Oxford University Press, 1972). For other appraisals, consult the relevant parts of Alice Kessler-Harris, *Out to Work: A History of Wage-Earning Women in the United States* (New York: Oxford University Press, 1982), and Rosalind Rosenberg, *Divided Lives: American Women in the Twentieth Century* (New York: Hill and Wang, 1992), as well as Susan M. Hartmann, *The Homefront and Beyond: American Women in the 1940s* (Boston: Twayne, 1982); and D'Ann Campbell, *Women at War with America: Private Lives in a Patriotic Era* (Cambridge: Harvard University Press, 1984).

Richard Rhodes, *The Making of the Atomic Bomb* (New York: Simon and Schuster, 1986) provides a definitive account of the scientific, technological, political, and economic aspects of the Manhattan Project. See also the official Atomic Energy Commission history, Richard B. Hewlett and Oscar E. Anderson Jr., *The New World, 1939/1946* (University Park: Pennsylvania State University Press, 1962). On the complicated role of the bomb in the war's endgame, including both the Japanese decision to surrender and U.S. relations with the Soviet Union, see Gar Alperovitz's tendentious *The Decision to Use the Atomic Bomb and the Architecture of an American Myth* (New York: Knopf, rev. ed., 1995); Martin Sherwin, *A World Destroyed: The Atomic Bomb and the Grand Alliance* (New York: Knopf, 1975); the relevant chapters in McGeorge Bundy, *Danger and Survival: Choices about the Bomb in the First Fifty Years* (New York: Random House, 1988); and the articles by Barton J. Bernstein cited in the footnotes for Chapter 22. The definitive account of Japan's final capitulation is Robert J. C. Butow, *Japan's Decision to Surrender* (Stanford: Stanford University Press, 1954).

The sixteen million Americans who served in the armed services during the war have been extensively studied, starting with Samuel Stouffer, *The American Soldier* (Princeton: Princeton University Press, 2 vols., 1949). See also Lee Kennett, *G.I.: The American Soldier in World War II* (New York: Scribner's, 1987); Geoffrey Perrett, *There's a War to Be Won: the United States Army in World War II* (New York: Random House, 1991); and Gerald F. Linderman, *The World Within War: America's Combat Experience in World War II* (New York: Free Press, 1997), as well as the several volumes dealing with troop enlistment, training, and deployment in the Army's official history. Also valuable, though not always fully reliable, are the accounts of accredited war correspondents, including Ernie Pyle, *Brave Men* (New York: Holt, 1944); John Steinbeck, *Once There Was a War* (New York: Viking, 1958); John Hersey, *Into the Valley: A Skirmish of the Marines* (New York: Knopf, 1943); Richard Tregaskis, *Guadalcanal Diary* (New York: Random House, 1943); Robert Lee Sharrod, *On to Westward* (New York: Duell, Sloan and Pearce, 1945), and his *Tarawa: The Story of a Battle* (New York: Duell, Sloan and Pearce, 1944). Their reportage is strongly criticized in Paul Fussell, *Wartime* (New York: Oxford University Press, 1989).

I have been able to sample only a few of the countless memoirs by servicemen: E.B. Sledge, *With the Old Breed at Peleliu and Okinawa* (Novato, Calif.: Presidio, 1981); Harry H. Crosby, *A Wing and a Prayer: The "Bloody 100th" Bomb Group of the U.S. Eighth Air Force in Action over Europe in World War II* (New York: HarperCollins, 1993); Samuel Hynes, *Flights of Passage: Reflections of a World War II Aviator* (Annapolis: Naval Institute Press, 1988); Alvin Kernan, *Crossing the Line: A Bluejacket's World War II Odyssey* (Annapolis: Naval Institute Press, 1994); William Manchester, *Goodbye, Darkness* (Boston: Little, Brown, 1979); and Audie Murphy, *To Hell and Back* (New York: Henry Holt, 1949).

WORLD WAR II: EUROPEAN THEATER

FINLAND

Leningrad

ESTONIA

Moscow

LATVIA

Baltic Sea

LITHUANIA

U.S.S.R.

Volga

E. PRUSSIA

Vistula Warsaw

• Kursk

Don

Stalingrad

Volga

POLAND

• Kiev

Neisse

CZECHOSLOVAKIA

Don

HUNGARY

Sea of Azov

ROMANIA

Ploesti

Black Sea

Danube

YUGOSLAVIA

BULGARIA

ALBANIA (IT.)

TURKEY

GREECE

Athens

SYRIA (FR.)

CRETE

CYPRUS

LEBANON

Mediterranean Sea

PALESTINE (BR.)

TRANS-JORDAN (BR.)

El Alamein • Cairo

LIBYA

EGYPT (BR.)

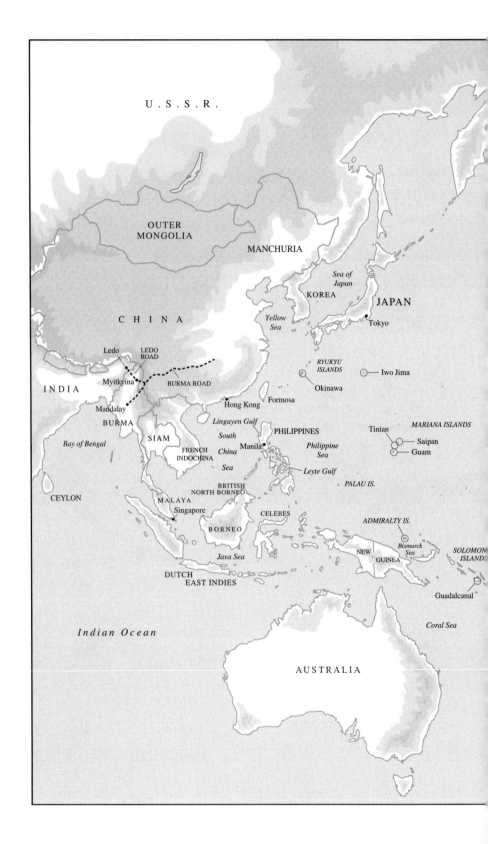

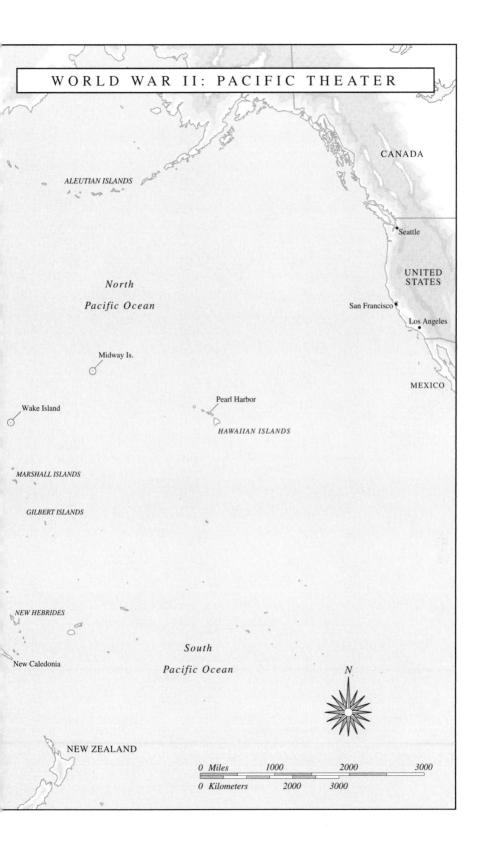

WORLD WAR II: PACIFIC THEATER

CANADA

ALEUTIAN ISLANDS

Seattle

UNITED
STATES

North

Pacific Ocean

San Francisco

Los Angeles

Midway Is.

MEXICO

Pearl Harbor

Wake Island

HAWAIIAN ISLANDS

MARSHALL ISLANDS

GILBERT ISLANDS

NEW HEBRIDES

New Caledonia

South

Pacific Ocean

N

NEW ZEALAND

| 0 Miles | 1000 | 2000 | 3000 |
| 0 Kilometers | 2000 | 3000 | |

Index

188; and British strategy, 151, 160, 188; and Casablanca commitments, 162, 165, 170; Churchill's views about, 257–59, 274–75; Eisenhower as commander of campaigns in, 264–65; and European balance of power, 160; FDR's views about, 25; German successes in, 68, 70; length of campaign in, 276; and Overlord/Anvil, 255–56, 274–75, 276; and second front, 151, 162; Stalin's/ Soviet views about, 186, 188, 256, 258; and Teheran Conference, 255–56, 257–59, 276. *See also* Italy; North Africa; Sicily

Mercer, Lucy, 383

Merchant marine: British, 63; Japanese, 397–98n; and legacies of World War II, 432; U.S., 9, 42, 74. *See also* Convoys

Mers el-Kebir (Algeria), 27

Messenger (Randolph newspaper), 338

Messerschmitt fighters (German), 183

Mexican-Americans, 345

Mexico, 352

Meyer, Dillon S., 329, 330

Middle East, 149n, 151, 381

Midway Island, 108–9, 110–19, 130, 385

Migration: of blacks, 343–44; during World War II, 322–23

Mikawa, Gunichi, 124, 125–27

Military, Japanese, government role of leaders in, 78–79

Military manpower, U.S.: needs for, 205–12. *See also* Selective service

Military training, U.S., 51–52, 181, 183, 202, 203, 286–87, 290, 291, 346. *See also* Pilots: training of

Military, U.S.: blacks in, 286, 287, 339, 340, 342, 345–48, 392, 423; brutality of, 387–88, 430; and elections of 1944, 362–64; first enter Germany, 368; Japanese-Americans in, 330, 347; mobility of, 290; order of battle for, 288–89; and profile of average GI, 285–86; term of service in, 287; Truman desegregates, 348; views about rearmament of, 22; women in, 285. *See also specific person, battle/ campaign, or branch of service*

Milward, Alan, 223

Mindanao (Philippines), 105, 397, 398

Minimum wages, 358

Missouri (U.S. battleship), 427–28

Mitchell, Archie and Elsie, 423–24

Mitchell, Billy, 92, 178

Mitsubishi A6M fighters. *See* Zeros

Mobility: and Battle for Northwest Europe, 298, 299, 299n, 302–3, 316–17; of civilians during World War II, 322–23, 357; of military, 290; of tanks, 299, 299n. *See also* Mechanized warfare

Mobilization: administration for, 194–95; and aerial warfare, 205, 206, 229–30; agencies for, 53; and assembly line, 224–29; and civilian consumption, 193, 220–21; complete versus progressive, 26, 34; and economy, 191–93, 197–98; efficiency in, 223–30; as end of Great Depression, 192, 194; FDR's views about, 4, 52–53, 70; and Feasibility Dispute, 202–3, 205, 206; goals for, 193, 198; and isolationism, 194; and labor, 53; and Lend-Lease, 53–54; and mass production, 224–30; and material shortages, 202–4; New Deal compared with, 197–98; and Pacific War, 55; political aspects of, 204–5; and quantity versus quality, 223–24, 229; and Red Army's entrance into Europe, 188; resources for, 222–23; and Soviet aid, 60; and Soviet staying power, 205–6; and unemployment, 192; and U.S. strategy, 25–26, 193–94, 203; and Victory Program, 60–63, 206; in World War I, 192. *See also* Contracts, military; Rearmament

Model, Walter, 305

Molotov, Vaycheslav, 149–50, 154–55

Molotov-Ribbentrop Pact (1939), 10, 47, 187, 336

Mongolia, 84, 380

Monnet, Jean, 3, 4

Monroe Doctrine, 67

Monte Cassino (Italy), 173–74, 279

Montgomery, Bernard: and Battle for Northwest Europe, 298, 301–2, 305, 309–10, 312, 320; and Eisenhower, 265, 309–10; and Italian campaign, 173; at Normandy, 272; in North Africa, 156, 158, 159, 272; and Overlord, 271–72, 293; on Rommel, 270; in Sicily, 167, 168; on Stalin, 376; style of, 271–72; tactics of, 297

Montgomery Ward Company, 217

Morale: and aerial warfare, 177, 177–78n, 178, 179; Allied, 292, 307; and Battle of Britain, 28–29; and Battle for Northwest Europe, 307, 313, 318–19; and bombing, 4, 177, 177–78n, 178, 279–80, 318–19; British, 28–29; FDR's views